Contents

Introduction

Demolishing clichés

First of all, to dispense with a misleading term of reference. 'Classical music' conjures up all the wrong associations, not least enforced education, a sedentary lifestyle and what I can only coin as 'old fogeyism'. 'Concert music' is hardly ideal, but it's better. 'Great music', however, is better still – certainly for the purposes of a book that purports to deal with 'a thousand masterpieces'. Great music has the potential to change your life. It can heighten your religious sensibilities (Bach's *St Matthew Passion*, Bruckner's symphonies or Schoenberg's *Moses und Aron*), bring history alive (certain Shostakovich symphonies), address your inner conflicts (Tchaikovsky's Fourth or Mahler's Sixth Symphonies), expose you to the elements (Sibelius's *Tapiola*) or transport you to realms far beyond the reach of normal consciousness (Beethoven's last string quartets).

The idea that listening to great music has to be either 'relaxing' or 'intellectual', the exclusive province of fireside home-birds, bespectacled professors or the perennially middle-aged, has led many potential fans to ditch the idea as passive or snobbish. However, if you've ever flown skywards on a Beethoven symphony, or experienced the full force of a Wagner music drama, you will know that great music is infinitely more meaningful than the delusions that its less sincere fans harbour about themselves. In a sense, even the composer ceases to matter. His work is everything, a nourishing narcotic – imaginative, compelling and, above all, urgently relevant.

My own baptism into the world of great music was as a sick child confined to bed with a set of records that alternated jazz and classical tracks. I'd borrowed the discs primarily to hear Artie Shaw, Glenn Miller and Duke Ellington, but when the Italian conductor Arturo Toscanini lit up the sky with the Third Act Prelude from Wagner's *Lohengrin*, I gatecrashed a world that has held me in its thrall ever since. Part of the seduction was in the music's physical impact, its bold, brave spirit. Anyone intent on demolishing the 'relaxation' myth surrounding great music should grab a CD of Bartók's Fourth String Quartet and play the fifth movement – a fiercely rhythmic onslaught that also puts paid to the rumour that chamber music is tame.

Virtually every genre featured in this book embraces a diverse range of musical experience: while Bartók stamps and rages, Mozart seduces us with aching understatement. His G minor String Quintet holds at its core the most profoundly beautiful slow movement this side of Heaven.

Great music, the emotions and the spirit

Anyone who has watched a Hollywood movie will know that the musical soundtrack is as much a part of the overall experience as the plot, direction or acting. The riveting scores that Erich Wolfgang Korngold composed for *Elizabeth and Essex*, for example, or the passionate violin concerto that Alfred Newman wrote into *Wuthering Heights* (the version starring Laurence Olivier and Merle Oberon) activate the tear-ducts with as much power as the most seductive big-screen embrace. Space precludes inclusion of these wonderful scores in this context, and yet if you're sensitive to musical influences you will hear them anyway - in the music of Richard Strauss, Wagner and Tchaikovsky.

The pages that follow include countless works where scorching musical narrative triumphs on its own terms. Who could 'miss the point' of Tchaikovsky's *Romeo and Juliet* Fantasy Overture, with its restless alternations between tender entreaty and blood-curdling conflict: the fact that Montagues and Capulets are involved is hardly the point - the music could just as well be about your family and the family of your own partner or lover. And when Salome is presented with the severed head of John the Baptist, Richard Strauss's goggle-eyed music expresses unmistakable titillation tinged with shame. It is one of the supremely erotic moments in music; you'd probably react even without knowing the story.

Love is a constant pretext in the selections that follow, from the sultry world of Debussy's *Prélude à l'après-midi d'un faune* to the unmasked violence of Stravinsky's *Rite of Spring* where, amidst vivid scenes from Pagan Russia, a young virgin dances herself to death. And then there are the operas – Puccini's impoverished lovers in *La bohème*, or the rapturous exchanges of Wagner's *Tristan und Isolde*. Has anyone expressed the delirium of erotic longing more powerfully than Wagner does in the Third Act of *Tristan*? Absolutely not. Come to think of it, few composers have voiced a more touching farewell than Bach did when he penned a mini-drama for a brother about to depart for foreign climes, his *Capriccio on the departure of his beloved brother* (you'll find it under "Bach Solo").

The expressive scope of great music is limitless. Reams have been written on the psychological significance of musical notation, chords and sounds, of how – and why – great works are composed the way they are, why they so often pull at our heartstrings. The manner of music's making is infinitely mysterious, but the sum effect of a masterpiece defies precise analysis. Take a work like Tchaikovsky's

Fourth Symphony – music filled with echoes of a destiny that its composer viewed with both forbearance and fear. The Fourth's first 20 minutes grapple with inner conflicts that, in Tchaikovsky's particular case, mirrored a confrontation with homosexuality. The blaring fanfares that dominate the work symbolize the stark inevitability of Fate, rallying beyond dreams of repose, bouts of fantasy and breezy trips out among the people.

Likewise in the case of Danish composer Carl Nielsen's Fifth Symphony where a lone side-drummer enters into battle against the entire orchestra: the grim forces of war versus 'the good', and the good wins. The *Guinness Classical 1000* is rich in parallel experiences.

Then there's the spiritual dimension, although not all spiritual music travels the conventional channels of religious worship. It is of course true that Bach, Handel, Mozart and the various Renaissance church masters wrote within the context of an active liturgy. Having said that, it is difficult to think of, say, Beethoven's epic *Missa solemnis* in terms of churches or cathedrals. The *Missa* seems like music of the sky, the ether, or the theatre of the mind. Some of the greatest spiritual works sidetrack specific liturgy in favour of abstract forms – the late quartets of Beethoven, for example, or the symphonies of Anton Bruckner.

What is a masterpiece?

"A production surpassing in excellence all others by the same hand ... a production of masterly skill." So states the *Shorter Oxford English Dictionary* concerning a word that has its origins in the seventeenth century. "Surpassing ... all others" does of course suggest an order of rank, and although none of the works included in the *Guinness Classical 1000* falls below a minimum high level of artistic attainment, there are many hundreds (perhaps even thousands) more that – given the space and extended editorial brief – could have been added. It is also worth pointing out that 'masterpiece' in this context can refer either to a 15-hour epic (Wagner's *Ring* cycle) or a single, three-minute Scarlatti harpsichord sonata. Joy is as much a part of our programme as pain, comedy as much as tragedy (well almost as much) and although it's inevitable – given the riches of a 500-year time span – that most of our selections are drawn from the musical past, there's some impressive representation from the post-war period (Messiaen, Reich, Pärt, Bryars, Adams, etc).

How I chose the 'Guinness Classical 1000'

Bach composed over 200 sacred cantatas, Scarlatti 555 solo sonatas, Haydn over 100 symphonies, Schubert over 600 songs. You see the problem? A thousand might seem like a generous selection, but when you actually confront the amount of great music available on disc, choosing becomes a major challenge. Being the product of a single mind, the *Guinness Classical 1000* does, to some extent, reflect a personal bias. Any one of our readers might justifiably harbour resentment over this or that omission but not, I hope, doubt the breadth or variety of the final product.

My criteria for selection have been, in the main, twofold: first, to include every one of the very greatest masterpieces – I mean the towering 'milestones' like Beethoven's Ninth Symphony and late string quartets, Bach's *St Matthew Passion*, Wagner's *Ring* cycle, etc. Were I to limit the book to those works only, I would – like a literary anthologist whose parallel project would embrace Shakespeare, Goethe and few other masters – be content with around 300 works, or less. Masterpieces are plentiful, but milestones are conspicuous by their rarity. Secondly, my intention here is to represent the whole spectrum of great music, from the Masses of the sixteenth-century English composer William Byrd to the most powerfully communicative compositions of the 1990s. Some readers might complain that while including a work like Gavin Bryars' *Jesus' Blood never failed me yet* (an extraordinarily moving narrative that not everyone rates as highly as I do) I omit certain Verdi operas and some of Haydn's greatest string quartets. But, to return to the point I raised earlier, a truly comprehensive survey of masterpieces would run to many hundreds of pages. The further you venture from an elevated 'core' of great works (a canon of sorts), the broader your potential terms of reference. As a matter of interest, my own personal 'core canon' of great Western musical masterpieces is as follows:

Bach St Matthew Passion
Bach Goldberg Variations
Beethoven Missa solemnis
Beethoven Piano Sonata No. 32
Beethoven Diabelli Variations
Beethoven String Quartet No. 14
Beethoven Symphony No. 9
Bruckner Symphony No. 9
Mahler Symphony No. 9
Mozart String Quintet in G minor
Mozart The Magic Flute
Mozart Piano Concerto No. 22
Schubert String Quartet No. 15
Schubert Piano Sonata in B flat
Sibelius Symphony No. 7
Wagner Tristan und Isolde

Where to find what you're looking for

Although this is emphatically not a book on musical history, it does attempt to investigate the greatest works composed in a particular genre by placing each composition in some sort of chronological context. In so doing, it offers a birds' eye view of the development of, say, the symphony, the tone-poem, the string quartet or Italian opera. We start among concertos, then move on to the symphony, the tone-poem, orchestral variations and suites, chamber music, songs, opera and ballet. Each section is subdivided, for example – "Chamber Music" starts with music for two musicians, then adds a third for "three's a crowd", shifts to the string quartet and ends up with "The more, the merrier". You can then peruse either a genre or the various categories within that genre. You can also enjoy flipping from, say, German Song to French song, or from Italian opera to German opera, etc. Each subdivision is prefaced by a very brief introduction.

Chronological versus alphabetical order

As to an 'order', all composers are arranged chronologically; thereafter their works are listed either chronologically (i.e. Sonata No. 1 is before Sonata No. 2) or alphabetically – which means that although Verdi was born before Puccini, his operas are listed in alphabetical order. We therefore combine historical perspective with relatively easy access. However, anyone who is as yet unfamiliar with composer chronologies and simply wants to locate a particular work quickly should turn to the Index of the *Guinness Classical 1000* where composers and titles are listed in alphabetical order.

Choosing the recordings

If you open the current edition of the *Gramophone* CD catalogue and turn to the voluminous section devoted to Beethoven, look under the 'symphonies' section and you'll find roughly 90 separate recordings of Beethoven's *Choral* Symphony. Some are brand-new, others reissued from stereo recordings from the 1960s, 1970s or 1980s, while there are some that hark back to the far-off days of mono LPs and 78s. How do we choose between them? Does 'newest' mean 'best', and do the vintage releases survive simply because older collectors insist on re-visiting the recordings that they grew up with? The answer to the first question – i.e. whether newest means best – is a resolute 'no'. It is of course true that digital technology has allowed us living-room access to the kind of sound we'd previously experienced only in the concert hall; and, yes, old recordings rarely deliver the volume, depth or spatial information that nowadays we more or less take for granted. But although technology has taken us from hazy reproduction to virtual reality, true musicianship doesn't 'date' and some older performances are so powerfully communicative that they triumph through the passage of 40, 50 or even 60 years. Which brings me to my own criteria for selection. Where a digital recording sweeps the board – either unconditionally or when weighed against the relative pros and cons of older rivals – then I give it pride of place. For example, Sir Colin Davis's Philips CD of Beethoven's *Choral* Symphony is deeply considered, beautifully played and superbly recorded, virtues that combine for a musical experience that should satisfy either novices or seasoned *aficionados*. However, there are some older performances that take a stronger interpretative stand in one direction or another – Arturo Toscanini, for example, is more overtly dramatic; Wilhelm Furtwängler centres more on the score's mystical elements; and Rafael Kubelík suggests a very personal brand of lyricism. So while Davis is my primary recommendation (and the latest CD catalogue number for his recording is the one that's quoted in our Index to the *Guinness Classical 1000*), the paragraph dealing with 'the best recording' of the *Choral* Symphony also mentions various alternatives – firstly, because no recording, however great, can be considered definitive (musical performance is an interpretative art and is therefore self-renewing) and, secondly, because there's always the chance that our chosen recording will be deleted (see below) and it's important to offer quality alternatives. One none the less assumes that performances of stature – which is what the vast majority of our selections are – will always be in demand and therefore justify more-or-less constant availability.

Will our recommendations be available in the shops?

Even as I write this, the recording industry is regularly being accused of merciless over-production. CDs are brought on to the market one month, withdrawn the next and then reissued again three months later. An exaggeration? Perhaps – but it does go some way towards explaining why certain of our recommendations will be unavailable by the time this book is published. However, don't despair. The record numbers listed in our Index to the *Guinness Classical 1000* merely represent the latest CD incarnation as we go to press, and there's little doubt that – even if temporarily 'off the shelves' – the majority of the records listed will be reissued again and again. If in doubt, quote the relevant record number to your dealer and add the disc content information – i.e. Sir Colin Davis's digital Philips recording of Beethoven's *Choral* Symphony with the Dresden Staatskapelle (so as not to confuse it with any other Sir Colin Davis recording of the *Choral* that may have been issued since). Secondary recommendations (where record numbers are not quoted) will assure you of a worthy 'runner-up' or a significant historical alternative.

Mono, analogue and digital – three stages in the development of hi-fi

Sound-wise, our recommendations are divided into just three categories: digital, which means that a digital stereo tape recorder was used for the sessions, the mixing and/or editing and mastering (for CD); analogue, which – in this context – means a pre-digital stereo recording that has been digitally remastered (sometimes 're-mixed' from the original tapes); and mono which is a single-channel (analogue) recording, sometimes digitally refurbished and taken either from tape or from 78rpm masters/discs.

'Digital' is considered state-of-the-art and has the potential to reproduce a lifelike dynamic range with maximum clarity but no 'tape hiss'. Analogue recordings (which can be either AAD [analogue mix and digital mastering] or ADD [digital mix and digital mastering] – terms I don't use here) reproduce a stereo panorama but with a less extreme dynamic range than digital recordings and varying degrees of tape hiss. Mono recordings condense the entire sound picture into a single channel, often to surprisingly good effect. Judicious microphone placing and sensitive balancing (between soloists and orchestra, for example) are very much of the essence, which is why some (well balanced) analogue recordings are preferable to various of their more dynamic – but less well-balanced – digital 'successors'. Attitudes to the transfer of old 78s to CD tend to vary from company to company, some of whom employ surface-noise reduction and 'mock-stereo' techniques, while others keep the sound much as it was on the original discs. Not wanting to complicate the issue, I have kept sound references merely to 'digital, analogue, mono', unless the CD in question requires further comment.

How to read the "Guinness Classical 1000"

To recap briefly, the *Guinness Classical 1000* opens amongst concertos, symphonies and orchestral works, slims down for chamber music and instrumental solos, then explores the vocal worlds of song and opera before ballet music and the final curtain. The first paragraph of each entry is entirely devoted to the music; the second documents the selected 'best recording', and the third discusses that recording and refers to any significant CD rivals (sometimes quoting older recordings that are not as yet on CD). The only CD numbers listed are in the index and opus numbers quoted in the main text refer, in many cases, to the most up-to-date catalogues of a composer's work – for example, I use 'BWV' numbers for Bach, 'K' numbers for Mozart, 'FS' numbers for Nielsen, 'B' numbers for Dvořák, 'Sz' numbers for Bartók, etc. Otherwise, I used the standard opus number. A simple glossary (printed towards the end of the book) should help explain various musical terms used within the main text.

In compiling the *Guinness Classical 1000*, I have attempted to convey some of the joy, excitement and profound stimulation that recorded music has offered me over the years. It is, of course, as much a personal statement of artistic faith as a resumé of great music and I hope you will forgive the occasional spot of enthusiastic 'overkill'. As a devoted recorded music reviewer (primarily for *Gramophone* and *The Independent*), I spend most of my working life listening, absorbing, comparing and weighing the relative advantages and disadvantages of musical performances. It is a charmed life, and I couldn't have lived it without the loving support of my wife Georgie and my two daughters, Francesca and Victoria. This book is therefore dedicated to them.

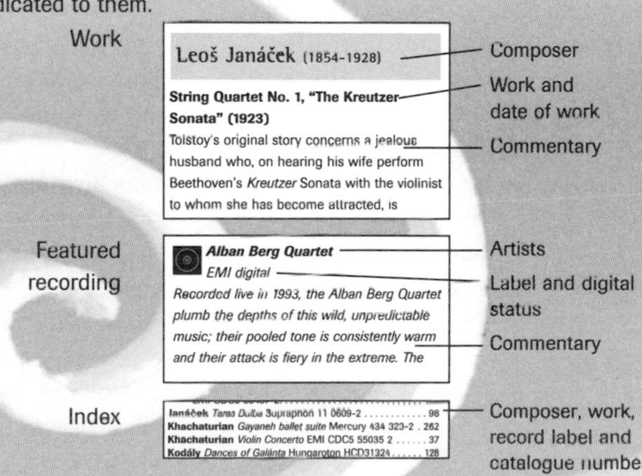

Early Concertos – A Baroque Bouquet (1714-1739)

'Concerto' originally meant 'playing together', but by the seventeenth century it implied a work where a small group of instruments is heard either in alternation or in combination with a larger group. This category contains some of the most joyous works in the repertory, from Bach's multi-coloured *Brandenburg Concertos*, through Handel's regal *Concerti grossi* to the buoyant rhythms of Vivaldi's *Four Seasons.*

Arcangelo Corelli (1653-1713)

Concerto grosso in G minor, Op. 6 No. 8, "Christmas Concerto" (published 1714)

It is said that Arcangelo Corelli always wore black and collected paintings that he never paid for. That aside, he was largely responsible for the development of the *Concerto grosso* form – a dialogue between small and large orchestral forces, the "concerto" being a small group of instrumentalists (in this case, two violins and a cello), and the "grosso", the 'answering' orchestra. The *Christmas Concerto*'s Italian folk-music origins are made manifest in a swaying *siciliano* (shepherds' music) and a bass-line that evokes a folk bagpipe.

I Musici
Philips digital

Versions of the Christmas Concerto abound, from Herbert von Karajan (DG, analogue) and Guido Cantelli (Music & Arts, mono) to Sir Neville Marriner (Decca, analogue) and period-instrument groups (La Petite Bande on DHM, analogue, and the Brandenburg Consort on Hyperion, digital). The last named present the whole opus, but I Musici is especially successful in balancing interpretative finesse, textural warmth and a sense of style. They present all of Op. 6's 12 concertos and perform on modern-day instruments. My advice is to go for broke and invest in 'the 12' – they're really beautiful works.

Antonio Vivaldi (1678-1741)

Concerto for violin and strings in E minor, Op. 11 No. 2 (RV277), "Il favorito" (published *c*1729-30)

Vivaldi composed numerous concertos for solo or multiple violins, most of which emanate from the 1720s. This particular piece is one of 12 concertos that he presented to Emperor Charles VI. The hub of the work is an exquisite *Andante* where the violin sings an extended line to a gentle accompaniment. The finale's opening recalls "Autumn" from *The Four Seasons.*

Concerto in C major for two flutes (or recorders), two theorbos, two mandolins, two chalumeaux, two violins, cello, strings and continuo, "con molti stromenti", RV558 (1740)

One of a group of works aptly named *concerti con molti stromenti* (which can be irreverently translated as "everything but the kitchen sink"). This particular piece was composed for a visit to the Pietà of Friedrich Christian, the then-new Electoral Prince of Saxony. It's among the most joyous concertos in the entire Baroque repertory, a sort of 'Seventh *Brandenburg*' (see under Bach, below) that vies with its twentieth-century successors in terms both of rhythmic thrust and varied tonal colouring.

Arthur Grumiaux (violin), Staatskapelle Dresden/Vittorio Negri
Philips analogue

Grumiaux's poetic reading of the Violin Concerto must be counted as one of the most beautiful Vivaldi recordings ever made: the slow movement in particular is touched by a rare and subtle expressiveness. RV558, on the other hand, is given with enormous gusto and the 1970s sound remains excellent. Viable alternatives (in RV558) include one by Leonard Bernstein with members of the New York Philharmonic (easygoing, a mite heavy-handed, but tremendous fun – Sony, analogue) and the superb period-instrument Il Giardino Armonico (Teldec, digital).

The Four Seasons ("The trial between harmony and invention", Op. 8: Concertos Nos. 1-4) (*c*1720)

Probably conceived as a court entertainment, Vivaldi's most popular masterpiece (itself a fourfold extraction from his most descriptive set of concertos) was based on four colourful sonnets by an unknown author. *The Four Seasons* is rich in graphic tone-painting, from bird-song in "Spring", through thunder, barking dogs, "balmy zephyrs", "a multitude of winds", dozing drunkards, rifle shots and dogs, a chase, fleeing wild animals and wild winds.

Enrico Onofri (violin), Il Giardino Armonico/Giovanni Antonini

Teldec digital

Performances of The Four Seasons tend to fall into one of two camps – the warm, elegantly tailored modern-instrument versions (exemplified by I Musici on Philips and Karajan on DG), and the raw, primary-coloured period-instrument versions, of which Il Giardino Armonico is among the most characterful. Nigel Kennedy's famous digital EMI recording brings 'period' wildness to a modern instrument, while Nikolaus Harnoncourt (Teldec, analogue) and Nils-Erik Sparf (BIS, digital – both are on period instruments) are probably the wildest of all.

Johann Sebastian Bach
(1685–1750)

Six Brandenburg Concertos (1708–21)

The most colourful, tuneful and texturally varied set of Baroque concertos and a watershed in the genre's development. Although written for the court orchestra at Cöthen (where Bach was Chapel-Master), the Concertos were dedicated to the Margrave Christian Ludwig von Brandenburg. At the time, they were neither as fashionable nor as widely discussed as the *Concerti grossi* of Corelli, Vivaldi and Handel (see above and below), but nowadays the *Brandenburgs* are among the most frequently performed (and recorded) instrumental works in the entire Baroque repertory.

Brandenburg Concerto No. 1 in F major for violin, oboes, horns, bassoons and strings, BWV1046 (1717)

Aside from its colourful scoring, the First *Brandenburg* is unusual in that the finale is a sequence of dances (a minuet and a polonaise, plus their respective 'trio' sections). The slow movement is a grave, extremely memorable *Adagio*.

Brandenburg Concerto No. 2 in F major for recorder/flute, oboe, trumpet, violin and strings, BWV1047 (1718)

The most festive-sounding of the six concertos, with clearly defined contrasts between soloists and a 'backing' group consisting of strings and a harpsichord. Bach wrote the virtuoso trumpet part so that his trumpeter at the Cöthen Court – one Johann Ludwig Schreiber – had some colourful display material to work with.

Brandenburg Concerto No. 3 in G major for strings, BWV1048 (1711–13)

A relatively concise, fiercely rhythmic composition, brilliantly written so that the three solo groups work in and around the main ensemble, sometimes adding to them, and sometimes highlighting just one player. The first movement has tremendous impetus, while the second is slighter and swifter – and probably never more so than in our recommended recording.

Brandenburg Concerto No. 4 in G major for violin, two recorders/flutes and strings, BWV1049 (*c*1720)

A delightful piece, pastoral in mood and additionally available in an alternative guise for harpsichord and strings (in F major, BWV1057). As with the Second and Fifth Concertos, Bach maximizes contrasts between the soloists and the tutti string band. The outer movements feature virtuosic violin writing and winsome work for duetting recorders.

Brandenburg Concerto No. 5 in D major for harpsichord, violin, flute and strings, BWV1050 (1720–21)

The first true keyboard concerto in the history of music features a vigorous opening *Allegro* that blossoms into a fully-fledged solo harpsichord cadenza. The skipping third movement – another *Allegro* – shows Bach at his most tuneful and extrovert.

Brandenburg Concerto No. 6 in B flat major for violas, cellos and double-bass, BWV1051 (1708–10)

A sombre instrumental line-up and in marked contrast to its brighter-toned companions. It's worth noting that Bach's employer at Cöthen was himself a viola da gamba player (the precursor of the modern cello) and, contrary to court etiquette, enjoyed joining in. The Sixth *Brandenburg* is the most sonorous of the group and includes what is surely the most beautiful slow movement of them all.

Musica Antiqua Köln/Reinhard Goebel

Archiv digital

With lean-sounding period instruments, quick-wristed virtuosity and some alarmingly fast tempos, these performances will either strike a sympathetic chord (as they do with me) or send you racing back to the shop for a refund. Those in search of a more temperate period-instrument statement might prefer either the generally lively Trevor Pinnock (with The English Concert – also DG Archiv, digital) or Sigiswald Kuijken's extremely musical Petite Bande set (Deutsche Harmonia Mundi, digital); whereas modern-instrument devotees are well served by Szymon Goldberg's deeply expressive accounts with the Netherlands Chamber Orchestra (Philips, analogue) and Karl Richter's incisively dispatched Munich Bach Orchestra set (DG Archiv, analogue).

All these recordings should yield a high level of musical satisfaction.

Concerto in C minor for two keyboards and strings, BWV1060 (*c*1732)

The leading attraction here is an especially beautiful *Adagio*, cool as spring air with the two players responding to each other over a warm accompaniment of plucked strings. However, although the scoring sounds absolutely right for the music, it wasn't Bach's first choice. The missing 'original' had the two solo parts allotted to oboe and violin (a later reconstruction has since become quite popular).

Robert and Gaby Casadesus (pianos), Zurich Chamber Orchestra/Edmond de Stoutz

Sony Classical analogue

Old-fashioned or not, the Casadesus (a husband and wife team) play with an elegance, warmth and Gallic charm that make the most of Bach's timeless score. Edmond de Stoutz directs a solid accompaniment, but those who prefer the 'authentic' sound of harpsichords might investigate Trevor Pinnock and Kenneth Gilbert on DG Archiv (digital).

Double Concerto in D minor for two violins, strings and continuo, BWV1043 (1717-23)

Bach's most celebrated concertos for violin – the ones included here – were the first concertos that he composed. His precedent had been the violin concertos of Vivaldi (*L'estro armonico* in particular, published in 1711), six of which he later transcribed for different instruments. The so-called Double Concerto features much excited contrapuntal interplay between the two soloists (specifically in the outer movements) and what is perhaps the best-known – and best-loved – of all Bach's instrumental slow movements.

Arthur Grumiaux and Herman Krebbers (violins), Solistes Romands/Arpad Gerecz

Philips analogue

The main problem with the Double Concerto is in achieving a balance between stylish restraint and romantic expression, something Grumiaux, Krebbers and the orchestra do with what sounds like unconscious facility. Rivals are plentiful (most of the best are analogue), notably David and Igor Oistrakh (DG, analogue), Yehudi Menuhin with George Enescu (EMI, mono) and Henryk Szeryng with Maurice Hasson (Philips, analogue). Alice and Nikolaus Harnoncourt (Teldec, analogue) provide a robust – and often startling – period-instrument alternative in all three violin concertos.

Harpsichord Concerto in D minor, BWV1052 (date unknown)

The most dramatic of all Bach's solo concertos opens with a stern *Allegro* – immensely powerful music with a strong rhythmic impetus. The slow movement features solo writing of almost operatic eloquence, flanked either side with a chant-like melody played on full strings. The finale – another urgent *Allegro* – revisits the uncompromising mood of the first movement, then climaxes to a fiery solo cadenza that builds in intensity before descending into a virtuoso maelstrom.

Karl Richter (harpsichord), Ansbach Bach Week Soloists/Karl Richter

Teldec mono

Most of the great D minors are played on the piano – Glenn Gould's performances (Sony, analogue) being among the most charismatic (at least three Gould alternatives have been released on CD). Richter's playing of the outer movements is appropriately muscular, although the Adagio is notably poetic. Teldec's mono sound is more than adequate.

Violin Concerto No. 1 in A minor, BWV1041 (1717-23)

The A minor Violin Concerto is characterized by great expressivity of tone (especially in the *Andante*) and a lilting, gigue-style third movement. Like its companion in E major (see below), it also exists in a version for keyboard and strings.

Jascha Heifetz (violin), Los Angeles Philharmonic Orchestra/Alfred Wallenstein

RCA mono

Those who suspect that Heifetz might overdose on emotion (he was, after all, one of the century's most vibrant virtuosos) should hear this poignant – and beautifully shaped – account of the A minor Concerto's Andante. Heifetz's tone is subtly inflected, his phrasing a model of poise and restraint. Fine analogue alternatives are legion, with Arthur Grumiaux (Philips) and David Oistrakh (DG) among the best. Simon Standage and Trevor Pinnock (DG Archiv, digital) lead the period-instrument field.

Violin Concerto No. 2 in E major, BWV1042 (1717-23)

The sunny first movement of the E major Violin Concerto – a vigorous *Allegro* – is virtually as long as the other two movements put together, whereas the expansively rhapsodic *Adagio* approximates Bach's Passion music at its most introspective. The finale is a spirited *Allegro* in triple time.

 ***David Oistrakh (violin), Royal Philharmonic Orchestra/Sir Eugene Goossens***

Deutsche Grammophon analogue

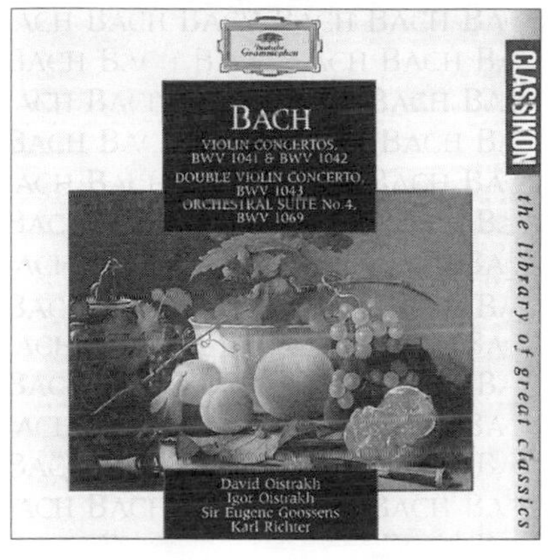

Warm, urbane playing, firmly accompanied and cleanly recorded. Oistrakh was the most thoughtful of virtuosos and yet his Bach has both spirit and heart. Heifetz (RCA, mono) is marginally more intense and Grumiaux (Philips, analogue) more wistful, but Oistrakh's interpretation is full of significant musical insights. However, those with a taste for 'old-style' Baroque should try and search out marvellous pre-war (mono) recordings by Mischa Elman (Pearl) and Bronislaw Huberman (APR).

George Frideric Handel
(1685-1759)

Concerti grossi, Op. 6 (1739)

The *Concerto grosso* is in effect a dialogue between a small group of players (or "concertino", consisting here of two violins and cello) and a larger band (usually strings, and known as the "ripieno"). There were basically two types – Vivaldi's, which were usually in three movements (fast-slow-fast, as utilized by Bach), and Corelli's (see above), which contained between four and eight movements. Handel followed Corelli's models, although his own very distinctive style shines through in music that is at once regal, buoyant and nobly lyrical.

Concerto grosso No. 5 in D major for two solo violins, solo cello, strings and bass continuo (with optional oboes and bassoons)

One of the two most famous concertos in the series, cast in six movements with an imperious opening *Larghetto e staccato*, a balletic *Presto* and a stately *Minuet: Un poco larghetto* to close.

Concerto grosso No. 7 in B flat major for strings and bass continuo

A particularly original statement, one that – some 200 years later – Arnold Schoenberg re-fashioned as a "Concerto for string quartet and orchestra". No. 7, which is in five movements, opens to a noble *Largo* and concludes with a pair of varied dance movements, a minuet style *Andante* and a lilting *Hornpipe*.

Concerto grosso No. 12 in B minor for two solo violins, solo cello, strings and bass continuo

The other familiar piece in the series, concise in its design and harbouring one of Handel's best-known melodies outside of *The Water Music* and *Messiah* – a beautiful Aria marked *Larghetto e piano*.

 ***Academy of St Martin in the Fields/ Sir Neville Marriner***

Decca analogue

Marriner, like Raymond Leppard before him (English Chamber Orchestra, Philips, also analogue), employs modern instruments for readings that combine elegance, rhythmic vitality and a certain stylistic decorum. Those who prefer a tougher, more blatantly assertive approach might try Nikolaus Harnoncourt and Concentus Musicus Wien (Teldec, digital – and on relatively thin-sounding period instruments), whereas Karl Richter's Munich Bach Orchestra (DG Archiv, analogue) is clean-cut and grandly imperious. Trevor Pinnock's English Concert (DG Archiv, digital) – again, on period instruments – is spirited and urbane, while the Orpheus Chamber Orchestra (DG, digital) offer an effective balance between light 'authentic-style' textures and the more familiar sonorities of modern instruments.

Organ Concerto No. 5 in F major, Op. 4 No. 5 (1735-36)
According to a contemporary report, Handel the organist had "a fine and delicate touch, a *volant* finger, and a ready delivery of passages the most difficult ...". He wrote his organ concertos primarily for his own personal use. There are two sets of six (plus various individual pieces), the second set (Op. 7) having been written during the composer's last creative period. Op. 4 No. 5 is a transcription of a Handel Flute Sonata (Op. 1 No. 11) and is among the loveliest of the series, opening with a serene *Larghetto*, followed by a perky *Allegro*, a lilting *Alla siciliana* and ending with a festive *Presto*.

Organ Concerto No. 6 in B flat major, Op. 4 No. 6 (1735-36)
The Sixth Organ Concerto is an absolute delight. Cast in three movements, it also exists in arrangements for harp (an especially popular transcription), harpsichord and recorder. The first movement is a piping *Andante-Allegro*, the second a *Larghetto* dialogue between organ and strings and the third an elegant *Allegro moderato*.

Ton Koopman (organ), Amsterdam Baroque Orchestra
Erato digital
As ever, Koopman's performances generate tremendous enthusiasm and the Erato recordings (made at St Bartholomew's Church, Beek-Ubbergen, Holland) are quite superb. Alternative versions include the flamboyant Herbert Tachezi under Nikolaus Harnoncourt (Teldec, digital) and a breezy, bright-toned Czech set by Jaroslav Tuma and the Virtuosi di Praga (Supraphon, analogue). Those who fancy the harp version of Op. 6 No. 6 are directed to Marisa Robles with the Academy of St Martin in the Fields under Sir Neville Marriner (Decca, analogue).

Classical Dialogues (1775-1806)

The concertos of Haydn and Mozart generally subscribe to the 'three movement' (fast-slow-fast) design already used by, say, Vivaldi. But although Baroque composers often hinted at what we'd now loosely call 'romantic' writing (especially in their slow movements), the concertos of Mozart and the young Beethoven explored new levels of invention.

Joseph Haydn (1732-1809)

Piano Concerto in D major, HobXVIII:II (1784)
The most popular of Haydn's numerous keyboard concertos opens with a sparkling *Vivace* – the sort of quick-witted, elegant Classicism that cries out for a pianistic colourist. There's a song-like slow movement that, although not quite on a par with 'top drawer' Mozart, has genuine charm, and a lively final rondo marked *all'Ungarese* (referring to its gipsy music allusions).

Martha Argerich (piano), Württemberg Chamber Orchestra, Heilbronn/Jörg Faerber
Deutsche Grammophon digital
Argerich treats Haydn's D major as something of an organized firework display: her finger-work is immaculate, her touch feather-light and her sense of rhythm (and style) impeccable. She plays a second-movement cadenza by the great Polish-born harpsichordist Wanda Landowska and indeed Landowska's own recording is well worth hearing, as is Arturo Benedetti Michelangeli's (both are EMI analogue recordings – Landowska's in mono, Michelangeli's in stereo).

Trumpet Concerto in E flat major, HobV11e/1 (1796)
One of two well-known Classical concertos for keyed trumpet (the other is by Johann Nepomuk Hummel), Haydn's E flat is trim and tuneful. The first four notes of the *Andante* anticipate Haydn's *Emperor* String Quartet of three years later (the one which uses the Austrian National Anthem in its slow movement) and there's a sparkling *Allegro* to close.

Håkan Hardenberger (trumpet), Academy of St Martin in the Fields/Sir Neville Marriner
Philips digital
A brilliant though warm-toned rendition by the leading trumpeter of the 1990s (he also contributes his own first-movement cadenza). Marriner and his band provide a predictably pert orchestral backdrop and Philips's disc also includes the Hummel E major, Hertel's Concerto in D and a first recording of a reconstructed concerto by Johann Stamitz.

Wolfgang Amadeus Mozart
(1756-1791)

Clarinet Concerto in A major, K622 (1791)

The clarinettist Anton Stadler was a member of Mozart's Masonic lodge; he even travelled with Mozart to Prague to perform in the opera *La clemenza di Tito*. Stadler was an astonishing virtuoso who pioneered the so-called basset clarinet (which extended the range of the regular instrument downwards by four semitones) and it was for him – and it – that Mozart composed his great Clarinet Concerto, the slow movement of which is especially sublime.

Ernst Ottensamer (basset clarinet), Vienna Philharmonic Orchestra/Sir Colin Davis

Philips digital

Warmth of tone, ease of delivery and an instrument that realizes the full tonal range of Mozart's original inspiration make this a particularly winning account of the Clarinet Concerto. Older (analogue) alternatives featuring the incomparable Jack Brymer (under Beecham on EMI, or Davis and Marriner on Philips) are also strongly recommended.

Concerto for flute, harp and orchestra in C major, K299/297*c* (1778)

A concerto that was fashioned specifically for the Duc de Guines (a former French Ambassador to England) and his daughter. "The Duc plays the flute incomparably," Mozart wrote to his father, "and his daughter … plays the harp *magnifique*." The real prize here is the tender slow movement – so romantic in its harmonic language and yet cast well within the bounds of Classical propriety.

Joshua Smith (flute), Lisa Wellbaum (harp), Cleveland Orchestra/ Christoph von Dohnányi

Decca digital

Such beautiful music seems almost to play itself – or at least that's the impression one gets from an unselfconsciously musical performance such as this. 'Classical' or 'poised' would be fair descriptions of Dohnányi's conducting, while Decca's well-balanced sound is an extra bonus. Worthy analogue alternatives include Sir Thomas Beecham (EMI, mono) and Sir Neville Marriner (Philips).

Concerto for two pianos and orchestra in E flat major, K365/316*a* (1779)

Mozart composed his delightful two-piano Concerto on returning to Salzburg after an extended visit abroad. He was in the service of the Prince-Archbishop at the time and envisaged performances with his sister Nannerl. In fact, the exuberant finale is based on one of Nannerl's favourite melodies. As with the great *Sinfonie concertante* for violin and viola (also in E flat major, see below), the first movement is especially majestic, while the *Andante* slow movement is rich in exquisite musical dialogue.

Robert and Gaby Casadesus (pianos), Philadelphia Orchestra/Eugene Ormandy

Sony Classical analogue

Husband and wife invest Mozart's score with maximum sparkle and although Ormandy's Philadelphia accompaniment is somewhat heavier than we're used to nowadays, it's still pretty boisterous. The 1960 recording reports a slightly shallow piano sound, but is otherwise perfectly acceptable. Viable alternatives include Alfred Brendel and Imogen Cooper (Philips, analogue) and Daniel Barenboim with András Schiff (Decca, digital).

Horn Concerto No. 3 in E flat major, K447 (1787)

There are four completed Mozart horn concertos (they were originally composed for a valveless or 'natural' horn), three of which are in the key of E flat. All were probably written for Joseph Leutgeb, a 'hunting-horn' player and fellow-Mason. The Third is scored for clarinets, bassoons and strings and includes an especially lovely *Romanze*. Both the Third and the Fourth Concertos are well-known primarily for their catchy finales.

Dennis Brain (horn), Philharmonia Orchestra/Herbert von Karajan

EMI mono

Recommending the late Dennis Brain in the Mozart horn concertos has become something of a critical cliché, and yet the playing is so deft and polished, the accompaniments so discreetly musical, and the 1953 recordings so very good for their age, that the recommendation still stands. However, there are countless worthy rivals, not least Barry Tuckwell with The Academy of St Martin in the Fields under Sir Neville Marriner (EMI, digital).

Piano Concerto No. 9 in E flat major, K271, "Jeunehomme" (1777)

The first great Mozart piano concerto, named after the French pianist who premièred it.

The second movement – one of Mozart's darkest – is full of anguish, while a *Cantabile* Minuet suddenly appears mid-way through the *Presto* finale. Mozart composed three separate sets of cadenzas for this concerto, and our chosen pianist (Andreas Staier) uses the second of them.

Andreas Staier (fortepiano), Concerto Köln
Teldec digital
Like Géza Anda (DG, analogue), Daniel Barenboim (EMI, analogue) and various other top-ranking pianists, Andreas Staier directs the orchestra (in this case, an on-the-ball period-instrument band) from the keyboard. His is a vital, highly spontaneous account, warmly shaped in the slow movement and with a range of expression that's particularly rare on fortepiano recordings (the instrument's sound falls mid-way between a harpsichord and a piano). Clara Haskil (Philips, mono) provides a fine historical alternative, while András Schiff (Decca) dominates the digital field – on a standard modern piano, that is.

Piano Concerto No. 15 in B flat major, K450 (1784)

A marked advancement over its immediate predecessors in that Mozart granted important parts to oboes and bassoons (his previous four piano concertos offered the option of an all-strings accompaniment). The first movement is playful and ebullient, the second an ornamental theme and variations and the occasionally martial finale (which introduces the flute for the first time) recalls the spirit of the hunt. K450 is one of two concertos that Mozart thought would "make one sweat" (the other is K451).

Alfred Brendel (piano), Academy of St Martin in the Fields/ Sir Neville Marriner
Philips digital
A crisp, keenly articulated reading, urgent though never hard pressed. Marriner's mastery of dynamics is especially effective in the finale and the sound is very well balanced. Fine alternatives include Géza Anda (DG, analogue), Robert Casadesus (Sony, analogue) and an especially distinguished mono recording by the great Arturo Benedetti Michelangeli (EMI).

Piano Concerto No. 17 in G major, K453 (1784)

One of the works that Mozart composed for Barbara Ployer, and one of six masterly concertos that were crafted during 1784 (the others being K449, 450, 451, 456 and 459). It's the sort of piece that operates on various levels – easygoing on the surface, but with a certain resilience and a great strength of purpose (Beethoven must surely have been influenced by it). The aria-like slow movement is among Mozart's loveliest, while the delightful theme-and-variations finale starts out to a melody that anticipates *The Magic Flute*'s "Bird-catcher's aria".

Géza Anda (piano), Salzburg Mozarteum Camerata Academica
Deutsche Grammophon analogue
With breezy, open sound, a sweet (though occasionally rather thin) string tone, pert woodwinds and habitually elegant turns of phrase, this remains among the finest performances in Anda's admirable cycle (it was in fact the first complete set of the concertos to be recorded in stereo). Finger-work is supple and left-hand counter-melodies subtly underlined. As to rivals – Maria João Pires (DG digital), Brendel (Philips, analogue) and Andreas Staier (fortepiano – Deutsche Harmonia Mundi, digital) lead the ranks.

Piano Concerto No. 19 in F major, K459 (1784)

The last of the great '1784' concertos is notably rich in orchestral incident (the highly contrapuntal finale is remarkable in this respect). However, for this writer, it's the slow movement that most haunts the memory – especially the tragic 'falling' sequence approximately 40 seconds from the opening. Mozart was highly adept at making the soloist 'first among equals' (his own status in performance), and this particular concerto is a fine example of his dialogic mode of writing.

Clara Haskil (piano), Berlin Philharmonic Orchestra/ Ferenc Fricsay
Deutsche Grammophon mono

A pianist who was noted for her beautiful tone, control of musical line, perceptive phrasing (which was neither cold nor overly expressive) and unassuming virtuosity. This is a very famous performance, stylishly conducted by Fricsay (a regular musical collaborator) and very well recorded for the 1950s. As to competition, Brendel (Philips,

analogue – there's also an earlier Vox recording) and Christian Zacharias (EMI, digital) are among the best.

Piano Concerto No. 20 in D minor, K466 (1785)

The first of Mozart's concertos where the *Allegro* tutti (purely orchestral writing) and solo work are in marked contrast to each other. The opening is quiet, tense and tragic in tone (not unlike the G minor Symphony), whereas the ensuing solo suggests an inward lament. The eloquent second movement is interrupted half-way through by an anguished faster section while the finale returns us to the sombre mood of the first movement.

Clara Haskil (piano), Berlin RIAS Orchestra/ Ferenc Fricsay

Deutsche Grammophon mono

Haskil was one of the century's greatest Mozartians and her account of the Concerto's central Romance has a unique poise and sensitivity. Fricsay's accompaniment is admirably discreet, but if it has to be stereo (this version was recorded in mono in 1954), then Brendel (Philips), Anda (DG) or indeed Haskil's own stereo remake (slightly inferior to this, under Markevitch and issued on Philips) should fit the bill. All are analogue recordings.

Piano Concerto No. 21 in C minor, K467, "Elvira Madigan" (1785)

Although employment in a film soundtrack might seem a flimsy excuse for appending an ephemeral title to a major masterpiece, there can be little doubt that the film *Elvira Madigan* did more to popularize Mozart than anything prior to Peter Schaffer's 1979 play *Amadeus*. The Concerto's opening *Allegro* is rich in varied material while its central *Andante* – the movement used in the film – is a sublime solo melody set against quiet string triplets. The finale is irrepressibly joyful.

Géza Anda (piano), Salzburg Mozarteum Camerata Academica

Deutsche Grammophon analogue

Anda is a prime recommendation in Mozart (he recorded all the concertos and his performances are among the best available), but this reading is special, not only because it is the actual version used in the film Elvira Madigan (and therefore the best known recording of all), but – more significantly – it represents Anda's Mozartian style at its most elegant and beguiling. As to alternative versions, Robert Casadesus (Sony, analogue) and Alfred Brendel (Philips, digital) warrant serious consideration.

Piano Concerto No. 22 in E flat major, K482 (1785)

A work that marks the meeting of two worlds – the outwardly ceremonial (the first movement's majestic demeanour) and the infinitely reflective (the expansive slow movement, with its tragic episodes in C minor). Woodwinds are important throughout, the clarinets especially although a baleful bassoon plays a prominent role in the second movement. The closing Rondo is unusual in that roughly half-way through, the initial, child-like first theme gives way to a far slower, minuet-style idea that's treated to an especially wide range of instrumental colours.

Annie Fischer (piano), Philharmonia Orchestra/Wolfgang Sawallisch

EMI analogue

Fischer's Mozart is forthright but never overbearing, delicate but never merely 'pretty'. It's Mozart as viewed from a Beethovenian standpoint, although there's filigree detail to spare and Sawallisch's accompaniment is consistently sensitive. Viable stereo alternatives include Brendel (Philips, analogue) and Christian Zacharias (EMI, digital), with Rudolf Serkin (Sony), Edwin Fischer (EMI, 'live' from Salzburg – the slow movement is truly wonderful) and Artur Schnabel (Music & Arts) offering strong reportage from the mono era.

Piano Concerto No. 23 in A major, K488 (1786)

The first of three concertos that have frequently been compared with the last three symphonies (the others are K491 and K503): in both cases the middle work – the one in the minor key – has a basically tragic demeanour. The A major, which was completed just prior to the première of *The Marriage of Figaro*, suggests a mood of quiet contentment, while the central *Adagio* opens to a melody of such extraordinary beauty that one is at a loss as to imagine how Mozart could possibly maintain his inspiration. Of course he does – first with a delightful second subject and then with an ebullient Rondo finale.

Robert Casadesus (piano), Columbia Symphony Orchestra/George Szell

Sony Classical analogue

A Gallic approach to Mozart – cool, elegant and with a buoyant accompaniment under Szell: the finale, in particular, is admirably crisp and well articulated. The analogue recording is very clear, though perhaps a little too bright for some, which is why I'd be tempted to consider András Schiff (Decca, digital), Alfred Brendel (Philips, analogue) and Daniel Barenboim (Teldec, digital) as viable alternatives.

Piano Concerto No. 24 in C minor, K491 (1786)
Beethoven considered this to be Mozart's finest concerto. In fact, he once told his pupil Ries "we shall never write anything like this" (even though Beethoven's own C minor – his Third Concerto – runs it pretty close). And you can certainly understand his fascination with the first movement's questioning opening melody, its whispering coda, the deceptively simple slow movement and the earnestness of the *Allegretto*'s variations.

Wilhelm Kempff (piano), Bamberg Symphony Orchestra/Ferdinand Leitner
Deutsche Grammophon analogue
It takes a great Beethovenian to bring out Mozart's anticipations of the mature Beethoven's style and Wilhelm Kempff certainly has the credentials for the job. His is a finely sculpted account, thoughtful though never ponderous – but there are other good C minors from Casadesus (Sony, analogue), Annie Fischer (EMI, analogue), Clara Haskil (Philips, analogue) and Daniel Barenboim (EMI, analogue).

Piano Concerto No. 25 in C major, K503 (1786)
Again, the first movement is a positively Beethovenian statement – strong and heroic and mirrored by a carefree but relatively restrained closing *Allegretto*. The heart of the work, however, is a serenely peaceful *Andante* with subtly interweaving themes. This was the last of the 12 magnificent concertos that Mozart composed between 1784 and 1786, although – and here I quote Alfred Einstein – "in no other concerto does the relation between the soloist and the orchestra vary so constantly and so unpredictably".

Alfred Brendel (piano), Academy of St Martin in the Fields/Sir Neville Marriner
Philips analogue
Typically intelligent playing, sensitively phrased and acutely responsive to every unexpected twist in Mozart's dialogue. Fine accompaniments, too, very well recorded – but there's a first-rate digital option from András Schiff and Sándor Végh (Decca).

Piano Concerto No. 26 in D major, K537, "Coronation" (1788)
An assertive though fairly conventional concerto that proclaims its operatic points of reference loud and clear (the deceptively simple *Larghetto* is reminiscent both of *The Magic Flute* and *Don Giovanni*). The title reminds us that on October 15th, 1790 Mozart played the work (together with his Concerto No. 19) at the Coronation of Emperor Leopold II in Frankfurt.

Friedrich Gulda (piano), Royal Concertgebouw Orchestra/Nikolaus Harnoncourt
Teldec digital
Two famous 'enfants terribles' in full cry, Gulda tickling the solo line with sundry embellishments (he plays along with the orchestra too, as per the traditions of the day), and Harnoncourt responding with some manfully assertive conducting. The sound is superb – but those in search of something a little more orthodox are directed either to Robert Casadesus (Sony, analogue) or Christian Zacharias (EMI, digital).

Piano Concerto No. 27 in B flat major, K595 (1791)
Mozart's last piano concerto mixes melodic serenity with moments of profound disquiet. Best-known is the central *Larghetto*, which opens with child-like simplicity (the soloist plays alone) only to be greeted – at around two minutes into the movement – with relatively dark orchestral textures. The finale's main theme recalls an eighteenth-century music-box, though much of the writing that follows is extremely brilliant.

Emil Gilels (piano), Vienna Philharmonic Orchestra/Karl Böhm
Deutsche Grammophon analogue
A musical partnership that captures the music's autumnal hues without compromising its gaiety. Both Gilels and Böhm were accomplished classicists (Böhm was in any case a famous Mozartian), the Vienna Philharmonic play like angels and the recording retains the full measure of its original bloom. Favoured alternatives include Casadesus (Sony, analogue) and Barenboim (Teldec, digital).

Sinfonia concertante in E flat major for violin, viola and orchestra, K364/320*d* (1779)
The finely tensed opening and ensuing crescendo suggest a work of symphonic proportions and indeed Mozart sets virtuoso duetting against an immensely strong orchestral backdrop. The slow movement, composed around the time that Mozart lost his mother, is a heart-rending elegy and the finale an exuberant *Presto*. This is unquestionably one of Mozart's greatest concertos.

Igor Oistrakh (violin), David Oistrakh (viola), Moscow Philharmonic Orchestra/Kyrill Kondrashin
Decca analogue
Father and son in earnest dialogue, characterfully supported by what was at the time (early-1960s) one of Soviet Russia's two greatest orchestras. Earlier analogue rivals include three fine versions featuring the great

Scottish-born violist William Primrose – with Jascha Heifetz (RCA, analogue), Isaac Stern (Sony, mono) and Albert Spalding (Biddulph, mono – and perhaps the most eloquent of the three). The finest digital recording is by Gidon Kremer and Kim Kashkashian conducted by Nikolaus Harnoncourt (DG, digital).

Violin Concerto No. 3 in G major, K216 (1775)

When Mozart wrote to his father boasting that he had played the violin "as if I were the greatest fiddler in all of Europe", his father wrote back urging even more energy and dedication. It seems almost certain that the five authenticated violin concertos (there are at least two more of doubtful origin) were written primarily for the composer himself to play. The Third is the most popular of the set, its central *Adagio* serving as the very epitome of Mozartian elegance and tunefulness.

 ***Arthur Grumiaux (violin), London Symphony Orchestra/Sir Colin Davis***

Philips analogue

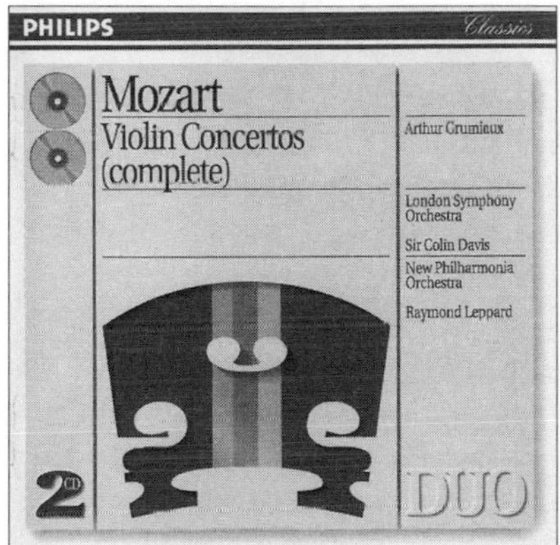

Grumiaux was the ultimate in refined musicianship, an immaculate player whose sweet, though never overbearing tone was ideal for Mozart. This particular version is included as part of a complete set of the concertos, currently accommodated on two CDs and including the great Sinfonia concertante in E flat for violin and viola plus shorter works. There's also a superb historic recording of the Third Concerto by the young Yehudi Menuhin (Biddulph, mono).

Violin Concerto No. 5 in A major, K219, "Turkish" (1775)

The nickname *Turkish* originates from Mozart's employment of exotic dance-like material for the closing Rondo – similar in outline to the lively Turkish-style music he later composed for his opera *The Abduction from the Seraglio*. The Fifth is probably the finest of Mozart's violin concertos and, like the Third, has a sublime *Adagio* at its core.

 ***Jascha Heifetz (violin), Chamber Orchestra***

RCA analogue

A tough, assertive performance with a seductively sweet centre: Heifetz extracts more expressive potential from a single bar of the Adagio than most other violinists manage for the entire concerto. He recorded the work three times, but this is his most invigorating version. However, Grumiaux (Philips, analogue) remains a delightful first option for those in need of all five concertos.

Ludwig van Beethoven
(1770–1827)

Concerto for violin, cello, piano and orchestra in C major, Op. 56, "Triple" (1803-04)

Composed for the Archduke Rudolf and two musicians who were in his service, the Triple Concerto is anything but a virtuoso *tour de force*. Neither is it particularly profound, and yet its winsome ideas, lusty orchestral writing and general sense of well-being (especially in the first movement) make it a joy to encounter. The slow movement is short and sweet (just five or so minutes), the finale a vigorous Rondo in the form of a polonaise.

 ***Eugene Istomin (piano), Isaac Stern (violin), Leonard Rose (cello), Philadelphia Orchestra/Eugene Ormandy***

Sony Classical analogue

There have been many glitzy Triples but none that quite rivals the warmth, vitality and sheer physical thrust of this superb performance under Ormandy. Sony have also issued another, rather more intimate account with Rudolf Serkin, Leslie Parnas and Jaime Laredo (under the excellent Alexander Schneider), but this version – by a bona fide piano trio – has a grandeur all its own.

Piano Concerto No. 1 in C major, Op. 15 (1797)

A brief look at the heading tells us that, like Chopin's two piano concertos, Beethoven's 'official' first and second are numbered according to publication date rather than to their date of composition. What's doubly confusing is that the First so obviously marks an advance over its predecessor, what with its expansive orchestral introduction, thematic variety (especially in the first movement), poetic slow movement and lively, syncopated finale.

 ***Maurizio Pollini (piano), Berlin Philharmonic Orchestra/Claudio Abbado***

Deutsche Grammophon digital

Recorded live during 1992, Pollini's second Beethoven concerto cycle marks something of an interpretative advance on his already excellent first (also out on CD). The First Concerto is played with sovereign authority and great technical aplomb, although I wouldn't want to forego earlier recordings by Géza Anda (in the studio on EMI mono, or live on Orfeo analogue), Sviatoslav Richter (Preludio, Praga or RCA, analogue mono/stereo) or Wilhelm Kempff (1953, DG, mono).

Piano Concerto No. 2 in B flat major, Op. 19 (1793, revised 1794-95)

The Second is – as I've already implied – the first of Beethoven's five piano concertos, although there was an even earlier piece, dating from the composer's fifteenth year. The B flat, however, is sprightly, tuneful and very securely based on Mozartian models. The Concerto's most celebrated movement is its gaily rocking finale, a brief but fetching Rondo.

 ***Leon Fleisher (piano), Cleveland Orchestra/George Szell***
Sony Classical analogue

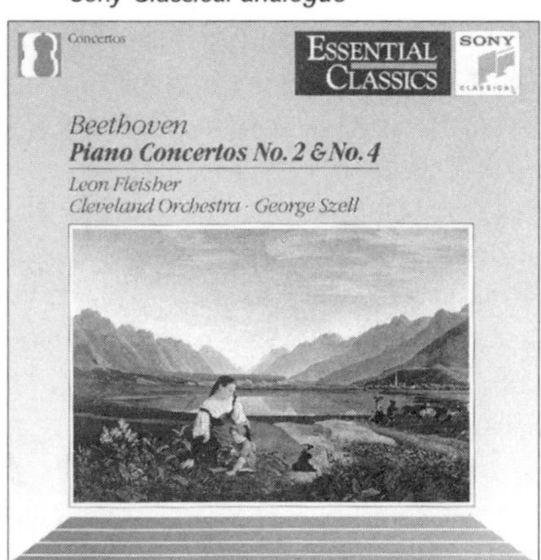

Cerebral but incredibly alive, with superb orchestral support under Szell. The whole cycle is worth hearing, but the Second is especially good. Viable analogue alternatives feature the unpredictable but brilliant Glenn Gould (behaving himself, on Sony, mono), Rudolf Serkin (Sony again – they have something of a monopoly on this piece) and Martha Argerich (DG, digital).

Violin Concerto in D major, Op. 61 (1806)

An 'anti-virtuoso' violin concerto, large-scale and intense (the long orchestral introduction is immensely strong), with a sublime slow movement and a lively Rondo. It's little wonder that early audiences were confused and that at the Concerto's first performance, soloist Franz Clement lightened the atmosphere by interpolating acrobatic solos between the movements!

 ***Gidon Kremer (violin), Chamber Orchestra of Europe/Nikolaus Harnoncourt***
Teldec digital

This Violin Concerto's recorded past is studded with miracles – Joseph Szigeti (Pearl, Sony, mono), Bronislaw Huberman (APR, mono), Fritz Kreisler (Biddulph, Pearl, Grammofono, mono), Jascha Heifetz (RCA – under Charles Munch analogue, or Toscanini, mono), David Oistrakh (EMI, analogue), have all achieved marvels of perception and technique. Gidon Kremer is their modern counterpart, a lean, agile interpreter who refuses to dawdle and adds interest by transcribing the cadenza that Beethoven originally wrote for his piano transcription of the score. But of the historic league, Huberman is the boldest and Szigeti the most thoughtful.

The Great Romantics (1800-1909)

Mozart had already anticipated the 'Romantic Revolution' in his 22nd and 24th Piano Concertos, but it was Beethoven who built triumphant orations into his Third, Fourth and Fifth Piano Concertos. Thereafter, Romanticism was in full cry and if the heart sometimes ruled the head, the greatest composers effected a balance between musical structure and emotion. This is the era that saw the birth of virtuoso extravagance – Paganini, Tchaikovsky, Rachmaninov, fabulous fingers and a plethora of musical legends. Here, as in "The Twentieth-Century Concerto" (see below) we also include some shorter works that are more concertos than not.

Ludwig van Beethoven
(1770-1827)

Piano Concerto No. 3 in C minor, Op. 37 (*c*1800)

Mozart's influence might at first suggest we place this great work under "Classical Dialogues", except that here the Mozartian axis centres more on melodrama: we'd probably be more justified in placing Mozart's 24th Concerto (on obvious forerunner of Beethoven's Third) under "The Great Romantics". The first movement's extended introduction is full of storm and stress, while the *Largo* slow movement has a lyrical intensity that borders on the operatic. The finale is a dancing Rondo.

Rudolf Serkin (piano), New York Philharmonic Orchestra/Leonard Bernstein

Sony Classical analogue

Forceful and passionate, though Serkin – a fine Beethovenian by any standards – treats structure as a leading priority. A personal favourite has Arturo Benedetti Michelangeli on resplendent form (as recorded live under Giulini, on DG, analogue), though some will find his tempi too slow and the piano too closely balanced. Wilhelm Kempff (DG, his mono recording) and Clara Haskil (Philips, analogue) are also superb, though rather less assertive than Serkin.

Piano Concerto No. 4 in G major, Op. 58 (1805-06)

The pianist raises the curtain with a quiet, pious statement of the first movement's principle motive. Thereafter it's a combination of Classical simplicity and the most musical manner of pianistic display, with running passages that approximate strings of pearls and beautifully arched phrases. The slow movement begins by alternating stern orchestral statements and humble solo responses while the joyful finale – which is cast in Beethoven's most dramatic vein – is full of urgent dialogic cross-fire.

Radu Lupu (piano), Israel Philharmonic Orchestra/Zubin Mehta

Decca analogue

Wonderfully sensitive playing, intelligently supported by Mehta and the orchestra. Again Serkin provides an essential option (preferably under Toscanini, on RCA, mono) and so do Leon Fleisher (under Szell, Sony, analogue) and Murray Perahia (under Bernard Haitink, Sony, digital). Schnabel's 1942 recording (under Frederick Stock, RCA, mono) is interpretatively superb while Pollini's digital live recording (under Abbado, DG) also has many unforgettable moments.

Piano Concerto No. 5 in E flat major, Op. 73, "Emperor" (1809)

Although by the time he wrote his Fifth Piano Concerto Beethoven had lost his admiration for Napoleon (the original dedicatee of the *Eroica* Symphony), the *Emperor* nickname remains justified. The very opening is both regal and heroic: full orchestral chords interspersed with brief solo cadenzas lead to an imperious orchestral tutti and 20 minutes of animated dialogue. The slow movement ranks with that of the Violin Concerto as being among Beethoven's finest; then, beyond a teasing introduction, the brilliant finale provides ample opportunity for (musical) pianistic display.

Leon Fleisher (piano), Cleveland Orchestra/George Szell

Sony Classical analogue

A grand, fairly 'central' reading, strong in every department. But competition here is especially fierce, not least from Murray Perahia (under Haitink, Sony, digital), Vladimir Horowitz (under Fritz Reiner, RCA, mono), Alfred Brendel (under James Levine, Philips, digital) and Artur Schnabel (under Stock, RCA, mono)

Niccolò Paganini (1782-1840)

Violin Concerto No. 1 in E flat major, Op. 6 (*c*1817)

Paganini's First Concerto (there are six in all) is a feast of simple but attractive ideas, sugary tunes and wrist-twisting solo writing. Although composed in the key of E flat, Paganini wrote the violin part in D minor with the instruction that the soloist tune the violin's open strings a semitone higher than usual – a ploy which, in addition to facilitating a match with the orchestral key, lends considerable brilliance to the solo part.

Shmuel Ashkenazi (violin), Vienna Symphony Orchestra/Hermin Esser

Deutsche Grammophon analogue

Ashkenazi's sweet-toned Paganini First is one of the most enjoyable of the stereo era. However, there's an even more brilliant account – albeit one that's over 60 years old – from the 16-year-old Yehudi Menuhin (EMI or Biddulph, mono), a miracle of spontaneous playing and virtually on a par with Menuhin's legendary account of the Elgar Violin Concerto (see below).

Carl Maria von Weber
(1786 1826)

Clarinet Concerto No. 1 in F minor, J114 (1811)

Weber composed the finest clarinet concertos after Mozart and before Copland (they were written specifically for the great Munich clarinettist Heinrich Baermann). The First has the attraction of an especially sublime second movement where mid-way through (2'45" on track 2 of our chosen recording), the orchestra falls silent and three horns provide a warming backdrop for the soloist to continue. It is an unforgettable moment in a concerto that also boasts a vigorous though lyrical Rondo finale.

Sharon Kam (clarinet), Leipzig Gewandhaus Orchestra/Kurt Masur

Teldec digital

If you want to hear some really exceptional clarinet playing, then listen from 4'50" into the second movement where Sharon Kam ushers back the Adagio's principal theme. It's pure magic! The Leipzig orchestra's warm-textured accompaniment is well-nigh ideal, and so is the recording. No need to look further – though if perchance you need to, Charles Neidich and the Orpheus Chamber Orchestra (DG, digital) should also give much pleasure.

Felix Mendelssohn (1809-1847)

Violin Concerto in E minor, Op. 64 (1844)
Mendelssohn composed this concerto (his second) for Ferdinand David, leader of the Leipzig Gewandhaus Orchestra – although another virtuoso, the young Joseph Joachim, provided additional inspiration. The Concerto is fashioned very much 'of a piece', with a substantially eventful *Allegro molto appassionato* placed first (the second theme is one of Mendelssohn's loveliest), a songful *Andante* and – beyond a tender Introduction – a glittering, elfin finale.

 ***Arthur Grumiaux (violin), Concertgebouw Orchestra/Bernard Haitink***
Philips analogue
Interpreters of the Mendelssohn concertos can be roughly divided into two camps, the musical virtuoso (Heifetz, Stern, Milstein, Gitlis, Vengerov, Perlman, etc) and the virtuoso musician (Kreisler, Szigeti, Francescatti, Suk and, of course, Arthur Grumiaux). Grumiaux's performance is tender, poised and warmly phrased, with excellent orchestral support under Haitink – but all the above named deserve to be heard, Heifetz (RCA, 1959 stereo recording) and Kreisler (Pearl or Biddulph, mono), especially.

Fryderyk Chopin (1810-1849)

Piano Concerto No. 1 in E minor, Op. 11 (1830)
Chopin's Second Piano was actually composed before his First, the reverse numbering having been prompted by a publishing technicality. Musically, the First is proud, lyrical and decorative, with sturdy (rather than particularly inspired) orchestration and an especially fetching central *Romance*. The finale is a delightful, dance-like Rondo.

 ***Maurizio Pollini (piano), Philharmonia Orchestra/Paul Kletzki***
EMI analogue

Recorded in the wake of his victory at the Warsaw Chopin Competition in 1960, Pollini's account of the First Concerto has all the hallmarks of his mature Chopin style (several examples of which serve as fill-ups on the CD) – namely control, sculpted phrasing, immaculate timing and consumate musicianship. Technically, it's a superb reading – although Artur Rubinstein (RCA analogue or EMI mono) is unrivalled for aristocratic wisdom and Moritz Rosenthal (a very old recording on Pearl Opal, mono), for stylish bravura.

Piano Concerto No. 2 in F minor, Op. 21 (1829)
Comparing the first of Chopin's piano concertos (this one) with its successor ('No. 1', see above) reveals a more lyrical strain in the earlier work, especially its first movement (the E minor is relatively imperious). However, it's the magical *Larghetto* that makes the most powerful effect – much as it did when Chopin premièred the Concerto in March 1830.

 ***Artur Rubinstein (piano), Philadelphia Orchestra/ Eugene Ormandy***
RCA analogue
Rubinstein surveys the glorious Larghetto with matchless poise and tonal warmth; his rubato is wholly natural, his technique perhaps not quite as agile as it once was (in three earlier recordings of the work) but the performance scores by dint of its elegance, solid accompaniment and full-bodied sound. Krystian Zimerman provides a cultivated alternative to Rubinstein (DG, digital, coupled with Concerto No. 1), while the 'old school' is eloquently represented by Alfred Cortot's memorable pre-war (mono) EMI recording.

Robert Schumann (1810-1856)

Cello Concerto in A minor, Op. 129 (1850)
Schumann in the late autumn of his composing career, reflective, mellow and alternating bold resolution (orchestral episodes) with an intimate brand of poetry (the slow movement is especially lovely). He was himself an amateur cellist and his knowledge of the instrument adds a further perspective to a work that, in addition to its own perennial qualities, anticipates Elgar's great Concerto of almost 70 years later.

Heinrich Schiff (cello), Berlin Philharmonic Orchestra/Bernard Haitink
Philips digital

Music-making of the highest order, with a terrific sense of give-and-take, vibrant in tone (Schiff achieves fever-pitch intensity in the slow movement) though always warmly considered. Older alternatives include a passionately emphatic performance by Casals (Sony, mono) and the more refined – but technically infallible – János Starker (EMI, Mercury or Philips, all analogue).

Piano Concerto in A minor, Op. 54 (1841-45)

"The Concerto is something between a symphony, a concerto and a large sonata," wrote Schumann to his wife Clara; "I find I cannot write a concerto for virtuosos." In fact the first movement started life as a separate *Rhapsody* for piano and orchestra (1841). The dramatic opening immediately draws the pianist into the fray and although Schumann's reluctance to compose a 'virtuoso' concerto guarantees a high quota of musical poetry, the first movement cadenza is among the most riveting in the Romantic repertoire. Schumann's songful muse dominates a brief *Intermezzo* that in turn leads to a lilting though vivacious finale.

Dinu Lipatti (piano), Philharmonia Orchestra/Herbert von Karajan
EMI mono

Schumann's best-known concerto calls for a maximum of musical perception, and Lipatti's inward, though technically brilliant, performance satisfies on all counts. The mono sound may be relatively constricted (although it's better than Lipatti's live Swiss recording under Ernest Ansermet – Decca, mono), but the playing has a luminosity and precision that transcend its primitive aural setting. The most impressive digital alternative features the flamboyant Martha Argerich under Nikolaus Harnoncourt (Teldec), while there are countless quality vintage rivals including Fleisher (Sony, analogue), Richter (DG, analogue), Cortot, (Biddulph, mono) and Haskil (Philips, mono).

Violin Concerto in D minor (1853)

Long considered a pathological symptom of artistic decline, Schumann's Violin Concerto is a work of rare expressive richness. The violinist Joachim owned the manuscript and banned performance until 100 years after Schumann's death, but when Joachim's grandniece 'heard' protests on the concerto's behalf from the ghosts of both her uncle and Schumann himself, the ban was lifted and plans for a 1937 première put in motion. Yehudi Menuhin was chosen to do the honours but then the Nazis stepped in and, for reasons of national pride (not to mention anti-semitism), had 'their' Georg Kulenkampff pip him to the post.

Henryk Szeryng (violin), London Symphony Orchestra/Antál Dorati
Mercury analogue

A tough, resilient performance, warm-toned and masterfully conducted by Dorati. The slow movement is extraordinarily moving, but one shouldn't forget either the important première (mono) recordings by Menuhin (Biddulph) and Kulenkampff (Teldec), or Gidon Kremer's perceptive 1995 live recording (Teldec, digital) where Schumann's controversially slow metronome markings are scrupulously observed.

Franz Liszt (1811-1886)

Piano Concerto No. 1 in E flat major, S124 (1849, revised 1853, 1856)

Imagine how this Concerto's dramatic opening (now almost a musical cliché) must have sounded back in 1855, the year of its première – when Berlioz conducted and the playful triangle that announces the last movement was considered extremely perplexing. As much a tone-poem as a concerto, Liszt's E flat is none the less a rewarding vehicle for anyone with the imagination and technique to tackle its many challenges.

Piano Concerto No. 2 in A major, S125 (1839, revised 1849-61)

Unlike the First Concerto, the Second opens quietly with a song-like clarinet melody before the piano enters with a tender yet simple first variation. The work falls into four distinct movements, two of which – the first and third – are further subdivided. Liszt's Second Concerto is generally more reflective than his First, and far more mellow in tone.

Sviatoslav Richter (piano), London Symphony Orchestra/ Kyrill Kondrashin
Philips analogue

Richter offers brilliant, perceptive and above all dignified readings, keenly supported by th LSO in 1961 recordings that, as digitally refurbished by Philips, have tremendous presence (they were actually engineered by a top-notch American team). There are earlier live performances by Richter of the First Concerto (Praga and Multisonic – and ruled more by head than heart) while Alfred Brendel (Philips, analogue) provides a more thoughtful alternative in both works.

Henri Vieuxtemps (1820-1881)

Violin Concerto No. 5 in A minor, Op. 37 (1861)

One of the most stylish and subtly expressive of Romantic virtuoso violin concertos, concise (it is cast in a single movement and plays for something under 20 minutes), poised and melodically attractive. Vieuxtemps was a Belgian violinist and composer who achieved considerable success both in Russia and America and whose shorter works are staples of the virtuoso's repertory.

Jascha Heifetz (violin), New Symphony Orchestra/ Sir Malcolm Sargent

RCA analogue

The second of Heifetz's two recordings (the first, also under Sargent, dates from 1947) boasts excellent stereo sound and enshrines a performance that is both technically brilliant and interpretatively refined. The only drawback is that some of Vieuxtemps' orchestral writing has been cut – though the excisions are fairly judicious. Those who require the uncut score should opt for Arthur Grumiaux (Philips, analogue).

César Franck (1822-1890)

Symphonic Variations for piano and orchestra (1885)

A skilfully-wrought set of six variations on a somewhat sombre theme, starting with a dialogue between piano and orchestra then alternating brilliant pianistic embellishments with passages of great beauty and simplicity. The extrovert finale – one of Franck's most memorable ideas – provides a breezy summation of everything that has gone before. The *Symphonic Variations* is César Franck's most popular work beyond the Symphony in D minor and *Panis angelicus.*

Artur Rubinstein (piano), Symphony of the Air/Alfred Wallenstein

RCA analogue

Rubinstein was a keen Francophile and his elegantly turned readings of major French repertoire have enjoyed justifiable record-catalogue longevity. His Symphonic Variations are sculpted, aristocratic and warmly accompanied by Wallenstein and his orchestra (actually Toscanini's recently-dispanded NBC Symphony working under a pseudonym).

Edouard Lalo (1823-1892)

Symphonie espagnole, Op. 21 (1873)

Lalo had a marked predilection for the foreign and exotic, having composed – in addition to this masterly five-movement symphony-cum-concerto – a *Concerto Russe* for violin and orchestra and a *Rapsodie Norvégienne.* The *Symphonie,* however, is his best-known work, a Spanish-tinted *tour de force,* championed by the great violinist/composer Sarasate and still incredibly popular today.

Yehudi Menuhin (violin), Paris Symphony Orchestra/ Georges Enescu

EMI mono

It was Yehudi Menuhin who first recorded the five-movement version of the score (most of his contemporaries omitted the powerful "Intermezzo") and this 1933 classic – made when the violinist was still in his teens – should keep you poised on the edge of your seat. Jascha Heifetz (RCA, mono) is even more dashing, though somewhat less spontaneous, while Isaac Stern (Sony, analogue) leads the stereo field.

Johannes Brahms (1833-1897)

Concerto for violin, cello and orchestra in A minor, Op. 102 (1887)

When the violinist Joseph Joachim divorced his wife, Brahms took her side and the two musicians were subsequently estranged. This Concerto – that last that Brahms composed – helped to effect a reconciliation; its intimate character, glowing melodies and symphonic proportions are wholly characteristic, although the instrumentation has a certain autumnal quality that is fairly typical of late Brahms.

Nathan Milstein (violin), Gregor Piatigorsky (cello), Robin Hood Dell Orchestra/Fritz Reiner

RCA mono

Although recorded as long ago as 1951, Reiner's performance has a lyrical warmth and sense of inevitability that none of his rivals quite equals: both soloists are superb (they were in any case great friends) but if stereo is essential, then try Isaac Stern, Leonard Rose and the Philadelphia Orchestra under Eugene Ormandy (Sony, analogue). Another significant historical recording, under Wilhelm Furtwängler (EMI, mono), underlines the concerto's more reflective side.

Piano Concerto No. 1 in D minor, Op. 15 (1854-58)

To think that at its first performance, the Concerto's first two movements were greeted with total silence (not in those days a mark of respect). Originally conceived as a symphony, then as a sonata for two pianos, Brahms's First Piano Concerto alternates mammoth gestures (the massive orchestral opening) with sublime poetry (the *Adagio* slow movement) and the spirit of the dance (the closing Rondo).

Artur Rubinstein (piano), Chicago Symphony Orchestra/Fritz Reiner

RCA analogue

Rubinstein's elegant though energetic performance has the added advantage of a keenly assertive orchestral backdrop. Emil Gilels (DG, analogue) offers a more leisurely alternative, Sir Clifford Curzon (Decca, analogue) more in the way of personal reverie while the digital age is very well served by Alfred Brendel with the Berlin Philharmonic under Claudio Abbado (Philips)

Piano Concerto No. 2 in B flat major, Op. 83 (1878-81)

This "symphony with piano obbligato", as the Austrian music critic Eduard Hanslick once described it, is cast in four rather than the usual three movements. It's a huge piece, gnarled and heroic, with an expansive first movement, a passionate Scherzo (that's the 'extra' movement), a grave *Andante* that opens to a particularly beautiful cello solo and then a graceful finale that one of Brahms's biographers described as "gracious as a ballet, as witty as a comedy, as sensitive as a pastoral play and as intoxicating as champagne."

Emil Gilels (piano), Chicago Symphony Orchestra/Fritz Reiner

RCA analogue

With lean, muscular support from the Chicago Symphony under Reiner, Gilels's first version of the B flat (his second, under Eugen Jochum - DG, analogue - trades fire for finesse and extra breadth) combines power and poise in equal measure. A more rugged alternative is provided by Rudolf Serkin (Sony, analogue), while Brendel's latest recording (under Abbado, for Philips) is a firm digital first choice. Leon Fleisher (under the baton of that great Brahmsian George Szell on Sony, analogue) is another strong contender in both concertos.

Violin Concerto in D major, Op. 77 (1878)

Once pigeonholed as a concerto against the violin, Brahms's Op. 77 is, in the words of Bronislaw Huberman (one of its greatest interpreters) "neither against the violin nor for the violin with orchestra; it is a concerto for violin against orchestra - and the violin wins!". A momentous first movement finds both sides on fighting form, whereas the second opens to a gorgeous oboe solo and the third has the overall feel of a gipsy dance.

David Oistrakh (violin), French Radio National Orchestra/ Otto Klemperer

EMI analogue

Here the violin 'wins' by the subtlest means, namely, a rounded tone, warmly cultivated phrasing and perceptive musicianship. Klemperer's marmoreal accompaniment makes for a formidable confrontation, but the Concerto's lyrical soul is never compromised. Incidentally, there's a wonderfully supple live Oistrakh performance on Telstar's Revelation label (mono). However, those in search of a faster, more intense account will probably prefer Jascha Heifetz with Fritz Reiner conducting (RCA, analogue).

Camille Saint-Saëns
(1835-1921)

Introduction and Rondo capriccioso for violin and orchestra in A minor, Op. 28 (1863)

Originally hailed as "the new Mozart" (he gave a piano recital at the Salle Pleyel when he was ten years old), Saint-Saëns was a consummate craftsman with a good ear for melody and an orchestral palette much influenced by Beethoven. His *Introduction and Rondo capriccioso* opens to a slow, quintessentially French melody before breaking into the Rondo proper - a pert, breezy tune that breaks half-way for a melancholy interlude.

Jascha Heifetz (violin), RCA Victor Symphony Orchestra/William Steinberg

RCA mono

The second of Heifetz's two recordings (1951 in preference to 1935 on Biddulph - which is virtually as good) is poised, perfumed and extremely brilliant. Others have approximated its qualities, though none quite equals them.

Cello Concerto No. 1 in A minor, Op. 33 (1872)

Cast in a single movement with three distinct sections, Saint-Saëns's First Cello Concerto is among the jewels of the cellist's repertoire. The opening *Allegro* is blustery and vividly coloured, whereas the central 'movement' has the soloist play a songful melody over a delicate accompaniment and the 'finale' (which returns us to "Tempo 1") incorporates a sequence of beautiful melodies.

 ***André Navarra (cello), Lamoureux Orchestra/Charles Munch***
Erato analogue
Absolutely unrivalled. Navarra's playing combines tonal bloom with great intensity while Munch's accompaniment is both forceful and shapely. The 1965 stereo sound is dry but extremely clear. Reliable rivals are plentiful, with János Starker (Mercury, EMI, analogue) leading the field by a considerable distance.

Piano Concerto No. 2 in G minor, Op. 22 (1868)
The somewhat severe opening cadenza soon gives way to a generous, big-hearted melody and a host of elegantly crafted ideas, the sort that Saint-Saëns could write in his sleep. The Concerto's most famous movement is a bubbly Scherzo that opens to rocking timpani and rather resembles (in effect if not thematic profile) Henry Litolff's celebrated *Scherzo*, while the finale approximates a breathless helter-skelter.

 ***Artur Rubinstein (piano), Symphony of the Air/Alfred Wallenstein***
RCA analogue
A famous CD, and a favourite Rubinstein party piece (he often played it in concert and there are it least three separate recordings of his felicitously phrased interpretation). However, those intent on digital sound should be pleased with the version by André Watts (Telarc).

Piano Concerto No. 4 in C minor, Op. 44 (1874)
Roughly half-way through a fairly sombre first movement, Saint-Saëns hints at the noble chorale theme that will dominate the finale. Thereafter, the material becomes progressively more varied, with Lisztian virtuoso writing and many moments of great delicacy. The Scherzo recalls Brahms in playful mood while the finale – which follows the Scherzo without a break – is an action-packed Rondo that anticipates, melodically if not structurally, Saint-Saëns' Third Symphony (composed two years later).

 ***Robert Casadesus (piano), New York Philharmonic Orchestra/Leonard Bernstein***
Sony Classical analogue
As with Rubinstein in the Second Concerto (see above), Casadesus sounds as if he's really enjoying himself – and so do Bernstein and the orchestra. The current couplings includes a portentous account of the Third Symphony, but there are fine alternatives from Pascal Rogé (Decca) and Aldo Ciccolini (EMI), both of them analogue recordings.

Violin Concerto No. 3 in B minor, Op. 61 (1880)
Saint-Saëns' Third Violin Concerto, composed during the 1880s for the great Spanish virtuoso Pablo de Sarasate, combines dramatic impulse (a particularly assertive first movement), graceful melodic invention (the wistful *Andantino*) and bravura (a dashing, tarantella-like finale). A confirmed Classicist, Saint-Saëns incorporates a plethora of memorable musical ideas into a sound though supremely elegant structure.

 ***Pierre Amoyal (violin), Montreal Symphony Orchestra/Charles Dutoit***
Decca digital
An agile, gracefully phrased performance, stylishly accompanied and very well recorded. Charismatic vintage alternatives abound, with Nathan Milstein (EMI, analogue) and Louis Kaufman (Biddulph, mono) leading the ranks, and Yehudi Menuhin (EMI, mono) a technically fallible but deeply musical fourth option.

Henryk Wieniawski
(1835–1880)

Violin Concerto in D minor, Op. 22 (1862)
Wieniawski was one of the founding members of a Russian violin school that went on to spawn countless great virtuosos (Heifetz being perhaps the greatest of all). His output includes countless charming *morceaux*, but his Second Violin Concerto is his masterpiece. Its three movements include a famous *Adagio* (a popular encore in its own right) and a fiery gipsy-style finale.

 ***Jascha Heifetz (violin), RCA Victor Symphony Orchestra/Izler Solomon***
RCA mono
To say that Heifetz is heard "in his element" might seem faintly patronizing (he was equally "in his element" in unaccompanied Bach), but there can be no doubt that for technical wizardry, tonal allure and sheer style, there's

nothing to touch this particular recording (an earlier pre-war [mono] version, under Barbirolli – EMI, RCA or Biddulph – is brilliant, but not quite so intense).

Max Bruch (1838-1920)

Scottish Fantasy for violin and orchestra, Op. 46 (1880)

Perhaps the finest of all Bruch's many works for violin and orchestra, dedicated to Pablo de Sarasate and stuffed full of memorable tunes. The orchestration features a prominent harp part (underlining the Celtic element) while, beyond a solemn introduction, four movements parade a varied sequence of Scottish-style melodies – the most beautiful of which are featured in the *Adagio*.

Jascha Heifetz (violin), Osian Ellis (harp), New Symphony Orchestra of London/Sir Malcolm Sargent

RCA analogue

The second of two superb recordings by Heifetz, utterly inimitable for its sweetness, 'speaking' eloquence (an invariable virtue on all Heifetz's records) and breathtaking virtuosity. With fine sound (1961) and lively orchestral playing (Sir Malcolm Sargent was a superb accompanist), this ranks as the best-ever version of a much-loved work.

Violin Concerto No. 1 in G minor, Op. 26

Dedicated to the great violinist-composer Joseph Joachim, Bruch's best-known Violin Concerto – the first of three – was once described by Leopold Auer (teacher of, among others, Heifetz, Elman and Milstein) as the composer's "artistic declaration of independence". Its themes are indelibly memorable, its orchestration Brahmsian in the extreme and its most familiar feature is a sweet-centred *Adagio* that seems to epitomize the spirit of the Romantic violin concerto.

Isaac Stern (violin), Philadelphia Orchestra/Eugene Ormandy

Sony Classical analogue

Stern's full, muscular tone and warm-hearted musicianship assure an impassioned Bruch G minor, sumptuously accompanied by the Philadelphia Orchestra – but anyone investing in Heifetz (his stereo RCA version), Menuhin (his childhood version under Landon Ronald, EMI or Biddulph, mono), Arthur Grumiaux (Philips, analogue), Alfredo Campoli (Pearl, mono) or Ivry Gitlis (Vox, mono) should be more than satisfied. All are analogue recordings.

Pyotr Il'yich Tchaikovsky (1840-1893)

Piano Concerto No. 1 in B flat minor, Op. 23 (1874-75)

When composer-pianist Anton Rubinstein deemed this Concerto "unplayable", who would have guessed that he'd soon be both playing and conducting it! A brilliant fusion of folk music, virtuoso piano writing and creative daring (what other concerto opens with such uncompromising grandilo-quence?), Tchaikovsky's B flat minor – together with Grieg's A minor – represents the ultimate popular archetype of 'The Concerto'.

Vladimir Horowitz (piano), NBC Symphony Orchestra/ Arturo Toscanini

RCA mono

A 1943 concert performance that raised a fortune in war-bonds and that even today remains the most hair-raising Tchaikovsky First ever committed to disc. But it certainly doesn't tell the whole story. A far slower, darker and more thoughtful alternative is provided by Victoria Postnikova, the Vienna Symphony Orchestra and Gennadi Rozhdestvensky (Decca, digital), but if fast speeds and visceral excitement are your main priorities, then Martha Argerich, Claudio Abbado and the Berlin Philharmonic (DG digital) are almost as exciting as Horowitz and Toscanini.

Piano Concerto No. 2 in G major, Op. 44 (1879-80)

A very different proposition to the First Concerto, though hardly less original: if uncut (which, unfortunately, it rarely is), the Second Concerto features a 16-minute *Andante non troppo* that's all but a self-contained 'piano trio' (piano, violin and cello). The majestic first movement makes wrist-breaking demands on the pianist, but the joyful finale is one of Tchaikovsky's most ebullient inspirations.

Victoria Postnikova (piano), Vienna Symphony Orchestra/Gennadi Rozhdestvensky

Decca digital

A much-underrated performance that balances perception and bravura within the framework of some exceptional piano playing. The coupling is a particularly sympathetic account of the flawed but often powerful one-

movement Third Concerto. If available, you should also try and hear Shura Cherkassky's hair-raising (cut) mono DG recording of the Second Concerto.

Violin Concerto in D major, Op. 35 (1878)
A far lighter, less monumental piece than any of the piano concertos, lyrical in style and imbued with a feeling of folk music (especially in the finale, with its polonaise-style second idea). Tchaikovsky composed his Violin Concerto in the wake of emotionally crippling angst: he had recently emerged from one of the most difficult periods of his life, which included a disastrous marriage. Originally deemed unplayable by violinist and pedagogue Leopold Auer, it was subsequently premièred by Adolf Brodsky and has since become a repertory mainstay.

 ***Jascha Heifetz (violin), Chicago Symphony Orchestra/Fritz Reiner***
RCA analogue
Great Tchaikovsky fiddle concertos are legion – Huberman (EMI, mono), Elman (Pearl, mono), Milstein (EMI or DG, analogue), Oistrakh (Melodiya, Russian Disc, Sony or DG, analogue mono/stereo), Stern (Sony, analogue), you name them! Heifetz recorded the work three times and although some favour the more restrained manner of the 1937 and 1950 mono recordings (both are on RCA), this 1957 stereo remake is more subtly expressive – and better conducted – than either of the earlier ones.

Further listening *Jascha Heifetz's discography features many enjoyable Romantic concertos, including Wieniawski's Second, Bruch's Second and the concise but touching Concerto by Julius Conus. All are mono and are issued as part of RCA's multi-volume "Heifetz Collection".*

Antonin Dvořák (1841-1904)

Cello Concerto in B minor, B191 (1894-95)
Dvořák composed the greatest of all cello concertos between America and Prague and dedicated it to Hanus Wihan, founder of the Bohemian String Quartet. The first movement opens to an expansive orchestral introduction and bids the soloist enter in the style of a fiery improvisation; the lyrical slow movement is based on one of Dvořák's songs and the vivacious finale closes to a long and loving farewell.

 ***Pablo Casals (cello), Czech Philharmonic Orchestra/George Szell***
EMI mono
Idiosyncratic though it is, Casals's legendary 1937 recording is so passionate, personal and eloquently phrased that comparison with other versions seems tantamount to heresy. And yet there are good stereo rivals – Pierre Fournier, for example (again under Szell, DG analogue), Heinrich Schiff under Sir Colin Davis (Philips, digital) or either of János Starker's analogue recordings (EMI or Mercury).

Violin Concerto in A minor, B108 (1880, revised 1882)
Imagine a concerto that combines the energy of Dvořák's *Slavonic Dances* (last movement), the lyricism of his best quartets (slow movement) and the drama of his later symphonies (first movement) and you'll have some idea of what to expect from this delightful though still-underrated work. It was originally intended for the great Joseph Joachim (Brahms's friend and musical collaborator), though Joachim's suggestions for 'improvements' encouraged Dvořák to re-fashion the piece – albeit in his own inimitable style.

 ***Josef Suk (violin), Czech Philharmonic Orchestra/Karel Ančerl***
Supraphon analogue
The composer's great-grandson has recorded this concerto at least three times (the last, on an analogue Orfeo d'Or CD, is a riveting live performance), but his first version is both the freshest and the sweetest version available. Ančerl's conducting is consistently on the ball and there's a gorgeous makeweight in Dvořák's Romance for violin and orchestra.

Edvard Grieg (1843-1907)

Piano Concerto in A minor, Op. 16 (1868)
Second only to Tchaikovsky's First Piano Concerto in popularity, Grieg's A minor is infused with the spirit of Nordic song. The opening timpani crescendo and succeeding solo cadenza have become synonymous with its composer's name while, viewed as a whole, the Concerto is both structurally sound and musically appealing. It's no surprise that it brought Grieg worldwide fame.

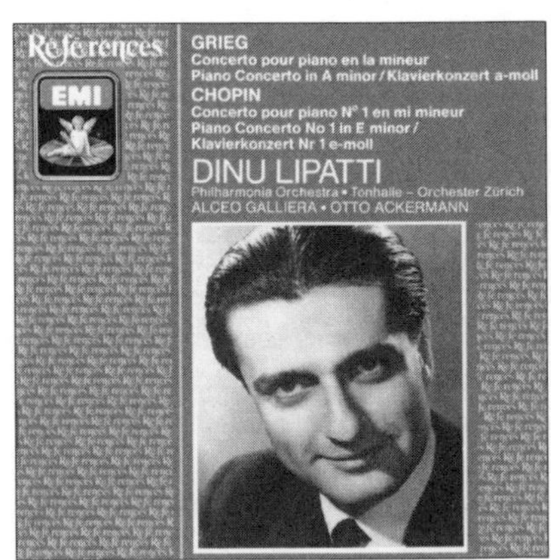

 ***Dinu Lipatti (piano), Philharmonia Orchestra/Alceo Galliera***

EMI mono

Lipatti's Grieg Concerto is a perfect synthesis of poetry, warmth and forthright virtuosity. The Philharmonia Orchestra (then merely a year or so old) offer him sterling support and the 1947 recording leaves no grounds for complaint. However, those in search of a stereo alternative should be happy with Géza Anda (DG), Sir Clifford Curzon (Decca) or, if digital sound is required, Murray Perahia (Sony).

Ernest Chausson (1855-1899)

Poème for violin and orchestra, Op. 25 (1896)

Chausson's *Poème* was inspired by both the playing and the compositions of the great Belgian violinist Eugène Ysaÿe (Ysaÿe's own similarly structured *Chant d'hiver* actually pre-dated it). Although popularly treated as a violin showpiece, *Poème* is in fact a lyrical narrative that makes maximum expressive capital of a small but characterful roster of themes. It opens and closes in a spirit of veiled mystery.

 ***David Oistrakh (violin), Boston Symphony Orchestra/Charles Munch***

RCA analogue

Oistrakh's rise to fame was initially prompted by his success in the 1937 Ysaÿe Competition in Brussels, although his subsequent reputation rested more on perceptive musicianship and a warm, highly cultivated tone. He was particularly well suited to the wistful world of Chausson's Poème, though Arthur Grumiaux (Philips, analogue) and Yehudi Menuhin (EMI, pre-war, mono) offer imaginative alternatives, while Jascha Heifetz (RCA, mono) is unrivalled for drive and passion.

Alexander Glazunov (1865-1936)

Violin Concerto in A minor, Op. 82 (1904)

Glazunov dispenses with the standard orchestral introduction, launching his Concerto (and the soloist) on one of the loveliest themes in the repertory, a winding lament set over gently pulsing woodwinds. There are three sections that are played without a break; the stylistic bias is lyrical throughout (very much in the manner of Glazunov's best ballet music) and the trumpeting finale is especially vivacious.

 ***Jascha Heifetz (violin), London Philharmonic Orchestra/ Sir John Barbirolli***

Pearl analogue

Heifetz played the Glazunov Concerto on the occasion of his bar mitzvah (the Jewish 'coming of age', at 13), under the composer's direction. His lean, sweet tone and lightning inflexions are heard to better advantage in this 1934 recording than in an equally stunning – though somewhat less reposeful – 1962 stereo remake. I would also recommend keeping an eye out for David Oistrakh's lustrous recordings (Revelation and Monitor, both mono).

Serge Rachmaninov (1873-1943)

Piano Concerto No. 2 in C minor, Op. 18 (1900-01)

A glorious re-affirmation of creativity, the composer having recently suffered crippling depression. The première of his First Symphony had been a fiasco and Rachmaninov sought therapy through hypnosis and auto-suggestion. The creative upshot of his treatment is a richly romantic Concerto that rivals Tchaikovsky's First in terms of grandeur and melodic appeal and that later made its mark on the film industry (*Brief Encounter* uses the second movement for its soundtrack). Rachmaninov dedicated his Second Concerto to the doctor who helped to re-build his self-confidence.

 ***Sviatoslav Richter (piano), Warsaw Philharmonic Orchestra/Stanislaw Wislocki***

Deutsche Grammophon analogue

Richter makes a mountainous crescendo of the Concerto's famous opening chords though his playing elsewhere is notably lyrical, even delicate. It's a superb performance, warmly accompanied – though the composer's own interpretation (as heard in his second recording, made in 1929) remains uniquely compelling (RCA, mono).

Piano Concerto No. 3 in D minor, Op. 30 (1909)

This work came within a hair's breadth of qualifying for inclusion in with the modern concertos, not because it lacks big tunes or lavish gestures (quite the contrary), or even because of its date of composition – but because here more than anywhere else in Rachmaninov's concertos, the style of writing suggests an uninterrupted stream of consciousness. There are three well-structured movements, two of which (the second and third) play without a break. The Third Concerto's moods range from a wistful opening theme to a grandly opulent finale, whereas the slow movement resembles a passionate improvisation.

 ***Vladimir Horowitz (piano), RCA Victor Symphony Orchestra/Fritz Reiner***

RCA mono

Many collectors will prefer to stand by

Rachmaninov's own performance, a hell-for-leather affair, taken down in Philadelphia in 1939-40. However, Horowitz's 1951 recording is a veritable showcase for some astonishing pianism. The mono recording may be a trifle clangorous, but the performance displays an executive brilliance and musical sophistication that even the composer himself failed to match. Earl Wild (Chandos, analogue) offers the most impressive stereo option.

The Twentieth-century Concerto (1903-1993)

This section is both exciting and paradoxical. The paradoxes emerge with composers like Elgar and Samuel Barber, both of whom wrote concertos that hark back to the heyday of the great Romantics. The excitement is in a plethora of colours – from the acid statements of Igor Stravinsky and the pungent rhythms of Bartók or Prokofiev to the quiet innovations of the young American composer John Adams.

Sir Edward Elgar (1857-1934)

Cello Concerto in E minor, Op. 85 (1919)

Elgar's last major work ponders the loss and futility of war, the Great War – not in any obvious way, but through a certain nostalgia and sense of longing. The stern opening spells wounded pride, while the ensuing melody – so melancholy and world-weary in spirit – rises to a magnificent climax. Like the Violin Concerto, the Cello Concerto saves its most powerful gestures until the last movement, where the music seems to lose itself in painful reverie before drawing to a brief but triumphant conclusion.

Jacqueline du Pré (cello), London Symphony Orchestra/ Sir John Barbirolli
EMI analogue

It would be all too easy to use this wonderful work as a musical meditation on Jacqueline du Pré's tragically truncated life (she died of multiple sclerosis, aged only 42), especially as the performance itself is notably vibrant and intense. Taken on its own terms, however, it is one of the finest Elgar recordings of the stereo era, with only Casals (under Boult, EMI) and possibly Beatrice Harrison (under Elgar himself, also EMI) – both mono – as inspired forebears.

Violin Concerto in B minor, Op. 61 (1909-10)

A concerto with the impact of a symphony, such is its size, emotional range and power of expression. Elgar's orchestral writing has a boldness, even defiance that contrasts with a heart-rendering solo line. Towards the end of the work, the soloist intones a long cadenza backed by the eerie murmur of plucked strings playing *tremolando* (an atmospheric effect that's normally achieved with the bow).

Yehudi Menuhin (violin), London Symphony Orchestra/Sir Edward Elgar
EMI mono

Love at first hearing, captured on the wing in a performance that even after 60-odd years, remains unrivalled. Menuhin was 16 at the time, Elgar 75, and yet the sheer energy and emotional charge generated between them defies description. A later recording with Menuhin and Sir Adrian Boult (EMI, analogue) should please the 'anti-scratch' brigade, as will Dmitry Sitkovetsky's sympathetic digital version (Virgin) with Menuhin conducting.

Frederick Delius (1862-1934)

Violin Concerto, RTVII/6 (1916)

Delius's finest Concerto falls into three distinct sections, with an unaccompanied cadenza at its centre. Verdant, wistful and aromatic, it is a particularly warming essay, quintessentially English in spirit and fully deserving of Sir Thomas Beecham's praise. "It has considerable melodic beauty," wrote Beecham on one occasion, "and is structurally entirely logical and effective."

Jean Pougnet (violin), Royal Philharmonic Orchestra/ Sir Thomas Beecham
EMI mono

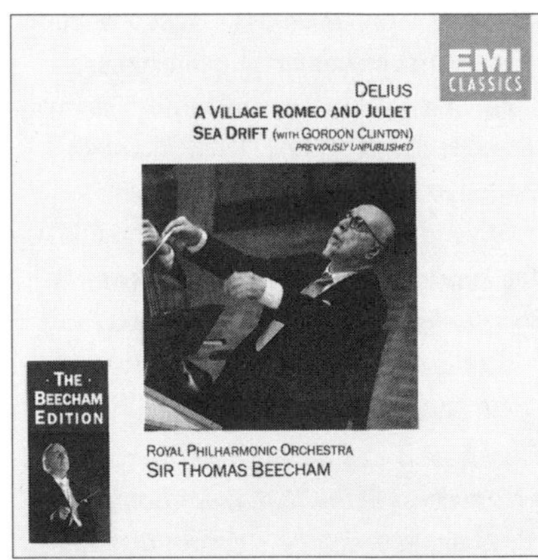

Although both Tasmin Little (Argo, digital) and Yehudi Menuhin (EMI, analogue) have made excellent stereo versions of the Delius Violin Concerto, the oldest recorded interpretations remain the most idiomatic. Albert Sammons (Testament, mono) was the work's dedicatee but although his performance is extremely eloquent, Jean Pougnet's is equally so and has

the added advantage of Sir Thomas Beecham's wonderfully supple conducting.

Carl Nielsen (1865-1931)

Clarinet Concerto, FS129 (1928)

A single-movement Concerto in four sections with two solo cadenzas which – like the Flute Concerto (see below) – was composed for a member of the Copenhagen Wind Quintet (in this case Aage Oxenvad). Nielsen develops his material with the utmost skill, centring more on bold harmonies and expressive nuances than on overt technical display. It is not an 'easy' work (at one point, Nielsen has his soloist confront a hyper active side-drummer) and yet its many secrets are easily accessed by patient performers (and listeners).

Flute Concerto, FS119 (1926)

Nielsen composed his playful and in many ways elusive Flute Concerto for a member of the Copenhagen Wind Quintet (Holger Gilbert-Jespersen). The writing itself is lean, quixotic and often rather beautiful (sample the serenely lyrical passage 4'46" into our recommended version), while the more disquieting second movement hints at Danish folk-song. Nielsen revised the Concerto's ending after the Paris première on October 20th, 1926.

Julius Baker (flute), Stanley Drucker (clarinet), New York Philharmonic Orchestra/Leonard Bernstein

Sony Classical analogue

One can easily imagine Bernstein revelling in Nielsen's many tricks and surprises. There's an exploratory excitement about both performances, while the soloists (front-desk men from the New York Philharmonic) are superb and the recordings extremely good for their mid-1960s vintage. Compelling historical options are available featuring the clarinettists Louis Cahuzac (Clarinet Classics) and Ib Erikson (a live recording on Danacord or a studio one on Dutton, both mono) and the Flute Concerto's dedicatee Gilbert-Jespersen (Dutton, mono).

Violin Concerto, Op. 33 (1911)

The Violin Concerto is far more accessible than either the Flute or Clarinet Concertos – less playfully disruptive, too. An extremely underrated work, it has its own unique brand of poetry, most especially in the *Poco adagio* slow movement, one of the loveliest passages in Nielsen's orchestral output. The first movement's wistful second idea (1'33" into our recommended recording) recalls the pure and breezy world of Nielsen's songs while the quizzical closing Rondo accommodates two contrasting episodes. A fine, bracing concerto, full of inspired ideas.

Maxim Vengerov (violin), Chicago Symphony Orchestra/Daniel Barenboim

Teldec digital

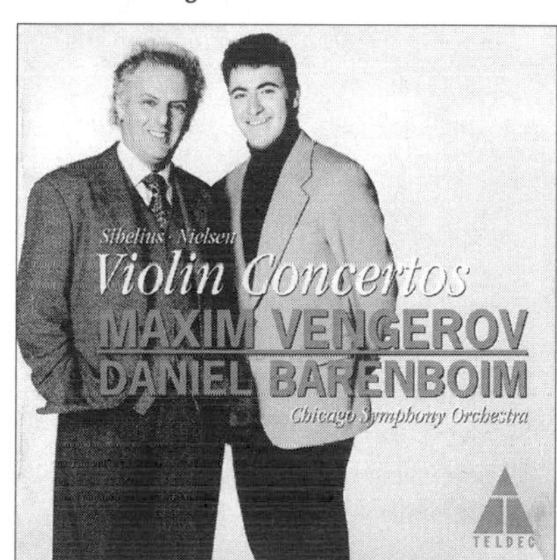

Quite simply the best recording that this marvellous work has ever had, technically brilliant, tonally pure and sensitively conducted by Barenboim. The orchestral playing is both elegant and powerful, and the recording wholly excellent. Vengerov's only serious rival is Nielsen's son-in-law Emil Telmányi on an old 78rpm recording (Danacord, mono).

Jean Sibelius (1865-1957)

Violin Concerto in D minor, Op. 47 (1903, revised 1905)

One of the fledgling century's great concertos. The opening suggests mysterious half-lights and the first theme a plaintive aria, although the drama soon increases with luscious orchestration and wildly outspoken writing for the soloist. The slow movement is a warmly romantic *Adagio di molto*, whereas the finale resembles a rhythmic dance. Sibelius – himself a violinist – conducted the first performance and subsequently subjected the work to wholesale revisions.

Jascha Heifetz (violin), Chicago Symphony Orchestra/Walter Hendl

RCA analogue

With a tone of molten silver, an incredible technique and faultless intonation, Heifetz provides what is probably the most focused interpretation that the work has ever had. Hendl's conducting is cleanly dramatic and the 1959 recording more than passes muster. Viable alternatives include Ivry Gitlis under Jascha Horenstein (Vox, mono), David Oistrakh under Eugene Ormandy (Sony – or under Gennadi Rozhdestvensky, Melodiya – both are analogue) and the historic 1945 performance by Ginette Neveu under Walter Susskind (EMI, mono). Heifetz's pre-war version with Sir Thomas Beecham conducting (EMI, Biddulph) is also worth searching out, although his later recording (the one recommended here) is more keenly inflected.

Ferruccio Busoni (1866-1924)

Piano Concerto (1903-04)

"The title concerto is used here in its original sense, signifying a co-operation of different means of producing sound" (Busoni – as quoted from the programme-note for the first performance). The very opening has a grandeur equalled only by the First Piano Concerto of Brahms whereas the ensuing four movements (which play without a break and which add up to a total timing of some 70 minutes) incorporate a Scherzo, a 20-minute *Pezzo serioso*, a tarantella and a choral finale that sets the words (translated from the Danish poetry of Oehlenschläger) "Lift your hearts to the eternal power/feel near to Allah, observe His work!". Long though it is, Busoni's immensely eventful Piano Concerto makes for a compelling listening experience.

 ***John Ogdon (piano), Men's voices of the John Alldis Choir, Royal Philharmonic Orchestra/Daniell Ravenaugh***

EMI analogue

Anyone who sets out to survey this, the most massive of all piano concertos, needs to be something of a pianistic philosopher and Ogdon's insight, concentration and obvious sense of mission fit the bill perfectly. The 1967 recording stands up extremely well, but I would also recommend a highly impressive – but controversially expansive – reading by Victoria Postnikova under the commanding baton of Gennadi Rozhdestvensky (Erato, digital).

Arnold Schoenberg (1874-1951)

Piano Concerto, Op. 42 (1942)

Don't be put off by the fact that this Concerto is based on a specific 'tone row' (a series of 12 notes, each of which is granted equal importance in the composing process – something that can lead to profound, though superficial, 'disharmony'). The music itself is so strong and eventful that the "unifying impact" (Brendel) of its material need not be analysed in detail. Schoenberg's Piano Concerto is a taut, often profoundly lyrical dialogue that features powerful orchestral writing (the brass are used to tremendous effect). It falls into four distinct sections that can be roughly explained – according to Schoenberg himself – by the titles "Life was so easy", "Sudden hatred broke out" (the Nazis, most especially), "A grave situation was created" and "But life goes on". It's not difficult to marry the images with the music, but neither is it necessary.

 ***Alfred Brendel (piano), South West German Radio Symphony Orchestra/Michael Gielen***

Philips digital

Brendel and Gielen play this concerto as if it were Mozart or Brahms – with absolute mastery and naturalness of expression. No other recording approaches it (not even a much earlier recording by the same artists), though it would be unfair to forget an epoch-making analogue version by Glenn Gould (Sony).

Maurice Ravel (1875-1937)

Concerto for piano (left hand) and orchestra (1931)

Ravel composed his Left Hand Concerto – an immensely powerful work suggestive of passion, struggle and a carping cynicism – for the pianist Paul Wittgenstein (brother of the philosopher Ludwig), who lost his right arm during the First World War. By covering the entire range of the keyboard very early on in the piece, Ravel creates the illusion of two hands working overtime, while the central crescendo (shorter than in his *Boléro*, but even more effective) is built on a seedy jazz theme.

 ***Samson François (piano), Paris Conservatoire Orchestra/André Cluytens***

EMI analogue

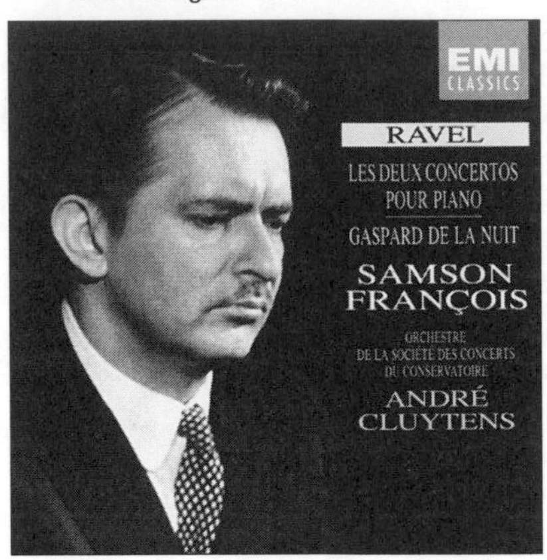

A confrontational performance, muscular and defiant, with a strong, albeit somewhat reedy orchestral backdrop under Cluytens. There are very good – though not quite so charismatic – digital alternatives from Leon Fleisher and the Boston Symphony under Seiji Ozawa (Sony) and Zoltán Kocsis with the Budapest Festival Orchestra under Iván Fischer (Philips, and including some jazzy instrumental solos).

Piano Concerto in G major (1931)

Ravel's two-hand Concerto is very different in spirit to its gnarled successor – lighter, brighter and with a saucily playful *Presto* finale. Jazz is an obvious influence throughout, while the slow movement opens to one of Ravel's longest – and coolest – melodies. The Concerto was premièred by Marguerite Long in January 1932.

 ***Arturo Benedetti Michelangeli (piano), Philharmonia Orchestra/Ettore Gracis***
EMI analogue

Marguerite Long herself made a fairly distinctive recording of the Concerto (set down pre-war for EMI, mono), but Michelangeli's is perhaps the most celebrated version of all – justly so with its delicacy, lightning reflexes, incredibly fluid touch and absolute control in the languorous slow movement. The orchestra is on top form, the conducting sympathetic and the 1957 sound still pretty good, although there are fine rivals from Martha Argerich (DG, analogue) and Zoltán Kocsis (Philips, digital).

Manuel de Falla (1876-1946)

Nights in the gardens of Spain – symphonic impressions for piano and orchestra (1907-16)

An evocative tone-poem-cum-concerto, piquantly orchestrated and describing – in three separate movements – the hillside gardens in Generalife near the Alhambra in Granada, a Distant [Moorish] Dance and the gardens of the Sierra de Córdoba. As the composer himself wrote in a programme-note for the première, "... since these symphonic impressions ... have realized their purpose, the citation of their titles should be a sufficient guide for listening".

 ***Eduardo del Pueyo (piano), Lamoureux Orchestra/Jean Martinon***
Philips analogue

A classic 1955 performance that conveys a vivid sense of atmosphere. The solo playing is both delicate and colourful, the conducting likewise (the first movement's principal climax is generously expansive) and the actual sound quality remains remarkably impressive. Viable alternatives include Gonzalo Soriano with Rafael Frühbeck de Burgos conducting (EMI, analogue), Alicia de Larrocha and Ernest Ansermet's Suisse Romande Orchestra (Decca, analogue) and Artur Rubinstein under the baton of Vladimir Golschmann (RCA, mono).

Ernest Bloch (1880-1959)

Violin Concerto (1937-38)

This most Jewish of composers opens his Violin Concerto with an American Indian motif, although material used later on in the work suggests inward communing and cantorial pleading. The first movement features 'David and Goliath' confrontations between soloist and orchestra; the second is a lyrical *Andante*, and the third intimates a spirit of optimism.

 ***Yehudi Menuhin (violin), Philharmonia Orchestra/Paul Kletzki***
EMI analogue

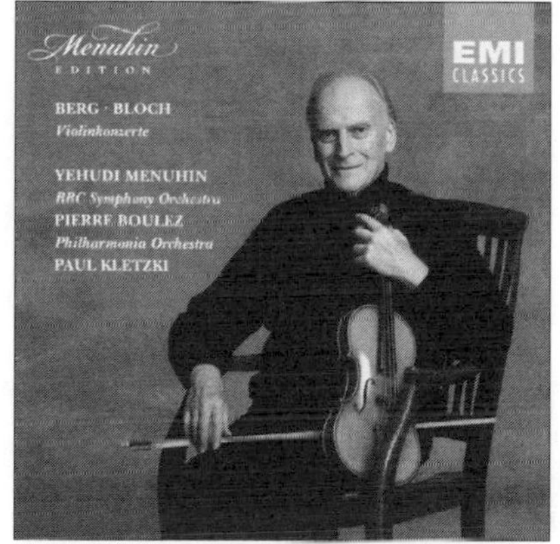

It was perhaps surprising that the man who recorded Bartók's great Violin Concerto (his Second) not long after it was written took so long to record Bloch's concerto masterpiece (Menuhin had befriended both composers). And yet this 1963 classic shows Menuhin at the height of his powers, although discerning listeners should also investigate the magnificent late-1930s recordings with Joseph Szigeti – on Pearl (studio) under Charles Munch or Music & Arts (live) under Willem Mengelberg, both of them in mono.

Béla Bartók (1881-1945)

Piano Concerto No. 1, Sz83 (1926)

The most formidable of Bartók's three piano concertos – an angular, hard-hitting and often colourful essay that calls on numerous solo instrumentalists and protests modernism in virtually every bar. The *Andante* is a sort of ritual in waltz-time (the slow-burning climax is quite hypnotic), while the finale – with its battling percussion and sliding brass – is a fierce-fisted *Allegro molto*.

 ***Peter Donohoe (piano), City of Birmingham Symphony Orchestra/Sir Simon Rattle***
EMI digital

Donohoe and Rattle make great play with the First Concerto, especially in the hectic first movement (a riot of colour) and the artfully calculated Andante. The recording is one of EMI's best, although there are fine analogue alternatives from Rudolf Serkin (Sony, an incredibly bald statement of the score) and Géza Anda (less forbidding than Serkin, but equally effective).

Piano Concerto No. 2, Sz95 (1930-31)

Bartók's greatest instrumental Concerto boasts numerous unique features including a first movement that dispenses with strings, a second that re-employs them to magical effect (adding a top-speed central section where woodwinds suggest insects scurrying at midnight) and a powerfully rhythmic finale. The dialogue between piano and orchestra is unusually taut.

 ***Géza Anda (piano), Berlin Radio Symphony Orchestra/Ferenc Fricsay***

Deustche Grammophon analogue

A real classic. Anda's 1959 recording has an urgency, clarity and pianistic finesse that no other version even approaches, while Ferenc Fricsay's consistently on-the-ball accompaniment makes for meaningful dialogue with the whole concerto – and of the first movement in particular. Those in search of a digital option should be happy with Zoltán Kocsis (Philips) who, like Anda and Donohoe, programmes all three piano concertos on a single CD.

Piano Concerto No. 3, Sz119 (1945)

Left uncompleted at the time of Bartók's death (Tibor Serly orchestrated the last 17 bars), the Third Concerto marks a lightening of spirit and easing of tempo. The first movement is wistful and transparent, the second, a sublime *Adagio religioso* (again the strings are eloquently used) and the third, a carefree *Allegro vivace*, takes a sideways glance at the equally invigorating *Concerto for Orchestra.*

 ***Zoltán Kocsis (piano), Budapest Festival Orchestra/Iván Fischer***

Philips digital

Kocsis has made a close study of Bartók's own recorded performances, although in this particular case there is no composer-interpreted 'prototype' to compare him with. However, he does manage to suggest the warmth and flexibility of Bartók's own playing style and the orchestral accompaniment is excellent. I'd also recommend a light, fresh-faced analogue alternative by the fine Czech pianist Eva Bernáthová (Supraphon)

Violin Concerto No. 2, Sz112 (1937-38)

Symmetrical in design and infused with the spirit of folk-song, Bartók's Second Violin Concerto is both highly accessible and musically substantial. It opens to a harp accompaniment (the violin's first entry parades an endless line of Hungarian-style melody) then embarks on a highly eventful journey, one that Bartók both revisits and revises for the finale. The second movement is a brilliant set of variations that frolics, teases and cries.

 ***Thomas Zehetmair (violin), Budapest Festival Orchestra/ Iván Fischer***

Berlin Classics digital

The fieriest, most agile Bartók Second Concerto available, keenly inflected, superbly accompanied under Fischer and vividly recorded. Bartók himself was a great admirer of Yehudi Menuhin's playing; he even wrote a Solo Violin Sonata for him (one of the his greatest 'late' works – see under "A sense of daring", below). Menuhin actually recorded the Second Concerto four times, but his first version (1946 – RCA, mono) is easily his finest. Other notable recordings of the work include those by Isaac Stern (Sony, analogue), Christian Tetzlaff (Virgin, digital) or Anne-Sophie Mutter (DG, digital)

Igor Stravinsky (1882-1971)

Concerto in D major for string orchestra, "Basle Concerto" (1946)

A study in rhythm and string sonorities – balletic, breathless, frequently dissonant and extraordinarily eventful (for example, the dramatic darkening that occurs three-quarters of the way through the first movement – 3'17" into our recommended recording). The Concerto's slow movement is an elegant *Arioso*, whereas its finale is an eerie Rondo in perpetual motion. The "Concerto in D" (as it's most commonly known) was commissioned by the Swiss conductor and new-music entrepreneur Paul Sacher to celebrate the twentieth anniversary of the Basle Chamber Orchestra.

 ***Columbia Symphony Orchestra/ Igor Stravinsky***

Sony Classical analogue

Stravinsky lays bare every twist and turn in his acerbic harmonic world and his players respond with impressive precision (at least for most of the time) and plenty of rhythmic bite. The 1963 New York recording delivers every detail intact, though digital-only collectors are well served by the Norwegian Chamber Orchestra under Iona Brown (Virgin).

Violin Concerto in D major (1931)

Composed during the height of the Depression, Stravinsky's Violin Concerto is a chirpy, neo-Baroque piece that opens to astringent chords and proceeds through a jog-trot Toccata. The work's lyrical core is found in two intensely-voiced arias, whereas the finale is a sprightly Capriccio. Stravinsky disliked all the standard violin concertos, bar those by Schoenberg and Bach. It was the latter's Double Concerto that suggested the duet with violin featured in the last movement of the present piece.

 ***Isaac Stern (violin), Columbia Symphony Orchestra/Igor Stravinsky***

Sony Classical analogue

Tough, energetic and idiomatically accompanied. The sound is excellent for its period (1960) while Stern's characteristically vibrant tone is an added attraction. Worthy digital rivals include Frank Peter Zimmermann (EMI) and Anne-Sophie Mutter (DG).

Karol Szymanowski (1882-1937)

Violin Concerto No. 1, Op. 35 (1916)
Had Scriabin written a violin concerto, it may well have sounded like Szymanowski's First. How best to describe it? Lyrical it certainly is, and lavish too – though never gratuitously so. It's almost as if each major climax is a composite of a thousand luminous jewels, so dazzling is its range of tone and colour. The Concerto was written for the great Polish violinist Paul Kochanski and makes considerable demands on the soloist. It is cast in a single movement that falls into three sections.

 ***Thomas Zehetmair (violin), City of Birmingham Symphony Orchestra/Sir Simon Rattle***
EMI digital

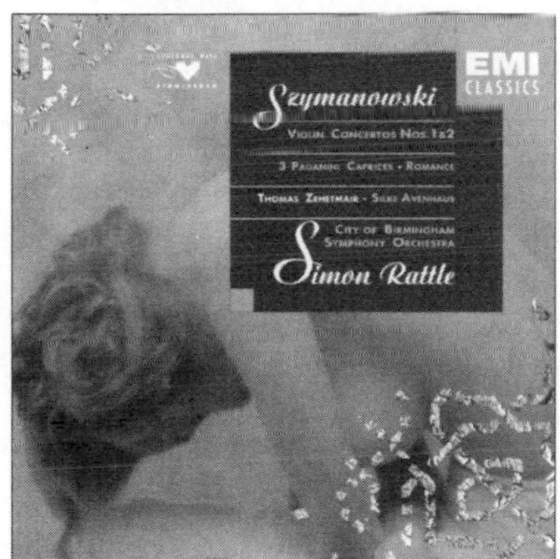

Zehetmair's expressive agility and Rattle's ear for timbre combine for a reading that, in terms of colour and sheer physical impact, is unrivalled. The recording is dynamically expansive, but there are one or two notable older recordings, the best of which feature Wanda Wilkomirska (Polskie Nagrania [Muza], analogue) and David Oistrakh (Melodiya or Chant du Monde, mono)

Alban Berg (1885-1935)

Violin Concerto, "To the memory of an Angel" (1935)
The angel in question was Manon Gropius, the 18-year old daughter of Alma Mahler (by her second husband, a famous architect). Berg completed his Concerto tribute shortly before his own death, fashioning a poignant essay that combines Mahlerian intensity with skilful use of 12-tone techniques. It is perhaps the most accessible of so-called '12-tone' or 'serial' works, not least on account of the appearance – towards the end of the initially fraught second movement – of Bach's chorale melody *Es ist genug* ("It is enough! Lord, if it pleases you, take off my yoke!").

 ***Josef Suk (violin), Czech Philharmonic Orchestra/ Karel Ančerl***
Supraphon analogue
Suk's warmth of tone and felicitous phrasing, combined with a refusal to overstate the case (very important in such an incredibly intense piece) is fully matched by Ančerl's beautifully shaped account of the orchestral score. Worthy rivals include Arthur Grumiaux (Philips), Henryk Szeryng (DG) – both are analogue – and Frank Peter Zimmermann (EMI, digital).

Frank Martin (1890-1974)

Petite Symphonie concertante for harp, harpsichord, piano and string orchestra (1944-45)
A modern follow-up to the Baroque *Concerto grosso*, spiky, highly original in design (although the actual scoring recalls Bach's *Brandenburg Concertos*), darkly coloured and with occasional echoes of jazz. The *Petite Symphonie* is just one in a series of works that was commissioned by the Swiss conductor Paul Sacher. There are three movements, the first of which – a pained *Adagio* leading to a propulsive *Allegro con moto* – is longer than the other two put together (cf Bach's Fifth *Brandenburg Concerto*).

 ***Pierre Jamet (harp), Germaine Vaucher-Clerc (harpsichord), Doris Rossiaud (piano), Suisse Romande Orchestra/Ernest Ansermet***
Decca mono
Although recorded as long ago as 1951, Ansermet's classic performance remains especially convincing. Digital-only collectors are advised to investigate a fine recording by the London Philharmonic under Matthias Bamert (Chandos).

Bohuslav Martinů (1890-1959)

Double Concerto for two string orchestras, piano and timpani (1938)
A grim sister to Bartók's similarly antiphonal *Music for strings, percussion and celesta* (composed two years earlier), tough, tense, propulsive and with urgent dialogue between the two string orchestras. Martinů's style straddles the borders of the neo-Baroque (like Frank Martin, he was influenced by the *Concerto grosso* form), though the darkly spiralling *Largo* wrestles at the limits of tonality.

 ***Jan Panenka (piano), Josef Hejduk (timpani), Czech Philharmonic Orchestra/Karel Sejna***
Supraphon analogue
Karel Sejna started his career among the double-basses of the Czech Phil. He knows the orchestra from the bottom up (so to

speak) and his style is characterized by a firm rhythmic grip (so important in this work), clarity of vision and a sure sense of structure. The 1958 recording was always excellent, but sounds even better in Supraphon's superb analogue transfer.

Sergey Prokofiev (1891-1953)

Piano Concerto No. 2 in G minor, Op. 16 (1912-13, revised 1923)

"The devil take this futuristic music!" Not the ideal reaction to a concerto-epic by an outrageously talented 22-year old, and hardly indicative of the work's Romantic nature. As it happened, the manuscript was destroyed and Prokofiev re-wrote the concerto some ten years later. It's a brute of piece, extravagant (the first movement features a massive solo cadenza), beefy (try the 'fee-fi-fo-fum' opening of the "Intermezzo"), lyrical and witty.

Victoria Postnikova (piano), USSR Ministry of Culture Symphony Orchestra/Gennadi Rozhdestvensky

Melodiya/BMG analogue

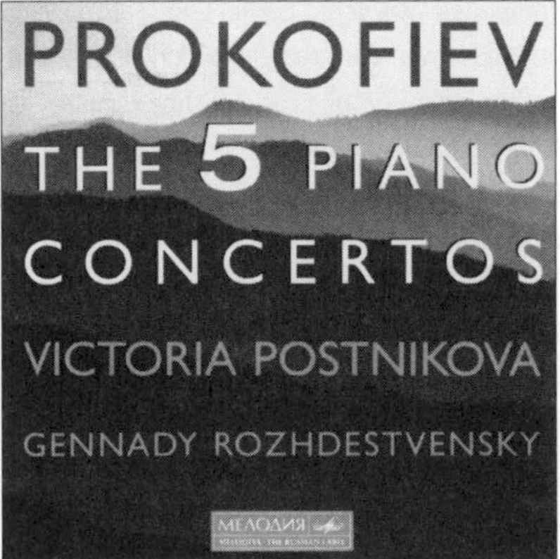

Postnikova is a big player and her full-blooded style finds its musical match in Prokofiev's most expansive piano concerto. Rozhdestvensky supports her with characteristic care over detail and although the recording tends to spotlight solos (especially among the woodwinds), its close-set, fairly aggressive profile suits the music.

Piano Concerto No. 3 in C major, Op. 26 (1917-21)

A radiant, good-humoured concerto that starts quietly, frisks to a lively *Allegro* and features a colourful theme-and-variation second movement. The finale opens to a cheeky, march-style idea but breaks off mid-way for a romantic interlude. Prokofiev's Third Piano Concerto – by far the most popular of the five – is a favourite display piece for virtuosos and ends in a mood of heady excitement.

Victoria Postnikova (piano), USSR Ministry of Culture Symphony Orchestra/Gennadi Rozhdestvensky

Melodiya/BMG analogue

As in the Second Concerto, Postnikova and Rozhdestvensky make real music where others are content merely to hammer the notes. Some chosen tempos are unusually broad, but the tension never flags and the recording, although occasionally 'rigged', is very lifelike. Viable, more orthodox alternatives are on offer from Martha Argerich and Evgeni Kissin (both DG – analogue and digital, respectively), while the composer himself (EMI or Pearl, mono) is effortlessly musical and William Kapell (RCA, mono) is astonishingly brilliant.

Concerto No. 4 in B flat major for piano (left-hand) and orchestra, Op. 53 (1931)

Originally composed for the one-armed pianist Paul Wittgenstein (brother of the philosopher Ludwig), the Fourth Concerto combines lyrical intensity with a consistently gripping sense of struggle. The two outer movements are fast and frothy (they share the same basic material), while the *Andante* harbours one of Prokofiev's finest melodies and the playful third movement alternates grandeur with a disruptive brand of playfulness.

Yefim Bronfman (piano), Israel Philharmonic Orchestra/ Zubin Mehta

Sony Classical digital

A cool, stylishly sculpted reading, though amply responsive to the fourth movement's fun and games. Sony's recording is more refined than Melodiya's (for Postnikova, the next best option), but discerning collectors should also consider the older but equally charismatic Rudolf Serkin version with Eugene Ormandy conducting (again for Sony and recorded back in 1958, analogue).

Piano Concerto No. 5 in G minor, Op. 55 (1931-32)

Both Stravinsky and Schoenberg were present at the Fifth Concerto's première and may well have approved (either overtly or covertly) of Prokofiev's audacious piano writing, its flair and barely contained aggression. The hypnotic slow movement recalls Slavic folk music, while the provocative second movement struts its stuff with maximum force. The finale follows both the Second and Fourth Concertos in relaxing for quieter material, although the Fifth alone ends with a jovial march.

Victoria Postnikova (piano), USSR Ministry of Culture Symphony Orchestra/Gennadi Rozhdestvensky

Melodiya/BMG analogue

Easily the finest version of the Fifth currently available – punchy, incisive and carefully calculated, but with real heart in the

Larghetto. The sound is typically analytical, even a mite coarse, but the overall effect is highly dramatic. Older rivals worth noting include Richter (DG or EMI, analogue) and Vladimir Krainev (Teldec, digital).

Violin Concerto No. 1 in D major, Op. 19 (1916-17)

A concerto that begins like a fairy tale – quietly and to an accompniment of shimmering strings, while the soloist enters with a seamless 'once upon a time'. Things soon hot up, however, with much pungent passagework in the first movement, an icy, reptilian *Scherzo* and a passionate third movement that dies away to memories of the opening *Andantino*.

Frank Peter Zimmermann (violin), Berlin Philharmonic Orchestra/ Lorin Maazel

EMI digital

Zimmermann is a highly intelligent player with a formidable technique and a genuine sense of style. He has the greatest respect for his fêted forebears but is very much his own man. Mention must also be made of such old-world masters as David Oistrakh (a supreme interpreter of this work, though his Russian recordings are best) and Joseph Szigeti (EMI, mono). Both are of course analogue.

Violin Concerto No. 2 in G minor, Op. 63 (1935)

Prokofiev was a dab hand at re-fashioning musical material: his Second Violin Sonata started life as a flute sonata and his Second Violin Concerto was first conceived as a concert suite for violin and piano. The heart of this Concerto is in the long, winding melody that dominates the second movement while the finale is a rowdy waltz-burlesque (with plenty of work for the bass drum).

Jascha Heifetz (violin), Boston Symphony Orchestra/Charles Munch

RCA analogue

Heifetz's is the sweetest, freshest and most poignant 'Prok 2' on disc – the second movement suggesting just a hint of a 1930s-style popular song. Munch conducts a vigorous accompaniment, but there's an equally fine predecessor with the same soloist (the concerto's first-ever recording, in fact), also from Boston, under Serge Koussevitzky (Biddulph or RCA, mono).

Paul Hindemith (1895-1963)

Violin Concerto (1939)

By scoring the opening bars for solo timpani, i.e. reminding us that Beethoven's Violin Concerto starts in a similar fashion, Hindemith shows his affection for past masters. The Concerto's lilting first minutes tell us that this will be one of the composer's more approachable works, while the lyrical strain reaches a new level of intensity for the second movement and the finale is dry, boisterous and entirely characteristic (its breezy extroversion and poetic interludes remind us that Sir William Walton's music is heavily influenced by Hindemith).

Isaac Stern (violin), New York Philharmonic Orchestra/ Leonard Bernstein

Sony Classical analogue

Superb solo work from Stern, keenly accompanied by Bernstein and captured in typically 'wide-screen' Sony sound. The keenest rivalry comes from David Oistrakh, preferably under the composer's baton (Decca, analogue) and André Gertler under Karel Ančerl (Supraphon, analogue).

Erich Wolfgang Korngold (1897-1957)

Violin Concerto, Op. 35 (1945)

Get the tissues ready for a concerto that revisits all those vintage Hollywood weepies with their gorgeous, heart-rending soundtracks. Korngold uses material that he had already employed for the films *Another Dawn*, *Juarez*, *Anthony Adverse* and *The Prince and the Pauper*. The first movement opens with one of Korngold's loveliest melodies, but it is the central *Romance* that really tugs at the heart-strings. Everything is beautifully written – as indeed one might expect from a prodigy whose early works were championed by some of the greatest conductors of the day.

Jascha Heifetz (violin), Los Angeles Philharmonic Orchestra/ Alfred Wallenstein

RCA mono

"The work was contemplated for a Caruso of the violin rather than a Paganini," wrote Korngold. "It is needless to say," he continued, "how delighted I am to have my Concerto performed by Caruso and Paganini in one person: Jascha Heifetz." A less sympathetic commentator complained that the work contains "more corn than gold" – but that was at a time when musical snobbery was more prevalent than it is now.

George Gershwin (1898-1937)

Piano Concerto in F major (1925)

Gershwin's largest-scale instrumental work is a colourful narrative in three movements that sings 'America' every inch of the way. The opening uses timpani to dramatic effect, and thereafter blues, swing and romantic melodiousness (the sort that's well-known from *Rhapsody in Blue*, see below) predominate. The slow movement is a soulful elegy interrupted by a cheeky dance tune, while the finale is a pianistic speed-track.

Daniel Wayenberg (piano), Paris Conservatoire Orchestra/Georges Prêtre
EMI analogue
Nimble pianism from Wayenberg backed by French orchestral sonorities (c1960) that sound absolutely right for the score (the Parisian brass sport an authentically 1920s-sounding vibrato, while the woodwinds are tart and reedy). Those preferring something a little less idiosyncratic might like to try the excellent analogue alternatives from Eugene List (Mercury) and André Previn (EMI).

Rhapsody in Blue (1924)

Gershwin gatecrashes the classical foyer with a showpiece that combines aspects of jazz with virtuoso piano writing on a Lisztian scale. "No set plan was in my mind, no structure to which my music would conform," he once said; "... I was summoned to Boston ... It was on the train with its steely rhythms, its rattlety-bang that is so stimulating to a composer ... I frequently hear music in the very heart of noise. And then I suddenly heard – and even saw on paper – the complete construction of the *Rhapsody*, from beginning to end ... as a sort of musical kaleidoscope of America."

George Gershwin (piano), Columbia Jazz Band/Michael Tilson Thomas
Sony Classical analogue
Rhapsody in Blue was orchestrated by Ferde Grofé, initially for jazz band (and Paul Whiteman's band in particular), then for full symphony orchestra. This particular recording employs a 1925 piano roll as 'backed' by a zippy 1970s performance of the original jazz orchestration. The sound is excellent, the playing rumbustious in the extreme – although one shouldn't forget Leonard Bernstein's lovingly indulgent Sony (analogue) recording from some years earlier.

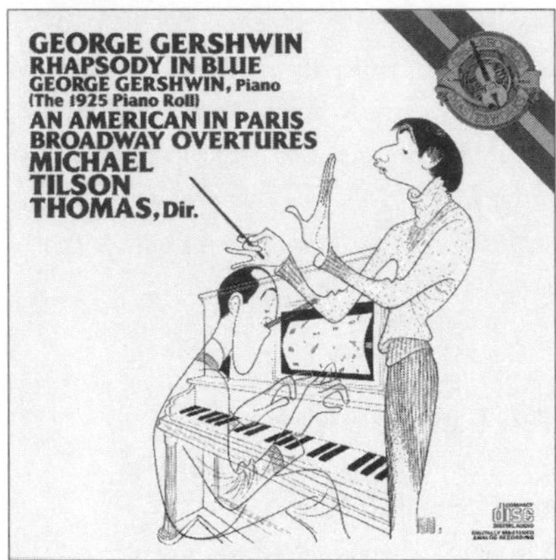

Francis Poulenc (1899-1963)

Concerto in G minor for organ, strings and percussion (1938)

A riot of a piece composed at the near edge of world catastrophe and opening to a harshly dissonant solo cadenza. Poulenc's design incorporates four movements in one and embraces a wide range of mood and expression, from gruelling drama to an almost religious intensity and sweet, salon-style melodies. It certainly gives the lie to those who accuse Poulenc of perfumed superficiality.

Berj Zamkochian (organ), Boston Symphony Orchestra/Charles Munch
RCA analogue
Charles Munch conducted the Concerto's public première (in 1941) and his obvious authority is fully matched by the commanding virtuosity of Berj Zamkochian, who summons a massive sonority from Boston Symphony Hall's superb organ (with its 4,802 pipes). The orchestra, one of America's finest, responds excitedly to Munch's flamboyant direction.

Concerto for two pianos and orchestra in D minor (1932)

A punchy opening has both pianists showing their technical mettle, while the ensuing theme – one of Poulenc's best – crosses Mozartian elegance with Bachian severity. Thereafter, adorable varieties of musical silliness (frothy tunes that stick their tongues out) give way to what sounds like an imitation of Balinese gamelan music. The wistful *Larghetto* features more Mozartian references, whereas the kitsch-style finale (hints of *Pale Hands I Loved*, and much else) returns us to a mood of playful exuberance.

Francis Poulenc, Jacques Février (pianos), Paris Conservatoire Orchestra/Georges Prêtre
EMI analogue
Février was a long-term friend of the composer; in fact, it was he who partnered Poulenc for the 1932 première. Thirty-odd years later and the two men were still playing with immense vitality. There are other good versions around (Gold and Fizdale under Leonard Bernstein – Sony, analogue – being among the most strongly-characterized) but Février and Poulenc are still the best.

Aaron Copland (1900-1990)

Concerto for clarinet and string orchestra, with harp and piano (1947-48)

It would be difficult to imagine a more serenely peaceful musical interlude than the opening of Copland's Clarinet Concerto. There are basically two sections to the work, the first of which is marked "Slowly and expressively", and the second (which is full of witty, Swing-inspired 'jazzisms'), "Rather fast". The Concerto was commissioned by the 'King of Swing' Benny Goodman.

Benny Goodman (clarinet), Columbia Symphony Orchestra/Aaron Copland

Sony Classical analogue

Goodman's second recording of the Copland Concerto is idiomatic, spirited and easygoing. The sound (dating from the 1960s) is remarkably good for the period, although there's a fine, easygoing digital alternative featuring the young French clarinettist Paul Meyer with the English Chamber Orchestra under David Zinman (Denon).

Joaquín Rodrigo (b1902)

Concierto de Aranjuez for guitar and orchestra (1939)

The *Concierto*'s heart is a beautiful, dreamy *Adagio* that the blind composer once referred to as an "elegiac dialogue". Rodrigo's wife recalls that the movement "was an evocation of the happy days of our honeymoon when we would walk through the parks of Aranjuez; at the same time it was a song of love". The outer movements are breezy, high-spirited and luminously scored. Rodrigo has composed at least 13 concertos, six of which involve the guitar.

Pepe Romero (guitar), Academy of St Martin in the Fields/Sir Neville Marriner

Philips digital

Romero's easy virtuosity is matched by quietly eloquent playing from members of the Academy (the cor anglais especially). It's a beautiful recording, while the appropriate couplings include the Fantasía para un gentilhombre (which is second only to the Concierto in popularity).

Sir William Walton (1902-1983)

Viola Concerto in A minor (1928-29, revised 1936 and 1961)

Among the earliest of Walton's major works, and one of the finest concertos for the instrument – mellow, inventive (the Scherzo has an almost Handelian exuberance), skilfully orchestrated and melodically distinctive. The last movement is especially beautiful. The Concerto was composed at Sir Thomas Beecham's behest and was originally intended for the noted British violist Lionel Tertis (who initially turned it down). In the event, it was the great German composer and violist Paul Hindemith who gave the world première – at a 1929 Prom.

Yehudi Menuhin (viola), New Philharmonia Orchestra/ Sir William Walton

EMI analogue

A warmly responsive reading, perceptively conducted and well recorded – although there's notable vintage (mono) rivalry from Frederick Riddle (Dutton) and William Primrose (Pearl), both under Walton's baton. There's also a pretty impressive stereo/analogue version by the fine Russian violist Yuri Bashmet under Gennadi Rozhdestvensky (Revelation – and coupled with Benjamin Britten's Spring Symphony sung in Russian!).

Violin Concerto in B minor (1938-39, revised 1943)

The melodies would be worthy of the great Romantics while Walton's colourful orchestration (as revised in 1943) bears the hallmark of a true master. One particular moment towards the end of the first movement (7'34" into the first track on this particular disc) has the soloist weave a soulful accompaniment for the return of the main theme (on the flute): it is among the loveliest moments in all twentieth-century music. The Scherzo is a real *tour de force*, both for the soloist and the orchestra.

Jascha Heifetz (violin), Philharmonia Orchestra/Sir William Walton

RCA mono

Jascha Heifetz commissioned the Walton Concerto; he also premièred it and recorded it twice (both times for RCA). His, it should be said, is a benchmark interpretation, although Aaron Rosand's loving rendition (Harmonia Mundi, digital) is captured in superior sound. There's also an extremely moving Sony (analogue) recording featuring Zino Francescatti as soloist (Eugene Ormandy conducts the Philadelphia Orchestra).

Aram Khachaturian (1903-1978)

Violin Concerto in D minor (1940)

The composer of the *Sabre Dance* opens his only Violin Concerto with a dramatic orchestral flourish and a propulsive, neo-

Baroque solo line. The second theme is haunting and lyrical, as indeed is the whole of the slow movement, whereas the *Allegro vivace* finale re-visits the fiery world of Khachaturian's *Gayaneh* ballet. The whole work has a decidedly Eastern flavour. David Oistrakh, our preferred soloist and the Concerto's dedicatee, helped mould the solo part.

David Oistrakh (violin), Philharmonia Orchestra/ Aram Khachaturian

EMI mono

David Oistrakh's self-effacing virtuosity and natural poise make the very best of a score that, in the wrong hands, can sound brash, even rather empty. There are various recordings with Oistrakh as soloist (most of them emanating from Russian sources), but this is the most polished and refined. Viable alternatives include Leonid Kogan with Charles Munch conducting (RCA, analogue), Julian Sitkovetsky (with a decidedly Eastern-sounding accompaniment under composer-conductor Taki Niyazi, Russian Disc, mono) and an elderly but sweet-centred performance featuring film soundtrack virtuoso Louis Kaufman (Biddulph, mono).

Sir Michael Tippett (b1905)

Concerto for double string orchestra (1938-39)

Although fairly complex in design, the Concerto presents such involving musical arguments that any listening difficulties (mostly to do with dissimilar instrumental lines converging) are dwarfed by the work's emotional thrust. The *Adagio cantabile* features a particularly powerful main theme (English through and through although universal in its appeal), while both outer movements are rich in lively rhythmic interplay.

Moscow Chamber Orchestra, Bath Festival Orchestra/Rudolf Barshai

EMI analogue

Tangible proof that great music transcends national borders. The two orchestras 'connect' as if they'd been playing together for years and although the recording is a little thin by today's highest standards, it's more than adequate. There's a fine digital alternative from the Academy of St Martin in the Fields under Sir Neville Marriner (EMI).

Dmitry Shostakovich
(1906-1975)

Cello Concerto No. 2 in G major, Op. 126 (1966)

Much as I hate generalizations, I'd suggest that while Shostakovich's warmly expressive First Violin Concerto is marginally greater than his more cynical Second, his predominantly acid Second Cello Concerto has the edge over his more accessible First. Here we have poetry, irony and a mounting anger that raises the alarm (on whooping horns) at the beginning of the last movement. The heat intensifies further as the movement progresses, and the overall effect is akin to the mysterious though often biting musical language of Shostakovich's last symphonies and string quartets.

Mischa Maisky (cello), London Symphony Orchestra/Michael Tilson Thomas

Deutsche Grammophon digital

Maisky tends the Concerto's lyrical sections with abundant affection (his soft playing is often breathtaking) and Tilson Thomas leads an alert, incisive accompaniment – though readers might also like to investigate recordings by Heinrich Schiff (with the composer's son Maxim conducting, Philips, digital) and the work's dedicatee, Mstislav Rostropovich (DG, analogue or even better – and if you can find it – live on Russian Disc, also analogue).

Piano Concerto No. 2 in F major, Op. 102 (1957)

Anyone sampling the disarmingly tender *Andante* could be forgiven for thinking in terms of Rachmaninov, or even Chopin. Shostakovich composed nothing else like it, but then he did write it for his (then) young son Maxim. Unashamedly popularist, the Second Concerto also features a mock-militaristic first movement with a prominent snare-drum part and a jokey, off-beat finale that habitually brings the house down.

Leonard Bernstein (piano), New York Philharmonic Orchestra

Sony Classical analogue

A famous musical balancing act where Lenny displays double-barrelled virtuosity and the recording – made just a year after the work was composed – stands up remarkably well. Viable alternatives include Eugene List (best under Maxim Shostakovich's direction, Melodiya, analogue) and the composer himself (EMI, mono).

Violin Concerto No. 1 in A minor, Op. 99 (1947-48, revised 1955)

A noble but defiant Concerto, composed for David Oistrakh in the wake of Stalin's repressive dictates on art and rich in meaningful allusions – not least in the Scherzo, where Shostakovich's use of his own musical 'signature', D. Sch. – the notes D-E flat ("Es" in German)-C-B ("H" in German). The first movement is a brooding Nocturne, the Passacaglia third movement opens with a broad-shouldered brass theme, while the finale suggests forced jollifications in the face of humiliation and persecution (most especially of the Jews).

Maxim Vengerov (violin), London Symphony Orchestra/Mstislav Rostropovich

Teldec digital

A palpable triumph from the young Vengerov, and one of the best recordings of the work to have come our way since David Oistrakh's magnificent mono recording of the 1950s (under Dimitri Mitropoulos – Sony, and still an essential document). Vengerov's friend, contemporary and colleague Vadim Repin has also made a fine digital CD of the piece (under Kent Nagano, Erato).

Samuel Barber (1910-1981)

Violin Concerto (1939-40)

A fully-fledged Romantic concerto, as you can easily discover by sampling either the opening few minutes or the emotionally charged *Andante*. The man who commissioned the concerto (Samuel Fels) initially thought it insufficiently technically demanding for his adopted prodigy (Iso Briselli) but, after a certain amount of to-ing and fro-ing, Barber's masterpiece finally saw the light of day. Few twentieth-century concertos are as accessible or as instantly lovable as this.

Itzhak Perlman (violin), Boston Symphony Orchestra/Seiji Ozawa

EMI digital

Perlman's warmth of tone and personality suit this work perfectly. The recording is clean and luminous, while the all-American couplings (which include Bernstein's fine Serenade) are highly appropriate. Older versions worth noting feature Isaac Stern (Sony, analogue) and Louis Kaufman (the luscious-sounding soloist on the film soundtrack of Gone with the Wind, Music & Arts, mono).

Benjamin Britten (1913-1976)

Violin Concerto in D minor, Op. 15 (1939, revised 1958)

The very opening (a pivotal motive scored for timpani, cymbal and sensually sliding strings) is instantly arresting. And yet there's even better to come. A mischievous *Scherzo*, for example, and a cadenza leading to a wonderful Passacaglia (varied repetitions of the one theme) – an idea that Shostakovich followed in his First Violin Concerto, but in reverse. The closing pages of the Concerto are among the most haunting in the twentieth-century orchestral repertory.

Nora Grumliková (violin), Prague Symphony Orchestra/Peter Maag

Supraphon analogue

A recording that represents a considerable achievement – not only for the soloist (fine though she is), but also for the Prague Symphony Orchestra and Peter Maag. The performance suggests an intuitive grasp of what this work is all about (and it's often about profound emotional discomfort), though if you have difficulty in tracking it down, then Mark Lubotsky's Decca analogue recording (under the composer's baton) is a worthy second choice.

John Adams (b1947)

Violin Concerto (1993)

Mysterious, mobile and delicately scored, Adams's Violin Concerto is a subtle study in musical movement. The tone of the work seems to touch on various styles from earlier in the century – Alban Berg (more of the opera *Wozzeck* than of the Violin Concerto) and Sibelius in particular. The evocative second movement is entitled "Body through which the dream flows", after a poem by Robert Haas. The work is dedicated to the late David Huntley, a quiet force in the promotion of twentieth-century music in America. It is possibly the finest violin concerto of the last 50 years.

Gidon Kremer (violin), London Symphony Orchestra/Kent Nagano

Nonesuch digital

Kremer's silvery tone and agile bowing could hardly be more gainfully employed, while Nagano's accompaniment is both responsive and discreet. The recording is excellent.

Classical models (1772-1801)

The Greek word 'symphony' means 'sounding together' but in terms of music, it has meant different things to different eras (and to different countries – in America, for example, the word also denotes a full orchestra). As to Classical symphonies, most consist of four movements, the first of which subscribes to 'sonata form', where an initial 'first subject' (or theme) is developed or 'worked out' then summoned back for a 'recapitulation'. The second movement is usually slow, the third a lighter-hearted Minuet (later – as in Beethoven's symphonies – a Scherzo) and the finale fairly fast and dramatic. The ever-inventive Joseph Haydn was the Classical symphony's true father, and Beethoven its wildest young son.

William Boyce (1711-1779)

Eight Symphonies, Op. 2 (published in 1760)

"Symphonies" here means – roughly speaking – "Overtures", being eight extremely attractive but relatively short pieces cast in either two or three movements (some early Mozart symphonies follow a similar pattern). Much of the material was taken from Boyce's odes, masques and incidental music while the symphonies themselves straddle Baroque and Classical styles, combining (again roughly speaking) the noble gait of Handel's concertos, the liveliness of Vivaldi and the high energy level of early Haydn.

Academy of St Martin in the Fields/Sir Neville Marriner

Decca analogue

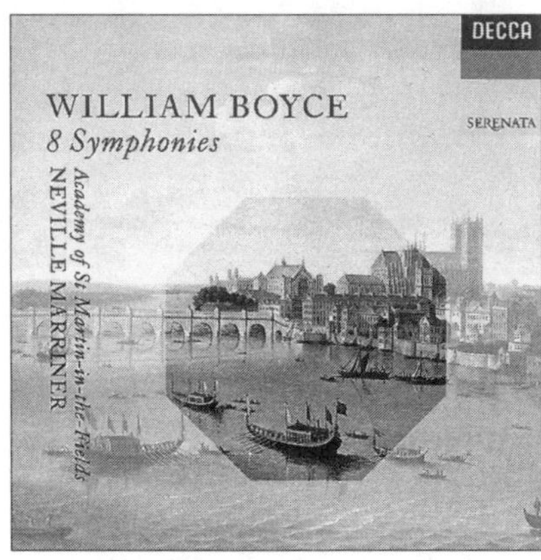

The Academy's performances are typically clean, incisive and warmly phrased, very much along the lines of their equally accomplished recordings of (say) Handel's Concerti grossi, Op. 6 (see "A Baroque Bouquet", above) and Haydn's "Paris" Symphonies (see below). The recordings are excellent.

Joseph Haydn (1732-1809)

Symphony No. 44 in E minor, "Trauersymphonie" (1772)

Haydn's *Sturm und Drang* ("Storm and Stress") symphonies (1760s-1770s) hail from a period that witnessed a new level of pathos and disquiet in European literature (Rousseau, Goethe, Schiller, etc). The music itself is invariably tense, driven and markedly Romantic in spirit; the level of invention (and wit), astonishing even by Haydn's standards. The *Trauer* or "Mourning" Symphony – one of the darkest of the series – is so-called because Haydn is said to have wanted the tender *Adagio* to be performed at his own funeral (it was actually played at a Haydn memorial concert in 1809).

Symphony No. 45 in F sharp minor "Farewell" (1772)

The very opening suggests breathless urgency and a vivid premonition of Mozart's Symphony No. 40. However, the work's title refers specifically to the witty *Adagio* finale where one musician after another finishes his part, packs up his music and departs, leaving just two violinists on stage (this 'phased' instrumentation is written into the score). Haydn's gesture reminded Prince Eszterházy (in whose household he served as Kapellmeister) that his players were homesick after an extended stay at his castle at Einsenstadt.

Symphony Orchestra of Radio Zagreb/Antonio Janigro

Vanguard Classics analogue

Two highlights from a pioneering set, recorded in the former Yugoslavia during 1963 and featuring Symphonies Nos. 44 to 49. Janigro was a master cellist much admired by the conductors Fritz Reiner, Erich Kleiber and Igor Markevitch, and his conducting style blends rhythmic verve with a genuine sense of Classical style. The sound too remains full-bodied and lifelike.

Symphony No. 48 in C major, "Maria Theresia" (1768)

A bright, festive piece composed in honour of the Empress Maria Theresia who had visited Eszterháza castle in September 1773. The opening *Allegro* sizzles with life, the *Adagio* is both mobile and elegant, the Minuet lightly imperious and the finale a robust *Allegro* with lively work for the oboes.

Symphony No. 49 in F minor, "La Passione" (1768)
The sombre opening *Adagio* seems to anticipate Schubert's *Death and the Maiden* Quartet (certainly in its opening phrase), whereas the ensuing *Allegro di molto* has an urgency that's fairly typical of Haydn's work of this period. There's a melancholy Minuet and a *Presto* finale full of dramatic dynamic contrasts.

 ***Orpheus Chamber Orchestra***
Deutsche Grammophon digital

The conductorless Orpheus Chamber Orchestra plays like an augmented string quartet, with keen articulation, fine orchestral discipline and a warm pooled tone. Anyone suspecting that the lack of a maestro means a lack of personality will be pleasantly surprised. The state-of-the-art recordings were made in 1986 at the Arts Center of the New York State University.

Symphony No. 60 in C major, "Il Distratto" (1769)
An ingenious and amusing creation in six rather than the usual four movements – all of which served as incidental music to Jean François Regnard's play about a hapless individual whose persistent absent-mindedness gets him into all sorts of trouble. Haydn's score reflects the character's predicament in various ways – by loud outbursts, sudden digressions, unexpected changes of key, and more.

 ***The Eszterházy Orchestra/David Blum***
Vanguard Classics analogue
An extremely fine orchestra, originally formed to commemorate Haydn's 30 years' residency as Kapellmeister to the Court of Eszterháza. Blum's performances are both scholarly and immensely vital, while our enjoyment is further enhanced by the conductor's highly intelligent booklet-essay. The recordings date from the mid-1960s and sound quite superb.

The "Paris" Symphonies
The "Paris" Symphonies (Nos. 82-87) were the fruits of a commission from Le Concert de la Loge Olympique and marked a significant step forward in terms of Haydn's symphonic development. Furthermore, the Paris orchestras were much larger than the Eszterháza court band that Haydn was used to and therefore facilitated greater colour, weight and brilliance.

Symphony No. 82 in C major, "The Bear" (1786)
The nickname originates in the finale's bagpipe-style principal tune which is said to have reminded Paris audiences of a dancing bear. The slow movement is in variation form, while the Minuet – one of Haydn's most substantial – is especially imperious. The "dancing bear" finale marries the expected wit with a fair degree of urgency.

Symphony No. 83 in G minor, "The Hen" (1785)
The high-powered opening recalls Haydn's *Sturm und Drang* manner of some years earlier (see above), whereas a contrasting 'clucking' second idea explains the *Hen* nickname. The *Andante* slow movement combines lyricism with drama, the Minuet is both warm and expansive and the finale (cast in 12/8 metre) resembles a vigorous jig (with more than a hint of "she cut off their tails with a carving knife"!).

Symphony No. 84 in E flat major (1786)
The slow opening has an airy, quasi-operatic nature, whereas the ensuing *Allegro* is almost Handelian in its robust cheerfulness. The *Andante* opens darkly but blossoms to a fairly colourful series of variations and the Minuet employs the so-called 'Scotch snap' (where 'dotted' notes are reversed, i.e. the short note comes first instead of last).

Symphony No. 85 in B flat major, "The Queen" (1785)
A favourite of Queen Marie-Antoinette that opens to a noble *Largo* and then switches to a vigorous *Allegro*. The second movement is a set of variations on an old French song *La gentille et jeune Lisette* (it was this movement that apparently inspired the Queen's admiration) and the Minuet incorporates rustic *sforzandi* ('forced' accents).

Symphony No. 86 in D major (1786)
After a brightly-lit slow introduction, Haydn launches the most excitable *Allegro* of the set (varied colours add considerable interest to the argument). The poignant slow movement is unusually free in form (Haydn called it a "Capriccio"). The Minuet has a Viennese-style 'trio', while the finale is especially impressive in its urgency and rock-solid structure.

Symphony No. 87 in A major (1785)
One of the first movement's main ideas is an amusing combination of two scale-like motives – one climbing up, the other down.

The slow movement incorporates a brief cadenza for flute and oboe, the Minuet is perhaps the most gracious of the six and the finale is typically rich in thematic variation.

Austro-Hungarian Haydn Orchestra/Adám Fischer

Nimbus digital

Fischer's orchestra is absolutely right for these big, texturally varied pieces: there's weight, clarity and impressive depth to the sound (Nimbus's characteristically reverberant style of recording is here kept well in check). The performances have considerable personality but analogue rivalry includes impressive – albeit occasionally heavy-handed – readings under Bernstein (Sony, in rather opaque sound), Karajan (DG), Menuhin (EMI) and Marriner (Philips).

Symphony No. 88 in G major, "Letter V" (*c*1787)

When Brahms heard the *Largo*, he is reported to have said "I want my Ninth Symphony to sound like that". And little wonder, given its glorious principal melody and solidly dramatic interjections. The vigorous first movement opens to a commanding *Adagio* introduction, while the Minuet is especially rugged (the trio – or central – section suggests the drone of bagpipes) and the finale is exceedingly dramatic. The nickname harks back to a time when Haydn's symphonies were identified by letters of the alphabet rather than by numbers.

La Petite Bande/Sigiswald Kuijken

Virgin Classics digital

Crisp and lean, with plenty of telling detail and very well judged tempos (the finale isn't rushed off its feet, as is sometimes the case). Kuijken conducts a period-instrument orchestra, but there is strong modern-instrument rivalry from Leonard Bernstein (DG, digital, or Sony, analogue) and – provided you can take extremes of tempo (a very slow Largo, a very fast finale) – Toscanini (RCA, mono).

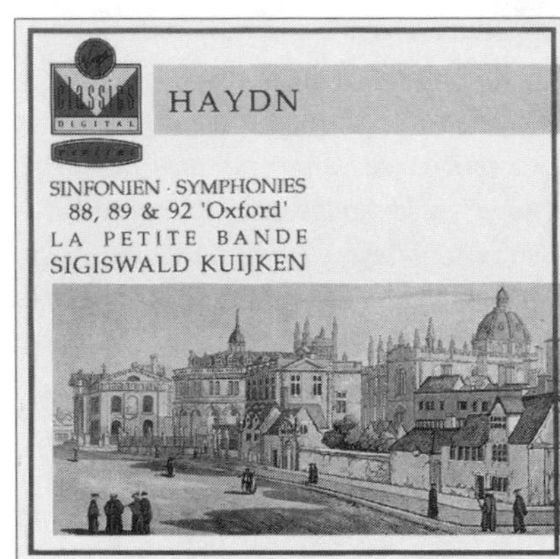

Symphony No. 92 in G, "Oxford" (1789)

The *Oxford* nickname originates from a simple ceremony. Haydn used the symphony to mark his capping as an honorary doctor at Oxford University – albeit some two years after it was composed. As with so many of his later works, Haydn sets things in motion with a broad introduction, whereas the main *Allegro spiritoso* is spiced by off-beat accents and the slow movement is one of the composer's loveliest (its closing moments are particularly touching).

Royal Concertgebouw Orchestra/Sir Colin Davis

Philips digital

The expected virtues of clarity, incisiveness and warmth are as much in evidence here as in Sir Colin's superb set of "London" Symphonies (see below). Both playing and recording are of the highest order and the current coupling for the performance is another fine work, Haydn's Symphony No. 91 in E flat major.

The "London" Symphonies

Like all great masterpieces, Haydn's "London" Symphonies can be appreciated on various levels – as tuneful, beautifully crafted musical entertainment; as harbingers of Beethoven's standard-bearing 'Nine' (see below and "The Romantic Revolution"), or as the innovative, witty and often profound late fruits of a musical genius. The "London" label is easy to explain. In 1790, Haydn's employer Prince Nikolaus Eszterháza died; his successor was less interested in music, and it seemed an opportune time for "the Shakespeare of music" (as Haydn was called) to visit the British capital. He travelled in response to requests from the German violinist, impresario and composer Johann Peter Salomon, first in 1790-91 and again in 1794-95. Indeed, it was for Salomon's London concerts that Haydn composed what, in the event, turned out to be his last 12 symphonies.

Symphony No. 93 in D major (1791)

The first numbered "London" Symphony was not the first to be written but was actually intended for the opening concert of the 1792 season. A noble introduction gives way to a breezy, folk-like *Allegro assai* that, in turn, generates an infectious sense of well-being (note the merrily chugging 'second subject'). The second movement opens blandly before darkening significantly and ending with a joke where bassoons blare out a rude bottom C. The somewhat hefty Minuet features a trio for drums and brass.

Symphony No. 94 in G major, "Surprise" (1791)

The nickname originates from an unexpected loud chord in the theme-and-variations slow movement which was designed, according to Haydn's biographer, not to awaken his sleeping public but to surprise them with something new. The earthy Minuet is unusually fast and bucolic (*Allegro molto*) – rather like a musical representation of a Breughel painting – while the finale is one of Haydn's wittiest.

Symphony No. 95 in C minor (1791)
The highly dramatic first movement glances back at minor-key Mozart (the great G minor Fortieth Symphony was composed three years earlier) and forwards to the assertive world of Beethoven (the Fifth Symphony is written in the same key). Haydn described the second movement as "a little *Andante*"; the Minuet opens in an uncommonly pensive mood and the finale's initial phrases suggest the gracefulness of a lyrical aria.

Symphony No. 96 in D major, "Miracle" (1791)
The earliest of the "London" Symphonies is also among the most inventive. Listen, for example, to the fiercely Beethovenian drama that characterizes the first movement's closing bars, or the quietly held intensity of the helter-skelter finale (where Haydn himself requested the "softest possible *piano*"). In this particular case, the nickname is mistakenly applied: the 'miracle' refers to a chandelier that came crashing down during a concert that included Symphony No. 102, not No. 96.

Symphony No. 97 in C major (1792)
One of the least-known "London" Symphonies, but a real cracker all the same (it is, together with No. 98, the greatest of those written during Haydn's first London visit). The slow introduction slides imperceptibly into a boldly battling *Vivace*, whereas the second movement – a theme with variations – makes novel use of *sul ponticello* (bowing 'on the bridge' and producing a thin, glassy sound). The Minuet suggests Handelian pomp, and the finale the gruff humour of the young Beethoven.

Symphony No. 98 in B flat major (1792)
The solemn opening makes a dark, even intimidating statement of the theme that – moments later – dominates the principal *Allegro*. This wind-blown first movement is followed by a profoundly Mozartian *Adagio* (with coincidental echoes of *God Save the Queen*) where great depth of feeling suggests a possible tribute (Mozart had died the previous year). The gaily skipping finale is full of novel effects.

Symphony No. 99 in E flat major (1793)
One of the brightest, most expressive works in the series, with a particularly droll first-movement 'second subject'. The *Andante* includes a trio for woodwinds; the Minuet's opening approximates a humorous 'question and answer' and the finale is hyperactively contrapuntal. After the first performance, the *Morning Chronicle* wrote "the overture, being performed with increasing accuracy and effect, was received with increasing rapture".

Symphony No. 100 in G major, "Military" (1793-94)
Nothing could be less military than the pleading sentiments of the opening *Adagio*, but when it comes to the *Allegretto* second movement Haydn employs a line-up of triangle, cymbals and bass drum to create a 'Turkish' effect that was popular at the time (and which he reintroduces in the finale). A contemporary correspondent described the Symphony as "rather less learned and easier to take in than some other recent works [of Haydn's], yet is just as rich in new ideas".

Symphony No. 101 in D major, "Clock" (1793-94)
This particular 'clock' runs for the duration of the *Andante* (the clock's mechanism is personified by the 'tick-tock' accompaniment to the main theme), though, as a symphonic movement, it's by no means lacking in drama. The opening *Adagio* is one of Haydn's finest, and the ensuing *Presto* especially dynamic. The Minuet is the longest of any in the "London" Symphonies, and the finale is notably rich in tonal contrasts.

Symphony No. 102 in B flat major (1794)
One of the most harmonically daring and structurally sophisticated works in the series: the urgent first movement is rich in ear-catching accents and dramatic hesitations – again, Beethoven springs to mind. The slow movement is especially beautiful – anyone not convinced of the lyrical powers of Haydn's muse should hear it – and the vigorous finale has a definite sense of 'outdoors'.

Symphony No. 103 in E flat major, "Drum Roll" (1795)
The solo drum roll marks the Symphony's mysterious opening, whereas a little later there's an unmistakable premonition of the introduction to Beethoven's First Symphony (heard among the woodwinds). The first movement *Allegro* has tremendous panache (it is marked *con spirito*, or "with spirit"), the second movement is darkly ceremonial – at least initially – and the finale (again, marked *con spirito*) opens to a bracing call to arms on the horns.

Symphony No. 104 in D major "London" (1795)
The beefiest of Haydn's first-movement slow introductions prefaces one of his finest symphonic structures. The *Andante* has a

genuine sense of tragedy at its core (evident roughly half-way through the movement), the Minuet includes further examples of the amusing 'false stops' that Haydn had employed in various earlier works and the finale combines long-breathed lyricism (the dreamy second subject) with great cumulative excitement – especially from the strings.

 ***Royal Concertgebouw Orchestra, Amsterdam/Sir Colin Davis***
Philips analogue/digital
Naturalness is the key word here, a fluent, unforced and consistently satisfying series of performances that point and illuminate the individual characteristics of each work without resorting to caricature (a frequent interpretative vice in Haydn symphonies). Davis had forged a genuine rapport with his marvellous Dutch players and is rightly proud of these sessions, while the extremely lifelike recordings – whether analogue or digital (as in Symphonies Nos. 93 and 94) – vividly mirror his warm and witty interpretative stance. However, those who favour a more highly-coloured option are directed either to the robust period-instrument cycle under Frans Brüggen (Philips, digital), the endearingly imperious Herbert von Karajan (DG, analogue), Sir Thomas Beecham's warmly characterized set (EMI, mono and analogue/stereo) or the quirky but frequently arresting New York recordings of Leonard Bernstein (Sony, analogue).

Wolfgang Amadeus Mozart
(1756-1791)

Symphony No. 25 in G minor, K183/173*dB* (1773)
The first genuine augury of Mozart's mature symphonic style, often known as the 'little' G minor to distinguish it from the bigger and better-known G minor of 1788 (see below). Urgent in tone and mood (this was, after all, Mozart's 'tragic' key), its prophetic nature extends further to a Minuet that anticipates the parallel movement in another great late work – again in G minor – the String Quintet, K516. Mozart's No. 25 was exclusively used in the film *Amadeus*.

 ***Royal Concertgebouw Orchestra/Nikolaus Harnoncourt***
Teldec digital
Harnoncourt's Mozart is cast very much in a 'post-Amadeus' mould – in other words, dramatic and sharply attenuated rather than merely elegant. His 'little' G minor is admirably assertive, although Benjamin Britten's more temperate performance (Decca, analogue) provides a perceptive alternative.

Symphony No. 29 in A major, K201/186*a* (1774)
Mozart's A major Symphony possesses a particularly winning first idea in an ardently repeated phrase underpinned by a noble, rising accompaniment: the effect is quietly exhilarating, while the remainder of the movement bristles with life (the development section especially). There's a tender *Andante* (it could almost come from one of the operas), a gallant Minuet and a vigorous, good-humoured finale.

 ***English Chamber Orchestra/Benjamin Britten***
Decca analogue
A bright, intelligently phrased performance, beautifully played and with an underlying humanity that illuminates every bar. Abbado and the Berlin Philharmonic (Sony) provide a fine digital alternative, while Ton Koopman (Erato, digital) tops the period-instrument stakes. There's also a punchy though rather mannered version under Pablo Casals (Sony, mono).

Symphony No. 31 in D major, K297/300*a*, "Paris" (1778)
There are various theories as to exactly what it was that so excited the Paris audience at the première of this Symphony. Furthermore, Mozart wrote two *Andantes* and there's still debate as to which one should be performed. The Symphony itself is full of vigour and inventive ideas, not least in the first movement. There is no Minuet.

 ***Royal Concertgebouw Orchestra/Nikolaus Harnoncourt***
Teldec digital
A vivid, highly inflected performance, one that's especially sensitive to the dramatic key change that sits at the heart of the first movement. It also includes a performance of the alternative Andante. Orchestral playing is precise and the sound is appealingly 'open', but collectors with a taste for vintage performances will find either of Beecham's recordings (LPO or RPO, EMI or Sony, both mono) to be full of character.

Symphony No. 33 in B flat major, K319 (1779)

The last movement is irresistible, a jig-like *Allegro assai* ("very cheerful") with plenty of bustling counterpoint. The Symphony was originally cast in three movements, but when Mozart moved to Vienna (from Salzburg) he added the Minuet and Trio. It is believed that the work was originally intended for a theatrical troupe of actors, dancers and singers.

 ***Cleveland Orchestra/George Szell***

Sony Classical analogue

Szell's performance bristles with life: the finale in particular benefits from crisp articulation and elegant phrase-shaping. The dry but lively 1962 recording remains extraordinarily clear, but if digital sound is a prerequisite, then Sir Charles Mackerras (Telarc) and Michael Gielen (Intercord/EMI) provide viable options.

Symphony No. 34 in C major, K338 (1780)

The last symphony that Mozart composed in Salzburg opens with a martial gesture. There are just three movements (again, the finale is especially delightful) and although the first was originally followed by a Minuet (the initial 14 bars of which were written on the back of the last page of first movement), it was subsequently torn from the manuscript score.

 ***Concertgebouw Orchestra/George Szell***

Philips analogue

One of the finest of Szell's Concertgebouw recordings - superbly played, keenly characterized and captured in clear, spacious sound. Harnoncourt's digital Concertgebouw recording (Teldec) makes an excellent second choice but - as with most of the symphonies - Sir Neville Marriner's Academy of St Martin in the Fields is consistently 'on the ball' (there are two different sets - the 'complete' symphonies on analogue Philips and the major works only on digital EMI. The Philips performance is marginally superior).

Symphony No. 35 in D major, K385, "Haffner" (1782)

As originally composed (i.e. to celebrate the ennoblement of Mozart's friend Sigmund Haffner the younger), the *Haffner* Symphony incorporated both a March and a first-movement 'repeat' (where the initial arguments should be played a second time). However, Mozart's final plan dispensed with both. The Symphony opens with a commanding flourish and ends with a witty finale.

 ***Berlin Philharmonic Orchestra/Claudio Abbado***

Sony Classical digital

A lean, well-crafted interpretation, skilfully conducted and extremely well recorded. The Haffner has been especially lucky on disc, with estimable alternatives under Marriner (EMI, digital or Philips, analogue), Harnoncourt (Teldec, digital), Karl Böhm (DG, analogue) and two notable mono recordings under Toscanini - one with the New York Philharmonic Symphony (1929, RCA or Pearl - and very flexible in its phrasing) and the other with the NBC Symphony (1946 and much 'straighter').

Symphony No. 36 in C major, K425, "Linz" (1783)

The second of the six 'late' symphonies opens with a noble *Adagio*, then edges in to a particularly exhilarating *Allegro spiritoso*. The slow movement is among Mozart's loveliest and the finale among his most brilliant. Mozart had just married Constanze and was travelling to Salzburg to introduce her to his family. *En route*, he was shown great kindness by Count Thun in Linz. "On Tuesday November 4 [1783] I am giving a concert in the theatre here", wrote Mozart to his father; "and as I have not a single symphony with me, I am writing a new one at breakneck speed".

 ***Bavarian Radio Symphony Orchestra/Rafael Kubelík***

Sony Classical digital

Those who prefer a lyrical, unforced approach to Mozart symphonies will surely enjoy Kubelík's Bavarian Radio Symphony set of the 'last six', a warm-hearted production that's every bit as a poetic as Bruno Walter's version if not quite as overtly affectionate. As to Walter himself, his famous New York Philharmonic (mono) recording is coupled with an extensive - and highly revealing - rehearsal sequence, "The Birth of a Performance".

Symphony No. 38 in D major, K504, "Prague" (1786)

The very first bars have an unmistakably Beethovenian ring to them: you immediately sense that this is something quite new in Mozart's symphonies - darker in tone, more dramatic and more deeply felt than before (the opening *Adagio's* ritual-style timpani writing sounds especially ominous). And yet the elegance is still there, the *joie de vivre* (especially in the first movement's main *Allegro*). The Symphony No. 38 was composed between *The Marriage of Figaro* and *Don Giovanni* and completed on 1st December 1786, though it was actually intended for a concert in Prague during the following month. Unusually, there is no Minuet third movement.

 ***Royal Concertgebouw Orchestra/Nikolaus Harnoncourt***
Teldec digital

Harnoncourt directs a taut, highly characterful performance, using mainly modern instruments but with a period-instrument sense of style. Viable modern-instrument alternatives include Rafael Kubelík and the Bavarian Radio Symphony Orchestra (Sony or Orfeo [live], digital) and Klemperer's first [mono] Philharmonia recording (originally EMI and in urgent need of a CD reissue.

Symphony No. 39 in E flat major, K543 (1788)

Mozart's last three symphonies were composed in just six weeks - without either a commission or any known plans for performance (although some experts speculate that Mozart may have lived to conduct them). Each work marks a dizzying high point of the symphonic repertory and has its own unmistakable personality, the E flat being distinguished by a noble *Adagio* introduction, a songful *Allegro*, a questioning slow movement, a rustic Minuet with a folk-style trio (lovely writing for the clarinet) and a quicksilver finale.

 ***Chamber Orchestra of Europe/Nikolaus Harnoncourt***
Teldec digital

Harnoncourt views the last three symphonies as a cycle. "I think it is important for once to perform them together, for a special occasion, uncut," he writes; "giving them their full importance, almost as if they were a single work." His E flat is typically lithe and inflected, with all repeats observed, a bracing Minuet and a vigorous account of the finale. The current coupling includes Symphonies Nos. 39-41 and could well serve as a prime recommendation for all three works.

Symphony No. 40 in G minor, K550 (1788)

A miracle within a miracle (Mozart's late and largely unexplained symphonic trilogy), the 'great' G minor lays claim to being the finest of all Classical symphonies - even though, in terms of mood and colouring, it seems to straddle the borders of Classicism and Romanticism. The first movement in particular suggests restlessness, conflict and an unstoppable inward drama: the pace is (or should be) swift, the argument unrelentingly urgent and the melodic material, tragic in tone (save, perhaps, for a consolatory second subject).

 ***English Chamber Orchestra/Benjamin Britten***
Decca analogue

Intuitively musical, intensely dramatic yet finely proportioned and with all repeats observed, Britten's G minor seems to satisfy most schools of interpretative thought - save, perhaps, those who favour digital sound and period instruments (who are in any case well served by John Eliot Gardiner's English Baroque Soloists on Philips). Furtwängler's incredibly urgent mono Vienna Philharmonic recording (EMI) is another absolute 'must'.

Symphony No. 41 in C major, K551, "Jupiter" (1788)

Possibly the most heroic symphonic statement prior to Beethoven's *Eroica* and certainly one of Mozart's most exhilarating creations. The *Jupiter* features forcefully argued outer movements (the finale is in itself an inspired example of dramatically employed counterpoint), a slow movement that reaches operatic levels of lyrical intensity and a highly eventful Minuet.

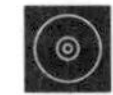 ***Orchestra of the Eighteenth Century/Frans Brüggen***
Philips digital

A veritable epic of a performance (it plays for some 40 minutes), lively but broadly paced, generous with repeats and employing period instruments to dramatic effect. Brüggen seems to approach the score from a Beethovenian axis, but if you prefer a swift modern-instrument approach then George Szell and the Cleveland Orchestra (Sony, analogue) should fit the bill - their top-gear account of the finale is simply mind-blowing. Sir Neville Marriner (Philips, analogue) and Lord Menuhin (Virgin, digital) offer somewhat milder modern-instrument options.

Ludwig van Beethoven
(1770-1827)

Symphony No. 1 in C major, Op. 21 (1800)

Beethoven's symphonic début takes up the story where Haydn left off, although robust good humour and strength of design are common to both composers. The First Symphony features a keenly cantering Scherzo (already an advance on Haydn's Minuet) and an ingenious finale where a halting *Adagio* suddenly transforms to an ebullient *Allegro molto e vivace*.

Orchestra of the Eighteenth Century/Frans Brüggen
Philips digital
Let me say straightaway that Beethoven symphony recordings habitually generate furious controversy among critics – and the relatively 'Classical' First Symphony is certainly no exception. Those who swear by the period-instrument revolution will surely agree that Brüggen's version marked something of a watershed: it was one of the very first 'period' Beethoven orchestral recordings that actually sounded like a real performance (rather than like a historical experiment). Nikolaus Harnoncourt is trim and stylized (Teldec, though not on period instruments), while leading representatives of the Old School still lay claim to unmatched greatness – Arturo Toscanini (RCA or Biddulph, mono), Wilhelm Furtwängler (EMI, Tahra or Music & Arts, mono) and Bruno Walter (Sony, analogue) are, respectively, fiery, elemental and loving. however, their recordings all sound old.

Symphony No. 2 in D major, Op. 36 (1801-02)

"It was only my art that held me back," wrote Beethoven in the "Heiligenstadt Testament" (that despairing confession of his deafness, written in October 1802 to his brothers and named after the town in which he was living at the time). It was during this period that Beethoven completed his epoch-making Second Symphony, a much bigger piece than the First – though it still has one foot in the Classicism camp. The first movement, in particular, is immensely forceful, while the *Larghetto* anticipates the balmy world of the *Pastoral* Symphony and the bucolic finale is rich in mischievous surprises.

NBC Symphony Orchestra/Arturo Toscanini
RCA mono
Yes, an old mono recording (1949-51) – but a performance of such clarity, rhythmic verve and cauterising intensity (the violins in the first movement have to be heard to be believed) that the one-dimensional sound soon ceases to be an issue. However, those averse to single-channel sonics are advised to try Frans Brüggen (Philips, digital), Nikolaus Harnoncourt (Teldec, digital), Pierre Monteux (Decca, analogue) or George Szell (Sony, analogue)

The Romantic Revolution (1804-1911)

It was Ludwig van Beethoven who forged the most imposing bridge between Classical and Romantic symphonic writing (others hinted this way or that, but none to such devastating effect). 'Romantic' in this context ranges from the epoch-making *Eroica* Symphony to the first works in symphonic cycles that were destined to come into our next category, "The New Symphony" (Nielsen, Sibelius, etc). And although Sir Edward Elgar's symphonic masterpieces are, chronologically 'of the twentieth-century', their Romantic soul places them securely within the Romantic Revolution. Conversely, there are some nineteenth-century works that are so profoundly forward-looking (early Mahler, primarily), that we couldn't possibly place them here.

Ludwig van Beethoven
(1770-1827)

Symphony No. 3 in E flat major, Op. 55, "Eroica" (1804)

The Romantic symphony's rightful father, Promethean in its scope, revolutionary in its structure and with an implied moral subtext: Beethoven's first impulse was to name Napoleon Bonaparte as dedicatee, but when Napoleon named himself Emperor – Beethoven destroyed the dedication. The *Eroica*'s ground-plan incorporates a mighty first movement (that plays for anything up to 20 minutes), a noble Funeral March, an effervescent Scherzo and a colourful theme with variations. Beethoven's Third Symphony exceeds the length of his Second by roughly half as much again.

Cleveland Orchestra/George Szell
Sony Classical analogue
With nearly 100 CD versions to choose from, the Eroica will not be pinned down to (or indeed comprehensively represented by) a single interpretation. Szell's performance is stronger, more precise, better played and better balanced than most, but I'd be irresponsible not to mention Toscanini (especially his shattering 1939 RCA recording, mono), Furtwängler (a mighty reading, but only as recorded live – preferably the 1952 version on Tahra) or Klemperer (stoical and strong, especially in his 1955 EMI recording). All three are in mono. There are others, too (Nikolaus Harnoncourt [Teldec]

and Sir Colin Davis [Philips] offer the best digital versions), but you won't go far wrong with our four basic recommendations.

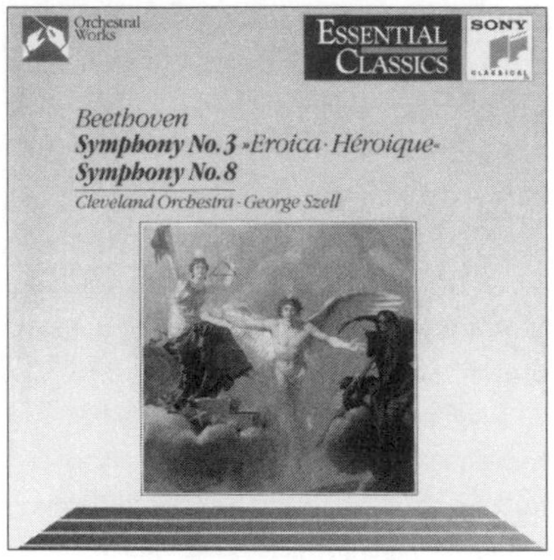

Symphony No. 4 in B flat major, Op. 60 (1806)

Schumann's much-quoted description of the Fourth as a "slim Greek maiden between two Norse giants" has become something of a critical cliché and yet it hardly suggests the exhilaration one feels when, say, the mysterious opening *Adagio* suddenly leaps into a joyful *Allegro vivace*. The Fourth is chock-full of surprises (the first movement especially), while the slow movement's principal theme wouldn't be out of place in an early-Romantic Italian opera.

 ***North German Radio Symphony Orchestra/Günter Wand***

RCA digital

'Balance' is the key-word here, with fine articulation, intelligent phrasing, warm orchestral textures and a sure sense of structure (habitual virtues in Wand's Beethoven). However, the Fourth yields singular secrets to different conductors and I'd additionally commend Furtwängler (DG or Grammofono, mono) for mystery, Toscanini (preferably his 1939 NBC broadcast on Relief or Music & Arts, mono) for a singing line and athletic rhythms and Pierre Monteux (Decca, analogue) for perennial freshness.

Symphony No. 5 in C minor, Op. 67 (1808)

'Fate knocks at the door' with one of the most famous motives in all music: four notes hammered out *Allegro con brio* – proud, defiant and dramatic. The four-note signature crops up again and again in Beethoven, but the Fifth has another striking feature in a rumbustious Scherzo that quietens to an echo before transforming into a triumphant finale and returning again, deathly quiet this time, mid-way through the movement. The *Andante con moto* is in variation form and the Symphony's closing pages race home for an exultant C major peroration.

 ***Vienna Philharmonic Orchestra/Carlos Kleiber***

Deutsche Grammophon analogue

Like father like son, Carlos Kleiber follows Erich (on Decca, mono) with a performance of tremendous vitality. He scores an immediate 'extra' by observing the finale's repeat, but then Kurt Masur (a more temperate view – Philips, digital) adds a rarely observed repeat in the Scherzo. The Fifth has been retold many times on disc; significant historic mono alternatives include the galvanizing Toscanini (RCA – 1939 version, preferably), the elemental Furtwängler (DG or Music & Arts, 1943 or 1947 – both live), the sleek but powerful Karajan (DG, 1962 version – analogue) and the majestic Klemperer (EMI, 1955, mono).

Symphony No. 6 in F major, Op. 68, "Pastoral" (1808)

Beethoven's five-movement structure was something of a novelty at the time, while the programme itself remains self-explanatory: "Pleasant feelings on arriving in the countryside" (a hearty tune, a constant pulse and a hypnotic development section); a songful "scene by the brook"; peasants' merrymaking (with the village clarinettist on great form), a violent storm (Wagner beckons from the distant horizon) and, finally, gratitude for delivery from the storm and a serene Shepherd's Hymn. The *Pastoral* Symphony forged a clear pathway for Berlioz's five-movement *Symphonie fantastique* (see below).

 ***Cleveland Orchestra/George Szell***

Sony Classical analogue

Szell's every brush-stroke is precise, finely graded and colour-sensitive. True, the 1960s recording is beginning to sound its age (it'll be rather too clinical for some), but the performance itself is superb. Viable historic mono alternatives range from the lean and energetic Toscanini (1952, and with a lightning storm) to Furtwängler's leisurely sightseeing tour (1954, Tahra). Sir Colin Davis's beautifully played Staatskapelle Dresden recording (Philips, digital) is also well worth considering.

Symphony No. 7 in A major, Op. 92 (1812)

Wagner described it as "the apotheosis of the dance" – and with good reason. Here Beethoven breaks with conflict to inaugurate a veritable dance festival. The first movement opens majestically but soon skips into a foot-tapping 6/8; the second is a noble *Allegretto* that rather resembles a passing processional; the Scherzo is boundlessly energetic (although the folk-like trio's effect rests largely on the conductor's choice of tempo) and the stamping finale climaxes in whirlwind dialogue between first and second violins.

Vienna Philharmonic Orchestra/Carlos Kleiber

Deutsche Grammophon analogue

Another top-grade production from Kleiber and the Vienna Philharmonic, boundlessly energetic, superbly played and coupled with an equally riveting account of the Fifth (see above). Other notable Sevenths include Toscanini with the New York Philharmonic Symphony (RCA, mono), Kubelík with either the Bavarian Radio Symphony or the Vienna Philharmonic (DG, analogue) and Sir Colin Davis with the Staatskapelle Dresden (Philips, digital).

Symphony No. 8 in F major, Op. 93 (1812)

The brightest and most playful of the nine symphonies, bucolic in the extreme and with a finale that combines mischievous hesitations with an unrelenting energy. The first movement flies into action with one of Beethoven's most robust themes, then builds with the utmost confidence and expertise, while the two middle movements – a tongue-in-cheek *Allegretto scherzando* and a rustically rolling *Tempo di menuetto* – can't fail to raise a smile.

Vienna Philharmonic Orchestra/Pierre Monteux

Decca analogue

A fresh, eminently straightforward account, joyfully projected and superbly played. Monteux lets the music speak for itself, but for a more characterful rendition you might try either the vigorous period-instrument recording under Roger Norrington or the bluff humour of Otto Klemperer (both are on EMI, the Norrington being digital, the Klemperer analogue).

Symphony No. 9 in D minor, Op. 125, "Choral" (1822-24)

That mysterious happenings are afoot is obvious even from the opening bars: a jagged motive on strings set against a restless accompaniment. The Ninth's first movement is a vehement, profoundly futuristic statement and while the wildly cantering Scherzo and relatively peaceful *Adagio* suggest at least a semblance of normality (though even there, surprises abound), the big shock comes with a choral finale that – at a single stroke – changed our perceptions of the symphony for ever. The words, an "Ode to Joy", are by Schiller and Beethoven's excited treatment of them embraces us with a candour and ingenuity that, even today, sounds strikingly innovative.

Sharon Sweet (soprano), Jadwiga Rappé (contralto), Paul Frey (tenor), Franz Grundheber (bass-baritone), Dresden State Opera Chorus, Staatskapelle Dresden/Sir Colin Davis

Philips digital

The beauty of Davis's account is as much in the sound quality as the performance: every detail registers while tempi are more-or-less ideal and the singing generally excellent. However, the Ninth is bigger than all of us and there are many past interpreters who are – in a sense – 'bigger' than Davis, pre-eminently the matchlessly mysterious and deliriously joyful Furtwängler (either 1951, EMI or 1954, Tahra – both are live), the fiery Toscanini (1939, Naxos), or the incomparably lyrical Kubelík (DG analogue or a live recording on Orfeo). Don't shrink from trying as many versions as you can lay your hands on: for example, Norrington (EMI), Gardiner (DG Archiv) and Harnoncourt (Teldec) – all of them digital – are leading exponents of the period-instrument school (although Harnoncourt uses mostly modern instruments).

Franz Berwald (1796-1868)

Symphony No. 3 in C major, "Sinfonie singulière" (1845)

Born the year before Schubert but destined to live 40 years longer, Sweden's greatest composer was both a rich fund of invention and a superb craftsman. He was also something of a medical pioneer, having founded an orthopaedic institute and devised some of the apparatus used therein. There are four mature symphonies, each of which has a subtitle. *The Sinfonie singulière* features a remarkably expressive slow movement (which incorporates a lively Scherzo) as well as audible premonitions of a later Scandinavian master, Carl Nielsen.

Gothenburg Symphony Orchestra/Neeme Järvi

Deutsche Grammophon digital

A fine performance presented as part of a neatly-packaged complete cycle and skilfully remastered from the original digital tapes. Järvi and his Swedish players are captured here in full cry, doing what they're especially good at, i.e. promoting the cause of significant but little-known Scandinavian music.

Franz Schubert (1797-1828)

Symphony No. 4 in C minor, D417, "Tragic" (1816)

The writer Clive Brown has suggested a parallel between this, Schubert's most overtly dramatic Symphony, and Beethoven's similarly restless Fourth String Quartet (also in the pensive key of C minor). Mozart's G minor Symphony (No. 40) is another point of reference, not only in its 'tragic' mood (the two first movements are especially similar), but in that both works were composed relatively quickly. Schubert's outer movements are urgent yet Classical in design, whereas the rustic Minuet anticipates Schumann.

Berlin Philharmonic Orchestra/Nikolaus Harnoncout
Teldec digital
Harnoncourt stresses the 'tragic' nature of Schubert's Fourth (the opening Adagio molto is immensely powerful), but leavens the weight with wide dynamics and a characteristically light touch elsewhere. The Scherzo is particularly meaty and Harnoncourt's scholarly instinct draws out the parallels with Mozart and Beethoven.

Symphony No. 5 in B flat major, D458 (1816)
Schubert's Fifth is among the most luminous, tuneful and brightly scored of early Romantic symphonies (Dvořák's Fifth is another); it also employs a smaller orchestra than its companions. The first movement features felicitous woodwind scoring, the *Andante con moto* has a song-like profile and the finale returns us to the spring-like exhilaration of the first movement.

Chamber Orchestra of Europe/Claudio Abbado
Deutsche Grammophon digital
A trim, nicely poised reading, beautifully paced and incisively phrased. Nikolaus Harnoncourt's Royal Concertgebouw recording (Teldec) provides a good digital alternative, while earlier (analogue) 'classics' include a warm, easygoing account under Bruno Walter (Sony) and Sir Thomas Beecham's charming rendition with the Royal Philharmonic (EMI).

Symphony No. 6 in C major, D589 (1817-18)
The Cinderella of Schubert's symphonies, even though its musical value far exceeds its reputation. The opening *Adagio* suggests a lyrical narrative, whereas the jaunty *Allegro* anticipates Schubert's *Great* C major of seven years later (this work is often referred to as the "Little" C major, to distinguish it from its epic successor). The *Andante* is tuneful and uncomplicated, with a more animated central section, while the *Scherzo* recalls the parallel movement in Beethoven's First Symphony and the closing *Allegro moderato* resembles an elegant Minuet (although the closing pages offer an unmistakable anticipation of the *Great* C major).

The Chamber Orchestra of Europe/Claudio Abbado
Deutsche Grammophon digital
As with Abbado's Fifth, this recording was the first to be based on the autograph manuscript. Musically, it remains one of the most stylish and persuasive interpretations on disc, although Frans Brüggen's period-instrument digital Philips version is an excellent alternative.

Symphony No. 8 in B minor, D759, "Unfinished" (1822)
Speculation as to precisely why Schubert never completed his great B minor Symphony has long been debated by both musicologists and music-lovers. One possible reason is that he was working on it in the same year that he contracted syphilis and that his emotional state caused him to abandon a work that must after all have been closely associated – in chronological if not in spiritual terms – with the diagnosis. However, like Bruckner's similarly incomplete Ninth Symphony, the *Unfinished* stands on its own terms – a powerful, two-tier essay, rich in contrasts and ending on a note of unequivocal peace.

Orchestra of the Eighteenth Century/Frans Brüggen
Philips digital
A period-instrument performance that has all the grandeur, menace and atmosphere of such old-world analogue masters as Furtwängler (DG, mono), Klemperer (EMI), Bruno Walter (Sony) and Toscanini (RCA, mono) – although it doesn't actually supersede any of them.

Symphony No. 9 in C major, D944, "Great" (1825-28)
The *Great* C major vies with Beethoven in both stature and impact, and yet when Mendelssohn rehearsed it in London, uncomprehending musicians actually laughed at the trio of the last movement. The opening horn solo signals a broad introduction that in turn leads to a bright but expansively argued *Allegro*. The second movement's opening seems jaunty enough, and yet its later episodes are dominated by wild fanfares shared between trumpets and horns. There's a bucolic Scherzo and a top-gear finale dominated by an indelible little tune that underpins the whole movement.

 ***Cleveland Orchestra/George Szell***
Sony Classical analogue
Szell paces the opening Andante to perfection and his pointing of detail thereafter is a delight in itself. This is a lean, Classical account of the score, less volatile than Furtwängler's famous Berlin studio recording (DG, mono) and less fiery than Toscanini's with the Philadelphia Orchestra (RCA, mono – but in rather poor sound). Sir Georg Solti and the Vienna Philharmonic (Decca) offer a good digital alternative, and there are other excellent digital Ninths under Günter Wand (RCA), Nikolaus Harnoncourt (Teldec) and Claudio Abbado (DG).

Hector Berlioz (1803-1869)

Symphonie fantastique, Op. 14 (1830)
Just look at the date of composition! Wagner was still a teenager (and still a fair distance from even his earliest masterpieces) and yet Berlioz's madcap tone-poem about sexual obsession, with its reveries and passions, distant thunder, march to the scaffold and witches' sabbath anticipates not only Wagner himself (Berlioz's harmonies and orchestration are highly adventurous), but twentieth-century Expressionism. As musical narratives go, this is definitely one of the most exciting.

 ***Lamoureux Orchestra/Igor Markevitch***
Deutsche Grammophon analogue
I choose this 1961 (stereo) recording because it strikes a fine balance between poise and interpretative daring. Markevitch is a red-blooded exponent of the Symphonie, whereas John Eliot Gardiner (Philips, digital) presents a 'straighter' though still exciting account on period instruments and Sir Colin Davis (Philips again – either his analogue LSO and Concertgebouw versions or his digital one with the Vienna Philharmonic) brings out both the Classical and the Romantic aspects of the score. Bernard Haitink (Vienna Philharmonic, Decca, digital), on the other hand, offers the darkest and in many respects most disturbing option.

Harold in Italy – symphony for viola and orchestra, Op. 16 (1834)
Paganini commissioned Berlioz to write a viola concerto and the result was this inspired symphony concerto, where the soloist projects Byron's Childe Harold in all his vicissitudes of mood and temperament. Harold wanders through the mountains, he witnesses the evening prayers of the Pilgrims (a hypnotic March), hears the Abruzzi Mountaineer serenade his lover and finally succumbs to a terrifying "Orgy of the Brigands".

 ***William Primrose (viola), Boston Symphony Orchestra/Serge Koussevitzky***
Biddulph mono
Another 'oldie' I'm afraid (it was recorded way back in 1944), but a performance of such searing heat and intensity that even the best of its successors seem tame by comparison. Still, there are some fairly good analogue alternatives, not least William Primrose's third recording (under Charles Munch, RCA), Yehudi Menuhin under Sir Colin Davis (EMI) and Donald McInnes with Leonard Bernstein conducting (EMI).

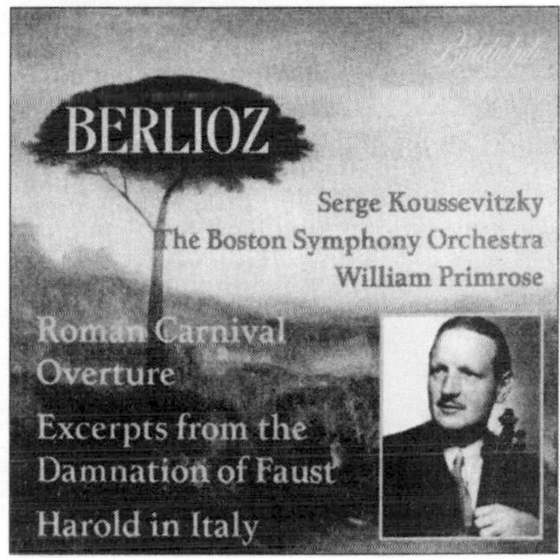

Roméo et Juliette – dramatic symphony for soloists, chorus and orchestra, Op. 17 (1839)
The most direct musical route to the heart of Shakespeare's tragedy, starting with a furious fugato that re-enacts the battle between the Montagues and the Capulets and incorporating a rousing "Feast of the Capulets", a gossamer "Queen Mab" Scherzo and one of the most glorious love scenes in the entire repertory – an exquisite tone-poem, eloquent beyond words and a sure-fire influence on Wagner's *Tristan und Isolde*. However, perhaps the score's most striking episode is entitled "Romeo at the Capulets tomb: Invocation – Juliet's re-awakening – Frenzled joy, despair – Final agony and death of the two lovers": tragic chaos reflected in music that, in terms of sheer originality, is light years ahead of its time.

 ***Gladys Swarthout (mezzo-soprano), John Garris (tenor), Nicola Moscona (bass), Chorus, NBC Symphony Orchestra/Arturo Toscanini***
RCA mono
Originally broadcast in the late 1940s,

Toscanini's performance has an intensity and expressive ardour that burn through the limitations of old (though perfectly clear) mono sound like a laser. Pierre Monteux's stereo LSO recording (Millennium, analogue) makes for a good second choice, while the digital field is dominated by a fine Philips recording with the Vienna Philharmonic under Sir Colin Davis.

Felix Mendelssohn (1809-1847)

Symphony No. 1 in C minor, Op. 11 (1824)

The teenage Mendelssohn already had 12 vivacious string symphonies under his belt when he composed his First Symphony 'proper', a dramatic piece with more than a hint of Mozart's G minor (see "Classical models", above). Other influences abound – for example, the urgent first movement is Schubertian in its thematic complexion but Beethovenian in impulse, whereas the second is a quintessentially Mendelssohnian 'Song without words'.

Symphony No. 2 in B flat major, Op. 52, for soloists, chorus and orchestra, "Hymn of Praise" (1840)

In terms of style, Mendelssohn's Second falls somewhere between a symphony and an oratorio (here Beethoven's Ninth – see above – is an obvious forebear) and features three winsome instrumental movements followed by a huge choral finale. In fact, the finale is so varied in style and effect (its various solos and choruses remind us of Mendelssohn's major choral works) that it's sometimes performed out of context. Mendelssohn composed the Symphony in honour of the 400th anniversary of the invention of printing.

Symphony No. 3 in A minor, Op. 56, "Scottish" (1842)

When, in 1829, the 22-year-old Mendelssohn visited Edinburgh's Holyrood Palace he wrote home to his family, "I believe I have found today the beginning of my *Scottish* Symphony". However, the resultant masterpiece – Mendelssohn's greatest symphony – was a long time in the making. The first movement starts slowly, then edges into a moody *Allegro* that becomes, by turns, agitated and animated. The overall effect is similar to that of the equally elemental *Hebrides* Overture (also known as "Fingal's Cave" – see "Narratives in Sound") while the Scherzo is all gossamer lightness.

Symphony No. 4 in A major, Op. 90, "Italian" (1833)

Mendelssohn was relatively unhappy with what was to become his most popular symphony. Although he revised the work on at least two occasions, he never actually published it – which is why it's known not as his Second Symphony (its rightful chronological position), but his Fourth. The prompting inspiration was Mendelssohn's Italian travels of 1830-31 and the resulting masterpiece, one of the sunniest symphonies in the repertory, opens with a vivacious *Allegro* and closes with a fiery *Saltarello*.

Symphony No. 5 in D major, Op. 107, "Reformation" (1829-30)

Mendelssohn's Fifth Symphony was composed in 1830 to celebrate the 300th anniversary of Melanchthon's *Confessio Augustana* ("Augsburg Confession"), although Mendelssohn subsequently renounced and even considered burning the score. The Fifth is festive in spirit and utilizes both the so-called "Dresden Amen" (used later by Wagner in his opera *Parsifal* – see "Twilit Catastrophes") and the Lutheran chorale *Ein' feste Burg*. It is full of typically Mendelssohnian turns of phrase, not least the frothy Scherzo and the lyrical *Andante*.

Celestina Casapietra, Adele Stolte (sopranos), Peter Schreier (tenor), Leipzig Radio Choir, Leipzig Gewandhaus Orchestra /Kurt Masur
RCA analogue

The orchestra that Mendelssohn himself conducted in performances that combine warmth, reserve and a notably unaggressive brand of vitality. Kurt Masur went on to record the cycle again (digitally, for Teldec and with the same orchestra), but this earlier cycle – although marginally less dynamic – retains an appealingly gentle demeanour. Single recommendations include Wolfgang Sawallisch's Berlin Second (EMI digital – his New Philharmonia analogue cycle on Philips is also well worth hearing), Sir Georg Solti's Chicago Symphony Fourth (Decca, digital), Peter Maag's London Symphony Orchestra Third (Decca, analogue) and Toscanini's NBC Symphony Fifth (RCA, mono).

Robert Schumann (1810-1856)

Symphony No. 1 in B flat major, Op. 38, "Spring" (1841)

The majestic opening fanfare was conceived with specific words in mind: "Im Tale zieht der Frühling auf" (In the valley spring is approaching). Schumann's idea was to evoke a sound 'from on high', with movements that were originally designed to reflect, respectively, the beginning of spring, evening, "Cheerful play fellows" and the height of spring. Although Schumann later excised these images from his ground-plan, they serve as a fairly accurate guide to the music's mood and demeanour.

Symphony No. 2 in C major, Op. 61 (1845–46)

Illness provides the subtext for this, Schumann's greatest symphony. In fact, it is quite likely that he was already suffering from the syphilis that would eventually claim his life; "the work is stamped with melancholy", he once wrote, and yet there are many radiant passages, not least the surging climaxes of the glorious *Adagio espressivo*. The first movement opens darkly, but soon engages a tough, strongly argued *Allegro*, and there's a vivacious Scherzo. The finale puts on an extremely brave face.

Symphony No. 3 in E flat, Op. 97, "Rhenish" (1850)

Schumann penned his *Rhenish* (or "Rhine") Symphony after he had been appointed music director at Düsseldorf. The score itself spells joy and gratitude, initially with an ebullient first movement (the very opening is one of Schumann's boldest inspirations), then with a Scherzo-cum-waltz, a poetic interlude marked simply "not fast", an imposing musical evocation of an enthronement at Cologne Cathedral and a breezy, upbeat finale. The *Rhenish* is as brightly affirmative as the Second is torn with conflict.

Symphony No. 4 in D minor, Op. 120 (1841, revised 1851)

Schumann's D minor Symphony (the shortest and most popular of the four) harbours four movements within a single, sweeping structure. All the material generates from the thematic idea heard at the work's outset: there's a robust first movement, a homely *Romanze*, a muscular Scherzo and an energetic finale. In recent years the first, more concise version has gained new-found credibility but the 1851 revision remains the more familiar of the two.

Staatskapelle Dresden/Wolfgang Sawallisch

EMI analogue

Sawallisch's 1972 set has become something of a standard recommendation, though not without good reason: the playing is consistently keen, the interpretations fresh and intelligent and the recordings present a fine orchestra in well-judged perspective. Some 20 years on and Giuseppe Sinopoli conducted the same orchestra for his digital set (DG), a fine production though not quite up to Sawallisch's standard, while George Szell and the Cleveland Orchestra (Sony, analogue) offer disciplined execution and quietly individual interpretation and Rafael Kubelík's Bavarian Radio Symphony Orchestra cycle (Sony) is uniquely perceptive (it's my own personal favourite) – but it will prove too wilful and soft-grained for some. Essential historic options for individual symphonies include Hermann Abendroth in No. 1 (Tahra, mono), Ernest Ansermet in No. 2 (Decca, analogue), Bruno Walter in No. 3 (Sony, mono) and Wilhelm Furtwängler in No. 4 (DG, mono).

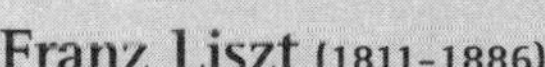

Franz Liszt (1811–1886)

A Dante Symphony, S109 (1855–56)

Prior to composing his *Dante Symphony* Liszt had already produced the first version of his raging *Dante Sonata* (see "Mighty Monologues"). The Symphony, however, is no less impressive. There are three sections: a violent Inferno (which suggests, in purely musical terms, the words that Dante placed over the Gates of Hell, "Abandon hope all ye who enter here …"), a twilit Purgatorio (that anticipates the mysterious musings of Liszt's later style) and a luminous Magnificat.

Volker Arndt (treble), Mathias Eisenberg (organ), Choir of St Thomas's, Leipzig, Leipzig Gewandhaus Orchestra/ Kurt Masur

EMI analogue

An extremely gripping performance – fiery, dynamic and tonally solid (the close-balanced recording lends an almost tangible 'edge' to the double-basses). There's an exciting digital alternative under Daniel Barenboim (Teldec) which sensibly couples the Dante Symphony with the Dante Sonata (played by Barenboim himself). However, Masur's interpretation of the Symphony is rather more imposing.

A Faust Symphony, S108 (1854–57)

Dedicated to Berlioz, whose *Damnation of Faust* provided Liszt with his prompting inspiration, *A Faust Symphony* opens among Faust's unpredictable mood-swings, progresses to Gretchen's homely sweetness, then pays a visit to the infinitely mischievous Mephistopheles before climaxing in a choral apotheosis. Although influenced by Wagner, Liszt's finest Symphony vies with the best of his tone-poems in its energy, poetry and cumulative effect.

 ***Boston Symphony Orchestra/Leonard Bernstein***

Deutsche Grammophon analogue

Bernstein had a special affinity with this work; his first recording (with the New York Philharmonic, for Sony) was justly famous and this superior 1976 remake was awarded the coveted "Grand Prix du Disque" in 1978. It's an immensely exciting performance, biting in the outer movements and with a tender account of "Gretchen" at its core. The recording, too, stands up remarkably well. Giuseppe Sinopoli and the Staatskapelle Dresden (DG) provide Bernstein's hottest digital rival, with Sir Simon Rattle and the Berlin Philharmonic (EMI) following close behind.

César Franck (1822-1890)

Symphony in D minor (1886-88)

The opening minutes glower rather in the manner of Wagner, though the first movement's principal theme is bright and heroic. The second movement features some shimmering writing for strings, while the finale builds to a towering penultimate climax that resolves the arguments with consummate skill. The Symphony's first audiences were perplexed by its daring character (Franck was 65 when he wrote it), though nowadays the 'Franck D minor' is widely considered to be the founding monument of the French symphonic school.

 ***Chicago Symphony Orchestra/Pierre Monteux***

RCA analogue

A bold, big-hearted performance, structurally sound and with a stereophonically informative orchestral layout (first and second violin desks are separated left and right, which is particularly effective in the second movement). Willem van Otterloo and the Concertgebouw (Philips, analogue) offer a fine alternative, while the same orchestra under the charismatic baton of Willem Mengelberg (Biddulph or Philips, mono) leads the historic field.

Anton Bruckner (1824-1895)

Symphony No. 1 in C minor (Linz version, 1865-66)

The first of Bruckner's numbered symphonies (Nos. '0' [a fine piece] and '00' lie outside the official canon) is untypical in that it opens with a firm marching tread rather than quiet, shimmering strings (as is the case with virtually all the other symphonies). The slow movement, however, is especially poignant and there's a vigorously stamping Scherzo. Bruckner later went on to tone down his earliest masterpiece, but this original version is far more effective.

 ***Chicago Symphony Orchestra/Sir Georg Solti***

Decca digital

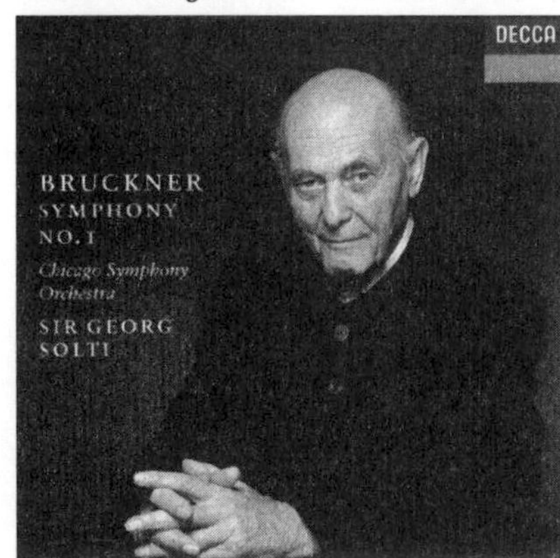

Solti's Bruckner can sometimes tend towards excessive brusqueness, even impatience, but this is an extremely fine performance, powerfully played and superbly recorded. The best earlier rival features the great Brucknerian Eugen Jochum conducting the Berlin Philharmonic (DG, analogue).

Symphony No. 2 in C minor, (1871-72, revised 1875-76, 1877)

Composed between the Symphonies Nos. 1, "0" and 3, Bruckner's Second was rejected by the Vienna Philharmonic as "nonsense" and "unplayable". And yet, as is so often the case with musical invective, contemporary judgement proved cruelly misleading. The restless, cello-led opening is especially rich in atmosphere while the ensuing first-movement arguments – urged on by heralding brass – are among the strongest in all of Bruckner's output. Like the First and Sixth Symphonies, the Second relies less on shimmering string *tremolandos* (a Brucknerian speciality) than clear-cut drama.

 ***Chicago Symphony Orchestra/Sir Georg Solti***

Decca digital

As with the Solti's account of the First Symphony, the Second is admirably forthright, very well played and superbly recorded. Best among Solti's rivals are Bernard Haitink (Philips, analogue), Eugen Jochum (preferably his DG version, also analogue) and Riccardo Chailly (Decca, digital).

Symphony No. 3 in D minor (1873-77, revised 1888-89)

Dedicated to Wagner, the Third was originally dominated by Wagner quotations. However, subsequent pruning established both a finer structural balance and leaner orchestral textures; but there's still the thorny problem of sorting through various editions of the score. Best is Bruckner's 1877 first revision, though the first version of all – completed at the end of 1873 – remains compulsive listening despite its obvious excesses. The Symphony itself is highly dramatic with a slow movement that opens somewhat in the manner of Mozart.

 ***Bavarian Radio Symphony Orchestra/Eugen Jochum***

Deutsche Grammophon analogue

The greatest virtue of Jochum's performance is its high inspirational flight. The first movement is immensely exciting, the finale (with its charming polka) both spontaneous and easygoing. Haitink (Philips, analogue) – a fine performance, though not quite as fiery as Jochum's – uses the preferable 1877 edition of the score, while Eliahu Inbal (Teldec, digital) gives us the full measure of Bruckner's extravagant first thoughts.

Symphony No. 4 in E flat major, "The Romantic" (1874-86)

Bruckner's best-known – and probably best-loved – Symphony suggests a chivalrous spirit adventuring among the elements. The hushed and mysterious opening is dominated by a distant horn melody that reappears for the Symphony's blazing home straight. There's also a piously processional *Andante*, a boisterous 'hunting' Scherzo (with a middle section that anticipates Mahler) and a dark-hued finale.

 ***San Francisco Symphony Orchestra/Herbert Blomstedt***

Decca digital

Herbert Blomstedt's reading is very a much a thinking-man's performance, beautifully considered, often dramatic and superbly played but with a sense of humility that is essential for any effective Bruckner interpretation. It's a cumulatively powerful reading, one that's based on the first 'definitive' version of the score. Viable alternatives include Furtwängler's vintage Berlin broadcast (DG, mono) and Michael Gielen's South West German Radio Symphony Orchestra recording (EMI, digital) of Bruckner's expansively discursive – and musically quite different 'original' version. The present writer considers that the 'original' Fourth is musically more interesting than its better-known revision (especially the Scherzo).

Symphony No. 5 in B flat major (1875-76)

Possibly the most imposing of all Bruckner's symphonies, not least for a 24-minute finale that includes a compelling 'double fugue' (one half massive, the other comparatively ethereal) and a blazing peroration where various salient themes are rendered triumphant on a full compliment of brass. The slow movement features a glorious arch of melody (played by the strings), while the Scherzo consists of a restless sequence of dramatic incidents.

 ***Royal Concertgebouw Orchestra/Riccardo Chailly***

Decca digital

One of the most difficult choices in the whole book, mainly because this writer has the nerve to disagree with virtually all Bruckner's interpreters! Chailly's is the most transparent version available, a beautifully played account that suggests selfless dedication to the score. Eugen Jochum's Munich recording (DG, analogue) is its nearest rival and although Furtwängler (DG, mono – a thrilling wartime Berlin broadcast) and Klemperer (EMI, analogue) have much to say about the score, both are rather too idiosyncratic to merit primary recommendation. Karajan (EMI or DG, analogue) will please those who favour size over subtlety.

Symphony No. 6 in A major (1879-81)

It was Mahler who premièred the Sixth with the Vienna Philharmonic, albeit with various cuts and instrumental alterations. As it happens, this is one of the few symphonies that avoids the drastic revisions that transformed various of its stablemates – the Third, Fourth and Eighth Symphonies in particular. The Sixth is also among the most concise and clear-cut of Bruckner's works, with an especially gripping first movement (the main theme of which isn't unlike Maurice Jarre's *Lawrence of Arabia*) and a slow movement that anticipates Elgar's mature style.

 ***Bavarian Radio Symphony Orchestra/Wolfgang Sawallisch***

Orfeo digital

A strong, well-lit performance, outgoing in spirit and yet with a warmly expressed Adagio. Viable analogue rivals include Eugen Jochum (DG, EMI or Tahra – the DG is probably the best) and Heinz Bongartz (Berlin Classics) while Herbert Blomstedt (Decca) leads the digital field.

Symphony No. 7 in E major (1881-83)

Artur Nikisch's 1884 première of the Seventh helped launch Bruckner to worldwide fame. It's said that the long opening theme came to the composer in a dream, while the glorious *Adagio* is imbued with the spirit of Wagner ("it is possible, I thought ...", wrote Bruckner not long after writing the movement, "that the master will not live much longer – and it was then that the C sharp minor *Adagio* came to me"). The Scherzo resembles a lilting peasant dance while the finale includes a noble chorale. Those seeking a 'doorway' to Bruckner symphonies should approach the Seventh first.

 ***New York Philharmonic Orchestra/Kurt Masur***

Teldec digital

Masur's performance is warm, seamless and beautifully played. However, strong (analogue) rivals are plentiful, with Furtwängler's mono Berlin Philharmonic broadcasts (EMI, DG and Music & Arts – preferably the EMI) and Jochum's Berlin Philharmonic recording (DG) being among the most impressive.

Symphony No. 8 in C minor (1884-87, revised 1889-90)

An elemental outpouring on a vast scale: jagged, noble and grounded in an unshakeable religious faith. Bruckner was evidently excited by the first version of his score, though when the conductor Hermann Levi criticized it, he instigated wholesale alterations (some of which, admittedly, worked to the Symphony's advantage). However, the end result remains overwhelming. The heart of the Eighth is an other-worldly *Adagio* which contrasts with the storm, stress and exultation of its musical surroundings.

 ***Concertgebouw Orchestra/Eduard van Beinum***

Philips mono

Some conductors make Bruckner sound expansionist and self-obsessed (especially those who slow the pace), but van Beinum's approach is swift and athletic. The sound is rather dated, but the performance has tremendous impetus (van Beinum uses the old Haas editon of the score). Wilhelm Furtwängler's broadcast relays (1949, EMI/Music & Arts or 1944, Music & Arts, mono) combine rapt spirituality with Dionysian impulse, while Karajan (EMI or DG, analogue) offers a broad, granitic statement of the score. Readers who fancy sampling the densely packed original version are directed to Eliahu Inbal and the Frankfurt Radio Symphony Orchestra (Teldec, digital).

Symphony No. 9 in D minor (1891-96)

Bruckner's furthest flight to the beyond, a magnificent essay that was left incomplete (although sketches for the finale do exist) but that still serves as a profound epitaph to a great symphonist. The first movement oscillates between rage and repose, the second is a pounding Scherzo with a sylph-like Trio and the *Adagio* harbours the most devastating climax in the whole of Bruckner's output.

 ***Bavarian State Orchestra/Wolfgang Sawallisch***

Orfeo digital

A strong, committed performance: assertive, spiritually responsive and with the requisite level of nervous intensity. Bruckner's Ninth has inspired numerous distinguished readings, but the finest of all is Wilhelm Furtwängler's 1944 Berlin Philharmonic broadcast (Music & Arts, DG, mono) – a terrifying memento from a nation that was poised on the brink of catastrophe. Two later BPO recordings are also well worth hearing – under Eugen Jochum (DG, analogue) and Daniel Barenboim (Teldec, digital) – while speculative performing versions of the finale have been recorded by Eliahu Inbal (Teldec) and Yoav Talmi (Chandos). Both the latter are digital.

Alexander Borodin (1833-1887)

Symphony No. 2 in B minor (1870-76)

Borodin's Second presents the most bullish opening of any Russian Romantic symphony, a pounding eight-note motive that completely dominates the first movement. The filigree Scherzo features a flurry of repeated notes (especially treacherous for the horns), while the lyrical third movement has a serene, folk-like melody (first played by the horn) as its principal theme and the finale generates excitement reminiscent of the *Prince Igor* Overture.

 ***London Symphony Orchestra/Jean Martinon***

Decca analogue

Although some 36 years old, Martinon's performance has impressive cut and thrust: the playing is absolutely spot-on, the recording extraordinarily dynamic (try the very opening) and the transfer to CD is first-rate. Alternatives include a rather more lyrical performance under Evgeni Svetlanov (Melodiya/BMG, digital) and a mono thriller under the great Nikolai Golovanov (c1950, Multisonic, mono).

Johannes Brahms (1833–1897)

Symphony No. 1 in C minor, Op. 68 (1855–76)

The pounding heartbeat that opens Brahms's First Symphony establishes a level of inspiration that remains constant throughout the cycle. A long time in the making, the First is the most exultant of the four, a heroic affirmation that takes Beethoven's mantle (note how the finale's 'big tune' recalls the "Ode to Joy") and builds to a mighty structure. The first movement strides purposefully, the second suggests the world of song, the third is a gracious *Intermezzo*, while the variegated finale is an epic in itself.

Vienna Philharmonic Orchestra/Wilhelm Furtwängler
EMI mono

Wilhelm Furtwängler's 1952 broadcast performance features huge brush-strokes, flexible tempos and white-hot playing. It's a truly inspired vision, though alternative live recordings with the Berlin Philharmonic (DG, mono) and North German Radio Symphony Orchestra (Tahra, mono) are just as good and there's an equally imposing 1940 performance – much 'straighter' but no less intense – under Toscanini (Music & Arts, mono). Major analogue rivals include Herbert von Karajan with the Berlin Philharmonic (DG – his 1963 recording) and George Szell with the Cleveland Orchestra (Sony).

Symphony No. 2 in D major, Op. 73 (1877)

If the First Symphony suggests momentous events, the Second seems more in touch with nature – a subtle, mellow narrative where the first movement's principal theme recalls Brahms's celebrated *Lullaby* and the musical argument unfolds with organic inevitability. The predominantly dark slow movement inhabits a more questioning environment than its predecessor (the brass suggest sinister portents) although a lilting *Allegretto grazioso* lightens the mood and the Symphony ends with a blazing (albeit occasionally pensive) *Allegro spirito*.

London Symphony Orchestra/Pierre Monteux
Philips analogue

Pierre Monteux's clear-headed account suggests a warm heart and a positive interpretative stance that doesn't overplay the work's 'autumnal' axis. What is more, Monteux is one of the very few conductors who observes the first movement's important repeat, and his recording has the added advantage of placing the first violins on the left, the seconds on the right – a real advantage for those who like to follow the stereophonic interplay of Brahms's writing. Furtwängler (EMI, mono) is perhaps more volatile and Toscanini (RCA, mono) more physically exciting, but Monteux's balanced approach remains immensely satisfying.

Symphony No. 3 in F major, Op. 90 (1883)

It's interesting to note that while Brahms's even-numbered symphonies open with a sigh, his First and Third storm the heavens. The Third's introduction takes flight among the brass then rushes headlong among the strings for one of Brahms's most glorious themes. Thereafter, and there's a marked contrast between the outer movements' momentous happenings and the relative calm of the central *Andante* and *Poco allegretto* – the latter, with its passionate cello theme, being one of the cycle's most familiar single movements.

Berlin Philharmonic Orchestra/Wilhelm Furtwängler
EMI mono

Furtwängler's finest broadcast Third (recorded in 1949) is quite remarkable: the opening bars rocket to the stars and although tempos thereafter are extreme, the sum effect is utterly compelling. If, however, stereo is essential, then Bruno Walter (Sony), Fritz Reiner (RCA) and George Szell (Sony) are among the finest analogue rivals. No digital contender comes close.

Symphony No. 4 in E minor, Op. 98 (1884–85)

As is so often the case, 'last' here means 'greatest'. Brahms was by now a master-builder and his final symphonic structure allows a wilting first theme (such a powerful but mysterious opening) to blossom, gain momentum, reflect on itself and then triumph in a brilliant coda ('tail' or peroration). The slow movement twice visits one of Brahms's most heart-rending melodies, while the fiery Scherzo positively bounds with energy and the finale – a boldly uncompromising Passacaglia, or 'theme with variations' – proves, like its First Symphony predecessor, massively conclusive.

Cleveland Orchestra/George Szell

Sony Classical analogue

George Szell's reading is at once superbly played, powerfully built, generously expressive (try any of the slow movement) and physically exciting. And although the sound is quite dry, stereophonic definition is remarkably clear. As to alternatives, Toscanini's live 1935 recording of the Fourth (EMI, mono) features a positively coruscating finale, but if 78rpm surface hiss worries you, try the fierily assertive Carlos Kleiber with the Vienna Philharmonic (DG, analogue).

Piano Quartet No. 1 in G minor, Op. 25 (1861, orchestrated by Arnold Schoenberg in 1937)

Schoenberg was 19 when Brahms died and his lifelong devotion to the older composer's music is evident throughout his entire output. This orchestration – which has been referred to as "Brahms's Fifth" (jokingly, by Schoenberg himself) and which eschews any suggestion of mere 'cleverness', is remarkably vital and full-bodied, especially in terms of its string writing. The score includes colourful percussion and a highly imaginative re-creation of the Quartet's closing pages. The slow movement could easily be part of a lost Brahms symphony, while the finale is a fiery gipsy-style Rondo. It's a hugely appealing work.

SWF Symphony Orchestra Baden-Baden/Michael Gielen

Intercord digital

Easily the best recording that this Quartet-Symphony has ever had, a passionate, forthright and meticulously detailed affair, very well engineered. Gielen excels in the overt musical drama of the first and last movements, but if his recording proves to be difficult to obtain try Christoph Eschenbach and the Houston Symphony (RCA, digital).

Camille Saint-Saëns
(1835-1921)

Symphony No. 3 in C minor, Op. 78, "Organ" (1886)

A symphonic spectacular that's highly unusual on a number of counts: first, for accommodating four 'movements' within a two-tier structure, then by employing an organ to bolster an already strong orchestral sonority, and lastly, for the skilful interweaving of the Scherzo and finale (a valiant *Maestoso* followed by a hectic fugal development and culminating in a triumphant closing section).

Berj Zamkochian (organ), Boston Symphony Orchestra/Charles Munch

RCA analogue

Recorded in 1959, but still something of a blockbuster, Munch's account of the Organ Symphony features silky strings, refined woodwinds (a familiar feature of the Boston Symphony), biting brass and a remarkably lifelike organ sonority. More recent alternatives include Daniel Barenboim and Herbert von Karajan (both DG, the former analogue, the latter digital), while Toscanini's classic 1952 NBC broadcast (RCA, mono) gives even Munch a run for his money.

Pyotr Il'yich Tchaikovsky
(1840-1893)

Manfred Symphony Op. 58 (1885)

There was a time when Tchaikovsky thought *Manfred* his "best symphonic work" (that was before he'd composed his Fifth and Sixth Symphonies). The first movement suggests Manfred's tormented wanderings (its closing pages are among Tchaikovsky's most dramatic); there's a fairy-like Scherzo, a simple *Pastorale* and a versicoloured finale that recalls Arimanes' subterranean palace, Astarte's shade and Manfred's death.

Concertgebouw Orchestra/ Bernard Haitink

Philips analogue

Manfred is extremely prone to cuts in performance – so be careful about your choices of recording (Toscanini [RCA or Music & Arts, mono], so fine in most respects, is a prime offender). However, Haitink's 1979 recording scores an all counts. The pacing is absolutely right, the 'feel' of the performance dark without being excessively gloomy, the playing superb and the sound first-rate. Evgeni Svetlanov (Melodiya, analogue) is marginally more red-blooded while Mikhail Pletnev (DG, digital) keeps textures light and transparent.

Symphony No. 1 in G minor, Op. 13, "Winter Daydreams" (1866, revised 1874)

If ever a Symphony's first pages suggested intimations of magic, then this is it. *Winter Daydreams* opens to shimmering strings and pert woodwinds, though what comes next is fairly dramatic and the slow movement's principal theme recalls the world of Russian folk-song. Other highlights include a charming third movement central section or 'Trio' (reminiscent of the waltz-themes in Tchaikovsky's great ballets) and an unexpected slow (*Andante*) episode in the finale – dark, melancholy music and deeply prophetic of the composer's full maturity.

Symphony No. 2 in C minor, Op. 17, "Little Russian" (1872, revised 1879)

Tchaikovsky's *Little Russian* is imbued with a feeling of folk music. It is also highly original, with a cheeky march taking the place of the expected slow movement and a boisterous set of variations placed fourth. However, the most original movement is the darkly intense Scherzo, with its powerful crescendos and vivid interplay between string sections. The 1872 original version (recorded by Geoffrey Simon for Chandos, digital) is very different to the revision – although, ultimately, the latter is more musically satisfying.

Symphony No. 3 in D major, Op. 29, "Polish" (1875)

Still much underrated, the *Polish* Symphony (so-named because its finale is a vigorous *Polonaise*) has all the charm and melodic appeal of Tchaikovsky's ballets and Orchestral Suites. It is also structurally unusual in having five movements rather than the usual four (in this respect it rather resembles Schumann's *Rhenish* Symphony.

London Symphony Orchestra/Igor Markevitch

Philips analogue

A composer himself, Igor Markevitch was able to 'reach the parts' that other conductors failed to touch – underlining salient details, phrasing imaginatively, tracing Tchaikovsky's balletic soul and occasionally bending the musical line (his handling of the Third Symphony's introduction is second to none). The LSO's response is keen, painstaking and technically accomplished, while the 1960s recordings (part of a fine – if sometimes wayward – complete Tchaikovsky symphony cycle) stand up remarkably well. Viable alternatives are Bernard Haitink (Philips) and Evgeni Svetlanov (Melodiya), though mention should also be made of Antál Dorati's roughly contemporaneous LSO recordings (Mercury, and, like those of Markevitoh, full of interest) which will soon be available again. All are analogue.

Symphony No. 4 in F minor, Op. 36 (1877)

The Fourth was written in the wake of the composer's disastrous marriage to Antonina Milyukova; it opens dramatically, with a powerful horn theme that suggests "the fatal force which prevents our hopes of happiness from being realized". The entire first movement (Tchaikovsky's finest) is marked by passionate alternations between anguish, reverie and repose, while the extrovert finale represents Tchaikovsky attempting to regain a sense of joy through the rejoicing of others.

Leningrad Philharmonic Orchestra/Evgeny Mravinsky

Deutsche Grammophon analogue

Mravinsky's performance is distinguished by a combination of refinement and virtuosity. The playing is certainly magnificent, but those in search of a more flexible, re-creative approach are directed to analogue rivals from Igor Markevitch (with the LSO, Philips, analogue) or, pre-eminently, Willem Mengelberg (a stunning pre-war recording with the Amsterdam Concertgebouw, Pearl or Music & Arts, mono). Seiji Ozawa and the Saito Kinen Orchestra (Philips) provide a fine live digital option.

Symphony No. 5 in E minor, Op. 64 (1888)

"I have come to the conclusion that it is a failure. There is something repellent, something superfluous, patchy and insincere, which the public instantly recognizes." So wrote Tchaikovsky to his patron Nadezhda von Meck soon after the Fifth Symphony's première. And although he did change his mind ("I no longer find it bad but love it once again"), one wonders how the composer of such a powerful, emotionally candid and ultimately triumphant piece could have fallen so seriously "out of love" with his own inspired creation. The Fifth features a binding 'motto' theme, while the ardent slow movement is the best-known of the six.

London Symphony Orchestra/Igor Markevitch

Philips analogue

Markevitch charts the Fifth Symphony's volatile course with impressive imagination, although he keeps things moving and rarely indulges the moment at the expense of the whole. Mravinsky (DG, analogue) is more dynamic, and Stokowski (his 1935 Philadelphia recording, Biddulph, mono) more overtly glamorous, but Markevitch achieves the best balance overall.

Symphony No. 6 in B minor, Op. 74, "Pathétique" (1893)

Tchaikovsky's 'real' Sixth (parts of which have turned up both as a Third Piano Concerto and a 'reconstructed' Seventh

Symphony) was abandoned in favour of this, his last and most tragic symphonic work. The idea of a programme was the composer's own (" ... let them guess it who can"), but the title *Pathétique* wasn't used until after the first performance. A shattering experience, the *Pathétique* combines thunder (parts of the first movement), malevolence (the second), brave resolve among the people (third) and tragic resignation (the finale).

 ***Leningrad Philharmonic Orchestra/Evgeny Mravinsky***

Erato digital

The fourth and last of Mravinsky's 'officially released' Pathétiques is among the most devastating performances on disc – the first movement especially. Less tightly disciplined than its immediate predecessor (DG, analogue), it tells an even more powerful tale. Essential vintage options include Furtwängler (1938 recording, EMI or Biddulph, mono), Mengelberg (1937 recording, Music & Arts, mono) and Václav Talich (Supraphon, mono) – all of them offering highly imaginative slants on a single musical tragedy.

Antonin Dvořák (1841-1904)

Symphony No. 5 in F major, B54 (Op. 76) (1875)

The breeziest of Dvořák's mature symphonies; one might even call it his 'Pastoral'. The opening woodwind-calls, which suggest bird-song in spring, lead directly to an animated though lyrical *Allegro* and a fairly mobile slow movement; then there's a dance-like Scherzo (which follows the slow movement without a break) and a dramatic finale.

 ***Czech Philharmonic Orchestra/Karel Sejna***

Supraphon mono

An extraordinarily fresh performance. The woodwinds are clear and characterful, the strings keen-edged and Sejna's choice of tempos well-nigh ideal. The coupling is something of a rarity, Dvořák's three tuneful Slavonic Rhapsodies. A more overtly dramatic version of the Fifth dates from the 1960s and features the London Symphony Orchestra conducted by Witold Rowicki (Philips, analogue).

Symphony No. 6 in D major, B112 (Op. 60) (1880)

Dvořák's express intention was to compose a work "of indisputable vitality"; indeed his Sixth combines the pastoral qualities of the Fifth with a sense of musical architecture that anticipates the Seventh Symphony of four years later. The first movement opens to gently pulsing horns and a smiling melody shared between woodwinds and lower strings; the slow movement is among Dvořák's most lyrical, the Scherzo, a *Furiant* very much in the style of the *Slavonic Dances* while the finale is a noble though spirited *Allegro*.

 ***Czech Philharmonic Orchestra/Karel Ančerl***

Supraphon analogue

Everything about this performance seems right – the pacing, the phrasing, the chirpy Czech woodwind tone and the sense of release that greets the Symphony's joyous finale. A fine alternative is provided by the London Symphony Orchestra under Witold Rowicki (Philips, analogue). Neither recording has any serious digital rival.

Symphony No. 7 in D minor, B141 (Op. 70) (1884-85)

Dvořák's Seventh opens to a sombre motive on violas and cellos before swirling into action and rending the clouds to reveal sunlight. Thereafter, arguments alternate between heroic gesturing (the first movement's thrilling peroration), song-like reflection (the *Poco adagio*) and the lilt of the dance (third movement), while the finale – a suitable crown for Dvořák's greatest symphonic structure – sees all these elements combined.

Berlin Philharmonic Orchestra/Rafael Kubelík

Deutsche Grammophon analogue

A reading that combines fire, flexibility and a sure grasp of Dvořák's storm-tossed structure, as presented on two CDs together with Symphonies Nos. 8 and 9. The sound isn't brilliant (a touch of shrillness might worry some) and those who'd prefer a more temperate – and better recorded – option should consider Sir Colin Davis's similarly coupled package with Concertgebouw Orchestra (Philips, analogue).

Symphony No. 8 in G major, B163 (Op. 88) (1889)

The Eighth is as joyfully extrovert as the Seventh is darkly elemental – although both symphonies open to the strain of lower strings (here cellos take the lead). This time, however, the principal flute sets the mood for most of what follows: bouncing rhythms in the first movement, lyrical narrative in the second, a lilting violin melody for the third and a festive finale.

London Symphony Orchestra/Antál Dorati

Mercury analogue

A hugely energetic performance with incisive solo work, pungent rhythms and a lyrical flow to the slow movement. The recording is remarkably vivid for 1959, but hi-fi buffs might prefer the all-digital recordings (of Symphonies Nos. 7-9) by Christoph von Dohnányi and the Cleveland Orchestra (Decca).

Symphony No. 9 in E minor, B178, "From the New World" (Op. 95) (1893)

Although influenced by American popular song and black American spirituals (Dvořák was now Music Director of the New Conservatory of Music in New York), the so-called *New World* Symphony overflows with Czech resonances. The wistful *Largo* (much beloved of a certain brown bread manufacturer) is particularly famous, while the Scherzo and finale conjure up images of wide open spaces.

Concertgebouw Orchestra/Antál Dorati

Philips analogue

As bracing, powerful and sensitive a New World as any currently available. Dorati's speeds tend towards briskness (try the exhilarating Scherzo) and the late-1950s recording is astonishingly lifelike. The coupling is an excellent digital version of the contemporaneous Cello Concerto (with Heinrich Schiff), but digital fanciers might prefer the more relaxed Kyrill Kondrashin/ Vienna Philharmonic recording (Decca).

Nicolai Rimsky-Korsakov (1844-1908)

Symphony No. 2, Op. 9 "Antar", (1868, revised 1875 and 1897)

Musical narrative or symphony? 'Rimsky 2' is both. The 'story' concerns the hero Antar who sees a bird attack a gazelle, saves her and is rewarded with "revenge, power and love" when she reveals herself as the Queen of Palmyra. The Symphony reflects this narrative in a score that combines visceral drama with some exceedingly delicate scoring (the latter especially in the first movement).

Rotterdam Philharmonic Orchestra/David Zinman

Philips digital

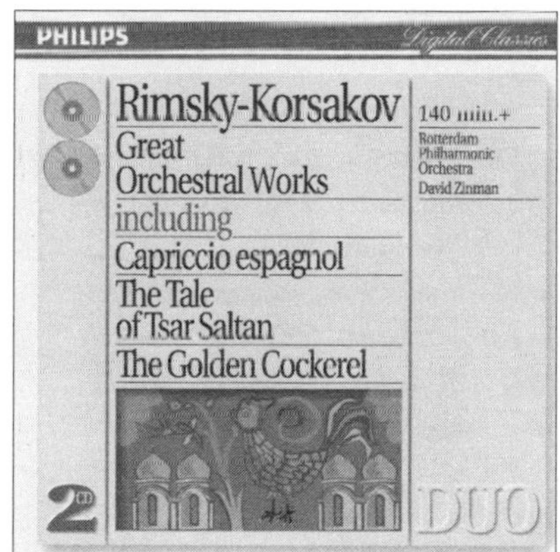

The best of Rimsky'-Korsakov's three symphonies receives an especially fine performance under Zinman – well played, judiciously paced, dynamically recorded and forming part of a useful all-Rimsky orchestral collection. There is a good digital CD of the slightly different 1875 score by the Russian State Orchestra under Evgeni Svetlanov (RCA), while Pierre Monteux's classic San Francisco Symphony recording (RCA, mono) is also well worth searching out.

Ernest Chausson (1855-1899)

Symphony in B flat major, Op. 20 (1889-90)

Chausson's Symphony goes one step beyond César Franck's D minor Symphony of the previous year in its explosive climaxes and the passionate sweep of its melodies (the two works share a darkly glowering countenance – see above). Although Wagner is an obvious influence (*Tristan* weeps audibly at the beginning of the second movement), the Symphony is marked by a delicacy of texture that's uniquely French.

Boston Symphony Orchestra/Charles Munch

RCA analogue

Munch brings a genuine sense of re-creative spontaneity into the studio while his Boston players respond with a level of enthusiasm that hasn't been matched in 35 years. The recording, too, is excellent – though an even earlier (1950) version, with the San Francisco Symphony under Pierre Monteux (RCA, mono) also vies for attention.

Edward Elgar (1857-1934)

Symphony No. 1 in A flat major, Op. 55 (1907-08)

The noble arch of melody that opens Elgar's First Symphony, although crucial to the argument, gives little indication of what follows – a many-hued 'round trip', rising or falling through a hugely eventful *Allegro*, firing on all cylinders for a quick-march Scherzo and then resting for one of Elgar's most lovingly extended slow movements. The bracing finale climaxes to an extravagantly embellished restatement of the opening melody.

 ***London Philharmonic Orchestra/Sir Adrian Boult***
EMI analogue
Elgar confided much interpretative advice to Boult, and this grand though infinitely subtle interpretation amply reflects a rare level of understanding. There are another two Elgar Firsts from Boult – the first in mono (Testament – forthcoming), the second recorded live at the Proms during the same period as our EMI recommendation (IMP, analogue) and extremely exciting. But on balance this studio version serves as the more considered statement. Those in search of a stronger emotional charge should consider Sir John Barbirolli's magnificent Pye recording (EMI Phoenixa, analogue).

Symphony No. 2 in E flat major, Op. 63 (1909-11)
Although dedicated to the memory of King Edward VII, Elgar's Second transcends temporal mourning (the second movement is in effect a noble funeral march) for 'the spirit of delight' the serves as the work's motto – both musically and spiritually. While the First Symphony starts quietly and ends in a blaze of light, the Second breezes forth only to end in a mood of Brahmsian tranquillity. Some consider it to be Elgar's greatest work.

 ***Hallé Orchestra/Sir John Barbirolli***
EMI analogue
A broad, loving and warmly played account, extravagant perhaps (the original occupied one and a half LP records) but so full of insight that the odd indulgence hardly seems to matter. However, if integrity, clarity and a certain 'stiff upper lip' seem more to the point, then you couldn't possibly do better than Sir Adrian Boult – particularly as recorded in 1944 (EMI or Beulah, mono). Andrew Davis and the BBC Symphony Orchestra provide the best digital altermative (Teldec).

Alexander Glazunov (1865-1936)

Symphony No. 5 in B flat major, Op. 55 (1895)
Glazunov was a Romantic 'throwback' whose symphony cycle (eight complete works and with a Ninth unfinished) is full of wonderful things, not least the winsome, tuneful Fifth, with its warming melodies, colourful orchestration (a cross between Tchaikovsky and Rachmaninov) and balletic mobility. In fact, the Scherzo could easily have come from one of Glazunov's ballets, while the heart of the Symphony is a memorable *Andante*.

 ***USSR Ministry of Culture Symphony Orchestra/Gennadi Rozhdestvensky***
Olympia digital
Rozhdestvensky's reading has great panache (it's part of a notable complete Glazunov cycle), although most listeners would be equally happy with Evgeni Svetlanov (Melodiya) or Evgeny Mravinsky (superbly played but less well engineered, on Russian Disc, mono). Olympia's recording (from a Melodiya original) is appropriately expansive.

Jean Sibelius (1865-1957)

Symphony No. 1 in E minor, Op. 39 (1898-99)
Berlioz's *Symphonie fantastique* was among Sibelius's prompting inspirations, as was the orchestral music of Borodin, Tchaikovsky and Bruckner. But listen to the opening bars – a desolate clarinet solo underpinned by quietly rolling timpani – and the composer's identity is immediately apparent. Sibelius's First alternates dark, melancholy music, economically scored, with red-blooded Tchaikovskian rhetoric – strings, brass and timpani being used to particularly impressive effect.

 ***Finnish Radio Symphony Orchestra/Jukka-Pekka Saraste***
Teldec digital
Recorded live in St Petersburg during May 1993, Saraste's fiery performance (included as part of his second Sibelius cycle with the Finnish RSO) combines sensitive phrase-shaping with youthful spontaneity; the highly dramatic slow movement is especially impressive. Saraste's earlier RCA (digital) recording is also recommendable, while analogue rivals include Lorin Maazel with the Vienna Philharmonic (Decca).

Sergey Rachmaninov (1873-1943)

Symphony No. 2 in E minor, Op. 27 (1906-07)
Having weathered critical slings and arrows for his daring First Symphony (1897), Rachmaninov was careful not to offend with his Second. He didn't, although had he followed his original path, this work might have been discussed under "Contemporary" rather than "Romantic". The resulting piece has a sombre, melancholy quality reminiscent of Tchaikovsky's Fifth (also in E minor, and an obvious influence).

Russian National Orchestra/Mikhail Pletnev

Deutsche Grammophon digital

Rachmaninov as conductor was no slouch and Pletnev's performance follows his lead with a taut, slimline and refreshingly un-indulgent reading. Some, however, will prefer a more relaxed and, dare I say, more 'purple' alternative (this is, after all, a romantic blockbuster). André Previn and the LSO (EMI, analogue) provide a sumptuous reading, and so does Lorin Maazel with the Berlin Philharmonic (DG, digital).

Carl Nielsen (1865-1931)

Symphony No. 1 in G minor, FS16 (Op. 7) (1890-92)

An ideal stepping-stone from Dvořák's *New World* to the world of Nielsen – fresh, open-air music, strong in profile, finely structured and keenly suggestive of Nordic landscapes. The first movement features a particularly urgent development section (where Nielsen further intensifies his already strong arguments); there's also a noble *Andante*, a pastoral third movement and a bracing finale.

London Symphony Orchestra/André Previn

RCA analogue

A lean, ardent performance, recorded at the outset of Previn's association with the LSO (a period that saw some of their best records). The recording is clean and well-balanced, the playing extremely polished and the current coupling, music from "Saul and David" and a rather raucous account of the great Symphony No. 4 under Jean Martinou. Digital alternatives under Herbert Blomstedt (Decca) and Paavo Berglund (RCA) are equally satisfying.

The new symphony (1884-1987)

Just as Beethoven had one foot placed firmly in the Classical camp, Mahler, Scriabin, Rachmaninov and Glière (to pick just four names out of a very big bag) often harked back to the heyday of symphonic Romanticism. However, the twentieth century has seen many innovations in symphonic form, from Mahler's and Shostakovich's expansive epics, through concise single-movement structures by Scriabin, Sibelius and Roy Harris, to the somewhat acerbic writing of Schoenberg's First Chamber Symphony and the hypnotic unfolding of Górecki's Third.

Gustav Mahler (1860-1911)

Symphony No. 1 in D major, "Titan" (1888, revised 1893, 1896-98)

Mahler raises the curtain on his First Symphony amidst nature and chirruping birdsong. The principal theme also turns up in his song-cycle *Songs of a Wayfarer* (the coupling on our recommended recording) while, thereafter, there's a rustic dance sequence, a sardonic mock-funeral march with a schmaltzy central section and an explosive finale that climaxes to battling brass and timpani. Mahler's original design incorporated a charming fifth movement, subtitled "Blumine", but most conductors stick to the four-movement revision.

Bavarian Radio Symphony Orchestra/Rafael Kubelík

Deutsche Grammophon analogue

Kubelík's recording (his second) is an irresistibly lyrical affair, lively, light-textured and sensitively phrased. Like Klemperer (see below), he divides his violins 'left and right'; but those in search of something rather more overtly dramatic should try Abbado and the Berlin Philharmonic (also on DG, digital).

Symphony No. 2 in C minor, "Resurrection" (1884-86, revised 1893-96)

"We are standing by the coffin of a loved one...", writes Mahler with reference to his searingly dramatic first movement; "...an awe-inspiring voice reaches our heart," he continues, "a voice which we do not hear amid the deafening bustle that normally surrounds us: What now?" The 'answer' arrives via a blissful memory (*Andante*), scepticism (scherzo), primaeval light (contralto solo) and, finally a vast, "Last Trump" finale that dissolves judgement and ends as "an all-powerful sense of love courses through us with blissful knowledge and being". The final chorus is especially moving.

 ***Elisabeth Schwarzkopf (soprano), Hilde Rössl-Majdan (mezzo-soprano), Philharmonia Chorus, Philharmonia Orchestra/Otto Klemperer***

EMI analogue

Strong, resolute conducting, with an ideal orchestral layout (violin desks are clearly divided left and right), fine singing and good, early-1960s sound. Best digital rivals are from Gary Bertini (EMI) and Claudio Abbado (DG), while Solti's 1966 LSO recording (Decca) is especially dramatic, and so is Mehta's Vienna Philharmonic recording of 1975 (also on Decca – both are analogue).

Symphony No. 3 in D minor (1893–96, revised 1906)

A vast, verdant world cast in two substantial sections, the first of which is a 35-minute "Summer's Noon Dream" (Mahler's own title) that opens to a commanding theme on horns (Pan awakes) before "summer marches in". The second part consists of a gentle Minuet "What the flowers tell me", a fanciful Scherzo (with post-horn solo) "What the beasts of the forest tell me", a Nietzsche setting for contralto "What man tells me", a delightfully festive "What the angels tell me" and finally "What loves tells me", one of Mahler's most sublime slow movements.

 ***Christa Ludwig (mezzo-soprano), New York Choral Artists, Brooklyn Boys' Chorus, New York Philharmonic Orchestra/Leonard Bernstein***

Deutsche Grammophon digital

A big, broad, rugged reading, less intense perhaps than Bernstein's admirable Sony recording (also from New York, albeit in analogue), less fresh-faced than Rafael Kubelík's version with the Bavarian Radio Symphony (DG, analogue), but a powerful statement none the less – and in superb sound.

Symphony No. 4 in G major (1892, 1899–1900, revised 1901–10)

Mahler's most amiable symphony opens to a gentle jog-trot and a melody of Mozartian elegance. Innocence, humour and a feeling of outdoors dominate the first movement, whereas the second is a sardonic "Dance of Death", the third a narrative in itself (starting with a glorious, long-breathed melody before breaking into laughter) and the finale, a charming song about "The Heavenly Life".

 ***Christine Whittlesey (soprano), South West German Radio Symphony Orchestra/Michael Gielen***

EMI digital

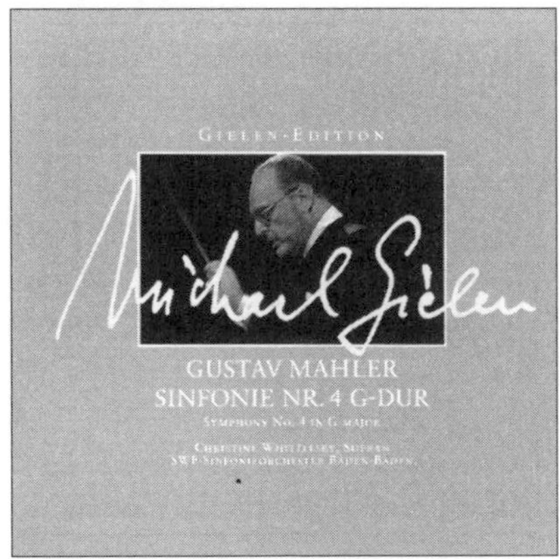

Michael Gielen scores on at least three significant counts: his choice of speeds is ideal, his characterization extremely vivid and his employment of string portamenti (sliding from one note to the next) – so important in Mahler – is consistently well judged. The slow movement, in particular, is unforgettable. George Szell's Cleveland recording (Sony) is a good analogue second choice and there are two important historic mono versions, the first by the Concertgebouw under Willem Mengelberg (Philips), the other by the Vienna Philharmonic under Bruno Walter (DG). Both conductors were friends of the composer.

Symphony No. 5 in C sharp minor (1901–02)

The Fifth opens to a sardonic funeral march then lunges into a stormy second movement ("Stormily agitated, with great vehemence") that runs the gamut from heavy-booted aggression to exultant affirmation. The bucolic Scherzo features a nostalgic central section; there's the famous *Adagietto* (a tender love-letter to the composer's wife) and a cheerful finale that's full of busy counterpoint.

 ***Bavarian Radio Symphony Orchestra/Rafael Kubelík***

Deutsche Grammophon analogue

Kubelík's 'funeral march' has a sense of irony and defiance that no other version quite matches, and although the recording is rather thin by modern standards (it dates from 1971), the playing has immense character. Fine second options include Bernstein (DG, digital or Sony, analogue), Leinsdorf (RCA, analogue), Haitink (Philips, his Royal Concertgebouw [analogue] recording) and Abbado (DG, his 1993 digital recording).

Symphony No. 6 in A minor (1904)

Grim resolve characterizes a first movement that sets out with marching feet before calming mid-way for a visit to the meadows and the gentle rattle of cow-bells. This is Mahler's most devastating symphony: the Scherzo stamps and snarls, the slow movement is tinged with melancholy and the turbulent finale – it plays for roughly half-an-hour – throws down the gauntlet and rises to a series of huge climaxes, two of which shatter to blows from a hammer. Mahler deleted a third blow (through superstition), though some conductors reinstate it.

Vienna Philharmonic Orchestra/Pierre Boulez

Deutsche Grammophon digital

Sampled at random, Boulez's performance might seem a trifle under-powered – and yet its cumulative effect is overwhelming. Kubelík (DG, analogue) provides a more bracing alternative, Bernstein (with the VPO, also on DG) a shattering – if occasionally overstated – second option. Those with an ear for historic performances should search out the expansive but profound Hans Rosbaud (last on Datum, mono).

Symphony No. 7 in E minor (1906)

A symphonic 'stream of consciousness': wry, inventive and harmonically sophisticated. The long first movement starts to a sullen tread but soon switches to the musical equivalent of a glorious sunset (the movement's central section). There are two 'Night Music' interludes (tenderness mixed with humour), a terrifying Scherzo and a rag-bag finale that has more method than its madness suggests.

Vienna Philharmonic Orchestra/Lorin Maazel

Sony Classical digital

Maazel's reading sometimes verges on caricature but the performance has real charisma and the playing is often superb. Kubelík (DG, analogue) offers a sprightlier, more lyrical alternative (his Scherzo is both malevolent and mischievous) while Michael Gielen (EMI, digital) and Pierre Boulez (DG, digital) are powerfully cerebral and Bernstein (either on DG [digital] or Sony [analogue]) typically characterful.

Symphony No. 8 in E flat major, "Symphony of a Thousand" (1906)

The very opening is unforgettable: "Come, Creator Spirit, Visit our Souls", and thereafter the first movement of Mahler's most densely populated symphony (at least in terms of the personnel required – the première employed a cast of 1003) suggests untold reserves of energy. The longer (and, to some, inferior) second movement sets the concluding scene from Goethe's *Faust*, and ends with the words "All that passes is a parable, all that is unattainable is a true event; the eternal feminine draws us near".

Heather Harper, Arleen Auger, Lucia Popp (sopranos), Yvonne Minton, Helen Watts (mezzo-sopranos), René Kollo (tenor), John Shirley-Quirk (baritone), Martti Talvela (bass), Vienna Boys' Choir, Vienna State Opera Chorus, Vienna Singverein, Chicago Symphony Chorus, Chicago Symphony Orchestra/Sir Georg Solti

Decca analogue

Mahler once said that all his work to date was but a prelude to the Eighth, although some commentators (including the present writer) feel that the symphonies that surround it somehow ring truer. Solti's performance has immense gusto and is nowadays accommodated on a single CD. Bernstein's vintage LSO Sony (analogue) recording is at times even more fervent (though the sound is rather dated), while Abbado's live Berlin Philharmonic recording (DG, digital) is interpretatively unfussy, well sung and beautifully engineered.

Das Lied von der Erde (1908-09)

Das Lied is one of Mahler's greatest symphonies (possibly the greatest after the Ninth), and it's lack of a 'series number' is due only to Mahler's superstition about the number '9' (remember that Beethoven's and Bruckner's Ninth Symphonies were also their last). The texts are based on German translations of classic Chinese T'ang dynasty poetry, while the music is boldly heroic (the "Drinking Song of the Earth's Sorrow"), exquisitely delicate ("Autumn Loneliness") and occasionally harrowing (the growling central climax of the 30-minute "Farewell" finale).

Ernst Haefliger (tenor), Mildred Miller (contralto), New York Philharmonic Orchestra/Bruno Walter

Sony Classical analogue

Walter conducted Das Lied's world première; he also recorded it three times (more, if you count 'pirate' issues), but this expansive stereo version presents a vast aural canvas that brings into focus every facet of Mahler's magnificent score. An earlier version with Kathleen Ferrier (Decca, mono) is preferred by some (though not this writer), while top-ranking rivals include Fritz Reiner (RCA, analogue) and a 1939 Concertgebouw broadcast under Carl Schuricht (Grammofono, Archiphon, mono) where, amidst the depths of "The Farewell", a Nazi zealot shouts out "Deutschland, über alles, Herr Schuricht!". Mahler was of course Jewish.

Symphony No. 9 in D minor (1909)

The ultimate distillation of Mahler's symphonic world, with a half-hour first movement that serves as both a watershed of musical late Romanticisim and a vivid augury of Alban Berg's inspired decadence. It is probably the finest first movement in the whole of twentieth-century symphonic music. There's also a boisterous *Ländler* tinged with irony, a savage *Rondo-burlesque* and a closing *Adagio* that climaxes powerfully before bidding us a long and profound farewell.

 ***Berlin Philharmonic Orchestra/Herbert von Karajan***

Deutsche Grammophon digital

Karajan at his most compelling, recorded in concert during the 1982 Berlin Festival. The string playing in particular has a burning intensity that is matched only by a famous pre-war Vienna recording (also live, and made on the eve of the Austrian Anschluss) under Bruno Walter (Dutton, EMI, mono). This particular reading underlines Mahler's anticipations of Alban Berg.
Other fine Mahler Nines include Sir Georg Solti's LSO recording (Decca, analogue) and Bruno Walter's American remake (with the Columbia Symphony Orchestra, Sony, analogue).

Symphony No. 10 in F sharp minor (1910) – incomplete

Mahler left the first movement, the second and 28 measures of the third fully orchestrated, whereas the rest survives only in 'short' score and is best-known nowadays in a fine performing version prepared by the British musicologist Deryck Cooke. Mahler's widow had originally put an embargo on public performances, but later rescinded her first decision. Musically, the opening *Adagio* is possibly the best movement (its last climax breaks on a frighteningly dissonant chord), though the long finale is especially poignant. Take note, however, that no performing version can ever be anything more than speculative.

 ***Philadelphia Orchestra/Eugene Ormandy***

Sony Classical analogue

Although both Riccardo Chailly (Decca) and Sir Simon Rattle (EMI) have made fine digital versions of the 'Cooke' Mahler Tenth and there are countless excellent versions of the Adagio alone (George Szell [Sony, analogue], Michael Gielen [EMI, digital] and Rafael Kubelík [DG, analogue] being among the best), Ormandy's première recording (not, it has to be said, of Cooke's 'definitive', i.e. last, performing version) has a missionary zeal that is consistently compelling. The string playing is especially fine.

Carl Nielsen (1865-1931)

Symphony No. 2, FS29, "The Four Temperaments" (1901-02)

A bracing series of musical reflections on pictures that Nielsen had discovered in a Zeeland village inn. Musical directions incorporate the names of the temperaments themselves, the first being an eruptive *Allegro collerico* leavened with lyricism (Nielsen envisaged a wild swordsman on horseback); the second, a lazy waltz (*Allegro comodo e flemmatico*), the third, a noble *Andante malincolico* (with "a hint of quiet melancholy", to quote Nielsen himself) and the last a confidently energetic *Allegro sanguineo*.

 ***Chicago Symphony Orchestra/Morton Gould***

RCA analogue

Rumbustious in the extreme, marvellously well played and excitingly recorded (the couplings, by the way, include Benny Goodman's version of Nielsen's Clarinet Concerto). Leonard Bernstein's wilful but gripping New York recording (Sony, analogue) makes a good second choice, while Herbert Blomstedt and the San Francisco Symphony (Decca) lead the digital stakes. There's also a fine vintage Danish recording under Nielsen-expert Thomas Jensen (Dutton, mono).

Symphony No. 3, FS60, "Sinfonia espansiva" (1910-11)

The Third Symphony's first movement opens to a jagged, accelerating repetition of a single A major chord, then swings into a joyful *Allegro espansivo* before climaxing like an epic extension of the *Carousel* Waltz. The idyllic second movement features two distant solo voices (singing a wordless vocalise); there's a sturdy though somewhat thoughtful Scherzo and a noble finale that Nielsen himself described as "a hymn to work and healthy enjoyment of daily life".

 ***Ruth Guldbaek (soprano), Niels Møller (tenor), Royal Danish Orchestra/Leonard Bernstein***

Sony Classical analogue

Bernstein sweeps through the first movement with immense gusto; it's a heroic reading, keenly played though rather crudely recorded. Paavo Berglund and the Royal Danish Orchestra (RCA) provide a good digital alternative, while there's a superb mono live performance (1959, on Danacord) by the Danish Radio Symphony Orchestra under an especially famous Nielsen advocate, Thomas Jensen.

Symphony No. 4, FS76, "Inextinguishable" (1914-16)

Nielsen's *Inextinguishable* doesn't so much 'start' as explode into action. The title refers to what has been described as "a subjective expression of the inextinguishability of life in its evolutionary process..." (Nicolas Slonimsky) while the Symphony's organic construction incorporates four harmonically bold movements that flow into each other without a break. The closing pages feature two timpani players placed at opposite ends of the orchestra and engaged in thundering drum warfare. It's a magnificent, life-affirming work.

 ***Royal Danish Orchestra/Paavo Berglund***

RCA digital

Berglund's recording – part of a recommendable complete cycle – generates considerable tension. Blomstedt (Decca) offers a powerful digital alternative (magnificently recorded, incidentally), while, once again, the Danish Radio Symphony Orchestra under Thomas Jensen (as heard live in 1952, Danacord, mono) are uniquely idiomatic.

Symphony No. 5, FS97 (1921-22)

While the Fourth Symphony has four movements played as one, the Fifth – arguably Nielsen's greatest work – has two, the first of which incorporates percussion writing that's prophetic of Shostakovich (note the sinister marching sequence roughly five minutes into the work) and a conflict-ridden climax where a lone side drummer tries to disrupt the orchestra's heroic forward momentum. The orchestra wins, though not without casualties (a clarinet suggests mourning) and the Symphony's ending is unequivocally triumphant.

 ***New York Philharmonic Orchestra/Leonard Bernstein***

Sony Classical analogue

Bernstein's 1962 Fifth, the first to be recorded in stereo, was something of a 1960s bombshell. The performance itself has a level of intensity that has never been matched (not even by the Danes themselves), although Rafael Kubelík's digital recording with the Danish Radio Symphony Orchestra (EMI) has a special nobility and Blomstedt's San Francisco version (Decca, also digital), interpretative intelligence and sonic splendour.

Symphony No. 6, FS116, "Sinfonia semplice" (1924-25)

If the Fifth Symphony anticipates Shostakovich, the sparer, livelier and even more harmonically audacious Sixth (completed merely days before its first performance) hints at Prokofiev style cynicism. The first movement starts brightly enough but soon darkens inexplicably although, Nielsen being Nielsen, there are elements of optimism later on. The brightly percussive second movement suggests mischievous provocation; there's a Bartókian *Adagio*, and Nielsen's boldest step towards a 'musical new order' ends with a versicoloured (if emotionally equivocal) theme and variations.

 ***Stockholm Philharmonic Orchestra/Gennadi Rozhdestvensky***

Chandos digital

It's hardly surprising that a master conductor of key twentieth-century Russian symphonic repertoire should excel in this, the most glacial (albeit the most lightly scored) of Nielsen's symphonies. If, however, you'd prefer to keep to digital cycles by Blomstedt (Decca), Berglund (RCA), Järvi (DG) or Myung-Whun Chung (BIS – both of the latter having much in their favour), then rest assured that each conductor has recorded an impressive version of the Sixth.

Jean Sibelius (1865-1957)

Symphony No. 2 in D major, Op. 43 (1901)

The greater part of the Second was conceived while Sibelius and his family were on a visit to Italy and although parts of the finale suggest a heroic processional (the closing minutes are crowned by a thrilling repetition of a victorious theme), much of the rest conveys a feeling of warmth and sunlight. The principal exception is the brooding, highly excitable second movement – said to be inspired by the darker aspects of Mozart's *Don Giovanni*.

 ***San Francisco Symphony Orchestra/Herbert Blomstedt***

Decca digital

A performance that's marked by a rare sense of musical logic, each phrase relating to the next with impressive inexorability. Although not as viscerally exciting as such analogue (mono) classics as Toscanini (RCA or Dell'Arte), Beecham (EMI) or Koussevitzky (RCA or Pearl), Blomstedt's reading remains

especially satisfying. Jukka-Pekka Saraste's live St Petersburg recording (Finlandia) provides a fine digital option.

Symphony No. 3 in C major, Op. 52 (1907)

The first movement is among the most joyful in Sibelius's symphonic output, a mobile, classically proportioned *Allegro moderato*, rather like a springtime canter across verdant plains. The second movement is a lilting, somewhat melancholy intermezzo, whereas the finale anticipates the Fifth Symphony in merging scherzo (a rather dark episode) and finale into a single thrilling unity. The closing pages are hypnotically propulsive.

Finnish Radio Symphony Orchestra/Jukka-Pekka Saraste
Finlandia digital

Saraste paces the Third to perfection, realizing its wide range of mood and colour (from joy, to quiet introspection, to heroic affirmation). The playing, too, is highly distinguished, while the phrasing is both luminous and affectionate. Best among Saraste's rivals are Sir Simon Rattle (EMI, digital) and fine historic (mono) recordings by Robert Kajanus (Finlandia) and George Szell (on the Cleveland Orchestra's own CD label).

Symphony No. 4 in A minor, Op. 63 (1911)

The bleakest and harmonically most adventurous of Sibelius's symphonies opens grimly among the low strings, scales ethereal heights and suffers ominous interjections from brass and timpani. The pensive Scherzo harbours powerful nightmare images (one instinctively thinks of Edvard Munch), before the *Largo* summons a spirit of eerie desolation and, beyond a huge climax, the finale ushers us out with quiet but stoical resolve. Biography gives some hint to the Symphony's spirit: Sibelius had recently been diagnosed as having a throat tumour.

Berlin Philharmonic Orchestra/Herbert von Karajan
Deutsche Grammophon analogue

Karajan steers a careful course between logic and feeling; his orchestra plays superbly and the 1965 recording still stands its ground – although there are excellent digital versions under Ashkenazy and Blomstedt (both on Decca).

Symphony No. 5 in E flat major, Op. 82 (1915, revised 1919)

A lone horn calls through the mists before Sibelius instigates one of twentieth-century music's most disorientating symphonic developments, desolate, elemental, noble then gradually accelerating for a triumphant close. The *Andante* hovers somewhere between dance and song, whereas the finale starts with a nervous shimmer and climaxes to a majestic though intensely lyrical brass theme.

Berlin Philharmonic Orchestra/Herbert von Karajan
Deutsche Grammophon analogue

Karajan's penchant for tonal blending precludes neither atmosphere nor tension, while the playing of the Berlin Philharmonic projects the full grandeur of Sibelius's vision. Herbert Blomstedt (Decca) offers a good digital alternative while, among older (mono) rivals, both Serge Koussevitzky (Pearl) and Sibelius's friend Robert Kajanus (Finlandia) are matchlessly idiomatic.

Symphony No. 6 in D minor, Op. 104 (1923)

The most lyrical and ethereal of Sibelius's seven symphonies, rich in expressive string writing (especially at the beginning and end of the piece) and transparently scored. Elusive at first, the Sixth is a mine of subtle musical activity which, although lacking the physical impact of, say, the Second, Fifth and Seventh Symphonies, suggests (in the words of Sibelius scholar Robert Layton) "powerful undercurrents just beneath the surface".

New York Philharmonic Orchestra/Leonard Bernstein
Sony Classical analogue

Some listeners might feel that Bernstein over-plays the expressive element (the Symphony's closing pages suggest an almost Tchaikovskian intensity), but the overall effect is undeniably moving. Subtler alternatives include Sir Simon Rattle (EMI, digital), Jukka-Pekka Saraste (Finlandia, live – also digital) and Sir Thomas Beecham (EMI, mono).

Symphony No. 7 in C major, Op. 105 (1923)

Sibelius had his Eighth Symphony destroyed (at least one witness attested to its astonishing quality), possibly because he sensed that it did not equal his towering Seventh. Although just 20-odd minutes in length, Op. 105 surveys a vast range of mood and colour, developing organically (it's conceived in a single movement) from an initial rising theme, through scherzo and storm to a sequential upheaval that equals, in its emotional intensity, the most harrowing moments in Mahler or Tchaikovsky. The final page witnesses a tortuous but heroic struggle towards the home key.

BBC Symphony Orchestra/Serge Koussevitzky
Pearl mono

The original LP reissue of Koussevitzky's white-hot 1933 broadcast performance carried a photo-reproduced endorsement from the composer himself. This is one of those 'once in a lifetime' recordings, the sort that sets impossibly high interpretative standards – although Karajan (DG), Mravinsky (Olympia) and Sir Colin Davis (his Boston recording on Philips), all of them analogue – still have plenty to tell us.

Albert Roussel (1869-1937)

Symphony No. 3 in G minor, Op. 42 (1929-30)

Roussel's intention was "to achieve... music which satisfies itself, music which looks to free itself from illustrative or descriptive elements ... I constantly try to obliterate from my mind the memory of objects and forms capable of being translated into musical effects." And yet the Third Symphony's pounding *Allegro vivo*, pensive *Adagio* (one of the high-spots of twentieth-century symphonic writing) and joyful Scherzo suggest, at least to this listener, a busy metropolis heading towards an uncertain future.

French National Orchestra/Leonard Bernstein

Deutsche Grammophon digital

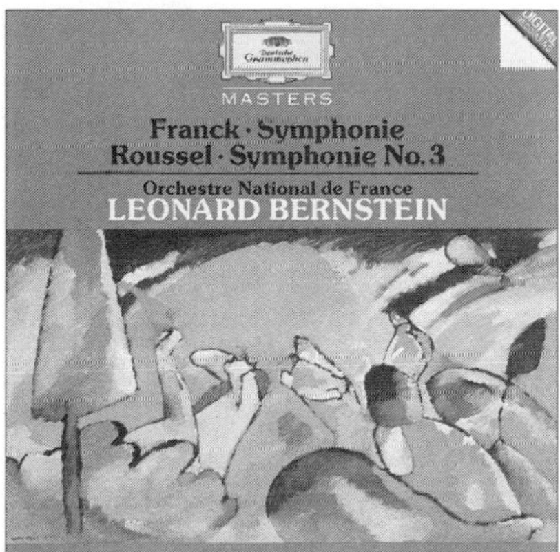

Although its release was unaccountably delayed by some 12 years, Bernstein's second recording of the score (his first, for Sony, was with the New York Philharmonic) generates tremendous power. A less charismatic performance with the French Radio Philharmonic Orchestra under Marek Janowski (RCA, digital) comes as part of a useful (and reliable) survey of all four symphonies, while Charles Munch's Erato (analogue) recording relates an especially intense first movement.

Alexander Zemlinsky (1871-1942)

Lyric Symphony, Op. 18 (1922-23)

One of two works that follow on the heels of Mahler's *Das Lied von der Erde* (the other is – at least in this writer's opinion – Shostakovich's *Michelangelo* Suite). But while Mahler set ancient Chinese poems, Zemlinsky turned to the Bengali poet Rabindranath Tagore. The seven songs suggest a discourse between a man and a woman (their subject-matter is, for the most part, love and longing) while the music inhabits a world filled with Mahler, Wagner and the dawning discoveries of Schoenberg and his school. Zemlinsky, a fine conductor, befriended Schoenberg and was encouraged by Mahler.

Deborah Voigt (soprano), Bryn Terfel (bass-baritone), Vienna Philharmonic Orchestra/ Giuseppe Sinopoli

Deutsche Grammophon digital

Passionate and perceptive, superbly played (the Vienna Philharmonic sounds absolutely right for this post-Mahlerian masterpiece) and memorably sung. Bryn Terfel in particular underlines the continuity between the Lyric Symphony and Das Lied. Rivals are plentiful (more so now than ever before) with Michael Gielen (Arte Nova, digital) and Riccardo Chailly (Decca, digital) as next-best to Sinopoli.

Alexander Scriabin (1872-1915)

Symphony No. 1 in E major for soloists and orchestra, Op. 26 (1899-1900)

"O wondrous image of divinity, pure art of harmony!" – rapturous words to greet a new century, with extravagant music to match. Scriabin's "Hymn to art" serves as the climax to a First Symphony where contrasts abound, from the pampered tones of the dreamy opening *Lento* to the stormy orations of the second and fifth movements and an expansive choral finale.

Symphony No. 2 in C minor, Op. 29 (1901)

Scriabin toughened up his act after the calorie-crazed excesses of his (gloriously OTT) First Symphony. And yet major stylistic preoccupations remain common to both works: a feeling for drama and landscape – the second movement suggests a hedonistic garden-scene rich in bird life – and a melodic distinctiveness that culminates in a grand finale and one of Scriabin's biggest and best tunes.

Symphony No. 3 "Divine Poem", Op. 43 (1902-04)

"The evolution of the human spirit" and "exhilarating affirmation" – ideas that send Scriabin's Third Symphony hurtling towards an all-embracing, universal music. The tone is darker than before, but the narrative is action-packed – starting with "the conflict between man as the slave of a personal God and man as God himself," then man "intoxicated and soothed by the voluptuous pleasures he has plunged into" and, finally, "The spirit... [which] abandons itself to the supreme joy of a free existence".

Symphony No. 4, Op. 54, "Poem of Ecstasy" (1905-06)

The ultimate musical foreplay – forging ahead one moment, holding back the next then teasing the listener with false starts and cunningly aborted climaxes. Scriabin deploys his forces with immense skill, leaving the longest and loudest until last; his express intention was to convey "the ecstasy of untrammelled action, the joy of creative activity".

Symphony No. 5 "Prometheus – Poem of Fire", for piano, chorus and orchestra, Op. 60 (1908-10)

Prometheus is a true augury of twentieth-century musical dissonance and opens to one of the most terrifying chords in all music, a murky flatland rent in two by the score's first violent eruption. A virtuoso pianist serves as commentator for a maniacal dialogue that climaxes with a chorus and (as originally intended) a light-projection show. A 'final act' follow-up work was left unfinished, although a speculative completion does exist (it's best on Russian Disc, under Kyrill Kondrashin, analogue).

Stefania Toczyska (soprano), Michael Myers (tenor), Westminster Choir, Dmitri Alexeev (piano), Philadelphia Orchestra/Riccardo Muti

EMI digital

Lavish canvases such as these cry out for the Philadelphia's opulent pooled tone and Muti avoids the temptation to inflate, exaggerate or over-dramatize. EMI offer wide-screen, ambient sound (again, appropriately) and Scriabin is handsomely served throughout. Bargain-hunters might also like to consider Dimitri Kitaienko and the Frankfurt Radio Symphony Orchestra (RCA, digital – and with a spurious choral ending to the Poem of Ecstasy), while Giuseppe Sinopoli's New York full-price coupling of the Third and Fourth Symphonies (DG digital) is also pretty sensational.

Ralph Vaughan Williams
(1872-1958)

Symphony No. 1, for soprano, baritone, chorus and orchestra, "A Sea Symphony" (1903-09, revised 1923)

The opening fanfare, one of Vaughan Williams's most inspired ideas, announces a maritime call to arms: "Behold, the sea itself…", proclaims the chorus (the words are by Walt Whitman), and the orchestra responds by painting the sea's "heaving breast". *A Sea Symphony* celebrates both the sea and man's journey towards eternity; there are four movements, the third being a playful Scherzo, the Fourth – and longest – a moving meditation on "The Explorers" – sea-borne or otherwise.

Felicity Lott (soprano), Jonathan Summers (baritone), London Philharmonic Choir, London Philharmonic Orchestra/Bernard Haitink

EMI digital

Haitink has the full measure of what is surely one of the finest representatives of a grand English choral tradition (the mature VW stands at the helm, Elgar at the stern). He chooses his tempos with care, braves some huge aural waves and has the benefit of a magnificent digital recording (the organ can be heard with amazing clarity). Haitink's finest analogue predecessors are Boult (Decca [mono] or EMI [analogue]) and Previn (RCA, analogue), while Andrew Davis's Teldec recording serves as a viable digital alternative.

Symphony No. 2, "A London Symphony" (1913, revised 1920 and 1933)

Mists at dawn and the distant pealing of Big Ben herald this, Vaughan Williams's most approachable symphony (it was one of his own favourites). Within minutes, we're thrown amidst the city's bustle, visit secluded churchyards, witness Bloomsbury Square in cold November (the Symphony's evocative slow movement), take a trip to the Embankment and overhear a cockney barrow boy before night falls and we're back on the shores of the Thames. All this colourful activity is forged in an artful four-movement structure and orchestrated with the utmost skill.

Philharmonia Orchestra/Leonard Slatkin

RCA digital

Leonard Slatkin's enthusiastic promotion of English music has benefited London audiences throughout the 1980s and 1990s, and his VW cycle has many peaks – this being one of the highest. It's a vigorous, well crafted reading, well played, warm-hearted and superbly recorded – but there's a whole roster of formidable rivals from, among others, Andrew Davis (Teldec, digital), Bernard Haitink (EMI, digital), Sir John Barbirolli (with the Hallé, EMI recorded in 1957), André Previn (RCA, analogue), Sir Adrian Boult (his superb 1952 mono recording) and Sir Henry Wood (a sparkling pre-war mono recording, Dutton). This is definitely the luckiest VW symphony on disc.

Symphony No. 3, "A Pastoral Symphony" (1921)

The title is VW's own and although many still view the Third as quintessentially 'English-Pastoral' (it tends to prompt those 'musical cow-pat' clichés), attentive listening will recognize moments of profound disquiet – especially in the last movement. But then one must not forget that the work was originally conceived amidst the horrors of the First World War. The very opening is pure magic (Ravel is an audible influence) while the finale incorporates a wordless soprano line. It's a reposeful, rather sad *Pastoral Symphony* to contrast with Beethoven's relative extroversion; it is also among the most haunting of all VW's compositions – in fact, his orchestral masterpiece (at least in this writer's opinion).

 ***Heather Harper (soprano), London Symphony Orchestra/André Previn***

RCA analogue

There's an exploratory, fresh-minted aspect to Previn's Pastoral that even now, some 25 years after it was recorded, suggests enthusiastic re-creation. Previn's love of French music helps to illuminate the Ravelian aspects of the score and the recording is both clear and beautifully balanced. Digital-fanciers might like to try Vernon Handley (EMI) or Leonard Slatkin (RCA).

Symphony No. 4 in F minor (1931-34)

"I don't know if I like it, but it's what I meant." VW's well-known comment on his own uneasiest symphony suggests unstoppable self-expression rather than a 'labour of love'. The Fourth is largely violent, disruptive and extraordinarily exciting (the very opening will either annoy you or grab you by the throat), though its actual structure is as sound as a bell. The present writer finds it very hard to take (too much flailing, too little substance) – but that's a personal reaction, one that many experts find inexcusable.

 ***BBC Symphony Orchestra/Ralph Vaughan Williams***

Dutton Laboratories mono

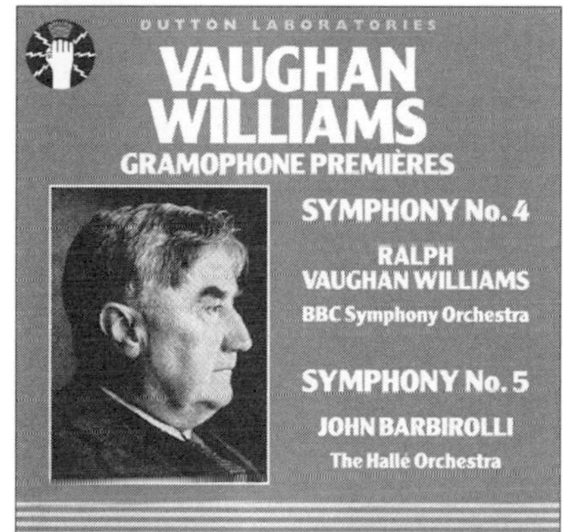

If VW's Fourth is going to work, there can be no holds barred. And of all the composer-conducted performances in the catalogue, this 1937 recording vies with Rachmaninov's account of his own Third Symphony (RCA, Pearl, mono) for 'first place'. Energy levels are high, the playing is white hot and the current transfer especially dynamic (though some of the quieter music sounds a mite synthetic). Good digital rivals include Leonard Slatkin (RCA) and Andrew Davis (Teldec).

Symphony No. 5 in D major (1938-1943, revised 1951)

Dedicated "in sincere flattery" to Sibelius, this work serves as the ideal gateway to Vaughan Williams's symphonic world. The opening horn calls – so mysterious, yet so sensuous – set the scene (Ravel's *Daphnis et Chloé* lies within earshot) while the Scherzo suggests animated twilight. The *Romanza* is at once both austere and bewitchingly romantic (the first few minutes are unforgettable) while the Symphony ends with a noble though variegated *Passacaglia*.

 ***London Symphony Orchestra/André Previn***

RCA analogue

Again, André Previn's Ravelian credentials serve this Symphony particular well, especially in the tranquil reaches of the first and third movements. His feeling for texture and control of line are admirable, although competition is hot, with fine versions from Sir John Barbirolli (EMI [analogue] or, even better, Dutton, 1944, mono), Sir Adrian Boult (Decca [mono] or EMI, analogue) and Bernard Haitink (EMI, digital).

Symphony No. 6 in E minor (1944-47)

The cataclysmic opening bars conjure disruption on a huge scale: massed strings shoot to the skies, only to be gunned down by thundering brass and timpani. Then comes the oafish, galloping second subject (a sort of malevolent *Sorcerer's Apprentice*) and an especially noble central theme (once used in the TV series "Family at War"). The pensive second movement suggests a finger poised dangerously near the button, the Scherzo anarchy or mob rule, and the eerie Epilogue, utter desolation visited by the briefest ray of light.

 ***London Philharmonic Orchestra/Sir Adrian Boult***

Belart mono

It would be difficult to imagine a more committed performance than this and, indeed, the composer himself says as much in a brief speech at the end of the CD. The playing has fire, clarity and great sensitivity (especially in the Epilogue) and the sound, although single-channel, is both dynamic and informative. Previn (RCA, analogue), Slatkin (RCA, digital) and Boult's impressive first recording (EMI, mono) provide viable alternatives.

Symphony No. 7 for soprano, women's chorus and orchestra, "Sinfonia antartica" (1949-52)

One of the repertory's great symphonic soundscapes, and fully on a par with Strauss's similarly graphic *Alpine Symphony* (see "Narratives in Sound"). Sample from 7'40" into track 3 on our recommended version ("Landscape") for a terrifying visitation by brass, percussion and organ – scenic aural majesty, and as imposing as anything in VW's symphonic output. Then there's the Epilogue's blizzard, the whales and penguins of the Scherzo and the Intermezzo's nostalgic oboe solo. *Sinfonia antartica* grew out of a score that Vaughan Williams had originally composed for the film *Scott of the Antarctic*, but listeners are strongly advised to forget its cinematic ground-springs and concentrate instead on its many purely musical virtues (especially its magnificent orchestration).

Sheila Armstrong (soprano), London Philharmonic Choir, London Philharmonic/Bernard Haitink

EMI digital

The feeling for texture and atmosphere that distinguish Haitink's recordings of Vaughan Williams's Sea Symphony and Fifth Symphony (also EMI, digital), are even better exemplified here, and the sound is remarkably vivid. True, there's significant rivalry from Boult (Decca [mono] and EMI) or Previn (RCA) – both include the optional narration Haitink excludes – but both are analogue and Sinfonia antartica cries out for the dramatic dynamic extremes afforded by good digital sound.

Symphony No. 8 in D minor (1953-56)

A colourful bridge from the scenic austerity of the Seventh Symphony to the disquieting commentaries of the Ninth. VW himself described the score as having been written for "what is known as a Schubert orchestra with the addition of a harp. Also there is a large supply of extra percussion, including all the 'phones and 'spiels known to the composer." There are also three tuned gongs. Of all VW's symphonies, this is the most abstract, the most experimental and the least pastoral. It is also, in some respects, the most fun (with a Scherzo for winds and an exotically percussive finale).

Philharmonia Orchestra/Leonard Slatkin

RCA digital

VW's dedication of his Eighth Symphony "for glorious John [Barbirolli] with love and admiration from Ralph" suggests that Barbirolli's own recording (EMI, analogue) – made in stereo in 1956 by top-flight engineers and still sounding excellent – should be our first choice. And yet Slatkin's intelligence and sense of colour, allied to first-rate digital engineering, make for an equally compelling experience.

Symphony No. 9 in E minor (1956-57, revised 1958)

Pastures new, strange and more than a little unsettling. The very opening suggests the Ninths of Bruckner and Beethoven while the presence of saxophones (always an ominous augury in VW) drags us from the countryside to the metropolis. True, there are glimpses of green and the odd whiff of fresh air, but they're few and far between. The second movement opens with a lonely flugelhorn solo, the third (a scherzo) features heavy brass and percussion and the equivocal slow finale is both mysterious and majestic.

London Philharmonic Orchestra/Sir Adrian Boult

Everest analogue

Recorded merely hours after Vaughan Williams died (the CD opens with a brief memorial speech by Sir Adrian himself), this fine performance bespeaks an unusual degree of dedication. Bryden Thomson (Chandos, digital) provides a swift and stimulating alternative.

Sergey Rachmaninov
(1873-1943)

Symphony No. 3 in A minor, Op. 44 (1935-36)

A Russian Romantic in America (Rachmaninov's home when he wrote the work). All the old virtues are there – melodic fecundity, sumptuous orchestration, Tchaikovskian resonances – and yet the Third Symphony adds something extra, a touch of daring. There are three movements, the second of which (the supposed 'slow movement') incorporates a highly-coloured Scherzo. The very opening is unusual, too: clarinet, horn and muted cello lead to an unprecedented eruption which, in turn, gives way to a particularly beautiful string theme. It's a superb work, one that, together with the *Symphonic Dances* (see "Suites and Dances") and the *Isle of the Dead* (see "Narratives in Sound"), marks a high-spot in Rachmaninov's orchestral writing.

Royal Concertgebouw Orchestra/Vladimir Ashkenazy
Decca digital

One of Ashkenazy's finest achievements in the recording studio, a performance of great character and vitality set in the appropriately ambient acoustic of the Amsterdam Concertgebouw. The playing is superb, but there are fine rivals from the Berlin Philharmonic under Lorin Maazel (DG, digital) and – a little less glitzy, perhaps, but even more musical – the Rotterdam Philharmonic under Edo de Waart (Philips, analogue). Eugene Ormandy's sumptuous Philadelphia recording (Sony, also analogue) is a viable fourth option.

Charles Ives (1874–1954)

Symphony No. 2 (1898–1902)

If you're tired of Dvořák's *New World* Symphony (unlikely though that might be), Ives's Second will serve as a worthy 'New World-2'. Steeped in the idioms of Dvořák and Brahms (Ives's use of popular tunes is unmistakeably Dvořákian), it's none the less a highly original piece, rich in meaningful quotations (including *Camp Town Races*, *Columbia, Gem of the Ocean* and Beethoven's Fifth), often amusing and featuring some of the noblest orchestral writing ever to come out of America. If in doubt, try the fourth movement.

Royal Concertgebouw Orchestra/Michael Tilson Thomas
Sony Classical digital

It was Leonard Bernstein who premièred Ives's Second (in 1951) and although his 1958 Sony New York Philharmonic version still has plenty going for it, Tilson Thomas offers a rather fresher performance, lighter in touch than Bernstein's and far better recorded.

Symphony No. 3 "The Camp Meeting" (1904)

The Third and gentlest of Ives's symphonies (it's scored for a chamber orchestra) has a strong autobiographical element: all the movements are rich in musical quotations, often from the Presbyterian liturgy which Ives had known from his youth. When, on May 5th, 1947, Ives was told that his Third Symphony had won the Pulitzer Prize, he responded with the words "prizes are for boys – I'm grown up!"

New York Philharmonic Orchestra/Leonard Bernstein
Sony Classical analogue

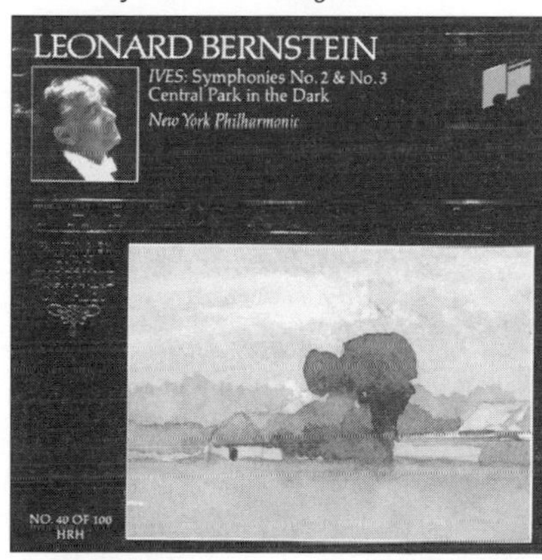

An especially intense reading, beautifully played and still sounding well in an excellent digital transfer. The CD also contains one of the better recordings of the Second Symphony and the riotous tone-poem, Central Park in the Dark. Michael Tilson Thomas's digital Sony recording (with the Royal Concertgebouw Orchestra) makes for a fine second choice.

Symphony No. 4 (1910–18)

An existential Symphony, part profound, part profoundly funny, and that leaves you feeling as if you've plunged headlong into your unconscious. The questions posed are the perennial 'what?' and 'why?', and the 'answer' or 'explanation' is suggested initially in a mysterious Prelude and a berserk *Allegretto* where wildly converging forces clash among marching tunes and songs of the day. The 'slow movement' is a hymn-like fugue and the ethereal finale (a slow processional) is one of Ives's most arresting inspirations. It's a work that has to be heard.

Chicago Symphony Chorus, Chicago Symphony Orchestra/ Michael Tilson Thomas
Sony Classical digital

Ives's canvas incorporates organ, piano, chorus and a huge orchestra; it cries out for an informative acoustic, and Chicago's Medinah Temple is as near-ideal as any. Tilson Thomas conducts a finely graded interpretation, but there's an equally cogent Cleveland reading under Christoph von Dohnányi (Decca, digital) while Leopold Stokowski's pioneering Sony (analogue) recording remains uniquely impressive. Tilson Thomas was the first to record the work using the Critical Edition.

Franz Schmidt (1874–1939)

Symphony No. 4 in C major (1932–33)

When Franz Schmidt lost his only daughter, he composed this Symphony as a requiem for her ("Requiem" is in fact its unofficial subtitle). Conceived in a single movement, it opens to a lonely trumpet solo then develops through four variegated sections, weeping, exulting, even occasionally forgetting - but always returning to its tragic subtext.

London Philharmonic Orchestra/Franz Welser-Möst

EMI digital

Schmidt's Fourth is what one might call an 'organically fashioned' symphony, being four movements cast in one. And because of that, any potential interpreter needs to view it as a whole, and not sectionalize it or indulge its various episodes. Welser-Möst offers a lean, impassioned and above all cogent reading, superbly played and warmly engineered. It is, in this writer's opinion, the finest available CD of Schmidt's music.

Arnold Schoenberg (1874-1953)

Chamber Symphony No. 1, Op. 9 (1906, revised 1922)

Schoenberg condenses a four-movement structure into a single unit, using just 15 solo instruments to create a highly dramatic - yet fundamentally optimistic - effect. Strauss and Mahler are audible influences (Mahler's Seventh Symphony is quoted fairly early on in the piece), but the entire work is studded with the kind of accessible complexities that make Schoenberg's best music so compelling.

Royal Concertgebouw Orchestra/Riccardo Chailly

Decca digital

Riccardo Chailly's penchant for fin de siècle masterpieces has resulted in an especially varied discography and this version of the Chamber Symphony is among the clearest, most impassioned and best played on record. Alternative versions include effective transcriptions for piano quintet (Gulda, Hagen Quartet on DG; Litwin, Arditti Quartet on Auvidis) and piano duet (Kocsis and Hauser on Quintana). All are digital.

Josef Suk (1874-1935)

Asrael Symphony in C minor, Op. 27 (1905)

A searingly intense musical essay and one of the pivotal post-Dvořák Czech symphonies. Suk's *Asrael* (the title refers to the Angel of Death) is in effect a requiem both for Dvořák himself (Suk was both his pupil and his son-in-law) and for Suk's wife (Dvorák's daughter) Otilka, who died while the original fourth movement was taking shape. The work also includes a highly inventive Scherzo, a tender musical portrait of Otilka.

Czech Philharmonic Orchestra/Václav Talich

Supraphon mono

Talich directs a powerful, sympathetic and finely-graded account of the score. The 1952 recording comes up extremely well on CD and the most recent incarnation appears on two discs in harness with Talich's equally distinctive account of Dvořák's memorable Stabat mater - itself a profound reaction to bereavement, in this case the triple-blow of losing three daughters. Talich's finest rival is Rafael Kubelík (a superb broadcast recording with the Bavarian Radio Symphony Orchestra - Panton, analogue).

Reinhold Glière (1875-1956)

Symphony No. 3 in B minor, Op. 42, "Il'ya Mouromets" (1909-1911)

A Symphony that's cast very much in the style of Scriabin and Rimsky-Korsakov (the sound palette is rich, the manner of its employment extremely dramatic), Glière's epic Third traces the colourful career of an eleventh-century Russian hero (Il'ya of Mourom), who remained motionless for 30 years until wandering pilgrims prophesied a dramatic future for him. There are four long movements, "Mourometz's Confrontation with a Rival", "The Highwayman named Nightingale", "At the Court of the Sun Prince Vladimir" and "The Heroic Exploits of Il'ya and his Petrification".

USSR Radio and Television Large Symphony Orchestra/Natan Rakhlin

Russian Disc analogue

Rakhlin was a highly skilled conductor who never appeared outside Russia but whose flair for the big Romantic masterpieces is effectively exemplified in this fine - if raucously recorded - performance. Alternatives include a stunning (albeit significantly cut) 1940 reading by Stokowski and the Philadelphia Orchestra (Biddulph) and a worthy BBC Philharmonic digital recording under Sir Edward Downes (Chandos).

Nikolai Miaskovsky (1881-1950)

Symphony No. 6 in E flat minor, Op. 23 (1921-24)

An extremely dramatic work cast in four movements, three of which play for over a quarter-of-an-hour apiece, and culminating in a radiant choral finale. Miaskovsky was a prolific symphonist (he wrote 27 in all) whose style combines the dramatic directness of, say, a Prokofiev with complex musical developments and an unmistakable Russian tone. The first performance inspired weeping, shouts for joy and a lengthy ovation. Some commentators went as far as to claim that Miaskovsky's Sixth was the first symphony after Tchaikovsky's Sixth to justify the name!

Yurlov Russian Choir, USSR Symphony Orchestra/Kyrill Kondrashin

Russian Disc mono

An extraordinarily intense performance (you could imagine that the première, under the great Golovanov, was similarly impressive), recorded back in 1959 and still sounding reasonably good. There are a couple of modern competitors but, quite frankly, they don't even begin to rival Kondrashin's mastery.

Arnold Bax (1882-1953)

Symphony No. 3 in C major (1929)

The opening bassoon solo is sad and doleful, although the ensuing *Allegro moderato* is both energetic and – on occasion (i.e. 6'53" into our recommended recording) – disarmingly tender. The slow movement features a memorable horn solo as well as much dark, typically Celtic tone-painting while the finale closes to a slow epilogue, "the basic idea of the music being adumbrated as through a dark haze". Although Bax's Third reflects weathered Northern climes, its language is frequently charged with emotion (Barbirolli's performance greets the light with special eloquence at 4'46" into the second movement).

Hallé Orchestra/Sir John Barbirolli

EMI mono

A real classic, and so much more impassioned than a worthy but generally less responsive reading by the London Philharmonic under Bryden Thomson (Chandos, digital). Sir John Barbirolli, an enthusiastic Baxian, had only recently taken over the Hallé Orchestra when this recording was made (it was in fact their first collaboration on disc). Virtually every minute of this exceptional performance is informed by an excited sense of exploration. The original 78s date from 1943-44.

Igor Stravinsky (1882-1971)

Symphony in C (1940)

Forged in the wake of both personal and political tragedy, Stravinsky's greatest symphony combines Neo-Classical restraint with a fervent dynamism that recalls Tchaikovsky (as do some of the harmonies). While working on the piece, Stravinsky lost both his wife and his eldest daughter to tuberculosis; in fact, he contracted the disease himself and had to recuperate at a sanatorium in the French Alps.

The Orchestra of St Luke's/ Robert Craft

Music Masters digital

Craft assisted Stravinsky on many of his own recordings and his mastery of texture, rhythm and dynamics – even at fast tempi (as here) – hightens an already intense musical drama. Digital sound and an extra dash of nervous energy (especially in the first movement) mark this recording as exceptional, although "Stravinsky conducts Stravinsky" (Sony, analogue) is an obvious second choice.

Symphony in Three Movements (1942-45)

The first movement – originally entitled a Symphony-Overture and recalling the violent gestures of Stravinsky's *Rite of Spring* ballet – was inspired by film footage of Japan's invasion of China, whereas the second (a pensive *Andante*) utilizes music originally intended for a film soundtrack (*Song of Bernadette*) and the third (*con moto*) revisits the disruptive spirit of the Symphony's opening.

Columbia Symphony Orchestra/ Igor Stravinsky

Sony Classical analogue

Much of this performance's impact is due to a stereo recording that, even after the passage of some 35 years, still sounds pretty amazing. Good digital alternatives are available from Robert Craft (Music Masters) and Charles Dutoit (Decca) – but Stravinsky's own version is still the most authoritative.

Symphony of Psalms for chorus and orchestra (1930, revised 1948)

An all-pervasive sense of ritual informs this, one of Stravinsky's greatest works. There are three movements that set verses from the Vulgate version of the Psalms, the last of which - "Alleluia, laudate Dominum" - being among the composer's most memorable pages. The *Symphony of Psalms* is one of many fine works that the Russian conductor Serge Koussevitzky commissioned for the fiftieth anniversary of the Boston Symphony Orchestra.

Boys' and Male Voices of the Russian State Academic Choir, Russian State Academic Orchestra/Igor Markevitch

Philips analogue

The fact that Igor Markevitch believed Stravinsky to be a deeply religious man is reflected in a performance that combines tonal austerity with a strong spiritual element and an unfailing sensitivity to detail (a regular feature of Markevitch's conducting).

The bold Russian voices are especially distinctive, but if this early-1960s recording proves difficult to locate (it is available at the time of writing), then there are fine alternatives under Leonard Bernstein (Sony) and the composer himself (his last version, with the Toronto Festival Singers - also on Sony). Both are analogue.

Karol Szymanowski (1882-1937)

Symphony No. 3 for tenor, chorus and orchestra, Op. 27, "The song of the night" (1914-16)

A Symphony that carries on where Scriabin's *Prometheus* (or Fifth Symphony - see above) left off. With massive, coruscating climaxes and a roster of instrumental timbres that approximates the most rarefied aural glitter, Szymanowski's Third is among the most potent - and most mystically poetic - symphonies of the early-twentieth century. The texts are taken from a Polish translation of the second Divan by the Persian mystical poet Jalal Ad-Din ar-Rumi.

Jon Garrison (tenor), CBSO Chorus, City of Birmingham Symphony Orchestra/Sir Simon Rattle

EMI digital

Sir Simon Rattle's love of Szymanowski tells in every bar, whether among the sustained quieter reaches of the closing movement or the huge waves of sound that precede it. Worthy alternatives include Antál Dorati (Decca, analogue) and Jerzy Semkow (EMI, analogue), but neither is quite in Rattle's class.

Bohuslav Martinů (1890-1959)

Symphony No. 3, H260 (1944)

Few of Martinů's works reflect the tragedy of war as vividly as this superb symphony. The highly mobile first movement marries mystery with climaxes of lacerating power; the beautiful slow movement treads a path from darkness to light, whereas the initially dramatic finale ends with a hymn-like epilogue. The Third's structure harks back to baroque models and the Corellian *Concerto grosso*.

Czech Philharmonic Orchestra/ Karel Ančerl

Praga analogue mono

Ančerl's account of the Third, which was recorded in concert during November 1966, has a special intensity - and little wonder considering that between the work's composition and its first performance (by the Boston Symphony under the great Koussevitzky) most of Ančerl's family was murdered in a Nazi concentration camp. The sound quality, although mono, is remarkably good.

Symphony No. 5, H310 (1946)

An amazing work that combines Neo-Classical delicacy (the second movement) with galumphing energy (the closing *Allegro*) and a quizzical, almost mystical, quality that seems to strengthen with each encounter. Martinů's Fifth was premièred at the 1947 Prague Spring Festival (under Rafael Kubelík) and was later promoted by Ernest Ansermet, who introduced it to American audiences - with considerable success.

Czech Philharmonic Orchestra/Karel Ančerl

Supraphon mono

Ančerl's reading is both texturally transparent and physically exciting - and although the recording is in mono, it's so spacious that you hardly notice a lack of stereophonic information. A thrilling live performance by the same artists is available from Multisonic (mono - but it's far less well recorded than the Supraphon CD).

Symphony No. 6, H343, "Fantaisies symphoniques" (1953)
The first two movements of Martinů's Sixth open to weirdly swarming winds and brass before contrasting themes are taken up by the strings. Darker than the Fifth, the Sixth shares with its predecessor an adventuring spirit and a predilection for bold colours and strong rhythms. *Fantaisies symphoniques* was composed for the Boston Symphony Orchestra and premièred by them in 1955 under Charles Munch (they also recorded the work for RCA).

Czech Philharmonic Orchestra/Karel Ančerl
Supraphon mono
It was Václav Neumann, Ančerl's successor at the Czech Philharmonic, who described this recording as "stunning … an amazing experience for all of us" – no mean compliment coming from a man who went on to record the work himself. The coupling is Martinů's delightful folk-cantata, A Bouquet of Flowers. However, you should also keep an eye out for Charles Munch's excellent Boston recording (RCA, analogue).

Sergey Prokofiev (1891–1953)

Symphony No. 1 in D, Op. 25, "Classical" (1916–17)
Prokofiev's First Symphony is an ingenious but respectful send-up of its Classical models (Haydn in particular), light, tuneful and spiced by pungent harmonies. The first movement is a sprightly *Allegro*, the second, an elegant *Larghetto*, the third a boisterous Gavotte (Prokofiev also uses it in his *Romeo and Juliet* ballet) and the finale a busily scurrying *Molto vivace*.

Czech Philharmonic Orchestra/ Karel Ančerl
Supraphon mono
Ančerl and his players don't miss a trick. Rhythms are taut, detail legion (instrumental interchanges are projected with extraordinary clarity) and the playing itself has immense vitality. However, Claudio Abbado and the Chamber Orchestra of Europe (DG) provide a stylish digital alternative.

Symphony No. 3 in C minor, Op. 44 (1928)
The very opening raises the alarm – shrill, primitivist music, forged (like virtually everything else in the score) from material that Prokofiev had already used in his opera *The Fiery Angel*. The mysterious *Andante* is followed by a chilly, reptilian Scherzo (eerily sliding strings help set the mood) and then there's the grotesque finale, a pitch-black processional with heavy brass and percussion – a sort of musical *Jurassic Park*, huge, forbidding and totally uncompromising.

Royal Concertgebouw Orchestra/Riccardo Chailly
Decca digital

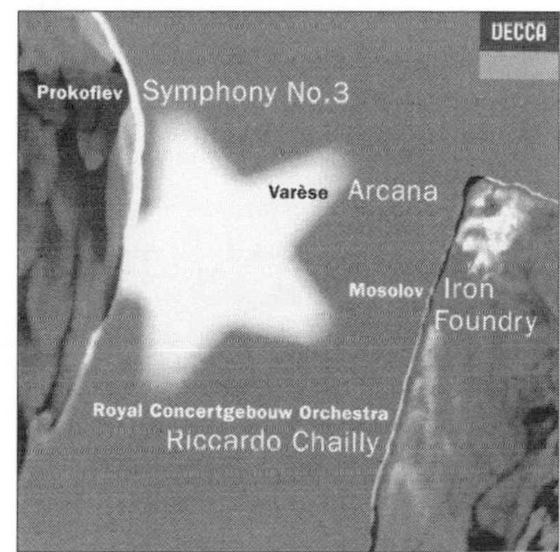

Not the wildest 'Prok 3' on disc, but certainly the best recorded and set within the context of a stylistically varied twentieth-century programme (Mosolov, Varèse). Zdenek Kosler's Czech Philharmonic recording (Supraphon, analogue) is made of tougher fibre, while Erich Leinsdorf and the Boston Symphony (RCA, analogue) lead the vintage field.

Symphony No. 5 in B flat major, Op. 100 (1944)
One of Prokofiev's strongest works, less disruptive than the more radical Second, Third and Fourth Symphonies, but hardly less imposing. The opening *Andante* is remarkably fluent; its course is clearly mapped, its final pages overwhelmingly powerful. The playful *Allegro marcato* Scherzo features a quacking trumpet trio, while – beyond an especially intense *Adagio* – Prokofiev rounds things off with an affectionate but madcap finale.

Berlin Philharmonic Orchestra/Herbert von Karajan
Deutsche Grammophon analogue
A grand, gleaming Fifth where the first movement's peroration is topped by a spectacularly well recorded tam-tam. Koussevitzky's 1946 Boston Symphony recording (RCA, mono) is perhaps slightly more intense, and Dorati's LSO version (Mercury, analogue) more tautly argued, but Karajan's is a powerful, extremely well balanced statement of the score.

Symphony No. 6 in E flat major, Op. 111 (1945–47)
The greatest of the seven symphonies, though the Union of Soviet Composers labelled it "utterly formalist". Prokofiev's opening gesture – a stinging march-like motif played on the brass – marks a descent into his longest and darkest symphonic movement, dominated (mid-way) by a sombre melody underpinned by a constant

'tick-tock' rhythm. The spacious *Largo* is full of pain and although the finale seems cheerful, at least initially, its later episodes suggest unchecked fury.

 ***Leningrad Philharmonic Orchestra/Evgeny Mravinsky***

Praga analogue

Electrifying! Mravinsky (who premièred the work) inspires a performance of unprecedented boldness and precision: sample the last movement's central section where all hell suddenly breaks loose – especially for the last five minutes. This 1967 live recording is notably superior to Mravinsky's 1959 studio version (Melodiya, etc). Seiji Ozawa and the Boston Symphony (DG) provide a worthy digital alternative.

Symphony No. 7 in C sharp minor, Op. 131 (1951-52)

A mystery that's very different in nature to another 'late' Op. 131 masterpiece in C sharp minor – Beethoven's Fourteenth String Quartet. Here, the music opens to a sinister chord and a melancholy string melody; there's waltz-like *Allegretto* that works itself into a delirious frenzy (recalling Prokofiev's great ballets), followed by a brief but tender slow movement and a vivacious finale that can end in one of two ways – either with a threat (a flash-back to the Symphony's opening mood) or a forced laugh. Prokofiev himself provided both options.

 ***Berlin Philharmonic Orchestra/Seiji Ozawa***

Deutsche Grammophon digital

Ozawa's balletic credentials (he has made excellent recordings both of Romeo and Juliet and Tchaikovsky's Nutcracker) are useful in this, the most balletic of Prokofiev's symphonies. However, also recommendable are recordings under either Gennadi Rozhdestvensky (Melodiya, analogue) or his father, Nikolai Anosov (Supraphon, mono), both of whom exhibit a special understanding of a great but underrated score. All three conductors opt for the quieter ending.

Arthur Honegger (1892-1955)

Symphony No. 3, H186, "Liturgique" (1945-46)

A poignant and powerful 'war memorial' that draws upon elements of the Catholic liturgy. Honegger's Third opens with a devastating vision of "The Day of Judgement"; there's a deeply expressive "De profundis clamavi", rich in counterpoint and with various instruments playing at the extremes of their range, and a sinister March that builds in muscle before breaking off for a gentle, strings-dominated *Adagio.*

Berlin Philharmonic Orchestra/Herbert von Karajan

Deutsche Grammophon analogue

A magnificent reading of a great work. Karajan's control never precludes drama, especially in the hard-driven outer movements. His handling of the quiet closing pages is wonderfully luminous and the recording – a 1969 analogue production – still sounds marvellous, especially as remastered on DG's original. The current couplings include the equally impressive Second Symphony.

Ernest John Moeran (1894-1950)

Symphony in G minor (1924-37)

Moeran was a musical craftsman whose influences number Delius and Sibelius among their ranks but whose natural propensity for creating vivid colours and incorporating musical aspects of his Celtic heritage led to some wonderful scores. The G minor Symphony is a vibrant, scenic essay, profoundly Sibelian in its 'climate' but strongly individual both in terms of its shape and its thematic complexion. It rather approximates a 40-minute ramble across thickets in autumn.

 ***Hallé Orchestra/Leslie Heward***

Dutton Laboratories mono

It was Walter Legge (producer of the present 1942 recording) who described Leslie Heward (1897-1943) as "musically speaking, the most satisfying conductor this country [England] has produced since Beecham". This particular performance – an inspired evocation, utterly natural both in phrasing and nuance, and greatly admired by the composer himself – caught Heward towards the very end of his career. Illness felled him merely months after the sessions were completed. A fine digital alternative is provided by Vernon Handley (Chandos) and one lives in hope that Sir Adrian Boult's superb Lyrita (analogue) recording will reappear before long

Paul Hindemith (1895-1963)

Symphony, "Mathis der Maler" (1934)

A symphonic distillation of music from Hindemith's part-autobiographical opera about a painter (Matthias Grünewald) who abandons his art, makes common cause with the oppressed and eventually learns that the artist who betrays his abilities is useless to society. Poised on the very edge of the Nazi era, *Mathis der Maler* is a noble expression of irreconcilable tensions, at once dramatic, serene and equivocally triumphant.

Berlin Philharmonic Orchestra/Claudio Abbado

Deutsche Grammophon digital

Abbado has made two recordings of Mathis (the first, for Decca with the LSO, was a benchmark production of the analogue stereo era), but this live performance is particularly majestic and beautifully engineered. Notable vintage recordings include versions under the composer himself (DG or Teldec, mono), William Steinberg and Herbert von Karajan (both EMI, analogue),

Erich Wolfgang Korngold (1897-1957)

Sinfonietta, Op. 5 (1912)

The most astonishing show of musical precocity ever, save for Mendelssohn's Octet. This is quality stuff, an ardent, uplifting epic (over 40 minutes in length), packed full of spellbinding melodies. Korngold was just 15 when he composed it; the Vienna Philharmonic premièred it and if you can resist the Scherzo's central 'big tune' (4'08" into our recommended version – and a vivid precursor of Korngold's luscious film scores), then you can't possibly be a genuine romantic!

Berlin Radio Symphony Orchestra/Gerd Albrecht

Varèse Sarabande digital

Gerd Albrecht is well known for his patronage of the rare and the exotic and he certainly does Korngold proud with a performance that combines bracing high spirits with great warmth of tone. The recording is spacious, but if you find the disc difficult to track down (you just might), then there's a good alternative under Matthias Bamert (also digital, Chandos).

Roy Harris (1898-1979)

Symphony No. 3 (1939)

Music of the open plains – big, chunky and with a generous melodic drift. Cellos set things in motion, then the brass join in and the mood switches from epic lyricism to breezy travel music, rumbustious horseplay and a tragic finale that recalls Sibelius's similarly structured Seventh Symphony (it's about the same length, too – that's about 18-20 minutes).

New York Philharmonic Orchestra/Leonard Bernstein

Deutsche Grammophon digital

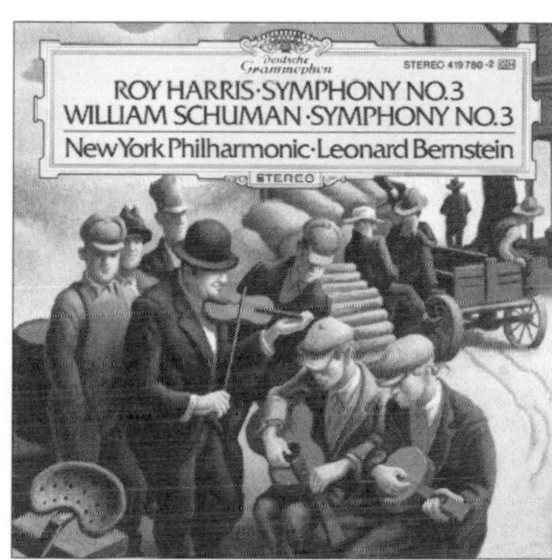

Anyone who attended Bernstein's American bicentennial performance at the Royal Albert Hall (also with the NYPO) will know what to expect – a sonorous, broad-shouldered account, as rugged and uncompromising as the music itself. Bernstein studied with Serge Koussevitky, the man who commissioned the Symphony (he too made a marvellous recording of it – the first ever, now out on a Pearl CD, mono).

Aaron Copland (1900-90)

Symphony No. 3 (1944-1946)

Readers in search of Copland's ubiquitous *Fanfare for the Common Man* need look no further: it turns up more or less intact in the fourth movement of the Third Symphony. The most popular American symphony after Roy Harris's Third (see above) combines the manly, 'open air' style familiar from Copland's cowboy ballets with occasional hints of jazz (and a touch of Prokofiev – especially in the second movement). Like so many American masterpieces of the 1930s and 1940s, it was first performed by the Boston Symphony under Serge Koussevitzky.

Dallas Symphony Orchestra/Eduardo Mata

EMI digital

In 1995 Eduardo Mata lost his life in a plane crash while still at the very height of his powers, and this expertly crafted performance (which is also magnificently recorded) shows his skills to fine advantage. It's smoothly executed without being slick, and expressive without slipping into emotional overkill. The best rivals are conducted by Leonard Bernstein (DG) and Leonard Slatkin (RCA) – both of which are digital recordings. Bernstein's earlier version (Sony, analogue) is also very impressive.

Kurt Weill (1900-1950)

Symphony No. 2 (1933-34)

If you're attracted to the caustic, unsettling world of Kurt Weill's music but you're uncomfortable with the stage/vocal works then this profoundly moving Second Symphony – which is something of a requiem for a Europe on the brink of self-destruction – should certainly appeal. The first movement recalls the energized though poignant world of *The Seven Deadly Sins* (the final moments are frighteningly abrupt); the *Largo* second movement suggests menace and sorrow (Hitler had recently been elected to power) and the finale, the cynical humour of *The Threepenny Opera.*

 ***BBC Symphony Orchestra/Gary Bertini***

EMI analogue

A sensitive, disciplined and vividly characterized performance. The 1967 recording still sounds impressive and the current couplings – Weill's First Symphony, plus Schoenberg and Busoni – are entirely apt. A rival version under Edo de Waart (Philips, analogue – again with the First Symphony), though not quite as impressive, is also recommendable.

William Walton (1902-1983)

Symphony No. 1 in B flat minor (1931-35)

The very opening gives the lead, a jagged, propulsively driven figure that underpins the entire movement and works towards a shattering climax. The Scherzo is a riot of colour, the *Andante* deeply melancholic in mood while the finale marks a truly heroic resolution. Some contemporary influences are discernible, but Walton's busily extrovert style registers throughout.

 ***London Symphony Orchestra/André Previn***

RCA analogue

An incisive, hard-driven performance though one that's always keenly responsive to the more lyrical aspects of the score. Previn went on to re-record the work (with the RPO – for Telarc, digital), but failed to achieve the white-hot excitement that he and his players generated for these benchmark 1966 sessions. There's also a fine 1950s recording under the composer's own baton (EMI, mono).

Karl Amadeus Hartmann (1905-1963)

Symphony No. 6 (1951-53)

A work of immense power by a composer who had resorted to 'inner emigration' under the Nazis. Hartmann had consistently refused to collaborate with the regime and when the war came to an end, he set to work refashioning some of his older material for a series of fine – and still – underrated symphonic masterpieces. The Sixth is cast in two sections – a highly dramatic *Adagio* followed by an often frenzied Toccata with three fugues. In addition to standard instrumentation Hartmann's scoring includes a varied line-up of percussion plus piano (all much in evidence in the second movement) while his musical language recalls the very different voices of Hindemith, Mahler and Martinů.

Berlin Symphony Orchestra/Günther Herbig

Berlin Classics analogue

A dedicated, perceptive performance, very well recorded and exceedingly well transferred to CD. Herbig was a pupil of the great Hermann Scherchen who had in turn encouraged Hartmann to see music as "a simile for humans and time". An alternative recording under Rafael Kubelík (Wergo, analogue) comes as part of a recommendable survey of Hartmann's complete symphonies.

Dmitry Shostakovich (1906-1975)

Symphony No. 1 in F minor, Op. 10 (1923-24)

The work of a precocious genius fresh out of the Leningrad Conservatory (Glazunov greatly admired the piece) and astonishingly prophetic of Shostakovich's later symphonies. In fact the quizzical first movement looks as far ahead as the Fifteenth, while there's a breakneck Scherzo that ends with a series of crashing piano chords, a haunting slow movement and a highly eventful finale that sounds like first rate film music.

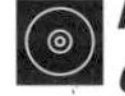 ***New York Philharmonic Orchestra/Leonard Bernstein***

Sony Classical analogue

Although Bernstein homes in on the First Symphony's humour, he also recognizes both its pathos and a certain wistful nostalgia (especially towards the end of the slow movement). He re-recorded the work in

Chicago (DG, digital) and there's a superb mono version by the Cleveland Orchestra under Artur Rodzinski (Sony or the Cleveland's own label – if you can find it!).

Symphony No. 4 in C minor, Op. 43 (1935–36)
Forged in an atmosphere of fear and oppression, Shostakovich's boldly out-reaching Fourth Symphony had to wait 35 years for its world première (the original first performance was aborted while at the rehearsal stage). Still, that's hardly surprising; had the Soviet authorities encountered its strident tones, overt cynicism and modernist techniques head on, Shostakovich's already insecure situation would have worsened considerably.

City of Birmingham Symphony Orchestra/Sir Simon Rattle
EMI digital
Shostakovich's Fourth is steeped in Mahler and so it's hardly surprising that its best interpreters – Bernard Haitink (Decca, digital), Kyrill Kondrashin (Melodiya, analogue), Eliahu Inbal (Denon, digital) and Sir Simon Rattle – are all distinguished Mahlerians. Rattle's is the most perceptive version around, a truly epic account of the score, studded in detail, magnificently played and expertly recorded.

Symphony No. 5 in D minor, Op. 47 (1937)
Shostakovich's opera *Lady Macbeth of Mtsensk* (see "Psychologists and Psychoses", below) had courted Stalin's displeasure and his Fifth Symphony – although filled with subtle anti-Stalinist allusions – earned his redemption. "The subject of my Fifth Symphony is the evolution of an individual," wrote the composer. The first movement's stern opening leads to an agitated *Allegro non troppo*; there's a sardonic (and very Mahlerian) Scherzo, a powerfully emotive *Largo* and a finale that suggests loud cheering through gritted teeth.

Leningrad Philharmonic Orchestra/Evgeny Mravinsky
Erato digital
Mravinsky conducted the world première and went on to promote the Symphony world-wide. There are numerous CDs of his keenly inflected interpretation, Erato's (taken from Russian tapes) being about the best recorded. However, Bernstein (Sony, analogue) is more outwardly emotive, and Haitink (Decca, digital) more thoughtfully introspective.

Symphony No. 6 in B minor, Op. 54 (1939)
The Sixth opens with an intense though desolate slow movement that's about as long as the other two movements put together. The centre-placed Scherzo jeers and caterwauls, and the finale is a brittle, high-speed *Presto*. Initial reactions to the score were cagey and uncomprehending – at least in Russia. Although not ranked as one of Shostakovich's 'war' symphonies, the Sixth is an unmistakable product of its time.

Leningrad Philharmonic Orchestra/Evgeny Mravinsky
Melodiya/BMG analogue
One of Mravinsky's greatest Shostakovich interpretations, with a frantic final Presto that pushes the Leningrad players to the very limits of their virtuosity (recorded live in 1972, it's the best of various Mravinsky Sixths that have been released on CD). Masterful alternatives include Leonard Bernstein (New York Philharmonic, on Sony, analogue), Fritz Reiner (Pittsburgh Symphony, Sony, mono) and Kyrill Kondrashin (Melodiya/BMG, analogue).

Symphony No. 7 in C major, Op. 60, "Leningrad" (1941)
A Symphony that, to quote Shostakovich himself, "is about the Leningrad that Stalin destroyed and that Hitler merely finished off". The long first movement features a banal marching tune that crescendos with cunning monotony, until wickedness confronts protest and "God exacts a grim vengeance for the blood that has been spilled". Shostakovich continued: "If people were to read the Psalms before attending any performance of the Seventh, there would perhaps be fewer silly statements about this Symphony".

London Philharmonic Orchestra/Bernard Haitink
Decca digital
Haitink's is a broad, sombre Seventh, one that eschews any hint of sensationalism. However, those who'd rather confront the 'big guns' are directed to either Evgeny Mravinsky and the Leningrad Philharmonic or Kyrill Kondrashin and the Moscow Philharmonic: both are analogue (Mravinsky's recording is in mono), and both on BMG/Melodiya.

Symphony No. 8 in C minor, Op. 65 (1943)
The most devastating of Shostakovich's three 'war' symphonies (i.e. Nos. 7-9): desolate, fraught with tension and opening to a meditative, half-hour *Adagio*. The third movement is a fiercely propulsive *Allegro non troppo* that climaxes among big drums and tam-tam before exploding into a noble passacaglia, whereas the finale, set in the optimistic key of C major, offers at least some semblance of hope.

Leningrad Philharmonic Orchestra/Evgeny Mravinsky

Philips digital

The Eighth Symphony is dedicated to Mravinsky: he conducted its world première and made its very first complete commercial recording (1947 – Melodiya/BMG, mono – a riveting experience). Mravinsky's perception and mastery of dynamics are everywhere in evidence, his sense of drama too, though Haitink (Decca, digital – a remarkably fine performance) is better recorded and Kondrashin (Praga, live – analogue) more viscerally exciting.

Symphony No. 9 in E flat major, Op. 70 (1945)

An ostensibly lighthearted Symphony that cries 'hidden subtext' in virtually every bar. Shostakovich's Ninth is cast in a "light and sunny mood" (the composer's own description), with a slapstick first movement, an *Adagio* that wears a very weary countenance, a galloping, catch-me-if-you-can Scherzo (a mini 'concerto for orchestra'), a desolate *Largo* that opens to glowering brass and a finale that starts with a cheeky bassoon solo and gradually gains in momentum until the final race home and an unmistakable grimace.

Moscow Philharmonic Orchestra/Kyrill Kondrashin

Melodiya/BMG analogue

Kondrashin conducts the Ninth with skill and cunning, exploiting its dramatic potential on all levels of meaning. The 1965 recording is reasonably good, although a contemporaneous Sony version under Leonard Bernstein is sonically superior. Other fine (analogue) alternatives include David Oistrakh (Russian Disc) and Efrem Kurtz (Sony, mono).

Symphony No. 10 in E minor, Op. 93 (1953)

It was in 1948 that Shostakovich was attacked by the Union of Soviet Composers as having "a propensity for the world of degenerate, repulsive and and pathological phenomena". He lost his professorships and hit hard times financially, but within a few years Stalin died and he was able to resume symphonic composition. In fact the Tenth includes a notorious 'Stalin' Scherzo – savage music, though incredibly exciting – as well as a powerfully structured (slow) first movement, a caustic third and an invigorating finale. This is one of the works that includes Shostakovich's own signature (worked out via keys and their German equivalents, i.e. D, Es, C and H – or DSCH).

Leningrad Philharmonic Orchestra/Evgeny Mravinsky

Praga analogue

One of numerous Mravinsky Tenths and fairly typical in its strength, refinement and orchestral discipline. A thrilling live recording, it's in a class of its own – although there are fine digital recordings under Stanislav Skrowaczewski (Carlton Classics) and Gennadi Rozhdestvensky (Olympia).

Symphony No. 11 in G minor, Op. 103 "The Year 1905" (1957)

A graphic tone-painting that commemorates the abortive Russian Revolution of 1905 (as opposed to the February uprising of 1917 and the Bolsheviks' seizing of power in November of the same year). The opening depicts the lonely "Palace Square" (popular tunes echo in the distance) while "January the Ninth" describes the murderous dispersal – by Tsarist troops – of the aggrieved crowd. There's "Perpetual Remembrance" (which quotes a revolutionary funeral march) and a fierce finale that bravely anticipates the heroic events of 12 years later.

Leningrad Philharmonic Orchestra/Evgeny Mravinsky

Praga analogue

Whatever one's feelings about Russian-Soviet history, there can be little doubt that Shostakovich's openly patriotic Symphony is a heartfelt celebration of an ideal (rather than a reflection on that ideal's distorted political realization). It needs to be played with an almost savage intensity and Mravinsky qualifies with honours (there are alternative versions by him on Melodiya and Russian Disc – both of them in mono – but this is the best).

Symphony No. 13 in B flat minor, "Babiy Yar" for bass, chorus and orchestra, Op. 113 (1962)

Dmitry Shostakovich and the (then) young non-conformist poet Yevgeny Yevtushenko collaborated for a powerful five-movement epic that chronicles Stalinist anti-semitism, the humiliating power of humour, the terrible times that women experienced in trying to feed their families, fear and the sardonic smile of careerism. However, when high-ranking Communists pointed out that not only Jews were killed at Babiy Yar,

Yevtushenko was obliged to supplement his text with references to Russians and Ukrainians. After the 1962 première, the Symphony wasn't heard again until 1965.

Arthur Eisen (bass), Choirs of the Russian Republic, Moscow Philharmonic Orchestra/Kyrill Kondrashin

Melodiya/BMG analogue

Kondrashin's performances of this harrowing work were always special events (his legendary 1962 first performance has been issued on Russian Disc) and Melodiya's 1967 recording is no exception. Arthur Eisen is a commanding bass soloist, but there's an extremely fine 1993 live recording (Decca, digital) with Sergei Aleksashkin under Sir Georg Solti who, at the time, had just discovered the work.

Symphony No. 14 for soprano, bass, strings and percussion, Op. 135 (1969)

Shostakovich's word-painting skills are every bit as effective as those of his friend – and the Fourteenth Symphony's dedicatee – Benjamin Britten. There are 11 movements to poems by Garcia Lorca, Apollinaire, Küchelbecker (a friend of Pushkin) and Rilke. Some are violent (the vicious "Malagueña" second movement or the wildly sarcastic "The Zaporozhian Cossacks' reply to the Sultan of Constantinople"); others – such as the opening "De Profundis" or the moving lament "O Delvig, Delvig!" – deeply introspective. Shostakovich's Fourteenth is, like his *Michelangelo* Suite (see "Across the Nations"), one of the finest orchestral song-cycles after Mahler's *Das Lied von der Erde*.

Evgenya Tselovalnik (soprano), Evgeny Nesterenko (bass), Moscow Philharmonic Orchestra/ Kyrill Kondrashin

Melodiya/BMG analogue

A pungent performance, bitingly incisive and with fine singing – especially from Nesterenko. There's an even more high-powered alternative under Rudolf Barshai (who conducted the world première – Russian Disc, analogue), while Bernard Haitink's fine Royal Concertgebouw recording (Decca, digital) has Dietrich Fischer-Dieskau and Julia Varady singing the poems in their original languages (an option that was authorized by the composer).

Symphony No. 15 in A major, Op. 141 (1971)

Shostakovich's last Symphony poses countless questions, all of which are left unanswered. The first movement parodies Rossini's *William Tell* Overture then flares to breathless rage, the *Adagio* is a sombre elegy, the bony Scherzo suggests mirthless laughter while the finale opens to the "Fate" motive from *Götterdämmerung*'s "Funeral Music" (one of Wagner's blackest pages and itself charged with dark historical associations) then swings into the main movement on the opening of *Tristan und Isolde*. There's a terrifying climax before the Symphony ends to the uncomfortable shuffling of tuned percussion.

Cleveland Orchestra/Kurt Sanderling

Erato digital

Sanderling's long association with this Symphony (he has conducted it countless times) tells in every bar. Some, however, will find it just too slow and introspective, and are therefore directed to Gennadi Rozhdestvensky (Olympia).

Olivier Messiaen (1908-1992)

Turangalîla Symphony for piano, ondes martenot and orchestra (1946-48)

"The *Turangalîla* Symphony is a love song ..." writes Messiaen, "... the *Turangalîla* Symphony is a hymn to joy." The title merges two Sanskrit words, the meaning of which corresponds almost exactly to Messiaen's own description. There's an important part for solo piano and the massive orchestration also employs an ondes martenot (a weirdly wailing electronic keyboard instrument) that weaves, snake-like, through the textures. *Turangalîla*'s language ranges from a deliriously affirmative "Joy of the Blood of the Stars" to the most exquisite love music.

Yvonne Loriod (piano), Jeanne Loriod (ondes martenot), Orchestre de la Bastille/Myung-Whun Chung

Deutsche Grammophon digital

Messiaen's own judgement cannot be taken lightly. "Coming after the many excellent interpretations that we already know," he writes in the CD booklet, "this new version, superb from every point of view, can be considered henceforth the definitive account." Quite an accolade, though Riccardo Chailly's Decca recording is even better in terms of sound and Sir Simon Rattle's EMI recording is also extremely effective (both are digital). Still, Chung's spontaneity and perception definitely earn him first place.

Alan Hovhaness (b1911)

Symphony No. 2, Op. 132, "Mysterious Mountain" (1955)

"Mountains are symbols, like pyramids, of man's attempt to know God," writes Hovhaness; "Mountains are symbolic meeting places between the mundane and spiritual worlds. To some, the *Mysterious Mountain* may be the phantom peak, unmeasured, thought to be higher than Everest, as seen from great distances by fliers in Tibet. To some, it may be the solitary mountain, the tower of strength over the countryside – Fujiyama, Ararat, Monadnock, Shasta or Grand Teton." *Mysterious Mountain* combines a feeling of ancient legend with delicate textures and a markedly individual melodic drift.

 ***Chicago Symphony Orchestra/Fritz Reiner***

RCA analogue

Reiner's refined though virtuosic approach lends an appropriate sense of tranquillity to the second movement's serene opening (a fine place to sample), while the fast writing thereafter is brilliantly realized. The 1958 recording has been effectively refurbished.

Benjamin Britten (1913-1976)

Sinfonia da Requiem, Op. 20 (1940)

A work of an enormous power (Britten composed it in the wake of his father's death), the first movement anticipating the war-torn world of Prokofiev's Sixth Symphony. The opening *Lacrymosa* is "a slow marching lament in a persistent 6/8 rhythm with a strong tonal centre in D"; the second, *Dies irae*, "a form of Dance of Death with occasional moments of quiet marching rhythm" and the deeply devotional *Requiem aeternam* finale opens "very quietly" while "over a background of solo strings and harps, the flutes announce the quiet D major theme, the principle motive of the movement." (The quotes are from Britten himself.)

 ***New Philharmonia Orchestra/Benjamin Britten***

London (Decca) analogue

Unlike certain other composer-conductors, Britten was always among the finest (some would say the finest) advocates of his own music. This particular performance never puts a foot wrong – whether in terms of its galvanizing climaxes or its judicious phrasing – but there are are some compelling rivals, not least those conducted by Sir Simon Rattle (EMI) and Libor Pešek (Virgin – both are digital recordings).

Simple Symphony for string orchestra, Op. 4 (1933-34)

Brilliant employment of child's play, Britten having utilized material that he originally composed between the ages of nine and 12. The *Simple* ground-plan incorporates a "Boisterous Bourrée", a "Playful Pizzicato" (the work's most famous movement), a "Sentimental Sarabande" that recalls Grieg's *Holberg Suite* and an energetic "Frolicsome Finale" to close. It's delightful stuff, very much on a par with Prokofiev's equally winsome *Classical* Symphony.

 ***English Chamber Orchestra/Benjamin Britten***

Decca analogue

Good versions of this Symphony are relatively plentiful, but this December 1968 recording has special claims to 'best ever' status, what with its chirpy characterization, easy virtuosity and fine sound. The couplings – all of which are conducted by Britten – represent English string music at its most appealing.

A Spring Symphony for soloists, chorus and orchestra, Op. 44 (1949)

The introduction, "Shine out, fair sun, with all your heat" traces the thaw from winter to spring, with boys' whistling, copious bird-song and ending with a wonderful setting of Milton's *Now the bright morning star*. The sultry slow movement sets Herrick and Vaughan and suggests the coming of war, while the beautifully orchestrated Scherzo gives way to a sun-drenched, swaying finale that Britten himself described as "a May-day festival, a kind of Bank Holiday". Like so many musical masterpieces of the 1940s, *A Spring Symphony* was commissioned by the conductor Serge Koussevitzky, although the actual first performance was given in Holland.

 ***Jennifer Vyvyan (soprano), Norma Procter (contralto), Peter Pears (tenor), Boys from Emanuel School, Wandsworth, Orchestra and Chorus of the Royal Opera House, Covent Garden/Benjamin Britten***

Decca analogue

Although habitually loath to append the word 'definitive' to any recorded performance, this superbly engineered 1960 production tempts me to relent. Singing, playing and recording are quite simply beyond praise, although historically-minded listeners would do well to investigate the actual world première performance (under Eduard van Beinum [with Kathleen Ferrier], also on Decca – though in pretty dire sound).

Witold Lutosławski (1913-1994)

Symphony No. 3 (1983)
Listening to Lutosławski Three is rather like venturing into a tropical forest alive with bird and insect life. There are two movements, the first of which alternates lengthening rhythmic units and slow refrains, the second being based – according to the composer himself – "on a slow singing theme and a sequence of rather dramatic recitatives played by the string group. A short and very fast coda ends the piece."

 ***Berlin Philharmonic Orchestra/Witold Lutosławski***
Philips digital
Lutosławski's recording has the advantage of orchestral refinement and superb sound. A rival version under Daniel Barenboim (with the Chicago Symphony – Erato, digital) is marginally more exciting, but the composer himself inspires that extra degree of concentration from the players.

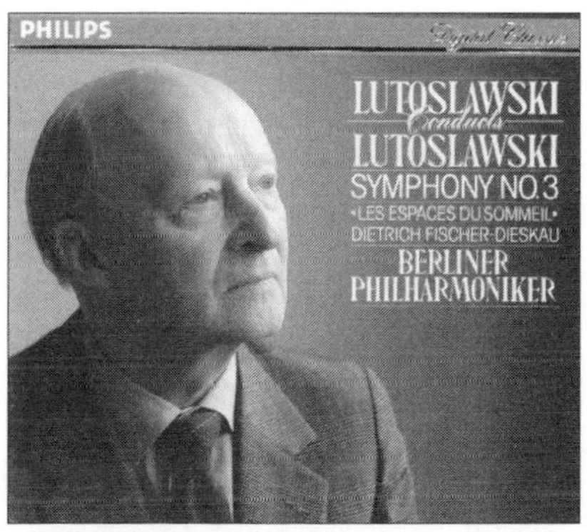

Leonard Bernstein (1918-1990)

Symphony No. 2, "The Age of Anxiety" (1947-49, revised 1965)
"The scene takes place in a bar where four lonely people, three men and a woman, find each other. Through alcohol they experience inner, semi-conscious adventures, a kind of spiritual journey to find a place where relationships can be formed and faith can be established" (quoted from Jack Gottlieb's annotation for DG). Bernstein's prime mover was the poetry of W. H. Auden and the Symphony's language ranges in style from the soulful Prologue to a jazzy "Masque" (marked "extremely fast") and an optimistic Epilogue. It's an extremely fine piece, one that's still somewhat underrated.

 ***Lukas Foss (piano), Israel Philharmonic Orchestra/ Leonard Bernstein***
Deutsche Grammophon analogue
A scintillating performance, much abetted by Foss's brilliant pianism (especially in the "Masque"). Bernstein's earlier New York Philharmonic recording (Sony) is marginally more brash (sometimes appropriately), though in most other respects this 1977 remake leads the field.

Robert Simpson (b1921)

Symphony No. 9 (1987)
Hyperion's annotator Lionel Pike says it all. "This symphony is not only a mighty study of musical motion ... it is also a study of the power of a simple musical germ to generate enormous paragraphs of music ... [It] is a giant written by a giant among symphonists." Too true, especially for those whose symphonic idols are Bruckner, Sibelius and Nielsen.

 ***Bournemouth Symphony Orchestra/Vernon Handley***
Hyperion digital
Recorded just a year after the Symphony's completion, Handley's CD première is a model of committed music-making: one immediately senses an important voyage of discovery. The sound is superb, and there's an invaluable bonus in a fascinating 18-minute illustrated talk by the composer himself.

Hans Werner Henze (b1926)

Symphony No. 4 (1955)
A darkly intense score, rich in atmosphere (its original stage-music context suggested forest life and the changing seasons) and full of finely-crafted instrumental detail. Contrasts abound: some of Henze's loveliest ideas alternate with moments of barely repressed violence. Although cast in a single movement, the Symphony falls into five distinct sections. The closing pages are extraordinarily compelling.

 ***Berlin Philharmonic Orchestra/Hand Werner Henze***
Deutsche Grammophon analogue
Part of a set that features Henze's first six symphonies (the first five have been recorded in Berlin in April 1964, the Sixth in London in April 1972). Playing, interpretations and engineering are wholly up to scratch – but the Fourth Symphony is something very special.

Henryk Górecki (b1933)

Symphony No. 3, Op. 36 (1976)
It was the launching of the British independent radio station Classic FM that catapulted 'Górecki Three' to fame, although the Symphony's earlier usage on a film soundtrack had already attracted an enthusiastic band of listeners. However, Górecki's hypnotic, artfully structured design and tragic subtext (which includes the prayer of an 18-year-old originally inscribed on the

wall of a Gestapo cell) gave birth to a work that, far from aiming at a 'popular market', is as sincere and moving as any Symphony composed since the Second World War. Tempos are slow and the last two movements feature a soaring soprano line.

 ***Dawn Upshaw (soprano), London Sinfonietta/David Zinman***
Nonesuch digital

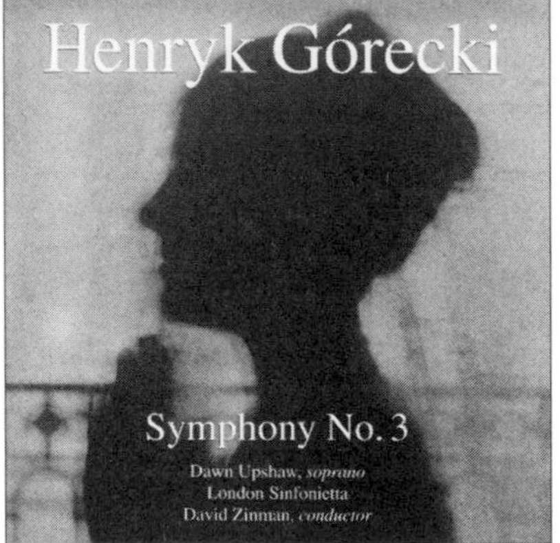

Other recordings preceded this one (a 1987 Olympia release under Katlewicz being among the best), and yet the combination of Upshaw's sweet soprano, Zinman's control of line and the London Sinfonietta's seamless playing remains irresistible. The recording is superb, and the booklet annotation (by Górecki expert David Drew), both sympathetic and intelligent.

Further listening *If you enjoy Górecki's Third Symphony, then you might explore the symphonies of Georgian composer Giya Kancheli (Olympia, digital), the Third Symphony of Howard Hanson (best conducted by Serge Koussevitzky, Biddulph, mono) and the music of Avro Pärt (especially his Tabula Rasa – on ECM, analogue).*

Curtain Up (1800-1901)

Overtures to operas and other large works have long provided orchestras with staple fare – either as 'curtain-raisers' or as encores. Many have a specific story to tell and therefore qualify for our "Narratives in Sound" (see below), whereas others are either pot-pourris of tunes used in the operas or single movements designed to establish particular moods.

Luigi Cherubini (1760-1842)

Anacréon, opéra-ballet (1803): Overture
Beethoven was among Luigi Cherubini's most ardent admirers though the older composer lived long enough to straddle the borders between Classicism and early-Romanticism. Cherubini's pre-Beethovenian *Anacréon* Overture opens with a slow introduction that recalls the world of Mozart's *Magic Flute* then proceeds with a principal theme that anticipates the "Leonore" motif from Beethoven's three celebrated concert overtures of the same name (composed just a couple of years later – see "Narratives in Sound").

NBC Symphony Orchestra/Arturo Toscanini
RCA mono
Even in his youth, Arturo Toscanini was an ardent champion of Cherubini's overtures (he performed a selection of them at the International Exposition in Turin as early as 1898). This particular broadcast performance, which dates from December 1949 and still sounds impressive, reveals the same muscular, tough-grained qualities that characterize Toscanini's finest Beethoven interpretations.

Ludwig van Beethoven
(1770-1827)

The Consecration of the House: Overture in C major, Op. 124 (1822)
Beethoven's last overture was composed for the then-newly-built Theater in der Josefstadt (in Vienna) and was first performed on October 3rd, 1822. It was Beethoven himself who claimed that the conception of the main theme was inspired by Handel. The very opening is especially regal, whereas the ensuing fugal passages are full of bubbling excitement. The Overture ends in a rush of contrapuntal activity that recalls the fiery finales of the great symphonies.

NBC Symphony Orchestra/Arturo Toscanini
RCA mono
A 1947 recording that enshrines a performance of remarkable brilliance and intensity – too much so for some, perhaps, in which case a calmer (though equally noble) alternative under Otto Klemperer (EMI, analogue) might prove more congenial.

The Creatures of Prometheus, Op. 43 (1800-01): Overture
A review of the first performance of *The Creatures of Prometheus* summed it up thus: "Prometheus banishes the state of ignorance, civilizing men through science and art and inculcating a sense of morality. This, in a word, is the subject matter." Beethoven's ballet music consists of 17 numbers plus the famous Overture – strong music that opens

to commanding chords then fires away rather in the manner of the first movement of the contemporaneous Second Symphony.

 ***Chamber Orchestra of Europe/Nikolaus Harnoncourt***

Teldec digital

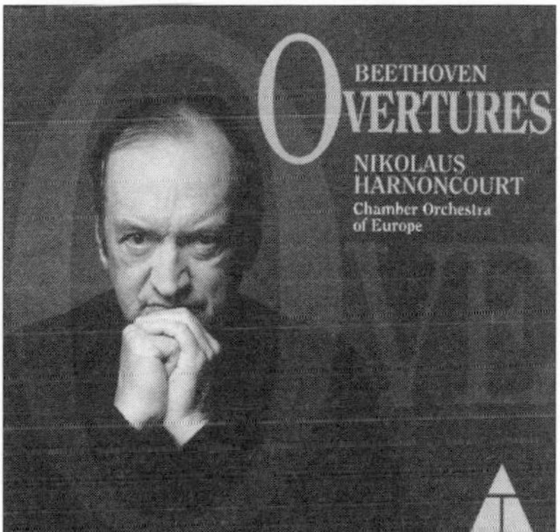

Harnoncourt clarifies the inner workings of Beethoven's score and prompts some vivid interplay between individual soloists. It's an agile, keenly inflected performance and has the added advantage of tailing the brief 'overture proper' with the ballet's dramatic "La tempesta" (a privilege usually reserved only for recordings of the ballet music). As to greats of yore, Toscanini (RCA, mono) and Klemperer (EMI, analogue) are among the best.

Carl Maria von Weber (1786–1826)

Oberon (1826): Overture

Weber's most imaginative overture raises the curtain on an opera based partly on Shakespeare's *A Midsummer Night's Dream* and partly on Wieland's epic poem *Oberon*. The story concerns the love of a knight for the Caliph's daughter, plus all manner of tribulations and a magic rescue operation. The Overture opens with the Knight's motive (on a solo horn), while the main body of the argument anticipates the fanciful happenings that follow.

 ***Bavarian Radio Symphony Orchestra/Rafael Kubelík***

Deutsche Grammophon analogue

Kubelík conjures up an appropriate sense of wonder: instrumental textures are crystal clear, the playing itself both spirited and poetic and the recording appealingly bright in tone. There's also a superb historic recording by the Concertgebouw Orchestra under Willem Mengelberg (Pearl, mono) – a little scratchy, perhaps, but musically more stylish than any made since the war.

Gioachino Rossini (1792–1868)

Semiramide, tragic melodrama (1823): Overture

The tragic tale of The Queen of Babylon who murders her husband, unwittingly marries her own son and is then killed by him as he tries to protect her from her lover. The Overture, perhaps Rossini's greatest, is a masterly synthesis of Classical lines (the opening sequence), delicate scoring (especially for winds) and slow-burning, stealthy crescendos.

 ***New York Philharmonic Symphony Orchestra/Arturo Toscanini***

RCA mono

Old it may be, and yet Toscanini's classic 1936 recording is among the most brilliant ever issued of a Rossini overture – taut, elegantly tailored and extraordinarily exciting. The playing has a dialogic quality that suggests chamber music, but if you'd prefer a modern recording, then Riccardo Chailly's latest version (with the La Scala Orchestra, Decca, digital) is a good choice.

The Thieving Magpie, melodrama (1817): Overture

An imperious opening (side drums announce a ceremonial theme for full orchestra) followed by witty writing for winds and some of Rossini's most dramatic crescendos. The melodrama's plot concerns the maid Ninetta, who is accused of stealing silver from her employer (a farmer, who also happens to be the father of her fiancé). Unfortunately for her, Ninetta has rejected the judge who in turn passes the death sentence on her – a most regrettable move given that the real thief turns out to be a magpie!

 ***Chicago Symphony Orchestra/Fritz Reiner***

RCA analogue

Reiner's orchestra at the very height of its powers, recorded in 1958 and still sounding remarkably fresh. As with Toscanini's Semiramide (see above), every player seems to be listening to his neighbour – which of course makes for tight ensemble and effortless transitions from one instrumental solo to the next. Strong rivals include Sir Thomas Beecham (EMI, analogue) and Claudio Abbado (with the Chamber Orchestra of Europe, digital).

Hector Berlioz (1803-1869)

Le carnaval romain: Overture, Op. 9 (1844)
Originally intended as an introduction to the Second Act of his opera *Benvenuto Cellini* (which, as it happened, had been a fiasco at its first performance), Berlioz's most popular overture has achieved a healthy life of its own. The opening flourish gives way to a tender cor anglais solo; there's a series of woodwind runs before the fiery saltarello (a theme from the opera) takes the lead. The orchestration is both original and dazzlingly colourful.

Le Corsaire: Overture, Op. 21 (1844)
The opening minute – a forceful 'rum-tum' followed by incredibly brilliant string writing, responsive woodwinds and a tender second theme on strings – mirrors the heady excitement of *Le carnaval romain*. A timpani roll gives way to teasing winds and delicate string figurations that announce a return of the first idea – now greatly embellished, with powerful brass and a rush of dramatic musical incident. Again, the orchestration is unbelievably bright and eventful (and way ahead of its time).

Paris Conservatoire Orchestra/Jean Martinon
Decca analogue
These scintillating performances were taped in 1958 by an orchestra that still retained striking national characteristics (horns that sound like saxophones, agile strings and reedy winds). Now available as part of Decca's Classic Sound series, the transfers have tremendous presence – but if you'd prefer something a little more refined (though still pretty exciting), try the Boston Symphony under Charles Munch (RCA, analogue).

Franz von Suppé (1819-1895)

The Beautiful Galathea (1865): Overture
Francesco Ezechiele Ermenegildo Cavaliere Suppé Demelli was born on board a ship just off the coast of Dalmatia. His prolific output includes numerous stage works, a few of which are nowadays remembered for their splendidly colourful overtures. *The Beautiful Galathea* concerns the sculptor Pygmalion who longs for the lovely Galathea (his own creation) to come to life; when she does, she steps down from her pedestal and takes part in the operetta's action.

Detroit Symphony Orchestra/Paul Paray
Mercury analogue
Paray's conducting combines French elegance with American-style virtuosity (the Detroit Symphony has never played better – at least not on disc). Mercury's current coupling includes more Suppé (Poet and Peasant, Light Cavalry, etc) as well as a selection of overtures by Daniel-François Auber.

Alexander Borodin (1833-1887)

Prince Igor, opera (1890): Overture
Borodin's only opera is best known for its *Polovtsian Dances* (which include a theme later popularized as "Stranger in Paradise") and its Overture, the latter having been reconstructed entirely from memory by Glazunov after Borodin's death (Glazunov had heard Borodin play it on the piano on numerous occasions). The construction is simple: various themes from the opera, skilfully knitted together into an expertly orchestrated, 12-minute pot-pourri.

London Symphony Orchestra/ Antál Dorati
Mercury analogue
Dorati's sparkling, incisively played 1959 account is presented alongside a strong though notably unfussy performance of Tchaikovsky's Fourth Symphony (plus the tone-poem Francesca da Rimini), whereas Sir Georg Solti's equally invigorating Decca (analogue) recording of 1966 shares a CD with other Russian fare. The digital field is led by the Russian National Orchestra under Mikhail Pletnev (DG).

Sir Edward Elgar (1857-1934)

Pomp and Circumstance March No. 1 in D major, Op. 39 No. 1 (1901)
Elgar's five masterly *Pomp and Circumstance* Marches are the British national equivalents of Dvořák's *Slavonic Dances*, Grieg's *Symphonic Dances* and the greatest of the Strauss family waltzes. The first two were premièred in 1901 by the Liverpool Orchestral Society, the D major featuring as its trio (or contrasting central section) a tune that was later known as *Land of Hope and Glory*. When asked whether a composer of stature should bother writing marches, Elgar replied, "Why should I write a fugue or something that won't appeal to anyone, when the people yearn for things that will stir them!".

BBC Symphony Orchestra/ Sir Edward Elgar
EMI mono
With estimable stereo versions available under the likes of Boult (EMI, analogue), Bernstein (DG, digital), Solti (Decca, analogue), and so on – why bother with a 1932 recording taken off a '78'? Because Elgar himself directs such a bracing, virile performance (you're instantly reminded of snappy 'newsreel' soundtracks)

that everyone else's sound stilted by comparison. Also, the actual recording still sounds astonishingly good – especially in EMI's latest 'state of the art' transfer.

Michael Torke (b1961)

Ash (1989)

Upbeat, fidgety, unpredictable and cast in the harmonic language – and orchestral dress – of Mendelssohn, Schumann or Weber. Torke takes simple tonic and dominant chords ("for me, the most pleasurable") and treats them to the sort of high-energy rhythmic treatment that we'd more commonly associate with Stravinsky. The result is both stimulating and disorientating.

 ***Baltimore Symphony Orchestra/David Zinman***

Argo digital

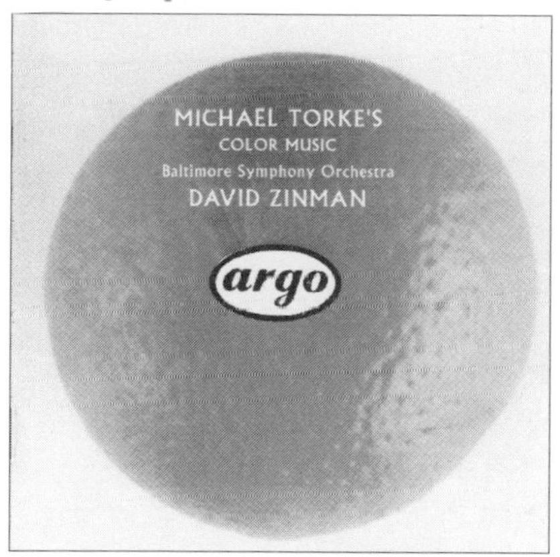

Part of a CD devoted to Torke's "Colour Music" (the other pieces are "Green", "Purple", "Ecstatic Orange" and "Bright Blue Music"). Each piece is quite different in style (usually more modern-sounding than "Ash"). David Zinman conducts a propulsive, well-disciplined performance and the sound is superb.

Narratives in sound (1673-1993)

Musical narratives date back to the time of Heinrich Biber (see below) and the German composer and theorist Johann Kuhnau (1660-1722, who wrote a series of programmatic Biblical Sonatas). We might also consider such vivid masterpieces as Vivaldi's *Four Seasons* and Beethoven's *Les adieux* or "Farewell" Sonata, both of which turn up elsewhere in this volume (i.e. in "Early Concertos" and "Mighty Monologues"). These, and works like them, attempt to tell a tale – either literally (as in the case of Dukas's *The Sorcerer's Apprentice*) or in terms of mood (Sibelius's *Tapiola*). The tone-poem or symphonic-poem originated in the dramatic overtures of Beethoven, was further developed by Liszt and Smetana and is still flourishing today. This section gathers together a wide variety of aurally suggestive compositions, from Biber's virtual-reality *Battalia*, through the bleak soundscapes of Sibelius to a minimalist essay based on the lonely tramp singing a religious song. Not all are orchestral, but all tell a story of one kind or another.

Heinrich Ignaz Franz von Biber (1644-1704)

Battalia in D major for 10-part strings (published 1673)

An Early Music blockbuster and one of the very first examples of descriptive programme music. *Battalia* conjures up – via extremely precise playing instructions – a military encampment, merrymakers, drunken musketeers (I defy anyone who doesn't already know it to identify this as seventeenth-century music) and 'snapping' strings in imitation of the cannon itself. The piece ends with a "Lament of the Wounded Musketeers". Biber employs various novel effects, such as affixing paper to the strings of the bass. If ever there was a musical case of 'back to the future', then this is it.

 ***Concentus Musicus Wien/Nikolaus Harnoncourt***

Teldec analogue

A performance that captures Harnoncourt and his players in full cry, superbly recorded. The current CD coupling is more innovative music by Biber and the disc might be said to represent the most potently re-creative employment of early instruments.

Ludwig van Beethoven (1770-1827)

Coriolan: Overture to von Collins' play, Op. 62 (1807)

Beyond a series of mighty hammer blows, Beethoven's most dramatic overture ushers in a restless staccato motive before the noble second theme – which reflects the gentler aspects of Coriolanus's nature – takes over. The main body of the Overture witnesses a mighty tug'o'war between these two themes (the passionate central section features strongly accented two-chord interjections), while the closing moments see the halting retreat of the restless first idea. Wagner thought that the Overture represented the meeting of Coriolanus with the two women at the gates of Rome.

 ***Berlin Philharmonic Orchestra/Wilhelm Furtwängler***
Grammofono mono
Devastating! Furtwängler's opening chords quite overpower early German tape technology, but the performance – taken down live during the darkest days of Nazi rule – reports an especially imposing tragedy. Not even Furtwängler himself surpassed it (i.e. in a better-known EMI [mono] studio recording from four years later). Fine stereo (analogue) alternatives under Fritz Reiner (RCA), Herbert von Karajan (DG) and Bruno Walter (Sony) are also recommended – but they're not in the same class.

Egmont – incidental music, Op. 84: – Overture (1810)
"I read the play with absorbing interest," wrote Beethoven to Goethe regarding the latter's tragedy, *Egmont*; "[I] thought it over, lived it through and then gave it musical expression." Beethoven's incidental music consists of an Overture and nine separate movements, but it's the Overture that's most frequently performed. Goethe's play concerns the Dutch Count Lamoral of Egmont, Governor of Flanders who helped to fight against the Duke of Alba and the Spanish Inquisition. Egmont was eventually executed (Beethoven recalls the terrible moment towards the end of the piece) though the Overture's closing moments suggest unequivocal victory.

 ***Philharmonia Orchestra/Otto Klemperer***
EMI analogue
A strong, stoical rendition, included as part of an abridged recording of the incidental music (with the soprano Birgit Nilsson). EMI's excellent 1957 stereo recording reports Klemperer's old-fashioned orchestral layout (double-basses on the left; violin desks separated left and right, etc) – but there's imposing mono competition from Toscanini (his 1939 [mono] broadcast recording, RCA) and Furtwängler (a 1953 Vienna Philharmonic live recording – Music & Arts, mono).

Leonore Overture No. 2, Op. 72*a* (1805)
Fidelio, Beethoven's only operatic masterpiece, was a long time in the making. Its prototype was the rarely-heard opera *Leonore*, for which Beethoven wrote no less than four overtures – one of which no longer survives. The concisely fashioned *Fidelio* Overture is generally used as a curtain-raiser to the opera itself, whereas the three *Leonore* Overtures are more in the manner of tone-poems – the Second and Third being far longer than the average opera overture. Both open dramatically and incorporate themes associated with the imprisoned Florestan (his great Second Act aria from *Fidelio*) and Leonore herself (a crescendoing *allegro*) as well as the trumpets of deliverance and an exultant finale. *Leonore* No. 2 is the most dramatic of the three.

 ***Berlin Philharmonic Orchestra/Wilhelm Furtwängler***
EMI mono
Furtwängler had a particular love for Leonore No. 2 and he performed it frequently. This recording dates from the last year of his life and relates the weight and commitment of his vision. However, there's also a live Berlin recording dating from 1949 (previously available on an LP from DG that, if it reappears on CD, should take pride of place). Other fine readings include Toscanini (his 1939 broadcast recording – RCA, mono), Otto Klemperer (EMI, analogue) and Herbert von Karajan (Berlin Philharmonic – DG, analogue).

Leonore Overture No. 3, Op. 72*a* (1805)
In case you're wondering why we haven't included the First *Leonore* Overture, it's because the narrative element is far stronger in the Second and Third. The Third is by far the most frequently played. It is also the most skilfully designed: less abrupt than the Second, marginally less theatrical, too – but with a symphonic sweep, formal polish and sense of exultation that suggest active parallels with the *Eroica* Symphony of two years earlier (Wagner thought it was the finest of the three).

 ***NBC Symphony Orchestra/Arturo Toscanini***
RCA mono
This is a live broadcast from 1939 and far more intense than Toscanini's studio recording (also on RCA, but dating from 1945). Just sample the heady excitement of the finale (the timpani crescendo is deafening, the rhetorical 'holding back' extremely effective) – but you should also try to hear Furtwängler with the Vienna Philharmonic (1944, DG, mono) and George Szell with the Cleveland Orchestra (Sony, analogue).

Orchestral works Narratives in Sound (1673–1993)

Carl Maria von Weber (1786–1826)

Invitation to the Dance, Op. 65 (1819 – orchestrated by Berlioz from Weber's piano original, 1841)

A key precursor of the Strauss family waltz-masterpieces, Weber's piano solo carried the title *Rondo brillant* and was dedicated to the composer's wife. Berlioz's colourful orchestration (which is topped and tailed by poignant cello solos) realizes the full measure of Weber's own programme about a gentleman's 'invitation to dance' and the gaiety of a ballroom in full swing.

Chicago Symphony Orchestra/Fritz Reiner

RCA analogue

Beautiful playing (especially from the lead cellist, János Starker) captured in an unexpectedly dynamic 1957 recording. Reiner's orchestra combines refinement of tone with executive virtuosity, but there are stylish (analogue) alternatives under Ferenc Fricsay (Belart), Wilhelm Furtwängler (Koch, mono), Arturo Toscanini (RCA, mono) and Erich Kleiber (Biddulph or Archiphon, mono). Clearly an affectionate 'old-world' style is most effective in this work.

Gioachino Rossini (1792–1868)

William Tell (1829): Overture

Rossini's Overture to his opera about a Swiss hero who fought against Austrian rule is also something of a miniature tone-poem. It opens to a cello melody (sometimes played solo) depicting sunrise over the Alps, then witnesses a thunderstorm (with a bass drum very much to the fore), visits herdsmen and their cattle (cor anglais and flute) while the final March – now virtually synonymous with the vintage TV hero "The Lone Ranger" – represents the overthrow of Austrian oppression by the Swiss.

World Orchestra for Peace/Sir Georg Solti

Decca digital

With players drawn from the world's greatest orchestras and Solti on top form, this proves to be the finest modern recording of Rossini's most popular overture. The recording is superb and the opening cello episode matchlessly eloquent, but it would be misleading to suggest that older recordings under Toscanini (NBC SO, 1952 – RCA, mono) and Fritz Reiner (RCA, analogue) haven't got at least as much to offer.

Felix Mendelssohn (1809–1847)

The Hebrides (Fingal's Cave) Overture, Op. 26 (1830)

Among the strongest and most atmospheric of soundscapes, not so much because of its orchestration (expert though that is) as through the sombre colouring of its thematic material. As Mendelssohn himself once wrote (in a letter to his family, dated "August 7th, 1829 – On one of the Hebrides"), "in order to make you understand how extraordinarily the Hebrides affected me, the following came into my mind there". 'The following' was the Overture's evocative first 20 bars.

Cleveland Orchestra/George Szell

Sony Classical analogue

Szell and the Clevelanders trace the contours of Fingal's Cave as with a single brush-stroke. The playing is superb, the climaxes carefully and brilliantly charted, and the recording, although fairly old (1962), possesses impressive clarity. The Overture's tranquil middle section is particularly beautiful, though Armin Jordan and the Suisse Romande Orchestra (Erato, digital) is virtually as successful – if marginally less refined and Wilhelm Furtwängler's two recordings (pre-war with the Berlin Philharmonic on Koch, post-war with the Vienna Philharmonic on EMI – both are of course mono) are very memorable.

Robert Schumann (1810–1856)

Manfred – incidental music, Op. 115: Overture (1852)

One of Schumann's darkest narratives, and one that rages wild (the final climax is positively defiant), dying among equivocal half-lights. Schumann himself described the Overture as one of his "most strapping children", though the despairing nature of the music (which reflects the complexion of Byron's poem, and which was written on the near side of mental illness) suggests melancholy, disquiet and vulnerability. The *Manfred* Overture precedes a sequence of incidental movements that, while often attractive, aren't really on the same inspirational plane.

Bavarian Radio Symphony Orchestra/Rafael Kubelík

Sony Classical analogue

Kubelík releases the full measure of Manfred's passion without overstating the case, and his handling of the closing pages has real pathos. Still, some may prefer the more overtly dramatic manner of Wilhelm Furtwängler (EMI or – preferably – DG live, both mono) or Arturo Toscanini (RCA, mono).

Orchestral works Narratives in Sound (1673-1993)

Franz Liszt (1811-1886)

The Battle of the Huns, S105 (1857)
A ghostly drama that recalls a specific battle where, in 451 AD on the Catalaunian Plains, Theodric led an army against the hordes of Attila the Hun. Liszt wanted the instruments to sound like ghosts and there's an remarkable passage mid-way through the work where repeated statements of a commanding, militaristic motive (played by the full orchestra) alternate with brief though ethereal organ solos. *The Battle of the Huns* recalls another Lisztian 'death ride', *Mazeppa*; it is the eleventh of 12 'numbered' tone-poems.

 ***Leipzig Gewandhaus Orchestra/Kurt Masur***
EMI analogue
Masur paces the battle to perfection, driving it hard yet allowing plenty of majesty in the central section. The sound, too, is extraordinarily vivid, though there's strong rivalry from Bernard Haitink and the London Philharmonic (Philips, analogue).

From the Cradle to the Grave, S107 (1881-82)
One of Liszt's strangest yet most compelling orchestral works and the very last of his tone-poems. The first movement, "The Cradle", suggests the mystery of life in embryo; the second, "The Struggle for Existence" is a violent onslaught strongly prophetic of Bartók, and the work ends with "The Grave, Cradle of the Future Life", a quiet though sinister movement that calls on earlier motives. Although less than a quarter-of-an-hour in length *From the Cradle to the Grave* is a profoundly disquieting experience, one that's especially rich in musical prophecies.

 ***NBC Symphony Orchestra/Arturo Toscanini***
Delle'Arte mono
Old though it is, Toscanini's riveting 1941 broadcast performance realizes the full mystery - not to say shock value - of Liszt's vision. However, panic not - there's lusty analogue back-up from Kurt Masur (EMI), Bernard Haitink (Philips) and Sir Georg Solti (Decca).

Mephisto Waltz (1880-81)
Liszt's dazzling orchestration of his First *Mephisto Waltz* for piano recalls a marriage celebration at an inn where, amidst dancing and laughter, Mephisto and Faust appear. Faust is persuaded to join in the fun; the village fiddler is dazed with wine, Mephisto commandeers his violin and then Faust - flushed with his newly recovered youth - enjoys a wild dance with a buxom maiden. The music fades to a nightingale's amorous song.

 ***Chicago Symphony Orchestra/ Fritz Reiner***
RCA analogue

Mephisto Waltz is an orchestral showpiece with a sinister edge that demands a combination of virtuosity and interpretative refinement (much as its piano counterpart does). Reiner is the perfect man for the job, although there's an almost equally good version (of similar vintage) by the Detroit Symphony Orchestra under Paul Paray (Mercury, and part of an imaginatively-planned programme called "Dances of Death" - see also Saint-Saëns' Danse macabre, below)

Les Préludes, S97 (1848, revised *c*1853)
Originally conceived as an overture to a choral work, Liszt's grandest and most popular tone-poem is based on an idea by the French poet, historian and statesman Lamartine. The 'programme' poses the question, "what is life but a series of preludes to that unknown song which Death so solemnly sings?", with the individual sections that include an Introduction ("Mankind, a Mortal Being"), Love's Happiness, Life's Storms, Back to Nature and - most famous of all - the stirring "Struggle for Freedom". Various distinctive themes serve as 'leading' motives.

 *Concertgebouw Orchestra/ Willem Mengelberg*
Pearl mono
If you're after the greatest Les Préludes ever recorded, then it simply has to be Mengelberg - a punchy, incisive reading, artfully shaped, magnificently played and in sound that is astonishingly good for 1929. Still, vivid stereo rivals are plentiful, with Leonard Bernstein (Sony) and Karel Ančerl (Supraphon) - both of them analogue - leading the field.

Richard Wagner (1813-1883)

Siegfried Idyll (1870)
Wagner's Christmas and birthday present to his wife Cosima was premièred at the family home in Villa Triebschen (by Lake Lucerne)

on Christmas morning, 1870. Wagner conducted a small orchestra on the staircase and Cosima must have been heartened, partly because the work marked a musical thanksgiving for their son Siegfried (who was just one year) and partly because the actual material mirrored the music drama *Siegfried* that Wagner was working on at the time. *Siegfried Idyll* is one of Wagner's gentlest inspirations; it's also one of his very few compositions for orchestra alone.

 ***Bavarian Radio Symphony Orchestra/Rafael Kubelík***

Sony Classical analogue

The subtle joys of Siegfried Idyll need affectionate coaxing, and Kubelík was the ideal man for the job. The performance is warm-hearted and the recording usefully transparent, but there are fine alternatives from, among many others, Sir Georg Solti (who employs the same number of instrumentalists as Wagner used for the Triebschen première – Decca, analogue) and Bruno Walter (Vienna pre-war on EMI mono, or America post-war on Sony analogue).

Bedřich Smetana (1824-1884)

Hakon Jarl, B118 (1860-61)

One of three symphonic-poems that Smetana composed while he was conductor of the Philharmonic Concerts in Gothenburg (the others – *Richard III* and *Wallenstein's Camp* – are also well worth hearing). *Hakon Jarl* deals with a Norwegian tyrant who tried to re-establish heathendom in the face of his country's conversion to Christianity. Smetana's score is tough, heroic and wildly animated – a vivid precursor of *Má vlast* (see below), and no less involving.

 ***Bavarian Radio Symphony Orchestra/Rafael Kubelík***

Deutsche Grammophon analogue

Kubelík's recording (his second – his first was made in Prague during the late-1940s) is highly dramatic and flexibly phrased. In its current incarnation, the CD also contains Smetana's other 'Swedish' tone-poems. The analogue sound quality is especially dynamic.

Má vlast (1872-79)

Má vlast consists of six symphonic poems which feature thrilling action music that was prototypical for generations of musical soundscapes and film soundtracks. Czech legend provides the subtext, initially through Vyšehrad Castle (*c*1872-4) with its memories of past glories, then the Vltava (Moldau, or Moldavia) River (1874), starting from two springs before flowing into the Elb. There's the amazon maiden Sárka (1875) who swears vengeance on the entire male race because of her husband's infidelity; the verdant richness of Bohemia's woods and fields (1875), and the final tone-poems Tábor (1878) and Blaník (1879) which recall the fearless Hussite bands and the resurrection of the Czech nation.

 ***Bavarian Radio Symphony Orchestra/Rafael Kubelík***

Orfeo digital

Kubelík taps the score's inspirational source with maximum spontaneity and a lyrical bias. He has recorded Má vlast no less than five times and although some will prefer his live Czech recording (made during a long-delayed return to his native Prague in 1990), this Munich set has the special virtue of balancing feeling and fire.

Johann Strauss II (1825-1899)

Emperor Waltz, Op. 437 (1889)

Composed in celebration of the fortieth anniversary (on December 2nd, 1888) of the accession of the Emperor Franz Joseph, The *Emperor Waltz* respects the often sorrowful life of its dedicatee with considerable majesty and a certain strain of melancholy. The opening measures are written in march-time, while the gently pulsing transition to the first waltz theme – one of Strauss's most evocative ideas – is pure magic.

 ***Vienna Philharmonic Orchestra/Herbert von Karajan***

Deutsche Grammophon digital

To hear the Vienna Philharmonic play Johann Strauss is to eavesdrop on a dialogue among friends; and when the conductor adds a measure of his own personality (which Karajan does, though never intrusively), the results are often spellbinding. This particular recording, one of Karajan's last, marks the high-point in an interpretation that evolved over a number of years. But there are many fine alternatives, not least Reiner (as part of his superb analogue Viennese anthology on RCA).

On the Beautiful Blue Danube, Op. 314 (1867)

Strauss had been commissioned to write "a lively and gay choral waltz" for a male-voice choir; the choir hated the words, but the conductor persisted and when Strauss himself conducted the work without a choir (in 1867 at the World Exhibition in Paris), it was tremendously successful. The music itself flows forth in colourful waves of different sizes – tuneful, vivacious and superbly crafted.

Chicago Symphony Orchestra/Fritz Reiner

RCA analogue

Fine Danubes have flowed forth even from the earliest days of recording, from Erich Kleiber's superb version for the acoustical recording horn (Archiphon, mono), through Clemens Krauss (Biddulph, mono), Toscanini (RCA, mono), Herbert von Karajan (EMI, DG, analogue) and this Reiner recording, possibly the most refined version in the catalogue. The orchestral playing is both subtle and idiomatic.

Alexander Borodin (1833-1887)

In the Steppes of Central Asia (1880)

Protected by Russian arms, camels and horses pass through the desolate wastes of the Steppes; an Oriental Melody and a Russian Song merge in an episode that dies away like an echo across the plains. Such is the ground-plan of Borodin's musical narrative, where a clarinet intones the Russian melody and a cor anglais, the Asiatic. Pizzicato basses suggest trotting horses and the high string writing echos the vastness of the Steppes.

Boston Pops Orchestra/Arthur Fiedler

RCA analogue

Fiedler's account is atmospheric, unaffected and very well played, though Neeme Järvi's excellent digital version with the Gothenburg Symphony Orchestra (DG) is also recommended, and so is a fine vintage stereo recording by the Philadelphia Orchestra under Eugene Ormandy (Sony, analogue).

Johannes Brahms (1833-1897)

Academic Festival Overture, Op. 80 (1880)

"A very lively pot-pourri of student songs *à la* Suppé." Brahms's own somewhat frivolous description underplays an artful design and some extremely dramatic writing. The Overture was composed as a token of gratitude to the University of Breslau, which had recently granted Brahms an honorary doctorate. The work ends with a rousing orchestration of the famous student song *Gaudeamus igitur* – "Let us live, then, and be glad/While young life's before us ...".

Tragic Overture, Op. 81 (1880, revised 1881)

It was an invitation to write incidental music for Goethe's *Faust* that prompted this, one of Brahms's greatest orchestral works. There is no programme as such, although conflict, repose and the shaking fist of some nameless authority seem central to its argument. The Overture is cast in the key of D minor (the same key as the equally dramatic First Piano Concerto) and was composed at Bad Ischl while Brahms was also working on his *Academic Festival Overture* (see above).

Vienna Symphony Orchestra/Wolfgang Sawallisch

Philips analogue

Sawallisch's pacing is more or less ideal and his players are totally atuned to Brahms's idiom. It's a fairly old recording (1961) yet the sound remains surprisingly dynamic. There is an equally fine contemporaneous performance by the London Symphony under Pierre Monteux (also Philips, analogue), while those in search of digital alternatives might care to try Kurt Masur and the New York Philharmonic in the Academic Festival Overture (Teldec) or Bernard Haitink and the Boston Symphony in the Tragic (Philips). Great mono 'oldies' – both of which are taken from 78s – include Mengelberg's Concertgebouw Academic Festival (Pearl) and Toscanini's BBC Symphony Tragic Overture (EMI).

Camille Saint-Saëns (1835-1921)

Danse macabre, Op. 40 (1874)

It's the dead of night: a distant bell chimes, then Death the fiddler waltzes through the rustling graveyard. Skeletons rattle around the tombstones until the oboe mimics the cock's crow and dawn breaks. *Danse macabre* was originally conceived as a song, but the tone-poem that Saint-Saëns fashioned from it soon became a prototype for all manner of spooky soundtracks.

Detroit Symphony Orchestra/Paul Paray

Mercury analogue

Paray's Danse macabre is taut, incisive, closely recorded and has great dramatic impact. It comes as part of an imaginatively planned album called "Dances of Death" (Liszt, Strauss and Schmitt are also included), but if you'd rather pursue the French connection, then Jean Martinon (Decca, analogue) offers an equally arresting performance in the context of an all-French programme.

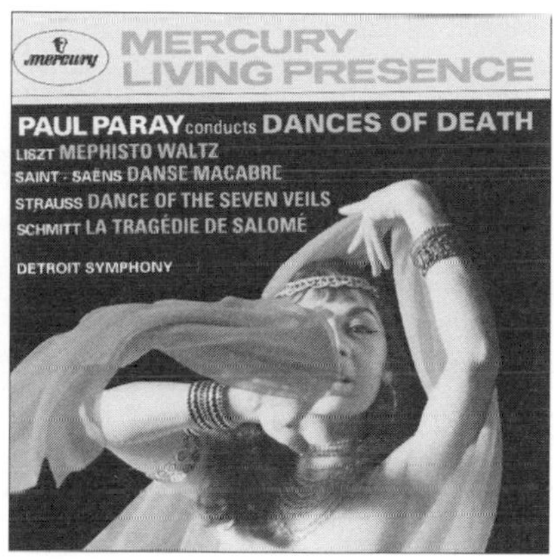

Mily Balakirev (1837–1910)

Tamara (1867-82)

The grizzly tale of an evil seductress who entices a traveller to her tower and, come morning, looks on as his corpse is borne down the river. Balakirev's symphonic-poem conjures the gloom and fantasy with consummate skill; it's an atmospheric and often exciting score, very Russian in profile, dedicated to Liszt (an obvious inspiration) and much admired by Rimsky-Korsakov.

 ***Royal Philharmonic Orchestra/Sir Thomas Beecham***

EMI mono

Beecham was a passionate advocate of the rare, the evocative and the unsung. He relishes Balakirev's piquant instrumentation and exotic colours (the opening pages are wonderfully evocative) and his coupling, Balakirev's winsome First Symphony – with its tacit references to Russian Church and folk music – is both enjoyable and appropriate. The best digital alternative features the Philharmonia conducted by Evgeni Svetlanov (Hyperion).

Modest Mussorgsky (1839–1881)

A Night on the Bare Mountain (1867, arranged and re-orchestrated by Rimsky-Korsakov in 1886)

The eerie swirling that opens *A Night on the Bare Mountain* depicts what Rimsky-Korsakov described as "the Assembly of witches, their talk and gossip". "Satan's Journey" is followed by "Obscene Praises of Satan" and then "Sabbath". Although the *Night* is best-known in a more colourful but less malevolent orchestration by Rimsky-Korsakov. Mussorgsky's stark but dramatic original (*St John's Night on the Bare Mountain*) is now gaining in popularity. The version used in the Disney film *Fantasia* was conducted and arranged by Leopold Stokowski.

 ***Chicago Symphony Orchestra/ Fritz Reiner***

RCA analogue

Brilliant in the extreme, though competition is strong – not least from the Philharmonia under Carlo Maria Giulini (EMI, analogue), Stokowski with the Philadelphia (from 78s, Dutton Laboratories, mono) plus Claudio Abbado's Berlin Philharmonic recording of Mussorgsky's St John's Night on the Bare Mountain (DG)

Pyotr Il'yich Tchaikovsky (1840–1893)

Francesca da Rimini – Symphonic Fantasia after Dante, Op. 32 (1876)

The most Lisztian of all Tchaikovsky's orchestral works, a sombre, impassioned tone-poem, skilfully orchestrated (horns and tam-tam are used to great effect) and with a glorious 'love theme' at its centre. The story concerns Francesca and Paolo whose forbidden love ends in Paolo's murder (by Francesca's husband) and permanent residence in the Second Circle of Hell. The inferno is depicted by swirling strings and blaring fanfares.

 ***New York Stadium Symphony Orchestra/Leopold Stokowski***

Dell'Arte analogue

Stokowski's second New York Philharmonic recording of the score (the orchestra is re-named for contractual reasons) and a long-time favourite – big-hearted, spontaneous and powerfully played. Evgeny Mravinsky's more stylized (though equally exciting) interpretation is issued on Russian Disc and Melodiya (in analogue or mono), while Gennadi Rozhdestvensky's Erato recording should please those who prefer digital sound.

Romeo and Juliet – Fantasy Overture after Shakespeare, Op. 67 (1869, revised 1879 and 1880)

Over a century on, and Tchaikovsky's *Romeo and Juliet* burns as brightly as ever – although the Overture we're familiar with is quite different to the version that Balakirev (*Romeo*'s dedicatee) criticized so harshly. Leopold Stokowski's recordings (on Cala and Pearl) revisit some of Tchaikovsky's earlier ideas, but the final version is by far the best – a supreme evocation of love and war, concisely structured and magnificently orchestrated.

Philharmonia Orchestra/Igor Markevitch

EMI analogue

An uncompromising recreation, urgent in the duel, passionate in the love music and superbly played throughout. Romeo has fared particular well in Britain, with the Royal Philharmonic (Rodzinski – EMI, analogue) and the LSO (Dorati – Mercury, analogue) vying with classic mono recordings under Toscanini (Music & Arts or RCA) and Willem Mengelberg (on Pearl – very old but the next best thing to Markevitch).

Emmanuel Chabrier (1841-1894)

España – rapsodie (1883)

Soon after Chabrier adopted music as a career, he travelled to Spain, collecting folk-songs, drinking manzanilla, befriending the dancers and generally having a fine time. His vivacious *España*, which includes a vigorous "jota" (the opening theme) and a sizzling "malagueña", is colourfully orchestrated. Emile Waldteufel's equally famous waltz of three years later uses virtually the same musical material.

London Symphony Orchestra/Ataulfo Argenta

Decca analogue

One the freshest Españas on disc, recorded in 1957 and for many years a popular stereo audio 'demonstration' item. The LSO brass excel, the strings have a keen edge and the sound – if just a tad dry – is still extraordinarily vivid. It is part of an all-Spanish programme, most of the music being by non-Spaniards.

Antonin Dvořák (1841-1904)

Carnival – concert overture, B169 (Op. 92) (1891)

Although known as 'concert overtures', Dvořák's Opp. 91-93 (all of which are represented in these pages) are cast more in the manner of tone-poems. The overall theme is "Nature, Life and Love" (Dvořák's own title) and *Carnival* is the "Life" component. It's an exuberant, top-gear affair that opens and closes in a mood of unstoppable excitement (the tambourine is very prominent). A more lyrical central section suggests life's tranquillity.

In Nature's Realm – concert overture, B168 (Op. 91) (1891)

The first instalment of the "Nature, Life and Love" triptych contains some of Dvořák's most arresting musical themes. The very opening alludes to a Nature *leitmotiv* (or "leading motive") that dominates all three overtures; we hear bird-song among the flutes and within moments the first theme blossoms into a full-blown climax. *In Nature's Realm* is a joyous musical 'high' that maintains its momentum throughout its quarter-of-an-hour duration.

Othello – concert overture, B174 (Op. 93) (1891-1892)

Othello is the most overtly dramatic piece in the "Nature, Life and Love" cycle. It deals with the "Love" element and reflects the full measure of Othello's conflicts. There's plenty of rigorous musical argument (the last section of the *Carnival* theme is skilfully refashioned) and Dvořák additionally uses an idea from his Requiem. Man is here seen as the victim of his passions, and therefore no longer in harmony with nature.

Czech Philharmonic Orchestra/Karel Ančerl

Supraphon analogue

Recorded in the early-1960s, Ančerl's performances have a freshness and precision that makes most rivals sound glumly under-vitalized. The spacious sound suits the music, but mention should also be made of Rafael Kubelík's excellent DG analogue recordings with the Bavarian Radio Symphony Orchestra and two superb performances of individual overtures – Karel Sejna's mono Czech Philharmonic version of In Nature's Realm (Supraphon), and Fritz Reiner's Chicago Symphony recording of Carnival. Both are analogue.

The Hussites – concert overture, B132 (Op. 67) (1883)

Fans of Smetana's *Ma vlást* (see above) will recognize the Hussite hymn *You are God's Warriors*, one of two national songs (the other is *St Wenceslas*) that Dvořák employs for this, perhaps his most tightly crafted concert overture. The furious development section has all the impact of a fully-fledged symphony (the great D minor Seventh Symphony was composed during the following year) and the closing pages spell 'triumph' in every bar. *The Hussites* was composed specifically for the opening of the new Czech Theatre in Prague.

 ***London Symphony Orchestra/ Witold Rowicki***

Philips analogue

Rowicki brings real grit to The Hussites and the LSO's playing has tremendous panache. The finest alternative recording (also analogue) is under Karel Ančerl (Supraphon) – a taut, incisive and magnificently played performance that bows to Rowicki only in terms of the latter's marginally more acute sense of drama.

The Water Goblin – symphonic-poem, B195 (Op. 54) (1896)

Dvorak composed four symphonic-poems after grisly, folk-inspired ballads by the Czech lyric poet Karel Erben. *The Water Goblin* is the liveliest of them and contrasts vivacious dance-style music (reminiscent of the *Slavonic Dances*) with passages of dark, brooding melancholy. This particular tale deals with a terrible water sprite who seeks vengeance when it believes itself to have been betrayed by a human being. Both Mahler and Janáček were hugely impressed by this vivid example of Dvořák's 'late' style.

 ***Czech Philharmonic Orchestra/Zdenek Chalabala***

Supraphon analogue

One of the most vivid performances of a Dvořák tone-poem ever recorded – especially where frisky, folk-like music takes the upper hand. The late-1950s sound is astonishingly vivid, but if the disc proves difficult to locate, then Kubelík's Bavarian Radio Symphony recording (DG, analogue) makes for an excellent second choice.

Nikolay Rimsky-Korsakov
(1844-1908)

Capriccio espagnol, Op. 34 (1887)

The opening "Alborada" (a lively morning song) sets the scene with generous splashes of festive colour. Rimsky had intended that his *Capriccio* – which he originally envisaged as being a *Concert Fantasy* for violin and orchestra – should "glitter with dazzling orchestral colour". He succeeded with a vengeance, not least through a virtuoso violin part and a heady sequence of five varied movements – "Alborada", "Variations", a return of the "Alborada", "Scena" and "Gipsy Song" and, to close, a thrilling "Fandango asturiano".

 ***London Symphony Orchestra/Ataulfo Argenta***

Decca analogue

The vital qualities that mark Argenta's highly spontaneous version of Chabrier's España (see above) apply in equal measure to this contemporaneous account of Capriccio espagnol. The best rival versions – all of them analogue – are from Kyrill Kondrashin (RCA), Karel Ančerl (Supraphon) and Igor Markevitch (Philips).

Russian Easter Festival Overture, Op. 36 (1888)

A vivid sense of ritual pervades Rimsky's "Overture on Themes of the Russian Church", although it's more a tone-poem than an overture in the familiar sense, one that recalls – according to its composer – the train of events from Passion Sunday to Easter Day. Rimsky's score evokes both the Orthodox Church and the heathenistic ethos from which it sprang. The orchestration is spectacular.

 ***Gothenburg Symphony Orchestra/ Neeme Järvi***

Deutsche Grammophon digital

Järvi's unbounded enthusiasm for pictorial Romantic scores strikes fertile soil in this particular work and the results are riveting. Older alternatives are legion, from the primitive-sounding but vividly narrated 1929 Stokowski recording (Biddulph, mono), to vintage analogue/stereo versions under Artur Rodzinski (EMI) and Igor Markevitch (Philips), both of them recorded in London.

Scheherazade, Symphonic Suite after "1001 Nights", Op. 35 (1888)

The Sultan Schahriar has sworn to execute each one of his wives after the first night, but the Sultana Scheherazade saves her own life by distracting him with one thousand and one nightly tales. He eventually abandons his plan, but not before hearing a plethora of stories, poems and folk-songs, some of which are painted in sound by one of the great orchestrators of the nineteenth century. The four movements describe the swell of the sea, Sinbad's ship, the story of the Kalandar Prince, the Young Prince and Princess, the Festival at Baghdad and the shipwreck.

 ***Chicago Symphony Orchestra/ Fritz Reiner***

RCA analogue

Scheherazade is primarily a programmatic 'concerto for orchestra', scenic in the extreme and with some highly distinctive solos (not least for the lead violinist – the voice of Scheherazade herself). Reiner's orchestra offers a brilliant though finely tapered account of the score, but there's strongly characterful competition from Nikolai Anosov (with David Oistrakh as violin soloist, Multisonic – mono), Kyrill Kondrashin (Philips) and Sir Thomas Beecham (EMI), all of them analogue.

Gabriel Fauré (1845-1924)

Pavane, Op. 50 (1887)

A touching narrative composed by Fauré during a summer break from his responsibilities as administrator and teacher. Fauré dedicated it to the Parisian hostess and patroness, the Comtesse Elisabeth Greffuhle and although he himself described it as "elegant, assuredly, but not particularly important" it has become by far his most popular orchestral work. It opens to a plaintive flute solo, with clouds gathering for a more dramatic central section. An optional choral part is included on some recordings.

French Radio National Orchestra/ Sir Thomas Beecham

EMI mono

An extraordinarily supple performance in good mono sound. Yan Pascal Tortelier's BBC Philharmonic recording (Chandos) provides the best digital alternative, whereas those who prefer the choral version are advised to investigate digital productions conducted by Seiji Ozawa (DG) and Charles Dutoit (Decca).

Leos Janáček (1854-1928)

Taras Bulba, Rhapsody for Orchestra after Gogol (1915-18)

Eighty years on and *Taras Bulba* still retains its ability to startle. Janáček's narrative is dynamic, colourful and brightly-lit, reflecting a story-line where the Cossack leader Taras Bulba and his two sons Andrij and Ostapov are killed in the 1628 war against the Poles. The first movement describes the battle at Dubno, the second the death of Ostapov and the third, Taras's capture, execution (at the stake) and victorious prophecies.

Czech Philharmonic Orchestra/ Karel Ančerl

Supraphon analogue

The familiar cliché that only Czech orchestras are capable of projecting Janáček's sound-world has been successfully countered by fine Taras Bulbas from, among others, the Royal Philharmonic (under Kubelík – EMI, analogue), Bavarian Radio Symphony Orchestra (under Kubelík – DG, analogue) and the Vienna Philharmonic (under Mackerras – Decca, digital). However, there can be little doubt that the sheer brilliance and character of Ančerl's classic reading justify a front-ranking recommendation.

Anatol Liadov (1855-1914)

Kikimora, Op. 63 (1909)

Liadov was the great miniaturist among musical tone-poets. His sense of atmosphere and piquant orchestral palette made for some truly magical evocations, *Kikimora* – a scherzo for orchestra – being among the most compelling. The story recalls the mischievous exploits of a dead (un-baptised) girl who was incubated in a crystal carriage tended by a cat. Liadov's use of woodwinds is especially imaginative.

Royal Philharmonic Orchestra/ Efrem Kurtz

EMI analogue

Vintage wine from an orchestra that was still under the magical influence of Sir Thomas Beecham (it was recorded back in 1957). Kurtz was an expert interpreter of Russian music and his subtly shaded though exciting rendition is indelibly memorable. Another great Kikimora finds Arturo Toscanini and the NBC Symphony Orchestra on great form (RCA, mono).

Edward Elgar (1857-1934)

Cockaigne, "In London Town" – overture, Op. 40 (1900-01)

Cockaigne (a mythical country) suggests – or at least suggested in 1901 – cockneys and the heady hubbub of city life. Elgar's nostalgic Overture opens with a perky little theme that recurs throughout the piece, relaxes for Londoners in love, features a development section that combines fanfares with a church service and ends in a mood of lavish ceremony. It's a masterly example of Elgar in tone-painting mode and combines the healthy jingoism of *Pomp and Circumstance* with the nostalgic reverie of the two symphonies.

London Philharmonic Orchestra/Eduard van Beinum

Beulah mono

Regal Cockaignes have come and gone (Beecham on Sony [mono] recording being

among the most distinguished), but van Beinum's has an excitement reminiscent of old newsreels that tops even Elgar's own (either 1926 or 1932, both on EMI mono). The 1949 Decca recording comes up as fresh as new paint, though stereo-only collectors might prefer Boult (EMI) or Solti (Decca) – both of them analogue.

Falstaff, symphonic study, Op. 68 (1913)

Possibly Elgar's greatest orchestral work and a piece of musical portraiture that's every bit as ingenious as Strauss's *Don Quixote* (see below). Shakespeare's lovable hero is epitomized by a wide-ranging bassoon cadenza marked "full tone, coarse", whereas the writing for strings (in particular) is extraordinarily brilliant. *Falstaff* reflects a very specific narrative, but its musical effect doesn't necessarily depend on knowledge of the character or story. The scoring is masterly (sometimes delicate, sometimes rumbustious) and the themes extremely characteristic.

London Philharmonic Orchestra/Vernon Handley

Classics for Pleasure analogue

A compelling but never overstated performance captured in fine sound. As ever, the composer himself provides strong competition (in a superbly refurbished 1931-32 mono EMI recording) and Sir John Barbirolli's affectionate 1964 EMI analogue recording is also something rather special.

In the South, "Alassio" – concert overture, Op. 50 (1903)

Elgar's most ambitious concert overture was inspired by a visit to Italy (Alassio) – where the weather was bad but the 'feel' of the country exhilarating – and opens in a mood of Straussian exuberance. The manuscript quotes "lands of palm and orange blossom" (Tennyson), "a land which was the mightiest in its old command" (Byron) while the piece itself recalls the powerful forces of ancient days (a grinding repeated theme in 3/4 time), a popular Italian song and impressive scenic grandeur.

Bournemouth Symphony Orchestra/Constantin Silvestri

EMI analogue

Perhaps it was the pines and palms of Bournemouth that inspired what is unquestionably the most exciting version of In the South since Elgar's own (1930, EMI mono). A good digital rival is provided by the Milan La Scala Philharmonic under Riccardo Muti (Sony), whereas Sir Georg Solti (Decca, analogue) revels in Elgar's Straussian orchestration.

Introduction and Allegro for strings (1904-05)

Ken Russell's TV Elgar documentary used this work as a soundtrack for cycle rides over the Malvern Hills – a good choice, given the music's rugged themes and bracing, open-air spirit. But there are other aspects to the score – its mystery, nobility and the many dramatic contrasts born of alternating a string quartet with a full string orchestra, a trick that Elgar had learned from the Handelian *concerto grosso* form.

English Chamber Orchestra/Benjamin Britten

Decca analogue

Elgar's music responds most readily to those who sense its delicate balance of reflectiveness and outward bluster. Benjamin Britten's perceptive re-creation touches the Introduction and Allegro's soul; it's a wonderfully comprehensive performance, superbly recorded (although some 30 years old) and placed within the context of a fine English string music miscellany. Other fine performances are conducted by Sir John Barbirolli and Sir Adrian Boult (both EMI, analogue).

Claude Debussy (1862-1918)

Images (1905-12)

Evocative sound-pictures of England, Spain and France. "Ibéria" – the third (and most famous) of the set – was composed first and consists of three sections, a carefree stroll through the Spanish countryside, a seductive night-scene and a mad-cap festival complete with guitar effects (the violinists strum four-part chords). The other movements are "Gigues" (which quotes *The Keel Row*) and the colourful "Rondes de printemps" ("Long live May, welcome May, with its wild banner").

London Symphony Orchestra/Pierre Monteux

Philips analogue

Monteux, a first-rate ballet conductor, fully understands Debussy's buoyant rhythms and colourful timbres. Textures are extremely luminous, the playing is first-rate and the 1963

recording superb. Bernard Haitink's somewhat later Concertgebouw version (analogue, also on Philips) provides an excellent alternative.

La Mer – three symphonic sketches (1903-05)

"You will say that the ocean doesn't wash the hills of Burgundy, and that what I am doing is like painting a landscape in a studio." Debussy had only limited experience of the sea, and yet his "three symphonic sketches" – "From dawn to noon on the sea", "The play of the waves" and "Dialogue of wind and sea" – are among the most powerfully descriptive seascapes in the repertory.

 ***Berlin Philharmonic Orchestra/Herbert von Karajan***

Deutsche Grammophon analogue

Karajan's first Berlin Philharmonic La Mer (1964 and still sounding excellent) suggests a cruise in mid-ocean – storm-tossed, yes, but totally secure. Alternative crossings find Fritz Reiner (RCA, analogue) weathering a more unpredictable climate, Toscanini (RCA, mono) facing the sunlight head-on and Bernard Haitink (Philips, analogue) suggesting more in the way of clouds and brine.

Trois Nocturnes (1900)

No finer sound-painting exists than "Nuages", the first *Nocturne* and a desolate evocation of floating clouds – or, to quote the composer himself, "the immutable aspect of the sky and the slow, solemn motion of the clouds, fading away in grey tones lightly tinged with white". "Fêtes", or "Festivals", conjures up "the vibrating atmosphere with sudden flashes of light" interrupted mid-way by rallying trumpets and a colourful procession, whereas the ethereal last *Nocturne*, "Sirènes" suggests an enigmatic song wafting across the waves "silvered by moonlight".

 ***Amsterdam Collegium Musicum, Concertgebouw Chorus and Orchestra/Bernard Haitink***

Philips analogue

Haitink's judgement of aural perspective, tempos and atmosphere is second to none, while the 1979 recording (it's just pre-digital) is a model of sensitive engineering. Good alternatives are plentiful, with Armin Jordan (Erato), Michael Tilson Thomas (Sony) and Pierre Boulez (DG) leading the digital stakes. There are also highly distinctive recordings of the first two Nocturnes under Pierre Monteux (Decca, analogue) and Arturo Toscanini (RCA, mono).

Prélude à l'après-midi d'un faune (1892-94)

The title *Prélude* recalls the suite of three pieces that Debussy planned but never composed, whereas the manifest tone-poem – a seminal work in the development of so-called musical Impressionism – reflects Stéphane Mallarmé's poem about a faun who recaptures fleeting images of nymphs, swans and garden lilies. Manet illustrated the published poem while Debussy's exquisite music is at once playful, romantic and subtly erotic.

 ***Royal Concertgebouw Orchestra/Carlo Maria Giulini***

Sony Classical digital

An artfully shaped reading, beautifully played and superbly recorded. However, there are countless top-ranking alternatives, most of them somewhat older than Giulini's, including Stokowski (Biddulph and EMI, mono/stereo), Toscanini (RCA, mono), Karajan (DG, analogue), Haitink (Philips), Cantelli (Testament, mono) and Beecham (EMI). All of them succeed in conveying a fanciful and evocative tale.

Frederick Delius (1862-1934)

Brigg Fair – An English Rhapsody, RTVI/16 (1907)

A bewitching theme with 17 variations, interrupted by a sublime string melody (between Variations 6 and 7) and peaking to a full-bodied climax. The first verse of the prompting folk-song tells us that "It was on the fift' of August, The Weather fine and fair, Unto Brigg Fair I did repair; For love I was inclined". *Brigg Fair* lays claim to being Delius's finest orchestral work and provides an enticing introduction to his aromatic style of writing.

 ***Royal Philharmonic Orchestra/ Sir Thomas Beecham***

EMI analogue

Recommending Beecham in Delius has become something of a critical cliché, and yet no one quite captures Delius's exquisite tonal world with as much subtlety or imagination. The playing, too, has a uniquely expressive quality. A fine, though broader-paced alternative (also analogue and on EMI) has Sir John Barbirolli conducting the Hallé Orchestra.

On hearing the first cuckoo in spring, RTV1/19 (1912)

A gently lilting narrative, more a memory or even a dream than an explicit description. The music suggests a quiet English meadow, but the actual material is based on a Norwegian folk-song and the harmonic language harks back to German late-Romanticism. Furthermore – and to remind you further of Delius's international standing – the world première was given under the baton of the great Dutch conductor, Willem Mengelberg.

 ***Hallé Orchestra/ Sir John Barbirolli***

Dutton Laboratories analogue

One of Barbirolli's most affecting Delius performances, recorded in Manchester's Free Trade Hall during early summer 1956. The sound has been expertly refurbished, but there are plenty of fine alternatives – not least Sir Thomas Beecham's stereo EMI (analogue) recording, Barbirolli's EMI remake (analogue) and the Academy of St Martin in the Fields under Sir Neville Marriner (either Decca, analogue, or Philips, digital).

Paris (The Song of a Great City), RTVI/14 (1899-1900)

It's hardly surprising that Delius's musical portrait of the French capital teems with Debussian points of reference (the dawn-like opening recalls both the mist-shrouded Seine and Debussy's *Images*) and just occasionally recalls the music of Ernest Chausson and Richard Strauss. However, the voice, or 'style', is still unmistakable – most especially in terms of the fragrant melodies, felicitous woodwind writing and the overall transparency of Delius's scoring. *Paris*, a truly gorgeous score, is cast in four distinct sections that play without a break.

 ***Royal Philharmonic Orchestra/Sir Thomas Beecham***

Sony Classical mono

Beecham lingers longingly over Paris's many solos (the RPO strings are especially tender). He also eases the passage of musical transitions and brings real brio to the faster, more extrovert music. The 1955 recording sounds reasonably well, but if it has to be digital then Andrew Davis and the BBC Symphony (Teldec) provide an enjoyable alternative.

The Song of the High Hills, RTII/6 (1911)

Hill-top breezes are almost tangible – distant mists, too, and voices drawn from the ether. Delius himself says it best. "I tried to express the joy and exhilaration one feels in the mountains," he once wrote; "and also the loneliness and melancholy of the higher solitudes, and the grandeur of the wide, far distances. The human voices represent Man and Nature ...". Which is why the work features here, under "Narratives in Sound", rather than in our choral section. Delius uses a soprano, tenor and chorus as wordless instruments on an expansive though restless canvas.

 ***Freda Hart (soprano), Leslie Jones (tenor), Luton Choral Society, Royal Philharmonic Orchestra/ Sir Thomas Beecham***

EMI mono

As with certain contemporaneous black and white movie classics, Sir Thomas's vintage evocation is especially strong in atmosphere. And although there are worthy digital alternatives under Eric Fenby (Unicorn-Kanchana) and Sir Charles Mackerras (Argo), this 1946 recording touches the work's soul with unique authority.

Richard Strauss (1864-1949)

Also sprach Zarathustra, Op. 30 (1895-96)

Thus spake Zarathustra was "freely composed after [the book by] Friedrich Nietzsche" but, rather than make any misguided attempt at 'musical philosophy', Strauss took Nietzsche's profoundly poetic imagery as a starting point for a highly original (and often unfairly maligned) tone-poem. Best-known is the spectacular Sunrise (used by Stanley Kubrick in his film *2001*), whereas subsequent episodes reflect on various of Nietzsche's themes – Forest Dwellers, Joys and Passions, the Sciences, the Convalescent, the Dancing Song and the Nightwalkers' Song. The ending is as mysterious as the opening is triumphant.

 ***Chicago Symphony Orchestra/ Fritz Reiner***

RCA analogue

There are two Chicago/Reiner recordings of Also sprach, this being the earlier (1954) version. In fact it was one of RCA's very first stereo sessions – and it still sounds spectacularly impressive (especially in RCA's

Living Stereo CD transfer). The performance itself combines clarity and virility, but there are fine analogue alternatives under Herbert von Karajan (BPO 1973 on DG and VPO 1959 on Decca) and Bernard Haitink (Philips)

An Alpine Symphony, Op. 64 (1911-15)
Night greets both the opening and closing sections of this, Strauss's last major tone-poem, and yet what scenic grandeur lies between: sunrise, the ascent, the forest, a brook and a waterfall; happy spells among meadows and thickets; then the summit, a storm and sunset. An object-lesson in descriptive orchestration (fledgling film composers lap it up), *An Alpine Symphony* provides nourishing repertoire for the mind's movie-screen.

San Francisco Symphony Orchestra/Herbert Blomstedt
Decca digital

Herbert Blomstedt is a first-rate musical mountaineer: his pace is well judged; he takes in plenty of detail and keeps a careful eye on the distant horizon. It's an admirably clear-headed performance, superbly played and captured in demonstration-class sound. The coupling is a highly recommendable version of Don Juan (see below).

Death and Transfiguration – tone-poem (1888-89)
The title is in some respects misleading, although Strauss's stated programme – the final illness, memories of life, hallucinations and the ultimate fight against death – feeds a highly dramatic musical narrative. What it doesn't presuppose is the glorious music of the 'transformation' itself, one of Strauss's richest melodies, sumptuously scored and culminating in an overwhelmingly powerful climax.

NBC Symphony Orchestra/ Arturo Toscanini
RCA mono
Toscanini's 1952 broadcast performance reigns supreme, even through old (though perfectly adequate) sound. The final climax builds inexorably and the tender closing pages are further intensified by the soft, frail singing of Toscanini himself. Among more recent (analogue) alternatives, Karl Böhm in Vienna (DG) and Rudolf Kempe in Dresden (part of his admirable complete survey of the tone-poems, EMI) are well worth considering.

Don Juan – tone-poem after Lenau, Op. 20 (1888)
Blatantly post-Wagnerian, *Don Juan* is the ultimate swashbuckling orchestral narrative, an exuberant, big-hearted display and not without touches of humour. Although based on a specific literary work, "study of the whole poem will be much more illuminating in the light of the music than study of the music in the light of the poem" (Sir Donald Tovey).

San Francisco Symphony Orchestra/Herbert Blomstedt
Decca digital
An affectionate look at a notorious rake, passionate though admirably transparent and with expansive climaxes – the recording boasts a level of realism that's exceptional even by Decca's habitually high standards. Still, do keep an eye out for Fritz Reiner's first Chicago Symphony recording (1954, RCA, analogue): it's a real stunner!

Don Quixote – fantastic variations for viola, cello and orchestra, Op. 35 (1896-97)
Anyone wanting solid proof of Strauss's orchestral mastery need look no further than *Don Quixote*, a brilliant set of variations "on a theme of knightly character" with star parts for solo cello (portraying the Walter Mitty-style Don) and viola (Sancho Panza). Individual tone paintings range from a "Battle with Sheep" (their bleating has an almost expressionist ring to it), a meditation on the virtues of the Don's ideal lady (Variation 5), "The Ride through the Air" (complete with wind machine) and a heart-rending finale.

Giusto Cappone (viola), Paul Tortelier (cello), Berlin Philharmonic Orchestra/Rudolf Kempe
EMI analogue
Tortelier's eloquent reading is represented on a number of discs (three of them with Kempe conducting), but this 1958 recording has a degree of wit, humanity and refinement that proves irresistible. A fine digital version with Heinrich Schiff as the Don and the Leipzig Gewandhaus Orchestra under Kurt Masur (Philips) is also well worth searching out.

Ein Heldenleben, Op. 40 (1897-98)
Strauss saw his *Hero's Life* as a sort of latter-day *Eroica* but there can be little doubt that it's also part-autobiographical – the long third section, for example, "The Hero's Wife" (with its intricate violin solo). Less subtle than *Don Quixote* and less concise than *Don Juan*, *Ein Heldenleben* is none the less full of

top-drawer musical material, not least the rapturous seventh and eighth sections, "The Hero's Works of Peace" and "Renunciation". Other episodes include "The Hero's Adversaries" (muttering critics, uproariously scored for woodwinds) and a stampeding "Hero's Battlefield".

Chicago Symphony Orchestra/ Fritz Reiner

RCA analogue

My first instinct is to forget about sound quality altogether and recommend a fabulous 1928 mono recording conducted by Heldenleben's dedicatee, Willem Mengelberg (RCA, Biddulph [a 'second' recording made up of alternative takes]). Still, knowing that many people will not want to brave pre-war sonics (though please do give Mengelberg a try), Reiner's early stereo recording – which still sounds amazingly lifelike – makes for a confident second choice.

Metamorphosen – study for 23 solo strings, AV142 (1944-45)

With Germany in ruins all about him, Strauss pondered the fate of a land that had seen some of his greatest triumphs. *Metamorphosen* is an "in memoriam" for Munich; in fact, one of his original sketches is actually headed "Mourning for Munich". This sombre, heavily contrapuntal score (it plays for around half an hour) employs ten violins, five violas, five cellos and three double-basses. One of its key thematic germs recalls the Funeral March from Beethoven's *Eroica* Symphony.

Berlin Philharmonic Orchestra/Herbert von Karajan

Deutsche Grammophon analogue

It was Herbert von Karajan who made the very first studio recording of Metamorphosen (EMI, mono – one of the finest ever) but this, his first version with the Berlin Philharmonic (1969), has the advantage of superior sound. An even older recording – live, this time – reports an especially intense performance by the Berlin Philharmonic under Wilhelm Furtwängler, a superb conductor whose fraught existence under Nazi rule lends his interpretation an ironic 'authenticity'. A texturally transparent digital alternative is provided by the Cincinnati Symphony Orchestra conducted by Michael Gielen (Vox).

Symphonia domestica, Op. 53 (1902-03)

"What can be more serious than married life?" wrote Strauss, with reference to his Op. 53; "I want the *Symphonia* to be understood seriously". The programme portrays various aspects of family life, including the parents alone with their child, 'seeing and doing', the love of mother and child, a lively row and a happy conclusion with stormy family scene. And yet the work can be appreciated just as well without the programme, i.e. purely as a vigorous, warm-hearted and often exciting adventure in sound.

Chicago Symphony Orchestra/ Fritz Reiner

RCA analogue

Virtuosic, tender and astonishingly well recorded for the mid-1950s, Reiner's Domestica is – like so many of his Strauss recordings – a cut above the rest. Historic rivals include charismatic wartime versions under Furtwängler (Arabesque, DG, etc, mono) or Strauss himself (DG, mono), while there are fine stereo alternatives under George Szell (Sony, analogue) and Wolfgang Sawallisch (EMI, digital – a definite digital top choice).

Till Eulenspiegels lustige Streiche, Op. 28 (1894-95)

Strauss opens his most amusing tone poem with a gentle 'once upon a time' played on strings, then traces Till's various antics (decimating a market, dressing up as a priest, starting arguments, etc) until, beyond his arrest, the drum rolls and the hangman's rope tightens. Till Eulenspiegel (or Till Owlglass, as he was known in England) was a fourteenth-century German peasant whose escapades were directed against authority.

Berlin Philharmonic Orchestra/Rudolf Kempe

EMI analogue

You'd have a hard job finding a bad Till Eulenspiegel on disc: conductors love it, orchestras revel in it and, in any case, Strauss's writing is so unequivocally graphic that an interpretative misfire would be virtually impossible. However, Kempe's characterizations are exceptional even in a crowded field (the playing, too, is marvellous), and the 1958 recording stands up remarkably well. Toscanini (RCA, mono) provides a riveting second choice.

Paul Dukas (1865-1935)

The Sorcerer's Apprentice (1897)

Although nowadays invariably associated with Mickey Mouse (i.e. in Walt Disney's animation masterpiece *Fantasia*), Dukas's "scherzo on a ballad by Goethe" does indeed describe the broomsticks and floods of water that Disney conjured up for the screen. Goethe's poem was drawn from one of the *Dialogues of the Gods* by the second-century Greek writer Lucian of Samosata about the sorcerer Pancrates and his apprentice Eucrates. Dukas's orchestration is masterly, with the narrative sequence of events painted in vivid primary colours.

 ***The Netherlands Radio Philharmonic Orchestra/Jean Fournet***

Denon digital

The great beauty of this performance is that it's slow enough to allow the subtler aspects of Dukas's orchestration to register, and sufficiently well-recorded for us to hear those details with stunning clarity. Furthermore, Denon provide copious index points (most CD players should register them) that follow each stage of the story: you can therefore check the music against the synopsis provided in the booklet. However, those who'd prefer a more virtuoso reading are directed to Igor Markevitch (EMI, mono), Toscanini (his 1950 recording, RCA, mono) or Leopold Stokowski (his 1937 Philadelphia recording, Biddulph, mono – it was of course Stokowski who conducted the Fantasia soundtrack).

Carl Nielsen (1865-1931)

Helios Overture (1903)

A sunrise to compare with Strauss's in *Also sprach Zarathustra* – starting among brass and the lower strings, then working its way through the orchestra until the pace increases and the ringing of trumpets announces a blazing first climax. Nielsen's inspiration was the rising sun over the Aegean Sea, and the Overture's closing pages suggest a maritime sunset.

 ***Gothenburg Symphony Orchestra/Neeme Järvi***

Deutsche Grammophon digital

Not the tidiest performance on disc (the strings have a job keeping up during the Overture's excited central section), but certainly one of the most spontaneous. Those who don't mind analogue sound should keep an eye out for Eugene Ormandy's stereo Sony recording with the Philadelphia Orchestra or Erik Tuxen's live Danish Radio performance on Danacord (mono – a contemporaneous studio recording on Dutton isn't as good).

Jean Sibelius (1865-1957)

En Saga, Op. 9 (1892, revised 1902)

When you first hear *En Saga* live, the one aspect of the scoring that strikes home more or less immediately is that there are no timpani – just a strategically employed bass-drum. The 'Saga' itself is somewhat non-specific, though the sense of journeying – sometimes slowly among mists, sometimes at top speed in the blazing heat – is powerfully conveyed. The pulse is more or less constant, the orchestration exceedingly atmospheric. The Swedish title reminds us of the pivotal role that Swedish culture played in Finland before the First World War.

Philadelphia Orchestra/ Eugene Ormandy

Sony Classical analogue

Although recorded as long ago as 1963, Ormandy's En Saga still sounds impressive and the performance itself is quite superb – exciting though never too hard-driven, incisive and notably sensitive in the lyrical passages (the solo string writing at 10'55", for example). My only complaint is that some of the softer playing doesn't sound soft enough. Best among Ormandy's rivals is Herbert von Karajan, whose Berlin Philharmonic (analogue) recording on EMI features an extraordinarily intense closing clarinet solo.

Finlandia, Op. 26 (1899, revised 1900)

Forged under the yoke of Russian oppression, Sibelius's best-known (and most patriotic) work features fist-shaking fanfares, earthy stamping and a noble central theme. "It was a long time before *Finlandia* was performed under its present title," wrote Sibelius; "It was presented in Scandinavia as *Suomi*; in Germany it was called *Vaterland*, and in France *La patrie*. In the Russian empire it could only be played under a title which would give no hint of its patriotic nature ...". Some performances (notably Ormandy's for Sony) incorporate a chorus.

 ***Berlin Philharmonic Orchestra/Herbert von Karajan***

Deutsche Grammophon analogue

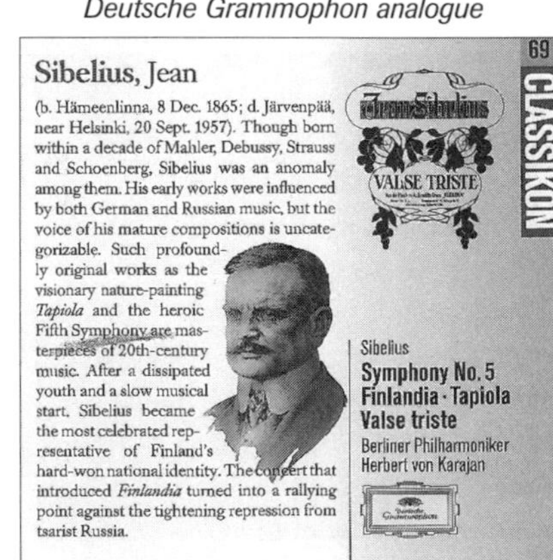

Fine Finlandias are virtually two-a-penny (including famous mono recordings under Toscanini [RCA] and Hans Rosbaud [DG] and a fine analogue version under Bernstein on

Sony), but Karajan's is one of the best – a thrilling, beautifully controlled performance, superbly played. The 1964 recording still sounds well.

Lemminkäinen Legends, Op. 22 (1893-95, revised 1897, 1900 and 1939) – including The Swan of Tunonela

The most underrated of Sibelius's masterpieces is based on tales from the Finnish national epic *Kalevala*, a work where – according to Sibelius himself – "the action is always subordinated to the feelings". The four movements are: "Lemminkäinen and the Maidens of Sari", a 16-minute love poem that swells with Wagnerian resonances; "Lemminkäinen in Tuonela", where the hero's body is carried to the Underworld amidst coldly shimmering strings and savage brass; The "Swan of Tuonela", who inhabits the river surrounding the dead and sings her song on a cor anglais against a floating backdrop of strings, and lastly, "Lemminkäinen's Return", where the hero arrives to a mood of festive excitement. Throughout this cycle (the greatest series of tone-poems beyond Smetana's *Má vlast*), Sibelius's imaginative use of the bass drum is especially remarkable.

Helsinki Philharmonic Orchestra/Leif Segerstam

Ondine digital

Segerstam is himself a composer and revels in Sibelius's cinematic narrative and pungent harmonies. Some tempos are slower than usual, but it's an amazingly powerful performance, superbly recorded (just try the last two or three minutes of "Lemminkäinen and the Maidens of Sari", say from 14'09" into track 1). Alternative recommendations are conducted by Paavo Järvi (Virgin, digital) and Jukka-Pekka Saraste (RCA, digital).

Pohjola's Daughter, symphonic fantasia, Op. 49 (1906)

One of Sibelius's most riveting orchestral works takes as its starting point a passage from the Finnish national saga, the *Kalevala*, where Pohjola represents Lapland (whose daughter's symbol was a spinning-wheel). The story concerns the hero Väinämöinen who sees Pohjola's daughter on a shining arc in the sky. She agrees to become his bride only if he can make a boat of her spinning-wheel and put it into the water without touching it. The opening cello solo is so eloquent it virtually speaks to you, while the ensuing events employ the full range of Sibelius's considerable orchestral skills.

New York Philharmonic Orchestra/Leonard Bernstein

Sony Classical analogue

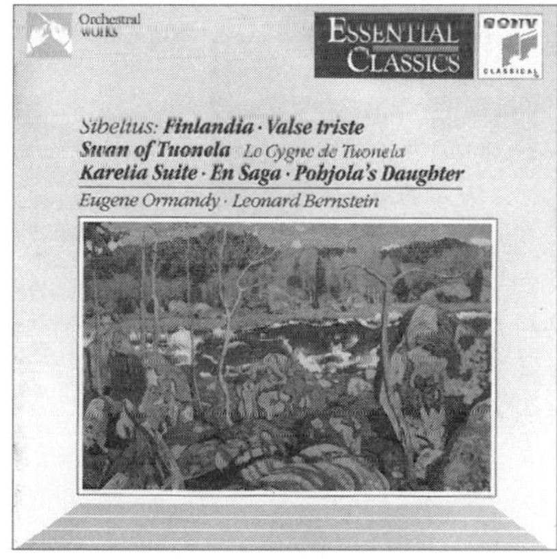

The very best recordings of Pohjola emanate from America – although Robert Kajanus, the work's dedicatee, made an impressive London recording back in 1932 (Koch, mono). Bernstein's 1964 recording combines the drive of Toscanini (recorded in New York with the NBC Symphony in 1940 and issued on CD by RCA, mono) with the lustre and drama of Serge Koussevitzky (whose 1936 Boston recording is available on Pearl, mono). Sony's vintage stereo relates a highly theatrical sound-stage.

Tapiola – tone-poem (1926)

There is no place in music more vast, more chilling or more awe-inspiring than *Tapiola*, a magnificent essay that barely escaped being sent back to its composer, or worse (luckily for us, the publishers had already engraved the work when the self-critical Sibelius asked for its return. The completed Eighth Symphony wasn't so fortunate: Sibelius had it destroyed). The score itself suggests "the Northlands dusky forests", "savage dreams" and a great, all-devouring wind.

Berlin Philharmonic Orchestra/Herbert von Karajan

Deutsche Grammophon analogue

Karajan allows "the Forest's mighty god" free reign, yet his control over the orchestra is never in doubt. Listeners in search of an even more ferocious onslaught should try Serge Koussevitzky's 1939 Boston Symphony recording (Pearl, mono) while an earlier version with the Berlin Philharmonic (also DG, mono) has the estimable Hans Rosbaud summon the elements and there's a fine digital recording under Herbert Blomstedt (Decca).

Florent Schmitt (1870-1958)

La tragédie de Salomé, symphonic suite Op. 50 (1910)

Evocative and sensual, poised somewhere between the worlds of Ravel (luminous textures), Roussel (taut rhythms) and Stravinsky (apocalyptic climaxes). The scenes and situations depicted include Herod's palace, Salomé adorning herself with jewels, Herod's lascivious thoughts, Salomé's emergence from the Dead Sea (where the music at times seems to echo Vaughan Williams), a grisly commotion with John the Baptist's severed head and – to end – a frenzied dance of terror.

Walther Straram Concert Orchestra/Florent Schmitt

EMI mono

It's amazing to think that at the time of writing this powerful though undeniably elderly contender (it was recorded in 1930) has the field to itself. Schmitt inspires a hugely enthusiastic performance (Straram's excellent orchestra was highly adept at performing the new music of the day), though readers should keep an eye out for excellent – though currently unavailable – analogue/stereo alternatives under Antonio de Almeida (RCA) and Jean Martinon (EMI).

Ralph Vaughan Williams (1872-1958)

The lark ascending (1914, revised 1920)

A highly evocative, achingly beautiful tone-poem for violin and orchestra, originally composed in 1914 for the British violinist Marie Hall. George Meredith sets the scene: "He rises and begins to round/He drops the silver chain of sound/Of many links without a break/In chirrup, whistle, slur and shake ... Till lost on his aerial rings/In light, and then the fancy sings."

Hugh Bean (violin), New Philharmonia Orchestra/ Sir Adrian Boult

EMI analogue

The lark ascending is an extremely difficult work to bring off. Over-project the violin part, and it begins to sound like a series of scales and exercises; underplay it, and you risk sounding effete. But if the balance is right – as it is here – then the effect is spellbinding. Hugh Bean becomes the lark, Boult and his orchestra, the landscape and sky. A benchmark recording.

Sergey Rachmaninov (1873-1943)

The Isle of the Dead (1909)

Arnold Böcklin's painting of a ghostly passenger *en route* to a mysterious island dominated by tall cypresses inspired one of Rachmaninov's greatest works. The dark opening suggests the gentle rocking of waves, while the main body of the piece contrasts the grimness of fate (underpinned by Rachmaninov's use of the *Dies irae* plainchant for the dead) with a lyrical, soaring melody that recalls the light and, one presumes, life itself.

South West German Radio Symphony Orchestra/ Michael Gielen

EMI digital

The opening bars pinpoint Rachmaninov's imaginative use of irregular rhythm: the bass line is strong and the ensuing climaxes, immensely powerful. Analogue rivals, all on RCA, are conducted by Fritz Reiner, Serge Koussevitzky (mono) and the composer himself (also mono, with the Philadelphia Orchestra – a 'must' for all fans of the piece).

Gustav Holst (1874-1934)

The Planets, H125 (Op. 32) (1916)

Ground-breaking in its day (certainly in terms of British music), Holst's seven-stage galactic journey reflects both a strong interest in mystical religion and an amazingly vivid musical imagination. Mars "the bringer of war" is its fiercest (and most celebrated) ambassador, with Venus the serene "bringer of peace" and Jupiter, "bringer of jollity" reporting half-way for a noble melody that's also known as "I vow to Thee my Country". Magic and mystery prevail in the other planets: Mercury, Saturn, Uranus and Neptune, perhaps the most haunting one of all.

Montreal Symphony Orchestra, Women's Chorus of the Montreal Symphony Orchestra/Charles Dutoit

Decca digital

Sir Adrian Boult gave The Planets its first (private) performance and many will prefer to stand by his strong, matchlessly idiomatic reading (there are various analogue versions to choose from). However, Dutoit's seamless, dynamic and magnificently recorded version packs a powerful punch – while Venus sounds especially beautiful. Other personable guides include Karajan (his 1961 Vienna recording, Decca) and Bernstein (Sony) – both analogue.

Arnold Schoenberg (1874-1951)

Pelleas und Melisande, symphonic poem, Op. 5 (1902-03)

A vast aural canvas populated with all

manner of strange but powerful sonorities, including seedy trombone slides [Golaud and Pelleas descending into the castle vaults], disruptive wallops on the bass drum, etc. Melisande herself is represented by an oboe or cor anglais (she has at least that much in common with her alternative selves as composed by Sibelius and Fauré) and the various characters and situations each have their own 'leading motives' – Pelleas, Melisande, Golaud, fate, jealousy, Melisande's falling in love, and so on. The story concerns the love of a woman for her husband's brother, fratricide and the woman's death of a broken heart. Musically, Schoenberg's score recalls the *fin de siècle* worlds of late Wagner and Richard Strauss.

Berlin Philharmonic Orchestra/Herbert von Karajan

Deutsche Grammophon analogue

Karajan's ear for sound, his innate musical refinement and sense of musical architecture inform what is unquestionably one of his greatest stereo recordings. The playing is generally superb and the analogue sound still fairly impressive. Fine digital alternatives are available under Pierre Boulez (Erato), Michael Gielen (Intercord/EMI) and Zubin Mehta (Sony).

Maurice Ravel (1875-1937)

Alborada del gracioso (1905, orchestrated 1918)

The "Morning song of the jester" is one of Ravel's most ingenious creations, having been orchestrated from one of his piano *Miroirs* and alternating frisky high spirits with a dark, sombre central section that suggests a sad face behind the mask. *Alborada* is a masterly example of how a relatively large orchestra can be used with maximum economy: Ravel employs each instrument with a fastidious awareness of its individual colour and yet the overall effect is extremely dramatic.

Suisse Romande Orchestra/Armin Jordan

Erato digital

Erato's recording combines spaciousness with respect for detail: listening to it is rather like observing a great painting from the near distance – the overall effect is overwhelming, and yet you're close enough to observe a wealth of detail. Fine alternatives are available under Gianluigi Gelmetti (a superb reading with the Stuttgart Radio SO on EMI digital) and Fritz Reiner and the Chicago Symphony (RCA analogue, very well played though perhaps just a little too highly-charged).

Boléro (1928)

The idea for a Spanish dance sequence came from the great Franco-Russian dancer Ida Rubinstein, and Ravel's original scheme was to orchestrate piano pieces by Albéniz – an option that was scuppered by potential legal complications. *Boléro* was the novel solution, one that – to quote Ravel himself – has "no form, in its usual meaning, no [or almost no] modulation". It's a slow-building 'concerto for orchestra' set to a constant drummed rhythm and takes around 14-17 minutes to climax. It is also immensely popular, although Ravel considered its success to be "only a fashion".

London Symphony Orchestra/Claudio Abbado

Deutsche Grammophon digital

As fine a version as any, very well played and superbly recorded – although when it comes to alternatives, the choice is virtually limitless, from the sultry Bernstein (his French recording, on Sony, analogue), to the high-powered Paul Paray (Mercury, analogue) and the first recording all, a highly characterful affair supervised by Ravel and conducted by Piero Coppola (Koch or EMI, mono).

Pavane for a dead princess (1899, orchestrated 1910)

The original French title of *Pavane pour une infante défunte* is poetry in itself; in fact, Ravel chose it more for the words than for the actual meaning. Originally written for solo piano, the *Pavane* is a gentle, flowing elegy which, in its orchestral guise, features felicitous writing for horn, strings and winds. It is among Ravel's most popular works (the most popular perhaps, after *Boléro*). As to its ideal interpretation, Ravel was careful to stress that it is "a pavane for a dead princess, not a dead pavane for a princess".

Chicago Symphony Orchestra/ Fritz Reiner

RCA analogue

Reiner at his most expressive, with especially warm playing from the Chicago strings and flexible, almost ecstatic phrasing. The basic tempo is ideally judged (this is certainly no 'dead pavane') and the 1957 recording is given a new lease of life thanks to the late John Pfeiffer's expert Living Stereo transfer. Pierre

Orchestral works Narratives in Sound (1673-1993)

Monteux's LSO recording (Decca, analogue) makes for an excellent second choice. The great French pianist Robert Casadesus offers one of the most beguiling versions of the solo piano version (Sony, mono).

Rapsodie espagnole (1895-1908)
The "Prélude à la nuit" and "Habanera" are among the most sultry and evocative movements in Ravel's output, while the "Malagueña" and closing "Feria" drape native Spanish rhythms in stylishly tailored orchestral garb (the percussion employed is particularly colourful). The "Habanera" was composed much earlier than the rest of the work (1895), while Ravel completed the orchestration (1908) in the company of Ralph Vaughan Williams.

London Symphony Orchestra/ Pierre Monteux
Decca analogue

Monteux's 1961 recording (a superb production for its years) enshrines a performance that's characterized by clarity, precision and immense enthusiasm. If, however, you'd prefer a digital version (an understandable option in this most sensuous of scores), then Kent Nagano's recording with the same orchestra (Erato) is particularly rich in atmosphere.

La valse – choreographic poem (1920)
The opening moments are pitch black. Spectres appear – shimmering, elegant, decadent, dancing to waltz fragments from Old Vienna (the scene is an "Imperial Court about 1855"). The tension mounts but the ending is both catastrophic and horribly prophetic of Europe's forthcoming collapse. Ravel himself spoke of "whirling clouds giving glimpses, through rifts, of couples waltzing. The clouds scatter little by little. One sees an immense hall peopled by a twirling crowd. The scene is gradually illuminated. The light of chandeliers burst forth in *fortissimo*."

Suisse Romande Orchestra/Ernest Ansermet
Decca analogue
Ansermet's mastery of texture makes for a pellucid presentation of a skilfully crowded score: no other performance is quite as effective in projecting the eerie opening bars or the more sinister aspects of Ravel's instrumentation (the chaotic ending rivals Stravinsky's Rite of Spring in its violent effect). The 1964 recording still sounds pretty spectacular. Eduardo Mata (RCA, digital) and Leonard Bernstein (Sony, analogue) conduct compelling alternatives.

Valses nobles et sentimentales (1911)
Ravel stated his intention of composing a chain of waltzes, "following the example of Schubert", although the sum effect is more Parisian in spirit – a heady sequence ending with a flurry of motives whispering by, rather like stray snapshots blown along a deserted street at night. *Valses* is the subtlest of evocations which, like the *Rapsodie espagnole*, started life as a piano work, albeit for two rather than four hands. Some commentators find the original more convincing.

Chicago Symphony Orchestra/ Fritz Reiner
RCA analogue
An irresistible combination of virtuosity and delicacy, with Reiner pointing or caressing each detail as if his life depended on it. There are more seductive versions around (Nagano's digital version on Erato, for example), but Reiner's is certainly the most brilliant. Those in search of the piano original are directed to either Pascal Rogé (Decca) or Jacques Rouvier (Calliope). Both are analogue recordings.

Ottorino Respighi (1879-1936)

Fountains of Rome – symphonic-poem (1914-16)
Respighi's intention was (and here I quote him) "to give expression to the sentiments and visions suggested [to the composer] by four of Rome's fountains, contemplated at the hour in which their character is most in harmony with the surrounding landscape or in which their beauty appears most impressive to the observer" – which, in this case, means the Fountain of Valle Giulia at Dawn, the Triton Fountain at Morning, the Fountain of Trevi at Midday and the Villa Medici Fountain at Sunset.

Pines of Rome – symphonic-poem (1924)
The most famous and instantly appealing of Respighi's historic Italian soundscapes (the so-called "Roman Triptych") opens among the parks and gardens of the Villa Borghese, then progresses to the orderly pines of the Roman campagna, the thick groves on the Janiculum hill at night and, lastly, to the pines of the Appian Way, so redolent of ancient Rome and her marching legions. Respighi's "Pines of the Appian Way" has served as a prototype for countless epic film scores.

Chicago Symphony Orchestra/ Fritz Reiner

RCA analogue

Consummate virtuosity from the Chicago Symphony Orchestra and a 1959 recording that even after a passage of nearly 40 years, remains among the most vivid in the catalogue. However, some will insist on digital sound (as well they might given the graphic nature of the repertoire), in which case I'd also recommend the New York Philharmonic under Giuseppi Sinopoli (DG).

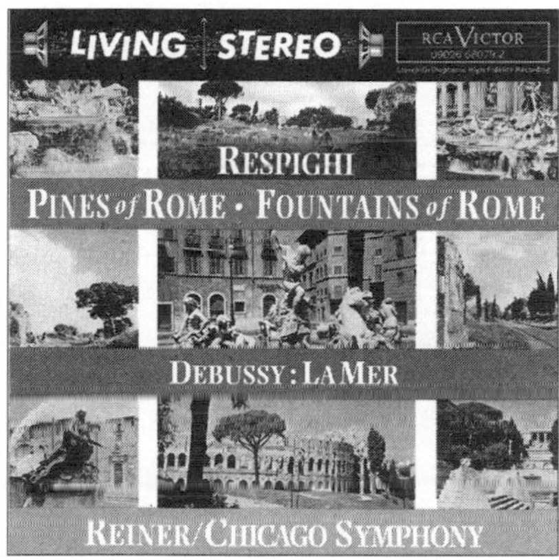

Ernest Bloch (1880-1959)

Schelomo, Hebrew Rhapsody for cello and orchestra (1915-16)

Although inspired by a wax sculpture, Bloch's tone-poem about King Solomon breathes a sensual, agitated world draped in aural glitter. Solomon is represented by the soloist, his concubines by the orchestra. "It is not my purpose, not my desire, to attempt a reconstitution of Jewish music," wrote the composer; "it is the Jewish soul that interests me, the complex, agitated soul that I feel vibrating throughout the Bible."

Emanuel Feuermann (cello), Philadelphia Orchestra/ Leopold Stokowski

Biddulph mono

Anyone in search of tangible proof that great music-making transcends the vintage sound-barrier should hear this recording. Feuermann's soulful, 'inward' narrative contrasts with a fervent and astonishingly colourful orchestra backdrop. It is a virtuoso performance with a deeply emotional core and the 1940 sound is more than adequate. The best stereo (albeit analogue) recording features André Navarra with the Czech Philharmonic Orchestra under Karel Ančerl (Supraphon).

Arnold Bax (1883-1953)

The Garden of Fand (1913-16)

A typically atmospheric score (Bax was a master tone-painter), touched with magic and orchestrated with the utmost subtlety. *The Garden of Fand* is an enchanted patch of sea where a beautiful Irish girl captures the hero Cuchulain and his crew and causes all to sink amidst dance and revelry. The musical style is mildly suggestive of Delius, Sibelius and Scriabin.

Royal Philharmonic Orchestra/ Sir Thomas Beecham

EMI mono

Piquant, wistful and beautifully phrased, Beecham's performance realizes the full measure of Bax's pastel-shaded evocation (the narrative element is vividly conveyed). Those in search of a stereo version are directed to either Sir Adrian Boult (Lyrita, analogue) or Bryden Thomson (Chandos, digital).

Edgar Varèse (1883-1965)

Arcana (1925-27)

A galactic blockbuster that employs a large string section, augmented winds and 39 percussion instruments. Punchy, impulsive and dazzlingly colourful, *Arcana* is a modernist masterpiece that plays high among the stars – the apocalyptic star, the ascending star, the elemental stars and "still another star, imagination, which begets a new star and a new heaven" (part of a quotation that heads the full score). Varèse's essay is a revolution in sound that continues to reverberate among the music of our own time.

Los Angeles Philharmonic Orchestra/Zubin Mehta

Decca analogue

A strong production, with glinting high frequencies, a big, solid bass and useful couplings that include more Varèse – most notably the hypnotic, all-percussion Ionisation. A modern (digital) alternative has Riccardo Chailly conducting the Royal Concertgebouw Orchestra (Decca, coupled with our recommended version of Prokofiev's Third Symphony).

Heitor Villa-Lobos (1887-1959)

Chôros No. 10 (1926)

A bold, primitivistic essay, cast in five separate sections, the first being an evocation of jungle life (forests, rivers, birds, animals, etc), the second a rhythmic "Batucada". The following sections recall the rain forests and ritual dancing, with lusty singing from the choruses, strumming guitars and a percussive (often syncopated) pulse that grows more exciting by the minute.

Chôros No. 10 is just one of a series of 15 like-titled works that were composed between 1920 and 1929, each one being quite different from the others.

Schola Cantorum de Caracas, Orfeón Universitario Simón Bolívar, Simón Bolívar Symphony Orchestra of Venezuela/Eduardo Mata
Dorian digital
A powerful performance – surely the best ever – recorded with maximum presence. The chorus is set to the rear of a vast sound-stage, with plenty of heavy brass and percussion for company.

Sergey Prokofiev (1891-1953)

Peter and the Wolf – a tale for children with narrator and orchestra, Op. 67 (1936)
A listener-friendly guide to how instrumental sonorities can conjure up colourful images, or in this case the characters of a specific story – be it a bird (flute), a duck (oboe), a cat (clarinet), a wolf (horn), a grandfather (bassoon), a group of hunters (timpani) or Peter himself (full string band). Prokofiev's score is witty, mischievous and cleverly constructed.

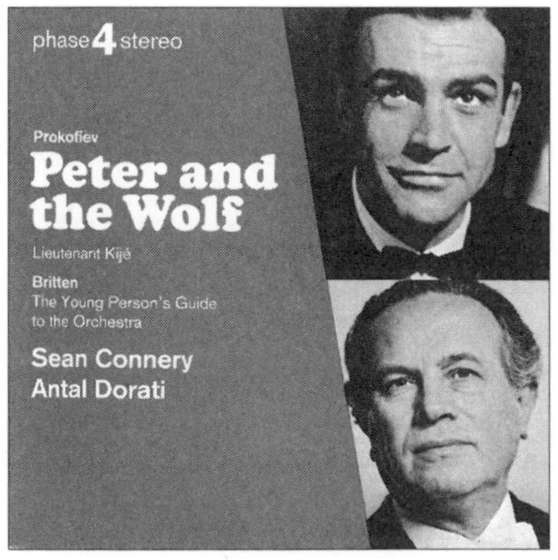

Sean Connery (narrator), Royal Philharmonic Orchestra/Antál Dorati
Decca analogue
Sean Connery delivers a stylish though refreshingly natural account of Gabrielle Hilton's revised narrative (so much better than the rather stilted original) while Dorati's conducting has plenty of sparkle. The recording makes a dramatic virtue of channel separation, but if you fancy a karaoke Peter and the Wolf (with no dialogue), then Leonard Bernstein and the New York Philharmonic provide one (Sony, analogue).

Arthur Honegger (1892-1955)

Pacific 231, H53 (1923)
A train journey in sound that, in the words of the composer, opens to "the quiet breathing of the engine at rest", then traces "its struggle to get underway, the gradual increase in speed leading to the lyrical or emotive state of the 300 ton train hurtling through the darkness." *Pacific 231* is the first of three vivid "Symphonic movements", the second of which, *Rugby*, depicts "attacks and counter-attacks that occur during the game".

ORTF National Orchestra/Jean Martinon
EMI analogue
Martinon's 1971 performance is both rugged and vigorous, qualities that apply in equal measure to "Rugby" (which is on the same CD). Those requiring all three "Symphonic movements" are directed to Charles Dutoit on Erato (digital), while there are gripping historic recordings under Piero Coppola (Koch, mono) and the composer himself (Music & Arts, mono).

George Gershwin (1898-1937)

An American in Paris (1928)
When Gershwin approached Ravel for tuition in composition, the wise Frenchman is alleged to have replied, "why would you want to become a second-rate Ravel when you could be a first-rate Gershwin?". *An American in Paris* more or less proves the point, what with its graphic evocation of Paris at work (blaring taxi horns suggest hectic traffic) and its sensual reportage of her night-life. The narrative is vivid and the tunes superb.

New York Philharmonic Orchestra/Leonard Bernstein
Sony Classical analogue
Bernstein's famous recording is a delightful combination of kitsch and camp, but rather than test one's patience (as so many over-the-top recordings do) it seems to grow more appealing on each hearing. Fine analogue alternatives feature Eugene Ormandy (Sony), Arturo Toscanini (in an uncharacteristically unbuttoned mood, RCA mono) and Nat Shilkret (with Gershwin himself on celesta – recorded in mono way back in 1929, Pearl). No digital rivals are quite as good as these.

Silvestre Revueltas (1899-1940)

Sensemayá (1938)
A highly dramatic musical re-enactment of a snake-killing ritual condensed into a mere six minutes – savage, sleek and mercilessly percussive. Revueltas was educated amongst gangsters, fought for the Republicans in the Spanish Civil War, spent time in mental institutions, was assistant conductor of the Mexico Symphony Orchestra and died young. *Sensemayá* was originally composed for

chamber orchestra but the 'full' version calls for 27 winds, 14 percussion and strings. The rest of Revueltas's output is equally colourful and is surely due for a revival.

New Philharmonia Orchestra/Eduardo Mata
BMG Catalyst digital
The late Eduardo Mata recorded Sensemayá three times, though only two versions are widely available, that listed above and one with the Dallas Symphony Orchestra (Dorian, digital). All three are extraordinarily gripping (if you can find the Dorian disc, it's well worth hearing), but there's also a riveting analogue recording (Sony) from the New York Philharmonic under Leonard Bernstein.

Alexander Mosolov (1900-1973)

Zavod (Iron Foundry) (1926-28)

A Futurist miniature that packs a whole symphony's worth of musical dynamism into a mere three-and-a-half minutes. *Zavod* evokes the rhythmic cacophony of steel production (Mosolov actually uses a metal sheet to help simulate the sound of clashing iron and steel), but although a celebration of the Soviet's then-new programme of industrialization, it was daubed 'naturalistic' by the authorities who forced its composer to follow a more conservative path.

Royal Concertgebouw Orchestra/Riccardo Chailly
Decca digital
Chailly directs a thrilling performance while Decca's spectacular recording reports the full range of Mosolov's thunderous orchestration. The current couplings includes contemporaneous works by Prokofiev and Varèse. Not one for those with sound-sensitive neighbours!

Olivier Messiaen (1908-1992)

Et exspecto resurrectionem mortuorum for wind, brass and percussion (1964)

Messiaen's popular large-scale work was envisaged in terms of – and here I quote the composer himself – "large spaces: churches, cathedrals, and even out of doors among high mountains". Each section is headed by a salient Biblical quotation and dramatic high points include the stark percussion crescendos that dominate the third movement, "the hour is coming when the dead shall hear the voice of the Son of God" and the deathly closing processional, "And I heard as it were the voice of the great multitude ...".

Cleveland Orchestra/Pierre Boulez
Deutsche Grammophon digital
A meticulous, finely-graded reading, one that, while avoiding undue exaggeration, never compromises on the score's considerable physical impact. The recording is both dynamic and refined.

Samuel Barber (1910-1981)

Adagio for strings (1937)

A beautiful theme that rises and falls, gradually gaining in intensity until suddenly the music stops – only to start up again for a reflective fade-out. Barber fashioned his *Adagio* from a String Quartet in B minor, and it was Arturo Toscanini – whose NBC Symphony Orchestra had just been formed – who conducted the world première. Barber's Adagio is a key work in the current classical music revival; it has been used on various film soundtracks (including *The Elephant Man*).

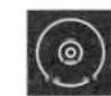

Los Angeles Philharmonic Orchestra/Leonard Bernstein
Deutsche Grammophon digital
Bernstein conducted the Adagio in observance of Barber's death (that was with the New York Philharmonic) and his performance carries the level of conviction you'd expect. Best among alternative versions is Toscanini's burningly intense world première recording (RCA mono).

Leonard Bernstein (1918-1990)

Symphonic Suite from the film "On the Waterfront" (1955)

Once described as "a musical portrait of life and love in New York", Bernstein's score was an essential component of Elia Kazan's magnificent film about power and corruption among the New York docklands. Bernstein intended to re-deploy material that, by his own admission, "would otherwise have been left on the floor of the dubbing-room" and although by no means fully representative of the original score (many wonderful moments are unique to the film soundtrack), this Symphonic Suite remains colossally impressive – the opening and closing minutes in particular.

Israel Philharmonic Orchestra/Leonard Bernstein

Deutsche Grammophon digital

Although labelled a 'Suite', On the Waterfront plays continuously – in fact, it's more like a tone-poem, which is how Bernstein conducts it. A tougher-grained New York recording (Sony, analogue – also under the composer) is marginally more idiomatic, though it cannot match the Israeli production's wide dynamic curve.

Einojuhani Rautavaara (b1928)

Cantus arcticus (1972)

Imagine being marooned on a grey, Arctic flatland, surrounded by sea-birds – thousands of them, crying and warbling among themselves, their multifarious messages the only sounds in an otherwise uninhabited landscape. Finland's most communicative living composer takes their taped cries as a starting point for a mysterious, sensitively scored narrative in three movements – "The Bog", "Melancholy" and "Swans Migrating". The second movement in particular is among the most haunting passages in post-war twentieth-century music.

Leipzig Radio Symphony Orchestra/Max Pommer

BMG Catalyst digital

Pommer is a staunch supporter of Rautavaara's music, a fact that is borne out in a number of excellent recordings. This particular production (which is also on Ondine should the BMG version be unavailable) merges bird cries and orchestra with considerable skill while the current couplings – which include Rautavaara's Fifth Symphony – exhibit further aspects of a major creative talent.

Karlheinz Stockhausen (b1928)

Gesang der Jünglinge (1956)

Taped children's voices singing musical fragments are merged within a hyperactive array of electronic sounds. The sheer variety of timbres and aural perspectives still retains the power to move and surprise, even after so many years (and a good deal of musical development of Stockhausen's part). *Gesang der Jünglinge* is an example of what Nicolas Slonimsky terms as 'Infantiloquy', where the onomatopoeic use of children's voices incorporates all manner of instrumental or (as in this case) electronic imitation. It also provides an extremely accessible introduction to the world of electronic music.

Stockhausen

Stockhausen 3 analogue

A recording that was originally issued on a Deutsche Grammophon LP (coupled with the equally absorbing Kontakte) but that has long been domestically unavailable. This particular CD, issued on Stockhausen's own label, will probably be difficult to locate – but the piece itself is significant enough to justify a fairly rigourous search. Hopefully by the time this book appears, someone will be thinking in terms of a further reissue – but, whatever the case, do try and hear it. As to rivals, there's no contest: the composition is the performance.

Henryk Górecki (b1933)

Kleines Requiem für eine Polka (1993)

A mystery narrative that opens to a gently tolling bell, weeps inwardly on piano and strings, switches suddenly to a savage *Allegro impetuoso*, quietens again, and then – strangest of all – raises the alarm with a relentless, lunatic polka. The effect is frightening, surreal, maniacal – a nightmare interlude in a work that also contains some of Górecki's most contemplative music. As to actual the title – i.e. why this is "a Requiem for a polka" and whether the polka is associated with anyone in particular – Górecki tells us nothing.

Schönberg Ensemble/ Reinbert de Leeuw

Philips digital

A keenly spontaneous performance, marginally less well-drilled than a fine rival version under David Zinman (Teldec, digital), but more appreciative of the work's alarming contrasts. The recording is admirably dynamic and comes as part of a fascinating all-Górecki programme.

Krzysztof Penderecki (b1933)

Threnody for the Victims of Hiroshima (1959-61)

A blinding light, a sickly held chord, the dizzy sliding from side to side, panic, commotion – all is terrifyingly conveyed in one of the most devastating musical narratives of the last half-century. Penderecki's *Threnody* is scored for strings and although the players themselves are given a certain amount of creative leeway (this freedom is often described as 'aleatoric'), the overall effect – from searing pain to utter desolation – is carefully gauged. But be warned, it's a profoundly abstract piece and there are no themes to cling on to. You're thrown straight into the thick of it all!

 ***Polish Radio National Symphony Orchestra/Krzysztof Penderecki***

EMI analogue

Fine sound, idiomatic playing and a sensible (all Penderecki) CD programme context.

Louis Andriessen (b1939)

De Stijl (1984-85)

Originally conceived as part of a larger work (*De Materie*), *De Stijl* – a funky-style music drama set to a constant rhythmic pulse – deals with the relationship between matter and spirit in art. The actual title recalls an art movement and magazine that were founded in 1917 by a group of Dutch artists that included Piet Mondrian. In fact, Mondrian dominates the middle section of the work, where spoken reminiscences of the artist fit to a fast, boogie-style piano accompaniment. *De Stijl* wields enormous power and although it calls on a number of 'pop' instruments – including electric guitars and 'heavy metal' percussion – the overall effect is profoundly humorous, moving and disquieting.

 ***Gertrude Thoma (voice), Schönberg Ensemble with Asko Ensemble/Reinbert de Leeuw***

Nonesuch digital

Superb in every way: fiery, loose-limbed, funky and powerfully recorded. A Dutch recording also exists (where the spoken interlude is delivered in Dutch), but it hasn't the punch of this Nonesuch production.

Gavin Bryars (b1943)

Jesus' Blood never failed me yet (1971, revised 1993)

A homeless old man sits at the edge of a pavement quietly singing to himself. The song is a religious ballad called *Jesus' Blood never failed me yet*, which Bryars repeats again and again to a slowly evolving accompaniment. After a minute or so, a handful of strings provide the old man with a warm aural blanket – softly at first, then slowly intensifying (the instrumentation gradually extends to full strings, brass, etc) until the singing takes flight against a full-textured orchestral backdrop. It's an amazing journey – humbling, comforting and deeply affecting.

 ***Old man (taped voice), chorus, string quartet, organ and orchestra with Tom Waits (additional vocalist)***

Point Music digital

The first (analogue) version of Jesus' Blood never failed me yet – made for Brian Eno's Obscure Records label – was shorter and didn't have the additional vocal part (Tom Waits wafts in towards the end of the piece with his own gravelly version of the song). However, the 'remake' provides the profoundest manner of minimalism, i.e. taking a strong single theme, repeating it and treating it to a lengthy (in this case a 75-minute) sequence contextual variations. Like Steve Reich's Different Trains (see "New Voices"), performance and composition are virtually indivisible.

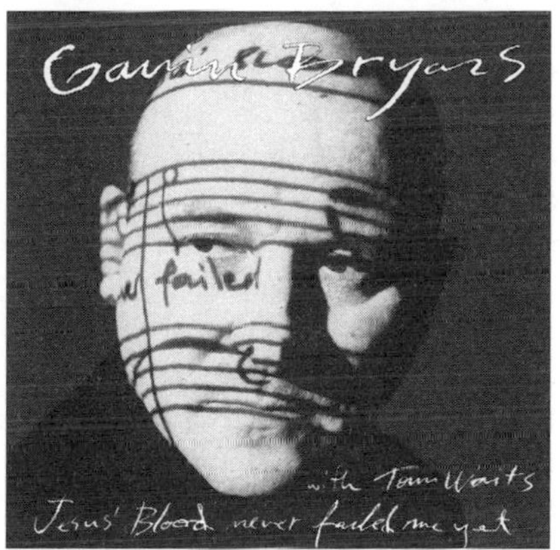

Further listening *Other works by Gavin Bryars include the Cello Concerto (played by Julian Lloyd Webber on Philips, digital), the two string quartets (Balanescu Quartet, Argo, digital) and After the Rain featuring guitarist Bill Frisell (ECM, digital).*

Variations on a Theme (1873-1953)

The idea of stating a theme and then varying it in subsequent musical episodes goes back to the baroque and before, and virtually every section in the current volume includes impressive examples of variation technique (especially "Mighty Monologues", see below). However, in this particular context we look at some of the many orchestral works that use the variation form primarily to explore different instrumental sonorities. They include some of the finest compositions in the orchestral repertory.

Johannes Brahms (1833-1897)

Variations on a Theme by Haydn, "St Antoni Chorale", Op. 56*a* (1873)

"The Variations are unbelievable! I do not know what to admire most – the characterization in each single variation, the magnificent interchange of grace, power and depth, or the effective orchestration ... This is in Beethoven's spirit from first to last." Clara Schumann's reaction to the first performance says it all, save that the theme is by Haydn and that the finale is a noble passacaglia built on a shortened version of the theme, which is repeated 18 times.

 ***Cleveland Orchestra/George Szell***
Sony Classical analogue

Szell's performance is presented in the context of his superb set of the complete Brahms symphonies; it's a beautifully moulded, well drilled account but there are other fine versions available under Herbert von Karajan (DG, analogue), Arturo Toscanini (RCA, mono), Wilhelm Furtwängler (a particularly searching interpretation, EMI, Tahra or DG, all mono) or Sir Adrian Boult (EMI, analogue).

Pyotr Il'yich Tchaikovsky (1840-1893)

Variations on a Rococo Theme in A major for cello and orchestra, Op. 33 (1876)

Tchaikovsky's love of the Classical style is evident throughout his entire output, not least in his *Mozartiana* Orchestral Suite (which includes a setting of Mozart's late choral masterpiece *Ave verum corpus* – see below under "Suites and Dances") and these charming variations on an elegant Rococo theme. The orchestral part is trimly tailored, whereas the soloist is challenged with expressive solo cadenzas and all manner of technical demands.

 ***Mstislav Rostropovich (cello), Leningrad Philharmonic Orchestra/Gennadi Rozhdestvensky***
Melodiya/BMG analogue

Captured here at the very height of his powers, Rostropovich combines effortless virtuosity with a characteristic warmth of tone. Rozhdestvensky draws a pert accompaniment from the Leningrad Philharmonic (also in prime condition at this time) and the stereo recording, although a little constricted by modern digital standards, is more than adequate.

Antonin Dvořák (1841-1904)

Symphonic Variations, Op. 78 (B70) (1877)

It seems quite inconceivable that this many-hued set of variations is less well known than those by Brahms and Elgar. All Dvořák's fingerprints are there: breezy dance sequences (there's a delicious variation in waltz-time), lyrical interludes (a gorgeous violin solo), masterful writing for brass and – to end – something of a rarity in Dvořák, a vigorous fugue.

 ***Czech Philharmonic Orchestra/Karel Sejna***
Supraphon mono

The sound might be dated (there's the occasional audible tape edit) but the playing is wonderfully assured: bright, buoyant, stylish and unmistakably idiomatic. Karel Sejna was originally a double-bassist with the Czech Philharmonic and one senses his 'inside knowledge' at virtually every juncture. The couplings, by the way, are the Ten Legends – which are a bit like soft-option Slavonic Dances.

Sir Edward Elgar (1857-1934)

Variations on an Original Theme, "Enigma", Op. 36 (1898-99)

"One evening after a long and tiring day, I lit a cigar and sat down at the piano. A theme came to me. My wife looked up and asked

'What is that?' 'Nothing,' I replied, 'but perhaps it can be made into something …" Elgar's own words trace the genesis of 14 variations, each of which sketches a particular character in sound (the composer himself, his wife and various friends – including A. E. Jaeger, the inspiration behind "Nimrod"). As to the theme itself (which Elgar himself never disclosed), various theories have circulated over the years – the most convincing of which postulates a particular passage from the slow movement of Mozart's *Prague* Symphony.

 ***Hallé Orchestra/Sir John Barbirolli***
EMI analogue
Barbirolli's 1956 Hallé version (a 1962 Philharmonia remake isn't quite so good) has the requisite warmth, liveliness and nobility, though I'd also recommend trying the composer's own (1926, mono) recording and extraordinarily fresh renditions under Toscanini (his 1951 NBC recording – RCA, mono) and David Zinman (Telarc, digital).

Frederick Delius (1862-1934)

Appalachia – variations on an old slave song, RTII/2 (1902)
The autograph score sets the scene. "*Appalachia* mirrors the moods of tropical nature in the great swamps bordering the Mississippi River," writes Delius, "which is so intimately associated with the life of the old negro slave population. Longing melancholy, an intense love of Nature, childlike humour and an innate delight in singing and dancing are still the most characteristic qualities of this race." Delius's score is at once wistful and ripely romantic, with minor contributions from a chorus and a solo baritone.

 ***Alun Jenkins (baritone), Ambrosian Singers, Hallé Orchestra/Sir John Barbirolli***
EMI analogue

An expansive, warmly voiced performance, recorded just a fortnight before Sir John Barbirolli died (in the summer of 1970). Beecham's edition of the score is used, and it is indeed Beecham himself who provides the best vintage alternatives (either with the LPO on EMI, or the RPO on Sony, mono).

Ralph Vaughan Williams (1872-1958)

Fantasia on a Theme by Thomas Tallis for double string orchestra (1910, revised 1919)
A passionate contrapuntal dialogue between full and solo strings, based on the third of eight settings of ecclesiastical modes composed by Thomas Tallis, "the father of English Cathedral Music", in 1567. Vaughan Williams employs much of Tallis's original harmonization, while the dynamic alternation of textures (intimate entreaties against the commanding, all-powerful sonorities of an orchestral string section) makes for some compelling – and often poignant – aural drama.

 ***Philharmonia Orchestra/ Leonard Slatkin***
RCA digital
Slatkin's second recording of the Fantasia (his first, made with the St Louis Symphony Orchestra, was for Telarc) parades a well-nigh perfect blend between string soloists and full orchestra, though some may find that it lacks the intensity of, say, Dimitri Mitropoulos with the New York Philharmonic (Sony, analogue) or a warmly cosseted reading with the English Sinfonia under Sir John Barbirolli (Classics for Pleasure, analogue).

Sergey Rachmaninov (1873-1943)

Rhapsody on a Theme of Paganini for piano and orchestra, Op. 43 (1934)
Brahms 'varied' themes by Paganini, and so did Schumann, Liszt and Lutosławski but Rachmaninov's masterpiece lays claim to being the greatest of them all. The most famous variation is the richly harmonized 'eighteenth' (which is often programmed as a separate piece, at least on record). The theme is from Paganini's A minor *Caprice* for solo violin and there are 24 variations, ranging in style from wistful reverie to virtuoso drama. The last climax blares out the *Dies irae* chant for the dead (a favourite motive with this composer), although the very last bars are very much 'off the cuff'.

 ***Sergey Rachmaninov (piano), Philadelphia Orchestra/Leopold Stokowski***
RCA mono
No one plays the Paganini Variations like the composer himself. Rachmaninov's powerful chords, lightning dynamics, improvisatory phrasing and effortless virtuosity are simply in a class of their own. Stokowski's conducting is

magnificent, as is the orchestral playing and the whole production sounds precisely what it is – fresh off the press (it was recorded straight after the work was completed, in 1934). However, if it has to be stereo, then Earl Wild is something of a Rachmaninov sound-alike (Chesky, analogue) and Mikhail Pletnev (Virgin, digital) is also pretty impressive.

Max Reger (1873-1916)

Variations and Fugue on a Theme of J. A. Hiller, Op. 100 (1907)

Max Reger's musical language combines the expansiveness of Bruckner, the warmth of Brahms and the wit of Richard Strauss. These particular variations are extraordinarily colourful; try, for example, the second, a gorgeous *Allegretto con grazia*, or the dreamy fifth, marked *Andante sostenuto*. The prompting theme was composed by Hiller, a one-time Cantor of St Thomas's, Leipzig who also happened to teach Beethoven's teacher.

Bavarian Radio Symphony Orchestra/Sir Colin Davis

Orfeo digital

One of Sir Colin's finest recorded performances. The Munich soloists are superb, the strings incisive and the sound quality 'open' and full-bodied. The coupling is Reger's delightful Ballet Suite – a listener-friendly corrective for anyone who anticipates a lack of melody or stodgy textures (unjustified accusations that are frequently levelled against Reger's music). Earlier alternatives worth hearing include an extraordinarily fine mono recording by the Berlin Philharmonic under Paul van Kempen (DG).

Variations and Fugue on a Theme of Mozart, Op. 132 (1914)

The theme is taken from the first movement of Mozart's Piano Sonata in A major (K331, itself the subject of variations), while the ensuing musical journey visits – like the *Hiller* Variations (see above) – all manner of harmonic territory, most of it strongly reminiscent of either Brahms or Bruckner. The work's lyrical core lies in variations Nos. 6-9, some of the tenderest, most atmospheric music in the entire late-Romantic repertory.

Bavarian Radio Symphony Orchestra/Sir Colin Davis

Philips digital

As with the Hiller Variations, Davis offers a sympathetic, highly responsive performance, one that's particlarly rich in poetic incident. Philips's sound is superb – though do keep an eye out for notable (mono) forebears under Karl Böhm (DG or EMI) and Hermann Abendroth (Tahra).

Arnold Schoenberg (1874-1951)

Variations for Orchestra, Op. 31 (1928)

The first of Schoenberg's orchestral works to be cast in the so-called '12-tone' idiom – i.e. forged with 12 notes that form an unbreakable sequence (whether as inverted, integrated in canon, or whatever: there are 48 different configurations). The orchestration includes a mandolin and flexatone and although the workings of the score are exceedingly complex, its actual sound is by turns delicate and exciting (try Variation 8 on track 24 of our recommended recording). Op. 31 consists of an Introduction and Theme, nine variations and finale.

City of Birmingham Symphony Orchestra/Sir Simon Rattle

EMI digital

A painstakingly crafted performance (Rattle attends to every tiny detail of the score) – dramatic, intelligently structured and superbly recorded. Fine digital alternatives include Michael Gielen (Wergo) and Pierre Boulez (Erato), while mono pioneers include Hans Rosbaud (Music & Arts) and Ernest Bour (Astrée).

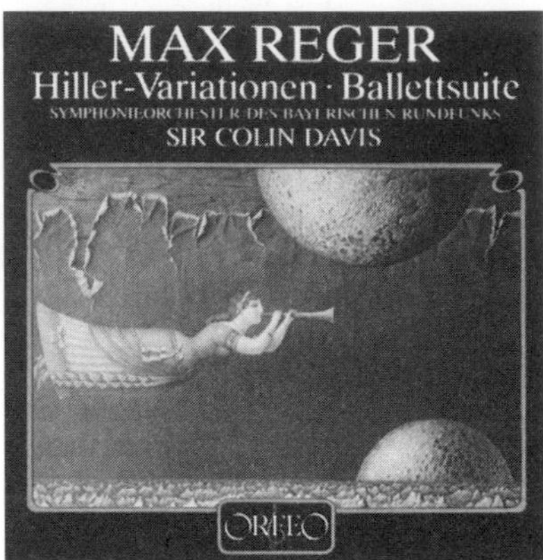

Ernö Dohnányi (1877-1960)

Variations on a Nursery Song for piano and orchestra, Op. 25 (1913)

You'd never guess from the portentously Wagnerian opening what's about to happen – *Twinkle, Twinkle, Little Star* followed by a warming (and often extremely humorous) series of variations. Dohnányi's most popular full-scale work is, after all, dedicated "to the enjoyment of lovers of humour and to the annoyance of others". The style is strongly reminiscent of Brahms, Strauss and Reger, and the overall mood of the piece, playfully romantic (the seventh variation is a delicious waltz).

Zoltán Kocsis (piano), Budapest Festival Orchestra/Iván Fischer

Philips digital

Dextrous pianism with vital, superbly recorded orchestral support under Iván Fischer. As it happens, Zoltán Kocsis – who is a fine scholar as well as an exceptionally gifted pianist – wrote the notes for the reissue of an extremely famous (and musically impressive) 1931 recording where the composer himself plays the solo part with the London Symphony Orchestra under Lawrence Collingwood (EMI, mono).

Zoltán Kodály (1882-1967)

Peacock Variations (1938-39)

Kodály's skilfully scored Variations "on a Hungarian folk-song" (the song is called *Fly, Peacock, Fly*) was composed for the fiftieth anniversary of the Amsterdam Concertgebouw Orchestra (see the CD review below). There are 16 variations in all, plus an introduction and finale. The musical style spices up a post-Impressionistic sense of colour with a generous pinch of paprika.

London Symphony Orchestra/Istvan Kertész

Decca analogue

Kertész conducts a vital, warmly-felt performance, very well played and extremely well recorded. It's also worth mentioning that this is one of the very few instances where an established masterpiece can be heard at its world première (which took place at the Amsterdam Concertgebouw in 1940 under the baton of Willem Mengelberg – Archive Documents mono. It's a terrific performance).

Anton Webern (1883-1945)

Fugue (Ricercata) from Bach's "Musical Offering" (1934-35)

Bach's sublime fugue is subtly re-tooled using different colours, types of articulation and tempo gradations. The effect is rather like an epic journey telescoped into a mere eight minutes (although Bach's original structure is in no way abridged). Furthermore, the orchestration changes in virtually every bar, illustrating – more accessibly than most of Webern's output – how a varied sequence of tiny musical cells can add up to a profoundly satisfying effect.

Vienna Philharmonic Orchestra/Claudio Abbado

Deutsche Grammophon digital

Abbado directs a smooth, effortless performance, pointing salient lines without disrupting the flow. The recording traces each line of the score with maximum fidelity, but those who prefer an all-Bach CD (this one also contains Schoenberg and 'original' Webern) might prefer to investigate an excellent digital alternative by the Boston Symphony Orchestra under Seiji Ozawa (Philips).

Passacaglia for orchestra, Op. 1 (1908)

Readers weaned on the idea that Webern is 'difficult' or 'obscurantist' should start here with Op. 1, a highly dramatic set of variations above or around a single line (here eight bars long), modernist in part – the scoring has a finely-honed, typically Webernian 'sting' – but with one foot placed securely in the world of Gustav Mahler. Ten minutes in length, the *Passacaglia* none the less contains a theme, 23 variations and a coda. It's a masterly example of concise musical narrative.

Vienna Philharmonic Orchestra/Claudio Abbado

Deutsche Grammophon digital

Abbado pulls no punches; he drives the music hard but relaxes into its more introspective variations with a genuine sense of repose. The Vienna Philharmonic remains the ideal instrument for Austro-German fin-de-siècle musical innovation and the recording is wholly excellent. First-rate alternatives are available under Christoph von Dohnányi (Decca, digital), Herbert von Karajan (DG, analogue) and Pierre Boulez (Sony, analogue).

Paul Hindemith (1895-1963)

Symphonic Metamorphoses on Themes of Weber (1943)

A mouthful of a title, but tremendous fun. Weber contributes the tunes and Hindemith provides the orchestral clothing – a lusty *Allegro*, a Chinese-style "Turandot" Scherzo that climaxes in swing mode, then a tender slow movement and a vigorous March. It's an appealing showpiece and serves as a welcoming doorway to Hindemith's multi-faceted musical world.

Cleveland Orchestra/George Szell

Sony Classical analogue

The Weber Metamorphoses is a sort of 'concerto for orchestra' and calls for consummate instrumental virtuosity. Szell's performance is spot-on in all departments, especially in the Scherzo, with its exotic percussion timbres and jazzy rhythms. The stereo recording, too, retains the full measure of its original impact – even after a passage of some 35 years.

Sir Michael Tippett (b1905)

Fantasia concertante on a Theme of Corelli (1953)

One of the most ingenious variation sequences in the repertory takes its cue from Corelli's *Concerto grosso*, Op. 6 No. 2 and calls for a *concertino* ensemble of two violins and cello in addition to full strings.

Tippett's design falls into five intricate parts, climaxing with the fourth (a fugue) and ending with a reference back to Corelli's *Adagio*. The *Fantasia concertante* witnesses an ecstatic interweaving of musical lines, a rich tapestry that pays repeated homage to its Baroque inspiration.

 ***Norwegian Chamber Orchestra/ Iona Brown***
Naim digital
A clear winner on all counts – in terms of clarity (Iona Brown and her players blend textures without obscuring individual lines), judicious instrumental balancing and superior recording quality. Best among studio rivals (Naim's version is live and includes audience applause) is Sir Michael Tippett's own recording with the Bath Festival Orchestra (EMI, analogue).

Benjamin Britten (1913-1976)

Variations and Fugue on a Theme by Purcell, Op. 34 (1946)
Sometimes known as *The Young Person's Guide to the Orchestra* – usually on occasions when it's performed with an educationally instructive narration – Britten's versicoloured variations treat Purcell's noble theme (drawn from the incidental music to *Abdelazer*) to a spectacular outing, working their way through the orchestra from woodwinds, through brass, strings and percussion until a thrilling fugue re-introduces the theme – this time in regal attire.

 ***London Symphony Orchestra/Benjamin Britten***
London/Decca analogue
The LSO plays its heart out in a performance that combines fine orchestral execution with great visceral excitement. Decca's 1963 recording still sounds pretty spectacular, though there's an equally compelling analogue recording with the Philharmonia Orchestra under Carlo Maria Giulini (dating from a year earlier). Best among the digital versions is Andrew Davis's Teldec recording with the BBC Symphony Orchestra.

Variations on a Theme of Frank Bridge for string orchestra, Op. 10 (1937)
Even more than his celebrated *Purcell* Variations, Britten's Op. 10 provides a dazzling *resumé* of the composer's creative style thus far. A masterpiece of skilful parody, individual variations range in style from "Aria italiana", "Wiener walzer", "Bourrée classique" and "Moto perpetuo", to a "Funeral march" and the magnificent "Fugue and finale". Premonitions of Shostakovich's later style abound.

Norwegian Chamber Orchestra/Iona Brown
Virgin Classics digital
The Bridge Variations are so multifarious in style and colour that opportunities for imaginative interpretation are virtually limitless. Iona Brown's performance is simply stunning, ranging in effect from the quietest (and most intense) of pianissimos to powerfully incisive faster variations. The recording, too, is outstanding, while the couplings – which include Britten's wonderful Lachrymae and the Simple Symphony – are excellent.

Suites, dances, etc (1733-1991)

A "suite" is an ordered set of pieces intended for a single performance, but current usage also includes orchestral suites distilled from larger works. This section features a plethora of colourful musical sequences, from the sprightly, dance-like inventions of Telemann, Dvořák and Tchaikovsky to compelling Concertos for Orchestra by Bartók and Lutosławski (i.e. orchestral works that don't fall readily into any other catgeory).

Georg Philipp Telemann (1681-1767)

"Darmstadt" Overture-Suite in D minor for three oboes, bassoon and strings, TW55: d min3 (*c*1760s)
Telemann, a self-taught musician, was exceptionally prolific. He referred to his overtures – he composed over 90 of them – as "overtures and their subsidiary pieces". In fact, they were much appreciated at the time (unlike Bach's Orchestral Suites) and no wonder, given their tunefulness, vivacity and masterly exploitation of contemporary

instrumental sonorities. The D minor Suite is one of many held at the State and University Library at Darmstadt and mixes sombre and bright colours – the closing Gigue being particularly striking.

Concentus Musicus Wien/ Nikolaus Harnoncourt

Teldec analogue

Stylish in the extreme and very well recorded. At the time of writing, there's no alternative version available (not that one's needed), but I'd also recommend investigating first-rate CDs of other Suites featuring, respectively, The English Concert (Archiv, digital) and the Freiburg Baroque Orchestra (DHM, digital).

Tafelmusik (Banquet Music) in three parts (published in 1733)

Telemann and Bach were friends; they often played together and Telemann was godfather to Bach's second son, Carl Philipp Emanuel. The title *Tafelmusik* was originally thought to denote "a collection of pieces intended for musicall entertainment during a banquet", but modern scholarship tends to think more in terms of a 'proving ground' for chamber ensembles. The "Banquet Music" tag was, it seems, little more than a sales gimmick. As to the music (a rich sequence of Suites, Quartets, Trios, and so on), such is its variety and pleasure-yield that the time (the total set lasts over four hours) seems to fly past.

Musica Antiqua Köln/ Reinhard Goebel

Archiv digital

Choosing between this superb production and a strong rival under Nikolaus Harnoncourt (Teldec – both employ period instruments) is difficult, but Goebel's wit, incisiveness and lightness of touch prove irresistible. The many dance movements are especially engaging.

Jean-Philippe Rameau
(1683–1764)

Les Boréades: Suite (1764)

Fiery descriptive music taken from a stage work that was virtually unknown until the mid-1950s. The Suite is full of amazing effects, including "Les Vents" which depicts how the wind god Boreus conjures up a fierce storm. The writing is rich in bustling crescendos, quite unlike the delightful "Air vif", an ebullient, swaying miniature and a cracking good tune to boot.

Orchestra of the Eighteenth Century/Frans Brüggen

Philips digital

Recorded live in 1986, Brüggen's performances – which are vividly realized on period instruments – are immediately engaging. The sound is spacious and full-toned, the playing deft, stylish and keenly animated. I can't imagine a more fetching – or, indeed, more dramatic – introduction to the world of Baroque instrumental music.

Johann Sebastian Bach
(1685–1750)

Orchestral Suite No. 1 in C major, BWV1066 (1720-25)

As a musical genre, the "Suite" had already established itself by around 1600, primarily as music for dancing – although it soon shifted closer to the sphere of 'art' music. Bach's Four Orchestral Suites open with lengthy Overtures (a term that's sometimes used generically for the whole work, i.e. instead of the word 'Suite'), followed by a series of dance movements. The First Suite, which dates from Bach's so-called Cöthen or early Leipzig periods, includes an especially attractive "Forlane" (fourth movement).

Orchestral Suite No. 2 in B minor, BWV1067 (1738-39)

Flautists world-wide (and James Galway in particular) have made extensive use of the famous "Badinerie" last movement, although the other pieces are scarcely less attractive. Suite No. 2 is the most mature of the four and was apparently influenced by chamber music. Aside from Bach's prominent use of the flute, the B minor Suite features an Overture that, in terms of design and metre, marks something of a formal advancement over similar pieces of the period.

Munich Bach Orchestra/Karl Richter

Archiv analogue

Karl Richter's performances are distinguished by rhythmic firmness and great clarity of line – qualities that pay especially high dividends in the First Suite. For those insistent on period instruments Nikolaus Harnoncourt's 1966 recording is the first choice (Teldec, analogue), with Ton Koopman and the Amsterdam Baroque Orchestra (Erato, digital) as a good second. Good modern-instrument alternatives include Lord Yehudi Menuhin (EMI analogue) and Sir Neville Marriner (EMI, digital).

Orchestral Suite No. 3 in D major, BWV1068 (*c*1723)

The fact that the Third Suite's celebrated second movement, a soothing "Air", has achieved a life of its own (most famously in a transcription known as "Air on a G String") is, in a sense, rather appropriate, given that the parent work was in all probability originally composed for solo violin, with wind instruments added later. Like the Fourth Suite, it contains five rather than seven movements although the tone – the "Air" excepted – is ceremonial.

Orchestral Suite No. 4 in D major, BWV1069 (*c*1723)

The most extrovert of Bach's Suites – timpani and brass are very much to the fore – was originally designed for two separate groups of instrumentalists (featuring oboes and strings, respectively), whereas the first movement also turns up as the introduction to Cantata No. 110. The final "Réjouissance" marks a joyous conclusion to the series.

Musica Antiqua Köln/ Reinhard Goebel

Archiv digital

Were it not for the fact that in Suite No. 2 Goebel uses just one instrument per part – a decision that some listeners will find quirky – I would probably make him my prime recommendation for all four. The Third and Fourth Suites are extremely vital, with lively tempos and the lean sonority of period instruments employed to splendid re-creative effect. Listeners who prefer modern instruments are directed to Richter (Archiv, analogue), Milan Munclinger (Supraphon, analogue) or Sir Neville Marriner (Philips, digital).

George Frideric Handel

(1685-1759)

Music for the Royal Fireworks, HWV351 (1749)

Grand, imperious music (cast in six varied movements) with an especially interesting history. *The Music for the Royal Fireworks* was a commission from King George II in celebration of the end of the War of Austrian Succession and the resulting peace treaty. The actual celebrations took place in London's Green Park; Handel's orchestra was accompanied by a 101-gun salute, but the planned fireworks display was a fiasco (the immensely successful rehearsal had caused a traffic jam on London Bridge).

The English Concert/Trevor Pinnock

DG Archiv digital

A performance of enormous vitality, superbly recorded. Modern-instrument alternatives include Karl Richter's splendid English Chamber Orchestra recording (Archiv, analogue), a gargantuan but hugely characterful 1961 account under Leopold Stokowski (RCA, analogue) and the ever-urbane Sir Neville Marriner with his Academy of St Martin in the Fields (Philips, digital).

The Water Music, HWV348-50 (c1715-17, revised 1736)

A musical apology from a moonlighting maestro. *The Water Music* was Handel's gift for King George I (originally the Elector of Hanover) who, while still in Germany, allowed him a 'short trip to England' which he (Handel) decided to 'extend' by a few years. When George succeeded Queen Anne to the throne, Handel was in disgrace, and it was this work – a mainstay of the Baroque repertory – that earned him forgiveness. And not only that, the King demanded to hear it three times!

Concentus Musicus Wien/ Nikolaus Harnoncourt

Teldec analogue

If you like your Water Music bright and breezy, then you'd do well to opt for Raymond Leppard or Sir Neville Marriner (Philips or Argo, respectively – both are analogue). Harnoncourt's is an aggressive, top-gear affair, with blaring (period) brass and attenuated strings. It's quirky, but it's tremendous fun.

Wolfgang Amadeus Mozart

(1756-1791)

Serenade No. 7 in D major, K250, "Haffner" (1776)

Wedding music on the grandest scale, Mozart having composed it for the marriage between Elisabeth Haffner (daughter of a wealthy merchant and banker who was also Burgomaster of Salzburg) and Franz Xavier Späth. The *Haffner* Serenade is preceded by a jaunty March (K249); there are no parts for cellos (cellists would have needed to sit down, and this was music that had to be played while standing) and none for timpani (they couldn't play on the march). The eight movements include a pensive G minor Minuet, a particularly beautiful *Andante* and a lively Rondo that is sometimes played as a violin solo (usually in Fritz Kreisler's arrangement).

Orchestra of the Eighteenth Century/Frans Brüggen

Philips digital

Lucy van Dael offers nimble performances of the important violin part, while Brüggen's period-instrument orchestra plays in a lively, spontaneous and pleasingly relaxed manner. The sound has plenty of bloom, but those who favour modern instruments might prefer the

Orchestral works Suites, dances, etc (1733–1991)

Vienna Mozart Ensemble under Willi Boskovsky (Decca, analogue).

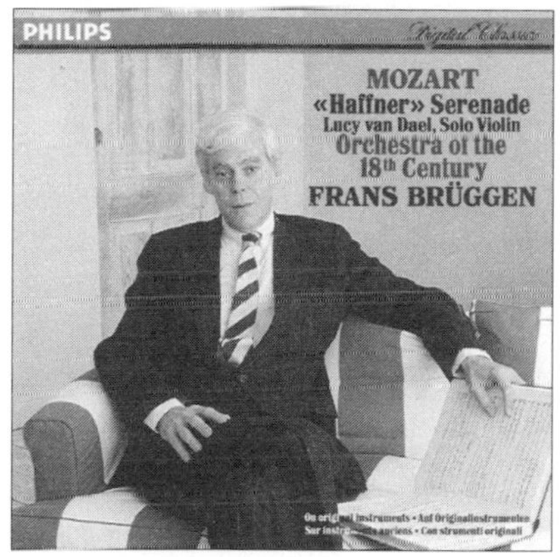

Serenade No. 9 in D major, K320, "Posthorn" (1779)

A large-scale, festive piece in seven movements, probably composed either for the nameday (or feast day) of the Archbishop of Salzburg or as University "Finalmusik". It's scored for flutes, oboes, bassoons, horns, trumpets, drums and strings, and contains one of Mozart's most gravely beautiful slow movements (the *Andantino*). The *Posthorn* nickname originates in Mozart's use of a 'corno di posto' in the second Trio of the second Minuet. Mozart also provided two attractive Marches to be played alongside the Serenade (both are included on our recommended recording).

Salzburg Mozarteum Camerata Academica/Sándor Végh

Philips digital

With a line-up of musicians that includes Aurèle Nicolet (flute), Heinz Holliger (oboe) and Klaus Thunemann (bassoon) – all of them among the finest living practitioners of their respective instruments – you could hardly go wrong. Végh's stylish conducting puts the icing on the cake and the recording is superb. High priorities among older versions are George Szell (Sony, analogue) and Ferdinand Leitner (DG, mono – not as yet on CD)

Serenade No. 10 in B flat major for 13 wind instruments, K361/370a, "Gran Partita" (1781–84)

"Today I also heard music for wind instruments by Herr Mozart, in four movements – glorious and sublime!" The quote is from Johann Freidrich Schink's *Literary Fragments*, although readers who remember the film *Amadeus* will also recall Salieri's similar reaction to the rapt *Adagio* (the third of the Serenade's seven movements). The *Gran Partita*, which Mozart composed after leaving Salzburg for Vienna, is unquestionably the greatest work ever written for wind ensemble.

Vienna Philharmonic Orchestra/Wilhelm Furtwängler

EMI mono

The principal reason for recommending this 1947 mono recording is Furtwängler's rapturous handling of the Adagio – surely the most beautifully shaped performance ever committed to disc. However, there are plenty of good digital alternatives, with the Bavarian Radio Symphony Winds under Sir Colin Davis (RCA) and the Chamber Orchestra of Europe under Alexander Schneider (ASV) being among the finest.

Serenade No. 13 in G major, K525, "Eine kleine Nachtmusik" (1787)

The four movements of what is undoubtedly Mozart's most popular work were originally five: a first Minuet and Trio has been lost. Of the rest, little need be said save that Mozart never heard the work performed in his lifetime and that a sprightly *Allegro*, a tender *Romance* (with a scurrying middle section), a bright though somewhat imperious Minuet and Trio and a gaily bustling finale *Eine kleine Nachtmusik* provide concise and delightful entertainment.

Concentus Musicus Wien/ Nikolaus Harnoncourt

Teldec digital

Harnoncourt observes all repeats, which means that the first movement plays for 8'27" rather than the usual 5-6 minutes. He takes the outer sections of the Minuet faster than the Trio (which he plays with much affection) and doesn't push the finale too hard. Period instruments are employed to fine effect, though readers who prefer standard modern instruments are well served by Sir Neville Marriner and the Academy of St Martin in the Fields (Philips, digital), the Columbia Symphony Orchestra under Bruno Walter (Sony, analogue) and numerous other good versions.

Felix Mendelssohn (1809–1847)

A Midsummer Night's Dream – incidental music to Shakespeare's play, Opp. 21 and 61 (1826 and 1842)

Mendelssohn was just 17 years old when he penned his magical Overture to this piece, but the incidental music – which actually makes use of some of the Overture's thematic material – was composed 16 years later in response to a commission from King Friedrich Wilhelm IV of Prussia. As to the music itself, there are miracles galore, including an elfin Scherzo, a pensive Intermezzo, a dreamy Nocturne and then one of the world's most celebrated Wedding Marches (the other, "Here Comes the Bride", is from Wagner's *Lohengrin* – see "Twilit Catastrophes", below).

Soloists, Finchley Children's Music Group, London Symphony Orchestra/André Previn

EMI digital

Previn conducts the complete score - which includes various shorter items that were for many years programmed only in the context of a theatre performance of the play. It's a warm, atmospheric production, beautifully balanced by the engineers, but it you require only the Suite (Overture, Scherzo, Nocturne, Wedding March, etc), then Armin Jordan and the Suisse Romande Orchestra (Erato, digital) offer a profoundly musical alternative.

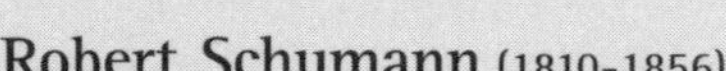

Robert Schumann (1810-1856)

Overture, Scherzo and Finale, Op. 52 (1841)

A super piece, written at a time when Schumann was in full creative flight (he had also composed the *Spring* and D minor Symphonies, as well as the first movement of the Piano Concerto in the same year). The Overture is bursting with *joie de vivre*, the Scherzo suggests an elfin "Ride of the Valkyries" (the scoring has a Mendelssohnian delicacy, the theme suggests definite premonitions of Wagner) while the Finale blazes with all the confidence of the Fourth Symphony's last movement.

Hanover Band/Roy Goodman

RCA digital

Bright-toned, vivacious and light in texture - virtues that particularly suit the breeziest of Schumann's orchestral works. Goodman's orchestra uses period instruments, whereas Wolfgang Sawallisch and the Dresden Staatskapelle offer a beefy modern-instrument (analogue) alternative (EMI).

Camille Saint-Saëns (1835-1921)

Carnival of the Animals (1886)

An amusing sequence of pieces written strictly for private amusement and which the composer himself banned from public performance during his lifetime. There are over a dozen animal characters, including Tortoises (a slow-motion version of Offenbach's celebrated "Can-Can"), braying donkeys, an elephant (thumping around on double-basses), a mysterious aquarium, a swan for cellists, a cuckoo in the depths of the wood - and that most annoying breed, the pianist (who drives us mad with the incessant practising of scales). Virtually every movement has become extremely well-known.

Martha Argerich, Nelson Freire (pianos), Gidon Kremer (violin), Mischa Maisky (cello) et al

Philips digital

A performance of tremendous vitality - witty, provocative, technically accomplished and superbly recorded. Rivals are plentiful, with such estimable zoo-keepers as Igor Markevitch (EMI, mono), Leopold Stokowski (Biddulph, mono), André Previn (Philips, digital) and Gennadi Rozhdestvensky (Erato, digital) being among the most imaginative.

Georges Bizet (1838-1875)

L'Arlésienne - concert suites from incidental music to Alphonse Daudet's play (1872)

A tale of love, despair and recovery from mental illness set within the landscape of Provence. Bizet composed his incidental music at breakneck speed and the two suites (the second is arranged by Ernest Guiraud) include a haughty Prélude, a vigorous Minuetto, a tender Adagietto, a chiming Carillon, a Pastorale, a Minuet and, to close, what is perhaps the most famous movement of all - the Farandole, which starts out by recalling the Prelude then switches to a wildly accelerating dance.

Lamoureux Orchestra/ Igor Markevitch

Philips analogue

Elegant, brilliant and pertly characterized performances, recorded back in 1959 but still sounding well. Antál Dorati recorded the same music with the same orchestra during the same year (for the same label!), and that's pretty exciting too - though there's formidable rivalry from Sir Thomas Beecham (EMI, analogue), Myung-Whun Chung (DG, digital) and Paul Paray (Mercury, analogue), all of whom are extremely stylish.

Modest Mussorgsky (1839-1881)

Pictures at an Exhibition (1874 - orchestrated by Ravel in 1922)

A witty, transparent and often dramatic orchestral version of Mussorgsky's famous picture gallery (itself inspired by Victor Hartmann's sketches and watercolours). Ravel's transparent orchestration lends extra malevolence to "The Gnome", nobility to "The Old Castle", humour to the "Ballet of the Unhatched Chickens", humanity to "Samuel Goldenburg and Schmuyle" and grandeur to "The Great Gate at Kiev".

Berlin Philharmonic Orchestra/Claudio Abbado

Deutsche Grammophon digital

A fine realization, superbly played and richly recorded, although two recordings by the Chicago Symphony – under Fritz Reiner (RCA, analogue) and under Rafael Kubelík (Mercury, mono) – are equally impressive (at least interpretatively). Those who fancy a more outrageous orchestration – a virtual caricature and with certain items cut – should try to hear Stokowski's spectacular 1940 Philadelphia recording (Dutton Laboratories).

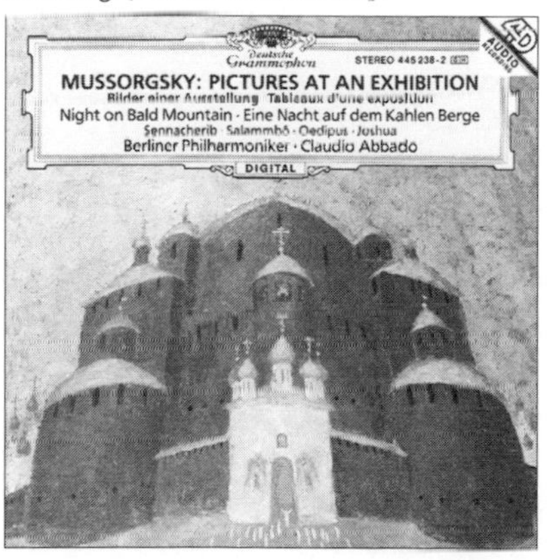

Pyotr Il'yich Tchaikovsky

(1840-1893)

Orchestral Suite No. 1 in D minor, Op. 43 (1878-79)

"I am completely finished as far as music is concerned," wrote Tchaikovsky around the time of his First Orchestral Suite – although Mme von Meck, his devoted patron and the work's dedicatee, helped to raise his spirits with a trip to Italy. Tchaikovsky's four Suites are extraordinarily inventive, the First opening with a desolate – almost Sibelian – introduction before progressing to a busy fugue and a varied sequence of balletic dance movements, the most famous of which is a *Nutcracker*-style "Marche miniature".

Prague Symphony Orchestra/ Jiří Bělohlávek

Supraphon digital

A fine performance, stylishly conducted and enthusiastically played. Evgeni Svetlanov's digital USSR Symphony Orchestra recording (Melodiya/BMG) is also excellent (though not quite so well recorded) and there's a masterly vintage account under Antál Dorati (Philips, analogue – and still sounding superb).

Orchestral Suite No. 2 in C major, Op. 53 (1883)

An absolutely marvellous work that opens in the manner of the *Serenade* for strings (though with sinister intimations thereafter) before launching into a highly dramatic fugue. The scoring recalls the pain-racked world of the Fourth Symphony and the Suite soars to a creative high point with the fantastical, stylistically advanced "Children's Dreams", a tone-poem that lasts nearly 15 minutes. There's also a harmonically audacious waltz, a playful "Scherzo burlesque" (with optional accordions) and a fiery "Danse baroque" to close.

New Philharmonia Orchestra/ Antál Dorati

Philips analogue

A thrillingly dynamic performance, one that includes the optional accordions in the "Scherzo burlesque" (Bělohlávek [Supraphon, digital] also includes them, but Svetlanov – in his Melodiya digital version – doesn't). The Mercury sound (Philips have issued the recordings under license) is extraordinarily lifelike.

Orchestral Suite No. 3 in G major, Op. 55 (1884)

Completed a year before the *Manfred* Symphony, Tchaikovsky's Third Suite is dominated by a highly eventful "Theme and Variations" that has been both performed and recorded separately. Yet there's far more to the Suite than an expansive last movement – a witty syncopated Scherzo, for example, and a "Valse mélancolique" whose central section anticipates mature Elgar. The opening movement is a heart-rending Elegy.

USSR Ministry of Culture Symphony Orchestra/Gennadi Rozhdestvensky

Erato digital

A supremely natural reading of the most popular Suite, supple in detail and execution and very well recorded. Bělohlávek's Prague recording (Supraphon) makes a good second digital option while the analogue field is dominated by a fine Sony version by the Los Angeles Philharmonic under Michael Tilson Thomas and Antál Dorati's famous New Philharmonia recording (Dorati's Scherzo features especially incisive woodwinds).

Orchestral Suite No. 4 in G major, Op. 61, "Mozartiana" (1887)

Tchaikovsky adored Mozart and so it's little wonder that he celebrated Vienna's best-loved musical son with a separate orchestral Suite – his express intention being to popularize various lesser-known Mozart miniatures. The most famous movement is a setting of the sublime *Ave verum corpus*, K618 whereas the Suite opens with the Gigue in G major, K574, continues with the Minuet from the Piano Trio, K355 and ends with a set of variations on a melody by Gluck that Mozart used for his Piano Variations, K455.

USSR Symphony Orchestra/ Evgeni Svetlanov

Melodiya/BMG digital

A fine, vividly characterized reading, though Bělohlávek's digital Prague recording makes a good second choice. Again, I must remind readers of a wonderful version of the Suites by the New Philharmonia Orchestra under Antál Dorati (Philips, analogue).

Serenade for strings in C major, Op. 48 (1880)

Tchaikovsky composed his adorable Serenade around the same time as his Second Piano Concerto and *1812* Overture. Prior to its publication, he wrote, "I am violently in love with this work and can't wait for it to be played". He also conducted it while on foreign tours. Of the Serenade's four varied movements, best-known are the charming Waltz and deeply moving Elegy.

Norwegian Chamber Orchestra/ Iona Brown

Virgin Classics digital

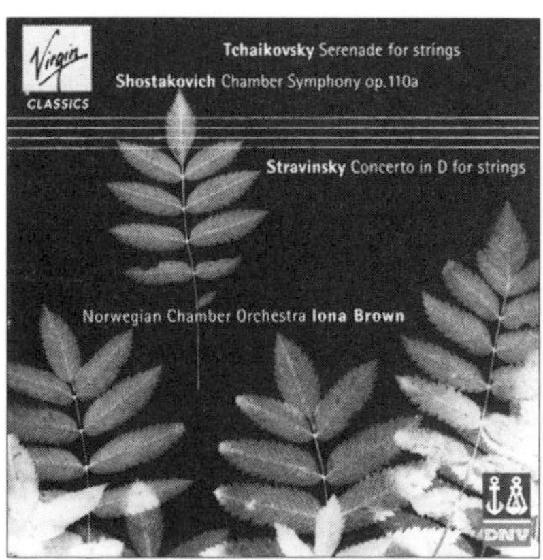

Brown's greatest virtue is the way she has her players shape their phrases: this is a real performance, vibrant both in detail and overall impact. The playing too is excellent, but there are at least two exquisitely expressive mono 'oldies' conducted, respectively, by Evgeni Mravinsky (Melodiya or Russian Disc) and Willem Mengelberg (Teldec or Biddulph).

Antonin Dvořák (1841-1904)

16 Slavonic Dances, B83 and B147 (Opp. 46 and 72) (1878 and 1886)

Each of these pieces should rightly have an entry to itself. All 16 *Slavonic Dances* are charming, colourful and singularly scored (and they're entirely the product of Dvořák's creative imagination – none of the Dances quote actual folk-songs). Both sets were commissioned by Dvořák's publisher, initially for piano duet, then for full orchestra. The first eight are the more extrovert, the second, marginally richer, even a little darker in character. The dance forms used include the Polka, Dumka and Furiant, and many individual pieces have become extremely popular.

Czech Philharmonic Orchestra/ Karel Sejna

Supraphon analogue

The most vivacious set of Slavonic Dances on disc, excellently recorded, idiomatically played and with due respect for the very individual character of each piece. Fine alternatives include Rafael Kubelík's superb Munich set (DG, analogue), Lorin Maazel's from Berlin (EMI digital – rather stylized but very musical) and a famous disc of the Cleveland under George Szell (Sony, analogue – affectionate, well-drilled and energetic).

Edvard Grieg (1843-1907)

Peer Gynt – incidental music to Ibsen's play (1874-75)

Although Grieg admired Ibsen's play (the two men were good friends), he experienced considerable difficulty in setting it to music. "It is a fearfully intractable subject," he once wrote, and after a successful first performance, set to add new numbers and re-orchestrate portions of the old score. *Peer Gynt* traces the downfall and redemption of a Norwegian peasant and the score (some of which is scarcely known away from its original theatrical context) includes the perennially popular "Morning" – not, as one might think, an evocation of Norwegian fjords, but of a morning scene in Africa!

Ilse Hollweg (soprano), Royal Philharmonic Orchestra/ Sir Thomas Beecham

EMI analogue

"The Beecham touch" informs every note of this delightful score, from Morning, through Ingrid's Lament and Anitra's Dance to Solveig's song and (much less well-known) Lullaby. Readers who would like to investigate

the complete score (a worthwhile adventure) are directed to Neeme Järvi's compelling DG recording (digital).

Nikolai Rimsky-Korsakov (1844-1908)

The Golden Cockerel, suite (1909)

Rimsky's opera – his last – about a lazy king and a cunning astrologer was first presented in Moscow in 1909. The orchestral suite (which was prepared by Glazunov and Maximilian Steinberg) is a veritable riot of colour and includes "King Dodon in his Palace", "King Dodon in the Battlefield", "King Dodon with Queen Shemakha" (the Queen sings the famous "Hymn to the Sun", though it's not featured in the Suite) and the glittering "Marriage Feast and Lamentable End of King Dodon", one of Rimsky's most spectacular orchestral showpieces.

London Symphony Orchestra/ Antál Dorati

Mercury analogue

A thrilling memento of a musical collaboration that produced some of the most exciting recordings of the 1950s and 1960s. These particular sessions date from 1956 and still sound remarkably effective – though there's a lively digital recording by the Bolshoi Symphony Orchestra under Alexander Lazarev (Erato).

Leoš Janáček (1854-1928)

Sinfonietta (1926)

Janáček's *Sinfonietta* opens like an Olympic celebration: fanfare trumpets ring resplendent, evoking an unmistakable sense of the outdoors. The ensuing movements (which employ the whole orchestra) survey an unusually wide range of moods – dance-like, playful, romantic and with a thrilling return of the opening fanfares for the home straight. Janáček's prompting inspirations included the "Sokol" gymnastics festival and the forthcoming Tenth Anniversary of the Czech Republic. This ebullient confession of youthful enthusiasm was in fact the work of a 72-year-old.

Bavarian Radio Symphony Orchestra/Rafael Kubelík

Deutsche Grammophon analogue

The Munich brass play their hearts out while Kubelík, as ever, fully connects with the score's emotional ground-springs. Other superb Sinfoniettas hail from Czechoslovakia (under Karel Ančerl, Supraphon, analogue) and Vienna (under Sir Charles Mackerras, Decca, digital).

Richard Strauss (1864-1949)

Le bourgeois gentilhomme – Suite of incidental music to Molière's play, Op. 60 (1918)

A delightful sequence that was originally planned to accompany a play within the context of Strauss's opera *Ariadne auf Naxos*. Sad to relate, the idea didn't catch on – but Strauss salvaged his incidental music (taken from two acts) for what turned out to be a very popular Suite. The Overture depicts an upstart posing as a nobleman; there are numerous colourful dance movements, and an enchanting "Dinner Music" episode full of Viennese charm.

Chicago Symphony Orchestra/ Fritz Reiner

RCA analogue

One of the great Reiner recordings and a dazzling showcase for individual Chicago Symphony players. Fine alternatives include memorable performances under Rudolf Kempe (EMI, analogue), Erich Leinsdorf (ASV, digital) and Strauss's friend and colleague Clemens Krauss (recorded in 1929, Koch, mono).

Alexander Glazunov (1865-1936)

From the Middle Ages – symphonic suite (1903)

A lavish orchestral evocation, the sort that could easily have accompanied a historical screen epic. There are four movements, the most overtly romantic being the Prelude (which harbours one of Glazunov's loveliest melodies) and an entrancing "Troubadour's Serenade". Also included are the colourful Scherzo and an expansive finale, "The Crusaders". Glazunov completed *From the Middle Ages* merely months after finishing his Seventh Symphony.

The USSR Symphony Orchestra/Evgeni Svetlanov

Melodiya digital

Recordings of this fine work have always been thin on the ground and although Svetlanov's high demonstrative account is the best we've had in years, it may well be difficult to find. Neeme Järvi's Chandos recording (also digital) isn't nearly so impressive, whereas the greatest recording of all – a much older [mono] Melodiya under the baton of Nikolai Golovanov – is exceedingly rare (at least at the time of writing). A third Melodiya recording, conducted by Vladimir Fedoseyev, is also worth looking out for.

Wilhelm Stenhammar
(1871-1927)

Serenade in F major, Op. 31 (1911-13)

This deceptively named *Serenade* looks back to Strauss (who conducted the young Stenhammer's Piano Concerto at the Berlin Philharmonie) and sideways to mature Sibelius. It is cast in five fairly substantial movements – an "Overture", "Canzonetta", Scherzo, "Notturno" and finale. The language is subtly evocative of the North and represents Sweden's leading Romantic composer at his most immediately appealing.

Gothenburg Symphony Orchestra/Neeme Järvi

Deutsche Grammophon digital

The sort of thing that Järvi does particularly well – energetic, outdoor music with a keen sense of fantasy and plenty going on. Playing, interpretation and recording are all first-rate and the Serenade comes packaged with the two symphonies and the symphonic overture "Excelsior!", all of which are well worth getting to know.

Sergey Rachmaninov
(1873-1943)

Symphonic Dances, Op. 45 (1940)

Rachmaninov's last orchestral work is also among his greatest. Meaningful self-quotation (most tellingly from the composer's First Symphony) lends a reflective air to certain passages, although the overriding impression is of immense physicality – especially in the martial outer sections of the First Dance and the thrilling peroration of the Third. The second, marked *Tempo di valse* recalls the opulent world of the great Tchaikovsky ballets.

Moscow Philharmonic Orchestra/Kyrill Kondrashin

Melodiya/BMG analogue

The beefiest Symphonic Dances around, with impressive weight in the outer pieces, a sweeping account of the second and due recognition of Rachmaninov's melancholy muse. The sound is a mite shrill, but there's impact to spare and Kondrashin allows the final tam-tam stroke to reverberate beyond the work's final chord (as per the composer's somewhat ambiguous instructions).

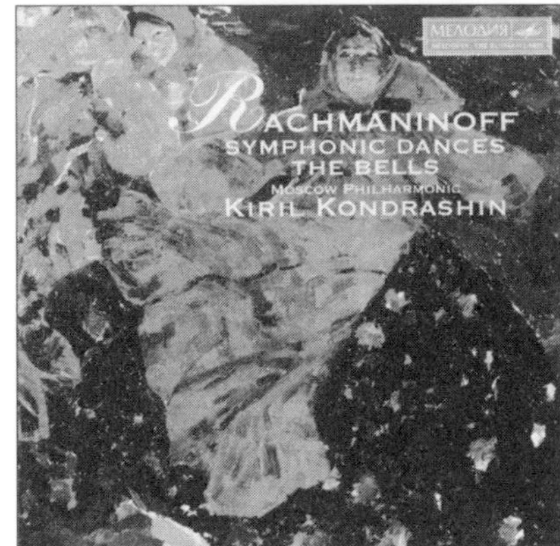

Max Reger (1873-1916)

A Ballet Suite, Op. 130 (1913)

Pure delight from beginning to end – and the best possible proof that Max Reger was anything but a dry, academic composer whose only joy was writing fugues. There are two aromatic slow movements ("Colombine" and "Pierrot and Pierrette") – both of them among the most haunting miniatures in the Romantic repertory – as well as an utterly seductive "Tempo di Valse", a burlesque-style Harlequin, an opening March and a closing *Presto.* Readers who fancy the idea of Impressionistic music with the odd sophisticated harmonic twist (Reger was a dab hand at modulating between keys) will adore Reger's Ballet Suite.

Staatskapelle Berlin/Otmar Suitner

Berlin Classics analogue

By far the best recorded performance of the Suite – stylish, warmly phrased and with some first-rate solo work (especially from the cellist and oboist in "Pierrot and Pierrette"). Digital rivals under Sir Colin Davis (Orfeo) and Horst Stein (Koch), although more than worthy, aren't nearly as charming or as characterful.

Arnold Schoenberg (1874-1951)

Five Pieces for orchestra, Op. 16 (1909, revised 1949)

"It was like a poem in Tibetan; not one single soul could possibly have understood it at a first hearing." So wrote *The Times* critic after the world première performance (in August 1912, under Sir Henry Wood) of these epoch-making pieces. Schoenberg had abandoned a 'tonal centre' and was reaching towards the "composition with 12 tones" that would dominate much of his later work. The music itself (which sounds relatively 'normal' by modern avant-garde standards) ranges in a style from scary "Premonitions", through a delicately tooled "Tone-colour melody" to an impetuous "Peripetia" ("the turning point of dramatic action").

London Symphony Orchestra/ Antál Dorati

Mercury analogue

A dramatic, clear-headed performance captured in a vintage stereo recording (1962) that has real 'edge' to the brass and string tone. The programme context is Vienna at the beginning of the twentieth-century (Schoenberg, Berg, Webern) but there are fine digital alternatives under Robert Craft (Koch) and Sir Simon Rattle (EMI).

Maurice Ravel (1875-1937)

Le tombeau de Couperin (1917, orchestrated 1919)

The carefree, skipping "Forlane" (an old Italian dance-form in 6/8 time) is perhaps the best-known item in this, Ravel's airy memorial to friends who had fallen in the First World War. *Tombeau* actually means 'tomb' or 'memorial' and the tribute extends, by dint of its elegant material, to the composer's great eighteenth-century French forebear, Couperin. It was originally a six-movement piano suite, but the orchestral version dispenses with two movements that Ravel deemed "too pianistic". What is left, however, is immensely charming and lovable.

Suisse Romande Orchestra/ Armin Jordan

Erato digital

A bright, transparent and nicely paced performance, superbly balanced by Erato's engineering team. There's a more rigorously rhythmic alternative under Paul Paray (Mercury, analogue), while Hugh Wolff and the Saint Paul Chamber Orchestra (Teldec, digital) are also recommended.

Ottorino Respighi (1879-1936)

Ancient Airs and Dances, Suite No. 3 (1932)

Charming and often vivacious transcriptions of French and Italian Renaissance lute music. There are three Suites in all, composed in 1917, 1924 and 1932 respectively. The Third Suite is scored for strings only and includes "Airs of the Court" by Jean-Baptiste Besard, a stirring Passacaglia (a sort of theme with variations) by Ludovico Roncalli and various pieces by anonymous composers, including a popular song and a Siciliana.

Philharmonia Hungarica/ Antál Dorati

Mercury analogue

A famous recording made in 1958 by a fine band of expatriot Hungarian musicians who subsequently went on to record all of Haydn's symphonies. The performances are supple, keen-edged and rhythmically alert and the sound itself closely balanced (very much in Mercury's familiar recording style).

Béla Bartók (1881-1945)

Concerto for Orchestra (1943-45)

Bartók's ground-plan was to provide the Boston Symphony Orchestra (whose conductor, Serge Koussevitzky, commissioned the piece) with a showcase concerto that would allow its players to shine. It was Bartók's last orchestral work, and still ranks as his most popular. Taken as a whole, the *Concerto for Orchestra* is probably the nearest Bartók came to writing a fully-fledged symphony. The first movement is immensely purposeful, the second a playful "Game of Pairs", the third an intense elegy, the fourth takes a pot-shot at Shostakovich's wartime *Leningrad Symphony* (which Bartók hated) and the finale is a joyous amalgam of folk-style tunes and vivid orchestral colours.

Chicago Symphony Orchestra/ Fritz Reiner

RCA analogue

Fritz Reiner, a friend of Bartók, helped to secure the Boston commission and his Chicago Symphony interpretation has a charisma that's reminiscent of Koussevitzky himself (whose interpretation is preserved via an old broadcast). Brilliant, refined and keenly inflected, it still sweeps the field – although Herbert Blomstedt's San Francisco recording (Decca) serves as a beautifully considered digital alternative.

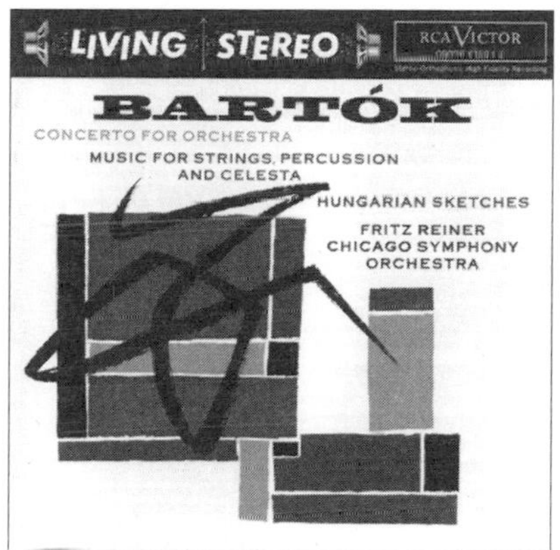

Dance Suite, Sz77 (1923)

Right from the opening 'growl' (tuba, piano, bassoon, cellos, double-basses and side-drum), you can sense that this is going to be something very special. And although the *Dance Suite* was originally composed to mark the 50th Anniversary of the unification of Buda with Pest, its range of influences includes motives based on Arabic, Slovakian and Romanian musics as well as Hungarian. The dances themselves are by turns darky insinuating, frisky, tense and riotously exciting – each being joined by a lyrical returning theme, or 'ritornello'.

Philharmonia Hungarica/ Antál Dorati

Mercury analogue

Dorati's pacing is uniquely authoritative, whether in the stealthy first dance, or in the wild syncopations that introduce the finale. He recorded the Dance Suite twice with Philharmonia Hungarica, but this version – the earlier of the two (the other was for Philips, analogue) – generates the most tension. Viable options include Sir Georg Solti and the

Orchestral works Suites, dances, etc (1733-1991)

Chicago Symphony (Decca digital) and the Berlin RIAS Orchestra under Ferenc Fricsay (DG, mono).

Divertimento, Sz113 (1939)
Although notably Hungarian in spirit, Bartók's string-orchestra masterpiece recalls the *concerto grosso* style of various Baroque composers (i.e. by having a small of group of strings enter into active dialogue with the full string band). The boisterous first movement exploits this technique to the full, whereas the *Molto adagio* has a tense, nightmarish quality that recalls the *Music for strings, percussion and celesta* (see below) and the finale is in the manner of a Hungarian dance (with an hilarious send-up of a Classical minuet towards its close).

BBC Symphony Orchestra/ Antál Dorati
Mercury analogue

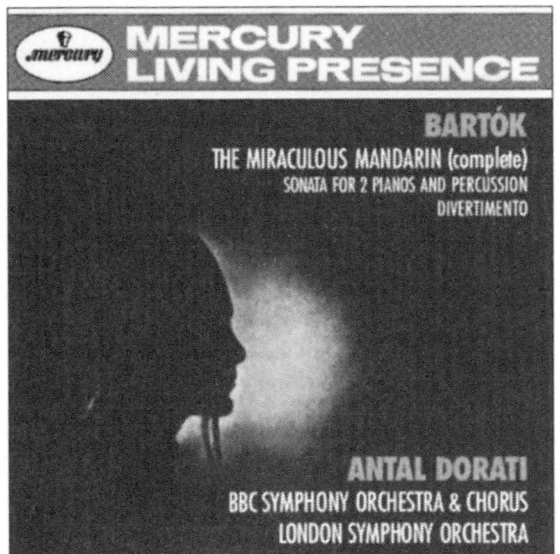

Rhythmically taut, incisively played (as per Dorati's usual manner with Bartók) and clearly - if rather drily - recorded. Good digital rivals include Pierre Boulez (DG) and Sir Georg Solti (Decca), though connoisseurs of stylish Bartók conducting will want to own a famous Berlin recording under the composer's noted compatriot Ferenc Fricsay (DG, mono).

Music for strings, percussion and celesta, Sz106 (1936)
Two groups of strings in taut dialogue, with piano, celesta and percussion to spice the action. The first movement is a mysterious canon, the second an urgent *Allegro*, the third - another slow movement - features eerily sliding strings and a ferocious climax and the fourth is a suite in itself that juxtaposes a whole sequence of Eastern European-style dance rhythms. *Music for strings, percussion and celesta* is a lean, highly atmospheric musical drama, a mite strange at first perhaps, but indelibly memorable.

Chicago Symphony Orchestra/ Fritz Reiner
RCA analogue
Although Reiner knew Bartók and championed his music, he didn't actually conduct this work until the month in which he recorded it - December 1958. It's a thrilling performance: dynamic and incisive, while the sound remains astonishingly lifelike. Other notable versions include a stunning (if occasionally fallible) live performance under Evgeny Mravinsky (Praga, analogue) and a fine digital version, also from Chicago, under Sir Georg Solti (Decca).

Zoltán Kodály (1882-1967)

Dances of Galánta (1933)
A colourful sequence of dances, some slow and melancholy, others fast and fiery. Galánta is a village in Pozsony in Hungary where Kodály and his family lived towards the end of the last century and it was there that he heard the playing of some famous gipsy bands. Later in life he utilized some of what he heard (Hungarian folk tunes as played by the gipsies), prompted by his discovery of a printed volume of melodies "after several gipsies from Galánta".

Dances of Marosszék (1930)
Similar in style to the *Dances of Galánta*, the *Marosszék* Dances were orchestrated for the great Italian conductor Arturo Toscanini from a work that was originally composed for solo piano. It was Toscanini who conducted the world première in 1930. Kodály drew his material from traditional tunes that he had collected in the Marosszék district (which is located between the Maros and Szamos Rivers).

Budapest Festival Orchestra/ Iván Fischer
Hungaroton digital
While some conductors treat these dances as orchestral showpieces, Fischer and his players perform them with genuine gipsy-style abandon - not too quickly and with real swagger. The recordings are good though fairly dry but there's compelling analogue rivalry from Antál Dorati (Mercury, in both sets of Dances), Ferenc Friscay (DG mono, in the Marosszék Dances) and Fritz Reiner (Sony mono, in the Galánta Dances).

Háry János Suite: Op. 15 (1927)
Háry János is a sort of Hungarian Don Quixote, boastful but loveable and full of tall stories. Kodály's *Singspiel* (ballad opera) tells how he tames wild horses, captures Napoleon, rescues a princess from a dragon but still remains faithful to his 'local' beloved. The Suite from the opera (of Kodály's own making) features six varied movements, including an ingenious, percussion-led "Viennese Musical Clock", the "Battle and Defeat of Napoleon", a vigorous (and famous) Intermezzo and a resplendent "Entrance of the Emperor and his Court".

Orchestral works Suites, dances, etc (1733-1991)

 ***London Symphony Orchestra/ István Kertész***

Belart analogue

Keenly played, vividly engineered (though there's a small degree of tape hiss) and characterfully conducted – but if you'd prefer to experience the whole work (a very worthwhile diversion), then try Decca's dazzling 1968 (analogue) recording, again with Kertész and the LSO, featuring a virtuoso, multi-role performance by Peter Ustinov. Sir Georg Solti's Chicago recording of the Suite (Decca, again) leads the digital field.

Anton Webern (1883-1945)

Five Pieces for small orchestra, Op. 10 (1911-13)

At just 19 seconds, the fourth of these highly condensed miniatures is probably the shortest work in the entire orchestral literature. The longest of the five, however, is the third, with its gently pulsing accompaniment and twinkling celesta – rather like a brief musical reflection on timelessness. Played as a whole, Op. 10 lasts for something in the region of four-and-a-quarter minutes. In addition to standard instruments the scoring includes a harmonium, a guitar, a mandolin and sheep bells.

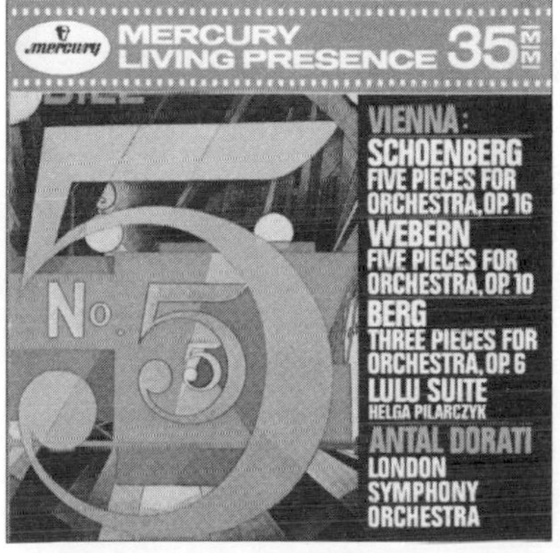

 ***London Symphony Orchestra/ Antál Dorati***

Mercury analogue

Dorati gauges the pulse of each piece with great expertise and Mercury's engineers capture every strand of Webern's subtle scoring. However, Webern responds particularly well to the quiet background afforded by digital technology and I would also recommend more recent digital recordings by Abbado (see below) and Boulez (both on DG).

Six Pieces for large orchestra, Op. 6 (1909)

Dedicated "in greatest love" to Arnold Schoenberg, "teacher and friend", Webern's *Six Pieces* have virtually every note painted in a different colour. They're rather more accessible than the *Five Pieces* of Op. 10, with a long (by Webern's standards) Funeral March placed fourth. Here tension is maintained through an artful control of timbre and dynamics, while the climax is colossal – certainly if heard live or in a good digital recording. If you don't as yet know any Webern, this is one of the better places to start.

 ***Vienna Philharmonic Orchestra/Claudio Abbado***

Deutsche Grammophon digital

Deutsche Grammophon effect an immense dynamic curve – especially in the Funeral March – while Abbado's ear for textural detail inspires a reading that combines clarity and warmth. The CD also includes a fine performance of the Five Pieces, Op. 10 (see above).

Alban Berg (1885-1935)

Three Orchestral Pieces, Op. 6 (1914-15)

One step beyond the bleakest moments in Mahler's Ninth Symphony, opening on a dark sigh of un-pitched percussion, and ending with a huge, gnarled march. Berg's *Three Orchestral Pieces* are complex, self-absorbed and cast in the most amazing array of tonal colours. Brass and lower strings have a field day, although there's plenty of delicacy and numerous pointers towards the nearby world of dramatic film music.

Vienna Philharmonic Orchestra/Claudio Abbado

Deutsche Grammophon digital

Abbado's second DG recording of the Three Orchestral Pieces (his first was with the LSO) has the benefit of an orchestra supremely suited to the job: cellos in particular project a glorious body of tone, while brass and percussion jump out at you with terrifying dynamism. The performance is both beautifully balanced and extraordinarily exciting.

Eric Coates (1886-1957)

London Suite (1932)

A sparkling evocation of London during the 1920s and 1930s, first with "Covent Garden" and a warming recollection of *Cherry Ripe*, then among the Elgarian strains of "Westminster" (Big Ben sounding close to hand) and lastly, the bustling excitement of "Knightsbridge". Make no mistake, Coates's nationalistic masterpiece is fully on a par with the best light music of Dvořák or Johann Strauss.

 ***London Philharmonic Orchestra/ Eric Coates***

Conifer mono

Another example of the composer's own recording topping the list. With spot-on playing, clear (albeit) constricted sound and a genuine sense of period, Coates' own London

Orchestral works Suites, dances, etc (1733-1991)

Suite is a sure-fire winner. But if it has to be stereo, then Sir Charles Groves (Classics for Pleasure) provides a warm-hearted alternative.

Sergey Prokofiev (1891-1953)

Lieutenant Kijé – concert suite from the film score, Op. 60 (1934)

Although *Lieutenant Kijé* started life as a film score (1933), its five relatively short movements are descriptive enough to survive their divorce from the screen. The vivacious "Troika" is the best-known, but the most ingenious is "The Death of Kijé" where various themes heard earlier in the Suite cross each other like wistful images in a dream.

 ***Chicago Symphony Orchestra/Claudio Abbado***

Deutsche Grammophon analogue

Abbado's Kijé has always served as a hi-fi demonstration disc and its analogue status certainly doesn't detract from its sonic impact. The performance itself is both sensitive and rumbustious although there are a few others that are equally worth noting (all analogue – though none of them quite so well recorded as Abbado) under, respectively, Fritz Reiner (also Chicago, RCA), Erich Leinsdorf (Boston, also RCA) and George Szell (Sony).

Scythian Suite, Op. 20 (1915)

Subtitled "Ala and Lolli", the *Scythian Suite* – a Diaghilev commission that never saw the stage – tells of an ancient slave warrior who saves the sun-god Ala from darkness. The music combines a sense of ritual with uncompromising violence, the second movement being a ferocious "Dance of the Spirits of Darkness", the coruscating finale, "The Glorious Departure of Lolli and the Sun's Procession".

 ***Chicago Symphony Orchestra/Claudio Abbado***

Deutsche Grammophon analogue

Again, Abbado and the Chicago Orchestra come up trumps with a performance of rare brilliance and virtuosity, stunningly well recorded. If, however, you fancy an even more incisive (mono) alternative, try and track down Karel Ančerl's live Czech broadcast (Czech Philharmonic, Praga) – surely the most riveting Scythian Suite on disc.

Arthur Lourié (1892-1966)

A Little Chamber Music (1924)

A pungent, harmonically adventurous essay, just eight minutes in length and that anticipates – sometimes in astonishing stylistic detail – the lean, Neo-Classical world of Stravinsky's *Apollo* ballet of four years later (see "Puppets and Pagans"). Lourié was a musical beacon for Russian Futurism before the First World War, but left for the West in 1922 and subsequently became a 'non-person' in his homeland. *A Little Chamber Music* was composed in Paris and Wiesbaden (where our recommended recording was made) and is one of the great unknown masterpieces of early twentieth-century music.

 ***Thomas Klug (violin), Deutsche Kammerphilharmonie/Gidon Kremer***

Deutsche Grammophon digital

Further evidence of Kremer's devotion to the lesser-known byways of twentieth-century music, superbly played, brilliantly recorded and included as part of a fascinating all-Lourié programme. The disc also features Lourié's setting of T. S. Eliot's "Little Gidding" and his Concerto da Camera.

Peter Warlock (1894-1930)

Capriol Suite (1926)

A delicious cross-breed of sixteenth-century dance tunes and twentieth-century musical sensibilities. It was in 1926 that Peter Warlock (the pseudonym of Philip Heseltine) was invited to contribute a preface for a translation of Thoinot Arbeau's *Orchesography* (a treatise on the art of dancing set out in the form of a dialogue between the author and his pupil, Capriol). Warlock's *Capriol Suite* uses several of Arbeau's dance tunes.

 ***Guildhall String Ensemble/ Robert Salter***

RCA digital

An extremely alert performance that underlines the odd little quirks in Warlock's subtle re-workings of Arbeau's tunes. The recording, too, is quite superb, but there are plenty of good alternatives around – not least a famous analogue recording by the Academy of St Martin in the Fields under Sir Neville Marriner (Decca).

Paul Hindemith (1895-1963)

Concert Music for brass and strings (1931)
Anyone who has visited the vast open-air music shed at Tanglewood, near Boston Massachusetts can imagine how this hugely sonorous essay – which was actually composed for Koussevitzky and the Boston Symphony – must sound like in that expansive acoustical environment. It's a fabulous piece: grand, extrovert and beautifully crafted. There are two movements, each of which are subdivided – the first into fastish and slow, the second into fast, slow and fast.

 ***San Francisco Symphony Orchestra/Herbert Blomstedt***
Decca digital

Charting the varied course of Hindemith's Concert Music – with its vivid alternations of sombre and bright, fast and slow – demands secure direction from the rostrum, fine orchestral playing and high quality sound. Blomstedt, the San Francisco Symphony and Decca provide all three in abundance, though it would be unfair to forget William Steinberg's superb analogue Boston Symphony recording (DG) or Hindemith's own 1955 recording with the Philharmonia (EMI analogue).

Duke (Edward Kennedy) Ellington (1099-1974)

Black, Brown and Beige – Suite for jazz band (1942-43)
Who knows what the current complexion of American serious music would be had the musical establishment encouraged Duke Ellington to follow the path of his *Black, Brown and Beige* (which Ellington himself called "a parallel to the history of the American Negro") – an astonishing work, as probing, sophisticated and profoundly beautiful as any music of the period. But a large proportion of the American press thought Ellington was being over-ambitious. The recording – made some 11 months after the première – is a 'pared down' version of the Suite and consists of "Work Song", "Come Sunday", "The Blues" and "Three Dances".

 ***Duke Ellington and his Orchestra***
RCA mono
The ultimate 'authentic' performance, naturally responsive to every heart-rending modulation, every rhythmic 'kick' in what should rightly be considered a seminal twentieth-century masterpiece. Ellington went on to record it again (for Sony) and there is the US Prestige CD release of the first performance, replete with Ellington's own introduction and a good deal of music excised from the Suite (44 minutes as opposed to the Suite's 18!).

Olivier Messiaen (1908-1992)

Éclairs sur l'au-delà (1987-91)
An inspirational monument, and one of the greatest orchestral compositions of the post-war period. *Éclairs sur l'au-delà* ("Illuminations of the Beyond") was Messiaen's last completed major work; it encapsulates all his strongest stylistic attributes, whether in the broadly spaced, monolithic gestures of "Apparition of Christ in Glory" or the timeless serenity of "Abide in Love". Messiaen employs an orchestra of nearly 130 players and yet the end result is both extraordinarily transparent and unexpectedly accessible. There are 11 varied movements that play for around 65 minutes.

 ***Orchestra of the Opera Bastille/ Myung-Whun Chung***
Deutsche Grammophon digital

A rival (live) recording by the Katowice Radio Symphony Orchestra under Antoni Wit (Jade, digital) is marginally more ethereal, but Chung's superb performance has superior brass and a bolder tonal profile.

Witold Lutosławski (1913-1994)

Concerto for Orchestra (1950-54)
The opening Intrada – a gritty, gangland-style processional – suggests the influence of Bartók, although subsequent episodes are highly original. There's a feather-light, spectral Scherzo and a closing "Passacaglia,

Toccata e Corale", the theme for which is first stated on a plucked double-bass (strings enter quietly and a solo piano gives the odd growl) and then makes its way through the whole orchestra. The theme is repeated no less than 18 times and the cumulative effect is very exciting. The *Concerto for Orchestra* is Lutosławski's earliest masterpiece.

Symphony Orchestra of the National Philharmonic, Warsaw/Witold Rowicki

Philips analogue

Although there have been numerous digital recordings of the Concerto for Orchestra (including worthy versions by Dohnányi on Decca and Barenboim on Erato), Rowicki's remains the most natural and, in many ways, the most compelling. It was recorded in 1964 and there is an alternative transfer on Muza/Olympia.

Baroque models (1620-1747)

'Chamber music' is one of the most widely-misunderstood terms in the so-called classical repertory – primarily because the actual word 'chamber' suggests amateurism or dull domesticity. The Australian composer Percy Grainger preferred 'room music', but even that hardly does credit to a corpus of work that – at its best – boasts at least as much incident, subtlety, passion and inventiveness as, say, symphonic or operatic music. We start our survey among some of the earliest examples of music employing relatively small groups of instrumentalists.

Orlando Gibbons (1583-1625)

Fantasias in three parts (*c*1620)

The sixteenth-century English composer Thomas Morley described the 'fantasy' as "the most principal and chiefest kind of music which is made without a ditty" (*Plain and Easy Introduction to Practical Music* – 1597) and Gibbons' *Fantasias* exhibit a mastery of the medium, with much contrapuntal interplay, surprising dissonances, variations, changing time signatures, fetching dance rhythms, and so on. But above all, they provide an oddly moreish listening experience.

Fretwork (six viol players)

Virgin Veritas digital

A homogeneous blend of tones, beautifully recorded and a fine programme that includes, in addition to the three-part Fantasias, Fantasias in two, four and six parts, plus organ solos, a three-part Galliard and both parts of "The Cries of London" (with Red Byrd) – an amusing and evocative work that incorporates London street cries.

Johann Pachelbel (1653-1706)

Canon and Gigue in D major (late-1600s)

The German composer and organist Johann Pachelbel was notably prolific (his output included around 70 organ chorales and 95 *Magnificat* fugues), but it is this delightful *Canon* – a musical form where each re-statement of the tune begins before the previous one has finished – that has become synonymous with his name. It gives ample scope for nifty team-work, whereas the light-hearted *Gigue* provides a skipping encore in a similar vein.

Musica Antiqua Köln/ Reinhard Goebel

Archiv analogue

Most versions of the "Canon and Gigue" (Karajan on DG, Leppard on Sony, Marriner on Philips, etc – all analogue – not to mention countless CDs that feature the Canon on its own) are for a conventional modern-instrument band, but Goebel's is a vivacious period-instrument alternative, stylishly embellished, brilliantly played and very well recorded.

Henry Purcell (1659-1695)

15 Fantasias (1680)

Any well-to-do sixteenth- or seventeenth-century English musical household might have possessed a chest of viols. Chamber music was in those days a peculiarly British province and Purcell's wonderful *Fantasias* – the last works to be composed for a viol consort – incorporate references to another English musical master, John Dowland. The *Fantasias* are at once intimate, profound and powerfully compelling as a cumulative musical experience.

Concentus Musicus Wien/ Nikolaus Harnoncourt

Archiv analogue

Not all pioneering early music sessions stand up to present-day critical scrutiny, but Harnoncourt's concentrated, intensely-voiced set of the Fantasias is one of the few that does. With intimate sound, clear internal textures and beautifully tapered phrasing, these 1963 recordings still prove highly competitive. An excellent digital alternative is provided by Jordi Savall (Astrée).

Johann Sebastian Bach
(1685-1750)

The Art of Fugue, BWV1080 (*c*1745-50)

Bach's sublimely harmonious *Art of Fugue* marks the culmination of a life-long preoccupation with counterpoint, although it is doubtful whether Bach ever intended the work to be performed in public. And it certainly wasn't an instant hit: in the first five years after the composer's death, only 30 copies of the printed edition were sold. But listening to it now, we cannot but marvel at the humbling impact of its multi-layered textures.

Juilliard String Quartet

Sony Classical digital

Being a great work of theory as well as a great work of art, BWV1080 offers countless performing options – from solo organ or piano to orchestra, wind band and string quartet. The Juilliard's great virtues are tonal warmth, internal clarity and an unstinting level of concentration. The crowning Contrapunctus XIV is left as it was, unfinished – but the Juilliards also include Bach's last chorale, "I herewith step before thy throne".

Musical Offering BWV1079 (1747)

Summoned to the Court of Frederick the Great, Bach was asked to improvise *fantasias* on various of the King's 15 keyboard fortepianos. The King then obliged Bach by providing a 'Royal Theme' that "the greatest organ and keyboard virtuoso in Germany" immediately built into a three-part fugue. Bach's noble offering to Frederick the Great consists of two magnificent *Ricercars* (literally, to 'look' or 'search for' – a form of fugal composition), *Canons* on the Royal Theme and a splendid *Trio Sonata* for flute, violin and harpsichord.

Barthold Kuijken (flute), Sigiswald Kuijken (violin), Wieland Kuijken (viola da gamba), Robert Kohnen (harpsichord)

Deutsche Harmonia Mundi digital

A supremely natural period-instrument performance, beautifully recorded. Those with a taste for 'orchestral' Bach might like to try Igor Markevitch's highly imaginative re-creation (EMI, mono), while Karl Münchinger and the Stuttgart Chamber Orchestra (Decca, analogue) provide the most musical modern-instrument alternative. Recordings of the Musical Offering tend to vary considerably in terms of chosen instrumentation (there are many theories as to what sounds best and why) – so read the notes carefully, and sample before you buy.

On equal terms (1784-1975)

Had space permitted, I would have launched this particular section with some of Bach's memorable sonatas for violin or cello (viola da gamba) and keyboard. As it is, we run the gamut from classically-crafted Mozart and Beethoven (where the centre of musical interest is as much with the piano as with its string-instrument colleague) to the intensely private narratives of Prokofiev and Shostakovich.

Wolfgang Amadeus Mozart
(1756-1791)

Violin Sonata No. 32 in B flat major, K454 (1784)

Mozart composed this grand sonata in the spring of 1784 when he met the violinist Regina Strinasacchi, a native of Mantua. "She has a great deal of taste and feeling in her playing," wrote Mozart, who performed the piano part from memory (he hadn't had time to write it down!). Aside from a noble *Largo* introduction and an especially ebullient first-movement *Allegro*, the Sonata is distinguished by a very fine *Andante*, one of Mozart's loveliest.

Jascha Heifetz (violin), Brooks Smith (piano)

RCA mono

Heifetz had that rare ability to infuse each phrase with a wealth of expressive meaning without bending the musical line. This was his second recording of the B flat major Sonata (his first, made in 1936 [Biddulph or RCA], is a little sweeter but marginally less assertive) and features some of the most stylish classical fiddle-playing on disc. However, Arthur Grumiaux and Clara Haskil (Philips, mono) offer a more balanced artistic partnership.

Violin Sonata No. 33 in E flat major, K481 (1785)

The opening *Molto allegro* represents Mozart at his most confident and fluent, while 4'07" into the same movement (on our recommended recording) there is an unmistakable anticipation of the *Jupiter* Symphony's finale. The *Adagio* is marked by breathtaking key changes and the finale – a set of variations – by an effortless stream of inventiveness.

Violin Sonata No. 35 in A major, K526 (1787)

The late A major Violin Sonata – possibly Mozart's finest work in the genre – is distinguished by considerable contrapuntal ingenuity, an especially virtuosic violin part and tremendous nervous energy (it was composed at around the same time as the opera *Don Giovanni*). The *Andante* has been compared with the finest slow movements in the great "Haydn" Quartets (see "Classical Quartets") and the finale is an exciting and brilliantly written *Presto*.

Arthur Grumiaux (violin), Walter Klien (piano)

Philips digital

Grumiaux as captured on tape towards the end of his distinguished career. The tone is characteristically 'pastel-shaded', the manner of phrasing infinitely subtle and the musicianship immaculate. These recordings are presented as part of a systematic survey of Mozart's mature violin sonatas and have the added advantage of Walter Klien's estimable pianistic artistry. Grumiaux's strongest rival is his younger self, with the great Clara Haskil as pianist (also on Philips, though in mono).

Ludwig van Beethoven
(1770–1827)

Cello Sonata No. 3 in A major, Op. 69 (1807–08)

One of Beethoven's most mellifluously melodious works, dedicated to his cellist friend Baron Ignaz von Gleichenstein. Although the Sonata is contemporary with the heroically gesturing Fifth Symphony, the Scherzo's central section is more anticipatory of the first movement of the Seventh (also in the key of A major), while the finale's principal theme recalls the Seventh String Quartet of a couple of years earlier.

Emanuel Feuermann (cello), Dame Myra Hess (piano)

EMI mono

Feuermann's seamless phrasing is a miracle to behold, while his tone is both firm and seductively warm. Superbly partnered by Dame Myra Hess, this great yet ill-fated cellist (he wasn't yet 40 when he died) is an ideal interpreter of Beethoven's best-known Cello Sonata, although Casals (EMI, Pearl, mono) and Rostropovich (with Sviatoslav Richter on Philips, analogue) are also excellent.

Cello Sonata No. 5 in D major, Op. 102 No. 2 (1815)

Beethoven dedicated his final two – and possibly greatest – cello sonatas to the quartet cellist Joseph Lincke. Although the Fourth (Op. 102 No. 1) is an extraordinarily fine piece, the sheer dynamism of the Fifth's opening movement is especially arresting, while its mysterious *Adagio* (the only true slow movement in the series) spells 'late' Beethoven in every bar. The powerful finale is a fairly rigorous fugue.

Mstislav Rostropovich (cello), Sviatoslav Richter (piano)

Philips analogue

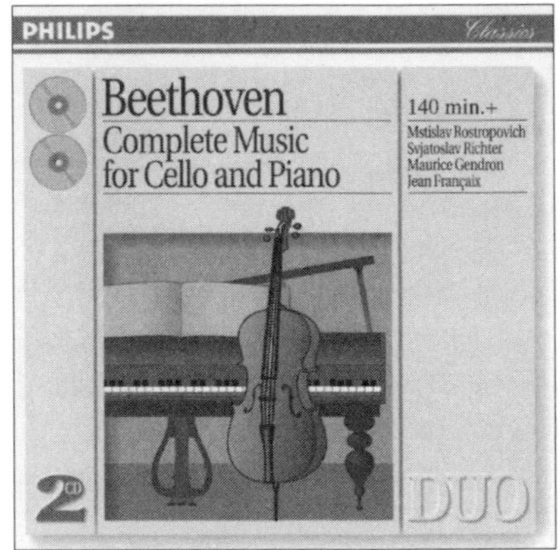

The combination of Rostropovich's full tone and Richter's intelligent though muscular pianism particularly suit this most intransigent of Beethoven's cello sonatas. Fine analogue options (in all the sonatas) include Pierre Fournier with Kempff (DG, analogue), Gulda (DG, analogue) or Schnabel (EMI, mono), Erling Bløndal Bengtsson with Anke Blyme (Danacord, analogue) and János Starker and György Sebok (Erato, analogue).

Violin Sonata No. 4 in A minor, Op. 23 (1800)

Beethoven's earliest violin sonatas are, for the most part, lyrical and elegantly tailored (the first three form a single opus, Op. 12). The A minor is an urgent, fast-moving work –

certainly the darkest of the first four, with a tense opening *Presto*, a playful (almost tongue-in-cheek) *Andante* and a pensive finale.

Arthur Grumiaux (violin), Clara Haskil (piano)

Philips mono

A wonderful partnership, and an appropriately lean performance of this particular sonata. Like most of my Beethoven violin sonata recommendations, this one comes from a highly distinguished complete cycle. Grumiaux's tone is expressive yet never over-sweet, while Haskil supports him with the utmost poise and finesse. Heifetz (RCA, mono) provides a roughly contemporaneous option (and a very exciting one), while Gidon Kremer and Martha Argerich (DG, digital) generate a high a level of tension.

Violin Sonata No. 5 in F major, Op. 24, "Spring" (1801)

Like so many of Beethoven's most appealing works, the *Spring* Sonata took time to germinate (note, by the way, that it's in F major – the same key as the *Pastoral* Symphony). It is also the first of the violin sonatas to be cast in four movements – in this case, a winsome opening *Allegro* (with a winding, song-like opening theme), an *Andante cantabile* in variation form, a saucy little Scherzo (it plays for a mere minute or so) and a bright closing *Allegro*.

Jascha Heifetz (violin), Emanuel Bay (piano)

RCA mono

Heifetz's celebrated 'speaking' tone (the sort you habitually encounter on vintage American film soundtracks) is particularly suited to the opening movement, while the Scherzo is thrown off with great aplomb. Violinistically, you'd be hard put to beat this performance although Gidon Kremer and Martha Argerich (DG digital) parade a more equal partnership.

Violin Sonata No. 7 in C minor, Op. 30 No. 2 (1801-02)

The C minor is to the 'middle' violin sonatas what the A minor (No. 4) is to their youthful predecessors, a swirling 'storm' after the sunnier climes of the *Spring* Sonata (its predecessor bar one). The richly harmonized slow movement draws an almost Mahlerian sigh (especially in its opening measures), while – as with the *Spring* Sonata – there's a cheeky Scherzo, rather longer this time and with mischievous, mock-dramatic fanfares.

Adolf Busch (violin), Rudolf Serkin (piano)

EMI mono

The leader of the fêted Busch Quartet as heard with his regular duo-partner (and subsequent son-in-law) Rudolf Serkin. They made numerous recordings together, of which this is one of the most distinguished: a passionate, highly animated account, tightly controlled yet with plenty of expressive inflexion. Joseph Szigeti and Claudio Arrau (recorded live, Vanguard, mono) provide a perceptive alternative while Gidon Kremer and Martha Argerich (DG, digital) combine thoughtfulness with impressive spontaneity.

Violin Sonata No. 9 in A major, Op. 47, "Kreutzer" (1803)

Beethoven himself described this Sonata as "written in a very *concertante* [concertizing] manner, almost like a concerto". Written at breakneck speed, the *Kreutzer* (named after its dedicatee, the Frenchman Rodolphe Kreutzer) opens with an imposing slow introduction before launching into a particularly fierce *Allegro* (albeit one that's frequently interrupted by reflective slow passages). There's an expansive, theme and variations second movement and a turbulent, dance-like *Presto* to close.

Gidon Kremer (violin), Martha Argerich (piano)

Deutsche Grammophon digital

A tremendous performance, full of 'storm and stress' yet with some ravishingly beautiful soft playing (much the same can be said about the rest of the Kremer/Argerich cycle). There are numerous historic alternatives, not least an elemental reading by violinist Bronislaw Huberman and pianist Ignaz Friedman (Biddulph, mono), two star musicians of the pre-war period whose combined personalities created aural lightning. Every self-respecting Beethovenian should hear it.

Violin Sonata No. 10 in G major, Op. 96 (1812)

Beethoven's last violin sonata is also his subtlest and suggests calm composure, even a certain sense of nostalgia. Like the Fifth and Seventh Sonatas, it features a Scherzo – in this case a witty, off-the-cuff outgrowth of the glorious *Adagio espressivo* slow movement. However, the biggest surprise comes in the closing variations where, quite without precedent, Beethoven slows the pace for an other-worldly *Adagio* and a brief reflection on the slow movement.

Joseph Szigeti (violin), Claudio Arrau (piano)
Vanguard Classics mono
Two musical thinkers engaged in genuine dialogue, a classic of its kind although the recording (taken from a live 1944 broadcast of the complete cycle) is rather murky. Kremer (DG digital), Heifetz (RCA, mono) and Grumiaux (with Clara Haskil – Philips, mono) provide fine alternatives.

Franz Schubert (1797-1828)

Fantasy in C major for violin and piano, D934 (1827)

A strange yet compelling piece that alternates boisterousness with passages of incandescent beauty. The main body of the *Fantasy* is a set of variations on Schubert's song *Sei mir gegrüst!* ("I greet you!"), while the joyful finale is prefaced by a recapitulation of the opening theme (cast very much in the manner of Schubert's ethereal 'late' style) and one of the most thrilling transition-passages in the chamber music repertory. Schubert's C major *Fantasy* is the greatest Classical-Romantic work for violin and piano after Beethoven's mature sonatas.

Adolf Busch (violin), Rudolf Serkin (piano)
Pearl mono
For Adolf Busch and Rudolf Serkin, classical poise, expressive warmth and inner vitality were major interpretative priorities. This particular performance is probably their finest on disc. As to rivals, Gidon Kremer and Valery Afanassiev (DG digital), Max Rostal and Colin Horsley (Symposium, mono) and Jascha Heifetz with Brooks Smith (RCA, analogue) are among the most impressive.

Fantasie in F minor for piano duet, D940 (1828)

One of a sequence of masterpieces that crown Schubert's final year. It was dedicated to his former pupil the Countess Caroline Esterházy and suggests, at least in its gently imploring opening idea, a confessional narrative. Cast in four sections that play without a break, the *Fantasie* is also extraordinarily dramatic (try the beginning of the *Largo*), with an assertive Scherzo and a finale that ends in a mood of tortured defiance.

Anne Queffélec and Imogen Cooper (piano duet)
Erato analogue

A performance that acknowledges the Fantasie's emotional weight without compromising its structure. This version is currently available as part of a set which includes all of Schubert's greatest piano duet music, but there's also an extraordinarily dramatic reading by Leonid Hambro and Jascha Zayde (MCA, analogue) and Music & Arts have issued an especially perceptive performance by Benjamin Britten and Sviatoslav Richter (analogue – and not universally available).

César Franck (1822-1890)

Violin Sonata in A major (1886)

Possibly the greatest of all Romantic violin sonatas, written for the composer, violinist and conductor Eugène Ysaÿe, who also gave the first performance (although, for most of the work, the piano is securely 'on top'). The opening movement ushers in a quietly conversational theme that prompts the pianist to respond with unprecedented grandeur. The *Allegro* second movement is mostly tempestuous, the third – a "Recitativo-fantasia" – suggests an impassioned operatic *scena*, while the finale opens to a long-breathed theme reminiscent of Fauré (and of the parallel movement in his First Violin Sonata – see below).

Arthur Grumiaux (violin), István Hajdu (piano)
Philips analogue
A Belgian himself (like the composer), Grumiaux always excelled in this Sonata. His elasticity of phrasing, subtly inflected tone and judicious choice of tempos are as natural as they are memorable and Hajdu proves a fine partner. Still, older masters also make their claims – not least Jacques Thibaud and Alfred Cortot (whose inspired account of the piano part has a breadth and passion that are second to none – Biddulph, mono), Jascha Heifetz and Brooks Smith (that's Heifetz's later [stereo] recording, on RCA, analogue) and Yehudi Menuhin with his sister Hephzibah (Biddulph, mono).

Johannes Brahms (1833-1897)

Cello Sonata No. 1 in E minor, Op. 38 (1862-65)

Brahms dedicated the first of his two cello sonatas to Josef Gänsbacher, but although the first two movements were written in 1862, the fugal finale wasn't completed until three years later. The E minor Sonata opens like a song: mellow, winding and introspective, whereas the second movement – a gentle Minuet – muses quietly and the finale is a fiery *Allegro*. It's a profoundly personal statement that yields its secrets only to its most persuasive interpreters.

János Starker (cello), György Sebok (piano)
Mercury analogue
One of at least four extant Starker recordings of the Brahms cello sonatas and possibly the best, not least because of Sebok's sympathetic piano playing (he also partners Starker on a rather earlier Erato recording). Starker's approach is lean, intense and appropriately intimate, though I would also recommend a warmly projected performance by Esther Nyffenegger on Divox (digital).

Cello Sonata No. 2 in F major, Op. 99 (1886)

The 'Eroica' of cello sonatas leaps from the speakers in a spirit of unprecedented boldness, at least in the first movement. The second plumbs the depths, especially during its poignant central episode, whereas the Scherzo is cast in Brahms's quizzical 'intermezzo' style and the finale suggests an unequivocally happy ending. Brahms had been enjoying congenial surroundings in Switzerland and was inspired to produce, in addition to this Sonata, his Second Violin Sonata (see below) and Third Piano Trio (see under "Three's a crowd", below).

Pablo Casals (cello), Mieczyslaw Horszowski (piano)
EMI mono
Casals lunges at the opening with the energy of a prize fighter, though the core of his performance – one of the greatest ever recorded – is an eloquently voiced account of the slow movement. The 1930s sound is still acceptable, though János Starker's more contained 1959 performance for Erato (analogue) has plenty to commend it. Starker's more lustrous first [mono] recording (with Abba Bogin on Saga) is also worth searching out.

Violin Sonata No. 1 in G major, Op. 78 (1878–79)

Possibly the finest of Brahms's violin sonatas (certainly the longest in terms of playing time) and an almost exact contemporary of the great Violin Concerto. The very opening is among the composer's most lyrical ideas, whereas the *Adagio* is deeply introspective (its closing pages, especially) and the finale quotes two of Brahms's songs, *Regenlied* – which is why the work is sometimes known as the *Regen* or "Rain" Sonata – and *Nachklang*.

Violin Sonata No. 2 in A major, Op. 100 (1886)

As in the First Sonata, song sits at the base of this work; the first movement's second idea reflects the beautiful Lied *Wie Melodien zieht es mir entgegen*. Another point of reference is at the very opening of the piece, which rather resembles the "Prize Song" from Wagner's opera *Die Meistersinger*. Lyrical in spirit and extremely concise, the revised Second Sonata features a soaring finale – though Brahms's first thoughts were far more expansive.

Violin Sonata No. 3 in D minor, Op. 108 (1886–88)

Premièred by Brahms and his great friend Joachim and dedicated to the conductor Hans von Bülow, the Third Sonata is a great favourite among virtuosos. Its earnest, driving spirit is evident right from the start although the noble *Adagio* is perhaps the most celebrated of Brahms's duo-sonata movements. The D minor Sonata is also the only one of the three that includes a Scherzo.

Isaac Stern (violin), Yefim Bronfman (piano)
Sony Classical digital
Warm, intimate readings, with a gently brushed violin tone from Stern and refreshingly direct piano playing from Bronfman. Viable analogue alternatives include an earlier set by Isaac Stern (fuller in tone than this digital remake, but musically rather less perceptive – with Alexander Zakin, also on Sony), while fine analogue versions by Arthur Grumiaux (Philips) and Josef Suk (Decca) stand alongside fiery historic recordings by Adolf Busch (EMI and Music & Arts, mono).

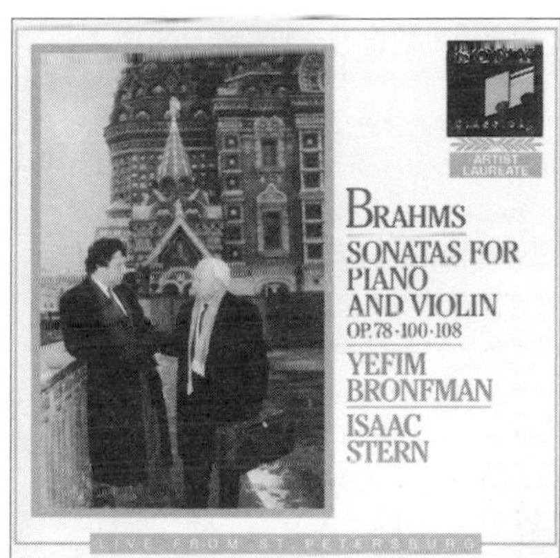

Gabriel Fauré (1845–1924)

Cello Sonata No. 2, Op. 117 (1921)

The tragic *Andante* second movement is a free transcription of a *Chant funèbre* that Fauré had previously composed to mark the centenary of the death of Napoleon I. It is among the most noble pages in all of Fauré (not unlike the famous *Elégie* in spirit, though sparer in tone), whereas the finale is an exhilarating, multi-coloured Scherzo. Fauré's two cello sonatas are late works that repay the most painstaking scrutiny.

Paul Tortelier (cello), Jean Hubeau (piano)

Erato analogue

It would be difficult to imagine finer performances than these (both cello sonatas are included on this CD, plus the Elégie). Tortelier gauges every bar with a sure instinct; his tone is warm, his phrasing 'inward' in precisely the right way. Jean Hubeau proves a quietly supportive partner and the 1962 recordings are first-rate.

Violin Sonata No. 1 in A major, Op. 13 (1875-76)

Fauré wrote his first chamber work while he was courting the daughter of Pauline Viardot (one of the great mezzos of the day) and it bespeaks an especially warm-hearted disposition. The opening *Allegro molto* is full of youthful passion; the *Andante* suggests melancholy reflection, the mischievous Scherzo features a sweet, song-like 'trio' section and the finale opens with one of the longest, most sinuous themes in the violinist's repertory.

Pierre Amoyal (violin), Pascal Rogé (piano)

Decca digital

Amoyal, a Heifetz pupil, combines Gallic charm with executive intensity while Rogé is among the most intuitively musical masters of French instrumental repertory. However, major historical forebears are very much of the essence, with Jacques Thibaud and Alfred Cortot leading the ranks (EMI, mono) and two recordings by Jascha Heifetz (both on RCA, mono) following close behind – the first (with Emanuel Bay, set down in 1936) being especially dynamic.

Claude Debussy (1862-1918)

Cello Sonata (1915)

Debussy himself is said to have provided the following programme: "Pierrot wakes up with a start and shakes himself violently. He runs off to serenade his lady love who, in spite of his supplications, remains indifferent to him. He consoles his lack of success by singing a freedom song." Debussy also insisted that "the pianist should never forget that he is not fighting the cello, but accompanying it". This is one of three late sonatas that would have become six (the fourth was to be scored for oboe, horn and harpsichord) had Debussy lived longer.

Paul Tortelier (cello), Jean Hubeau (piano)

Erato analogue

Tortelier and Hubeau invest the music's 11-minute course with a wealth of varied inflexion. It's a superb performance in every way (the disc also includes the two Fauré sonatas, see above).

Violin Sonata (1916-17)

Tragedy provides the subtext for this bittersweet though essentially playful masterpiece. Intended "as a secret, fervent tribute to the youth of France mown down by the scythe of war" (to quote Debussy's biographer Léon Vallas), the Sonata is – like the others in the series – dedicated to the composer's mother. Debussy himself gave the première (Gaston Poulet was the violinist) although he was by then critically ill with cancer. The Sonata sighs, cajoles, teases and reflects; it's a miracle of subtle musical suggestion and responds to a wide variety of interpretation.

Jascha Heifetz (violin), Emanuel Bay (piano)

RCA mono

I choose Heifetz because of his achingly beautiful tone and notably sophisticated phrasing. Heard purely as violin-playing, there's no one to touch him – although Arthur Grumiaux (either of his Philips recordings) and Joseph Szigeti (with Andor Foldes, Biddulph or with Béla Bartók, Vanguard or Hungaroton, mono) – both of them analogue – are also hugely distinctive. Jacques Thibaud and Alfred Cortot (EMI, Pearl or Biddulph, mono) offer the most strikingly characterful duo-partnership.

George Enescu (1881-1955)

Violin Sonata No. 3 in A minor, Op. 25, "dans le caractère populaire romain" (1926)

In the right hands, Enescu's Third Sonata sounds like organized improvisation. The themes have the unmistakable 'major-to-minor' flavour of gipsy music, although there's also plenty of muscle – especially in the last movement. It's a passionate, free-flowing piece, frequently touched by mystery and often redolent of similarly folk/ethnic-inspired works by Bartók and Bloch.

Yehudi Menuhin (violin), Hephzibah Menuhin (piano)

EMI mono

Recorded when Menuhin was 19 and still heavily influenced by Enescu's playing and personality, this benchmark performance is in a class of its own – though a slightly later rival where Enescu himself is partnered by Dinu Lipatti (Electrecord, mono – not as yet on CD) runs it pretty close. A tougher-grained version by Isaac Stern (Sony, analogue) offers a further perspective on a fine piece, but Menuhin's surging lyricism and intuitive understanding of Enescu's style pay the highest dividends.

Sergey Prokofiev (1891-1953)

Violin Sonata No. 1 in F minor, Op. 80 (1938-46)

One of Prokofiev's greatest compositions and a sobering reflection not only on the horrors of war but of crippling oppression under Stalin's rule. The musical material is shared evenly between the two players and features an austere first movement (one particular passage suggests, in Prokofiev's own words, the "wind in a graveyard"), a violent *Allegro brusco*, an ethereal but emotionally intense third movement and a fiery finale that finds time to re-visit material from earlier on in the work.

Vadim Repin (violin), Boris Berezovsky (piano)
Erato digital

Repin is one of the most gifted violinists of the younger generation, though he's no mere clone of David Oistrakh or Gidon Kremer (to mention just two of this sonata's most perceptive interpreters – the former on Praga or Melodiya, analogue, the latter on DG, digital). Repin's is a fairly intimate approach to a monumental score and contrasts well with the assertiveness of Berezovsky's piano playing. The recording is excellent.

Dmitry Shostakovich (1906-1975)

Viola Sonata, Op. 147 (1975)

As with the Fifteenth Symphony, the Viola Sonata – Shostakovich's last completed work – makes meaningful use of musical quotation. In this case it's the first movement of Beethoven's *Moonlight* Sonata, which haunts the Viola Sonata's final movement. Although predominantly mellow, the Sonata does incorporate a certain element of humour (the central *Allegretto*). It is dedicated to Feodor Druzhinin, the viola player of the Beethoven Quartet (could that be the reason for the *Moonlight* quotation?).

Shlomo Mintz (viola), Victoria Postnikova (piano)
Erato digital

A work such as this needs interpretative flexibility and a warm touch if it's to avoid sounding excessively stark. Mintz's performance is both tonally alluring and extraordinarily intense, while Postnikova gives him strong, though never over-bearing, pianistic support. The recording is superb – but one must not forget an impressive live performance (1985) by violist Yuri Bashmet and Sviatoslav Richter (MK, digital).

Three's a crowd (1788-1946)

A trio can denote any three performers playing together – either vocal or instrumental – but here refers mainly either to the string trio (violin, viola, cello) or the somewhat illogically named piano trio (piano, violin, cello). Again, the greatest trios feature music that quite transcends the modesty of the medium.

Wolfgang Amadeus Mozart (1756-1791)

Divertimento for string trio in E flat major, K563 (1788)

The greatest string trio of all, with only those of Beethoven and – many years later – Schoenberg falling anywhere near it in terms of quality. The *Divertimento* was composed in the wake of the last three symphonies; it is cast in six movements, with a glorious *Adagio*, a graceful finale and two Minuets flanking an *Andante* theme and variations. Although generally sunny in spirit, K563 has a sublime beauty that's as deeply affecting as virtually anything else in Mozart's output.

Jascha Heifetz (violin), William Primrose (viola), Emanuel Feuermann (cello)
RCA mono

Not just an old friend, but an indescribably eloquent performance – heartfelt, incisive and featuring string playing that has never been equalled (this particular recording was made back in 1941). The transfers from 78s are acceptable (a Biddulph transfer is virtually as good), but if stereo sound is required, there's a superb analogue recording by the Grumiaux Trio (Philips).

Ludwig van Beethoven
(1770-1827)

Piano Trio No. 5 in D major, Op. 70 No. 1, "Ghost" (1808)

Beethoven's Fifth Piano Trio opens with an extraordinarily high-powered *Allegro vivace e con brio*, its principal theme being one of the most unequivocally triumphant in Beethoven's output. The somewhat paradoxical *Ghost* title applies to the slow movement (where a ghostly atmosphere predominates), but high spirits return come the closing *Presto*.

 ***Stern-Rose-Istomin Trio***
Sony Classical analogue

Exciting isn't the word! Isaac Stern's regal threesome attacks the music with tremendous gusto and yet their handling of the central Largo could hardly be more sensitive. The present coupling is Op. 70's companion piece, in E flat major (No. 2), another masterpiece, one that features a particularly high quota of dramatic incident. Viable alternatives include a vintage performance led by Adolf Busch (also on Sony, mono) and the Beaux Arts Trio (Philips, analogue).

Piano Trio No. 7 in B flat major, Op. 97, "Archduke" (1811)

The title refers to the work's dedicatee, Archduke Rudolf of Austria. Musically, Op. 97 is Beethoven's greatest and most expansive piano trio. The amiable first movement is followed by a mischievous Scherzo; then there's a lengthy *Andante* (with variations) based on one of Beethoven's noblest melodies and a playfully tripping *Allegro* finale.

 ***Stern-Rose-Istomin Trio***
Sony Classical analogue

Wit and warmth predominate, while the three instruments are granted a very clear sound-stage. Currently this version is coupled with the full run of Beethoven's piano trios, but if you only require the Archduke you might like to consider either the Beaux Arts Trio (Philips, analogue) or the historic 1928 recording by Alfred Cortot, Jacques Thibaud and Pablo Casals (EMI, mono) – possibly the finest version on disc.

Franz Schubert (1797-1828)

Piano Trio No. 1 in B flat major, D898 (1827)

It was Robert Schumann who, after Schubert's death, wrote that "a glance at Schubert's [B flat] Trio and all miserable human commotion vanishes, and the world shines in new splendour". The opening theme is among the grandest in the repertoire, while the song-like second theme has the cello play the main theme to flowing piano triplets. However, the heart of the Trio is an *Andante* slow movement of such calm and beauty that it could almost stand on its own. The third movement is a light-hearted Scherzo and the finale an easygoing Rondo.

 ***Jacques Thibaud (violin), Pablo Casals (cello), Alfred Cortot (piano)***
EMI mono

Don't be put off by the 1926 recording date: this is among the most spontaneous, most lyrical and most profoundly eloquent chamber-music recordings ever made, and the sound – although undeniably constricted – is astonishingly good for the period. Major rivals include Heifetz, Feuermann and Rubinstein (RCA, mono), Schneider, Casals and Istomin (Sony, mono) and the Stern-Rose-Istomin Trio (Sony, analogue [stereo]). No modern recordings can quite rival any of these older versions.

Piano Trio No. 2 in E flat major, D929 (1827)

Schubert's relatively austere Second Trio is made of far sterner stuff than his First. The trenchant first movement suggests Beethovenian resolve (Schubert actually took part in a public performance of the Trio on the first anniversary of Beethoven's death), with a second theme reminiscent of the song-cycle *Winterreise* and the last String Quartet. The march-like second movement takes a side-glance at the *Great* C major Symphony (its ethereal principal theme is said to be based on a Swedish folk-song), whereas the gentle Scherzo is followed by a cheery, *echt*-Schubertian finale.

 ***Alexander Schneider (violin), Pablo Casals (cello), Mieczyslaw Horszowski (piano)***
Sony Classical mono

One of the most perceptive Schubert

recordings in the catalogue, distinguished by wistful playing from Casals and an especially poignant account of the second movement. There's strong rivalry from a famous pre-war recording by the Adolf Busch Trio (Pearl, EMI, mono), while the stereo field is well served by the Stern-Rose-Istomin Trio (Sony, analogue).

Robert Schumann (1810-1856)

Piano Trio No. 1 in D minor, Op. 63 (1847)

The D minor Trio's opening is among the most passionate pages in all of Schumann, while the ghostly chorale-theme that appears roughly half-way through the first movement (played, initially, by the cellist) is pure inspiration. A lighthearted Scherzo gives way to a typically introspective slow movement (again, the cello plays a major role) and a sunny, almost Mendelssohnian finale. Within weeks of completing this lovely work, Robert and Clara Schumann lost their youngest child.

 ***Beaux Arts Trio***
Philips digital

A very lucky work on disc. The Beaux Arts offer a typically stylish, well-balanced reading, sumptuously recorded, though it would be unfair to ignore a plethora of noteworthy alternatives – a fine performance from the 1970s, for example, led by pianist Jean Hubeau (Erato, analogue) or a classic 'oldie' with Jacques Thibaud (violin), Alfred Cortot (piano) and Pablo Casals (cello) – set down as long ago as 1928 but still as eloquently communicative as ever (Biddulph, EMI, mono). A 1952 (mono) Sony recording, also with Casals, is equally perceptive but rather less forceful.

Bedřich Smetana (1824-1884)

Piano Trio in G minor, B104 (1855, revised 1857)

A grand memorial for Smetana's second daughter Bedriska and a work of unprecedented emotional power. The passionate first movement is said to incorporate one of Bedriska's favourite tunes; there's a lively second movement with a tender trio and a fiery finale – again featuring a deeply nostalgic (and in this case almost Chopinesque) middle section. The G minor Trio ranks with the finest works in the medium and should be far better known.

 ***Guarneri Trio***
Supraphon digital

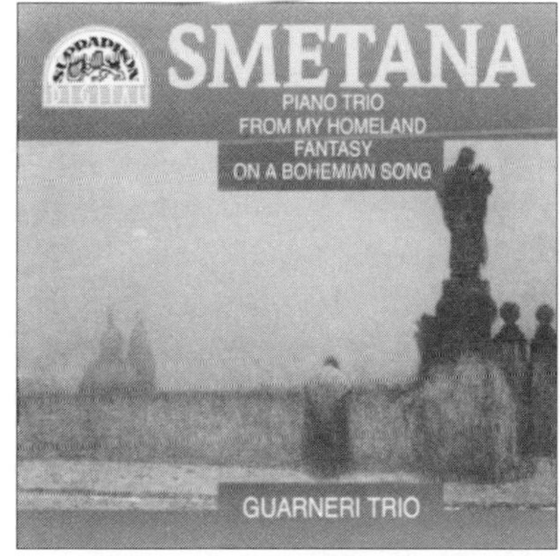

A highly spontaneous performance, forceful yet lyrical and granted an extremely immediate recording. Supraphon's makeweights are two memorable works for violin and piano (also by Smetana), but an alternative coupling by the same group (again on Supraphon) offers Dvořák's masterly Dumky Trio instead.

Johannes Brahms (1833-1897)

Horn Trio in E flat major, Op. 40 (1865)

The opening violin melody is especially haunting, while the horn's response (as from across some woodland glade) is wonderfully evocative. There's a cantering Scherzo, an *Adagio molto* in the manner of a sombre nocturne and an energetic, hunting-style finale. Brahms played both horn and piano and wrote his Trio in the wooded area of Baden-Baden; in fact, the first movement is said to have come to him from high among the hills and fir trees.

 ***Aubrey Brain (horn), Adolf Busch (violin), Rudolf Serkin (piano)***
EMI mono

Aubrey Brain, father of Dennis Brain (a great horn player who died prematurely), was among the finest wind players of his generation and his partnership with Busch and Serkin resulted in a performance of great poise and expressive power. The 1933 mono recording still sounds reasonably good, though there's a fine stereo option featuring the Nash Ensemble (CRD, digital).

Piano Trio No. 1 in B major, Op. 8 (1853-54, revised 1889)

Chamber music in the grand manner, although the composer's first thoughts (1853-54) were even grander. Still, Brahms was uncomfortable with the original and, some 35 years later, decided – and here I quote him – "not to stick a wig on it, but at least comb its hair a little". The result is a marvellous fusion of youthful inspiration and mature wisdom.

 ***Stern-Rose-Istomin Trio***
Sony Classical analogue

The first movement is marked Allegro con

brio, the last, Allegro – fast directions that Isaac Stern and his colleagues re-interpret in the light of Brahms's mellow maturity. Theirs is a broad, loving view of the piece, tonally rich and with particularly perceptive accounts of the middle movements, an impish Scherzo and an expansive Adagio. The recording is an affectionate look back at an earlier era (1966), a time when stereo meant 'left, middle and right' – and nothing in between.

Piano Trio No. 2 in C major, Op. 87 (1880-82)

More subtle and elusive than the first Trio, Brahms's Second Piano Trio opens to an assertive, upwardly spiralling melody that seems endlessly to reflect on itself. The slow movement's principal theme recalls Hungarian gipsy music, the mysterious Scherzo scurries along as if in fear for its life before the joyful finale bursts forth with new-found confidence.

Stern-Rose-Istomin Trio

Sony Classical analogue

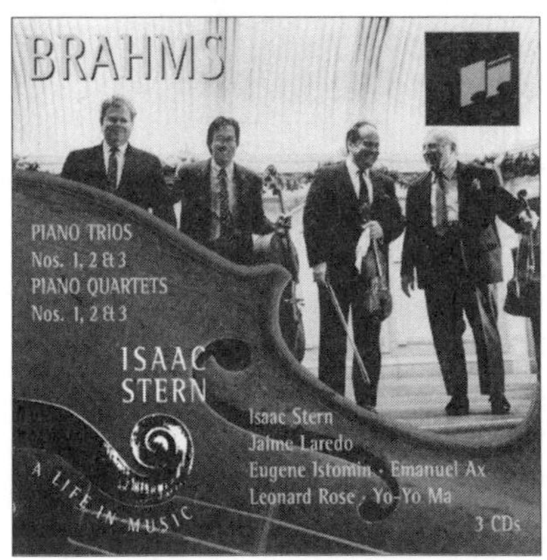

Another broad, strongly voiced performance from Stern, with a particularly passionate account of the finale. Those attracted to an earlier vintage could try Adolf Busch, Hermann Busch and Rudolf Serkin (also on Sony, mono) while Jascha Heifetz, Gregor Piatigorsky and Leonard Pennario (RCA, analogue) intensify the heat and the Beaux Arts Trio (Philips, analogue) achieve an effective interpretative middle-ground.

Piano Trio No. 3 in C minor, Op. 101 (1886)

A masterpiece of structural economy. The very opening suggests Olympian protest, whereas the secondary theme represents Brahms at his most candidly romantic. Strong, thoughtful and resolutely sure-footed, the Trio proceeds through a distracted Scherzo that Sir Donald Tovey likened to "a frightened child", a song-like slow movement that could serve as the child's lullaby and a big, beefcake finale.

Stern-Rose-Istomin Trio

Sony Classical analogue

Forceful, sonorous playing and fully up to the high standards set by the other performances in this splendid series. Stern and his team make no compromises and their efforts are captured in exceptionally vivid vintage sound (1966), beautifully remastered for the digital era.

Pyotr Il'yich Tchaikovsky (1840-1893)

Piano Trio in A minor, Op. 50 (1881-82)

When Nadezhda von Meck commissioned Tchaikovsky to compose a Piano Trio, she met with a negative response. But when the pianist and teacher Nikolay Rubinstein died, Tchaikovsky wrote his only Trio as a memorial. (Rachmaninov made a similar gesture when Tchaikovsky died). The A minor Trio is cast in two substantial movements – the first, a passionate *Pezzo elegiaco* (rich in top-grade Tchaikovskian melodies), the second, a theme with 11 variations, plus a finale and a coda.

Artur Rubinstein (piano), Jascha Heifetz (violin), Gregor Piatigorsky (cello)

RCA mono

Recorded in 1950, "the million dollar trio" (as it was known) parades a lustrous pooled string tone, although Rubinstein's playing hasn't the supple expressiveness of Vladimir Horowitz, whose uniquely compelling live recording of the first movement only (with Isaac Stern and Mstislav Rostropovich) is on Sony (analogue).

Antonin Dvořák (1841-1904)

Piano Trio in F minor, B130 (Op. 65) (1883)

Composed a year before the Seventh Symphony, Dvořák's Third – and greatest – Piano Trio has a good deal in common with its epic successor, not least a wealth of impassioned material. The first movement develops with storm and stress and although the delightful *Allegretto grazioso* marks a temporary lifting of tension, the slow movement sees sorrow return and the finale is a restless amalgam of folk-style motives.

Jascha Heifetz (violin), Gregor Piatigorsky (cello), Leonard Pennario (piano)

RCA analogue

Lightweight in tone, but emotionally intense and unfailingly lyrical (just sample Heifetz's sweetly turned account of the second subject in the first movement – at 2'31" – or the finale's second idea, at 1'49"). Those who prefer a more full-bodied sound should try either the Beaux Arts Trio (Philips, digital) or the Fontenay Trio (Teldec, digital).

Arnold Schoenberg (1874-1951)

String Trio, Op. 45 (1946)
When Schoenberg started work on his String Trio he had only just recovered from a heart attack (at one point, he had actually been pronounced clinically dead). He called the work a "humorous representation" of illness and recovery, although the actual music – a hugely gripping score composed in what one might vaguely describe as 'free atonality' – is anything but humorous. Highly concentrated and deeply personal, it suggests a subtle thematic link with the desolate world of Sibelius's Fourth Symphony (initially, nine seconds into the "First Episode" – or track 7 on our recommended recording). Coincidentally, Sibelius had, at the time of his Fourth Symphony, been diagnosed as suffering from a throat tumour.

Walter Levin (violin), Peter Kamnitzer (viola), Lee Fiser (cello)
Deutsche Grammophon digital

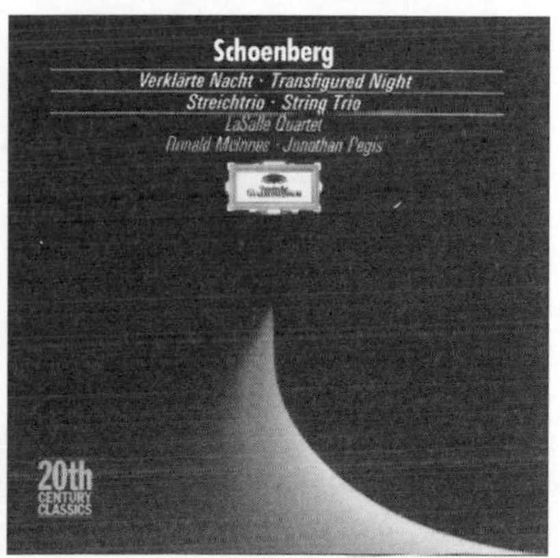

Keen, alert and finely-tensed playing by members of the LaSalle Quartet, expertly recorded. Schoenberg's Trio has been very lucky on CD, with two fine recordings by members of the Juilliard Quartet (one digital, the other analogue [coupled with Schoenberg's own recording of Pierrot lunaire]) and an impressive digital version with Gidon Kremer and members of the Hagen Quartet (DG).

Maurice Ravel (1875-1937)

Piano Trio in A minor (1914)
If you want to sample this wonderful work, try the noble *Passacaille* third movement first – a sombre near-relation to the *Pavane for a dead princess* and a telling reminder of the great French harpsichord composers. The second movement (the Trio's Scherzo) is named "Pantoum" after an ancient Malayan verse form that earlier French poets had adapted for themselves.

Artur Rubinstein (piano), Jascha Heifetz (violin), Gregor Piatigorsky (cello)
RCA mono
Rubinstein's mastery of the French idiom has been well displayed in his recordings of music by Debussy, Poulenc, Chabrier and indeed Ravel, whereas the tenderness and precision of Heifetz's playing suits Ravel's finely-sculpted style. The Passacaille is especially beautiful and the recording – although a little 'mono-dynamic' by today's best standards – is perfectly acceptable.

Dmitry Shostakovich (1906-1975)

Piano Trio No. 2 in E minor, Op. 67 (1944)
Ghostly string harmonics (a quiet, whistling sonority) inform the opening page of what is perhaps the greatest Piano Trio since Brahms. The first movement is mostly elegiac in tone; the second is a boisterous Scherzo with a joyful Trio, whereas the finale – a heart-rending passacaglia that opens to a series of commanding piano chords – leads directly into the finale, with its Yiddish folk melody (an unmistakable reference to Nazi atrocities that were taking place at the time). Shostakovich abhored anti-Semitism and this Piano Trio is in effect a musical tribute to a people who he always claimed could "express despair in dance".

Elisabeth Leonskaja (piano), Mikhail Kopelman (violin), Valentin Berlinsky (cello)
Teldec digital

Leonskaja is joined by the leader and cellist of the legendary Borodin Quartet for a performance that combines pathos (the Largo slow movement is filled with sorrow), drama and an incomparable command of the score's quieter passages. For a compelling historic version, try the David Oistrakh Trio (Praga or Multisonic, both mono).

The Classical string quartet (1772-1800)

Urgent discussions shared between four, with plenty of tonal variety (the instrumental equivalents of treble, tenor and bass-baritone voices) and endless potential for musical invention. The combination of two violins, viola and cello reached early maturity in the brilliant string quartets of Joseph Haydn, which in turn greatly influenced Mozart and the young Beethoven. All subscribed to 'sonata form' by stating, developing and recapitulating principal musical ideas.

Joseph Haydn (1732-1809)

String Quartet in C major, Op. 20 No. 2 (1772)

"With Op. 20 the historical development of Haydn's quartets reaches its goal; and further progress is not progress in any historical sense, but simply between one masterpiece and the next." So wrote the English music scholar, composer and pianist, Sir Donald Francis Tovey. Which makes any small selection of Haydn's quartets 'post Op. 20' seem merely arbitrary: truth to tell, they're all worth the closest scrutiny. The second of the six so-called *Sun* Quartets (named after the title-page design of their first edition) opens to a radiant *Moderato*, progresses to a virtually operatic *Adagio* (definite premonitions of Mozart in dramatic minor-key mode) with a soulful second section that leads to a chirruping Minuet and a contrapuntally dazzling finale.

String Quartet in A major, Op. 20 No. 6 (1772)

A boisterous, texturally varied first movement (so much musical incident would take a whole chapter to annotate) is followed by a bright, song-like slow movement (it could easily serve as an operatic aria), a Minuet rich in variety (the Trio middle-section is unexpectedly restrained) and a joyous fugal finale.

Hagen Quartet
Deutsche Grammophon digital

These remarkable recordings are included as part of a two-CD presentation of all six Op. 20 Quartets; they combine period-instrument-style leanness with tremendous executive vigour and feature a particularly effective account of the A major's last movement (some instruments playing with vibrato, others without).

String Quartet in G major, Op. 33 No. 5, "How do you do?" (1781)

Sir Donald Tovey once described Haydn's six Quartets, Op. 33 as "the lightest of all Haydn's mature comedies" and the first movement of the Fifth certainly describes high spirits and good humour (a pivotal four-note phrase suggests the words 'How do you do?', hence the nickname). The slow movement has a tender, quasi-operatic nature, the Scherzo is fairly typical in its rhythmic ambiguities and the finale is a lilting theme with variations tailed by a dashing *Presto*. Haydn dedicated his Op. 33 Quartets to Grand Duke Paul of Russia (later Tsar Paul II) which is why they're sometimes known as the "Russian" Quartets.

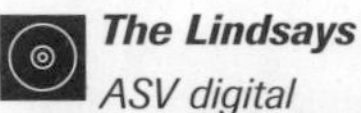

The Lindsays
ASV digital

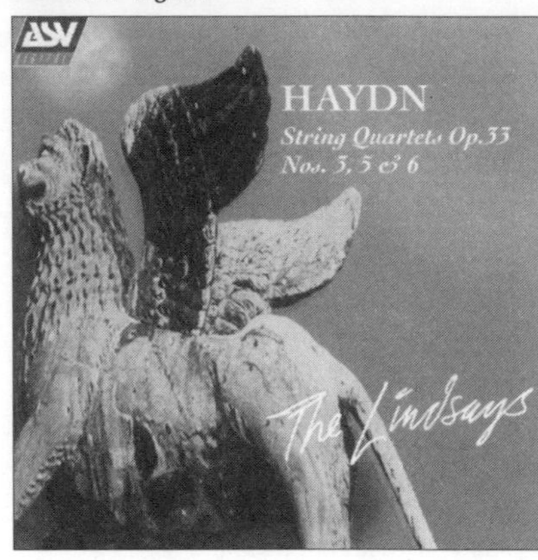

Boisterous playing, full of character yet never short on either warmth or tenderness. The recording is extremely vivid and the CD also includes fine performances of the Third and Sixth Quartets, Op. 33.

String Quartet in D minor, Op. 76 No. 2, "Fifths" (1797-99)

The nickname refers directly to the Quartet's use of the interval of 'a fifth' (a specific distance in pitch between two notes) which dominates the first movement. The opening *Allegro* is uncommonly urgent, while the elegant second movement again features a 'fifth' (this time between its first and second bars). After a terse, gnarled Minuet (where the principal theme is echoed between upper and lower strings) the finale returns us to the urgent mood of the first movement.

Takács String Quartet
Decca digital

Recorded in the generous acoustic of the Schubertsaal (Konzerthaus, Vienna), the Takács's performance – part of an excellent survey of the complete Op. 76 Quartets – sounds especially lustrous. The playing has energy, panache and warmth, but there's notable rivalry at super-bargain price from the Kodály Quartet (Naxos).

String Quartet in C major, Op. 76 No. 3, "Emperor" (*c*1799)

The opening *Allegro* is cast in Haydn's most buoyantly exciting style, sunny, extrovert and with a mass of colourful harmonic incident (even within the exposition, or initial arguments). The lovely second movement is a set of variations on the celebrated Austrian "Emperor's Hymn" (nowadays saddled with unfortunate wartime associations) that assigns important roles to all the instruments.

Amadeus Quartet
Deutsche Grammophon analogue
Haydn's music fares especially well in the hands of musicians schooled in a Viennese tradition of playing. The Amadeus Quartet was famous in its day for performances that combined elegance, a warm body of tone, piquant phrasing and interpretative spontaneity. This 1963 recording of the Emperor Quartet parades their finest qualities.

String Quartet in G major, Op. 77 No. 1, "Lobkowitz" (1799)

Initially conceived as the first in a set of six, Haydn's Op. 77 No. 1 was composed for Prince Franz Joseph Maximilian Lobkowitz whose patronage of Beethoven also inspired the latter's epoch-making Op. 18 Quartets (see below). In fact, Haydn specialist H. C. Robbins Landon surmises that it was Beethoven's achievement that convinced Haydn to stand aside for the sake of the new, which he did – save for a couple more movements from an uncompleted last quartet. The G major is distinguished by a witty opening *Allegro moderato*, a warm hearted *Adagio* and a gipsy-style finale.

Alban Berg Quartet
EMI digital
Supremely accomplished playing, well focused and extremely well recorded. Good alternatives are provided the Mosaïques Quartet (Auvidis Astrée, digital) and the vintage Amadeus Quartet (DG, as part of a collection of Haydn quartets). Fine older recordings are provided by the Pro Arte Quartet (Testament, mono) and the Vienna Konzerthaus Quartet (Preiser, mono).

String Quartet in F major Op. 77 No. 2, "Lobkowitz" (1799)

The second of Haydn's *Lobkowitz* Quartets was described by Sir Donald Tovey as "perhaps Haydn's greatest instrumental composition, with the two last symphonies to bracket with it". The F major is particularly ingenious, with a rhythmically inventive Minuet (full of built-in ambiguities) and a delightful theme-and-variations *Andante*.

Alban Berg Quartet
EMI digital
Very much along the same lines as the Alban Berg's stylish account of the G major (see above), with the Mosaïques (Auvidis Astrée) as a viable second choice. An elderly version by the Végh Quartet (DG, not yet on CD) would be well worth searching out. It's odd to think that, considering its high standing among connoisseurs, Op. 77 No. 2 has been so infrequently recorded.

Wolfgang Amadeus Mozart
(1756–1791)

The Six "Haydn" Quartets, String Quartet No. 14 in G major, K387 (1782)

Mozart completed his 15 early quartets before the age of 18, then abandoned the medium for a while; but when, in the early 1780s, he heard Haydn's latest quartets (probably Opp. 20 and 33 – see above), he was inspired to embark on a series of six works in homage. "I send my six sons to you, most celebrated and very dear friend," he wrote – and there can surely be no greater instance of musical flattery by imitation. The First Quartet in the series is especially winsome: witness, for example, its richly harmonized opening bars. There's a strongly accented Minuet, an *Andante* that opens like an accompanied violin solo and a finale that – like the parallel movement of the *Jupiter* Symphony – is rich in excited counterpoint.

String Quartet No. 15 in D minor, K421/417*b* (1783)

Mozart toiled over the Minuet of this sombre work while his wife Constanze was in labour, "rising from his desk to comfort her during her contractions and then returning to his work when they subsided". The child died and the entire work seems tinged with bitterness, not least in the pensive *Andante*, the painfully protesting Minuet (the outer sections especially) and the weirdly ambiguous set of variations that serves as the Quartet's finale.

String Quartet No. 16 in E flat major, K428/421*b* (1783)

The opening theme, written in octaves, is memorably intimate – but when repeated in harmony, it's as if monochrome has suddenly turned to colour. The *Andante* features sobbing inner voices that defy adequate description (the effect remains spellbinding, no matter how many times you listen to it) while the energetic Minuet offers light-hearted contrast, as does a vigorous but initially mock-hesitant finale.

String Quartet No. 17 in B flat major, K458, "Hunt" (1784)

The first movement's cantering rhythms, festive trills and horn-call sonorities explain the nickname, whereas the Minuet has an imperious gait that suggests a banquet after the hunt. The *Adagio* unfolds a simple but sublime narrative, and the finale – which Mozart refashioned from an earlier version – is full of Haydnesque surprises.

String Quartet No. 18 in A major, K464 (1785)

A Quartet imbued with the spirit of the Minuet, certainly in the first two movements – the second of which (the Minuet proper) seems to anticipate, at least initially, the second movement of Beethoven's great 'late' Quartet No. 15 (in A minor – see "The Romantic string quartet", below). The *Andante* is a set of variations, while the finale is a contrapuntal *Allegro non troppo* based on a 'falling' theme.

String Quartet No. 19 in C major, K465, "Dissonance" (1785)

A gently pulsing cello prompts a bitter-sweet harmonic sequence that seemed bizarre in its day (some even attempted to 'improve' on its dissonances), but that strikes most modern ears as among the quartet repertory's most exquisitely expressive pages. The ensuing *Allegro*, though thematically related to the opening, marks a lively contrast; the slow movement is songful, the Minuet mischievous and unpredictable, while the finale abounds in playful drama.

Emerson Quartet
Deutsche Grammophon digital

The Emersons are both elegant and assertive; they understand the strong though fragile nature of Mozart's melodies and make great play with the Quartets' many inventive episodes. An added attraction is their inclusion of Mozart's original finale for K464. However, competition is especially stiff in this repertory, not least from the Alban Berg Quartet (Teldec, part of an excellent set devoted to all ten of the mature quartets), the wonderfully mellow Budapest Quartet (recorded 1950-53 in mono, and issued on two discs – but omitting first movement repeats) and two sets by the Juilliard Quartet (Sony, the earlier of the two – from the 1960s – being the more striking). All quoted alternatives are analogue.

String Quartet No. 20 in D major, K499, "Hoffmeister" (1786)

A year after composing the Six "Haydn Quartets", Mozart set to work on a D major Quartet which was published in 1788 by a Viennese printer named Hoffmeister. K499 is distinguished by textural warmth, forward-sounding harmonies (Schubert is clearly within earshot) and an extraordinarily colourful Minuet.

String Quartet Nos. 21 in D major, K575, "Prussian" (1789)

Although Mozart had originally intended to write six quartets for King Friedrich Wilhelm II of Prussia, he only actually completed three. The King was an amateur cellist, and all three works feature prominent cello parts. Again, there is a plethora of novel sonorities and the quartets represent, with *Così fan tutte* and the Clarinet Quintet, a subtle advance on what was already a sublime musical style. The D major Quartet is unusual in that Minuet is placed second and not third, as in Mozart's previous quartets.

String Quartet No. 22 in B flat major, K589 (1790)

The soft, pastoral opening introduces a lovable movement that keeps the cello well to the fore. The *Larghetto* second movement again grants principal material to the cello, while the Minuet ends in a mood of great excitement and the feather-light finale is full of fascinating contrapuntal incident.

String Quartet No. 23 in F major, K590 (1790)

The concise first movement is notably intense, with significant interplay between the cello and the first violin. The *Allegro* is based almost entirely on the poignant melody stated at the outset, whereas the highly original Minuet features irregular phrase-lengths and some extremely unusual harmonies. This spirit of exploration extends further for a dramatic and harmonically inventive finale.

Melos Quartet
Deutsche Grammophon digital (K499, K575), analogue (K589, K590)

Poised, musically yielding and judiciously balanced, these remain among the most appealing Mozart quartet recordings of the late 'stereo analogue' – to 'early digital'. If, however, they prove difficult to locate, then you might try a similarly sympathetic collection by the Alban Berg Quartet (Teldec, analogue), the Amadeus Quartet (also DG, analogue) or indeed the highly responsive Quartetto Italiano (Philips, analogue – and part of the "Complete Mozart Edition").

Ludwig van Beethoven
(1770-1827)

String Quartet No. 1 in F major, Op. 18 No. 1 (1798-1800)

The first quartet of the series was substantially revised (the opening movement in particular) and although Haydn is clearly audible in the second and third movements, Beethoven's own voice is everywhere in evidence. The pensive second movement was apparently inspired by the "Tomb Scene" from Shakespeare's *Romeo and Juliet*.

String Quartet No. 2 in G major, Op. 18 No. 2 (1798-1800)

The very opening gives the game away – a playful gesture, happily employed for one of Beethoven's most genial first-movement developments. At first hearing, the lovely *Adagio cantabile*'s opening bars suggest a forethought of Wagner's *Tannhäuser*, whereas the frolicking Scherzo anticipates bigger, more serious jokes in the Quartets, Op. 59 No. 1 and Op. 127 (see "The Romantic string quartet", below).

String Quartet No. 3 in D major, Op. 18 No. 3 (1798-1800)

The D major is the earliest of the Op. 18 cycle. It opens to a neatly curled violin melody and develops fluently (with some very effective key transitions). The expressive second movement is full of inventive musical incident, the third is a rather pensive *Allegro* (replete with typically Beethovenian hesitations) and the finale a sprightly *Presto* that almost becomes a tarantella.

String Quartet No. 4 in C minor, Op. 18 No. 4 (1798-1800)

The Fourth Quartet opens to a dark, restless *Allegro ma non tanto* (don't forget that this is the key of the Fifth Symphony) but rather than follow with a profound slow movement, Beethoven teases us with a tongue-in-cheek, polyphonically inventive *Scherzo-Andante*. Next comes a Minuet tinged with tragedy (hardly a dance at all) and an impetuous finale.

String Quartet No. 5 in A major, Op. 18 No. 5 (1798-1800)

In total contrast to the Fourth Quartet, the Fifth opens with a decidedly happy countenance – although the first movement's ensuing arguments still suggest plenty of healthy tension. The second movement is a graceful Minuet (and a distant anticipation of the *Alla danza tedesca* from the Thirteenth Quartet – see "The Romantic string quartet", below), the third, a boldly out-reaching theme and variations and the finale a tersely argued *Allegro*.

String Quartet No. 6 in B flat major, Op. 18 No. 6 (1798-1800)

Beethoven's Sixth Quartet opens in the manner of a boisterous Mozartian operatic duet, while the vocal nature of the writing extends to a lyrical second movement. The cantering Scherzo suggests hunters on horseback while the finale opens – unusually, though not for the last time in the quartets – with a contemplative *Adagio* (entitled "La Malinconia"). The main body of the last movement, however, is disarmingly elegant.

Budapest Quartet
Sony Classical mono

It might seem something of an anachronism to choose a set of 1951 recordings, but the Budapest Quartet display such ease of expression and feeling for style that I couldn't in all honesty do otherwise. If, however, old sound really is a problem, then there are recommendable alternatives by the Emerson Quartet (DG, digital), the Vermeer Quartet (Teldec, digital), the Amadeus Quartet (DG,

analogue), the Talich Quartet (Calliope, analogue), the period-instrument Smithsonian Quartet (Deutsche Harmonia Mundi, digital) and the Alban Berg Quartet (EMI, preferably the versions recorded live in 1989, digital).

The Romantic string quartet (1798-1895)

There's a world of difference between the last of Beethoven's predominantly Classical Op. 18 String Quartets (see above), and the daring, deeply expressive world of his Op. 59 set. Thereafter and borders disintegrate, harmonic horizons widen and formal constraints relax considerably. This section includes works that signal new levels of creative freedom. It also harbours some extraordinarily beautiful music, especially among the various slow movements.

Ludwig van Beethoven (1770-1827)

String Quartet No. 7 in F major, Op. 59 No. 1, "Rasumovsky" (1798-1800)

A huge stride forward from the trimly-tailored (though stylistically bold) Six String Quartets, Op. 18, ambitious in scope and featuring an astonishingly playful Scherzo as well as one of Beethoven's longest and most affecting slow movements. The finale toys with a Russian folk-song – the reference being in honour of the Russian music patron Count Andrey Rasumovsky, to whom Beethoven dedicated all three of his Op. 59 String Quartets.

Talich Quartet

Calliope analogue

A warm-textured performance, keenly inflected and captured in a clear though intimate recording. The Budapest Quartet (Sony, analogue) offers a drier, more aggressive alternative and there are fine performances within the context of complete recordings by the Juilliard (Sony, digital), Amadeus (DG, analogue) and Alban Berg (EMI, live – digital) Quartets.

String Quartet No. 8 in E minor, Op. 59 No. 2, "Rasumovsky" (1805-06)

An abrupt opening sets the mood, and although lyricism breaks through thereafter, the ensuing development of ideas is extraordinarily tense. The slow movement scales ethereal heights (especially its second theme) while the Scherzo's central section features a Russian tune that Mussorgsky later worked into the "Coronation Scene" of his opera *Boris Godunov*. The finale skips along with ferocious energy, replete with mock-fanfares and furious counterpoint.

Budapest Quartet

Sony Classical analogue

The slow movement in particular is beautifully drawn, while the outer movements are wholly consistent with other performances in this series – forceful, tautly argued and closely recorded (the original tape was made in 1959). The Talich (Calliope, analogue) and Tokyo (RCA, digital) Quartets provide recommendable modern alternatives.

String Quartet No. 9 in C major, Op. 59 No. 3, "Rasumovsky" (1805-06)

The dogged opening idea is worked through with typical ingenuity and persistence, while the second movement has the character of a melancholic Slavic folk-song, richly harmonized and accompanied by a cello playing pizzicato. There's an elegant – though slightly quizzical – Minuet and a fiery fugal finale which maintains its momentum for a heady six minutes.

Budapest Quartet

Sony Classical analogue

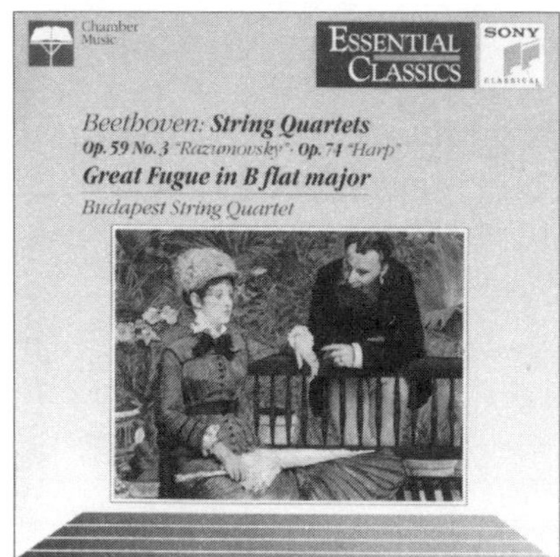

Although rather dry in tone, the Budapest Quartet parade a rugged intensity that suits the music (their recordings of the other Op. 59 Quartets display similar characteristics). Those in search of something a little sweeter are directed to the excellent Talich Quartet (Calliope, analogue), the fiery Emerson Quartet, digital) the Vermeer Quartet (Teldec, digital – their complete cycle is at budget price and is well worth acquiring) or the pre-eminent historical option, by the Busch Quartet (EMI, mono).

String Quartet No. 10 in E flat major, Op. 74, "The Harp" (1805-06)

High-points of Op. 74 include an eloquent introduction, an exultant first-movement climax (where the main argument blossoms to a swelling arpeggio – or harp-like –

accompaniment) and a fierce Scherzo that makes dramatic capital out of Beethoven's familiar 'four-note' rhythm (used to such effect in the Fifth Symphony). The *Harp* title was inspired by plucked arpeggio figures in the first movement.

Amadeus Quartet
Deutsche Grammophon analogue
Although currently available only as part of a seven-disc set devoted to the complete Beethoven quartets, the Amadeus's account of the Harp Quartet is especially urgent and impassioned: the Scherzo in particular has real panache, whereas the finale has a winning charm. Viable alternatives include the Talich Quartet (Calliope, analogue) and the Budapest Quartet (Sony, analogue).

String Quartet No. 11 in F minor, Op. 95, "Serioso" (1809)

The title, Beethoven's own, gives the clue; the opening flourish spells 'fury' in no uncertain terms. The desolate second movement descends to the strains of a solo cello, while the Scherzo (which follows without a break) starts to an anguished alarm. By way of contrast, the finale opens reflectively before breaking into a restless dance and ending – unexpectedly – in a brief flurry of Mendelssohnian busyness.

Végh Quartet
Auvidis Astrée analogue
Here there's energy to spare, though never to the extent that the work's more reflective elements are upstaged. The Végh Quartet phrase with great imagination; their playing is full of feeling, although occasional spots of sour intonation might worry some listeners. First-rate alternatives include the vintage Busch Quartet (EMI, mono) and the Alban Berg Quartet as recorded live in 1989 (EMI, digital).

String Quartet No. 12 in E flat major, Op. 127 (1823-24)

The first of Beethoven's 'late' quartets opens to majestic chords before sweeping into a richly romantic melody which, in turn, instigates a highly eventful development. The long, heart-rending slow movement reminds us that this Quartet followed the *Choral* Symphony, while the action-packed Scherzo recalls fun and games in the parallel movement in the Seventh Quartet (see above). The finale provides a further reminder of the Ninth Symphony in that its second theme recalls the "Ode to Joy" – though its mysterious closing pages transport us on to quite another plane.

Busch Quartet
EMI mono
Although recorded pre-war, the Busch are uniquely compelling in this, the most outwardly demonstrative of Beethoven's last quartets. The slow movement is especially memorable, but if digital sound is an essential prerequisite then the Emerson Quartet (DG) provide a good alternative.

String Quartet No. 13 in B flat major, Op. 130 (1825-26) – including the Grosse Fuge in B flat major, Op. 133 (1826)

Another of Beethoven's late 'tales of the unexpected', in this case a dazzling six-movement structure that has a plaintive *Andante con moto* placed third, flanked either side by impish faster movements and with large-scale essays at either end – the last being a huge, tragi-comic *Grosse Fuge*, or "Great Fugue", which is often performed separately. However, a timid publisher convinced Beethoven to substitute a lighter finale, which he did (it was the very last thing he composed); but the original is uniquely powerful both in its musical logic and its continuing capacity to surprise.

Emerson Quartet
Deutsche Grammophon digital
A finely graded, consistently alert interpretation, expressive without being overplayed, and elegant without being too well mannered. Furthermore, the Emersons score extra points by dispensing with Beethoven's 'second' (i.e. easier) finale altogether; many other groups haven't the nerve. Important older alternatives are by the Busch (Sony, Biddulph, Pearl – mono), Amadeus (DG, analogue) and LaSalle (DG analogue) Quartets.

String Quartet No. 14 in C sharp minor, Op. 131 (1826)

This is at once both the most ethereal and the most revolutionary of the 'late' quartets, a startling diversion from tradition in that its seven astonishingly varied movements play without a break. Wagner spoke of "a soul in distress", followed by "pleasant visions, a new yearning for life, beauty, gentleness, yearning, love, whims, humour, hilarity" and then "transition to resignation and painful renunciation" – one man's reaction and sure proof of the music's ability to evoke both strong emotions and powerful imagery.

Amadeus Quartet
Deutsche Grammophon analogue
The Amadeus recorded Op. 131 twice for DG, but this – the earlier of the two – shows a particularly strong grasp of Beethoven's spiritual orbit. So does the Végh Quartet (Auvidis Astrée, analogue), while the Busch Quartet (EMI, mono) make for an essential historical option and both Leonard Bernstein with the Vienna Philharmonic (DG, digital) and Sándor Végh with the IMS soloists (Capriccio, digital) offer a convincing case for playing Op. 131 with a full string band.

String Quartet No. 15 in A minor, Op. 132 (1825)

Beethoven had already sketched the A minor Quartet by the end of 1824, but illness delayed its completion until August 1825 (the work actually pre-dates Opp. 130 and 131, see above). The composer's recovery is poignantly celebrated in one of the longest and most profoundly moving of all his slow movements; it is, to quote Beethoven himself, "a hymn of thanksgiving in the Lydian mode [an old ecclesiastical musical mode] offered to God by a convalescent". The outer movements are superbly crafted, the passionate finale being preceded by a cheerful march.

Busch Quartet
EMI mono

A compelling (and by no means unique) example of top-grade vintage quartet playing. The pre-war Busch Quartet plumbs the very depths of Beethoven's most celebrated - and perhaps greatest - chamber-music slow movement. It's a truly remarkable recording, although the Végh (Auvidis Astrée, analogue), LaSalle (DG, analogue) and Alban Berg (EMI - their live 1989 recording, digital) all do this wonderful score justice.

String Quartet No. 16 in F major, Op. 135 (1826)

Beethoven's last Quartet (though not his last work for quartet - that was the 'replacement' finale of Op. 130, the *Grosse Fuge*, see above) is a typically oblique synthesis of darkness and light, with a playful *Allegretto* to start, a riotously syncopated Scherzo, a sublime slow movement that anticipates the last movement of Mahler's Third Symphony and a surprisingly extrovert finale, the initial slow phrases of which are headed with the words "must it be?", then "it must be!". Was this, as some say, a dialogue between Beethoven and his cook - or was it the composer's grateful anticipation of being released from what had become an intolerably painful life?

LaSalle Quartet
Deutsche Grammophon analogue

Intelligent, perceptive playing, notably respectful of both the soul and the humour of Beethoven's last Quartet. Again, the Busch Quartet (EMI, mono) offer unique insights while there are two effective orchestral versions, one of the complete quartet with the Vienna Philharmonic under Leonard Bernstein (DG, digital), the other of the Lento assai slow movement and Scherzo only, with the NBC Symphony under Toscanini (RCA, mono). Both are well worth hearing.

Franz Schubert (1797-1828)

String Quartet No. 13 in A minor, D804 (1824)

The most soulful and songful of Schubert's mature quartets opens to a melody of surpassing beauty and owes not a little to the late quartets of Beethoven (the passage just before the first movement starts to develop being a fair case in point - at 2'47" into our recommended recording). The *Andante* quotes a melody that's more famous in the context of Schubert's *Rosamunde* ballet music, the melancholy Minuet is based on a song composed some five years earlier while the finale has a definite whiff of paprika about it.

Melos Quartet
Harmonia Mundi digital

The best version currently available though if the Juilliard's version (Sony, analogue) - a cerebral performance with plenty of heart - reappears then snap it up. The Quartetto Italiano (Philips, analogue) is another recommendable alternative.

String Quartet No. 14 in D minor, D810, "Death and the Maiden" (1824)

Death as a consoling friend (at least that's the message of Mathias Claudius's poem), originally cast as a song, then treated to a highly imaginative sequence of variations in the context of Schubert's penultimate String Quartet. The remaining movements are, by turn, tensely dramatic, bracing (one of Schubert's finest Scherzos) and fast-driving.

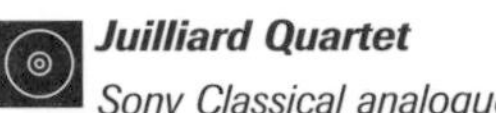

Juilliard Quartet
Sony Classical analogue

That Death and the Maiden treads a delicate path between Classicism and Romantic melodrama poses no obvious problems for the Juilliard Quartet. Their sense of form is impeccable, and yet they convey the music's underlying tensions - the eerie first statement of the song itself, for example, or the ghostly opening to the finale - with sure intuition. A more modern, digital alternative is provided by the Hagen Quartet (DG).

String Quartet No. 15 in G major, D887 (1826)

Glacial, taut and with a pained lyricism that threatens to fracture at any moment. In fact,

Schubert's last String Quartet approximates a terrifying glimpse into a hollow beyond. True, there are songful melodies (the first movement's 'second subject' and the main body of the second movement); but try the shuddering first five minutes (premonitions of Bruckner), or the stabbing dissonances that tear at the central section of the second movement and Schubert's newborn – and tragically short-lived – innovations will strike home with immense force.

Melos Quartet
Harmonia Mundi digital
A perceptive, fairly comprehensive rendition, very well recorded – also look out for the 1938 Busch Quartet (EMI, mono), a lyrical but uncompromising account, superbly played.

Felix Mendelssohn (1809-1847)

String Quartet in F minor, Op. 80 (1847)
A powerful corrective for those who imagine Mendelssohn's music to be all sweetness and light. The F minor Quartet was composed in a period of creative industry some months after the death of Mendelssohn's sister, Fanny; it's an ardent and energetic piece with an anxious, hard-driving third movement that is more suggestive of middle-period Beethoven than the untroubled composer of *A Midsummer Night's Dream*.

Melos Quartet
Deutsche Grammophon analogue
Recordings of Mendelssohn quartets are thicker on the ground nowadays than ever before, and yet these 1976-81 performances boast such a high level of insight and enthusiasm that most rivals sound glum by comparison. The three CDs feature all seven Mendelssohn quartets – the whole cycle is well worth getting to know – and the sound quality is excellent.

Bedřich Smetana (1824-1884)

String Quartet No. 1 in E minor, "From my Life" (1880)
A gripping musical autobiography that opens amidst the adventures and enthusiasms of youth, proceeds to a carefree polka (Smetana's favourite dance form), then a gorgeous love song to his wife and an ebullient finale – which suddenly stops dead with the onset of deafness (dramatically portrayed by a sustained 'whistle' on the first violin's E string).

String Quartet No. 2 in D minor (1882-83)
If the First Quartet is a focused recollection of life thus far, the Second throws us into a frenzied present – agitated, densely harmonized and drenched in nostalgia. It is a deeply disquieting piece, intensely lyrical featuring an almost schizoid sequence of mood-changes. It also contains what is surely the finest – and most complex – of Smetana's many polkas.

Talich Quartet
Calliope digital
Set in a warm acoustic, the Talich Quartet presents a vibrant, close-knit view of Smetana, strong in tone but never over-projected and with a lyricism that stays on the right side of sentimentality. Furthermore, there's a generous bonus in eight early piano polkas (excellently played by Radoslav Kvapil) that provide a revealing contrast with the mature pieces that Smetana wrote into his quartets.

Alexander Borodin (1833-1887)

String Quartet No. 2 in D major (1885)
Charm, delicacy and a more-or-less constant stream of melody characterize Borodin's most famous chamber work, composed during a summer spell in the country. Lovers of Broadway musicals will probably recognize at least two movements that were used in *Kismet* – "Baubles, bangles and beads" (Scherzo) and "And this is my beloved" (the celebrated Nocturne).

Borodin Quartet
EMI digital
Few quartet recordings are as alluringly sensuous – especially in the Nocturne, where first violin and cello sing their lines with maximum sweetness. The EMI recording is coupled with the more expansive (and marginally less memorable) First Quartet and there is fine mono recording by the dazzlingly brilliant Hollywood Quartet (coupled with Tchaikovsky and Glazunov, on Testament).

Johannes Brahms (1833-1897)

String Quartet No. 3 in B flat major, Op. 67 (1876)
The last, the most genial and the most Neo-

Classical of Brahms's three string quartets opens in the manner of a hunting call (Mozart's *Hunt* Quartet starts in a similar fashion) – though the plethora of ideas thereafter is typically Brahmsian both in terms of thematic warmth and contrapuntal ingenuity. The slow movement opens to a melody that recalls the finest of Brahms's Lieder; there's a gently questioning *Agitato* third movement (very much in keeping with the mellow spirit of the piece as a whole) and a winsome theme-and-variations finale.

Borodin Quartet
Teldec digital
Luminous playing – reflective, warm-hearted and with artfully blended instrumental lines. As to alternatives (not that you'll need them), the best are by the Juilliard Quartet (Sony, digital) and the eloquent pre-war Budapest Quartet (Biddulph, mono). Both the Juilliard and the Borodin have recorded all three of Brahms's quartets.

Pyotr Il'yich Tchaikovsky (1840–1893)

String Quartet No. 1 in D major, Op. 11 (1871)

One of Tchaikovsky's most beguiling early works, skilfully crafted and with an *Andante cantabile* at its centre that reduced Tolstoy to tears when he heard it. That particular movement is also available in countless arrangements (strings, violin and piano, etc), but the remainder of the Quartet consists of a vibrant first movement, a very Russian Scherzo and a vigorous finale. It is by far the best-known of Tchaikovsky's string quartets.

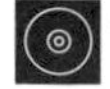

Hollywood Quartet
Testament mono
A fine example of the 'old' Russian-Jewish style of string playing otherwise exemplified by such violin virtuosos as Jascha Heifetz, Mischa Elman and others. The Hollywood Quartet gives a lean, fiery account of the score with a particularly eloquent Andante cantabile. The Borodin Quartet (Teldec) provides an excellent digital alternative; some may even prefer its fuller tone.

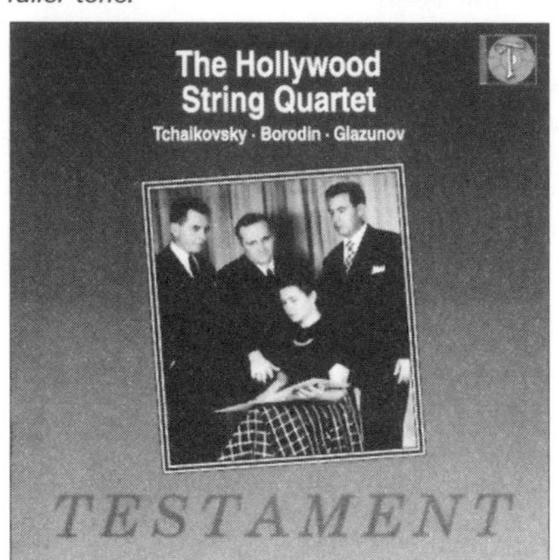

String Quartet No. 2 in F major, Op. 22 (1874)

A more questioning work than the First Quartet; more inventive too, although echoes of Russian folk-song are just as prominent (especially in the main body of the first movement – try 3'23" into the first track on the second disc of our recommended recording). The Second Quartet, the most harmonically adventurous of Tchaikovsky's chamber works, inhabits a warm emotional climate: the Scherzo jokes with a sigh, the slow movement is deeply elegiac and the finale, which is in the manner of a polonaise, incorporates some busy fugal writing.

Borodin Quartet
Teldec digital
Unquestionably the finest recording that this underrated work has ever had. The performance itself combines immense gusto and tonal lustre with an intuitive grasp of Tchaikovsky's harmonic language. It's more compelling than the Borodin Quartet's previous recordings (there are at least three, one of them live) and the digital sound is first-rate.

Antonin Dvořák (1841–1904)

String Quartet No. 9 in D minor, B75 (Op. 34) (1877)

Dvořák dedicated his Ninth Quartet – one of his loveliest though least-known chamber works – to Brahms. Although fairly melancholic in spirit (the composer had recently lost his first two children), there's also plenty of sunshine, not least in the folk-like melody that serves as the first movement's 'second subject', the lilting (almost Tchaikovskian) *Alla Polka* second movement and a finale that pays audible tribute to its dedicatee. However, the heart of the work is a glorious slow movement, the opening of which is among Dvořák's warmest inspirations.

Panocha Quartet
Supraphon digital
Finely-graded playing, unforced, yet stylish and notably well recorded. The CD is part of an impressive series that covers – or at least intends to cover – all of Dvořák's major chamber works. Its finest predecessor is by

the Prague Quartet (DG, analogue), also part of an excellent cycle.

String Quartet No. 12 in F major, B179 (Op. 96), "American", (1893)

One of three significant chamber works that Dvořák composed in America (the others are the String Quintet, B180 and the violin and piano Sonatina, B183). As with the *New World* Symphony, Dvořák called on the musics of the blacks and North American Indians – although none of these works contains direct quotations. The so-called *American* Quartet is redolent of both the American North and the open fields of Dvořák's native Bohemia.

Keller Quartet
Erato digital

A vital, loose-limbed performance, idiomatically phrased and with an eloquently voiced slow movement. Digitally speaking, it sweeps the board – though there are notable analogue forerunners from the Vlach (Praga, mono), Prague (DG) and Juilliard (Sony) Quartets – not to mention a fascinating (and matchlessly authentic) 1928 recording by the Bohemian Quartet (Biddulph, mono).

String Quartet No. 13 in G major, B192 (Op. 106) (1895)

Dvořák's penultimate chamber work (its immediate 'predecessor' was actually completed after B192) was partially composed in America, a fact that registers with considerable force at the beginning of the slow movement, which bears an unmistakable stylistic resemblance to the parallel movement in the *New World* Symphony. Beautifully crafted, with a plethora of winsome melodies (not least the first movement's second main idea), the G major also features a lilting Scherzo and a genial, folk-like finale.

Vlach Quartet
Praga mono

A notably Slavic style of playing tonally fulsome, highly dynamic and with an idiomatic turn of phrase. The broadcast recording, although hardly state-of-the-art, is more than acceptable (not to be confused with a version by the less exceptional 'new' Vlach Quartet on Naxos). Digital rivals include the fine Panocha Quartet (Supraphon) and the Lindsays (ASV), while the analogue field is dominated by the glorious 'old' Prague Quartet (Biddulph mono, recorded in 1933) and their latterday successor on DG (analogue, and included as part of a complete survey of all Dvořák's quartets).

String Quartet No. 14 in A flat major, B193 (Op. 105) (1895)

Taut arguments, sighing nostalgia and appreciative reminiscences of the American musical culture that Dvořák was about to leave characterize the first movement of this beautiful A flat major Quartet. There's also a carefree Scherzo (a *Furiant*), a poignant *Lento* (one of Dvořák's most heart-rending slow movements) and a finale that starts in a state of tension, swings into a Polka, tenses itself again, then proceeds to the end in high spirits. As with B192, composition this Quartet was begun in America and completed on home territory.

Barylli Quartet
MCA mono

You'd never believe that this recording was made as long ago as 1953, save that the sound is one-dimensional (and then you'll have to listen particularly hard for that fact to register). The Barylli's performance is broad, warmly expressive and full-toned – though there are fine stereo rival versions from the Lindsays (ASV, digital) and, especially, the Smetana Quartet (Testament, analogue).

Edvard Grieg (1843-1907)

String Quartet No. 1 in G minor, Op. 27 (1877-78)

Grieg's First Quartet (he actually wrote three-and-a-half, but this is the only one that was published) serves as an ideal introduction to the world of dramatic chamber music. Its opening movement is full of romantic gestures and coruscating climaxes, its *Romanze* second movement is a tender 'song without words' whereas further contrast is facilitated by a lilting, waltz-like "Intermezzo" and a finale that starts expressively and then sweeps into what sounds like a *Norwegian Dance*. You'd never guess that Grieg once claimed to have "great difficulty" with the quartet medium.

Budapest Quartet
Biddulph mono

It's always rather dangerous to recommend recordings that helped to form one's own musical tastes, but I can honestly say that this vibrant 1937 version of the Grieg Quartet has a degree of fire, intimacy and musical conviction that none since has rivalled. It still sounds excellent (the mono recording was judiciously balanced), but there's a listener-friendly digital option by the Guarneri Quartet (Philips).

New voices (1893-1988)

Beethoven had already intimated future trends in his ethereal late quartets (see above), but even he couldn't have imagined how far Bartók, Schoenberg and Steve Reich would develop the quartet medium. Here we deal with some of the most overtly demonstrative chamber music ever composed – from Janáček's intimate confessions to the Punk-like aggression of Bartók's Fourth Quartet.

Gabriel Fauré (1845-1924)

String Quartet in E minor, Op. 121 (1923-24)

Fauré's brand of modernity was subtle and unobtrusive. The String Quartet inhabits a rarefied atmosphere where, in the first and last movements especially, the melodic line seems constantly to rise, suggesting a kind of gravitational pull. It is fairly typical of Fauré's 'late' style – austere yet calming, inwardly intense yet almost completely free of neurosis. The second movement is notably eloquent and although the *Allegro* finale attempts to lighten the mood, an overall sense of sadness remains.

 ***Pro Arte Quartet***
Biddulph mono

Recorded just 11 years after the work was completed, this remarkably perceptive performance captures what was then 'new music' on the wing. The tone is intense, the ensemble watertight and although the sound is elderly, it conjures a feeling of intimacy that suits the music. Good modern rivals are relatively thin on the ground, but if you really can't face 78rpm transfers, then I'd recommend sampling the Parrenin Quartet (EMI, analogue).

Leoš Janáček (1854-1928)

String Quartet No. 1, "The Kreutzer Sonata" (1923)

Tolstoy's original story concerns a jealous husband who, on hearing his wife perform Beethoven's *Kreutzer* Sonata with the violinist to whom she has become attracted, is temporarily calmed by the music. Later, however, he chances upon the two together and, in a fit of rage, murders the woman he loves. Janáček's inclination was to side more with the wife (he was already deeply devoted to the young Kamila Stösslová) and his First Quartet protests her cause with unprecedented passion.

String Quartet No. 2, "Intimate Letters" (1928)

An irrepressibly youthful statement of passionate infatuation penned by a man of 74 and fashioned as a series of "Intimate Letters" to his adored Kamila Stösslová. There are four varied movements, but perhaps the most poignant is the third, a sad *Moderato* – part serenade, part lullaby, and strongly suggestive of a peasant mother with child in arms.

 ***Alban Berg Quartet***
EMI digital

Recorded live in 1993, the Alban Berg Quartet plumb the depths of this wild, unpredictable music; their pooled tone is consistently warm and their attack is fiery in the extreme. The Melos Quartet (Harmonia Mundi) provide a good second digital choice, while earlier recordings by such eminent string quartets as the Janáček (Supraphon, analogue), Smetana (Supraphon and Testament, analogue) and Hagen (their ECM version of No. 1, digital) serve the music with generous measures of intensity.

Claude Debussy (1862-1918)

String Quartet in G minor, Op. 10 (1893)

Although composed during the twilight of the last century and featuring a notably romantic *Andantino* slow movement (the closing moments of which are among the most beautiful in the entire quartet repertory), Debussy's G minor String Quartet anticipates various works composed early in the next century, including some of Debussy's own and the String Quartet of Maurice Ravel (see below). Leading features include relative harmonic sophistication and great rhythmic vitality – especially in the second and fourth movements.

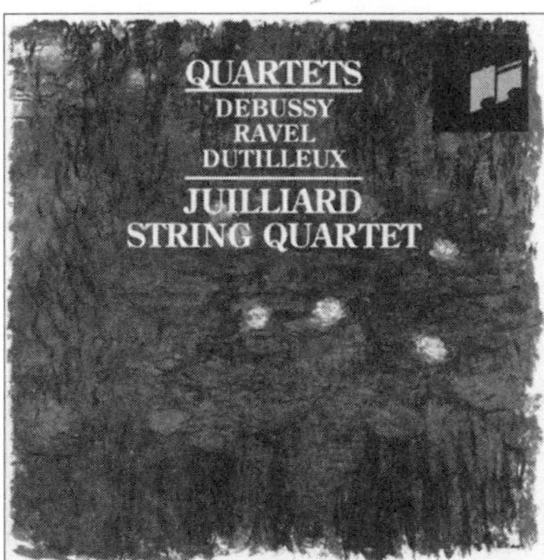

 ***Juilliard Quartet***
Sony Classical digital

The Juilliard's third recording of the Debussy Quartet has a warm tonal blend and an intuitive ease of delivery that mark it out as truly exceptional. Those who want something a little more sleek and attenuated are directed to the Emerson Quartet (DG digital), while there are compelling older recordings by the Capet and Pro Arte Quartets (both on Biddulph, mono).

Jean Sibelius (1865-1957)

String Quartet in D minor, Op. 56, "Voces intimae" (1908-09)

Sibelius fashioned this Quartet while working on his Third and Fourth Symphonies, and its intimate sound-world reflects the latter in particular (the two slow movements have much in common). The Quartet's first movement is taut and animated, the second all filigree scurrying, the third a desolate soundscape, the fourth suggestive of earth and air (the emphatic opening soon gives way to more ethereal writing) and the thrilling finale recalls the heady helter-skelter of "Lemminkäinen's Return" (see "Narratives in Sound").

Budapest Quartet
Biddulph mono

Brilliant playing – incisive but also sensitive to atmosphere (always essential with Sibelius) and wearing its 60-odd years with barely a wrinkle. Best among modern rivals is the Guarneri Quartet on Philips (digital) which, like this particular CD, couples the Sibelius D minor with Grieg's equally fine Quartet in G minor.

Arnold Schoenberg (1874-1951)

String Quartet No. 2 in F sharp minor, Op. 10 (1907-08)

An extraordinarily gripping work that witnesses a gradual retreat from a 'tonal centre' (it was the last of Schoenberg's works with a designated key signature). The fourth movement ushers in the words "I feel the air of another planet/the friendly faces that were turned toward me/but, lately, now are fading into darkness ...". Stefan Georg's poetry – sung by a soprano – provides a literary subtext for both the third and fourth movements. The second movement is cast in the form of variations, whereas the third recalls – in its veiled nostalgia – a Viennese song.

String Quartet No. 4, Op. 37 (1936)

Anyone needing confirmation that the mature Schoenberg could write music of great expressive power should sample the broad unison recitative at the opening of this Quartet's slow movement. The Fourth Quartet is rather less 'difficult' than the Third (a rigourously atonal composition); it opens dramatically then goes on to explore the medium's textural potential with a contrapuntal rigour that equals Brahms.

Dawn Upshaw (soprano), Arditti Quartet
Auvidis Montaigne digital

Few post-war string quartets have done more to spread the gospel of modern music than the Arditti Quartet. Their huge repertoire includes some of the most challenging works of the last 70 years and their performances of the Schoenberg quartets (these particular readings are part of a two-CD complete cycle) are informed by both scholarship and musical intuition. Dawn Upshaw is able to negotiate even the most demanding vocal writing and the recordings are excellent. However, those with a taste for interpretative adventure should investigate the Kolisch Quartet's 1936-37 set, recorded especially for Schoenberg (in Hollywood film studios – Archiphon, mono) and, although not without imperfections, extraordinarily compelling.

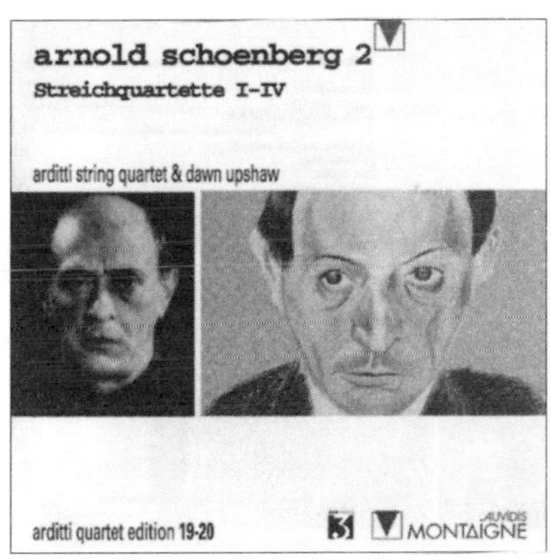

Maurice Ravel (1875-1937)

String Quartet in F major

The cool, gently hedonistic opening is the ultimate in musical escapism – although the action that follows is so full of innovative devices and shimmering excitement that it soon draws you into the fray. The second movement's pizzicato writing recalls Debussy's Quartet (see above); the *Très lent* slow movement is hauntingly atmospheric and the agitated finale unexpectedly dramatic.

Juilliard Quartet
Sony Classical digital

As in the Debussy Quartet, the Juilliard exhibits an intuitive grasp of the music's mood and arguments, easing from episode to episode with all the naturalness of seasoned jazz musicians. Rivalry is fairly fierce (the Debussy and Ravel Quartets are frequently coupled together on the same CD), with the Emerson Quartet (DG, digital) proving especially impressive.

Chamber music New voices (1893-1988)

Béla Bartók (1881-1945)

String Quartet No. 1, Sz40 (1908)
Written on the rebound from a failed love affair, Bartók's First Quartet commemorates its composer's obsession (the violinist Stefi Geyer, for whom he also wrote a violin concerto) by quoting 'her' theme in what he refers to, somewhat over-dramatically perhaps, as his "funeral dirge". Musically, Bartók the radical keeps one foot securely placed in the Impressionistic camp, although there are clear references to Hungarian folk-music.

String Quartet No. 2, Sz67 (1915-17)
Bartók's love of Debussy finds ardent expression in the opening *Moderato,* although the harmonic language is comparatively advanced and the wildly pulsing second movement - a fiery *Allegro molto capriccioso* - ends at top speed, scurrying insect-like in keen anticipation of the later quartets. The finale is mysterious, densely *hamornized* and subtly commemorative of themes heard earlier in the Quartet.

String Quartet No. 3, Sz85 (1927)
The shortest, most tightly constructed and possibly the most revolutionary of Bartók's six quartets (its raging narrative is condensed into a mere quarter of an hour). The Third is in effect a one-movement mini-drama that falls into four parts. Bartók forges his structure from carefully chosen thematic germs and the work culminates in a cataclysmic coda, where insistent rhythms and dramatic downward slides compound its impact.

String Quartet No. 4, Sz91 (1928)
Bartók out of doors, provoking us with obdurate themes and conjuring vivid images of wildlife at night (the third movement). The construction is 'arch-like' (fast-Scherzo-slow-Scherzo-fast), with a tactile second Scherzo (played pizzicato) that reflects the composer's love of insects and a stamping finale that rivals rock music in its untamed aggression and ferocious rhythms. Anyone requiring evidence of chamber music's ability to shock should start with the last movement of Bartók's Fourth String Quartet.

String Quartet No. 5, Sz102 (1934)
A half-way house between the primitivist protest of the Fourth Quartet and the relative serenity of the Sixth. The Fifth is in fact the longest of Bartók's quartets; its rhythms remain pungent and attractively upbeat while its emotional climate extends to a pair of mirroring slow movements. There's also a jazzy Scherzo and a furious finale that, near the end, suddenly cuts off for a cynical distortion of a Classical minuet. If the Third is the most radical of Bartók's quartets, the Fifth is surely the greatest.

String Quartet No. 6, Sz114 (1938)
The last Quartet is a profoundly inward narrative that anticipates - at least in mood - both the death of Bartók's mother and the tragedy of world war. It was probably the last of Bartók's 'Hungarian' works (he was soon *en route* to America) and although occasionally touched with humour, it marks a palpable turning from earth to spirit. Each movement starts with a sad motive while the Quartet's mysterious closing bars suggest a plethora of unanswerable questions.

Végh Quartet
Auvidis Astrée analogue
Sándor Végh's mastery in Bartók recalls the easy spontaneity and total involvement of key jazz musicians. Nothing sounds forced or superficial and although there are occasional pitch problems (Végh's intonation sometimes strays off the note), the sheer vitality, warmth and commitment of these performances easily win the day. A more 'hygenic' option is provided by the Emerson Quartet's Gramophone-Award winning digital set (DG) while the second of the Juilliard Quartet's three recordings (Sony, analogue) also warrants serious consideration.

Alban Berg (1885-1935)

Lyric Suite (1925-26)
Like Janáček's Second Quartet, Berg's *Lyric Suite* was born of a love affair (in Berg's case, involving the sister of the Expressionist writer Franz Werfel) and is rich in symbolic allusions. The title was inspired by Zemlinsky's *Lyric Symphony*, a quotation from which appears in the Suite's *Adagio appassionato* fourth movement. Berg's style of writing combines 12-tone techniques, colourful effects (the eerie sliding and tapping of the *Allegro misterioso* third movement) with richly harmonized passages that hark back to the heyday of late-Romanticism. The *Lyric Suite* is among the most inwardly compelling chamber works of the last 70 years. Berg subsequently arranged three movements for chamber orchestra, but the original remains uniquely powerful.

Juilliard Quartet
Sony Classical digital
A superb performance, spontaneous, intelligent and unstintingly expressive (just try the fourth movement). The sound is extremely full-bodied but there are fine alternative recordings by the LaSalle Quartet (DG, analogue), Arditti Quartet (Auvidis Montaigne, digital) and Alban Berg Quartet (Teldec analogue, or EMI digital).

Sergey Prokofiev (1891-1953)

String Quartet No. 2 in F major, Op. 92 (1941)

Prokofiev's enjoyable and provocative Second Quartet was forged very much in the style of Caucasian folk music. Best of all is the second movement, a shimmering *Adagio* interrupted by a perky little march tune (the closing pages are pure magic), whereas the 'folk' element is especially evident in the last movement – the principal subject of which is (or at least sounds) part 'stamping dance', part Charleston.

 ***Hollywood Quartet***
Testament mono

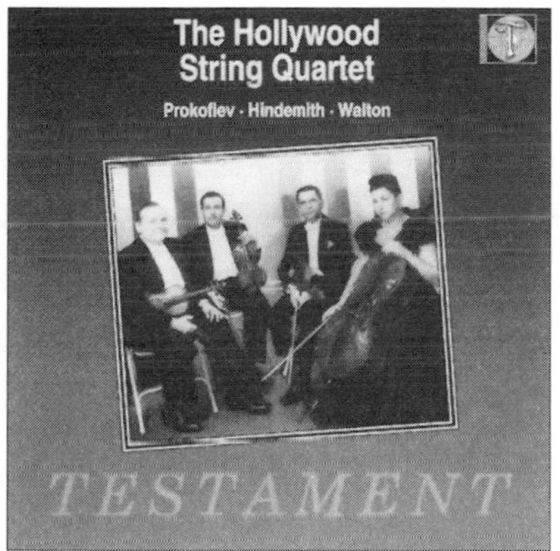

A benchmark interpretation, recorded just ten years after the work was completed. Felix Slatkin (father of the conductor Leonard Slatkin) leads a group where sweetness of tone (the sort that graces many a Hollywood film soundtrack), precision and virtuosity are tastefully employed. The Hollywood's account of Prokofiev's central Adagio must rank among the finest string quartet tracks ever recorded.

Pavel Haas (1899-1944)

String Quartet No. 2, "From the Monkey Mountains" (1925)

On October 16th, 1944 Pavel Haas travelled from the Nazi ghetto at Terezin (or 'Theresienstadt', as it was known to German-speakers) to the gas chambers at Auschwitz. Nine years earlier this immensely talented Janáček pupil had composed his mysterious quartet-suite, inspired by a visit to the Czech-Moravian Highlands which, in Brno, were sometimes known as the "Monkey Mountains". Haas's aim was to suggest the rhythm of the open countryside, bird-song, the irregular motion of village carts, revelry at night, etc. Composed mid-way between Janáček's two quartets, Haas's Second is surely their near-equal in terms of quality.

 ***Hawthorne Quartet***
Decca digital

Superb playing on a CD that also includes Haas's Third Quartet and a fascinating String Quartet (1921) by Hans Krása. The two composers travelled to their deaths on the same day.

William Walton (1902-1983)

String Quartet in A minor (1945-47)

Generally known simply as 'Walton's String Quartet', the A minor is in fact the second of two – its harshly dissonant predecessor (an undergraduate piece) having only recently been discovered. The 'Second', however, is among Walton's warmest creations – highly animated, bittersweet, wistful (not unlike the Violin Concerto in mood) and consistently melodic.

 ***Hollywood Quartet***
Testament mono

The Hollywood Quartet consulted Walton on matters of interpretation. In fact, the composer actually rejected their first tape (because of an omitted repeat in the Scherzo) but then went on to praise this particular recording. Three years later, they performed the work in Walton's presence: "I hope no one ever records my Quartet again, " he said, "because you captured so exactly what I wanted and yet we were 6,000 miles apart."

Dmitry Shostakovich (1906-1975)

String Quartet No. 8 in C minor, Op. 110 (1960)

Anyone doubting that chamber music can rival symphonic repertoire for descriptive or narrative power should sample this humbling masterpiece. Ostensibly inspired by the ruins of war-torn Dresden, the Eighth Quartet is a wordless indictment of war, violence, tyranny and oppression – whether personal or political. The music itself is rich in effects – from self-quotation, folk tones and gunfire to the notational equivalent of the composer's own signature (D Es C and H i.e. D. SCHostakovich), the German equivalents of our D, E flat, C and B.

 ***Borodin Quartet***
EMI analogue

Shostakovich's Eighth Quartet has become indelibly associated with the Borodin Quartet, who have recorded it at least four times (a Decca analogue recording from the 1960s is also well worth hearing). And the accolades are certainly justified, for their readings combine warmth, precision and an astonishing dynamism.

String Quartet No. 15 in E flat minor, Op. 144 (1974)
Six *adagios* in a row, each one quite different to its neighbours. Shostakovich's last Quartet takes its lead from Haydn's multi-slow movement *Seven Last Words of Christ* (also for string quartet). The first movement is like a liturgical chant, the second opens to rocketing *crescendos* on single strings, the third starts wildly before climbing quietly into the ether, the fourth offers pained respite, the fifth is a funeral march and the sixth recalls earlier motives (including a clear reference to the Eighth Symphony) before fading to a questioning void.

Beethoven Quartet
Praga analogue

The Beethoven Quartet was always closely associated with Shostakovich; the Fourteenth Quartet (1973) was dedicated to its cellist Sergey Shirinsky, who had died merely months after its first performance. This particular reading – which was recorded for Czech Radio in 1976 – is deeply introspective, though anyone with access either to a studio recording by the same ensemble (Consonance, analogue) or alternative versions by the Manhattan (Koch, digital) or Borodin (EMI, analogue) Quartets, not to mention a quartet led by Gidon Kremer (Sony, digital), should have no grounds for complaints.

Steve Reich (b1936)

Different Trains, for string quartet and tape (1988)
Take fragments of speech that recall the composer's earliest memories, replete with people and places;add the terrible spectre of the Nazi death camps; a screaming train siren, pounding rhythms and the intimate sonority of a string quartet – and you have a mini-drama that's part-documentary, part-chamber music and unquestionably a masterpiece. Reich's journey delivers us through innocence and tragedy to hope. It's a disquieting experience, full of unfamiliar sounds, but the effect is spellbinding.

Kronos Quartet
Nonesuch digital

The first and probably definitive recording, achieved in close collaboration with the composer. Hearing Different Trains on CD is actually more effective than hearing it in the concert hall.

The more, the merrier (1785-1976)

If the duo sonata represents chamber music as a more-or-less equal dialogue and the string quartet as an intimate conversation between four, our 'four or more' selection fattens textures further from the tonally sonorous string quintet (with either two violas or two cellos) to works with strings and piano and the sublime busyness of Mendelssohn's Octet for strings.

Wolfgang Amadeus Mozart (1719-1787)

Clarinet Quintet in A major, K581 (1789)
It was Mozart himself who named this work the *Stadler* Quintet, after his clarinettist friend Anton Stadler. Mozart had discovered the clarinet ten years earlier in Milan (the instrument's actual range reached lower then than it does now) and his Quintet exploits its expressive potential with consummate skill. The coolly sublime *Larghetto* is among the best-known movements in Mozart's output.

Jack Brymer (clarinet), Allegri Quartet
Belart analogue

Mozart's Clarinet Quintet calls for a combination of textural refinement and self-effacing musicianship, and Jack Brymer's stylish, mellifluous playing more than fits the bill, with nicely-turned support from the Allegri

Quartet. Those who fancy period-instrument sonorities and a basset-clarinet (the instrument that Mozart himself would have known) are directed to Alan Hacker and the Salomon Quartet (Amon Ra, analogue).

Piano Quartet No. 1 in G minor, K478 (1785)

A work that, like the G minor String Quintet (see below) and (late) G minor Symphony (see "Classical models", above), opens in a mood of considerable anguish. The first movement is dominated by a commanding unison theme that develops with great tension and considerable harmonic ingenuity; the graceful *Andante* is cast in Mozart's most lyrical vein and the finale includes a theme borrowed from J. C. Bach.

Piano Quartet No. 2 in E flat major, K493 (1786)

Mozart at his most confident and masterful – though the E flat major Quartet is quite unlike its G minor companion, certainly in the first movement, with its grand sonorities (the first theme especially) and sunny countenance. The *Andante* has a 'speaking' eloquence and the witty finale is marked by keen dialogue between piano and strings (the tender second theme – 1'28" into the relevant track on our recommended version – is especially memorable).

Quintet in E flat major, for piano, oboe, clarinet, horn and bassoon, K452 (1784)

"The best work that I have written so far in my life," is how Mozart described this Quintet to his father. And if you listen to the noble *Largo* introduction, you'll understand why. The *Larghetto* recalls the world of Mozart's wind serenades (the central section suggests parallels with the slow movement of his Piano Concerto No. 21 – from, say, 4'33") while the immensely eventful closing Rondo is rich enough in musical incident to stand alone.

Ingrid Haebler (piano), Michel Schwalbé (violin), Giusto Cappone (viola), Ottomar Borwitzky (cello), members of the Bamberg Wind Quintet

Philips analogue

Good though the accompanying artists are (the wind players especially), it's Haebler whose artistry shines brightest here. Her touch is firm but delicate, her phrasing characteristically flexible and she knows precisely when to assert herself and when to switch to an accompanying role. The excellent c1970 recordings have been beautifully refurbished.

String Quintet No. 2 in C minor, K406/516*b* (1788)

Mozart's Second 'viola' Quintet (the scoring – as in the rest of the series – is for two violins, two violas and cello) is actually his own arrangement of an earlier wind octet (known nowadays as K388). The very opening is darkly dramatic while the ensuing argument is leavened by a sweetly smiling 'second subject'. There's a gently flowing *Andante*, a tightly contrapuntal *Menuetto* and a theme with variations to close.

String Quintet No. 3 in C major, K515 (1787)

The opening is immediately distinctive: an upward stepping 'arpeggio' (harp-like figure) played on the cello and elegantly answered by the first violin. Once in motion, the genial though taut 'development' recalls the opera *The Marriage of Figaro* (which Mozart had recently completed). The *Andante* is an ardent dialogue between first violin and viola, the Minuet more sombre than the norm while the ebullient finale is the longest instrumental movement that Mozart ever composed (537 bars).

String Quintet No. 4 in G minor, K516 (1787)

Neither the Third not the Fourth Quintets were commissioned, so one might reasonably assume that Mozart was prompted by his own creative urges. And if the Third is relatively easygoing, the Fourth is an urgent forerunner of the late G minor Symphony, with an anguished opening *Allegro* (made all the more powerful by its rigorous structure), a melancholy Minuet (eased mid-way by one of Mozart's loveliest Trio sections) and a tragic *Adagio* introduction to the buoyant finale. But it is the heart-rending slow movement that bespeaks the deepest feelings: nothing else in Mozart quite matches it.

String Quintet No. 5 in D major, K593 (1790)

A reflective though immensely resourceful composition, its opening *Larghetto* recurring – subtly modified – after the main *Allegro*. The first measures of the slow movement unfold like the petals of a flower (there's also a hint of the Fourth Quintet's confessional eloquence) while the hugely eventful finale recalls Haydn at his most mischievously contrapuntal (note, too, an unmistakable reference to Mozart's own *Jupiter* Symphony of two years earlier).

String Quintet No. 6 in E flat major, K614 (1791)

The first theme is played by violas and treated to what seems like endless variation, whereas the opening measures of the *Andante* recall the *Romanza* from *Eine kleine Nachtmusik*. The Minuet features a particularly exquisite Trio, while the pert (though playfully halting) finale is refreshingly light-hearted.

Arthur Grumiaux, Arpad Gérecz (violins), Georges Janzer, Max Lesueur (violas), Eva Czako (cello)

Philips analogue

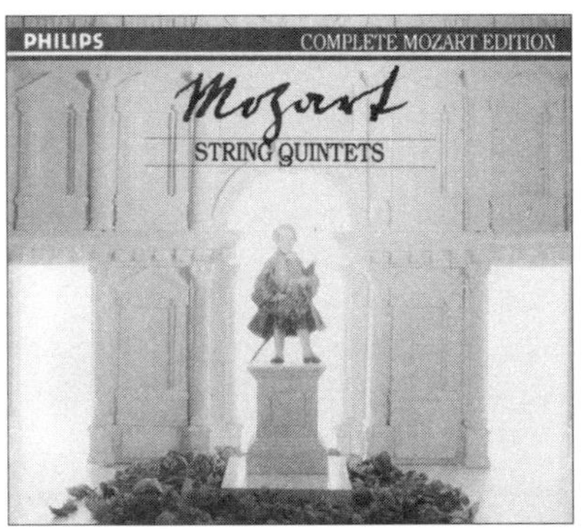

Reissued in Philips's acclaimed "Mozart Edition", Grumiaux's 1973 set of the Quintets (No. 1 is of course also included) boasts a conceptual intelligence and mellowness of tone that remain fairly unique – although Heifetz's recording of the Fourth Quintet (RCA, analogue) combines lyricism with great intensity (some will say too much intensity) and there's a wonderful pre-war recording of the Third Quintet with the augmented Pro Arte Quartet (EMI, mono).

Franz Schubert (1797-1828)

Octet in F major for two violins, viola, cello, double-bass, clarinet, bassoon and horn (1824)

The Octet is predominantly positive in spirit (it was modelled on Beethoven's Septet, albeit with a second violin added) but was actually composed during a period when Schubert was in deep despair: darker intimations trouble both the finale's chilling introduction and the fourth movement's minor-key variations. The work's six movements play for nearly an hour.

Vienna Chamber Ensemble

Deutsche Grammophon analogue

Top-ranking Viennese players in repertoire that must have been extremely familiar to them. The Adagio has a beguiling gracefulness, the finale's opening a grave intensity that anticipates Schubert's last String Quartet and the Allegro proper a wholly appropriate sense of well-being. The recording is excellent, but there are first-rate digital alternatives from the Berlin Soloists (Teldec) and the Berlin Philharmonic Ensemble (Denon).

Quintet in A major for piano, violin, viola, cello and double-bass, D667, "Trout" (1819)

Pure delight from start to finish, although there are also one or two references to the more introspective side of Schubert's nature. The *Trout Quintet* has a lively Scherzo as its centrepiece flanked either side by a lyrical slow movement, while the opening *Allegro vivace* is balanced by an equally buoyant *Allegro giusto* (literally 'strict' or 'just') finale. The work's title refers to Schubert's song *Die Forelle* ("The Trout") which serves as the basis for a lovingly embellished set of variations (in effect, the second of the two slow movements).

Ingrid Haebler (piano), Arthur Grumiaux (violin), Georges Janzer (viola), Eva Czako (cello), Jacques Cazuaran (double-bass)

Belart analogue

Intelligent, vivacious and with poetically expressive contributions from all the soloists (Grumiaux and Czako in particular). Philips have released a less sweet but marginally more thoughtful digital successor (Grumiaux's performance was originally a Philips release), led by Alfred Brendel (piano) and Thomas Zehetmair (violin).

String Quintet in C major, D956 (1828)

Unlike Mozart's and Brahms's string quintets (see above and below, respectively), which employ a string quartet plus a second viola, Schubert's uses a second cello – and that makes for some of the most voluminous sonorities in the chamber music repertory. The music itself approximates a sort of '*Great* C major Symphony among five' and features a serene *Adagio* that's suddenly interrupted by an anguished central interlude.

Isaac Stern, Alexander Schneider (violins), Milton Katims (viola), Pablo Casals, Paul Tortelier (cellos)

Sony Classical mono

Glorious music-making, led by the bright and intense violin playing of a (relatively) young Isaac Stern, with the wise and wistful Casals dominating the lower spectrum. The mono sound is perfectly adequate, but there is strong competition from Heifetz, Piatigorsky and friends (RCA, analogue), the Hollywood Quartet and Kurt Reher (Testament, mono), the Borodin Quartet with Mikhail Milman (Teldec, digital) and the LaSalle Quintet with Lynn Harrell (DG, digital).

Felix Mendelssohn (1809-1847)

Octet for strings (1825)

Probably the most perfect manifestation of teenage musical genius and an unremiting source of joy, whether for the players or for the listeners. The Octet is scored for a double string quartet – i.e. four violins, two violas and two cellos. Mendelssohn was just 16 years old when he wrote it and yet the work's expressive range incorporates an exhilarating opening *Allegro*, an *Andante* that sheds premature tears, a thistledown Scherzo (always a speciality with this composer) and a dazzling *Presto* to close.

Jascha Heifetz, Israel Baker, Arnold Belnick, Joseph Stepansky (violins), William Primrose, Virginia Majewski (violas), Gregor Piatigorsky, Gabor Rejto (cellos)

RCA analogue

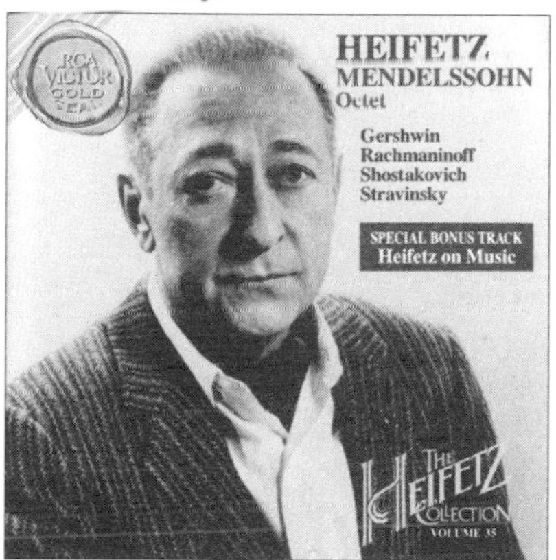

String virtuosity without peer, recorded during the summer of 1961 by a group of players who made the Octet something of a speciality. Sample the first five minutes or, better still, the Scherzo – and I challenge you to resist!

Robert Schumann (1810-1856)

Piano Quartet in E flat major, Op. 47 (1842)

The Piano Quartet is less extrovert in character than the Quintet (see below) but no less appealing. The slow movement sings a particularly soulful melody (it's very much in the manner of Schumann's more lyrical songs) and there's a fleet-footed, Mendelssohnian Scherzo.

Glenn Gould (piano), members of the Juilliard Quartet

Sony Classical analogue

Glenn Gould gives a clear-headed account of the solo part (quite unlike the zany excesses of some of his solo records) and his Juilliard collaborators (Robert Mann, Raphael Hillyer and Claus Adam) are all front-ranking players. There's also a coltish alternative from Alexandre Rabinovitch and friends (EMI digital), but the Gould-Juilliard Quartet alliance should more than fit the bill.

Piano Quintet in E flat major, Op. 44 (1842)

Possibly the most accessible chamber work of all. Schumann's Piano Quintet harbours a rich fund of melody, the first movement's second (lyrical) theme being especially memorable. There's also a galloping Scherzo and a march-like slow movement with deeply moving interludes. Schumann's friend and admirer Mendelssohn played the piano at the private première (Robert's most ardent interpreter, his wife Clara, was pregnant at the time).

Artur Rubinstein (piano), Guarneri Quartet

RCA analogue

Rubinstein's first recording of the Quintet (with the tonally glamorous Paganini Quartet, also for RCA) has long been deleted – but if it reappears while we're going to print, do snap it up. However, his later version – which is nearly as good – features buoyant pianism and warmly expressive string playing. There's also a wildly spontaneous live recording featuring pianist Martha Argerich (EMI, digital)

César Franck (1822-1890)

Piano Quintet in F minor (1878-79)

One of the supreme instrumental narratives of the Romantic era opens in a mood of pensive anticipation. The first movement alternates wan lyricism with tempestuous tonal storms; the second (marked *con molto sentimento*) has a fetching albeit fragile expressivity, while the whirlwind finale suggests a symphony in all but name. Saint-Saëns was the pianist in the first performance, and Franck subsequently dedicated the work to him (though the younger man left the hall without the precious gift that Franck had offered him – the Quintet's manuscript!).

Sviatoslav Richter (piano), Borodin Quartet

Philips digital

A perfect balance of structural solidity and tonal sweetness (Richter providing the former, the Borodins the latter): it's a powerful reading that never overheats, and the 1981 Russian recording has plenty of body. Good rival versions – and there are many – include the rightly famous Heifetz-Piatigorsky recording for RCA (analogue, and a performance that combines fire and elegance) and a compelling pre-war recording by Alfred Cortot and the International Quartet (Biddulph, mono).

Chamber music The more, the merrier (1785-1976)

Johannes Brahms (1833-1897)

Clarinet Quintet in B minor, Op. 115 (1891)

The sheer warmth of this wonderful Quintet tends to mask the ingenuity of its design. Brahms had been bewitched by the playing of clarinettist Richard Mühfeld, much as Mozart had been impressed by Anton Stadler (note his Quintet, see above), and the resulting masterpiece combines rhapsodic expressivity – the *Adagio* is rich in gipsy-style allusions – with a subtle but exhaustive use of variation.

Charles Neidich (clarinet), Juilliard Quartet

Sony Classical digital

A mellifluous, full-bodied reading, unhurried and eloquently phrased, especially by Neidich. The recording is notable for its integrated balance of textures but various older recordings also demand attention, not least Reginald Kell with the Busch Quartet (recorded in 1937 – Testament, EMI, mono).

Piano Quartet No. 2 in A major, Op. 26 (1861-62)

The second and greatest of Brahms's piano quartets opens to a restless, quizzical theme (not unlike the first subject of the Fourth Symphony), then goes on to use that same material as the basis for a tough, resilient musical argument. However, the very heart of the work lies in its *Poco adagio* slow movement, one of Brahms's most expressive utterances – a sweet and reflective essay punctuated by deeply moving outbursts.

Sviatoslav Richter (piano), Borodin Quartet

Philips digital

Richter's account of the solo part is cool, sensitive and uncompromisingly powerful while his Russian colleagues project a vibrant pooled tone (especially in the slow movement). There are a few minor slip-ups (this is a live recording) although the actual sound, which is set in a rather dry acoustic but has plenty of presence, is certainly more lustrous than its nearest rival – a 1932 set by Rudolf Serkin and the Busch Quartet (Biddulph, mono). There's another good digital version led by Isaac Stern (Sony, digital), but Richter and the Borodin Quartet remain a firm first choice.

Piano Quartet No. 3 in C minor, Op. 60 (1855-75)

The most intense of the three piano quartets. The first movement grows out of the little 'weeping' motive that dominates the introduction (there's a real battle of wills later on), whereas the Scherzo vies – in terms of excitement – with the parallel movement in the Piano Quintet (see below). There's a songful *Andante* and a finale that alternates lyricism (the opening theme is a little like the finale to the First Violin Sonata) with passages of unbridled passion (i.e. the tempestuous second idea). Brahms started this Quartet during the dark days of Schumann's final illness.

Jascha Heifetz (violin), Sanford Schonbach (viola), Gregor Piatigorsky (cello), Jacob Lateiner (piano)

RCA analogue

A performance where taut rhythms and a refusal to linger (so important in music that is already loaded with emotion) go hand in hand with an expressive power that is the special province of these players – Heifetz and Piatigorsky, in particular. For a more expansive, rather more relaxed approach, try the Beaux Arts Trio with Walter Trampler (Philips, analogue).

Piano Quintet in F minor, Op. 34 (1861-64)

The grandest of Brahms's mature chamber works originally started life as a string quintet for two cellos – although it's difficult to imagine the piano playing anything other than a dominant role. The Quintet's impact is that of a major dramatic symphony, the most thrilling movement being its proud, bracing Scherzo – just the thing for a musical pick-me-up, especially as the Trio or central section is one of the most gloriously effusive melodies in Brahms's output (it is in fact a cunning major-key transformation of the movement's principal theme).

Maurizio Pollini (piano), Quartetto Italiano

Deutsche Grammophon analogue

Pollini and his Italian colleagues deliver on all counts: theirs is among the strongest, most intense and best played versions ever recorded. However, the musical past provides – as ever – a significant storehouse of eminent rivals, not least Rudolf Serkin with the Budapest Quartet (Sony, analogue). There's also a fine digital alternative featuring pianist Elizo Virzaladze with the Borodin Quartet (Teldec) and a thrilling (though scratchy-

sounding) broadcast performance of Brahms's own two-piano version played by the composers Bartók and Dohnányi (Hungaroton, mono).

String Quintet No. 1 in F major, Op. 88 (1882)

The First Quintet's second movement is particularly striking: cast in five contrasted sections, it opens with a sombre theme strongly reminiscent of the Clarinet Quintet then twice takes flight with genial faster music. The first movement's radiant second theme is equally memorable while the Beethovenian finale represents Brahms at his most fiercely contrapuntal.

 ***Juilliard Quartet, Walter Trampler (viola)***

Sony Classical digital

The aural equivalent of vintage wine: distinctive, full-bodied and mildly intoxicating. True, leader Robert Mann does occasionally stray from the note's centre but, taken as a whole, this is a superb reading, beautifully recorded. The most engaging rival dates from before the Second World War and features an augmented Budapest Quartet (Biddulph, mono), while the Budapest's 1958 stereo remake (Sony, analogue) includes an especially riveting account of the finale.

String Quintet No. 2 in G major, Op. 111 (1890)

Just listen to the opening minute or so – an excited rush of string sound, grounded by the cello and dominated by a heroic theme that recalls the inspirational world of Brahms's Third Symphony. This is chamber music at its most charismatic: passionate, assertive and, once into the middle movements, quintessentially Brahmsian in its songful lyricism.

 ***Hagen Quartet, Gerard Caussé (viola)***

Deutsche Grammophon digital

A lean, fiery performance that comes coupled with a fine account of the First Quintet. There are inspired alternatives from the Budapest and Juilliard Quartets (both with Walter Trampler) and a star-studded string ensemble led by Isaac Stern (recorded in a church at the dead of night!). All three are on Sony Classical (the Juilliard is a digital recording – see above) but, being vaguely historical (they date from the 1950s), the Budapest and Stern recordings might prove rather difficult to locate.

String Sextet No. 1 in B flat major, Op. 18 (1856-60)

The sunniest of Brahms's chamber works opens in a spirit of sublime contentment, although subsequent arguments display a good deal of expressive instrumental interplay. The second movement – a theme with variations – harks back to the music of an earlier era: the theme itself resembles a noble slow march and the variations are dynamic and colourful (one in particular – a gorgeous interlude that occurs around half-way through the movement [5'33" into the relevant track on our recommended recording] – serves as a sort of 'Trio' section and anticipates the passionate worlds of the Fourth Symphony and the Piano Quintet).

 ***Isaac Stern, Alexander Schneider (violins), Milton Katims, Milton Thomas (violas), Pablo Casals, Madeline Foley (cellos)***

Sony Classical mono

Chamber-music playing of the highest order – wise, mellow, relaxed and graced with the inestimable bonus of having Pablo Casals 'lead' from the bottom end (so to speak). The second movement's ghostly closing moments are unforgettable, but there are fine, full-bodied alternatives from the augmented Amadeus or Alban Berg Quartets (DG analogue or EMI digital, respectively).

String Sextet No. 2 in G major, Op. 36 (1864-65)

If the First Sextet spells genial affirmation, the Second seems to represent a more negative train of feeling – heartache, reflectiveness, resignation. Or at least that's how it seems. Brahms had recently freed himself from an infatuation (the first movement incorporates the name 'Agathe' in musical notation), though he himself considered his G major Sextet to have the same "jovial character" as his First. Readers are advised to sample the *Adagio* third movement and judge for themselves.

 ***Jascha Heifetz, Israel Baker (violins), William Primrose, Virginia Majewski (violas), Gregor Piatigorsky, Gabor Rejto (cellos).***

RCA analogue

While Casals takes the lead on his recording of the First Sextet, here it's Heifetz's unmistakable 'speaking' tone that sets the mood. No stereo rival is in quite the same class (rarely has so much tonal variety been crammed into such a short time-span) though – as in the First Sextet – the Amadeus and Alban Berg Quartets (DG, analogue and EMI, digital) have much to offer. Collectors who don't mind vintage sound might also consider the augmented Budapest Quartet (Biddulph, mono), an especially perceptive reading which comes as part of an attractive Brahms chamber music collection.

Camille Saint-Saëns (1835-1921)

Septet in E flat major for piano, trumpet, string quartet and double-bass, Op. 65 (1881)

Unalloyed delight, with a proliferation of catchy tunes, craftsman-like instrumentation and buoyant rhythms. The Septet was commissioned by a Paris musical society called "La trompette" and although Saint-Saëns responded by saying that he'd rather write a concerto for 25 guitars (!), the resulting work – which is a mere quarter-of-an-hour in length – shows off his gifts to dazzling effect.

André Previn (piano), Thomas Stevens (trumpet), Julie Rosenfeld, Ani Kavafian (violins), Toby Hoffman (viola), Carter Brey (cello), Jack Kulowitsch (double-bass)

RCA digital

Relaxed, lively playing, superbly recorded; it's the sort of production that has the potential to lighten even the darkest mood. The current CD couplings includes Poulenc's equally winsome Sextet and Milhaud's popular La création du monde in a version for quintet.

Pyotr Il'yich Tchaikovsky (1840-1893)

Souvenir de Florence for string sextet, Op. 70 (1890, revised 1891-92)

Anyone expecting a chamber-music equivalent to the *Capriccio italien* is in for a shock. This is a big piece, with powerfully developed arguments (the first movement is especially bold) and a glorious slow movement that, half-way through (5'10" into the relevant track on our recommended recording), unexpectedly anticipates the shivering soundscapes of Sibelius. The *Souvenir de Florence* was composed in Russia during the summer months and was Tchaikovsky's last chamber work. Some would say that it is also his greatest.

Borodin Quartet, Yuri Yurov (viola), Mikhail Milman (cello)

Teldec digital

CD rivalry is especially strong in this work – largely because of an alternative version for full string orchestra (which, generally speaking, isn't nearly as effective as the sextet original). The augmented Borodin perform with their usual lustre, finesse and virtuosity, but there are other fine versions available, not least two analogue recordings featuring, respectively, Jascha Heifetz with Gregor Piatigorsky (RCA – intonation is slightly suspect, but it's an immensely vigorous performance) and Leonid Kogan with Mstislav Rostropovich (Multisonic, mono).

Antonin Dvořák (1841-1904)

Piano Quartet No. 2 in E flat major, B162 (Op. 87) (1889)

"As I expected, it came easily and the melodies just surged upon me, thank God." Dvořák's own words give us an idea of what to expect, though they hardly hint at the rapturous modulations (harmonic shifts) that occur towards the close of the first movement (from 7'38" into our recommended recording). The slow movement is one of Dvořák's finest (the opening theme suggests Wagner's vision of "endless melody"), the Scherzo is sunny and genial (with gipsy-style forays into the minor), and the folk-like finale is both vigorous and passionate.

Menahem Pressler (piano), Emerson Quartet

Deutsche Grammophon digital

A lean, lively performance characterized by intelligence, sweetness of tone and considerable technical polish, though I'm equally keen on a digital Supraphon recording led by violinist Josef Suk and a superb analogue Sony recording featuring the great Czech pianist Rudolf Firkušný and the Juilliard Quartet.

Piano Quintet in A major, B155 (Op. 81) (1887)

As with Dvořák's greatest symphonies, the Piano Quintet combines taut arguments with a healthy infusion of folk-inspired melody. In the case of the Piano Quintet, the "Dumka" second movement (Dumka is a Ukrainian term) alternates melancholy episodes with passages of tremendous vitality and the Scherzo reminds us of the most vivacious *Slavonic Dances*. The finale contains a veiled reference to the corresponding movement in Schumann's great Piano Quintet of 45 years earlier (i.e. at 2'09" into our recommended recording).

Rudolf Firkušný (piano), Juilliard Quartet

Sony Classical analogue

The elegance of Firkušný's playing combined with the Juilliard's fulsome tone makes for a fairly comprehensive interpretation, although there is powerful analogue rivalry from the Czech pianist Jan Panenka and the Smetana Quartet (Supraphon or Testament) and an especially high-powered reading that features pianist Jacob Lateiner, violinist Jascha Heifetz and cellist Gregor Piatigorsky (RCA, analogue).

Gabriel Fauré (1845-1924)

Piano Quartet No. 1 in C minor, Op. 15 (1876-79)

The opening has a positively Brahmsian exuberance, although Wagner would have served as a more understandable prompt – Fauré having recently returned from hearing *The Ring* in Germany. Personal anguish (a broken engagement) is reflected in the deeply melancholic *Adagio*, whereas a gossamer Scherzo and a stormy finale (again, Brahms's spirit beckons) provide plenty of contrast. Those who wish to explore Fauré's exquisite chamber music would do well to start with the C minor Piano Quartet.

Piano Quartet No. 2 in G minor, Op. 45 (1885-86)

Fauré's Second Piano Quartet opens in a mood of dark impetuosity. It was completed a year after Fauré composed his only symphony (which he subsequently destroyed) and seems to approximate orchestral sonorities. The first movement is full of romantic ardour, the sombre Scherzo features disquieting rhythmic ambiguities, the *Adagio* suggests the distant chiming of evening bells and the variegated finale recalls the worlds of Brahms (especially the second theme) and Schumann.

Jean Hubeau (piano), Raymond Gallois-Montbrun (violin), Colette Lequien (viola), André Navarra (cello)

Erato analogue

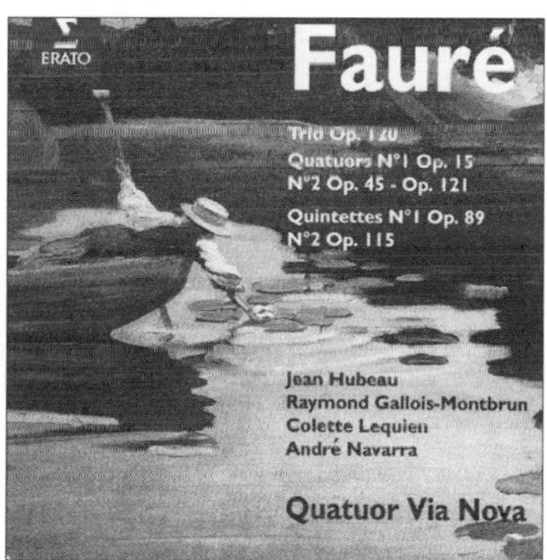

Both performances combine subtlety and ardour, while the recorded sound (1969-70) is warm and lifelike. Alternative analogue recordings with Jean-Philippe Collard (EMI) are also recommended, though readers who don't object to mono sound are urgently advised to investigate impassioned historic mono recordings featuring the great French pianist Marguerite Long (EMI – the Second Quartet, in particular).

Leoš Janáček (1854-1928)

Capriccio for piano (left hand) and seven wind instruments (1926)

With a brass ensemble that sounds like a group of heckling bystanders and an *Adagio* reminiscent of Chopin (at least in its opening bars), Janáček's highly original *Capriccio* isn't short of a surprise or two. Boisterous, lyrical, humorous and occasionally ominous-sounding, it was composed for the Czech pianist Otakar Hollmann, whose right hand was badly injured during the First World War. Some commentators hear *Capriccio* as a musical protest against the horrors of war.

Rudolf Firkušný (piano), members of the Czech Philharmonic Orchestra/Václav Neumann

RCA digital

Idiomatic in tone and style and very well recorded, although Firkušný's earlier DG (analogue) version, conducted by Rafael Kubelík is, if anything, even better (it isn't available at the time of writing). There's also a highly recommendable version with Paul Crossley and members of the London Sinfonietta (Decca, analogue) and a fairly stylish EMI digital recording with pianist Mikhail Rudy and members of the Paris National Opera Orchestra under Sir Charles Mackerras.

Ernest Chausson (1855-1899)

Concert in D major for violin, piano and string quartet, Op. 21 (1889-91)

Chamber music on a symphonic scale, composed by a man who once complained that "the red spectre of Wagner … does not let go of me". In some respects, it's rather like a violin concerto where a piano quintet plays proxy for the orchestra, although the balance between instrumental forces is far subtler - and more equal - than in the average virtuoso concerto (which is why Chausson preferred to use the eighteenth-century term of 'concert') . Chausson's dark, stormy narrative follows the lead of César Franck in recalling earlier themes for the finale.

Itzhak Perlman (violin), Jorge Bolet (piano), Juilliard Quartet

Sony Classical digital

A real partnership. Perlman blends effectively among his colleagues, Bolet is at his aristocratic best and the outer movements generate considerable urgency. It's by far the finest modern recording of the work, but there are at least two 'great' oldies - led, respectively, by Jascha Heifetz (RCA, mono) and Jacques Thibaud (with pianist Alfred Cortot - Biddulph, mono).

Sir Edward Elgar (1857-1934)

Piano Quintet in A minor, Op. 84 (1918-19)

The most ambitious of Elgar's chamber works is at once bold, lyrical, nostalgic and occasionally reminiscent of both Schumann and Brahms. George Bernard Shaw thought it the finest thing of its kind since [Beethoven's] *Coriolan.* "I don't know why I associated the two," he said, "but I did: there was the same quality."

Bernard Roberts (piano), Chilingirian Quartet

EMI digital

A dignified, 'inward' reading that captures the work's noble spirit perfectly. It's also beautifully recorded (1985 vintage) and comes appropriately coupled with Elgar's equally moving String Quartet. However, readers with an ear for musical history should investigate a fine performance that Elgar himself knew, featuring pianist Harriet Cohen with the Stratton Quartet (Dutton Laboratories mono - recorded in 1933). It was this recording that, together with a contemporaneous reading of the Quartet (included on the same disc), offered the composer some solace as he lay dying at his home in Worcester in 1934.

Arnold Schoenberg (1874-1951)

Verklärte Nacht for string sextet, Op. 4 (1899)

Richard Dehmel's poem *Transfigured Night* tells of a moonlit walk between two lovers, where the girl confesses to being pregnant by another man. Schoenberg's musical response is - like that of the lover himself - both tender and impassioned. The music looks back to the world of Wagner's *Tristan und Isolde* (the greatest musical love poem ever composed - see "Twilit Catastrophes", below) and forward to the relative complexities of Schoenberg's own later style. Although the full orchestral version could fit neatly under 'Narratives in Sound', the more intimate sextet 'original' is generally to be preferred.

Hollywood Quartet, Alvin Dinkin (viola) and Kurt Reher (cello)

Testament mono

Schoenberg himself attended the sessions of this classic 1951 recording. We're told that the 'difficult' composer - who was well-known for his exacting standards - listened through without comment. "Schoenberg didn't say anything at first." relates cellist Eleanor Aller, "he just looked at us and said 'it was good, very good ... in fact, I have nothing to say'." So good in fact that, 45 years later there's still nothing to say except that it's the best recording available. However, those intent on digital sound are directed to the augmented Juilliard Quartet (Sony).

Maurice Ravel (1875-1937)

Introduction and Allegro for harp, string quartet, flute and clarinet (1905)

If you enjoy Ravel's *Daphnis et Chloé* (see "Puppets and pagans", below) or Debussy's *Prélude à l'après-midi d'un faune* (see "Narratives in Sound", above), you'll surely adore this concise mini-narrative. The harmonies are lush though never overbearing (Ravel's innate good taste sees to that) and there's plenty of textural variety - so much so, in fact, that you could almost be listening to a small orchestra.

Ann Mason Stockton (harp), Arthur Gleghorn (flute), Mitchell Lurie (clarinet), Hollywood Quartet

Testament mono

All seven players excel in a performance that, although distinguished by a warm Hollywood-style 'sheen', lacks nothing in terms of either heart or intelligence. The mono recording is beautifully balanced and the other works on the CD highly colourful (Debussy, Turina, Villa-Lobos, Creston). Digital-fanciers are directed to an excellent Cala recording led by flautist William Bennett.

Béla Bartók (1881-1945)

Sonata for two pianos and percussion, Sz110 (1937)

Few piano works of the past 60 years have paraded the instrument's coloristic properties with as much imagination as this magnificent Sonata, while Bartók's use of percussion is both innovative and highly sensitive. The opening timpani roll is dark and ominous with sudden cymbal interjections and wild, scale-like passages from the pianists. The first movement is fiercely rhythmic, the second a mysterious nocturne with a menacing central climax while the third is unexpectedly light-hearted.

 ***Martha Argerich, Nelson Freire (pianos), Peter Sadlo, Edgar Guggeis (percussion)***

Deutsche Grammophon digital

A performance that suggests maximum spontaneity and a genuine sense of play. It was recorded live in 1993 and isn't exactly immaculate, but the spirit is right, the sound excellent and the overall effect consistently gripping. Argerich's analogue studio recording with Stephen Kovacevich (Philips) makes for a highly recommendable second option.

Paul Hindemith (1895-1963)

Kammermusik No. 1, Op. 24 No. 1 (1922)

"Dry as dust", "academic", "tuneless" – senseless clichés that have too often relegated Paul Hindemith to reference libraries and CD deletion racks. But try the opening movement of this *Kammermusik* or "Chamber Music" (scored for 12 instruments) and you're immediately startled by its nerve, originality and exuberance. Stravinsky's there, so is the spirit of the 1920s – and if you progress to the other six *Kammermusik*, you'll discover a veritable feast of invention, from Mahlerian irony to puckish good humour. The set also includes chamber concertos for winds, piano, cello, violin, viola, viola d'amore and organ.

 ***Royal Concertgebouw Orchestra/Riccardo Chailly***

Decca digital

A real showcase for members of the Royal Concertgebouw Orchestra, with additional help (in the other concertos) from the likes of cellist Lynn Harrell and violinist Konstanty Kulka. The sound is quite marvellous and the performances are consistently on-the-ball.

Dmitry Shostakovich (1906-1975)

Piano Quintet in G minor, Op. 57 (1940)

A big piece, composed on the eve of the Nazi invasion of Russia. Shostakovich's Quintet incorporates a tragic opening *Lento,* a massive, slow-moving fugue that harks back both to Bach and – in particular – to Beethoven, a spiky Scherzo, a sombre Intermezzo and finale that marks a half-hearted gesture towards reconciliation. It is a profoundly uneasy work, one that earned immediate acclaim among Russian audiences.

 ***Sviatoslav Richter (piano), Borodin Quartet***

EMI analogue

Shostakovich himself recorded the Quintet around the time of its first performance (Melodiya), but Richter's strong and noble reading is equally riveting and has the added benefits of superior sound and typically perceptive support from the Borodin Quartet. The couplings are significant: benchmark recordings of the Seventh and Eighth String Quartets (see above).

Steve Reich (b1936)

Drumming (1970)

An exhilarating journey set to a constant pulse, starting with a pair of tuned bongo drums, then switching to three marimbas plus women's voices, three glockenspiels (with whistling and piccolo) and climaxing in a final section where the entire community of instruments plays together. Reich has his rhythmic patterns (or 'processes') cross each other almost imperceptibly and the net result of *Drumming* is both stimulating and profoundly therapeutic. It is a seminal masterpiece of so-called Minimalism.

Steve Reich and Musicians
Nonesuch digital
Reich has made two commercial recordings of Drumming, the first (for DG, analogue) lasting some 85 minutes and the second (this one) around 55 minutes. The musical differences concern the time spent with each 'section' although this later recording is marginally more up-tempo than its predecessor. Confirmed Reichians should try to hear both.

Music for 18 musicians (1976)

The crowning glory of 1970s Minimalism and perhaps Steve Reich's greatest work. The opening 'pulse' sets the basic tempo for the entire piece; thereafter, related themes and ideas waft in, overlap with their successors then waft out. Far from being merely hypnotic experience, *Music for 18 musicians* is a painstakingly structured composition that can be appreciated either as a compulsive 'listen' (Reich's own definite priority) or as an elevated form of music therapy. Between them, the 18 musicians play violin, cello, two clarinets doubling bass clarinet, four women's voices, four pianos, three marimbas, two xylophones and metallophone (a vibraphone with no motor).

Steve Reich and Musicians
ECM analogue
Reich's concentration, precision and ease of delivery are available in two separate recordings, the first of which is marginally preferable. The sound is beautifully clear.

Early music solos (c1600-1770)

Our survey of solo instrumental masterpieces opens among some shorter works that are particularly difficult to date accurately. As to the music itself, there are can be little doubt that Scarlatti's vivacious keyboard sonatas approach – at least in terms of rhythmic and harmonic ingenuity – those of Mozart and occasionally even Beethoven.

William Byrd (1543-1623)

Sixth Pavan and Galliard

William Byrd was the most versatile English composer of his day and although he penned much fine vocal music (he was a pupil of Thomas Tallis), his instrumental works – which include many consort songs – are especially fine. This *Sixth Pavan and Galliard* exhibits Byrd's ornamental style at its most immediately appealing.

Glenn Gould (piano)
Sony Classical analogue
Glenn Gould (1932-82) was among the greatest exponents of Bach's keyboard works, and yet he claimed that his favourite composer was Orlando Gibbons (William Byrd's great contemporary). Gould's concentration, mastery of counterpoint and firm sense of rhythm made him the ideal interpreter of early keyboard music – a fact that is only partially compromised by his using a piano rather than a harpsichord or virginal.

Jean-Philippe Rameau (1683-1764)

Gavotte et doubles in A minor (1728)

Rameau on a 'high', stating a grand theme then treating it to a diverse yet forceful series of six variations. It may be that Handel's "Harmonious Blacksmith" Variations were an influence – or even the Passacaglia from Handel's G minor Keyboard Suite (see below) – but the elegance of the music, its Gallic charm and panache are typical of Rameau. The *Gavotte et doubles* is taken from *Nouvelles suites de pièces de clavecin*, Rameau's last harpsichord anthology.

Christophe Rousset (harpsichord)
L'Oiseau-Lyre digital

Brilliant playing – colourful, graceful, extremely musical and realized on an excellent Henri Hemsch harpsichord from 1751. It comes from a two-CD set that contains most of Rameau's principal harpsichord works and is superbly recorded. As to older rivals, my personal favourite is a thrilling mono recording by Fernando Valenti (Westminster) – hopefully due for reissue by MCA Classics. A fine version by pianist Robert Casadesus is also well worth searching out (Sony, mono – and long deleted).

George Frideric Handel
(1685–1759)

Keyboard Suite No. 7 in G minor (published 1720)

It is fairly certain that Handel used some of his Suites as teaching material (George II's daughters were among his few pupils). The Seventh – one of 16 – is built on an especially grand scale and it plays for some 23 minutes and is cast in six varied movements. The Ouverture recalls the Orchestral Suites of Bach and the closing Passacaglia (which stands handsomely on its own and which the composer Johan Halvorsen arranged very effectively for violin and viola/cello) generates great visceral excitement.

Andrei Gavrilov (piano)
EMI analogue

This thrilling performance – which is strong yet full of poetic incident – is included as part of a live recording that features all 16 Suites as shared between Gavrilov and his great compatriot, Sviatoslav Richter. There's an equally grand harpsichord version by Wanda Landowska (EMI, Pearl – mono) but those averse to 'romantic' Handel are directed to Bob von Asperen (Sony, digital). Incidentally, Handel's Fifth Keyboard Suite includes the celebrated theme and variations, "The Harmonious Blacksmith".

Domenico Scarlatti (1685–1757)

Domenico Scarlatti's keyboard sonatas are so rich in invention that to do them justice (there are around 555 of them) would take more them half of the present volume. Scarlatti's life was full of fascinating incident though the latter part of it was spent in Spain in the service of Princess Maria Barbara, a fact that is vividly reflected in his various Flamenco-flavoured compositions. So, rather than opt for a single-disc selection (the late Scott Ross's magnificent complete recording on Erato would justify at least two dozen pages of text), I thought it might be more useful to highlight four separate (and very different) sonatas in the context of four recommendable recitals, two each on piano and harpsichord.

Sonata in E major, Kk215
Andreas Staier (harpsichord)
Teldec digital

Scarlatti's harmonic boldness could, on occasion, approximate the dissonances of late Liszt and this particular Sonata features a jarring 'second half' (virtually all the sonatas are cast in 'binary' or two-part form) that has a decidedly contemporary feel to it. The rest of Staier's vividly recorded selection (there are 18 sonatas in all) is a mixture of the familiar and the unfamiliar and includes two pieces (Kk115 and Kk427) that further confirm Scarlatti's predilection for dramatic surprises. The playing is superb.

Sonata in E major, Kk380
Wanda Landowska (harpsichord)
EMI mono

This Sonata suggests a Spanish street processional and suits Wanda Landowska's extravagant, post-Romantic playing style. She performs on an elaborate twentieth-century instrument, one that, even as recorded in the 1930s and 1940s, projects a mighty welter of tone. Her programme is taken from a famous series of 78s and includes the wildly cascading Kk124, the impish Kk430 with its cuckoo-calls, Kk90 (sometimes known as Capriccio), the keenly cantering Kk519 and the stamping, Flamenco-style Kk141 with its treacherous repeated notes. Kk492 was one of a set recorded in Paris on March 8th-9th, 1940 and reproduces the distant thunder of anti-aircraft gunfire (Landowska had refused to abandon the session).

Sonata in A major, Kk39
Vladimir Horowitz (piano)
Sony Classical analogue

A dazzling flurry of repeated notes set within the context of a highly coloured programme. Horowitz habitually included Scarlatti sonatas in his concerts and this particular selection (based on a famous LP and augmented with extra items) includes Kk525, with its vivid suggestions of sudden gunfire, the meltingly gentle Kk466 and Kk162, where hunting horns join the fray. Everything is sculpted to perfection and there are pianistic fireworks galore.

Sonata in B minor, Kk87
Christian Zacharias (piano)
EMI analogue

Scarlatti at his most wistfully poetic (this particular Sonata – one of the most popular – is still sometimes referred to under the old Longo catalogue number of 'L33'). Zacharias's Mozartian axis pays highest dividends in the slower pieces (try Kk209), whereas there's more than a suggestion of Haydn in Kk322. The current issue includes 33 varied sonatas and might well prove a good place to start – even though the playing itself is a far cry from the guitar-like 'tang' of a harpsichord. Also, do keep an eye out for the discs of harpsichordist Fernando Valenti (Westminster, MCA); he recorded at least half the sonatas (some in mono, others in stereo) and his fiery temperament is effectively employed.

Antonio Soler (1729-1783)

Fandango (undated)
An infectious *tour de force* where strong Flamenco elements (the actual writing suggests strumming guitars) are married to a stream of musical variation. The work plays for around 11 minutes although, because the actual manuscript is fairly sketchy, certain points of detail vary from performance to performance. Soler was a Catalan composer and organist whose 120 keyboard sonatas vie with Scarlatti's (see above) for originality, rhythmic ingenuity and virtuoso challenges for the soloist.

Jonathan Woods (harpsichord)
Carlton Classics analogue
Technically brilliant, interpretatively individual and very closely recorded (the harpsichord is placed virtually in your lap). Wood's strongest rivals are Rafael Puyana (Philips or Mercury, analogue) and Nikita Magaloff, whose live 1962 Venice recording (Hunt, mono) shows a fine pianist at the height of his powers.

Further listening *Readers who appreciate the music of Domenico Scarlatti will probably enjoy a delightful set of concerto grossi that the Newcastle-upon-Tyne-born composer Charles Avison fashioned after various of Scarlatti keyboard sonatas. There's a digital set on period instruments available from Hyperion (Roy Goodman and the Brandenburg Consort) and, at mid-price on Philips, Sir Nevile Marriner's celebrated analogue recordings.*

Bach solo (1708-1742)

In planning our solo instrumental section, I thought it best to separate off a corpus of work that has been so variously interpreted and re-interpreted, arranged and re-arranged, recorded and re-recorded that it fully justifies a home of its own. Bach's works are so melodically rich, rhythmically invigorating and contrapuntally ingenious that they respond to all manner of musicianship – from the romantic excesses of harpsichordist Wanda Landowska (a personal favourite, and I shall not attempt to hide the fact), to the magisterial organ-playing of Helmut Walcha and the immaculate violin playing of Arthur Grumiaux. Controversy will continue to reign as to if – or how – this wonderful music should be played on instruments from Bach's own time, but whatever the outcome, the music itself suggests endless renewal.

Johann Sebastian Bach (1685-1750)

Capriccio in B flat major on the departure of his beloved brother, BWV992 (1704)
Departure here refers to a voyage rather than the 'final departure' of death. Bach was honouring his older brother Johann-Jakob, who was about to enlist in the King of Sweden's army band. The music, which is both charming and highly descriptive, mirrors Bach's efforts to dissuade his brother from travelling, then proceeds to a 'polyphonic' description of potential misfortunes, a lament from his friends, the final farewell and a trumpeting send-off.

Wanda Landowska (harpsichord)
RCA mono

Bach's colourful Capriccio would seem tailor-made for Landowska's flamboyant style of playing. The great Polish-born harpsichordist makes maximum dramatic capital out of each episode, though her powerful Pleyel instrument will not please those who insist on 'period' authenticity (Kenneth Gilbert, on Archiv digital, would suit them better). There are also numerous fine piano versions available, not least Rosalyn Tureck (VAI, digital), Jean-Bernard Pommier (EMI, analogue) and Wilhelm Kempff (DG, analogue).

Chromatic Fantasia and Fugue in D minor, BWV903 (*c*1720, revised *c*1730)
An astonishingly forward-looking piece that lends itself to all manner of interpretation. The 'Chromatic' label signals that the centre of interest lies among semitones, something that was far more common during the nineteenth and twentieth centuries. Bach's *Fantasia* visits harmonies that would not be

out of place in Liszt (some passages are decidedly spooky), while the fugue is among his grandest.

Andreas Staier (harpsichord)
Deutsche Harmonia Mundi digital
Staier is an imaginative harpsichordist whose sense of period style should assure him approval on all critical fronts. As to alternatives, Rosalyn Tureck (piano, VAI) is especially perceptive and there are wonderful old performances by Edwin Fischer (piano, EMI) and Wanda Landowska (harpsichord, EMI and Biddulph, mono), both of which explore the music's spiritual dimension.

Fantasia and Fugue in G minor, BWV542 (c1717-23)
The opening *Fantasia*, which was composed while Bach was Kapellmeister to Prince Leopold of Cöthen, is among the most immediately arresting musical episodes in the Baroque repertory. Its declamatory gestures, thundering bass pedal and all-pervading sense of inspired improvisation signal the radical harmonic innovations of a far later age. However, the merry Fugue provides a total contrast; it may have been based on a Dutch folk-song and was written before the *Fantasia*, at Weimar.

Helmut Walcha (organ)
Deutsche Grammophon analogue
Helmut Walcha was a superb organist who scaled the larger of Bach's structures like a master builder. As with various other of Walcha's recordings recommended here, this one features an especially fine instrument at St Laurenskerk, Alkmaar (in The Netherlands). The early-1960s sound remains highly impressive. As to rivals, Peter Hurford (Decca, analogue) and Marie-Claire Alain (Erato – either her analogue or digital recordings) offer interesting alternative interpretations.

French Suite No. 5 in G major, BWV816 (c1725)
One of Bach's earliest work's in 'suite' form, though the Fifth Suite – the best-known of the six – was written somewhat later than most of the others. While the first three Suites are cast in minor keys (their mood is correspondingly serious), the last three – all of them written in the major – are more joyful. Among the Fifth's seven movements is an especially bright Gavotte and a delightful Gigue.

Glenn Gould (piano)
Sony Classical analogue
The age-old dilemma of 'piano versus harpsichord' is habitually complicated by Glenn Gould, whose clean, precise and keenly articulated playing eschews any hint of romantic excess (and therefore resembles various early-keyboard performances). Gould's early-1970s recording of the Fifth Suite (part of a complete set of all Six French Suites) is close, clear and occasionally bothered by minor pitch problems. Gustav Leonhardt's BMG analogue recording is among the best of Gould's harpsichord rivals.

Goldberg Variations, BWV988 (1741-42)
A precious late fruit that grew from a Sarabande that Bach had originally included as part of a musical "Notebook" for his wife, Anna Magdalena. Bach is said to have composed the Variations to relieve the insomnia of his Dresden patron, Count Keyserlingk. They are named after Keyserlingk's harpsichordist, Johann Gottlieb Goldberg and represent a supreme example of variation form that culminates in a daringly romantic 25th Variation. Bach's *Goldbergs* represent the perfect balance of expressive power and contrapuntal ingenuity.

Glenn Gould (piano)
Sony Classical digital
Harpsichord or piano? Bach scholars will usually insist on the former, largely because its roster of tones and colours represents roughly what Bach had in his mind's ear when he composed the music. In which case Gustav Leonhardt (Deutsche Harmonia Mundi, analogue), Trevor Pinnock (Archiv, digital) or, for a generously expressive 'old-world' alternative, Wanda Landowska (EMI, Biddulph or RCA, mono), should fit the bill. Of piano versions (and there are a great many), Gould's last commercial recording (he made two) is particularly fluent, dextrous and invigorating.

Italian Concerto in F major, BWV971 (1735)
A vivacious work with a slow movement that suggests the expressive range of an operatic aria. The Concerto was originally published as part of the second volume of Bach's *Clavierübung* ("Keyboard Exercises"), 'Italian' and 'French' styles being all the rage at the time (also included is an expansive French Ouverture, a seventh Partita in all but name). Vivaldi was an obvious model, while the writing takes special advantage of the harpsichord's two manuals – one for 'full throttle' and solo voices, the other for softer accompaniments.

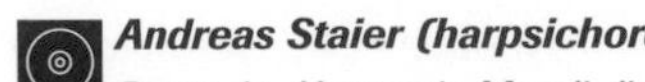

Andreas Staier (harpsichord)
Deutsche Harmonia Mundi digital
Staier combines rhythmic vitality with malleable phrasing, which means that although the performance is physically exciting, it never feels hard-driven. The sound is superb, but if you prefer your Bach on a piano, Glenn Gould (Sony, analogue), Arturo Benedetti Michelangeli (Teldec, mono), Marcelle Meyer (EMI, mono) and Jean-Bernard Pommier (EMI, analogue) should all give pleasure.

Partita No. 1 in B flat major, BWV825 (*c*1726)

Bach's Six Partitas (a seventh is entitled French Ouverture) are both the best-known and the richest of his multi-movement keyboard works, certainly in terms of invention and musical content. Given limitless space, I'd willingly recommend at least three versions of the whole set – but if one work has to suffice, the First (and most popular) Partita serves nicely, an elegant sequence of six movements with a noble Sarabande placed fourth and a cantering Gigue to close.

Dinu Lipatti (piano)
EMI mono
As near perfection as you could hope to hear: crisp but never clipped, responsive but never over-romanticized, reserved but never aloof. Glenn Gould (Sony, analogue) provides a fine if rather more stylized piano alternative, while András Schiff (Decca, digital) conjures up a world of Mozartian elegance. A fine digital harpsichord version by Andreas Staier is on Deutsche Harmonia Mundi.

Passacaglia and Fugue in C minor, BWV582 (*c*1708–12)

A palpable cathedral in sound, starting with the foundations (the majestic eight-bar main theme, initially stated in the bass), then working through a series of 20 magnificent variations and culminating in a mighty Fugue. Bach's *Passacaglia and Fugue* is a cornerstone of the organist's repertoire although it has been sumptuously orchestrated by both Leopold Stokowski (Pearl, mono) and Ottorino Respighi (Toscanini, on 'unofficial' CD labels, mono)

Ton Koopman
Teldec digital
Koopman is a daredevil among modern Bachians. One record company was so alarmed by his lavish embellishments that they edited them out, but Teldec give him his head for performances that combine grandeur, spontaneity and scholarship with the colourful tones of a fine eighteenth-century organ (Rudolf Garrels, Grote Kerk, Maassluis in The Netherlands).

Toccata, Adagio and Fugue in C major, BWV564 (1708–17)

Built on the scale of a concerto, this great work opens to a prelude for manual pedals and keyboards which in turn provides the basis for a powerful *Toccata*. The *Adagio* is a flowing meditation that recalls Bach's organ chorales and the finale – which makes creative use of short silences, or 'rests' – is a festive riot of counterpoint

Helmut Walcha (organ)
Deutsche Grammophon analogue
Walcha gives a vital, though stately reading on the amazingly colourful 'great organ' of the St Laurenskerk, Alkmaar in the Netherlands. The recording, which dates from the early-1960s, still sounds virtually as good as new, although digital-only collectors might prefer the more flamboyant Ton Koopman (Archiv or Teldec). There's also a fine piano solo arrangement of the Toccata, Adagio and Fugue by Busoni, brilliantly realized in a live recording by Vladimir Horowitz (Sony, analogue).

Toccata and Fugue in D minor, BWV565 (before 1708)

One can well imagine why Bach was criticized for improvising in church – especially if the results were as overtly dramatic as they are in this relatively early work. The *Toccata* (the most famous piece in the entire organist's repertory) falls into three varied sections, whereas the highly eventful *Fugue* climaxes among leaping figurations and an especially grand series of chords.

Helmut Walcha (organ)
Deutsche Grammophon analogue
Recordings of the Toccata and Fugue are legion, from Leopold Stokowski's famous orchestral transcription (as featured in the Disney film "Fantasia" – Pearl, RCA, EMI, Decca, etc – the old Philadelphia Orchestra recordings are best [Pearl, mono]), through the rugged though spiritually edifying Albert Schweitzer (Pearl, EMI, Sony, all mono) to the more overtly brilliant Ton Koopman (Teldec or Archiv, digital) and the crudely 'upbeat' rock violin version by Vanessa Mae (EMI, digital). Helmut Walcha – a great blind organist who recorded Bach's organ works twice over – is especially grand and the organ he plays, a Dutch instrument at St Laurenskerk, Alkmaar, is a source of pleasure in itself. The early-1960s recording remains highly impressive.

Trio Sonata No. 5 in C major, BWV529 (1730)

It is highly probable that Bach wrote his six colourful Trio Sonatas for his eldest son Wilhelm Friedemann, who was at the time poised to take up a post as organist in Dresden and who had actually been trained by his father. The term 'Trio Sonata' had previously been used exclusively for chamber music, but Bach extended the concept to embrace a solo work incorporating three independent parts. The Fifth Sonata is a real joy, its crowning glory being an extraordinarily expressive *Lento* slow movement.

Ton Koopman (organ)
Archiv digital

Supremely accomplished playing and less freely embellished than some of Koopman's other recordings of Bach's organ music. The organ is that of the Waalse Kerk in Amsterdam. Other fine versions are from André Isoire (Calliope, digital) and Helmut Walcha (DG, analogue).

Solo Cello Suite No. 3 in C major, BWV1009 (1720)

Composed while Bach was Kappellmeister at the Court of Cöthen, the Six Cello Suites were rediscovered for modern listeners by the great Catalan cellist Pablo Casals. Each work opens with a substantial Prelude and proceeds through a sequence of dance movements, the Sarabande serving as the 'slow movement'. No. 3's Prelude is especially grand (it opens with a lavish downward flourish), while the Bourrée (much beloved of the guitarist Segovia) is the most famous movement in the set.

Pablo Casals (cello)
EMI mono

Casals's pioneering set of the Six Cello Suites, recorded between 1936 and 1939, relates intense involvement, boisterous rhythms, poetically inflected phrasing and a tender, wistful tone. Those in a search of an off-the-cuff, period-instrument approach should investigate the excellent Anner Bylsma (Sony, digital).

Solo Cello Suite No. 5 in C minor, BWV1011 (1720)

The darkest of the Six Suites, where Bach asks the cellist to tune down the top string from A to G (a process known as *scordatura*). The sombre Prelude and Fugue set the scene, while the bleak Sarabande anticipates the great arias of the Passions and the closing Gigue has a halting, desolate air that suggests musical worlds far beyond Bach's own.

Heinrich Schiff (cello)
EMI digital

A particularly agile performance, one that gives the impression of spontaneous improvisation. Nikolaus Harnoncourt refers to Schiff's "irresistibly sprung, yet finely nuanced rhythm" in the Fugue, but discerning listeners should also hear Pablo Casals (EMI, mono) whose account of the Sarabande is especially poignant.

Solo Cello Suite No. 6 in D major, BWV1012 (1720)

Bach's Sixth Suite was originally intended for an instrument with five strings (quite common at a time when the 'thumb' position had yet to be established). Notable features included an ecstatically propulsive Prelude, a lengthy Allemande (the longest in the set) and a particularly vivacious pair of Gavottes.

János Starker (cello)
Mercury analogue

Starker has recorded the Suites several times, though the sheer consistency of his approach – with its dry tone, thrusting rhythms and expressively intense vibrato – is common to each set. The Mercury recordings – made while Starker was at the very height of his powers in the 1960s – are closely balanced and sharply focused, though their less well-recorded 1950s EMI (mono) predecessors are equally impressive.

Solo Violin Partita No. 2 in D minor, BWV1004 (1720)

Bach's Sonatas and Partitas for solo violin date from his period as church composer at Cöthen (1717-23). Bach was himself an accomplished string player (he played both violin and viola) and his mastery of the medium informs every note of these six works. The five-movement D minor Partita is the most famous of all, largely on account of a hugely ambitious "Chaconne" (a stately dance sequence where the main theme is subject to variations), one of the cornerstones of the violin repertoire and which lasts longer than the previous four movements put together.

 ***Arthur Grumiaux (violin)***
Philips mono
Let me say straight away that all violinists featured in these solo works have recorded the six unaccompanied pieces, and all might be considered 'first choices' for a complete recording. Grumiaux's virtues are technical excellence, immaculate musicianship and an 'inwardness' of expression that is particularly durable.

Solo Violin Sonata No. 2 in A minor, BWV1003 (1720)
Unlike the Partitas (which are, in the main, series of dance movements), the Sonatas subscribe to the slow-fast-slow-fast pattern that was already prevalent by the time Bach came to write these particular works. The main innovation here is a songful *Andante* where, through a skilful deployment of the bow, Bach has the violinist play both the melody and its gently pulsing accompaniment. The effect is entrancing.

 ***Nathan Milstein (violin)***
EMI mono
Milstein's silky tone and assured phrasing make for a supremely confident survey of this great Sonata. The mono recording is excellent but if stereo is required then his remake for DG is well worth considering (although it's not quite as good as this) and there's an excellent Erato (analogue) recording by the late Oleg Kagan. Period-instrument devotees should consider the excellent Sigiswald Kuijken (DHM, analogue), a fine player whose scholarly approach to articulation has much to teach us.

Solo Violin Sonata No. 3 in C major, BWV1005 (1720)
All three of Bach's solo violin sonatas feature brilliantly written fugues as their second movements. The Third Sonata has the biggest fugue of all, an expansive structure (it plays for anything between eight and ten minutes) that half-way through, turns the principal theme on its head and starts all over again. The *Largo* is one of Bach's great solo movements and the closing *Allegro* is particularly brilliant.

 ***Jascha Heifetz (violin)***
RCA mono
This set of the Sonatas and Partitas is essential listening for anyone in love with the violin. Heifetz's account of the C major Sonata is special even by his own exacting standards. There are two versions of it (an earlier performance from the 1930s is available on EMI, also mono), but this 1952 recording is utterly magnificent – vibrant, always spot-on the note and with a reading of the Fugue that is so accurate, expressive and exciting that after hearing it, no one else will do. It is, however, more a violinist's benchmark than a scholar's exegesis (for that, you'll need Sigiswald Kuijken, digital).

The Well-Tempered Clavier – 48 preludes and fugues for keyboard
First, to roughly explain the term "well-tempered": this is commonly used to signify a system of keyboard tuning suitable for all 24 keys, though it doesn't necessarily mean either equal temperament (standard modern tuning) or indeed any specific system of temperament. Bach's usage of the term refers to his first collection of 24 Preludes and Fugues, but nowadays "WTC" covers both sets. Book One is the better known of the two and opens with the C major Prelude that Gounod employed as an accompaniment to his rather sickly *Ave Maria*.

 ***Book One, BWV846-69 (1722)***
Friedrich Gulda (piano)
Philips analogue
Any attempts to outline WTC's expressive range in any detail would take up many pages and probably mean very little. Each work is a masterpiece in itself, whether in terms of (and here I refer specifically to Book One) exuberance (C sharp major Prelude), elegance (D major), rapt intensity (E flat minor) or the Fugue that Friedrich Gulda plays more slowly, more expressively and with greater control than anyone else I've so far heard: No. 18 in G sharp minor. The recordings are so close that your speakers virtually 'become' the piano, but period-authenticity devotees will probably be happier either with Colin Tilney (clavichord and harpsichord, Hyperion, digital) or Gustav Leonhardt (harpsichord, EMI, analogue), both of whom are excellent.

 ***Book Two, BWV870-93 (1738-42)***
Wanda Landowska (harpsichord)
RCA mono
WTC Book Two reflects stylistic advances that Bach had witnessed among his peers, and there are some differences in the way the fugues are constructed (i.e. the number of 'voices' or 'lines' employed). But from the listener's point of view, the appeal is much as before – great music and consummate counterpoint. The Book One recommendations will also stand for Book Two, except that I might add the provocative though perceptive Glenn Gould (piano, Sony, analogue), Samuel Feinberg (a magnificent Bachian, again on piano – Russian Disc, mono) and, pre-eminently, Wanda Landowska, whose regal playing of the D major Prelude conveys a unique – and typical – interpretative grandeur. Again, all the artists mentioned here have recorded both books.

Classical dramas (1778-1798)

The first flowering of the keyboard sonata witnessed significant works by, among others, Domenico Scarlatti (see "Early music solos", above) and one of Bach's best-known sons – Carl Philipp Emanuel. However, the greatest Classical sonatas were by the Italian-born English composer Muzio Clementi, Haydn, Mozart and the young Beethoven, all of whom significantly extended the language and scope of piano (formerly fortepiano) music.

Joseph Haydn (1732-1809)

Andante con variazioni in F minor, Hob XVII:6 (1793)

The opening theme is among the most tragic in Haydn's entire output, while the ensuing variations – perhaps the composer's finest – lead to a deeply melancholic coda. The work is said to have been written for a pupil of Mozart, although some suggest that it may also have been composed as a tribute to Haydn's close friend, Marianne von Genzinger, who had died earlier the same year. Certainly the work's sombre demeanour seems to reflect feelings of some considerable depth.

Piano Sonata No. 52 in E flat major (1794)

"No one can do it all – jests and thrills, laughter and deep emotion – and all as well as Haydn does." Such was the opinion of Wolfgang Amadeus Mozart, and this wonderful composition helps explain why. Haydn's last numbered Piano Sonata wasn't necessarily the last to be written (at least two others vie for that distinction), although it is surely his greatest work in the genre. Harmonically adventurous, it opens with a grand flourish and ends with one of Haydn's most brilliant *Presto* finales. The *Adagio* slow movement is especially beautiful.

Alfred Brendel (piano)
Philips (digital)

Playing that, in terms of phrasing, rubato and fluidity of touch, is truly in a class of its own. Brendel's native intelligence acknowledges both the profundity and the humour of Haydn's magnificent music. Both performances comes as part of a valuable four-CD collection of Haydn's major solo piano works, but readers who fancy something less probing and more overtly brilliant (in the Sonata, that is) are directed to Vladimir Horowitz (RCA or EMI, mono) or the ever-provocative Glenn Gould (Sony, analogue).

Wolfgang Amadeus Mozart (1756-1791)

Piano Sonata No. 8 in A minor, K310/300*d* (1778)

A work that inhabits the same troubled world as the late G minor Symphony (see "Classical models" above) and G minor Quintet (see "The more, the merrier", above). The first movement is dark and urgent, with insistent repeated chords and a powerful principal theme. The slow movement, initially so sublime, rises for a positively Gothic development (music that's almost Brucknerian in its breadth and impact) while the last movement revisits the urgency of the first.

Piano Sonata No. 11 in A major, K331/300*i*, "Turkish March" (1781-83)

The Sonata takes its name from its Rondo-finale, a witty, quasi-militaristic movement, complete with mock-reveilles. The expansive first movement (it plays for – on average – around a quarter-of-an-hour) is a gentle theme with colourful variations (Max Reger used it for his orchestral *Mozart* Variations – see "Variations on a theme", above) and there's a winsome Minuet. However, it is the variations that form the crux of the piece.

Piano Sonata No. 15 in F major, K533/494 (1786-88)

Mozart wrote nothing greater for solo piano than the *Andante* of this Sonata, a warmly pleading narrative that foreshadows Beethoven and even Brahms and contains some of the most daring harmonies in Mozart's keyboard output. The Sonata is actually a combination of two works – the Rondo finale having been added to the newly composed *Allegro* and *Andante*. The outer movements show Mozart at his most contrapuntally inventive.

Rondo in A minor, K511 (1787)

A work that vies with Haydn's *Andante con variazioni* in F minor (see above) as being one of the great 'single-movement' piano masterpieces in the Classical repertory.

Contrast is the key word here – principally between the tragic opening theme (a sort of swaying *siciliano*) and the more consolatory major-key episodes.

Mitsuko Uchida (piano)

Philips digital

No area of the repertory has proved more receptive to feminine musical intuition (if one can define such a phenomenon) than Mozart's piano sonatas. Viewed in musical terms, Uchida is at once sculptress, poet and a philosopher; her reading of the F major Sonata's slow movement is one of the greatest piano recordings ever made (a later, live recording [also for Philips], although superb, isn't quite so intense). However, I should also mention Lili Kraus (Sony, analogue), Maria João Pires (Denon or, preferably, DG – both are digital) and Alicia de Larrocha (RCA, digital), all of whom have, like Uchida, recorded distinguished complete cycles of the Mozart piano sonatas. The most memorable recordings of individual sonatas include Glenn Gould (Sony, analogue) or Dinu Lipatti (EMI mono) in No. 10, Horowitz in No. 11 (Sony, analogue) and two wonderful mono recordings of the A minor Rondo – Artur Schnabel (EMI) and Wanda Landowska (a great harpsichordist playing the piano – RCA).

Ludwig van Beethoven
(1770-1827)

Piano Sonata No. 3 in C major, Op. 2 No. 3 (1794-95)

The last and greatest phase of an astonishingly far-reaching Op. 2. Beethoven prepares us much as he does in the orchestral opening of his First Piano Concerto – majestically, with calm but strongly voiced musical paragraphs that bear extensive development later on. The *Adagio* is meditative and closes in a mood of serene peacefulness, the Scherzo romps buoyantly, offset by a darker Trio and the glittering finale features a noble, hymn-like melody.

Arturo Benedetti Michelangeli (piano)

EMI mono

Recorded in Milan during the dark days of 1941, Michelangeli's account is poised, resilient and tightly argued. The finale is nimble beyond belief while the sound – although fairly constricted – gives at least some idea of Michelangeli's vast dynamic range. Richard Goode (Nonesuch) and Alfred Brendel (Philips) provide the finest digital alternatives.

Piano Sonata No. 4 in E flat major, Op. 7 (1797-98)

The profound core of Op. 7 is a magnificent *Largo* which Harry Halbrecht has described as "the first of those great spiritual meditations in which Beethoven seems to sublimate the human passions in a contemplation of the harmony of the spheres". The first movement is a splendidly vigorous 6/8 *Allegro molto e con brio*, the third, a gently playful *Allegro* with an unexpectedly sombre Trio and the finale, a rondo that opens in the manner of a German art song.

Wilhelm Backhaus (piano)

Decca analogue

The great virtue of Backhaus's performance is its uncanny sense of improvisation: one imagines that Beethoven's own performances were similarly gruff and impetuous. The first movement works particularly well, though Sviatoslav Richter (Olympia, analogue) and Michelangeli (DG, analogue) are technically more accomplished.

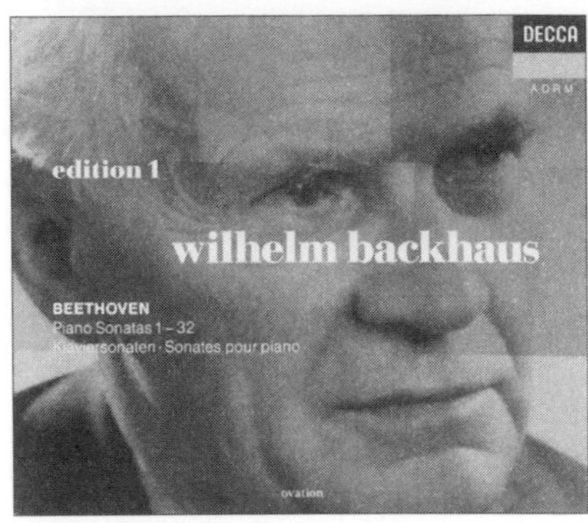

Piano Sonata No. 7 in D major, Op. 10 No. 3 (1797-98)

The exalted high point of Beethoven's early sonatas, and a work that could as easily have been included under our "Mighty monologues" (which follows this section). Op. 10 No. 3's first movement leaps upwards before vacillating excitedly and ushering in a restless but elegant second theme. Again, there's a sombre *Largo*, though this time Beethoven's writing ventures into harmonic realms that anticipate the Wagner of *Tristan und Isolde* (see "Twilit catastrophes", below). A cool Minuet and playfully hesitant Rondo round off Beethoven's most substantial Sonata prior to the *Pathétique* (see "Mighty monologues", below).

Vladimir Horowitz (piano)

RCA analogue

The finest of Horowitz's many Beethoven recordings, elegant and energetic in the outer movements and with a lean, melodramatic account of the Largo e mesto. Richter (Pyramid, EMI, Praga or Electrecord, digital/analogue) conjures up a more desolate atmosphere (specifically in the Largo) and Gilels (DG, digital), provides a more rounded tone.

Instrumental solos Mighty monologues (1798-1913)

Mighty monologues (1798-1913)

Here we witness a vast stylistic leap from Beethoven's trimly tailored early sonatas to the passion of his middle-period masterpieces and the ethereal narratives of his last years. We encounter some exquisite smaller forms by Mendelssohn, Chopin and Liszt, works that although relatively brief, provide vivid (and often highly dramatic) cameos from a musical revolution. We also find ourselves modifying the book's regular format by accommodating two or three pieces in a single entry (usually from a single opus number or genre, such as Chopin's Studies, Preludes and Polonaises). Anything less radical, and "Mighty monologues" would have dominated the whole volume!

Ludwig van Beethoven
(1770-1827)

Diabelli Variations in C major, Op. 120 (1822-23)

The original idea came from Anton Diabelli himself, an Austrian music publisher who invited a number composers to contribute a variation on what was, in all honesty, a rather innocuous little theme. Beethoven wasn't too keen initially, but eventually came up with his greatest and most audacious piano work – a sequence of 33 variations where Diabelli's waltz prompts all manner of miracles, from a parody on Mozart (Leporello in *Don Giovanni*), to *Prestos*, *Allegros*, *Andantes* and the deeply introspective trilogy of Variations 29-31. The closing sequence consists of a vigorous Fugue and a heart-stopping transition to an unexpectedly carefree Minuet. The cumulative effect of the *Diabellis* is overwhelming.

Alfred Brendel (piano)
Philips digital

You don't just play the Diabellis, you think them – and Brendel thinks more deeply than most. This is his third recording, and possibly his best. Other important (mostly analogue) contenders include Friedrich Gulda (Harmonia Mundi, albeit in acoustically dead sound), Artur Schnabel (Pearl, mono) and Sviatoslav Richter (Praga, Philips [digital], Arkadia).

Piano Sonata No. 8 in C minor, Op. 13, "Pathétique" (1798)

The title (which Beethoven authorized) is highly apt, and the sonata itself – which achieved instant popularity – epitomizes Romantic musical melodrama. The opening *Grave* suggests a fateful blow – doubly so when, minutes later and beyond the first statement of a furious *Allegro*, the repeat prompts its dramatic return. Beethoven's *Pathétique* revisits territory already charted in the great Sonata, Op. 10 No. 3 (see "Classical dramas", above), although the song-like *Adagio cantabile* is less sombre than the Seventh Sonata's *Largo e mesto*.

Rudolf Serkin (piano)
Sony Classical analogue

A forceful reading, superbly structured yet with a sensitive Adagio cantabile. The sound is rather harsh – so if that's a problem, best opt for Emil Gilels (DG, digital) or Radu Lupu (Decca, analogue), both of whom offer first-rate performances.

Piano Sonata No. 12 in A flat major, Op. 26, "Funeral March" (1800-01)

Beyond a winsome set of variations (the last of which look forward to Beethoven's Romantic successors), comes a lilting Scherzo with a richly harmonized Trio section and a "Funeral March on the Death of a Hero", initially suggested by Ferdinando Paer's opera *Achilles* (also the prompting inspiration for the *Eroica* Symphony's *Marcia funèbre*). The Sonata ends with a busily contrapuntal Rondo.

Wilhelm Kempff (piano)
Deutsche Grammophon mono

Singling out a Kempff performance for special comment is always difficult (his entire 1950s mono cycle is particularly rich in illuminating points of detail), but Op. 26 has a restrained grandeur that especially suits the work. Richter (Philips, Praga, Electrecord and Melodiya, analogue) offers an extraordinarily fine "Funeral March".

Piano Sonata No. 13 in E flat major, Op. 27 No. 1, "quasi una fantasia" (1800-01)

Beethoven again confounds expectations, this time with a novel, single-movement structure (hence the "sonata, almost a fantasia" reference) that falls into four distinct sections. The musical language is hugely varied, starting with a quizzical *Andante*, then proceeding through a galloping *Allegro*, a richly melodious *Adagio con espressione* and ending in jubilant mood with a boisterous *Allegro vivace*. There are surprises galore, but the music's design – is as clear as day.

Maurizio Pollini (piano)
Deustche Grammophon digital

Pianistic sculpture, immaculate musicianship and sensibly programmed with the Moonlight

Sonata (see below). Other excellent digital versions include Bernard Roberts (Nimbus, digital), Alfred Brendel (his second Philips recording) and Richard Goode (Nonesuch).

Piano Sonata No. 14 in C sharp minor, Op. 27 No. 2, "Moonlight" (1801)

Forget the highly inappropriate title which, as the Russian composer-pianist Anton Rubinstein rightly observed, "awakens a feeling of lyricism, while the music tells of a sky covered by heavy leaden clouds ". Like its companion piece (Sonata No. 13, see above), Op. 27 No. 2 is highly unconventional, with the famous *Adagio sostenuto* placed first, followed by a gently dancing *Allegretto* (described by Liszt as "a flower between two precipices") and a tempestuous finale – like "a storm bursting" (Rubinstein again).

Solomon (piano)
EMI mono

The most comprehensive interpretation available (recorded in 1945), sullen and wonderfully controlled in the first movement, elegant in the second and fiery in the third. A plethora of alternatives ranges from Paderewski (RCA, mono), Horowitz (RCA, mono and Sony, analogue) and Gilels (DG digital) to the more cerebral Brendel (Philips, his digital second recording).

Piano Sonata No. 15 in D major, Op. 28, "Pastoral" (1801)

A balmy interlude after the storm and stress of Op. 27 No. 2 (the so-called *Moonlight*, see above). The gently mobile opening *Allegro* is immediately warming; there's a rather melancholy *Andante* with a playful scherzo-style middle section (a favourite of the composer's, apparently), then a mischievous Scherzo-proper and an eventful folk-like finale to close.

Maurizio Pollini
Deutsche Grammophon digital

Pollini is again a noble commentator (he would in fact make an excellent first choice in any of the Sonatas Nos.13-15), though Wilhelm Kempff (DG, his 1951 mono recording), Gerhard Oppitz (RCA, digital) and Richard Goode (Nonesuch, digital) are equally arresting. Schnabel's 1933 mono recording is especially characterful, although the piano tone is rather 'pinched'.

Piano Sonata No. 16 in G major, Op. 31 No. 1 (1802)

The three Op. 31 Sonatas mark a further stylistic leap forward. They are contemporary with the so-called 'Heiligenstadt Testament' (Beethoven's confessions of deafness and intimations of death) and yet this particular Sonata opens to a humorous, syncopated *Allegro* – a little like a reveille – with a playful second theme. The elegant *Adagio* has an almost Chopinesque feel to it, while the finale is a pastoral interlude with a good joke or two up its sleeve.

Stephen Kovacevich (piano)
EMI digital

Re-creative music-making of the first order: spontaneous, thoughtful and beautifully recorded. Viable alternatives include Richard Goode (Nonesuch, digital) and the pre-war Schnabel (Pearl, EMI, mono), whose playful first movement can't fail to prompt a smile.

Piano Sonata No. 17 in D minor, Op. 31 No. 2, "Tempest" (1802)

Asked about the meaning of this Sonata, Beethoven once suggested reading Shakespeare's *The Tempest* – but the title was not his idea. The opening is remarkable: a slowly spread A major chord followed by a wildly animated *Allegro*. Come the development, and dream is wrecked again by the storm, before some quiet pleading and a menacing close. The *Adagio* second movement suggests utter stillness (at least initially), and the *Allegretto* finale, a lyrical canter.

Sviatoslav Richter (piano)
EMI analogue

The Tempest Sonata offers copious opportunities for tonal colouring and Richter's performance (his interpretation has been recorded a number of times) combines concentration with wide dynamic contrasts. Richard Goode (Nonesuch, digital) is also impressive, while Solomon (EMI, mono), Schnabel (Pearl, EMI, mono) and Kempff (DG, 1951, mono) head the 'old school'.

Piano Sonata No. 18 in E flat major, Op. 31 No. 3 (1802)

Here, a feeling of coolness predominates (the opening sounds almost like a pre-jazz improvisation), although the second theme – a real beauty – is cast more in the manner of Mozart. There's no slow movement, but a fetching Scherzo (an elegant scamper with good-humoured interjections), an idyllic Minuet and one of Beethoven's most affirmative finales – a wild, sunny tarantella that wouldn't be out of place in a Keystone Cops movie!

Stephen Kovacevich (piano)
EMI digital
As with No. 16, Kovacevich 'connects' with Beethoven's mischievous brand of invention. Here, however, I would especially urge sampling Schnabel (Pearl, EMI, mono): his finale has a reckless abandon that captures the music's spirit perfectly. Richard Goode (Nonesuch, digital) and Richter (Praga, analogue or Philips, digital) are also well worth hearing.

Piano Sonata No. 21 in C major, Op. 53, "Waldstein" (1803-04)

A contemporary of the *Eroica* Symphony and titled "Great Sonata" by Beethoven himself, this magnificent work also bears the name of its dedicatee, Count Ferdinand Waldstein (an amateur musician and patron of the composer). The opening idea suggests a rhythmically animated dawn chorus, while the first-movement development is as turbulent as anything Beethoven had composed up to that time. Again, there's no 'proper' slow movement, but a melancholy introduction to an expansive and technically demanding finale.

Richard Goode (piano)
Nonesuch digital
On disc as in concert, Richard Goode balances fire, precision and a genuinely Beethovenian ruggedness. His recorded rivals are many, from Solomon (EMI mono, and especially magical in the first movement), through the provocative Horowitz (preferably his 1972 Sony analogue recording) to Kempff (DG, 1951, mono) and the impulsive Schnabel (Pearl, EMI, mono).

Piano Sonata No. 22 in F major, Op. 54 (1804)

Sandwiched between two giants, Op. 54 is an underrated but sophisticated piece cast in just two movements (it usually plays for no more than 10 or 12 minutes). A sombre but harmonious introduction leads to a fairly fierce Toccata, while the *Allegretto* second movement seems to wander around in all directions - playful, wistful and yet supremely sure of itself.

Richard Goode (piano)
Nonesuch digital
Goode's performance has a relaxed, musing quality that suits the music especially well; it's a fairly intimate reading, but there are plenty of excellent alternatives, not least Brendel (Philips - either 1977, analogue or 1993, digital), Richter (Philips, digital) and Bernard Roberts (Nimbus, digital).

Piano Sonata No. 23 in F minor, Op. 57, "Appassionata" (1804)

The nearest thing to a 'Beethoven's Fifth Symphony' for piano - an "athletic body, without drapery, without ornament, in which everything is muscle and frame covered with hard, solid flesh, without any trace of flabbiness" (Romain Rolland). The first movement is a masterly synthesis of dynamic extremes, the second, a theme with three variations, and the finale a rolling monster - melodramatic, virtuosic and ending in a whirlwind *Presto*.

Sviatoslav Richter (piano)
Praga analogue
Richter goes hell-for-leather; it's a thrilling performance, indifferently recorded (live, in 1959) - although Richard Goode (Nonesuch, digital) suggests more in the way of structural sense and Kempff (DG, 1951, mono) is especially strong on nuancing. Other notable rivals include Rubinstein (RCA, analogue) and Gilels (DG, analogue).

Piano Sonata No. 24 in F sharp major, Op. 78 (1809)

The brief but lovely F sharp major Sonata provides something of a light interlude among the otherwise strongly assertive middle-period sonatas, and yet its concision, formal perfection and thematic attractiveness add up to something eminently appealing - especially in the hands of a fine interpreter. There are just two movements, a tightly structured *Allegro ma non troppo*, followed by a whimsical Rondo.

Robert Casadesus (piano)
Sony Classical mono
A fresh, transparent reading, typically Gallic in its elegance though rather harshly recorded. Richard Goode (Nonesuch) provides a fine digital alternative, and there's a superb pre-war recording - Classical in conception and stylishly phrased - featuring the hugely underrated Egon Petri (APR, mono).

Piano Sonata No. 26 in E flat major, Op. 81*a*, "Les adieux" (1809-10)

Imagine Beethoven sleeping in a cellar, his head wrapped in cushions to protect his ears from the noise of exploding mines (Napoleon's troops were advancing at the time). The title (the composer's own) mirrors the dedication to Beethoven's patron Archduke Rudolf, who had been forced to leave Vienna. The first three notes of the Sonata correspond to the German "Le-be-wohl" (farewell); there's a tense first-movement *Allegro*, a painfully disorientating slow movement and an exultant finale that marks the long-awaited 'return'.

Wilhelm Kempff
Deutsche Grammophon mono
Kempff showed an especial understanding of this piece; he would habitually penetrate its spiritual core (his stereo version is also very

fine) – although both Schnabel (EMI, mono) and Robert Casadesus (Sony, mono) make festive music of the finale, and there are fine alternative versions from Backhaus (Decca, analogue) and Goode (Nonesuch, digital)

Piano Sonata No. 27 in E minor, Op. 90 (1814)

Like Op. 78, Op. 90 is cast in just two movements, the first of which is headed "with vivacity and always with feeling and expression", the second, "not too fast and to be played in a very song-like fashion". The resolute opening is followed by a wistful response (this movement is said to represent "conflict between the heart and the head"), while the second movement ("conversation with the beloved") is intimate and sweet-centred.

Sviatoslav Richter (piano)

Olympia analogue

Richter's reading is distinguished by a combination of strength and delicacy (there are at least three alternatives to choose from), although Egon Petri (APR, mono), Solomon (EMI) and Charles Rosen (Sony) – all of them analogue – illuminate different aspects of this comparatively unfamiliar but attractive Sonata.

Piano Sonata No. 28 in A major, Op. 101 (1816)

The first – and most lyrical – of Beethoven's 'late' sonatas opens with a movement that, according to the composer himself, should be played in a "somewhat lively" manner but "with deepest feeling". The second movement is a sturdy March that anticipates Schumann, whereas the finale opens in a "slow and yearning" mood, before briefly recalling the first movement and launching into an ebullient finale, "swiftly, but not too much, and with determination"!

Richard Goode (piano)

Nonesuch digital

Beethoven's 'late' sonatas are regally served by a plethora of fine pianists, from Artur Schnabel (EMI, mono), Wilhelm Kempff (DG, from his earlier mono set) and Aldo Ciccolini (Nuova Era, digital) to Alfred Brendel (Philips, digital) and Maurizio Pollini (DG, analogue/digital). Richard Goode's characteristic feeling for structure and the precise mood of a piece is especially in evidence in Sonatas Nos. 28, 30 and 31.

Piano Sonata No. 29 in B flat major, Op. 106, "Hammerklavier" (1817-19)

The greatest of all piano sonatas is contemporaneous with at least three other Beethovenian monuments – the *Diabelli* Variations (see above), the *Missa solemnis* (see "The Symphonic Dimension", below), and the *Choral* Symphony (see "The Romantic revolution", above). The title means, literally, "hammer piano" or "piano forte" (at the time, Beethoven was keen on having titles written in German), but was also applied to the Sonata, Op. 101 (see above). There are four movements – an impulsive *Allegro* full of tonal conflict, a parodying Scherzo, an *Adagio* that unfolds one eloquent episode after another and a finale that, beyond a preparatory slow introduction, launches into a playful though complex fugue.

Alfred Brendel (piano)

Philips digital

Schnabel's incandescent slow movement is essential listening (Pearl, EMI, mono), but Brendel's naturalness of expression and intuitive grasp of Beethoven's harmonic language is also something very special. The live 1995 recording is excellent. Other fine versions of the Hammerklavier include Richter (Praga, analogue), Pollini (DG, analogue) and Solomon (EMI, mono).

Piano Sonata No. 30 in E major, Op. 109 (1820)

The final three sonatas form a sort of triptych, the first and last of them ending with a lengthy theme and variations. No. 30 opens to a gently rhapsodising first movement, then flies into a furious *Prestissimo* before the theme – which is noble and hymn-like in character – prompts a quarter-hour journey full of vivid tonal contrasts. The final climax is overwhelming, but the Sonata ends in a mood of sublime tranquillity.

Richard Goode (piano)

Nonesuch digital

An admirably clear-headed presentation with plenty of 'soul', though do keep an eye out for Stephen Kovacevich (Philips, analogue – though an EMI remake is also due) while, as in the other 'late' sonatas, Artur Schnabel's pre-war (mono) recordings are essential listening (Pearl's transfers are the best).

Piano Sonata No. 31 in A flat major, Op. 110 (1821-22)

Again, the first movement is wistful, romantic and free-flowing; and there's a fierce fast movement to follow (which, like that in Sonata No. 30, lasts only a couple of minutes). The third movement, however, is cast in six connected sections with a fugue at its core and an inversion of the fugue (i.e. the fugue turned upside-down) as its finale. One particular passage (it precedes the first statement of the fugue) seems to recall the aria "Es ist vollbracht!" from Bach's *St John Passion* ("It it is finished ... O rest for all afflicted spirits").

Richard Goode (piano)
Nonesuch digital

Goode has a special understanding of this piece, its endless modulations (shifting from one key to another) and multi-tier structure, most specifically in the finale. Other perceptive interpreters include Glenn Gould (Sony, mono), Mieczyslaw Horszowski (Vox or Relief, mono), Claude Frank (Music & Arts, analogue) and Bernard Roberts (Nimbus, digital).

Piano Sonata No. 32 in C minor, Op. 111 (1822)

The C minor Sonata's first movement epitomizes Beethovenian defiance, the opening *Maestoso* especially – except that, unlike certain earlier works, it seems to retreat, utterly broken, before returning with renewed resolve and a fiercely contrapuntal main Allegro. The second movement vies with the *Adagio* of the *Hammerklavier* in terms of length (both last for between 15 and 20 minutes), though Op. 111's noble *Arietta* instigates an astonishing sequence of variations, from boogie-style syncopations to celestial trills and the utter weightlessness of the closing minutes. There's nothing else in Beethoven's output that has quite the same effect.

Artur Schnabel (piano)
Pearl mono

Virtually all the pianists so far featured in our recommendations excel in Op. 111, Solomon (EMI, mono) and Richter (Philips, digital), especially. But Schnabel alone creates the illusion of having improvised the Sonata on the spot – no mean feat, given the stature of the music.

Franz Schubert (1797-1828)

Fantasie in C major, D760, "Wanderer" (1822)

As with Schubert's *Trout* Quintet (see "The more, the merrier", above), and *Death and the Maiden* Quartet (see "The Classical string quartet", above), the *Wanderer* Fantasie is so-called because a song sets the scene for a particular movement – in this case the *Adagio*, which embellishes a famous Lied that Schubert had composed six years earlier. Viewed as a whole, however, the *Wanderer* Fantasie alternates Beethovenian assertiveness with a spirit of songful reverie.

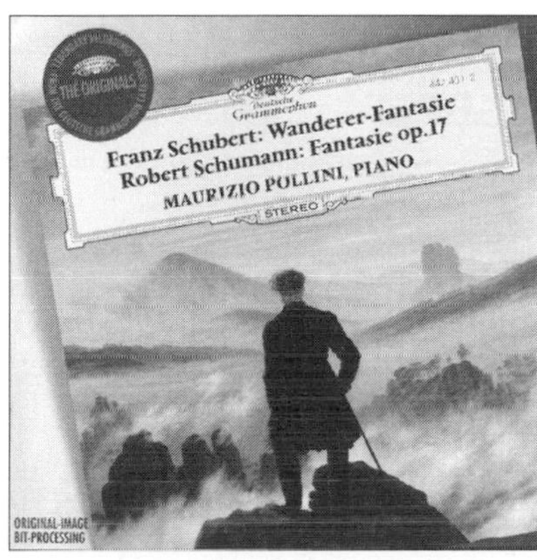

Maurizio Pollini (piano)
Deutsche Grammophon analogue

Pollini is a resilient Schubertian with a virtually infallible technique: his opening Allegro is strong but never percussive (as Richter's is sometimes prone to be), while he brings miracles of delicacy to the latter portions of the Adagio. Still, Richter's EMI recording remains a powerful rival, while Leon Fleisher (Sony, analogue) and Alfred Brendel (Philips) provide perceptive alternative versions – Brendel especially (his later digital recording).

Four Impromptus, D899 (Op. 90) (1828)

The first *Impromptu* opens to a masterful chord then switches to a wistful processional that suggests the melancholy narratives of Schubert's great song-cycles. The second and fourth pieces feature flowing passagework and contrasting middle sections, while the third – the most famous in the series – is a beautiful 'song without words' in G flat major.

Four Impromptus, D935 (Op. 142) (1828)

Schumann believed that parts of D935 must have originally belonged to a Sonata, so powerful is the music's overall design. The opening piece in F major has as its centre-piece an exquisite duet between upper and lower voices; the second is elegant and dance-like, the third – a delightful set of variations on a theme – recalls the world of Schubert's *Rosamunde* ballet, and the last is a highly audacious piece with a pronounced Hungarian flavour.

Alfred Brendel (piano)
Philips digital

Chosing between Brendel and his great teacher Edwin Fischer (APR, Pearl or Dante, mono) is difficult. Both play with the utmost imagination and sensitivity (Fischer is especially magnificent in the first of the D899 pieces), but Philips's superb digital recording must be counted a significant bonus. Other notable sets include Brendel's earlier (analogue) recordings (Philips and Vox), Artur Schnabel (EMI, mono) and Murray Perahia (Sony, digital).

Six Moments musicaux, D780 (1823-28)
Two of these exquisite pieces – the Second and Fourth – are subdivided into contrasting sections, the second resembling a Schubert Lied, the Fourth anticipating Chopin (at least in the opening section). The rest mix charm (Nos. 1 and 3), robust assertiveness (No. 5) and profound reverie (the last, No. 6 – which originally appeared as an independent piece called *Plaints d'un troubador*). Like so many of Schubert's miniatures, the *Moments musicaux* pack more meaning into a few minutes than many a lesser symphony manages in an hour or more.

 ***Alfred Brendel (piano)***
Philips digital
Brendel's eloquence never precludes a sense of appropriate style, and his charm is neither patronising nor superficial. Viable rivals include analogue recordings by Artur Schnabel (EMI, mono), Emil Gilels (Orfeo, analogue) and Sviatoslav Richter (Olympia, analogue), plus a whole plethora of pianists in individual pieces from the Moments musicaux.

Piano Sonata No. 19 in C minor, D958 (1828)
Schubert conceived his last three piano sonatas as a single collection; his original dedication was to Hummel, although they weren't actually published until 1838 when the dedication was transferred to Schumann. The first – and darkest – of them opens with grim resolve and develops adventurously (harmonic freedom being the particular of hallmark of Schubert's last phase) whereas the second movement is a haunting *Adagio* followed by a variegated Minuet and a fiery final movement that takes a side-glance at Schubert's last song, *Die Taubenpost*.

 ***Maurizio Pollini (piano)***
Deutsche Grammophon digital
Pollini's set of the last three sonatas is consistently strong, a marmoreal vision, technically impeccable and immaculately recorded. Brendel (Philips, digital) is perhaps a shade more 'giving' (some will prefer his more personalized – albeit equally cerebral – approach to the music), but Pollini's boldness and refinement yield very high dividends.

Piano Sonata No. 20 in A major, D959 (1828)
An astonishing piece that sports a bold chordal opening, followed by one of Schubert's loveliest 'second themes'. But the real surprise occurs in the *Adagio* where, amidst a sullen stream of melody, the music's harmonic core slowly disintegrates: arguments, modulations, even musical shape all wander in a confused delirium, until Schubert summons order and recaptures the movement's initial mood (the G major String Quartet pursues similar flights of fancy – see "The Romantic string quartet", above). Once sanity is restored, Schubert concludes his masterpiece with a skipping Scherzo and a consolatory closing *Allegro ma non troppo*.

 ***Maurizio Pollini (piano)***
Deutsche Grammophon digital
A superbly balanced account, but if you can track down Rudolf Serkin's Sony (analogue) recording, then snap it up: it's probably the greatest Schubert D959 on disc, although Artur Schnabel's 1930s recording (EMI, mono) runs it fairly close.

Piano Sonata No. 21 in B flat major, D960 (1828)
The B flat major is commonly considered to be Schubert's greatest piano sonata; it opens to a solemn melody punctuated by quiet, eerie trills in the bass and breathes an air of troubled resignation. The overall spirit is introspective, even dreamy, although the musical argument is every bit as original and outreaching as that in the previous sonatas. There's a desolate *Andante sostenuto*, a delicate Scherzo and a finale that is both light and restless.

 ***Sviatoslav Richter (piano)***
Olympia analogue
Richter is an uncompromising interpreter at the best of times, but his Schubert is especially stark. He observes the long first movement repeat, takes extremely slow tempos and suggests glacial wastes similar to those in Schubert's great song-cycle Winterreise (see "Wayfarers and wanderers", below). Warmer options include Brendel (Philips), Kovacevich (EMI) and Clara Haskil (Philips, analogue), while Artur Schnabel's 1939 recording (EMI, mono) and Andreas Staier's performance on a fortepiano (Teldec, digital) are especially perceptive.

Three Pieces, D946 (1828)
A profound, wind-blown appendage to the better-known sets of *Impromptus* (see above), the *Three Pieces* are more on line with the exploratory nature of the late

sonatas. The second, an *Allegretto*, includes some particularly turbulent writing, while the last of the series is in the manner of a *Hungarian Dance*.

Maurizio Pollini (piano)
Deutsche Grammophon digital
Pollini is a pianistic sculptor whose innate refinement, intellectual perception and control of line suit the bold but inscrutable contours of Schubert's last works. The fact that he is also deeply involved with certain branches of modern music helps to explain why he connects so strongly with the quasi-Expressionist aspects of these scores. Significant digital rivals include Brendel (Philips), Imogen Cooper (Ottavo), Andreas Staier (Teldec – very dramatic performances on a fortepiano) and Dirk Joeres (Carlton).

Felix Mendelssohn (1809-1847)

Prelude and Fugue in E minor, Op. 35 No. 1 (1837)

The Bachian title gives the game away, and when you listen to the Prelude – one of Mendelssohn's most beguiling single movements – you might catch a reference to Bach's First Keyboard Partita. The Fugue culminates in an ingenious (and inspired) reference to the Lutheran chorale *Ein feste Burg* (which Mendelssohn also used in his *Reformation* Symphony – see "The Romantic revolution", above).

Shura Cherkassky (piano)
Decca digital
Cherkassky's superior pedigree tells right from the Prelude's opening bars, a gorgeous melody cushioned by lovingly caressed arpeggios (a rapid, harp-like succession of notes). Benjamin Frith has made an extremely good recording of all six Preludes and Fugues (Naxos), but Cherkassky – whose disc, recorded live, consists of a mixed programme of Variations – remains uniquely satisfying.

Song without Words No. 14 in C minor, Op. 38 No. 2

"We went into the Drawing Room to see Mendelssohn and talked to him for some time," wrote Queen Victoria in her journal of May 30th, 1844; "He played to us beautifully – music from *A Midsummer Night's Dream* and two of his *Songs without Words*. He is such an agreeable and clever man and his countenance beams with intelligence and genius." There are eight books of *Songs without Words* ("Lieder ohne Worte"), plus an extra piece in G minor, Op. 49. No. 14, though hardly one of the most original in the series, is certainly one of the loveliest (you could well imagine the Queen adoring it). Other famous *Songs without Words* include the indelible "Spring Song" (No. 30) and the "Spinning Song" (No. 34).

Ignaz Friedman (piano)
Pearl mono
You could search far and wide for piano playing that's more sonorous, stylish and expressive than Friedman's. No one since 1930 has made more of these masterly miniatures and the recordings are among the finest of the period. As to 'complete' sets, Lívia Rev (Hyperion, digital) would be hard to beat.

Fryderyk Chopin (1810-1849)

Ballades – No. 1 in G minor, Op. 23 (1835); No. 2 in F major, Op. 38 (1840); No. 3 in A flat major, Op. 47 (1841); No. 4 in F minor, Op. 52 (1842)

Four fabulous flights of fancy, each lasting considerably longer than Chopin's three-to four-minute 'norm'. The First (in G minor) opens to a noble *Largo* and has at its centre one of Chopin's most exquisite melodies. The Second, in F major (although it ends in A minor), initially seems like a gentle boating song – that is until a violent *Allegro con fuoco* disrupts its tranquil mood. Then there's the Third and perhaps most popular *Ballade*, in A flat, which canters an astonishingly varied course with disarming ease, while the Fourth (in F minor, and, at roughly ten minutes, the longest) is a miracle of complex though carefully tooled counterpoint. All four works combine sophisticated design with an unprecedented harmonic and melodic richness.

Murray Perahia (piano)
Sony Classical digital
For years it seemed that the Ballades were out of season: there were plenty of good recordings around, but none that we might justifiably call 'great'. Then, in 1994, Murray Perahia came along with a set that is as fluent, as thoughtful and as comprehensively perceptive as any since Artur Rubinstein's (RCA, analogue). However, there are some important historic forebears in an unusually bold version by Sviatoslav Richter (Praga, mono) and the elegantly eloquent Alfred Cortot (EMI, Biddulph, mono). Perahia's programme couples the Ballades with other pieces by Chopin.

Barcarolle in F sharp major, Op. 60 (1845-46)

Ravel wrote of the *Barcarolle's* "continuous melodic line", "intensity" and "dazzling harmonies" (Debussy loved the piece too). It is indeed one of Chopin's most inspired narratives, a 'fifth *Ballade*' in all but name, densely populated with significant musical incident and harmonically prophetic of later styles. The term *Barcarolle* means, literally, 'boating-song', which in this case refers more to flowing rhythm than to a specific mood (in that respect at least, Chopin's title is as misleading as his use of the word *Scherzo* – see below).

 ***Maurizio Pollini***
Deutsche Grammophon digital

Pollini surveys the Barcarolle's structure like a master-builder – but without understating its emotional subtext. There are many fine alternatives, not least Artur Rubinstein (RCA, analogue), Benno Moiseiwitsch (APR, mono), Dinu Lipatti (EMI, mono) and Alfred Cortot (EMI, Biddulph, mono). All promote wholly natural though very different brands of pianistic poetry.

Four Mazurkas, Op. 33 (1837-38)

Chopin's *Mazurkas* are based on the old Polish national dance, the *Mazur*, from Mazovia, and yet their composition is so rich in harmonic and contrapuntal incident that to dismiss them as mere 'folk ditties' would be a profound mistake. All are well worth getting to know, yet this particular opus includes four of the finest: the first, in G sharp minor, opens in the manner of a gipsy melody, the second (D major) is carefree and extrovert, while the C minor (No. 3) wears a wistful demeanour and the fourth – the greatest of all (in B minor) – is a mini-drama that abounds in dynamic contrasts.

 ***Artur Rubinstein (piano)***
RCA analogue

Legend has it that Chopin himself never played a Mazurka twice in the same way, and similar claims might be made on behalf of Rubinstein whose mono recordings (EMI, pre-war and RCA, post-war) are crisper and generally less reflective than these mellow stereo remakes. Beautiful though they are, I'd also strongly recommend sampling the 12 Mazurkas that the great Ignaz Friedman recorded in 1930 (Pearl, Dante, mono) – fanciful, fiercely rhythmic performances that, once heard, haunt one's imagination forever.

Nocturnes Nos. 7 in C sharp minor and 8 in D flat major, Op. 27 Nos. 1 and 2 (1835)

It was the Irish composer John Field (1782-1837) who first introduced the *Nocturne* (French for "night-piece") as a genre, but it was Chopin who brought it to the acme of artistic perfection. The most famous Chopin *Nocturne* is No. 2 in E flat, Op. 9 No. 2, but the two Op. 27 pieces are among the greatest in the series. The outer sections of No. 7 feature a sombre melody set to a flowing accompaniment, whereas the far sweeter No. 8 is coloured with elaborate ornamentation. However, discerning listeners will want the whole collection (19 published *Nocturnes*, plus two posthumous pieces).

 ***Artur Rubinstein***
RCA analogue

Rubinstein recorded the Nocturnes three times – on 78s (EMI, 1936-37), on mono LPs (RCA) and, lastly, this famous stereo set from the 1960s. Admittedly, the sound will strike some as a little shallow (they may prefer the greater weight of Claudio Arrau's Philips set, also analogue), but the actual playing has a gracefulness and refinement that will appeal to most listeners. Rubinstein's pre-war set is for those who favour an extra shot of adrenalin.

Piano Sonata No. 2 in B flat minor, Op. 35, "Funeral March" (1839)

Schumann's jibe about Chopin binding together "four of his maddest children and thus smuggling them into a place which they could not have entered otherwise" says something about the Sonata's unorthodox design. And yet the first movement is a tower of formal strength, while Liszt wrote of the celebrated "Funeral March" – the Sonata's 'heart', which was composed first – that "one has the feeling of lamenting for the Death not of one hero ... but of a whole generation, which has in its passing left behind only women, children and priests".

 ***Vladimir Horowitz (piano)***
RCA analogue

Great performances of the "Funeral March" Sonata are legion, from the austerity of Rachmaninov pre-war (RCA, Pearl, transferred from 78s), to the poise of Rubinstein (RCA – elegant in the 1960s [analogue], more impassioned in the 1950s [mono]) and the more cerebral axis of Maurizio Pollini (DG, digital). Horowitz recorded the work twice, and while his later (analogue) Sony recording is extraordinarily fine, this 1950 mono predecessor is positively Gothic in its melodramatic emphases and intimidating virtuosity. You'll either love it or loathe it.

Piano Sonata No. 3 in B minor, Op. 58 (1844)

In marked contrast to the darkly brooding Second Sonata, the Third is at once both more majestic (the opening movement especially), more clearly structured and more affirmative in tone. The first movement is among Chopin's grandest inspirations, while the brief Scherzo cascades with colour, the *Largo* approximates the finest *Nocturnes* and the finale is fast and rhapsodic.

 ***Emil Gilels (piano)***
Deutsche Grammophon analogue
A more thought-provoking performance than most, with an especially broad account of the first movement (Gilels thought the Maestoso element to be of particular importance). Rubinstein (RCA, analogue) offers a more mainstream option (albeit one that's beautifully played), while Alfred Cortot's pre-war recording (Biddulph, EMI, mono) has a unique re-creative spontaneity and there's a massively stated, almost Beethovenian 1950s account from Claudio Arrau (EMI, mono).

Polonaises Nos. 6 in A flat major, Op. 53 (1842) and 7 in A flat major, Op. 61, "Polonaise-Fantasie" (1845-46)

Chopin wrote his greatest *Polonaises* while in exile (Poland was subordinated to Russia at the time), so rather than reflect the glittering world of aristocracy they protest an ardent patriotism. There are six mature pieces in all, including the two masterpieces included here. No. 7 is more a piano tone-poem cast in the form of a *Polonaise*; it's a red-blooded narrative that plays for some 13 minutes, and yet it is based on a tiny corpus of thematic material. No. 6, the so-called *Heroic* Polonaise, is the most famous of all, a proud and patriotic statement with stampeding octaves and a wealth of lyrical ideas.

 ***Artur Rubinstein (piano)***
RCA analogue
Rubinstein's playing combines a sense of pride and aristocracy with a brand of intuition that, while reflecting a natural feel for Polish dance rhythms, also conveys classical composure. His earlier recordings (1950s, RCA, or 1930s, EMI – both in mono) are somewhat bolder in spirit, while Vladimir Horowitz excels in Nos. 6 and 7 (Sony, analogue or RCA, mono/digital) and there's a fine alternative set of Nos. 1-6 from Lazar Berman (DG, analogue).

Preludes, Op. 28 (1836-39)

"Sketches, beginnings of studies, ruins, single eagle's-feathers in wild confusion" – Robert Schumann's review of the 24 Preludes, Op. 28 was at once deeply intuitive and partially misleading. Chopin's challenging sequence suggests a self-contained world where we hear and feel the gamut of emotions, from tenderness and laughter to fear and anguish. The music itself is perfectly crafted, its technical difficulties secondary only to its purely musical demands.

 ***Maurizio Pollini (piano)***
Deutsche Grammophon analogue

Being such personal music, Chopin's Preludes inspire widely divergent interpretations: no single version will please everyone. Pollini views the set as whole; his playing is strong, polished, immensely perceptive and technically masterful. Martha Argerich and Ivo Pogorelich are more volatile and Maria João Pires more outwardly expressive (all are on DG, digital), while Alfred Cortot (EMI, Biddulph) realizes the full range of the Preludes' terror and caprice.

Scherzos – No. 1 in B minor, Op. 20 (1831-32); No. 2 in B flat minor, Op. 31 (1837); No. 3 in C sharp minor, Op. 39 (1839); No. 4 in E major, Op. 54 (1842)

If ever a generic title gave the wrong impression, it is here – the term 'Scherzo' having previously been used to denote either a displaced minuet in a four-movement Classical work or a relatively lightweight miniature. Chopin's, however, not only break away from the classical pattern but are immensely wide-ranging both in style and expression. The First – perhaps the greatest of the four – is said to have been a musical reaction to the Tsar's repression of the Polish insurrection (the gentle central section quotes a Mazovian Christmas carol) whereas the Second opens to distant alarms then rolls forth with immense gusto. It, too, has a tranquil middle episode, as does the otherwise stormy Third *Scherzo*, although there a hymn-like central melody prompts cascading figurations that fall about it like wind-blown petals. The Fourth *Scherzo* is equally brilliant though rather less tense: here the earlier patterns are reversed in that the work's darkest moments reside more in its melancholy central section than in their relatively playful surroundings. In other respects, however, the Fourth is the most '*Scherzo*-like' of the four; it is also the most harmonically advanced.

 ***Maurizio Pollini (piano)***
Deutsche Grammophon digital
Given too much freedom, Chopin's Scherzos can easily run riot – but Pollini's control, allied to his intuitive musicality and infallible

technique, keep them well in check. These are among the strongest, most poised versions available although adventurous collectors will also want to investigate the more cerebral (and somewhat more detached) Sviatoslav Richter (Olympia, analogue), the 'two sides' of Artur Rubinstein (impetuous pre-war, EMI, mono – or aristocratic post-war, RCA, analogue), not to mention striking individual performances by Horowitz – Nos. 1-3 (RCA, mono) and No. 4 (EMI, mono).

Studies, Opp. 10 (1829-32) and 25 (1832-36)

Although aimed at tackling specific technical problems, Chopin's *Studies* broke new ground in that they challenged both the fingers and the poetic imagination. The first set includes such famous pieces as the lyrical E flat *Study*, also known as the song *Tristesse*, the stormy No. 4 in A minor (marked *Agitato*) and the most famous of all, the *Revolutionary Study* – Chopin's patriotic reaction to the news that Warsaw had been captured by the Russians (1830). The second set of *Studies* kicks up another storm with *Winter Winds* (No. 11) and includes one of Chopin's most personal and emotive utterances, the *Study* in C sharp minor, Op. 25 No. 7. Three additional or 'new' *Studies* were published posthumously but don't quite match the creative vitality of their dazzling predecessors.

Maurizio Pollini (piano)
Deutsche Grammophon analogue

Piano students will slink away, humbled by Pollini's awesome virtuosity. It's a tremendous achievement, though the brilliance is more than skin deep. And yet, as with all Chopin, there are important alternative viewpoints: Alfred Cortot's, for example, which trades technical polish for poetic insight (his recordings are on EMI or Biddulph, mono), then the flamboyant Earl Wild (Chesky, digital). And don't forget a plethora of great pianists in individual Studies – Vladimir Horowitz (RCA, EMI and Sony, mono/analogue), Ignaz Friedman (Pearl, mono), Moritz Rosenthal (APR or Opal, mono), Dinu Lipatti (EMI, mono), Sviatoslav Richter (Praga, mono) to name but a few.

Waltzes Nos. 2, 3 and 4, Op. 34 ("Valses brillants") in A flat major (1835), A minor (1831) and F major (1838)

It was probably a trip to Vienna and the experience of Johann Strauss's waltzes that inspired Chopin to try his own hand at the medium – although it was at that time (1829) that he wrote to his father claiming, "I have not learned anything especially Viennese, and am therefore still unable to play waltzes". Our chosen selection includes two or three of the most varied (the tender A minor *Waltz* is perhaps the loveliest of all) although, given a fine performance, all 14 waltzes (five posthumous pieces aren't quite as inspired) make for a pleasurable listening experience.

Dinu Lipatti (piano)
EMI mono

Chopin's Waltzes can be appreciated either as tuneful morceaux or as subtly inventive mini-narratives. Lipatti's 1950 performances take the latter option – they are quite simply the finest recordings of the Waltzes ever made (a slighter later set, recorded live shortly before Lipatti died of leukaemia a the age of 33, is rather less good). There's charm, panache, depth of feeling and a pianistic refinement that only Rubinstein (RCA, mono or stereo/analogue) approaches. Lipatti's only real rival is a hugely characterful pre-war recording by Alfred Cortot (Biddulph, mono). Fine older recordings of individual waltzes are legion (Ignaz Friedman's of the A minor [Pearl, mono] and Horowitz's of No. 7 in C sharp minor [RCA, mono or Sony, analogue] being fair cases in point).

Robert Schumann (1810-1856)

Carnaval, Op. 9 (1833-35)

For all its endless melody and surface glitter, *Carnaval* harbours a secret – the musical spelling of the German town of Asch (S is the German B flat, H, the German B natural), birthplace of a certain lady pupil with whom Schumann (whose own name is implied in the same letters) was falling in love. Musically, *Carnaval* is a dazzling sequence of memorable miniatures – playful, melancholy, resolute and with the odd meaningful caricature to further colour the mix.

Alfred Cortot (piano)
Biddulph mono

There's no escaping the 'golden oldies' in Carnaval. In addition to Cortot (possibly the most sympathetically characterized performance of all, albeit recorded as long ago as 1928), there's Rachmaninov (RCA), Godowsky (APR), Dame Myra Hess (Biddulph or Dutton) and Michelangeli (Testament) – all of course in mono. Mitsuko Uchida (Philips) and Gerhard Oppitz (RCA) provide interesting digital alternatives, but the real magic of Carnaval – its Romantic soul – cries out for a level of fantasy that was the special province of an older pianistic generation.

Carnival Jest from Vienna, Op. 26 (1839-40)

Schumann's mischievous resolve to sneak the *Marseillaise* into a city that had forbidden its performance (Vienna) helps to explain the rather strange title. However, *Faschingsschwank aus Wien* (as it's known to German-speakers) is in effect a fully-fledged Romantic sonata, powerful as well as playful, with the *Marseillaise* reference in the first movement and an aching Intermezzo – one of the most passionate movements in the repertory – placed fourth.

Arturo Benedetti Michelangeli (piano)
Testament mono

Recorded live the day before Michelangeli's fabled Ravel/Rachmaninov concerto coupling (EMI, analogue), this historic recording, recently released for the first time, is among the most impressive mementos of an exceptionally great pianist. The playing is stylish, dextrous and deeply poetic (what's more, the CDs also include a fascinating rehearsal sequence), but there is a fine digital alternative by Maria João Pires (DG) in the context of an all-Schumann programme.

Davidsbündlertänze, Op. 6 (1837)

When the Biblical David slew the Philistines he prompted a major nineteenth-century composer to pen 18 "Dances of the David Brotherhood". Schumann's Davidites defend the best of the musical past, present and future – they will have no truck with the hypocrisy of their lesser peers (Schumann was of course a canny music critic). This hugely enjoyable though somewhat cryptic sequence ends with a delicious waltz. "Quite superfluously Eusebius [the dreamer] made the following remarks," wrote Schumann above the music, "and his lips quivered painfully".

Rudolf Firkušný (piano)
EMI mono

Firkušný could on occasion be rather brusque, but here he employs a considerable range of pianistic colours and his characterizations are often exquisite (especially in No. 17, with its premonitions of Debussy's "Serenade for the Doll" from Children's Corner – 0'59"). Wilhelm Kempff's 1960s DG analogue version is typically thought-provoking and Alfred Cortot's classic 1937 account (Dante, Biddulph, Music & Arts, all mono) is the most spontaneous – and perhaps the least accurate – performance on disc.

Etudes symphoniques, Opp. 13 and posth (1834, 1873)

The original title was "Studies for piano of orchestral character by Florestan and Eusebius [Schumann's personification of the dreamer and the impetuous romantic]". The theme itself is dark and mysterious, while the highly contrasted sequence of variations culminates in a broad, swaggering finale. Many performers (including Richter) programme the five posthumous variations that were included in the 1873 edition. The *Etudes symphoniques* are extraordinarily inventive and tend to inspire hugely divergent readings, hence an abundance of stimulating recordings.

Sviatoslav Richter (piano)
Revelation analogue

Richter achieves maximum impact with what at first appears to be a minimum of means – not in any technical sense (his command of the keyboard is dazzlingly comprehensive), but more because he refuses to distort the music's shape. This is resolute, square-jawed playing, immensely strong in the more assertive studies and either ethereal or delicate elsewhere. In recording terms the 1972 live performance – Richter's best, at least on disc – leaves a lot to be desired (there are odd thumps here and there), so you might like to try the more temperate Rubinstein (RCA, analogue) or Brendel (Philips, digital). Mono historical options are plentiful, not least Alfred Cortot (Biddulph, Dante, Pearl), Percy Grainger (Biddulph) and Géza Anda (Testament). Digital-fanciers should be impressed by the marmoreal playing of Maurizio Pollini (DG).

Fantasie in C major, Op. 17 (1836-38)

"The most passionate thing I have ever composed – a deep lament for you." Schumann's confession to his beloved Clara places one of the piano repertory's key works in its proper autobiographical context. The very opening sets the mood with a yearning melody suspended over an undulating accompaniment, while the central movement is a stirring march and the closing slow movement (something of a rarity in a piece of this scale) suggests hard-won serenity.

Maurizio Pollini (piano)
Deutsche Grammophon analogue

Clarity of vision allied to pianistic finesse and a controlled response to the music's emotional climate. Pollini's performance is a model of intelligent interpretation, although there are recommendable alternatives from Sviatoslav Richter (Philips, digital; EMI, analogue or Praga, mono) and, especially, Benno Moiseiwitsch (Testament, mono – with a searing account of the opening movement).

Kinderszenen, Op. 15 (1838)

Schumann himself said it all in a letter to his fiancée Clara Wieck. "I was suddenly inspired to dash off 30 quaint little pieces," he wrote; "I have chosen a dozen of them... I am sure you will enjoy them; but to do so naturally you must forget you are a virtuoso." *Kinderszenen* ("Scenes from Childhood") are not so much 'for children' as for adults who wish to conjure up childhood memories. There are 13 pieces in all, the most famous of them being the Seventh, "Träumerei", or "Dreaming".

Vladimir Horowitz (piano)
RCA mono

Horowitz recorded Kinderszenen at least four times, starting with this entrancing 1950 mono version (his first), through the Sony (analogue) sessions of 1962, the live Royal Festival Hall concert performance of 1982 (RCA, digital) and an even later digital recording on DG. Each has its share of particular beauties, but the early RCA recording presents Horowitz's exquisite (though sometimes interventionist) tone-painting at its most colourful. Those in search of something a little less idiosyncratic – though just as poetic, in its own way – are directed to Radu Lupu (Decca, digital).

Kreisleriana, Op. 16 (1838)

Schumann's eight sketches of the fictional Kapellmeister Johannes Kreisler (a half-mad conductor-composer invented by E. T. A. Hoffmann [the subject of Offenbach's *Tales of ...*]) are also partly autobiographical. "Do play the *Kreisleriana* now and then," urged Robert to Clara, "a really wild love, as wild as can be, is in some of the movements – your life and mine, and many a flash of your eyes." *Kreisleriana*'s language is at once passionate, capricious, introspective and grand, a restless but inspired journey that, in the right hands, creates a particularly powerful impression.

Vladimir Horowitz (piano)
Sony Classical analogue

The work of a pianistic magician, mysterious one moment, impetuous the next and with an especially imaginative account of the last movement (where simultaneous themes demand the ultimate in concentration and control). Strong rivals include Radu Lupu (Decca, digital) and Alfred Cortot (Biddulph, Dante or Pearl – 1935, mono)

Papillons, Op. 2 (1829-31)

A wide-eyed sequence of miniatures and the first of Schumann's piano works to reflect quasi-literary/psychological preoccupations. *Papillons*, or "Butterflies", opens in the manner of a waltz, then flies into action with martial fanfares, commanding octaves, delicate traceries that seem to emerge out of the ether, romantic interludes and a nostalgically echoing finale.

Alfred Cortot (piano)
Biddulph mono

Schumann's piano music is full of fantasy and it takes a pianistic magician to realize the full measure of its expressive potential. Alfred Cortot's Papillons is magical in the extreme – quixotic, poetic, colourful, achingly expressive and indelibly memorable. It provides a guide-in-miniature both to Schumann's piano idiom and to Cortot's style of playing. The 1935 recording (which is also available on Pearl, Dante and Music & Arts) reports Cortot's bell-like tone with impressive clarity.

Franz Liszt (1811-1886)

Aux cyprès de la Villa d'Este: Thrénodie No. 1 (*c*1867-77)

My own favourite among Liszt's piano works takes just seven minutes to encapsulate the glorious final phase of an entire musical era (German late-Romanticism). It opens to a gentle rocking figure in the bass, then ranges across a variety of keys, themes, colours and dynamics with such immense depth of feeling – inwardly sobbing yet with great restraint – that by the time it has finished, you feel as if you've experienced a full-length music drama (Wagner's *Tristan* is hardly more effective). *Aux cyprès de la Villa d'Este* is taken from the Third and final book of Liszt's *Années de pèlerinage* ("Years of pilgrimage").

Alfred Brendel (piano)
Philips analogue

It would be difficult to imagine a more sensitive performance, one where the tone and pace of the piece is better judged. The sound is excellent, and the remaining works in the programme give further examples of Liszt's profound but austere 'late' style. Sviatoslav Richter's live mono version (Revelation) provides an inspired, if sonically inadequate, second option.

Ballade No. 2 in B minor, S171 (1853)

Like his *Vallée d'Obermann* (see below), Liszt's Second *Ballade* suggest a heroic narrative. Sacheverell Sitwell described it as "a really magnificent thing, not to be confused by its title with the *Ballades* of Chopin ... It is less passionate but more full-blooded, concerned, as it were, less with personal suffering than with great happenings on the epic scale, barbarian invasions, cities in flames – tragedies of public, more than private, import."

Vladimir Horowitz (piano)
RCA digital

Anyone who witnessed Horowitz's 1982 London performance of the Second Ballade will attest to its magnificence – and having heard this Met live recording soon afterwards, I can tell you that the two readings were virtually identical. In fact, I cannot think of any other CD track that so vividly captures the huge range of Horowitz's unmistakable sound.

Dante Sonata (Après une lecture du Dante – fantasia quasi sonata) (1837–49)

A thrilling narrative that opens among the swirling torrents of Hell and works its way towards the light. The *Dante Sonata* is among the most stirring and virtuosic of Liszt's middle-period works. It is in fact the last piece from the Second Book of his *Years of pilgrimage* (three separate collections that include, respectively, Swiss-inspired pieces, Italian-inspired pieces and miscellaneous 'late' works that were gathered together after Liszt's death).

Alfred Brendel (piano)
Philips analogue

Brendel's performance impresses on at least two counts – its overt brilliance and its profound musicality. Alternatives include a stormy though less thoughtful rendition by Daniel Barenboim (Teldec digital), usefully coupled with Liszt's Dante Symphony (conducted by Barenboim).

12 Études d'exécution transcendante, S139 (1851)

Liszt originally set out to compose "24 Grandes Etudes" (his very first plan stretched to as many as 48) but stopped short at 12. The result, however, is one of the high-points of his creative output, ranging in style from the heady helter-skelter of the First Study, through the pianistic drama of *Mazeppa* (which Liszt later orchestrated), to the defiance of *Eroica*, the romantic reflectiveness of *Ricordanza* and the harmonic daring of *Harmonies du soir*.

Lazar Berman (piano)
Melodiya/BMG analogue

Possibly the finest of Lazar Berman's various Liszt recordings, a seemingly effortless display of virtuosity imbued with grandeur and a sweeping, unforced lyricism. The mono recording is admirably clear, but one should also consider Cziffra (EMI, analogue) and Arrau (Philips, analogue), not to mention famous recordings of individual pieces such as Richter's of Harmonies du soir (Praga, mono; RCA or Philips, digital).

Funérailles (from Harmonies poétiques et réligieuses, S173 – 1845–52)

A dark processional that opens ominously in the bass, gradually gains in intensity then prompts a fierce calls to arms, a sombre, Hungarian-style melody and a tender lament. The central episode features a terrifying octave stampede – one of the most demanding passages in the piano repertory – whereas the closing bars are tersely conclusive. *Funérailles* is one of ten *Harmonies poétiques et réligieuses* that also include a magnificent *Bénédiction de Dieu dans la solitude*.

Vladimir Horowitz (piano)
RCA mono

Horowitz's second recording of Funérailles (his first, made pre-war, was for EMI, mono) is wilful, explosive and highly melodramatic. Technically, it's something of a tour de force (the stampeding octaves are positively manic), though some might find the 1950 mono recording rather too shallow in tone. Alfred Brendel (his 1991 digital recording, Philips) and Claudio Arrau (Philips, analogue) provide rather more temperate though equally powerful alternatives.

Piano Sonata in B minor, S178 (1852–53)

The greatest of all High Romantic piano sonatas is divided into three distinct sections yet plays for roughly half an hour without a break. The first episode opens to a quietly descending idea before breaking into a sudden, disruptive *Allegro* (marked *energico*); the second is a noble slow movement and the third ushers in a devilish fugue, builds to a thunderous final climax (where the principal melody rings out in a mood of uncompromising defiance) then calms to a mood of equivocal reflection.

Sviatoslav Richter (piano)
Philips digital

Richter thinks through the Liszt Sonata as if it were by Beethoven, summoning great reserves of power yet refusing to linger over the more romantic passages. Brendel (also on Philips, digital) offers an intelligent, fairly cool option while the 'Old School' has mighty exponents in Simon Barère (APR, mono – an especially fine reading), Vladimir Horowitz (his 1932 recording, APR or EMI, mono) and Alfred Cortot (Biddulph, Music & Arts or Pearl, mono).

Sonetto 104 del Petrarca (1837-49)

In their original form, the three *Petrarch Sonnets* are among Liszt's most beautiful songs. He re-worked the material during his years in Weimar, and the second of them – an especially passionate piece – evokes the ambivalence of love. The actual sonnet speaks of love's "freezing glow, its seeing blindness, and its weeping laughter", whereas the resigned epilogue relates "what you, my mistress, have done to me". *Sonetto 104 del Petrarca* represents the archetypal Romantic keyboard tone-poem.

 ***Vladimir Horowitz (piano)***
RCA mono

Horowitz's operatic demonstrativeness and lightning virtuosity make musical fireworks of the great central climax, but some will find his approach just a little too histrionic. Alfred Brendel (his first Philips recording, analogue) provides a perceptive though less volatile option, whereas the incredibly brilliant Simon Barère (APR, either his 1934 HMV recording or a broadcast recording from 1947 – both are in mono) takes the Horowitz approach a step further.

Vallée d'Obermann, S160/6 (1835)

Liszt's *Années de pèlerinage* ("Years of pilgrimage") – a journey of the soul rendered pianistic – span roughly 40 years of his career. There are three books that cover, respectively, Switzerland, Italy and a selection of miscellaneous themes (Third Book). *Vallée d'Obermann*, which is taken from the First Book, is one of the greatest works in the series. It was inspired by the composer's reading of *Obermann de Senancour* and is full of heaving climaxes, dramatic gear-changes, suspended motives and mystical interludes. The finale is a triumphant paean of joy.

 ***Vladimir Horowitz (piano)***
Sony Classical analogue

Horowitz makes a few 'choice' emendations to the score (something Lisztian purists will no doubt object to), but – viewed as a whole – his performance combines great emotional engagement with a virtually orchestral range of colours. The CD version of this 1966 live recording relates a few telltale tape splices, but the sound is otherwise fairly serviceable. Good 'straighter' options include Lazar Berman (DG analogue) and Alfred Brendel (Philips digital).

César Franck (1822-1890)

Prélude, choral et fugue (1884)

That Franck was an organist is fairly obvious from the rich sonorities of his piano masterpiece – and the fact that he was a teacher informs a sombre though rigorously worked fugue. The three-part structure was very typical of Franck (even his Symphony is in three – rather than the usual four – movements), whereas his piano writing owes something to the virtuoso heyday of Franz Liszt.

 ***Artur Rubinstein (piano)***
RCA analogue

Rubinstein's performance conveys the grandeur of the piece, whereas Richter (Melodiya, mono or Philips, digital) centres more on architecture. Other estimable performances include Jean Hubeau (Erato, digital), Aldo Ciccolini (EMI, analogue) and the matchlessly spontaneous Alfred Cortot (Biddulph, mono). There's also an orchestration of the piece by Gabriel Pierné (recorded by Koch, digital).

Johannes Brahms (1833-1897)

Piano Pieces, Op. 119 (1892)

These exquisite 'late' utterances spell loneliness, reflection and occasional defiance. Op. 119 is representative in that it suggests four very different moods (wistful, confessional, whimsical and heroic), but you could just as easily try any of the sets, i.e. Opp. 116, 117 or 118 (which contain a total of 20 pieces). All bear witness to maximum expressive power pared down to a minimum of notes.

 ***Wilhelm Kempff (piano)***
Deutsche Grammophon analogue

Extraordinarily fastidious playing, clipped, tonally bright and sculpted in every tiny detail. Kempff's tempos are faster – and his level of insight deeper – than the majority of pianists, although his pupil Gerhard Oppitz (RCA, digital) provides a warmer, more robust alternative. Furthermore, Kempff has the added advantage of accommodating all four sets of pieces on a single CD.

Piano Sonata No. 3 in F minor, Op. 5 (1853)

A formidable affirmation of youthful genius, huge in scale and assuming the mantle that Beethoven had bequeathed with his 'middle' and 'late' sonatas. The F minor is easily the finest of Brahms's three piano sonatas (all of which are early works) and, furthermore, it breaks with tradition by featuring five instead of the normal four movements – an epic *Allegro maestoso*, followed by a twilit *Andante*, an exuberant Scherzo, a thoughtful Intermezzo and an expansive finale.

Artur Rubinstein (piano)
RCA analogue

One of Rubinstein's finest stereo recordings and a particularly grand interpretation. Murray Perahia (Sony) and Gerhard Oppitz (RCA) provide the superior digital options, while there are striking earlier versions by Solomon (Testament), Harold Bauer and Percy Grainger (both on Biddulph, mono – and both from 78s).

Variations on a Theme of Handel, Op. 24 (1861)

Brahms composed his *Handel* Variations as a birthday present for the great love of his life, Clara Schumann. He took his theme from a keyboard movement that Handel himself had treated to a modest sequence of variations, then proceeded to fashion 25 of the most eventful and dramatic episodes in his keyboard output. The work culminates in a virtuoso fugue. There's also a highly effective orchestral version of the *Handel* Variations, prepared by the English composer Edmund Rubbra.

Gerhard Oppitz (piano)
BMG Eurodisc digital

Wonderful playing – thoughtful, spontaneous (the more forceful variations are played with spellbinding bravura) and performed on a brightly ringing Bösendorfer Imperial piano. But although I'd be more than happy to live with this excellent performance, I couldn't deny the virtues of older rivals by Solomon, Benno Moiseiwitsch (both Testament, mono) and Leon Fleisher (Sony, mono). Those who fancy the orchestral version are directed to the Cleveland Orchestra under Vladimir Ashkenazy (Decca, digital) or, better still, the thrilling world-première performance under Toscanini (Dell'Arte, mono).

Emmanuel Chabrier
(1841–1894)

Dix pièces pittoresques (1881)

If you can resist the elegant "Idylle" – the sixth piece in a series of ten and as haunting as it's pretty – then Chabrier is not for you. Other highlights include a robust "Danse villageoise" and an ebullient "Scherzo-valse". The great Swiss-French pianist Alfred Cortot aptly described these versicoloured *Dix pièces pittoresques* as having a "savoury and wholesome poetic quality", something he might also have claimed on behalf of the orchestral *Suite Pastorale* (four of the "Pièces" in orchestral guise – including the "Idylle").

Alain Planès (piano)
Harmonia Mundi digital

The finest digital CD of Chabrier's piano works available (virtually all of them are contained on a single disc): dapper, brilliant and admirably appreciative of the music's vivacious though bittersweet character. Notable forebears include Pierre Barbizet (Erato, analogue) and Marcelle Meyer (EMI, mono) – both of them unforgettably stylish (and unmistakably French). The most enjoyable recording of the Suite Pastorale is by the Detroit Symphony Orchestra under Paul Paray (Mercury, analogue).

Edvard Grieg (1843–1907)

Lyric Pieces, Op. 47: Nos. 2–4 (1887–88)

Grieg's ten books of *Lyric Pieces* span a period from 1867 to 1901 and encompass various moods and styles, from carefree dance, through wistful reflection to the deepest melancholy. Choosing between them is difficult, but this particular trio of pieces (selected, it should be said, partly because Emil Gilels' performances are so exceptional) is fairly typical: a tender "Albumblatt", an exquisite, sighing "Melody" and a strumming Norwegian dance called "Halling".

Emil Gilels (piano)
Deutsche Grammophon analogue
One could hardly imagine playing where heart, mind and technique are more sympathetically balanced. Gilels's performance of "Melody" (in particular) is a model of controlled expressive ardour, while the selection as a whole (the 20 pieces included are taken from all ten books) provides the best possible representation of a delightful corpus of miniatures. The 1974 recordings are fully up to present-day standards, but if you'd prefer to investigate the complete run of Grieg's Lyric Pieces then I'd recommend you try Gerhard Oppitz on RCA (digital).

Sergey Rachmaninov (1873-1943)

Piano Sonata No. 2 in B flat minor, Op. 36 (1913, revised 1931)

Rachmaninov's obsession with church bells colours the central section of the first movement (a stormy tolling that, in Horowitz's hands, sounds positively orchestral), while the second movement combines tranquillity with colourful fantasy and the finale is in the manner of a wild Scherzo. Possibly the most arresting of all Russian Romantic piano sonatas.

Vladimir Horowitz (piano)
Sony Classical analogue
Two points worth noting – firstly (and most significantly) that Horowitz's 1968 live recording is electrifying and, second, that he presents a composite of the original and revised versions of the score (sanctioned by the composer). A later RCA (digital) CD isn't quite so impressive, though Howard Shelley has made excellent studio recordings of both the original and the revised editions (Hyperion, digital).

A sense of daring (1888-1951)

Our earliest 'dares' are by the French composer Erik Satie, whose profound creative simplicity and pared-to-the-bone piano miniatures inspired many of his twentieth-century successors. Thereafter, and it's 'no holds barred' – from Debussy's Turner-esque soundscapes, through nature-loving Bartók (for piano or solo violin), cynical Prokofiev, mystical Scriabin and the luscious, *fin de siècle* effusions of Alban Berg.

Gabriel Fauré (1845-1924)

Barcarolle No. 12 in E flat major, Op. 106*a* (1915)

Fauré composed 13 *Barcarolles* between 1882 and 1921 and, like his *Nocturnes* (of which there are also 13 – see below), they cover a wide field of harmonic, rhythmic and tonal incident. The Twelfth opens prettily to a swift, lilting accompaniment (*Barcarolle* means "boating song") before progressing to a more advanced expressive world. The Third, Fourth and Fifth pieces in the series (all from the last years of the previous century) are among the finest of Fauré's earlier *Barcarolles*.

Nocturne No. 11 in F sharp minor, Op. 104 No. 1 (1913)

The Eleventh Nocturne seems to straddle the worlds of Schumann (of the C major *Fantasie* – "Mighty monologues", see above) and Debussy (of the more mysterious *Préludes*, see below); its aching melancholy, allied to great poise and restraint, is further intensified by the occasional spot of harmonic complexity. Other remarkable *Nocturnes* include Nos. 6 and 13, though anyone touched by No. 11 will probably adore the whole series. They mark the very apex of Fauré's piano output.

Jean Hubeau (piano)
Erato digital
Choosing between Jean Hubeau (a past-master in this repertory) and Kathryn Stott (Hyperion, digital) is difficult. Stott, being younger and technically more adroit, plays with marginally more fluidity, and yet Hubeau's performances are so naturally spontaneous and clearly formed (there's never the least hint of self-conscious 'point-making') that I couldn't in all honesty pass them over. The 'late' pieces are especially fine, but those who choose Stott – who is granted a marginally superior recording – should have little cause for complaint.

Leoš Janáček (1854-1928)

Along an Overgrown Path – 15 piano pieces (1901-08)

Janáček wrote these captivating miniatures when he was recovering from the death of his daughter Olga. Although deeply pondered and private in character, each piece from the first book (there are two books containing 15 pieces in all) carries a descriptive title. They range in character from the Grieg-like "A blown-away leaf", to the Dvořákian polka "Come with us", the atmospheric piping of "Madonna of Frýdek", the quiet terror of "Unutterable anguish" (which recalls the final phase of Olga's terrible illness) and perhaps, finest – and most haunting – of all, "The barn owl has not flown away!". According to Czech legend, a lingering barn owl is a sure prophecy of death and in this music Janáček audibly tries to shoo the owl away. It's an incredible piece of writing!

Sonata I. X. 1905, "From the street" (1905)

In 1905, the Czech town of Brno was largely German-speaking and when the Czechs demanded their own university, all hell broke loose. The ensuing demonstrations claimed the life of a young student – and Janáček's powerful Sonata recalls the place, date and cause of his death. There are just two movements (a third was destroyed by the composer), the second of which opens with a quietly repetitive theme that gradually intensifies until Janáček's anger reaches fever-pitch. This Sonata is perhaps his finest piano work.

 ***Rudolf Firkušný (piano)***
RCA digital
Firkušný, a Czech himself, knew Janáček well and received priceless tuition in how to play and interpret this captivating music. His booklet-notes are uniquely authoritative, while his performances combine gentleness, subtle drama and a warm, full tone. His earlier DG (analogue) recording is just as fine (some would say even more spontaneous, though this later set is perhaps marginally wiser) but not quite so well recorded.

Claude Debussy (1862–1918)

Children's Corner (1906–08)

Children's Corner bears a dedication "To my dear little Chouchou [Debussy's only child], with her father's most sincere apologies for what follows". Debussy bet a friend that he could make a joke out of one of Wagner's greatest melodies – and in "Golliwog's Cake-Walk", he plays havoc with a leading motive from *Tristan und Isolde*. The other movements – all of them ingeniously crafted – are "Doctor Gradus ad Parnassum" (a humorous look at piano practise), "Jimbo's Lullaby" (for a toy elephant), a "Serenade for the doll", "The snow is dancing" and "The little shepherd".

 ***Walter Gieseking (piano)***
EMI mono
Gieseking opts for relative understatement, though his playing of the slower pieces is rapturously beautiful. For a livelier option, try the habitually playful Alfred Cortot (Biddulph, mono), while Arturo Benedetti Michelangeli (DG, analogue) offers a unique degree of pianistic refinement. Also, one musn't forget Horowitz's magical renditions of "Serenade for the doll" (RCA, mono; Sony, analogue).

Estampes (1903)

Quintessential Debussy, awash with colour and rich in pictorial imagery. The oriental chiming of the first piece, "Pagodes", reflects the composer's love of Javanese gamelan music (so prophetic of post-war Minimalism), whereas the second *Estampe* ("Engraving"), "Soirée dans Grenade", is a refined evocation of Spain from a man who had never actually travelled there. The quixotic "Jardins sous la pluie" suggests the play of raindrops after a spring shower.

 ***Claudio Arrau (piano)***
Philips analogue
Perhaps the most spellbinding of all Arrau's Debussy recordings (there are a number of them, including earlier [mono] versions of these particular pieces) – sultry, subtle and colour-sensitive. Gieseking (EMI, mono) makes an obvious second choice.

Images (1905–08)

There are two sets of *Images*, the first of which has a broad, noble sarabande, "Hommage à Rameau", as its centrepiece. Before that comes a coolly improvisational "Reflets dans l'eau", whereas the third piece is a gently pulsing "Mouvement". The second set opens with the entrancing "Cloches à travers les feuilles", said to suggest church bells ringing from village to village on All Saints' Day; then there's the desolate, harmonically daring "Et la lune descend sur le temple qui fut" and the shimmering "Poissons d'or", a sophisticated mini-narrative, echoes of which can be detected in the jazz piano masters of a later generation – Oscar Peterson in particular.

Instrumental solos A sense of daring (1888–1951)

 ***Arturo Benedetti Michelangeli (piano)***

Deutsche Grammophon analogue

The greatest pianistic sculptor of the age was also a master of musical tension, and these readings of "Cloches à travers les feuilles" and "Et la lune descend sur le temple qui fut" are among the greatest ever made. I should also mention Artur Rubinstein's superb live recordings of "Hommage à Rameau" and "Poissons d'or" (recorded in concert at Carnegie Hall and issued on RCA, analogue), supremely natural performances, which sound almost like improvisations.

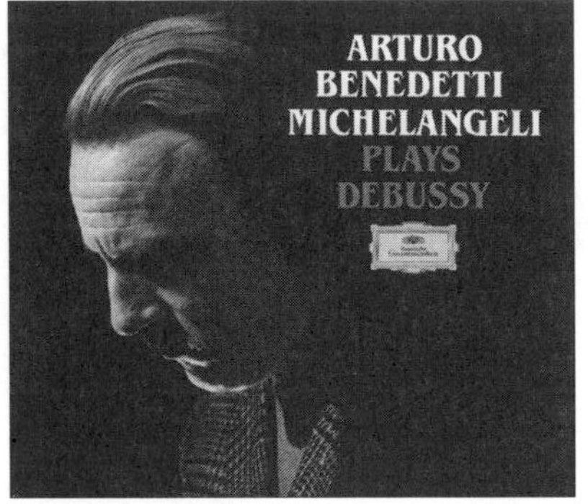

L'îsle joyeuse (1904)

L'îsle joyeuse opens with a trill and a series of ornamental flourishes, then ushers in a gentle, lilting melody, lavishly decorated. The main body of the piece (it plays for around six minutes) is reminiscent – on occasion – of Debussy's orchestral narratives *La mer* and "Fêtes" from *Nocturnes* (see "Narratives in Sound", above). Heat and brightness intensify as the journey progresses, culminating in cascades of notes and an exultant finale. *L'îsle joyeuse* is perhaps the most dazzlingly extrovert of all Debussy's major piano works.

 ***Vladimir Horowitz (piano)***

Sony Classical analogue

Horowitz's performance was recorded live at Carnegie Hall during 1966 and suggests a dozen pair of hands working overtime. True, you can hear some of the joins (edits), but the overall effect is unforgettable. Molinari's interesting orchestration of the piece is conducted by Geoffrey Simon on Cala (digital).

Préludes, Books One (1910) and Two (1913)

Like Turner at sea or Van Gogh inland, Debussy's piano *Préludes* conjure up images, colours, impressions and moods that utterly transcend the limits of language. There are 24 pieces in all, each suggesting a powerful, self-contained soundscape. The first *Prélude* recalls the vestal virgins of Ancient Greece, the second sailboats in a light breeze, and so on – through a wildly billowing West Wind, the mysterious spectre of a sunken cathedral, a coy Scottish maiden singing a simple (but beautiful) song, a musical reflection of the Grecian urn in Debussy's work room and a moonlit Buddhist temple in Indo-China. Then there's "Hommage à S. Pickwick, Esq., P.P.M.P.C" (with tongue-in-cheek support from *God Save the King*) and a wonderfully subtle firework display.

 ***Walter Gieseking (piano)***

EMI mono

One might also add the coolly sculpted Arturo Benedetti Michelangeli (Book One, DG, analogue) and the classically poised Robert Casadesus (Book Two, Sony, mono). However, Gieseking's 1950s set relates a strong re-creative involvement in each piece (Gieseking was himself a fine composer), a huge dynamic range (so vital in Debussy) and a fine – if occasionally fallible – technique. Krystian Zimerman, a refined virtuoso with a romantic turn of phrase, has made excellent recordings of all of the préludes (DG, digital).

Suite bergamasque (1905)

The great pianist Alfred Cortot described this delightful Suite as a "rather far-fetched combination of the modern and the old-fashioned which characterizes much of Debussy's later work. The old harpsichord-players whom Debussy regarded as the greatest of his musical predecessors appear like misty shadows. He revives their charm and their manner, but without making the work into a pastiche." The four movements are "Prélude", "Menuette", "Passepied" and what is perhaps the most famous musical evocation of moonlight ever composed, "Clair de lune".

 ***Walter Gieseking (piano)***

EMI mono

Gieseking's legendary control and feeling for nuance elevate his performance far above average, and while the 1950s mono recording is somewhat lacking in lustre, its musical virtues more than compensate for minor sonic shortcomings. There's a fairly sensitive orchestration of "Clair de lune" by Leopold Stokowski (conducted either by Stokowski himself [EMI, analogue or Biddulph, mono] or by Wolfgang Sawallisch [EMI, digital]).

Erik Satie (1866–1925)

Trois Gymnopédies (1888)

The diametric opposite of all that is grandiose, bombastic and overblown. Satie's deceptively simple piano music achieves its effect by the most economical means; most pieces are contemplative, slow-moving, serenely beautiful and melodically memorable, often tinged with Eastern overtones. Best-known are the exotic *Gnossiennes* and, in particular, the quietist *Gymnopédies*.

 ***Reinbert de Leeuw (piano)***
Philips digital

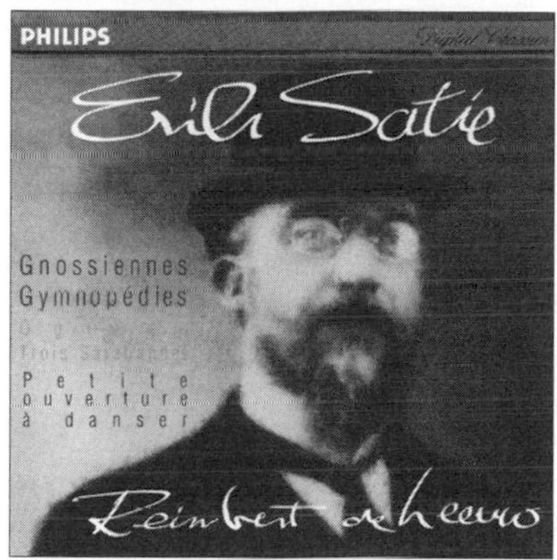

Satie's piano music might be relatively easy to play, but it's extremely difficult to interpret effectively. One needs, above all, a sensitive touch, an infallible sense of timing and a naturally artful rubato – qualities that Reinbert de Leeuw, a modern music specialist par excellence, consistently exhibits throughout this 67-minute Satie recital.

Enrique Granados (1867-1916)

12 Danzas españolas, Op. 37 (1892-1900)

Enrique Granados and his wife lost their lives when the S. S. Sussex was sunk by a German submarine between Folkestone and Dieppe. It was a tragic end to a career that had already enriched the repertory with a colourful Spanish treasury, the earliest significant jewels being 12 wonderful *Danzas españolas* that range in style from the exotic "Oriental", to the irrepressibly gay "Valencia" and the sultry – and extremely well-known – "Andaluza" (a piece that also exists in versions for guitar and orchestra).

Goyescas, (1911)

A suite of piano tone-poems inspired by the works of Goya. "*Goyescas* is a work forever, I am convinced of it ...", wrote Granados; "... they are the reward of my efforts to arrive ... I fell in love with Goya's psychology, his palette – with him and the Duchess of Alba; with his ladylike maja, with his models, his quarrels, his loves and courtships. The pinkish white in the cheeks in contrast with the black lace and embroidered velour ...". There are seven pieces altogether (that's if you count an 'appendix' "El pelele", or "The dummy") including "Conversations at the window grille" and "The maja and the nightingale". Granados also wrote a one-act opera *Goyescas* which includes a famous "Intermezzo".

 ***Alicia de Larrocha (piano)***
Decca analogue

Barcelona-born Alicia de Larrocha studied with Granados's disciple and collaborator Frank Marshall and her mastery of the idiom remains unchallenged – certainly in terms of the stereo and digital eras. She has recorded this repertory more than once (I have a great fondness for her wildly spontaneous but rather clangorous-sounding 1960s EMI analogue CDs), but these Decca sessions capture her art mid-way between youthful impetuosity and the relative wisdom of full artistic maturity.

Alexander Scriabin (1872-1915)

Piano Sonata No. 3 in F sharp minor, Op. 23 (1897-98)

A heroic four-movement work, awash with rich colours, grounded in Tchaikovskian rhetoric and full of extravagant dramatic gestures. A programme exists (it may or may not be Scriabin's own) that refers to "States of being" – starting with "the free, untamed soul passionately throws itself into pain and struggle", continuing with a soul that has "found some kind of momentary, illusory peace ...", "... floats on a sea of gentle emotion and melancholy ..." and, finally, "... struggles as if intoxicated ...". The Sonata's various themes are closely linked together.

 ***Marc-André Hamelin (piano)***
Hyperion digital

Hamelin manages to convey the Third Sonata's somewhat aromatic mysticism without distorting either its complex rhythms or its carefully fashioned structure. Available as part of a highly recommendable two-CD set of all nine Scriabin sonatas, Hamelin's recording none the less faces formidable competition from Vladimir Horowitz (RCA, mono) who offers a compelling but fairly idiosyncratic performance.

Piano Sonata No. 9 in F major, Op. 68, "Black Mass" (1912-13)

After the "mystical feeling [and] ... total absence of ... emotional lyricism" of the so-called *White Mass* Sonata (No. 7), the *Black Mass* is a highly condensed, Satanic onslaught (it plays for a mere nine minutes), quixotic, often dissonant and with searing climaxes, the last of which becomes a march that Scriabin himself described as a "parade of the forces of evil". The Ninth is the most famous of Scriabin's piano sonatas and is full of rattling trills and strange, half-lit harmonies.

Vladimir Horowitz (piano)
RCA mono
Horowitz's demonic reading seethes and spits as if the Devil himself were at the keyboard. Recorded in concert at New York's Carnegie Hall in 1953, it represents the fiery 'first phase' of a pianist who, shortly afterwards, took a 12-year sabbatical from the concert stage. His second recording (Sony, analogue) in fact marks his historic return to Carnegie Hall and although the demon was still in residence, he had by then moderated his gestures somewhat. Strongest among Horowitz's rivals are Sviatoslav Richter (Music & Arts, analogue) and the textually scrupulous Marc-André Hamelin (Hyperion, digital).

Maurice Ravel (1875-1937)

Gaspard de la nuit (1908)
One of the most disquieting piano works in the repertory. In fact, Ravel himself said "I wanted to compose a caricature of Romanticism," adding that "perhaps I went too far!". *Gaspard de la nuit* was inspired by a sequence of decadent prose poems by Aloysius Bertrand; its mood is schizoid and deeply unsettling, its pianistic demands often superhuman. There are three movements – "Ondine", the water nymph who turns to ice and melts; "Le gibet" (The gallows), full of terrifying hallucinations, and "Scarbo", a nightmarish elf.

Ivo Pogorelich (piano)
Deutsche Grammophon digital
Perhaps the most vivid performance of this work ever recorded, full of menace and exquisite refinement – although Michelangeli (Multisonic) is an essential mono option and there are finely-sculpted analogue alternatives from Robert Casadesus (Sony, also mono) and Jacques Rouvier (who offers an extraordinarily mobile account of "Ondine" – Calliope, analogue).

Béla Bartók (1881-1945)

Suite, Sz62 (Op. 14) (1916)
Anyone approaching Bartók's piano music for the first time could hardly choose a better 'boarding point' than this highly-coloured Suite. The first movement is playful and dance-like; the second, a burlesque-style Scherzo; the third, a fierce *Allegro molto* that recalls "The Chase" from *The Miraculous Mandarin* ballet (see "Puppets and pagans", below), and the fourth, a bleak, mournful elegy marked *Sostenuto*.

Zoltán Kocsis (piano)
Philips digital
Although Kocsis's performance reflects a thorough knowledge of Bartók's own recording of the work (available on CD from EMI, Pearl or Hungaroton, mono), it's no carbon copy. The playing is brilliant, attention to detail is invariably acute and the recording quality is superb. It comes as part of an ongoing series of all Bartók's major piano works.

Out of Doors, Sz81 (1926)
Uncompromising reportage of nature and her allies. The first movement is a savagely pounding study, "With pipes and drums"; the second is a sullen "Barcarolla"; the third, "Musettes", imitates bagpipes; the fourth is perhaps the most effective of Bartók's many "night music" studies (scurrying insects, bird cries, etc) and the Fifth is a virtuoso chase (again, vividly reminiscent of "The Chase" from Bartók's *The Miraculous Mandarin* ballet – see "Puppets and pagans", below).

Zoltán Kocsis (piano)
Philips
Zoltan Kocsis's recent recording of Out of Doors offers the most vivid characterization – although Claude Helffer (Harmonia Mundi, digital) and György Sandor (Sony, also digital), are keen rivals. So, for that matter, is a finely sculpted 1950s recording by the Hungarian pianist Andor Foldes (DG, mono).

Piano Sonata, Sz80 (1926)
A tough, high-energy masterpiece, formally watertight (Bartók respects the structural principles of his great Viennese predecessors) and rhythmically propulsive. The first movement has a barbaric intensity (more so, in fact, than Bartók's better-known *Allegro barbaro*), the second is a lament cast in stone while the third – a virtuoso *Allegro molto* – makes great play with folk-style themes.

Zoltán Kocsis (piano)
Philips digital
A stunning recording that combines great panache with a natural feeling for the music's Hungarian roots. For an alternative that can truly be called 'authentic'. György Sandor's second recording of the Sonata (Sony, digital) is also highly recommendable. Sandor knew Bartók personally and gave the première of his Third Concerto.

Sonata for solo violin, Sz117 (1944)
It was in 1943 that Bartók heard a performance of his First Violin Sonata played by Yehudi Menuhin. He also heard Menuhin perform a Bach Sonata for unaccompanied violin (the one in C major). Both interpretations left an indelible impression, so

that when Menuhin himself commissioned Bartók to write a solo sonata, the resulting masterpiece combined Bachian purity with red-blooded self-expression. In fact, it's probably the greatest unaccompanied violin sonata since Bach. The most affecting movement is a soulful "Melodia", but there's also a powerful Chaconne, a rigorous Fugue and a fast-moving finale.

Yehudi Menuhin (violin)
EMI mono
Menuhin's 1947 recording has a vivid, 'hot off the press' feeling that adds to the excitement: no other version quite equals its warmth, brilliance or sense of emotional involvement. Of more recent versions, György Pauk's digital Naxos CD is especially compelling – while analogue recordings by Sándor Végh (Valois, analogue) and Ivry Gitlis (Vox, mono) are also well worth considering.

Zoltán Kodály (1882-1967)

Sonata for cello solo, Op. 8 (1915)
The fact that this well-structured work resembles an epic folk improvisation shouldn't obscure its Bachian lineage (don't forget that Bach's unaccompanied Suites also employ copious dance rhythms). Kodály makes the cello sound like a guitar, a harp, folk pipes – indeed like an entire folk orchestra. These effects are achieved partly by selectively re-tuning the instrument, and partly by having the cellist pluck the strings, play whining harmonics, trills, stagger chords, and so on.

Erling Blöndal Bengtsson (cello)
Danacord digital
Bengtsson offers an especially uninhibited interpretation that stresses the improvisational elements in Kodály's work; his warm tone and highly personal brand of rubato contrast with the more formal readings of, say, János Starker (a brilliant and intense view of the piece, magnificently realized – on EMI analogue or Philips, mono) or Pierre Fournier (Praga, mono – recorded live).

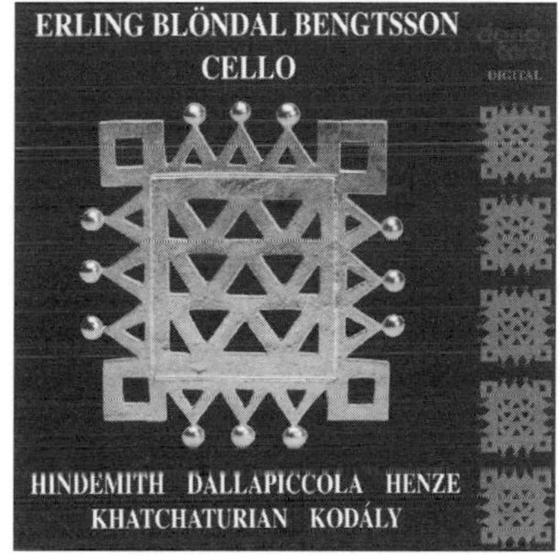

Alban Berg (1885-1935)

Piano Sonata, Op. 1 (1907-08)
An auspicious musical prophecy that none the less has its heart planted firmly among the final frontiers of late-Romanticism. The youthful Berg's harmonic language makes for some ravishingly beautiful sounds, far more so in fact than a sequence of even earlier pieces that pre-date this highly auspicious Op. 1. Pianist Alfred Brendel describes this rich but complex Sonata as "the most polyphonic string quintet ever entrusted to the piano".

Alfred Brendel (piano)
Philips digital
Brendel scores on all fronts – as a master of colour and nuance, as an informed commentator on structure, and as a knowing responder to musical modulation. The recording is superb, but there are other fine versions around – those by Glenn Gould (Sony, analogue) and Maurizio Pollini (DG, digital) being among the best.

Sergey Prokofiev (1891-1953)

Piano Sonata No. 6 in A minor, Op. 82 (1940)
The first of Prokofiev's so-called "War" Sonatas was apparently inspired, at least in part, by Romain Rolland's *Jean-Christophe* (a huge opus based on the life of Beethoven). However, the music itself is frequently relentless and implacable, not least in its insistent opening bars and a provocative Scherzo where the second theme suggests a crude, jeering folk dance – some say in imitation of Stalin himself. The smoky waltz-time slow movement is one of the most beautiful of all Prokofiev's instrumental movements.

Sviatoslav Richter (piano)
Praga analogue

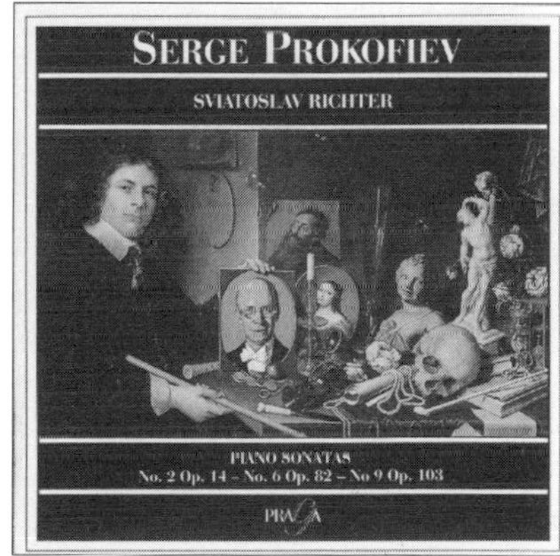

Richter gave the world premières of both the Sixth and Seventh Sonatas, while the Ninth – a milder, not to say, more equivocal piece – is actually dedicated to him. He is especially famous for his powerful account of the Sixth Sonata, and there are numerous alternative versions around, all of them live. However, this

1965 Czech broadcast is probably the best. There's also strong digital rivalry from Evgeni Kissin (Sony or RCA).

Piano Sonata No. 7 in B flat major, Op. 83 (1942)

Prokofiev's intention was to "write great music, in other words, whose ideas and technical realization reflect the momentum of the age". The Seventh Sonata – the most popular of the nine – features a curt, goose-stepping first theme, a casually romantic second movement (rather in the manner of top-grade salon music) and a wild, high-speed finale that suggests battling troops and shrill fanfares.

Sviatoslav Richter (piano)
Melodiya/BMG mono

Richter's 1958 recording of the Seventh Sonata is utterly relentless in its power and inspirational fervour, though there's estimable rivalry from Vladimir Horowitz (RCA, mono) and Glenn Gould (Sony, analogue).

Piano Sonata No. 8 in B flat major, Op. 84 (1944)

The last and longest of Prokofiev's "War" sonatas is also the most mysterious; it opens with a reflective *Andante dolce* (slow but sweet), then journeys through various related ideas before reaching the bittersweet slow movement – a rather lovely piece that wouldn't have been out of place in one of the composer's ballets. The scampering finale recalls, like the last movement of the Seventh Sonata, wild trumpet calls and the pounding of feet and drums – although this time the mood is more morose than frenetic.

Sviatoslav Richter (piano)
Deutsche Grammophon analogue

A noble encounter with what is perhaps the greatest of Prokofiev's piano sonatas, although the closing onslaught is incredibly brilliant. Best among Richter's peers is Emil Gilels, whose superb Melodiya recording (Vox, analogue) is second only to Richter's.

Aaron Copland (1900–1990)

Piano Sonata (1939–41)

Anyone familiar with Copland's orchestral works will have no trouble guessing who composed the Sonata's opening movement – big music, bold, statuesque and unmistakably American. The second movement is a catchy *Vivace* that leaps about the keyboard replete with echoes of both Stravinsky and jazz. The third and last movement is strong and simple, though it builds to a powerfully insistent central climax. Another remarkable aspect of Copland's Piano Sonata is its telling use of musical rests: it breathes easily.

Leo Smit (piano)
Sony Classical analogue

A fine reading from a man who knew Copland well and was a famous exponent of his piano works (this recording is part of a two-CD set containing the major portion of Copland's piano output). The sound might lack 'body', but the performance is profoundly idiomatic. Prominent among Smit's best rivals are Leonard Bernstein (RCA, mono) and a superb recording by the Hungarian-born pianist Andor Foldes (DG mono, but not as yet on CD).

Dmitry Shostakovich (1906–1975)

24 Preludes and Fugues for piano, Op. 87 (1950–51)

If there's any sense whatsoever in talking of a 'follow-up' to Bach's *Well-Tempered Clavier* (the *48* – see "Bach solo"), then Shostakovich's 24 Preludes and Fugues provide as good an excuse as any. Shostakovich took part in the Bach bicentennial commemorations in Leipzig (1950), performing his music with various colleagues. It was an experience that helped prompt a series of pieces that, in addition to exploring the harmonic potential of the various keys, conjures an exceptionally wide range of moods and shades. Furthermore, although Bach himself sits audibly in the background, each piece bears the unmistakable stamp of Shostakovich's mature creative personality.

Tatyana Nikolaieva (piano)
Melodiya/BMG digital

"I still have the impression that this music has just been written …" remarked Nikolaieva in an interview. She had premièred the work over the Christmas period in 1952 and her subsequent recordings – all of which relate both freshness and perception – have become legendary. This particular set is marginally superior to an even more famous recording that Nikolaieva made for Hyperion (digital). There are also impressive recordings of individual Preludes and Fugues by Sviatoslav Richter (Philips, Supraphon and Pyramid, analogue), Emil Gilels (Testament, mono) and the composer himself (EMI, Revelation, mono).

Olivier Messiaen (1908–1992)

Vingt regards sur l'enfant Jésus (1944)

These "20 glimpses of the Infant Jesus" form a compelling cycle (some 2 hours 20 minutess in length) that – like so much of Messiaen's work – attempts to reflect the full glory of God's creation. Four recurring themes inform a narrative that encompasses contemplation, joy, 'the all-powerful Word' (movement 12 – music that recalls Bartók at his most uncompromisingly percussive), Christ on horseback brandishing a sword amidst flashes of lightning (movement 18 – a positively terrifying vision) and the Church of Love. This glorious music has audible links with Debussy, Bartók, Schoenberg and Gershwin.

 ***Joanna MacGregor (piano)***
Collins digital

Anyone who has heard Joanna MacGregor convey the expressive range of Bach's Art of Fugue (preferably in concert) will not be surprised at this comprehensively sympathetic account of Vingt Regards. There's plenty of active rivalry (both digital and analogue), but the best of MacGregor's predecessors are Messiaen's wife Yvonne Loriod (Erato) and Michel Béroff (EMI). Both recordings are analogue.

Further listening *Prokofiev's piano music is immensely varied, and while the 'big' sonatas (see above) suggest a dramatic muse, many of the shorter pieces are both charming and atmospheric. Best, perhaps, are the twenty exquisite Visions fugitives, a dozen of which were recorded live by Artur Rubinstein (RCA, analogue).*

L'invitation au voyage (1840-1930)

The Romantic French art song began with Berlioz and reached its height with the inspired *mélodies* of Debussy, Duparc, Fauré, Ravel and Poulenc. Our selection barely scratches the surface of a bewitching and seductive genre (virtually all of Fauré's songs would justify inclusion on artistic grounds), but it does at least give some idea of the expressive range that these songs explore as a matter of course.

Hector Berlioz (1803-1869)

Les nuits d'été, Op. 7 (1840-41, orchestrated 1843 [No. 4] and 1856)

Perhaps the greatest *mélodies* of all, with poems by Théophile Gautier, achingly beautiful melodic writing (most especially in the second and fifth songs) and exquisitely tooled orchestration. There are six pieces in all: "Vilanelle", which tells of a lovers' spring-time walk through the woods; "Le spectre de la Rose" ("I am the phantom of the rose that you wore yesterday at the ball ... Here lies a rose, the envy of kings"), three laments – "Sur les lagunes" (On the lagoons), "L'absence" and "Au cimetière" – and, lastly, "L'île inconnu": "Take me ... to the faithful shore where love is eternal!".

 ***Régine Créspin (soprano), Suisse Romande Orchestra/Ernest Ansermet***
Decca analogue

A fine singer captured at the height of her powers and with luminous orchestral support under the ever-perceptive Ansermet, although Decca's earlier recording featuring Suzanne Danco (in mono, with the Cincinnati Symphony Orchestra) is equally fine. Those intent primarily on piquant orchestral sonorities are urgently directed to Fritz Reiner and the Chicago Symphony, stylish accompanists to a gloriously full-voiced but relatively unsubtle Leontyne Price (RCA analogue).

Gabriel Fauré (1845-1924)

La bonne chanson, Op. 61 (1892-94)

The subtlest, most aromatic of French song-cycles sets the words of Paul Verlaine. There are nine songs in all, each placing the idea of love in a separate thematic context – from the breaking of dawn and the pale star of morning, to moonlight, solitary walking and the end of winter. The version for voice, piano and string quartet (Fauré's own) was never published but adds extra warmth to the voice-and-piano original.

 ***Sanford Sylvan (baritone), David Breitman (piano), String Quartet***
Nonesuch digital

A most sensitive rendition, discreetly expressive and included as part of an imaginative all-Fauré programme consisting of other songs plùs two of the piano Nocturnes. As to older recordings, a pre-war set by Charles Panzéra and Alfred Cortot (EMI, Biddulph, mono) stands out as exceptional.

Henri Duparc (1848-1933)

L'invitation au voyage (*c*1870)

A mysterious, shimmering evocation by a composer who was stricken by illness at the height of his powers (his career ended long before the turn of the century). Duparc's invitation is extremely seductive. "My child, my sister," writes Baudelaire, "think of the sweetness of going to live there together, to love at our leisure, to love and to die in that land that resembles you ... There, all is order and beauty, luxury, calm and pleasure."

Charles Panzéra (baritone), Madeleine Panzéra-Baillot (piano)

Pearl mono

Panzéra sings with a directness and sincerity that contrasts markedly with the 'applied emotion' of various of his successors. The recording was made in 1935 and still sounds perfectly acceptable, though Pierre Bernac's recording from ten years later (EMI, mono) is also well worth hearing. The best modern recording is by José van Dam (Forlane, digital).

Claude Debussy (1862-1918)

Trois Chansons de Bilitis (1897)

Three settings of poems by Pierre Louÿs, the first ("Pan's Flute") dealing with music, love and the age-old problem of deceiving one's parents (i.e. "My mother will never believe that I spent such a long time looking for my belt"), the third, with the "Naiad's Tomb" at the dead of winter. But it is the second song, "La chevelure" that casts the strongest spell, what with its melding of erotic images and the subtle though explicit nature of its central climax.

Dame Maggie Teyte (soprano), Alfred Cortot (piano)

EMI mono

Dame Maggie Teyte sang Debussy mélodies to the composer's own accompaniments and her interpretations – so fresh and full of wonderment – remain unsurpassed. The great Swiss-French pianist Alfred Cortot is her consistently imaginative partner (his playing in "La chevelure" is extraordinarily responsive).

Maurice Ravel (1875-1937)

Histoires naturelles (1906)

A touching and often humorous cycle that tells of a peacock preening itself for a wedding that never takes place, a delicate cricket, a swan that dives under the lake, a kingfisher that lands on a fishing-rod and a clucking guinea hen. When the poet Jules Renard asked the composer what he had been able to 'add' to *Histoires naturelles*, Ravel answered that his intention had been "not to add something but [rather] to interpret".

Pierre Bernac (baritone), Francis Poulenc (piano)

Sony Classical mono

By the time these recordings were made (a few years after the Second World War), Bernac and Poulenc had refined their art to virtual perfection. True, the voice isn't quite what it had been in the mid-1930s, but Bernac's sensitivity to words and musical nuances serves as an object-lesson to all aspiring singers. The mono sound is excellent.

Joseph Canteloube (1879-1957)

Chants d'Auvergne (1923-30)

Canteloube drapes traditional Auvergne melodies in filigree orchestration, sometimes ornate ("L'Antouèno"), sometimes with the utmost delicacy (the famous "Baïlèro") and occasionally incorporating improvisatory instrumental solos ("Trois Bourrées"). The texts chosen tell of earthy folk and their amatory preoccupations, while the melodies themselves have a rambling, unfettered quality that sidesteps the more formal preoccupations of musical sophistication. There are 27 songs in all, about half-a-dozen of which have achieved lasting popularity.

Netania Davrath (soprano), orchestra/Pierre de la Roche

Vanguard Classics analogue

Davrath's bright soprano and vivacious characterizations are ideally employed – although those who crave something a little creamier might prefer Dame Kiri Te Kanawa (Decca, digital) or, if you'd rather a selection of favourites, either Victoria de los Angeles (EMI, analogue) or Anna Moffo with the American Symphony Orchestra under Leopold Stokowski (RCA, analogue). A marvellous pre-war selection with the soprano Madeleine Grey (EMI, mono) is forthright, passionate and uniquely idiomatic.

Further listening *Other fine interpreters of French mélodies include the baritones Bernard Kruysen (whose analogue recordings of Debussy, Ravel and Fauré are issued on Auvidis Valois CDs) and Gérard Souzay (various analogue selections have been issued on EMI and Philips). An analogue set of songs by Olivier Messiaen (EMI) features soprano Michèle Command and Reynaldo Hahn is well served by the tenor Martyn Hill (Hyperion, digital).*

Wayfarers and wanderers (1816-1948)

Although the earliest forms of Lied date from the fifteenth century, the term is most commonly used for the wonderful songs of Schubert, Schumann, Brahms, Wolf, Mahler, Richard Strauss and various other (usually lesser) composers. Beethoven's contribution to the genre was relatively modest (certainly in comparison with, say, Schubert and Schumann), but anyone investigating the length and breadth of German art song will encounter the most distinctive form of musical word-painting, from the tender entreaties of Schumann's *Dichterliebe* to the harrowing confrontations of Schubert's *Winterreise*. Even if you decide not to follow a translation, the music itself is invariably powerful enough to demolish even the most obdurate language barrier.

Ludwig van Beethoven (1770-1827)

An die ferne Geliebte, Op. 98 (1816)
A concise, elegant and endearing narrative, cast in a single 12-minute stretch but consisting of six separate songs bound together by brief but persuasive piano interludes. "To the Distant Beloved" joins the lover as he gazes into a hazy blue land, as he suffers inner torment and longing for the beloved, implores nature to carry his anguish to the lover's heart and bids her sing these songs, "for a devoted heart can reach the one it truly loves".

Ernst Haefliger (tenor), Erik Werba (piano)
Claves analogue
A model of sensitive, clearly articulated Lieder singing, expressively inflected and with excellent support from Erik Werba. Haefliger's voice is bright and finely tapered, but if you'd prefer a baritone, then there's the warmly communicative Gerhard Hüsch (Preiser, mono) or two excellent recordings by Dietrich Fischer-Dieskau – with Gerald Moore (EMI, mono) or Jörg Demus (DG, analogue), the EMI version being especially intimate.

Franz Schubert (1797-1828)

Du bist die Ruh, D776 (1823)
Friedrich Rückert's poetry inspired one of Schubert's most sublime songs (or Lieder): the piano writing suggests an angelic luminosity and the solo line soars aloft. "You are tranquillity, gentle peace," writes Rückert, "you are longing, and its assuaging". The poem ends with the words, "Your brightness alone lights the dwelling of my eyes – O fill it wholly!" This, together with *Ständchen* ("Serenade" – see *Schwanengesang*, below) and *Ave Maria* are probably Schubert's most famous Lieder.

Elisabeth Schumann (soprano), Karl Alwin (piano)
EMI mono
Even in middle age Elisabeth Schumann's soprano was bright, girlish and beautifully controlled. This wonderful performance is just one of around 50 Schubert songs that Schumann recorded during the 78 era and the album it's taken from contains them all.

Die schöne Müllerin, D795 (1823)
"The maid of the mill" is probably the most approachable of German Lieder-cycles. The story-line celebrates the love of a journeyman for the miller's daughter – although when a gamekeeper comes on to the scene and steals the maid's heart, the journeyman throws himself into the brook (his confidante throughout the cycle) and the brook remembers him with a beautiful lullaby. Schubert discovered Wilhelm Müller's *Poems from the Posthumous Papers of a Horn-Player* while on a visit to friends. The cycle's most popular songs include "Das Wandern" (The Rover), "Wohin?" (Wither?) and "Ungeduld" (Thine is my heart).

Aksel Schiøtz (tenor), Gerald Moore (piano)
Danacord mono
Yes, it's old – but Schiøtz's honeyed tenor creates an impression of wounded innocence that no other version quite matches and Danacord's transfer reveals the voice in its true glory. Those in search of more modern sound are directed to the tenors Ernst Haefliger (Sony, analogue) and Ian Bostridge (Hyperion digital, with baritone Dietrich Fischer-Dieskau reading the poems that Schubert never set to music). Fischer-Dieskau himself is best represented as recorded with Gerald Moore in 1961 (EMI, analogue).

Schwanengesang, D957 (1828)

Schwanengesang (literally "Swansong") isn't a song-cycle in the strictest sense of the term, but a two-volume collection of 14 songs published after Schubert's death. It makes for a riveting sequence, starting with "Liebesbotschaft" ("Love's message") and incorporating the celebrated "Ständchen" ("Serenade", Schubert's most popular song after *Ave Maria* and *Du bist die Ruh*), a terrifying "Doppelgänger" ("The Double") and the delightful "Die Taubenpost" ("Pigeon Post").

Hans Hotter (baritone), Gerald Moore (piano)

EMI mono

A Wagnerian god in an intimate musical context, although songs like "Am Meer" ("By the sea") and "Der Doppelgänger" respond well to Hotter's lyrical brand of vocal thunder. EMI's collection also includes such well-loved Schubert favourites as An die Musik ("To Music") and Im Frühling ("In Spring"), while the mono/stereo recordings – which date from between 1949 and 1957 – capture the voice with rare realism.

Vor meiner Wiege, D927 (1827)

Choosing individual pieces from Schubert's huge Lieder output (which includes over 600 individual songs, many of them masterpieces) is extraordinarily difficult. This particular Lied is one of the least-known. The poem, by Karl Gottfried von Leitner, recalls the cradle, motherly love and death: "once he has lost his mother," writes Leitner, "who then will lead him to his last and deepest sleep?". Schubert's music alternates a cradling peacefulness with startling pain. "Before my Cradle" is fully on a par with the best of the *Winterreise* song-cycle (see below).

Karl Erb (tenor), Bruno Seidler-Winkler (piano)

Preiser mono

Karl Erb was a famous Evangelist (St Matthew Passion – see "Passions and oratorios", below) and an eloquent Lieder singer. Modest, frugal (Erb would ride to concerts on his bicycle) and deeply religious, he was also devoted to his mother. His performance carries special conviction, although I wouldn't necessarily prefer it to a performance by Dietrich Fischer-Dieskau and Jörg Demus (DG, analogue), recorded at the same time as the Winterreise sessions noted below, but not as yet reissued on CD. That, too, is extraordinarily poignant, but Erb's recording (made in 1937 but still sounding well) should certainly be heard. There's also a fine version by soprano Elisabeth Grümmer with Gerald Moore at the piano (Testament, analogue).

Winterreise, D911 (1827)

"Today, I shall sing a cycle of awe-inspiring songs to you," said Schubert to his friend Josef von Spaun early in 1827; " … they have affected me more deeply than any other songs." And little wonder. Schubert had set 12 poems by Wilhelm Müller and would soon set 12 more. The narrative concerns a lovesick traveller on the verge of death. It's a harrowing but compelling tale and it matters not whether you join the hapless poet at the lime tree, the river bank, the village or the inn; whether you're contemplating frozen tears, courage, deception, a lone hurdy-gurdy player or a strange crow "intent to prey upon my body". *Winterreise* is probably the greatest song-cycle ever composed.

Dietrich Fischer-Dieskau (baritone), Jörg Demus (piano)

Deutsche Grammophon analogue

This is surely the finest of Fischer-Dieskau's numerous recordings of Winterreise, not least because the voice itself was in prime condition at the time (this was in 1965) and Demus provides an especially sympathetic accompaniment (Schubert's piano writing is in effect an additional commentary on the protagonist's plight). A good digital alternative features the baritone Wolfgang Holzmair with Imogen Cooper at the piano (Philips), while Gerhard Hüsch (Pearl, mono) offers the best vintage version.

Robert Schumann (1810-1856)

Dichterliebe, Op. 48 (1840)

The special charm of Schumann's songs resides mainly in their irresistible combination of exquisite melody and deeply poetic piano writing. Nowhere is this more in evidence than in the 16 songs that make up "Poet's Love", a consistently inspired cycle that opens in "the wondrous beauty of May" and ranges in mood from the brave resolve of "Ich grolle nicht" ("I am not bitter, even though my heart is breaking"), to the disorienting starkness of "Ich hab' im Traum geweinet" ("In my dreams I was weeping/I dreamt you lay in your grave") and the tender vision of "Allnächtlich im Traume seh' ich dich", where the lover again sees the beloved in a dream.

 ***Charles Panzéra (baritone), Alfred Cortot (piano)***

Biddulph mono

Although Panzéra is most widely celebrated as among the great interpreters of French song, his Dichterliebe (which was recorded in 1935) has a romantic ardour that no other version quite matches. Panzéra's diction is crystal-clear; his voice production mellow and vibrant and his 'accompanist' the most eloquent imaginable. Strong rivals include Dietrich Fischer-Dieskau (with Christoph Eschenbach, DG analogue) and Hans Hotter (Preiser, mono).

Frauenliebe und -leben, Op. 42 (1840)

"A woman's life and love" (to poems by Adalbert von Chamisso) is a supremely empathetic sequence that, if viewed as a 'male' commentary on 'female' emotions, still seems uncannily perceptive. Schumann traces a love affair from initial infatuation, through admiration, consummation, doubts and disillusionment (a poignant piano post-lude recalls the joy of times past). There are eight songs in all, the most famous of which is probably the second, "Er, der Herrlichste von allen" ("He, the most splendid of all").

 ***Brigitte Fassbaender (mezzo-soprano), Irwin Gage (piano)***

Deutsche Grammophon digital

Fassbaender achieves precisely the level of emotional engagement that is essential for an effective interpretation of this cycle, though she has a whole host of fine predecessors, not least Dame Janet Baker (Saga, analogue), Kathleen Ferrier (Decca, mono) and two great singers caught in the twilight of their careers, Elisabeth Schumann (EMI, mono) and Lotte Lehmann (with Bruno Walter, Sony or Pearl, mono).

12 Lieder, Op. 35 (1840)

The so-called "Kerner-Lieder" (named after the man who wrote the words, the Swabian poet Justinus Kerner) contain some of Schumann's most haunting songs. There's the tale of a young nun as seen through the eyes of a loving admirer (an especially touching narrative), a keen-eyed youth exploring the world and nature (the famous "Wanderlied") and "Silent Tears", a magnificent outpouring, fully on a par with Schumann's grandest piano pieces: "In the silence of the night many a man weeps away his grief," writes Kerner; "and then in the morning you would think his heart is always glad."

 ***Dietrich Fischer-Dieskau (baritone), Gerald Moore (piano)***

Orfeo mono

One of Fischer-Dieskau's most memorable interpretations, especially of the second song "Stirb, Lieb' und Freud!". This particular recording was made live in 1959 but there's an analogue successor with Christoph Eschenbach (part of a six-CD set devoted to Schumann's songs) and a wonderful earlier (mono) version, not as yet reissued on CD, with pianist Gunther Weissenborn (both are on DG).

Liederkreis, Op. 39 (1840)

Schumann wrote two *Liederkreis* (literally "Song-cycle"), one to words by Heine (Op. 24) and this, the more popular of the two, to poems by Josef von Eichendorff. There are 12 songs in all, the most famous of which is a magical nocturne ("Mondnacht", or "Moon-night") while the others include a haunting narrative about an old knight who keeps watch in an ancient castle ("Auf einer Burg") and an exhilarating "Frühlingsnacht" ("Spring Night") – which Liszt transcribed for solo piano.

 ***Dietrich Fischer-Dieskau (baritone), Christoph Eschenbach (piano)***

Deutsche Grammophon analogue

Fischer-Dieskau and Eschenbach are especially successful where Schumann's feelings run deepest ("Mondnacht" being a fair case in point): their poise, finesse and sensitivity to detail are consistently inspiring. Earlier classics include Erna Berger (DG, mono – though not available at the time of writing) and a fatherly Wagnerian bass-baritone, Friedrich Schorr (Pearl, mono).

Johannes Brahms (1833–1879)

Vier ernste Gesänge (1896)

Four Serious Songs is a masterly cycle based on biblical texts – although 'serious' by no means precludes 'tender' or 'beautiful', especially in the sullen first song, "For that which befalleth the sons of men", and the last, a manly affirmation of hope, ending with the words "And now abideth faith, hope, charity, these three; but the greatest of these is charity". Anyone wary of Lieder might profitably take these songs as a starting point.

 ***Kim Borg (bass), Eric Werba (piano)***

Finlandia analogue

The Finnish bass Kim Borg has a dark, vibrant voice, rounded in tone and here employed with the utmost sensitivity. These incomparable recordings come as part of a superb set "Kim Borg – Songs and Arias" which also includes songs by Schubert, Schumann, Wolf, Sibelius and Mussorgsky.

Gustav Mahler (1860–1911)

Des Knaben Wunderhorn (1888–89)

A colourful sequence based on German folk poetry (*Youth's Magic Horn*) and concerned largely with soldiers, their deaths, ghosts and sweethearts. Some songs – like the stern "Revelge" – relate a strong message (in this case, anti-war), whereas others are more lightweight in tone – the charming "Rheinlegendchen", for example, which tells of a song contest between a cuckoo and a nightingale. The twelfth song "Urlicht" (not included in our prime recommendation, although Bernstein habitually programmed it) was also used by Mahler in his *Resurrection* (Second) Symphony (see "The New Symphony", above).

Jessye Norman (mezzo-soprano), John Shirley-Quirk (baritone), Concertgebouw Orchestra/Bernard Haitink

Philips analogue

The combination of Jessye Norman's beautifully moulded mezzo and John Shirley-Quirk's strong though never hectoring characterizations fits well against a quietly perceptive orchestral backdrop. Haitink's principal rivals are George Szell (with Schwarzkopf and Fischer-Dieskau, EMI analogue) and Leonard Bernstein (with Christa Ludwig and Walter Berry, Sony analogue), though neither is quite as well recorded as these 1976 Philips sessions.

Kindertotenlieder (1901-04)

Mahler lost several of his brothers in childhood, and so it is hardly surpising to learn that he was drawn to Friedrich Rückert's poems about the death of children. The first song offers gentle consolation, the second is full of remorse and the third has the protagonist contemplate the spot where the daughter's face might have appeared. In the fourth song, the parent imagines that the children have merely gone out for a walk and the fifth effects a poignant transformation when, beyond regrets over letting the children go out in a storm (and some terrifying orchestral writing), the parent is comforted by the idea that they are now under God's protection.

Kathleen Ferrier (contralto), Vienna Philharmonic Orchestra/Bruno Walter

EMI mono

Bruno Walter had boundless admiration for the late Kathleen Ferrier, and his painstaking tuition paid high dividends in what is perhaps the finest recording they made together (although some would cite Mahler's Das Lied von der Erde – Decca, mono). The performances themselves are intensely expressed, though I wouldn't want to forego compassionate male alternatives from Dietrich Fischer-Dieskau (under Karl Böhm, DG analogue) or Bryn Terfel (under Giuseppe Sinopoli, DG digital).

Lieder eines fahrenden Gesellen (1884, revised 1892, 1896)

Beautifully crafted and scored with the utmost transparency, these four "Songs of a Wayfarer" constitute the finest of Mahler's early works. The texts are the composer's own and tell, respectively, of losing one's sweetheart to another, of love for nature, anxiety at missing the beloved ("When I look up at the sky, I see two blue eyes – alas, alas!") and wandering into the night with love and grief.

Dietrich Fischer-Dieskau (baritone), Bavarian Radio Symphony Orchestra/Rafael Kubelík

Deutsche Grammophon analogue

It's hardly surprising that the conductor whose grasp of Mahler's First Symphony is second to none should also have mastered the Symphony's nearest musical relation (the two first movements share similar material). And although Fischer-Dieskau made a famous mono recording under Wilhelm Furtwängler (EMI), this 1960s remake is both more imaginative and more spontaneous (and, dare I say it, more perceptively conducted).

Rückert-Lieder (1902)

Five further Rückert settings to add to the *Kindertotenlieder* (see above). All are informed by the spirit of the East (a perennial preoccupation with Mahler): the first recalls a fragrant lime tree, the second is a hymn to love and the third warns against curiosity about the creative process. The fourth song (and surely the most beautiful – "Ich bin der Welt abhanden gekommen") tells of the poet's renunciation of the world (it recalls, with unmistakable poignancy, the closing "Farewell" of Mahler's great Symphony-cum-Song-cycle *Das Lied von der Erde* – see "The New Symphony") and the fifth, midnight, suffering and death.

Christa Ludwig (mezzo-soprano), Berlin Philharmonic Orchestra/Herbert von Karajan

Deutsche Grammophon analogue

Just as Kathleen Ferrier's Mahler was inspired by a great Mahler conductor (Bruno Walter), so was Christa Ludwig's (Leonard Bernstein).

However, on this occasion, it is Herbert von Karajan who provides an orchestral accompaniment of the utmost clarity and refinement. An excellent digital alternative features baritone Thomas Hampson with the Vienna Philharmonic under Bernstein (DG), while no one plumbs the depths of "Ich bin der Welt abhanden gekommen" quite like Fischer-Dieskau (either under Karl Böhm [DG] or with Bernstein at the piano [Sony] – both are analogue).

Hugo Wolf (1860-1903)

Italian Songbook (1890-96)

"Love of life" might be an appropriate subtitle for this, Hugo Wolf's last song-cycle. The texts, which are based on Tuscan love-poems, are rendered into a miniaturist narrative that, to paraphrase the composer himself, runs from wrangling through reconciliation, pains of love, the lover's mental anguish, humour, helpless infatuation, and so on. The songs – 46 in all and commonly shared between soprano and baritone – are short, pithy, sardonic and often very beautiful.

Irmgard Seefried (soprano), Dietrich Fischer-Dieskau (baritone), Erik Werba (piano)

Orfeo d'Or mono

Fischer-Dieskau and Seefried invest each piece with a combination of sophistication and playful spontaneity. The recording was made live at the 1958 Salzburg Festival, but there is a studio alternative (where the piano part is shared between Werba and Jörg Demus) on Deutsche Grammophon (analogue), which was recorded during the same period.

Spanish Songbook (1889-90)

Wolf had a long-term fascination with Spain and his masterly collection of 44 songs – ten of which are 'sacred', and 34 'profane' – draws on, for example, Cervantes and Lope de Vega, as well as the German poets Geibel and Heyse (in Spanish guise) and various anonymous writers. The music itself is by turns, dialogic, playful, agonized, declamatory, mystical – and always acutely attentive to the power of the word. Good songs to sample include "Nun wandre, Maria" (Now onward, Mary), "In dem Schatten meiner Locken" (In the shadow of my tresses) and "Klinge, klinge, mein Pandero" (Ring out my pandura, but other thoughts are in my heart).

Anne Sofie von Otter (mezzo-soprano), Olaf Bär (baritone), Geoffrey Parsons (piano)

EMI digital

Subtle characterization, warm vocal projection and superb playing by one of the century's great accompanists. Neither singer indulges in excessive mannerism (as Dame Elisabeth Schwarzkopf, in her generally superb DG analogue recording with Dietrich Fischer-Dieskau, sometimes does) and the recorded balance is ideal.

Mörike-Lieder (1888)

Try the very first song, "The Convalescent's Ode to Hope" where the darkly Wagnerian introduction ("Deathly leaden loomed the morning") gives way to a triumphant "... the victory was won!". This brief passage from darkness to light is fairly typical in that Wolf's settings of Eduard Mörike survey all manner of moods, from the vibrant imaginings of "Daybreak", to the cheerful "Tramping" or the declamatory drama of "The Fire Rider". An evening spent with the *Mörike-Lieder* (good translations ease the passage for those of us without German) is tantamount to experiencing 50 exquisitely tooled tone-poems.

Dietrich Fischer-Dieskau (baritone), Gerald Moore (piano)

EMI analogue

Fischer-Dieskau relates each narrative as if it were a slice of personal reportage; his tone-production, phrasing and highly individual style of declamation spell 'authenticity' in its truest sense while Gerald Moore's accompaniments are both discreet and involving.

Richard Strauss (1864-1949)

Vier letzte Lieder (1948)

The *Four Last Songs* are the final and perhaps the richest fruits of Germany's greatest post-Romantic song-writer, piquantly orchestrated and recalling, respectively, sleep and "the magical circle of night", September wearily smiling "into the dying dream that was the garden", the "blissful presence" of spring and the "tranquil peace" of dusk. Strauss's *Four Last Songs* are among the most transparent, haunting and evocative Lieder ever composed.

Lisa della Casa (soprano), Vienna Philharmonic Orchestra/Karl Böhm

Decca mono

Although it was the great Norwegian soprano,

Kirsten Flagstad who premièred the Four Last Songs, the most celebrated recordings of the work are by Elisabeth Schwarzkopf (three separate versions, all on EMI) and Lisa della Casa. A fine Straussian (her Arabella was legendary), della Casa is here granted a particularly perceptive accompaniment from Strauss's friend and leading exponent Karl Böhm.

Arnold Schoenberg (1874-1951)

Pierrot lunaire, song-cycle for speaker and chamber ensemble, Op. 21 (1912)

Mad, distracted, compelling, mildly satirical and infinitely strange – *Pierrot lunaire* occupies a lonely territory mid-way between speech and song. The vocal line is composed in a style called *Sprechgesang*, or "speech-song" whereas the crystalline instrumentation represents the ultimate practical manifesto of musical Expressionism. The text is by the Belgian poet Albert Giraud (translated into German by Otto Erich Hartleben), and the poems themselves deal with the surreal exploits of an imaginary entertainer. Schoenberg described the work as "the solar plexus as well as the mind of twentieth-century music", whereas Pierre Boulez described it as "un cabaret supérieur". A 'difficult' listen, *Pierrot* is also a fascinating experience – provided you follow the text.

Barbara Sukowa (voice), Schönberg Ensemble/Reinbert de Leeuw
Koch Schwann digital
Sukowa's voice is pretty enough to suggest music through speech and powerful enough to project the full drama of the score's more aggressive episodes. It's certainly among the most animated Pierrots ever recorded. Reinbert de Leeuw directs a wonderfully supple accompaniment, well recorded by Koch Schwann, but there's significant competition from Phyllis Bryn-Julson with Peter Eötvös conducting (RCA, digital), Mary Thomas and David Atherton (Decca, analogue) and indeed the composer himself (with Erika Stiedry-Wagner as soloist, Sony, mono).

Kurt Weill (1900-1950)

The Seven Deadly Sins (1933)

Part song-cycle, part stage-work, Weill's political 'spectacle' (the original title was *The Seven Mortal Sins of the Petty-Bourgeois*) is humorous, sardonic, often extremely moving and very much a product of its time. Weill's melodies are highly distinctive and his word-painting as vivid as Mahler's or Schubert's. The words themselves are by Berthold Brecht and the story-line concerns a Louisiana girl who plies her profession to provide for her family but is railed against by the locals for immorality. Of the nine varied episodes included, one of the most characteristic (and perhaps the best place to sample) is "Anger", with its catchy tunes and upbeat instrumental interludes.

Angelina Réaux (soprano), Hugo Munday, Mark Bleeke (tenors), Peter Becker (baritone), Wilbur Pauley (bass), New York Philharmonic Orchestra/Kurt Masur
Teldec digital
Fine characterization from all concerned (Réaux, especially) and a discreetly spirited accompaniment under Masur. A strong digital rival with Anja Silja and her husband Christoph von Dohnányi conducting was issued as part of a Cleveland Orchestra 75th Anniversary Edition (on the orchestra's own label).

Accross the nations (1868-1974)

A brief international sequence, opening with Mussorgsky's affectionate and amusing *The Nursery* and closing with Britten's skilful and often beautiful settings of key British poets. The Americas are represented by Villa-Lobos in Bachian mode and Samuel Barber's touchingly simple evocation of childhood in a small, quiet town.

Modest Mussorgsky (1839-1881)

The Nursery (1868-72)

Mussorgsky was the ultimate 'realist' composer. "What I should like to do …", he once wrote, "… is to make my characters speak exactly as people speak in everyday life, without exaggeration or distortion, and yet write music which will be thoroughly artistic." This charming cycle depicts the child asking his nurse about the bogey man, then being punished for unravelling a ball of wool, discovering a beetle, playing with a doll, praying at evening, watching a cat scratching at a bird-cage and, lastly, riding a hobby-horse.

Marjana Lipovšek (mezzo-soprano), Graham Johnson (piano)

Sony Classical digital

Sensitive singing, subtle characterizations and accomplished, typically perceptive piano playing from Graham Johnson. Those who prefer a male version are directed either to Boris Christoff (EMI mono – although Christoff's 'child imitations' will strike some as decidedly camp) or Sergei Leiferkus (Conifer, digital).

Songs and Dances of Death (1875-77)

Four of Mussorgsky's greatest songs (with words by Golenischchev-Kutuzov) – although the original ground-plan made provision for no less than 12. Death is depicted as a "soft-hearted" friend at the side of a sick infant's cradle, as a "mysterious knight" singing to a mortally ill maiden, as dancing the Trepak among peasants and, finally, as a field marshall on horseback "flashing the white of his bones".

Boris Christoff (bass), French Radio National Orchestra/Georges Tzipine

EMI mono

Christoff acts out each song as if it were a scene from an opera; his voice is big, grainy and powerfully expressive, while the orchestral accompaniments – prepared by Rimsky-Korsakov and Glazunov – provide a dramatic aural backdrop. Shostakovich's orchestration is handsomely served by Sergei Leiferkus and Yuri Temirkanov (RCA, digital), while Kim Borg and pianist Erik Werba (Finlandia, analogue) offer a fine, albeit German-language version of the original.

Ralph Vaughan Williams (1872-1958)

Songs of Travel (1904)

Nine settings of poems by Robert Louis Stevenson, imbued with a genuine sense of wonder and a quiet originality, even though two of the songs recall existing tunes (Schubert and a Scots ballad). *Songs of Travel* is one of Vaughan Williams's earliest masterpieces. The ninth song – "I have trod the upward and the downward slope" – was found among VW's papers after his death and only later added to the cycle.

Bryn Terfel (bass-baritone), Malcolm Martineau (piano)

Deutsche Grammophon digital

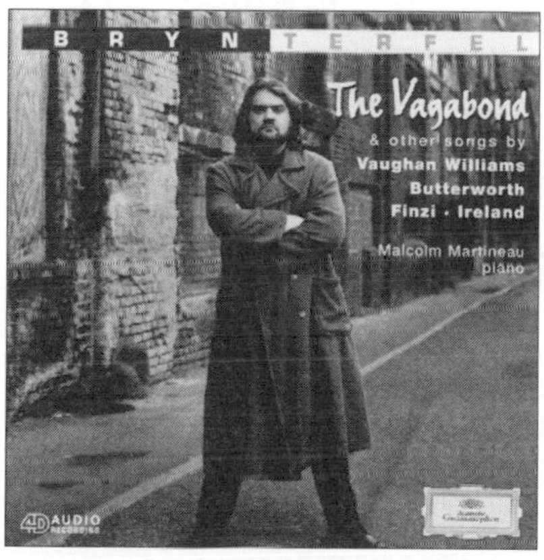

At long last a singer whose mastery of English repertory is fully on a par with the great national interpreters of German Lieder and French chanson. Terfel employs his dark, lyrical bass-baritone to superb effect while Malcolm Martineau – Terfel's regular accompanist – offers subtle and telling pianistic support.

Heitor Villa-Lobos (1887-1959)

Bachianas Brasileiras No. 5 for soprano, solo cello and cello ensemble (1938)

The opening Aria is a sinuous melody suspended over a gently mobile cello accompaniment, whereas – beyond a central Nocturne (with words by Ruth Valadares Corrêa) – the "Dansa" second movement incorporates fragments of imitated bird-song. Villa-Lobos (who was himself a cellist) had been fascinated by Bach's music since childhood and his *Bachianas Brasileiras* (literally "Brazilian Bach") meld Bachian influences with aspects of Brazilian folk music.

Dame Kiri Te Kanawa (soprano), Lynn Harrell (cello), Instrumental Ensamble

Decca digital

Te Kanawa conveys an appropriate feeling of gentle rapture while the accompaniment features a sensitive cello solo. Good rivals are plentiful, with the Brazilian singer Bidu Sayão (Sony, mono – though only the aria) leading the historical stakes (her voice is especially suited to the piece) and fine stereo recordings by Netania Davrath (under Bernstein, Sony – analogue) and Jill Gomez (Hyperion, digital). Victoria de los Angeles made a famous recording under the composer's own direction (EMI, mono).

Dmitry Shostakovich (1906-1975)

Suite on Verses of Michelangelo Buonarroti, Op. 145*a* (1974)

Magnificent music that feeds on feelings of regret, resignation and defiance. And yet the

Michelangelo Suite wears a quizzical, bemused countenance; it implies rather than states – whether about truth ("sword of justice and weight of wrath"), the beloved at morning, love itself, the "rough hammer" of creativity (thrillingly conveyed via thrashing percussion and whooping horns), death or immortality. It is Shostakovich's "Song of the Earth" (*Das Lied von der Erde*, see "The New Symphony", above).

Sergei Leiferkus (baritone), Gothenburg Symphony Orchestra/Neeme Järvi

Deutsche Grammophon digital

Leiferkus sings with aristocratic poise yet manages to convey feelings of anger, alienation, yearning and even torment. Järvi directs a strong, sensitive accompaniment, with beautifully judged tempos and very well played. The couplings are two other song-cycles – on texts by Japanese poets and Marina Tsvetayeva. But the Michelangelo Suite is the greatest masterpiece.

Samuel Barber (1910-1981)

Knoxville: Summer of 1915 (1947)

Barber's nostalgic essay for soprano and small orchestra relates the wonderment of a young child in a small, quiet town." It has become that time of evening when people sit on their porches, rocking gently and talking gently," (the words are by James Agee); " … People go by; things go by … After a little I am taken in and put to bed … But (no one) will … ever tell me who I am."

Dawn Upshaw (soprano), Orchestra of St Luke's/David Zinman

Nonesuch digital

The pretty, girlish quality of Upshaw's voice, allied to supreme verbal sensitivity and fine orchestral playing, make this one of the most touching accounts of Barber's quarter-hour masterpiece. The recording is excellent, but there are fine alternatives from Barbara Hendricks and Michael Tilson Thomas (EMI digital), Kathleen Battle with the Orchestra of St Luke's under André Previn (DG digital) and Eleanor Steber (her famous 1950 recording – Sony, mono).

Benjamin Britten (1913-1976)

Serenade for tenor, horn and strings, Op. 31 (1943)

Elevated word-painting and a work of great originality. The poems – by Cotton, Tennyson, Blake, Jonson, Keats and 'Anon' – deal with the theme of evening. Britten's masterful scoring incorporates a Prologue and Epilogue where the solo horn plays 'natural harmonics' – a brilliant effect that, when first heard, gives the disorienting impression of being unintentionally off-key. The moment when the Prologue ends and the strings usher in the first song, "Pastoral", is especially magical.

John Mark Ainsley (tenor), David Pyatt (horn), Britten Sinfonia/Nicholas Cleobury

EMI Eminence digital

The combination of John Mark Ainsley's lyrical singing and David Pyatt's accomplished horn playing make this one of the most satisfying Serenades available. Of course there are the famous recordings with Britten himself and Peter Pears (Decca, stereo with Barry Tuckwell or mono with the work's commissioning artist Dennis Brain) – both of them essential listening – but Ainsley and Pyatt are consistently effective.

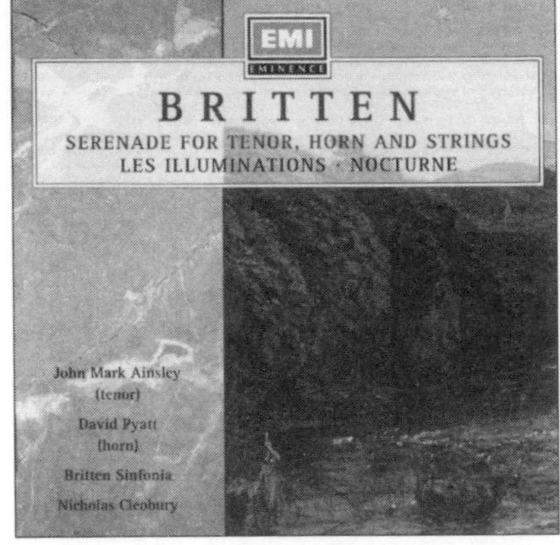

Sublime lamentations (1567-1610)

The chorus played a significant part both in Greek tragedy and in early Jewish worship, but our own appreciation of choral music has its roots in the polyphonic masterpieces by such Renaissance masters as Palestrina, Lassus and Byrd. It's a huge of field of repertory worthy of substantial representation and our chosen selection can only be treated as a tasty sampling. Renaissance choral music has a degree of harmonic sophistication that is especially appealing to modern ears.

Thomas Tallis (c1505-1585)

Lamentations of Jeremiah (*c*1567)

An extraordinarily powerful setting of two separate texts from the Book of Jeremiah, and one of the high points of Tallis's art. The despondent Jeremiah relates the wanderings and sufferings of Judah and implores his people to return to God. Tallis prefaces each set with a polyphonic "announcement", while the verses themselves (each of which is preceded by a 'sung' Hebrew letter) are exquisitely voiced.

 ***Theatre of Voices/Paul Hillier***
Harmonia Mundi digital
The evenness of these performances, their concentration, tonal fullness and perfect blend of voices could hardly be bettered – although, to be fair, The Tallis Scholars (Gimell, digital) are equally impressive. Harmonia Mundi's all-Tallis programme sets the Lamentations among motets and some rarely-heard string music. The recordings are outstanding.

Giovanni Pierluigi da Palestrina (1525/26-1594)

Missa Papae Marcelli (published 1567)
Palestrina was one of the major musical masters of the Renaissance. In fact, his fame and reputation were so great that he was asked to rewrite the church's main plainchant book. The Mass for Pope Marcellus is among his best-known works and makes fine use of the six 'voices' (or groups of voices) employed. The *Credo* (track 3 on our recommended recording) is especially impressive.

 ***Choir of Westminster Abbey/ Simon Preston***
Archiv digital
Recorded at All Saints' Church in Tooting, the Westminster Abbey Choir sounds as resplendent here as when in its home acoustical environment. Simon Preston directs a truly superb performance, judiciously balanced by the engineers – although anyone chancing upon The Tallis Scholars (Gimell, digital) will have no grounds for complaint.

Orlande de Lassus (1532-1594)

Missa super "Bella Amfitrit'altera" (published 1610)
Probably the best-known Mass by a Franco-Flemish composer whose immense output included over 2000 works – Masses, motets, psalms, hymns, responsorial Passions and various secular pieces. The mythical Amphitrite was the beautiful daughter of Oceanus, who became the wife of Neptune; she was also associated with Venice as the bride of the Adriatic. The music itself, which is notably spacious, direct and fresh-sounding, derives from the polyphonic madrigal.

 ***Regensburg Cathedral Choir, Archiv Produktion Instrumental Ensemble/Hans Schrems***
Archiv analogue
Beautifully sung, antiphonally recorded and performed with the aid of rich instrumental colouring (cornett, trombones, etc). Schrems' reading remains among the most persuasive on disc (it was recorded in 1968) although readers who would rather do without the instruments are advised to try the Christ Church Cathedral Choir, Oxford, under Simon Preston (Decca, analogue).

William Byrd (1543-1623)

Mass for five voices (*c*1595)
William Byrd's allegiance to the Catholic Church found profound expression in his three glorious Masses. "Nor did he ever lose sight of his debt to the great heritage of Tudor church music," writes John Milsom; "It is arguable that, in his Masses, he set out not only to provide his fellow Roman Catholics with works that were proud, defiant and thought-provoking, but also to pay homage to that musical heritage." The Mass in five parts is the most sonorous of the three. Like its companions, it is especially rich in closely-written counterpoint.

Mass for four voices (*c*1592-93)
The opening *Kyrie* is as good a place as any to sample the extraordinary beauty of this, the first of William Byrd's three Masses. Byrd was greatly influenced by the music of John Taverner (*c*1490-1545), one of the masters of Tudor church music, and he was proud to

contribute to that rich tradition. In fact it might even be said, with some justification, that Byrd's Masses crystallize an entire musical era.

The Tallis Scholars
Gimell digital
Supremely accomplished singing, stylish and scholarly and beautifully recorded in the mellow acoustic of Merton College, Oxford. Rival digital recordings by The Hilliard Ensemble (EMI) and King's College Choir (Decca) have many virtues, but The Tallis Scholars remain a secure first choice.

Claudio Monteverdi (1567-1643)

Vespro della Beata Vergine (Vespers of the Blessed Virgin) (published 1610)
Whether approached from a religious or an aesthetic standpoint, Monteverdi's forward-looking "Marian Vespers" (as they're sometimes known) remain among the most rapturously beautiful sacred pieces in the repertory. Monteverdi's design alternates choral settings of the psalms with concertos for solo voices, and there's a fine instrumental sonata placed at the work's centre. The Vespers, which lay neglected for many years, open with an exhilarating Toccata-style chorus, "O God, turn to me in my adversity".

Paul Esswood, Kevin Smith (countertenors), Ian Partridge, John Elwes (tenors), David Thomas, Christopher Keyte (basses) Regensburg Cathedral Choir, Hamburg Wind Ensemble for Early Music/Hans Martin Schneidt
Archiv analogue
Schneidt's recording dates from the mid-1970s and has a limpid, translucent quality that proves particularly satisfying. The singing is extremely accomplished, the direction spirited though unforced, but Archiv themselves have provided a strong digital successor under John Eliot Gardiner (his second recording of the work). Both versions exclude antiphons but include a second (alternative) version of the Magnificat.

Passions and oratorios (1707-1749)

It's here more than anywhere else in the book that the dictates of economy force an unhappy compromise. Bach's sacred cantatas – there are over 200 of them (and those are just the ones that survive!) – are abundantly rich in great music, and any self-respecting collection should, in all honesty, include at least half of them. Still, we do at least have a modest sampling, plus the inspirational peaks of the *St John* and *St Matthew Passions*, selective representation from Handel (another productive source of great religious music) and Pergolesi's adorable *Stabat mater*.

Johann Sebastian Bach (1685-1750)

Cantata No. 51, "Jauchzet Gott in allen Landen!", BWV51 (1730)
This life-affirming masterwork dates from the composer's Leipzig years (the period during which Bach wrote most of his church cantatas) and marks the Fifteenth Sunday after Trinity. The text, taken from St Matthew Chapter 6, opens with the words "Rejoice in the Lord in all lands" and the cantata includes a prominent trumpet part. The closing "Alleluja!" is among the most joyous movements in all of Bach's religious output.

Maria Stader (soprano), Munich Bach Orchestra/Karl Richter
Archiv analogue
Currently available only as part of a superb budget-price set containing 17 cantatas for the middle Sundays after Trinity, this remains the most beautiful recording of Cantata No. 51 ever made. Richter went on to record the work a second time, with Edith Mathis as soprano soloist (again for Archiv, analogue), and although the later version is even more exhilarating (especially the closing chorale and aria), Stader's pure-toned singing sways the balance in favour of its predecessor … just.

Cantata No. 80 "Ein feste Burg ist unser Gott", BWV80 (1724)
Reformation Day (October 31st) is one of the major events of the Lutheran year, and celebrates Martin Luther's historic nailing of his 95 Theses to the door of the church of

Wittenberg Castle. Bach's Cantata "A stronghold sure our God is still" is an affirmation of faith, with its resplendent opening chorus, its lilting first chorale (setting the words "And if the world were full of devils wholly to engulf us, then we'd not be at all afraid …") and the two closing movements, a duet for contralto and tenor and a majestic final chorale.

Edith Mathis (soprano), Trudeliese Schmidt (contralto), Peter Schreier (tenor), Dietrich Fischer-Dieskau (baritone), Munich Bach Chorus and Orchestra/Karl Richter

Archiv analogue

A performance that parades the various virtues that distinguish other fine performances in this inspired series – a lean though strong tonal profile, impressive executive discipline, superb singing and a devotional fervour that reaches to the very heart of Bach's music.

Cantata No. 82, "Ich habe genug", BWV82 (1727)

"Rejoicing do I greet my death/Ah, would that it had come already …". This comforting soliloquy on eternal rest was composed for the Feast of the Purification of the Virgin. Bach himself performed it on numerous occasions to considerable effect (using high, low or middle voices). BWV82's most heart-rending movement is the opening aria, where a swaying, plaintive melody is shared between oboist and vocalist.

Hans Hotter (bass), Philharmonia Orchestra/Anthony Bernard

EMI mono

Hotter scales down his powerful bass for a performance of rare sensitivity, while a like-minded Philharmonia Orchestra provides an eloquent accompaniment (Sidney Sutcliffe is the solo oboist). The mono recording is appropriately intimate, but those intent on stereo are directed to a fine alternative with John Shirley-Quirk and Sir Neville Marriner conducting (Decca, analogue).

Cantata No. 106, "Gottes Zeit ist die allerbeste Zeit", BWV106 (1707)

This funeral cantata, also known as "Actus Tragicus", opens with a solemn sinfonia featuring two recorders that weave and weep around each other with a hypnotic intensity that anticipates the Minimalists of 260 years later. The recorders then comment on the first chorus, "God's time is the best of all", while Bach's ethereal setting of the words "Lord Jesus" (in the fifth section) suggest the soul leaving the body. The closing chorus is a vigorous celebration of Divine Power.

Hertha Töpper (contralto), Ernst Haefliger (tenor), Theo Adam (bass), Munich Bach Chorus and Orchestra/Karl Richter

Archiv analogue

Although the two recorder players are beautifully blended, their subtly contrasting tones underline the 'duet' nature of the music. With distinguished singing, superb conducting and excellent sound, this remains among the finest of all Bach cantata recordings. Strong rivals include Gustav Leonhardt (Teldec, analogue) and an especially memorable 1954 Vanguard (mono) recording under Felix Prohaska.

Cantata No. 140, "Wachet auf, ruft uns die Stimme", BWV140 (1731)

One of the most noble works of Bach's Leipzig period, "Sleepers, awake" contains many inspired highlights, not least the long opening chorus – a piece to rank alongside the greatest choral movements from the Passions – and a duet between Jesus and the soul, scored for tenor and bass. The chorale "Zion hört die Wächter singen" (Zion hears the watchmen singing) is also famous in Bach's own organ transcription, as well as via TV advertising for a certain 'Black Horse' chain of banks. *Wachet auf* is a cantata for the 27th Sunday after Trinity.

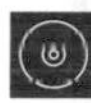

Edith Mathis (soprano), Peter Schreier (tenor), Dietrich Fischer-Dieskau (baritone), Munich Bach Chorus and Orchestra/Karl Richter

Archiv analogue

Some will object to Richter's slow tempi, and yet the opening chorus is given with such breadth and majesty that I can't imagine that many listeners will remain unmoved. For a total contrast, however (and a fine period-instrument performance on a smaller scale), try Nikolaus Harnoncourt (Teldec, analogue).

Christmas Oratorio, BWV248 (1734)

The *Oratorium Tempore Nativitatis Christi* (to quote Bach's own description of the work) consists of six separate parts written for the six festival days of the Christmas period. The themes covered include the birth of Jesus, the shepherds in the fields, the naming of Jesus and the Magi from the East. Musically, it's one of Bach's most popular and endearing works, with various highlights such as the exhilarating first chorus "Jauchzet, frohlocket, auf, preiset die Tage" (Rejoice, exult! up, glorify the days") and the lyrical Sinfonia that opens the second part.

 **_Gundula Janowitz (soprano), Christa Ludwig (contralto), Fritz Wunderlich (tenor), Franz Crass (bass), Munich Bach Chorus and Orchestra/ Karl Richter_**
Archiv analogue

Choosing between this famous 1965 recording and an immensely vital period-instrument performance under Nikolaus Harnoncourt (with Paul Esswood, Kurt Equiluz, Siegmund Nimsgern, Vienna Boys' Choir, Chorus Viennensis and Concentus Musicus Wien, Teldec analogue) was very difficult indeed – though, in the end, it was the superlative quality of the singing that inclined me towards this beautifully refurbished Archiv set. Richter's approach is incisive, clear-headed and deeply devotional.

Magnificat in D major, BWV243 (1723, revised 1728–31)

One of Bach's most immediately appealing sacred compositions, originally composed for Christmas 1723 then revised with added trumpets and flutes. Individual movements (12 relating the 10 verses of Luke's texts) are extraordinarily varied and frequently exciting, not least the ebullient opening "Magnificat" (My soul doth magnify the Lord) and the furiously fugal chorus "Fecit potentiam" (He has showed strength with His Arm). The final chorus is an exultant "Glory be to the Father".

 **_Maria Stader (soprano), Hertha Töpper (contralto), Ernst Haefliger (tenor), Dietrich Fischer-Dieskau (baritone), Munich Bach Choir and Orchestra/Karl Richter_**
Archiv analogue

Richter's performance is characterized by superb singing, clean execution and great firmness of rhythm. There's a fresh-toned digital alternative under John Eliot Gardiner (Philips, analogue), while Helmut Rilling's analogue recording for Sony rivals Richter's in its joyful exuberance.

Mass in B minor, BWV232 (*c*1748–49)

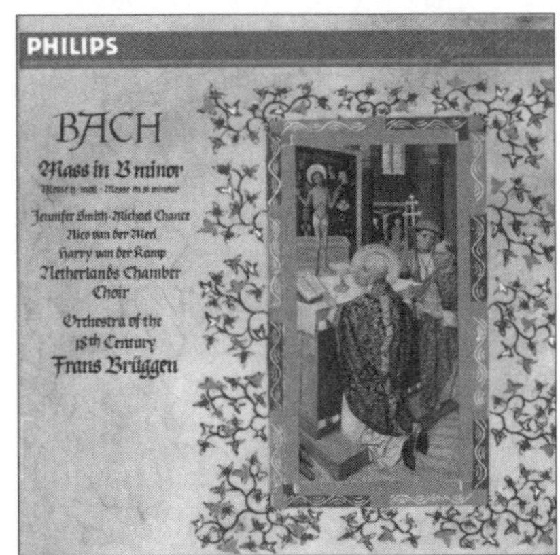

Bach compiled his "High Mass" (as it was known in the nineteenth century) from various existing works, though it is quite probable that the central section and *Sanctus*, both of which were appropriate to the Leipzig Lutheran church service, were specially composed. Although lacking the *St Matthew Passion*'s inward theatricality and sense of narrative, the B minor Mass none the less represents a high point (some would say the highest point) of Bach's choral style. Individual settings range from the long and sombre opening chorus to the pastoral "Domine Deus" for soprano, tenor, recorder and strings.

 **_Jennifer Smith (soprano), Michael Chance (countertenor), Nico van der Meel (tenor), Harry van der Kamp (bass), Netherlands Chamber Choir, Orchestra of the Eighteenth Century/Frans Brüggen_**
Philips digital

A live recording, made in Utrecht during March 1989, that combines inspirational fervour and informed scholarship. John Eliot Gardiner (Archiv, digital) is hardly less effective, whereas Karl Richter (Archiv, analogue) and Otto Klemperer (EMI, analogue) represent the 'old school' of broadly-paced, modern-instrument performances.

St John Passion, BWV245 (1724, revised *c*1730 and late-1740s)

The *St John Passion* is quite different to the majestic *St Matthew* (see below) in that it is shorter-breathed and more urgent – contrasts that are very well exemplified in the opening chorus "O Lord, our Sovereign" where the repetitions of the word "Herr" (Lord) suggest a desperate entreaty – quite unlike the noble unfolding of the *St Matthew*'s antiphonal "Come ye daughters, share my mourning…". It is a work more of community than of inward communion, but its restless spirit and glorious set pieces (especially No. 30, the alto aria "Es ist vollbracht" [It is finished], quoted by Beethoven in his Piano Sonata, Op. 110) prove consistently compelling.

Kurt Equiluz (Evangelist), Max van Egmond (Jesus), Bert van t'Hoff (tenor), Siegfried Schneeweis, Jacques Villisech (basses), soloists of the Vienna Boys' Choir, Concentus Musicus Wien/Nikolaus Harnoncourt

Teldec analogue

A pioneering, all-male production that recognizes the work's pensive spirit and features an extremely fine Evangelist in Kurt Equiluz. John Eliot Gardiner (Archiv) and Frans Brüggen (Philips) lead the digital field, while Benjamin Britten's 1971 English-language recording (Decca, analogue), although on modern instruments, displays a rare level of insight.

St Matthew Passion, BWV244 (1727)

With words by the Leipzig-based poet Christian Friedrich Henrici (known as Picander), Bach's mightiest work (which the conductor Otto Klemperer thought the greatest music ever composed) employs soloists and a double-chorus in relating the Gospel according to St Matthew, with contemplative references to the daughter of Zion, Mary and the faithful soul. The *St Matthew Passion*, which is in two parts, is so dramatic that, according to one report from the 1730s, a "pious, noble widow" was heard to scream "God save us, 'tis though one were at an opera or comedy"! The narrative is related by a tenor Evangelist, while Jesus himself, Peter and Judas are sung by baritone or bass soloists. Sample No. 63 in the score where "the veil of the temple was rent in twain" and the ensuing choral "Truly, this was the Son of God". Klemperer was surely right.

Ernst Haefliger (Evangelist), Kieth Engen (Jesus), Irmgard Seefried, Antonie Fahberg (sopranos), Hertha Töpper (mezzo-soprano), Dietrich Fischer-Dieskau (baritone), Max Proebstl (bass), Munich Bach Choir, Munich Children's Choir, Munich Bach Orchestra/Karl Richter

Archiv analogue

The sort of performance that changes lives – ardently sung, deeply devotional in spirit and with an evangelical zeal that sits at the very heart of Bach's inspiration. Klemperer's reading (EMI, analogue) is more stoical, Mengelberg's (Philips, mono – pre-war and heavily cut), more theatrical and John Eliot Gardiner's (Archiv, digital – on period instruments) more fleet of foot, but Richter's performance is in a class of its own. He recorded it twice and while his second version (with Dame Janet Baker, also for Archiv, analogue) is extremely fine, this earlier recording is far more compelling.

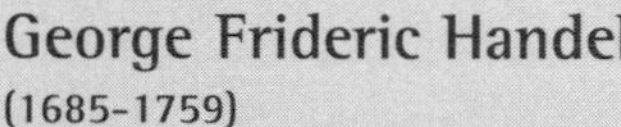

George Frideric Handel
(1685–1759)

Messiah, HWV56 (1742)

Unlike the Bach Passions, *Messiah* doesn't present a story; rather, it reflects on the events in an inspired sequence of set pieces. Handel himself conducted the work annually until his death for the benefit of the Foundling Hospital in London, to which he also gave his original manuscript. The many celebrated movements in *Messiah* include the tenor's "Comfort ye", the contralto aria "He was despised" and the soprano aria "I know that my Redeemer liveth". The many fine choruses are crowned by "Hallelujah": on composing it, Handel thought he saw all Heaven before him, "and the Great God himself".

Barbara Schlick, Sandrine Piau (sopranos), Andreas Scholl (alto), Mark Padmore (tenor), Nathan Berg (bass), Les Arts Florissants Chorus and Orchestra/William Christie

Harmonia Mundi digital

Having a male sing "He was despised" might surprise some, though even the briefest sampling of Andreas Scholl's performance should be enough to dispel any doubts. Christie's account (on period instruments) is fleet and dramatic, but there's strong competition from Ton Koopman (Erato, digital) and Sir Charles Mackerras (Mozart's orchestration, sung in German, on Archiv, analogue), not to mention magnificent vintage readings under Sir Thomas Beecham (RCA analogue, or – far older – Pearl, mono) and Hermann Scherchen (PRT, mono).

Zadok the Priest (Coronation Anthem No. 1, HWV258) (1727)

Handel's Coronation Anthems – there are three in all – celebrate George II's accession to the throne. In terms of aural splendour, they anticipate the glories of *Messiah*, *Belshazzar*, *Israel in Egypt*, *Saul* and *Samson*. *Zadok the Priest*, the most famous of the series, opens to an instrumental prelude full of excited anticipation before the principal melody (one of Handel's most noble inspirations) gives way to excited exclamations of "Alleluja" and "God Save the King".

Chorus and Orchestra of the Academy of St Martin in the Fields/Sir Neville Marriner

Philips digital

Marriner's performance combines vigour with fine singing while Philips's recording reports an appropriate degree of tonal weight. There are fine alternatives from Trevor Pinnock (DG, digital) and Sir David Willcocks (Decca, analogue).

Giovanni Battista Pergolesi (1710-1736)

Stabat mater for soprano, alto, strings and organ (1736)

A brief look at Pergolesi's birth and death dates shows us that the gods stole him young. And yet he had already made his mark with at least one significant innovation (the first *opera buffa* or comic opera). The *Stabat mater* is a consistently beautiful work that contrasts unpretentious creative novelty with music cast in a more conservative Baroque mould. There are 12 movements, which consist of a combination of arias and duets.

Mirella Freni (soprano), Teresa Berganza (mezzo-soprano), Naples Scarlatti Orchestra/Ettore Gracis

Archiv analogue

I make no apologies for choosing this warmly romanticized rendition of the Stabat mater (rather in the manner of the Italian Baroque modern-instrument group, I Musici). The style is supremely sensitive to the score's expressive language and the singing is absolutely superb. However, those who prefer 'authentic' timbres are directed to Nikolaus Harnoncourt, with Eva Mei and Sylvia McNair (Teldec, digital).

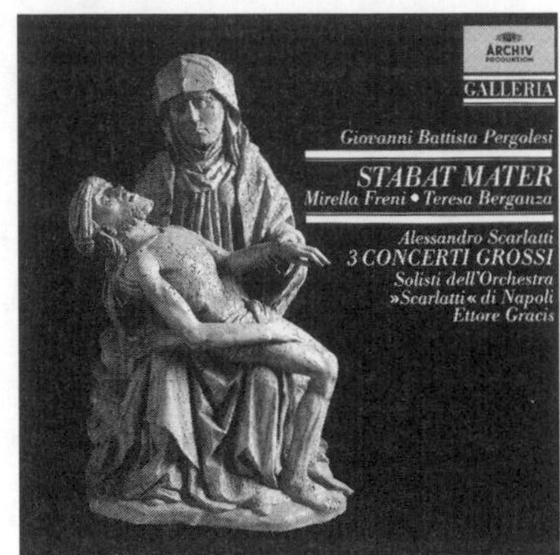

The symphonic dimension (1779-1900)

Haydn sets the scene with music that combines rigorous forms and great originality (the first few minutes of *The Creation* will confirm at least that much). However, some of Mozart's finest choral works pre-date Haydn's, whereas Beethoven's towering *Missa solemnis* forges a bridge between High Classicism and the Romantic choral masterpieces of Schubert, Brahms, Verdi, Fauré and Elgar. It might also be said that although religious denominational allegiances can (and often do) lend a certain justification to this and the surrounding sections of this book, they are by no means essential prerequisites for the appreciation of these wonderful works. Mozart, Haydn and Beethoven (to name but three) make their effect through purely musical means, while the precise complexion of their respective faiths – whether Catholic, Protestant, or whatever – can be treated as a totally separate issue.

Joseph Haydn (1732-1809)

Die Jahreszeiten (The Seasons), HobXXI/3 (1799-1801)

An exhilarating narrative on the cycles of life in nature as viewed by three peasants. Although Haydn initially found *The Seasons* hard work ("I ought never to have undertaken it," he once said; "it finished me off!") the resulting masterpiece is a radiant thanksgiving, with copious tone-painting (bleating sheep, rolling thunder, humming bees, a cock at dawn, etc) and a plethora of good tunes. It was Haydn's last large-scale work.

Gundula Janowitz (Hanne), Peter Schreier (Lukas), Martti Talvela (Simon), Chorus of the Vienna Singverein, Vienna Symphony Orchestra/Karl Böhm

Deutsche Grammophon analogue

Anyone who has heard rumours of Karl Böhm's 'dullness' (and, to be fair, there are enough recordings around to keep them alive) should hear this – one of the brightest, sweetest and most enthusiastic choral recordings in the catalogue. The singing is divine (especially from Janowitz), but be warned – the current reissue has neither texts nor translations. Sir Georg Solti (Decca) provides a good digital alternative.

Die Schöpfung (The Creation), HobXX1/2 (1796–98)

Quite what contemporary audiences made of Haydn's "Representation of Chaos" is anyone's guess: the music itself suggests total darkness, so that when the Command "Let there be Light" breaks through, the effect is breathtaking. The idea for *The Seasons* originated from Haydn's London impresario Salomon, the texts being based on a combination of the Book of Genesis and Milton in translation. Each day in the history of the Creation is musically represented, and the overall effect has a graphic vividness that borders on music drama.

Ruth Ziesak (Eva and Gabriel), Herbert Lippert (Uriel), René Pape (Raphael), Anton Scharinger (Adam), Chicago Symphony Chorus and Orchestra/ Sir Georg Solti
Decca digital

Decca's current booklet carries a testimonial by Sir Georg himself. "I was joined in my excitement and passion for this work by all my colleagues, soloists, orchestra and chorus alike," writes Solti; "rarely can I recall such exuberant joy and sheer enchantment as we shared during these Chicago concerts". That sense of involvement is vividly conveyed in the actual recording, although Leonard Bernstein's (DG, digital, or Sony, analogue) runs it close and Rafael Kubelík (Orfeo, digital) offers a profoundly poetic alternative option.

Mass No. 10 in C major, "Mass in Time of War" (Paukenmesse), HobXXII/9 (1796)

Haydn's exalted 'late' Masses (there are six of them in all) provide an essential supplement to the so-called "London" Symphonies (see "Classical models", above). The *Missa in tempore belli* (to give it its Latin title) is an extremely powerful work which reflects a period in history when Austria was at war with France and Napoleon's armies were poised for action. Haydn employs timpani and trumpets to thrilling effect.

Mass No. 11 in D minor, "Nelson Mass", HobXXII/11 (1798)

For some time it was assumed that the title reflected Haydn's gratitude to Admiral Nelson for winning the Battle of the Nile (he was thought to have been working on the Mass's "Benedictus" at the time). However, the "Nelson" reference is more likely to have honoured a four-day visit that the Admiral made some two years later. This *Mass in Distress* (its official title) is an especially brilliant work with the solo soprano taking a central role.

Patricia Wells, Judith Blegen (sopranos), Gwendolyn Killebrew (mezzo-soprano), Michael Devlin, Kenneth Riegel (tenors), Alan Titus (baritone), Simon Estes (bass), Norman Scribner Choir, Westminster Choir, New York Philharmonic Orchestra/Leonard Bernstein
Sony Classical analogue

Although somewhat questionable in terms of style (Bernstein was a decidedly 'romantic' Haydn conductor), both performances have a weight, vitality and dramatic fervour that elevate them far above the norm. The singing is generally fine while both performances suggest a genuine sense of occasion – in fact, the Mass in Time of War was recorded live in 1973 to coincide with a peace demonstration. The sound is extremely spacious, but those in search of a leaner, period-instrument account of the Nelson Mass are directed to Trevor Pinnock (Archiv, digital).

Wolfgang Amadeus Mozart
(1756–1791)

Ave verum corpus in D major for chorus, strings and organ, K618 (1791)

Just three minutes in length, *Ave verum corpus* is one of Mozart's most exquisite choral compositions, written for a church at Baden (a spar near Vienna where Mozart took the cure). The melody was originally conceived for clarinet and basset-horn and was to receive more lavish treatment when, some 96 years later, Tchaikovsky orchestrated it as part of his Fourth orchestral Suite, *Mozartiana* (see "Suites and dances", above).

Netherlands Chamber Choir, Orchestra of the Eighteenth Century/Frans Brüggen
Philips digital

An appropriately simple interpretation, sung in an unaffected and devotional manner and captured in a perfectly balanced recording. Ave verum corpus is one of Mozart's most oft-recorded compositions and there are many fine versions to choose from – from Leonard Bernstein (DG, digital) to Sir Neville Marriner and Sir Colin Davis (both Philips – digital and analogue, respectively) and William Christie (Erato, analogue).

Mass No. 16 in C major, "Coronation", K317 (1779)

Mozart's Sixteenth Mass was directed by Salieri at Leopold II's Coronation in 1791, hence the title – although the actual composition of the Mass dates from an earlier period when Mozart was court organist at Salzburg (and produced some of his finest church music). The *Coronation* Mass is concise, thematically varied and immediately appealing (sample the exhilarating *Credo* first).

Marinella Pennicchi (soprano), Catherine Patriasz (contralto), Zeger Vandersteene (tenor), Jelle Draijer (bass), Netherlands Chamber Choir, Orchestra of the Eighteenth Century/Frans Brüggen
Philips digital

Brüggen's vividly-inflected period-instrument performance certainly doesn't stint on energy and although some tempos are a mite extreme (the Credo's "Et incarnatus" episode is dramatically slow), the sum effect is both stirring and inspirational. There's also a fine modern-instrument version under Sir Colin Davis (Philips, analogue).

Mass No. 18 in C minor, "Great", K427/417*a* (unfinished) (1782-83)

Mozart's wife Constanze was fairly central both to the concept and the realization of this particular masterpiece. It was in 1782 that Mozart married her against his father's wishes and this Mass – the fulfilment of an earlier vow – served as something of an appeasement both to his earthly and his Heavenly fathers. Constanze sang the soprano part in the first performance and although originally planned on a Handelian scale, the C minor Mass remained uncompleted at the time of Mozart's death. The "Et incarnatus est" is especially beautiful.

Sylvia McNair, Diana Montague (sopranos), Anthony Rolfe Johnson (tenor), Cornelius Hauptmann (bass), Monteverdi Choir, English Baroque Soloists/John Eliot Gardiner
Philips digital

The singing is superb, the musical approach lean, dramatic and scholarly. Gardiner has made some corrections to Alois Schmitt's re-construction (principally to the Credo, with rewritten string parts for the "Et incarnatus est" that fit Mozart's style better than Schmitt's version). The recording is first-rate.

Mass No. 19 in D minor, "Requiem", K626 (1791)

A stranger dressed in grey visited the mortally ill composer to commission a Requiem, but wished to remain anonymous (we now know that this was Count Franz Walsegg-Stuppach, who regularly passed others' works off as his own). Convinced that the Requiem was for his own funeral, indeed that someone was trying to poison him, Mozart never completed the score and it was left to his pupil Süssmayr to add the finishing touches. Circumstances of composition apart, the Requiem remains among Mozart's most compelling and enduring works – the magnificent opening chorus being particularly impressive.

Rachel Yakar (soprano), Ortrun Wenkel (contralto), Kurt Equiluz (tenor), Robert Holl (bass), Vienna State Opera Chorus, Concentus Musicus Wien/Nikolaus Harnoncourt
Teldec digital

Startlingly dramatic and extremely well sung. Harnoncourt's 1980s (period-instrument) recording certainly pulls no punches, but competition is especially fierce in this work (its use in the film Amadeus granted it almost cult status) and there are fine rivals under Peter Schreier (Philips, digital), Sir Colin Davis (Philips, digital) and many others.

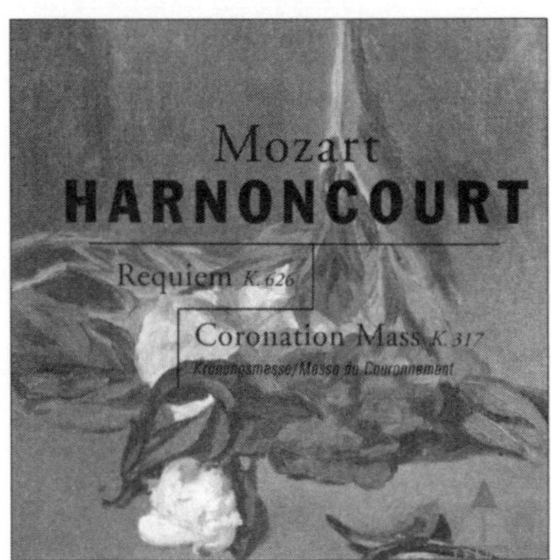

Ludwig van Beethoven
(1770–1827)

Missa solemnis in D major, Op. 123 (1818–23)

Beethoven's supreme vocal masterpiece makes considerable technical demands on its interpreters, yet its inspirational flight is so consistently high that performers invariably relish the struggle. The *Credo* in particular is unique in its fervent expression and forward momentum, while the *Benedictus* features a sublime violin solo (as beautiful as anything in the Violin Concerto) and the *Agnus Dei*, a manner of drama that one would normally expect only from an opera. The *Missa* is significantly indebted to early music, a fact that registers in some notably transparent counterpoint.

 ***Zinka Milanov (soprano), Bruna Castagna (alto), Jüssi Björling (tenor), Alexander Kipnis (bass), Westminster Choir, NBC Symphony Orchestra/Arturo Toscanini***

Music & Arts mono

Toscanini's drive is matched by an unerring sense of musical structure and some exceedingly fine singing. True, the 1940 recording is sonically somewhat compromised – but the performance itself is so compelling that you hardly notice. This is the second and best of Toscanini's three recordings of the Missa solemnis (1935, 1940, 1953), but if the mono sound proves problematic, you'll find excellent versions under John Eliot Gardiner (Archiv, digital), Leonard Bernstein (Concertgebouw, DG, or New York Philharmonic, Sony – both are analogue) and Rafael Kubelík (Bavarian RSO, Orfeo, analogue).

Franz Schubert (1797-1828)

Mass No. 6 in E flat major, D950 (1828)

The most striking anticipations here are of Anton Bruckner – especially at the start of the *Gloria* or the *Sanctus* (perhaps the most disquieting moments in the score). Schubert's last Mass inhabits the same dramatic and mysterious realms as his last quartets, piano sonatas and songs – although its melodic writing is often as distinctive as in the finest Lieder (try the *Rosamunde*-type melody 2'23" into the *Credo* on our recommended recording, or the start of the *Agnus Dei*, with its echoes of Schubert's late song "Der Doppelgänger" [from *Schwanengesang* – see "Wayfarers and wanderers", above]).

 ***Benjamin Schmidinger (treble), Albin Lenzer (alto), Jörg Hering (tenor), Kurt Azesberger (tenor), Harry van der Kamp (bass), Vienna Boys' Choir, Chorus Viennensis, Orchestra of the Age of Enlightenment/Bruno Weil***

Sony Classical digital

With fine (all-male) solo singing and the dramatic sonorities of period instruments ('authentic' timpani and brass underpin the terror), this must rank as among the most compelling versions of a very great score. Modern-instrument rivals under Wolfgang Sawallisch (EMI or Philips, analogue – I'd personally go for the earlier Philips recording) and Claudio Abbado (DG, digital) are also well worth considering.

Hector Berlioz (1803-1869)

L'enfance du Christ, Op. 25 (1850-54)

A work that marries delicacy, tenderness and drama (witness Herod's recitative – on track 3 of our recommended recording). Based mainly on the second chapter of the Gospel according to St Matthew, Berlioz's 'sacred trilogy' (the three parts are separated by an Overture and a Trio for two flutes and harp) replaces the Magi from the Orient with evil soothsayers from Judea – who hear the prophecy of Christ's destiny from Herod's lips (in a dream) and advise "The Massacre of the Innocents". Perhaps the work's most famous passage is the beautiful "Shepherds' Farewell", a choral-orchestral Overture that opens Part 2, "The Flight from Egypt".

 ***Cesare Valletti (Narrator and Centurion), Florence Kopleff (Mary), Gérard Souzay (Joseph), Giorgio Tozzi (Polydorus, Herod, The Father of a Family), New England Conservatory Chorus, Boston Symphony Orchestra/Charles Munch***

RCA analogue

My principal reason for choosing this nicely refurbished 1956 recording is Charles Munch, whose dedicated direction and faultless sense of line highlight all that is lyrical in this marvellous score. The Boston strings have a silken sheen while, among the singers, Souzay and Valletti are especially convincing. The chorus is ardently enthusiastic but rather closely balanced, which is why some readers may prefer the truer perspectives and greater atmosphere of Sir Colin Davis's first recording (Decca, analogue).

Grande messe des morts (Requiem), Op. 5 (1837)

Completed in just three to four months, Berlioz's *Grande messe des morts* was originally commissioned as a commemoration for those who had fallen in the July Revolution of 1830. It's therefore hardly surprising that this most ceremonial of Requiems calls for (and here I quote the composer's stated requirements) 108 strings, four flutes, two oboes, two cor anglais, four clarinets, eight bassoons, 12 horns (six in C and six in E flat), four additional brass groups and a huge chorus. The Requiem's most celebrated episode – the one that calls for deafening volleys for brass and big drums – is the "Tuba mirum" ("The trumpet ... summons all before the throne").

Ronald Dowd (tenor), Dennis Wick (trombone), Wandsworth School Boys' Choir, John Alldis Choir, London Symphony Chorus and Orchestra/Sir Colin Davis

Philips analogue

Sir Colin Davis is one of the most perceptive Berlioz conductors of the last 50 years and has achieved wide acclaim with his multi-CD Philips Berlioz cycle. This recording forms part of that worthy undertaking and is notable for its drama, clarity of vision and sense of atmosphere. Viable rivals include Charles Munch in Boston (RCA, analogue) and Lorin Maazel in Cleveland (Decca, analogue – and with an especially powerful "Tuba mirum").

Felix Mendelssohn (1809-1847)

Elijah (1846)

"I am jumping about my room for joy. If it only turns out to be half as good as I believe it is, how pleased I shall be!" So wrote Mendelssohn regarding a masterpiece that was commissioned by the Birmingham Music Festival and that the composer later presented to Queen Victoria. Post-Bachian in tone and dramatic impact, *Elijah* is rich in memorable solos, duets and choruses.

Theo Adam (bass), Elly Ameling (soprano), Peter Schreier (tenor), etc, Rundfunkchor and Leipzig Gewandhaus Orchestra/Wolfgang Sawallisch

Philips analogue

"Elijah" or "Elias" (as it's known in German) – which to choose? This is the latter, rendered German and given a positively thrilling performance. Sawallisch's direction is honest, wholesome, even exultant (try the chorus "Be not afraid"), but those requiring the English version should opt either for the gentler Rafael Frühbeck de Burgos (with Dame Janet Baker, EMI, analogue) or the vintage Sir Malcolm Sargent (Dutton, mono).

Giuseppe Verdi (1813-1901)

Messa da Requiem (1874)

Verdi's tribute to his compatriot, the poet Manzoni, is one of the true masterpieces of his later years; in fact, it's probably the greatest Mass setting after Beethoven's *Missa solemnis*. Often criticized for being "overly operatic", the Requiem suggests burning sincerity expressed without the least inhibition. Best-known is the searing *Dies irae*, with its thundering bass drum, but the score's lyrical portions – and there are many – are scarcely less impressive.

Maria Stader (soprano), Oralia Dominguez (mezzo-soprano), Gabor Carelli (tenor), Ivan Sardi (bass), St Hedwig's Cathedral Choir, RIAS Symphony Orchestra, Berlin/ Ferenc Fricsay

Deutsche Grammophon mono

Toscanini's searing interpretations of 1940 (Music & Arts, mono) and 1951 (RCA, mono) are among the most thrilling imaginable and to recommend another will strike some as simply perverse. And yet Fricsay's (beautifully sung) live recording, made when he was already mortally ill with cancer, has a power, humility and depth of perception that reach to the very heart of this marvellous work. Carlo Maria Giulini (EMI, analogue) is also impressive, while Claudio Abbado (DG) offers a fine digital option.

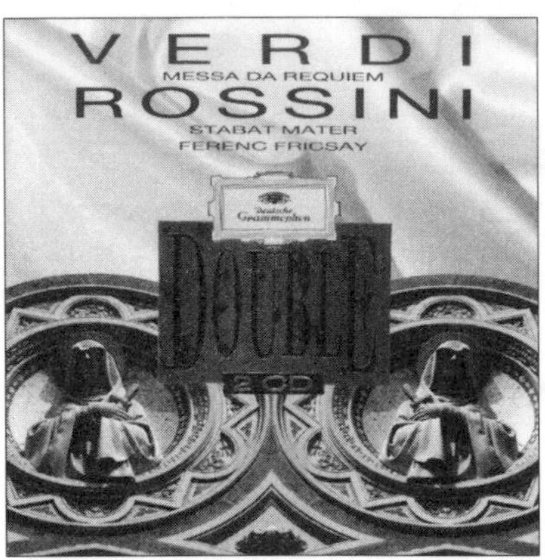

Anton Bruckner (1824-1896)

Mass No. 3 in F minor for soloists, chorus and orchestra (1868)

Long thought of as a pious, naïve figure with no life outside religion and music, Bruckner is now beginning to emerge as someone who enjoyed such 'profane' pleasures as dancing, swimming and the opposite sex. These are important considerations, especially when assessing a work – such as the great F minor Mass – that celebrates God in terms of both unshakeable faith and worldly affirmation. The musical language is rapt, mysterious and unstintingly bold, the sort with which fans of the great Bruckner symphonies will already be familiar (try the *Credo*'s mighty fugue – 8'27" into the relevant track on our recommended version).

 ***Maria Stader (soprano), Claudia Hellmann (contralto), Ernst Haefliger (tenor), Kim Borg (bass), Anton Nowakowski (organ), Bavarian Radio Chorus and Symphony Orchestra/Eugen Jochum***

Deutsche Grammophon analogue

The brothers Eugen and Georg Ludwig Jochum were well-known champions of Bruckner, Eugen being the more 'spiritual' interpreter (rather in the manner of Wilhelm Furtwängler), Georg Ludwig the more 'objective'. This particular performance marries devotional reverence with a wholly appropriate dynamism. The singing is excellent and the 1962 sound still extremely good. Franz Welser-Möst's highly mobile EMI (digital) recording makes for a satisfying second choice.

Te Deum (1881-84)

The sheer physicality of the opening pages recall the great Bruckner symphonies (the Eighth in particular) and it is therefore hardly surprising that, after Bruckner's death, the *Te Deum* was occasionally used as a 'finale' to the uncompleted Ninth Symphony (nowadays, of course, the 'real' finale is available in at least two reconstructions). Attentive Brucknerians will spot unmistakable references to the Seventh Symphony's *Adagio* in the *Te Deum*'s last movement.

 ***Jane Eaglen (soprano), Birgit Remmert (contralto), Deon van der Walt (tenor), Alfred Muff (bass), Mozart Chorus, Linz, London Philharmonic Orchestra/Franz Welser-Möst***

EMI digital

A hugely dynamic reading, very well sung (especially by the chorus) and with the 'ad libertum' organ part clearly audible. Welser-Möst's fondness for faster-than-usual tempos sends Bruckner sky-bound, but those who prefer a more 'churchy' alternative are directed to beautifully sung performances under Eugen Jochum (DG, analogue) or Rudolf Kempe (EMI, mono).

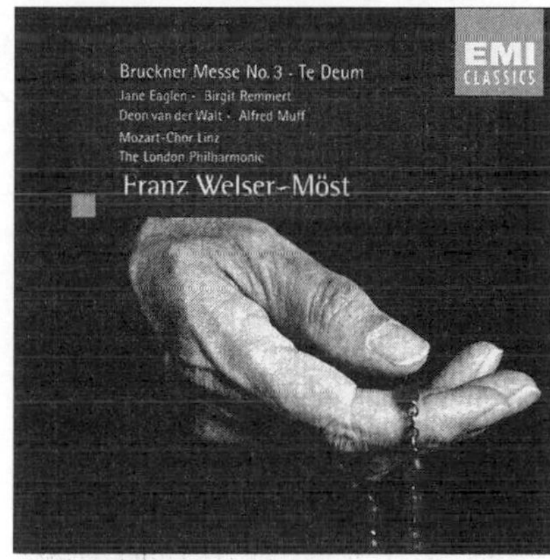

Johannes Brahms (1833-1897)

A German Requiem (Ein Deutsches Requiem), Op. 45 (1857-68)

An epic Requiem that, rather than concentrate on sin or punishment, comforts those who mourn, who suffer and who are in need of consolation. Brahms employs his large forces with the utmost restraint, although the dark, processional "Denn alles Fleisch ist wie Gras" (For all flesh is as grass - the second movement) is immensely powerful (it was originally intended as the slow movement to Brahms's First Piano Concerto - see "The Great Romantics", above). The texts, which were selected by the composer himself, are taken from the Lutheran Bible.

 ***Elisabeth Schwarzkopf (soprano), Dietrich Fischer-Dieskau (baritone), Philharmonia Chorus, Philharmonia Orchestra/Otto Klemperer***

EMI analogue

Klemperer's account has a sense of inevitability that is notably impressive in the second movement. The singing - both of the soloists and of the chorus - is superb, though earlier (mono) recordings by Bruno Walter (fiery and swift, Sony) and Rudolf Kempe (humble and warmly phrased, EMI) are equally valid. The best digital alternative - a dramatic rendition on period instruments - is conducted by John Eliot Gardiner (Philips).

Antonin Dvořák (1841-1904)

Requiem Mass, B165 (Op. 89) (1890)

It might seem odd to speak in terms of a 'sunny' Requiem and, to be sure, Dvořák's choral masterpiece does also contain many instances of overt drama (not least in an agitated *Dies irae*). However, the overriding impression is of faith, consolation and a characteristic oneness with nature, and never more so than a very poignant moment in the "Recordare" (disc 1, track 6 on our recommended recording) where - at 5'34" - the four soloists sing *a cappella* (unaccompanied) followed by a lyrical string passage that is quintessentially Dvořákian.

 ***Maria Stader (soprano), Sieglinde Wagner (contralto), Ernst Haefliger (tenor), Kim Borg (bass), Czech Philharmonic Choir, and Orchestra/ Karel Ančerl***

Deutsche Grammophon analogue

A superb line-up of singers (all of them mainstays of DG's catalogue of the time) join an orchestra-conductor combination that was responsible for some of the greatest Dvořák recordings of the stereo era. How could you go wrong? The late-1950s analogue sound is warm and spacious.

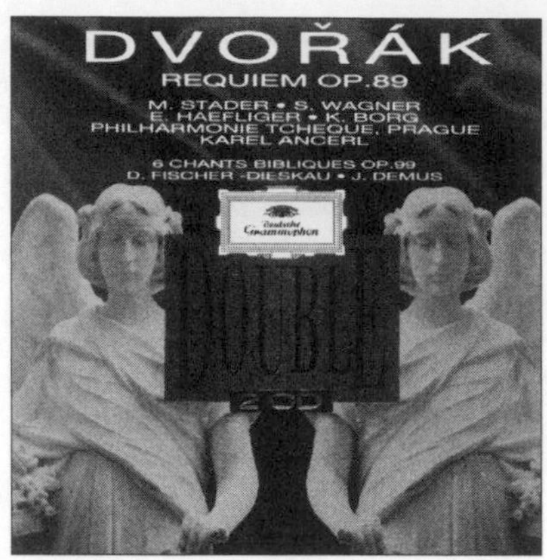

Gabriel Fauré (1845-1924)

Requiem for soprano, baritone, chorus and orchestra, Op. 48 (1888, revised 1890)
One of the most sublime religious works of the late-nineteenth century is best known to us in an orchestral version that's quite different to Fauré's comparatively dark-toned original. The edition performed here was premièred in 1888 and is scored for solo violin, divided violas and cellos (no massed violins), basses, a harp, timpani and organ. The "Offertory" and "Libera me" (which incorporates three trombones) were added a little later. The great beauty of Fauré's writing remains (note, in particular, "Pie Jesu" and "In paradisum") but textures are more sombre – and more dramatic – than we're used to.

 ***Catherine Bott (soprano), Gilles Cachemaille (baritone), Monteverdi Choir, Salisbury Cathedral Boy Choristers, Orchestre Révolutionnaire et Romantique/ John Eliot Gardiner***
Philips digital
A period-instrument performance that combines dramatic inflexion with sensitive phrase-shaping and fine singing. The recording, too, is first-rate, but if you'd rather stay with the brighter re-orchestration, then Charles Dutoit (Decca, digital) or Ernest Ansermet (Decca, analogue) provide two of the finest versions on disc.

Sir Edward Elgar (1857-1934)

The Dream of Gerontius, Op. 38 (1900)
Richard Strauss deemed Elgar's masterpiece about the soul's judgement and salvation as a "work of the first order almost throughout". Ernest Newman spoke of "a rounded completeness of vision that only comes when the artist sees his picture through and through in one white heat of imagination". Elgar himself wrote that "This is the best of me ... This I saw and knew; this, if anything of mine, is worth your memory." Among *Gerontius*'s greatest moments are the magnificent Prelude and the chorus "Praise to the Holiest".

 ***Peter Pears (Gerontius), Yvonne Minton (The Angel), John Shirley-Quirk (The Priest/The Angel of the Agony), London Symphony Chorus, Choir of King's College, Cambridge, London Symphony Orchestra/Benjamin Britten***
Decca analogue
Britten grants Gerontius dignity, spirituality and, above all, clarity. Peter Pears might not be everyone's ideal for the main protagonist (the voice, although used with supreme sensitivity, is a mite unsteady), but his responsiveness to Cardinal Newman's text is second to none. Britten's strongest rival is a 1945 recording under Sir Malcolm Sargent, with Heddle Nash as Gerontius (Testament, mono).

Modern man praises God (1915-1988)

The twentieth century has witnessed a crisis in religious faith, and with good reason: listen to Schoenberg's harrowing *A Survivor from Warsaw* (see below) and at least one of those reasons becomes abundantly clear. But there are also such inspirational flights of faith as Janáček's raw though immensely colourful *Glagolitic Mass*, Kodály's passionately patriotic *Psalmus hungaricus* and Steve Reich's foot-tapping *Tehillim* ("Psalms").

Leoš Janáček (1854-1928)

Glagolitic Mass (1926, revised 1929)
Janáček's late choral masterpiece (he was 72 when he composed it) is forged of earth and

spirit. Although set to Old Slavonic texts (hence the word 'Glagolitic'), it violated the Eastern Church tradition by including instruments along with the voices. In a good performance the Mass's sum effect is leapingly spontaneous: there are thrilling orchestral interludes, wild choral passages, haunting quiet episodes and a manic organ solo.

Tina Kiberg (soprano), Randi Stene (contralto), Peter Svensson (tenor), Ulrik Cold (bass), Danish National Choir, Danish National Radio Symphony Orchestra/Sir Charles Mackerras

Chandos digital

This is the original version of Janáček's score and very much more exciting than the more familiar revision (it includes some extraordinary timpani writing, plus other instances of striking instrumentation that Janáček had to modify because the performing resources at his disposal were relatively inadequate). The finest recordings of the more temperate revision are conducted by Karel Ančerl (Supraphon) and Rafael Kubelík (DG). Both are analogue, but Mackerras's performance is equally well conducted (if not quite as well sung).

Sergey Rachmaninov (1873–1943)

Vespers for unaccompanied chorus (1915)

I would challenge anyone to find a piece of unaccompanied choral music more beautiful or affecting than the *Gloria* or "Great Doxology" from Rachmaninov's Vespers (also known as the "All-Night Vigil"). The score incorporates authentic chant from the Russian Orthodox Church but, such is Rachmaninov's identification with the idiom, that only the most seasoned liturgical music experts will easily differentiate between 'ancient' and (relatively) 'modern'. Although *a cappella* (unaccompanied), the Vespers abound in tonal and melodic contrasts.

Swedish Radio Choir/Tõnu Kaljuste

Virgin Classics digital

An especially ethereal rendition, beautifully sung and superbly recorded. Those who prefer a more authentically Russian sound are directed either to the St Petersburg Capella (Chant du Monde "Russian Season") or the St Petersburg Chamber Choir (Philips). Both are digital recordings.

Arnold Schoenberg (1874–1951)

A Survivor from Warsaw for narrator, male voices and orchestra, Op. 46 (1947)

The real survivor had experienced the horrors of the Warsaw Ghetto and Schoenberg's harrowing narrative (just seven minutes in length) opens dramatically before instigating a painful procession of tortured victims. Within seconds, a brutal Nazi sergeant screams his orders and the hapless Jewish innocents are driven to their "final stampede". Schoenberg's mini-masterpiece (the text is his own) climaxes to the most important prayer in Jewish liturgy, "Shm'a Yisroël" – "Hear O Israel! The Lord our God, The Lord is One".

Gottfried Hornik (narrator), Male Choir of the Concert Chorus of the Vienna State Opera, Vienna Philharmonic Orchestra/Claudio Abbado

Deutsche Grammophon digital

Hornik's narration is chilling in the extreme while Abbado inspires an unusually expressive accompaniment: although the sum effect is powerful, one is left humbled rather than exhausted. Abbado and Hornik collaborate for what is surely the most profoundly poetic account on disc.

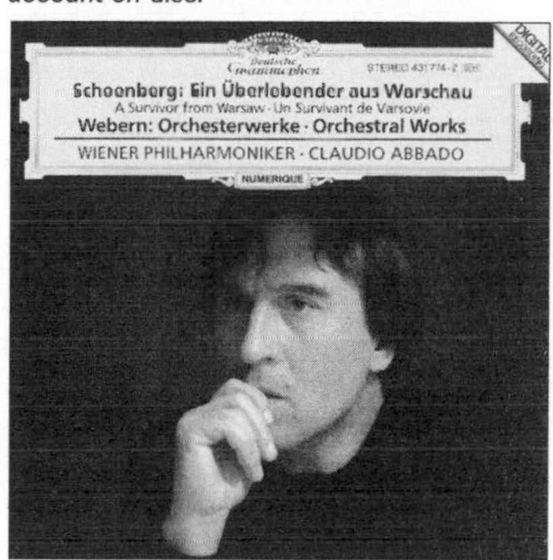

Zoltán Kodály (1882–1967)

Psalmus hungaricus (1923)

Kodály's masterpiece sets an old Hungarian text adapted from the Penitential Psalms and was composed in celebration of the fiftieth anniversary of the union of the cities Buda and Pest. The theme concerns David, who pleads with the Lord to deliver him from the persecution of his enemies. The second movement includes a chilling passage (2'14" into track 2 of our recommended recording) where the tenor soloist cries "May bitter death strike him down" [i.e. he who I thought to be my friend]. Both the music and the text reflect the political turmoil that Hungary was suffering at the time.

Lajos Kozma (tenor), Brighton Festival Chorus, Wandsworth School Boys' Choir, London Symphony Orchestra/István Kertész

Decca analogue

A performance of the utmost passion and intensity, beautifully sung and dynamically recorded. Good rivals are thin on the ground, but I would strongly recommend you hear a riveting 1959 German-language live recording with Ernst Haefliger, the St Hedwig's Cathedral Choir and the Berlin Radio Symphony Orchestra under the great Ferenc Fricsay (DG, analogue).

Sir William Walton (1902-1983)

Belshazzar's Feast, cantata (1930-31, revised 1948 and 1957)

The sheer physical excitement generated by *Belshazzar's Feast* (the score calls for antiphonal choruses plus multiple brass and percussion) has assured its lasting popularity with a wide public. Stravinsky, Elgar and plainsong are audible influences, but Walton's own sense of ceremony informs such memorable passages as the march "Praise ye the God of Gold" and the closing sequence "Then sing aloud to our God of strength": one single fanfare - and you immediately know the composer. *Belshazzar's Feast* opens to Isaiah's terrible prophecy and ends with the death of the Babylonian king and jubilation of the captives. The text was arranged from biblical sources by Osbert Sitwell.

 ***Gwynne Howell (baritone), Bach Choir Philharmonia Orchestra/ Sir David Willcocks***

Chandos digital

An extraordinarily fine performance, well balanced yet with plenty of weight from chorus and brass. The 1989 sound is superb, but those not averse to analogue sound should note that Walton's own (second) version from 30 years earlier is extremely exciting (EMI, analogue - although his first, made 16 years before that [also for EMI, but in mono] is more exciting still). I'd also recommend a fiery American recording with the Rutgers University Chorus and the Philadelphia Orchestra under Eugene Ormandy (Sony, analogue).

Benjamin Britten (1913-1976)

War Requiem, Op. 66 (1961)

The *Die irae* opens like an echo from some distant trench, then flares to a rage of drums and trumpets. It is one of the most chilling passages in a work that sets the text of the Latin Mass in combination with selected poems by Wilfred Owen. The *War Requiem* symbolizes the horror and the pity of war; it was first performed at the consecration of the new Coventry Cathedral (the old Cathedral was destroyed by bombs during World War Two) and owes something of its desolate power to the influences of Shostakovich and Mahler.

 ***Galina Vishnevskaya (soprano), Peter Pears (tenor), Dietrich Fischer-Dieskau (baritone), The Bach Choir, London Symphony Chorus and Orchestra/Benjamin Britten***

Decca analogue

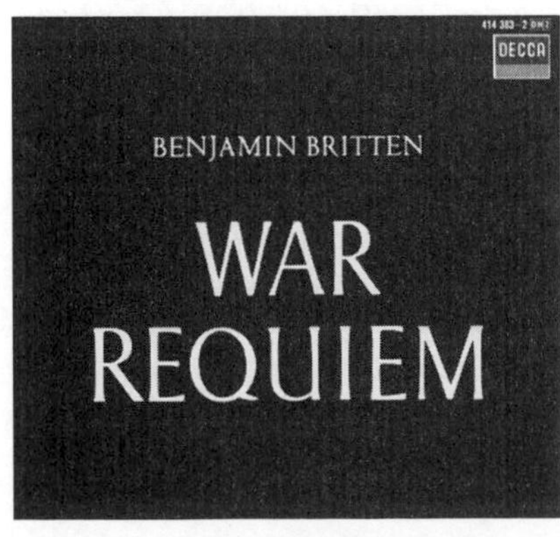

The combination of Britten's masterful conducting (where every nuance seems so exactly 'right') and supremely sensitive singing keep this superb 1963 recording securely in the front running - and that in spite of strong digital competition from Sir Simon Rattle (EMI) and Richard Hickox (Chandos).

Arvo Pärt (b1935)

Te Deum (1984-86)

It's as if the ancient past has suddenly invaded the present. Pärt's *Te Deum* steals the air over a bass pedal - sullen, powerful and full of longing. The style suggests Renaissance choral masters, the chiming of bells and the austerity of the Eastern Church. There are some fairly agitated string interludes and an especially riveting climax (from, say, 24'00" on our recommended recording) where a dark drone suggests some mighty power descended to earth. The closing pages are extraordinarily ethereal. *Te Deum* was commissioned by West German Radio.

 ***Estonian Philharmonic Chamber Choir, Tallinn Chamber Orchestra/Tonu Kaljuste***

ECM digital

A superb performance that's as much the result of imaginative production as of fine singing and playing. ECM's recording is an object-lesson in perfectly judged perspectives.

Steve Reich (b1936)

Tehillim (Psalms) for women's voices and instruments (1981)

One of the most approachable choral pieces

of the last 50 years. *Tehillim* (pronounced 'teh-hill-léem') opens as a solo with drum and clapping accompaniment, then adds a clarinet, a second voice, maracas, more voices, organ and so on, so that the texture becomes both fuller and more adventurous. There's a subdued slow movement and a catchy finale - a sort of Swingles-Stravinsky synthesis (very roughly speaking) and maddeningly moreish.

 ***Steve Reich and Musicians/George Manahan***

ECM analogue

A lean, lively performance and a good recording - although the bass-line is perhaps just a fraction lacking in body. There's a good digital alternative under Reinbert de Leeuw (Nonesuch) but Manahan's performance is the more incisive of the two.

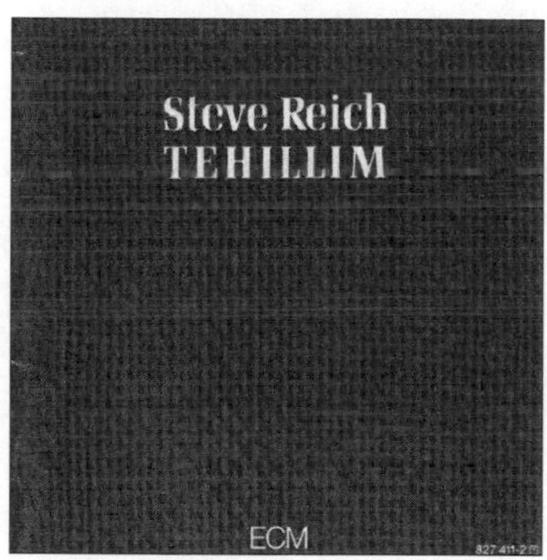

Further listening *Francis Poulenc's Gloria was one of the last - and finest - works by a twentieth-century master, and Leonard Bernstein's analogue Sony recording is among the best ever made. Avro Pärt's St John Passion is a rivetting masterpiece built on a minimum of musical material (Paul Hillier, ECM, digital) and Szymanowski penned a Sabat Mater that should be far better known (Sir Simon Rattle, EMI, digital).*

Voices out of church (1692-1941)

Weddings, wars and celebrations of all kinds, ranging in style from Purcell's Ode to the Patron Saint of music and a seven-minute "Chaldean incantation" by Prokofiev to the primitivistic stamping of Carl Orff's perennially popular *Carmina Burana*.

Henry Purcell (1659 1695)

St Cecilia's Day Ode, "Hail, bright Cecilia" (1692)

The patron saint of music was highly significant for Henry Purcell, who had commemorated her in various scores and actually died on the eve of her name day. Best-known among Purcell's Cecilian works is this 1692 Ode which, according to the *Gentleman's Journal*, was greeted at its première with "universal applause, particularly the second Stanza ['Tis Nature's Voice] which was sung with incredible Graces by Mr. Purcell himself". A heady sequence of solos, duets and choruses, the Ode's high point is the magnificent chorus "Soul of the World".

 ***Simon Woolf (treble), Paul Esswood, Roland Tatnell (countertenors), Alexander Young (tenor), Michael Rippon, John Shirley-Quirk (basses), Tiffin Choir, Ambrosian Singers, English Chamber Orchestra/Sir Charles Mackerras***

Archiv analogue

A strong, vigorous performance, expertly sung (Simon Woolf is especially agile), stylishly played and cleanly recorded. A rival recording under John Eliot Gardiner (Erato, digital) is also worthy of attention.

Johann Sebastian Bach (1685-1750)

Cantata No. 202, "Weichet nur, betrübte Schatten" (Wedding Cantata) (?1718-23)

Although this adorable cantata was originally composed as 'table' music for performance during banquets, it has a sublimity that quite transcends its domestic setting. There are five major arias, each with its attendant recitative and while it would be difficult to single out one movement as 'the best', "Sich üben im Lieben" (0'52" into track 10 on our recommended CD) is pretty irresistible.

 ***Kathleen Battle (soprano), soloists from the Ravinia Music Festival/James Levine***

RCA analogue

Quite aside from Battle's delightfully sweet-toned singing and the snug, closely balanced sound, this marvellous recording features superb instrumental contributions from such front-ranking players as Samuel Magad (violin), Frank Miller (cello), Ray Still (oboe) and Levine himself on harpsichord. As to viable rivals (Levine's performance isn't available at the time of writing), I'd go for Elly Ameling with Collegium Aureum (Deutsche Harmonia Mundi, analogue) or Barbara Hendricks with Peter Schreier conducting (EMI, digital).

Cantata No. 211, "Schweigt stille, plaudert nicht" (Coffee Cantata) (1734-35)

It may seem fickle to include this relatively

undemanding secular cantata when lack of space bars so many of Bach's great sacred cantatas the sheer wit and elegance of this celebration – and condemnation – of the "brown poison" earns it a justified place within our collection. The libretto concerns a daughter who agrees to give up coffee if her father agrees to find her a husband. Bach himself actually directed the work at Zimmermann's coffee house in Leipzig.

 ***Edith Mathis (soprano), Peter Schreier (tenor), Theo Adam (bass), Berlin Chamber Orchestra/Peter Schreier***

Archiv analogue

Stylish, even aristocratic singing (especially from the 'father' Theo Adam) although an earlier analogue recording (this one – which is excellent – dates from 1975) featuring Dietrich Fischer-Dieskau (EMI) is also well worth searching out. Gustav Leonhardt's digital Philips version (with Barbara Bonney) is another firm recommendation.

Hector Berlioz (1803-1869)

La Damnation de Faust, dramatic legend, Op. 24 (1854-56)

Berlioz himself describes Faust's birth-pangs: "It was during a concert tour of Austria, Hungary, Bohemia and Silesia," he writes, "... I journeyed along in my old German post-wagon ... writing when and where I could – in the coach, on the train, aboard ship". Ideas flooded forth and the resulting "dramatic legend" is among the composer's most compelling works. It opens on a plain in Hungary (Part One climaxes with the famous "Rakóczy March"), before Méphistophélès promises to fulfil all Faust's wishes, Faust falls in love with Marguérite, signs a pact with the Devil and descends to Hell while the Angels lead Marguérite to Heaven.

 ***Consuelo Rubio (Marguérite), Richard Verreau (Faust), Michel Roux (Méphistophélès), Pierre Mollet (Brander), Elisabeth Brasseur Chorale, RTF Children's Chorus, Lamoureux Orchestra, Paris/Igor Markevitch***

Deutsche Grammophon analogue

The most imaginative Damnation of Faust ever recorded, and singularly effective where ghostly spectres predominate (which they frequently do). Markevitch's conducting has real panache and the singing is largely above average, though there's a good digital alternative under Sir Georg Solti (with Frederica von Stade and Kenneth Riegel, Decca).

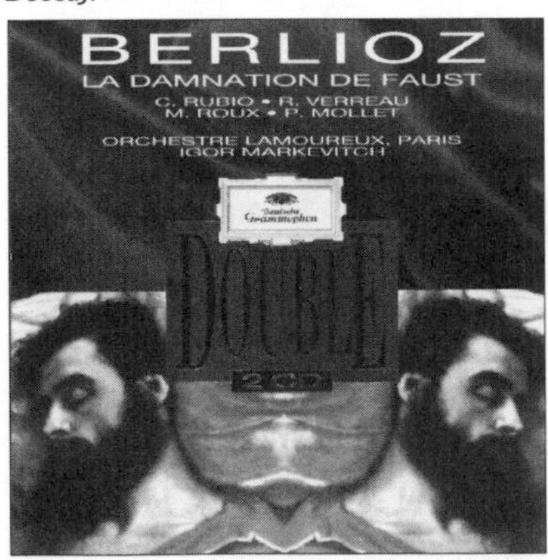

Johannes Brahms (1833-1879)

Alto Rhapsody for contralto, male voices and orchestra, Op. 53 (1869)

A wedding present for Clara Schumann's daughter, "but it is with bitterness that I write such a thing – in anger," wrote Brahms. Was he in love with her? The score itself – which sets words by Goethe about despair and potential sources of joy – opens to a forceful lunge on lower strings and a lonely alto monologue before the chorus enters with a particularly beautiful, hymn-like melody.

 ***Aafje Heynis (contralto), Vienna Symphony Orchestra/Wolfgang Sawallisch***

Philips analogue

A little-known singer whose tonal lustre rivals that of Kathleen Ferrier (Decca, mono) and whose feeling for words is especially acute. Sawallisch's accompaniment is warmly accommodating though there's an even finer (and earlier) Heynis recording, also for Philips (mono this time), with the Concertgebouw Orchestra under Eduard van Beinum. Of modern alternatives, I would particularly recommend the one with Jard van Nes under Herbert Blomstedt (Decca, digital).

Sir Edward Elgar (1857-1934)

The Music Makers, Op. 69 (1912)

"In interpreting the Ode [by Arthur O'Shaughnessy], I have felt that this 'music makers' must include not only poets and singers but all artists who feel the tremendous responsibility of their mission 'to renew the world as of yore'." Elgar's own words provide a conceptual subtext, while the score itself alternates deep introspection with what the composer himself described as "bursts of joy occasionally approaching frenzy". There are various self-quotations, including a particularly moving choral setting of "Nimrod".

Jean Rigby (mezzo-soprano), BBC Symphony Chorus and Orchestra/Andrew Davis
Teldec digital
Although both Sir Adrian Boult and Sir Malcolm Sargent gave fine performances of The Music Makers (both interpretations survive on analogue CDs, the former on EMI, the latter on Intaglio), Andrew Davis shows a particular understanding of the work's melancholic – even troubled – spirit. His handling of the quieter passages (of which there are many) is quite magical, and the recording is excellent.

Frederick Delius (1862-1934)

A Mass of Life, for soloists, chorus and orchestra, RTII/4 (1898, 1904-05)
A choral epic that combines moments of deep introspection with sudden, coruscating outbursts and many lyrical passages. Like Strauss, Mahler and various other composers of the period, Delius was both fascinated and exhilarated by the writings of Nietzsche. The *Mass of Life* (or "Eine Messe des Lebens", to give it its German title) uses texts from Nietzsche's philosophical poem *Also sprach Zarathustra*, and the musical style – which is typically Delian in its hedonistic harmonies – straddles the late-nineteenth and early-twentieth centuries.

Further listening *Lovers of Elgar's The Dream of Gerontius should enjoy The Kingdom (either under Richard Hickox, Chandos, digital, or Sir Adrian Boult, EMI, analogue), while Brahms's stirring Song of the Fates fares particularly well under Toscanini's baton (RCA, mono).*

Heather Harper (soprano), Helen Watts (contralto), Robert Tear (tenor), Benjamin Luxon (baritone), London Philharmonic Chorus and Orchestra/Sir Charles Groves
EMI analogue
A fine, well-sung performance, perceptively conducted by Groves. There's an older recording under Sir Thomas Beecham (Sony, mono) which, although undeniably impressive, has the solo voices balanced far too close to the microphones. We are sorely in need of a compelling digital version of this still-underrated score.

Sea Drift for baritone, chorus and orchestra, RTII/3 (1903-04)
The ineffable sadness of a young bird-watcher as he empathizes with a bird crying for its lost mate inspired Delius to unprecedented creative heights. This is the most exalted manner of tone painting, a passionate, tearful sigh though not without moments of drama. Furthermore, *Sea Drift* is among the most powerful musical expressions of personal loss ever composed (in that respect at least, it fully compares with the last movement of Mahler's *Das Lied von der Erde* – see "The new symphony", above). The words are taken from Walt Whitman's *Leaves of Grass* and their setting is surpassingly beautiful.

Gordon Clinton (baritone), Chorus, Royal Philharmonic Orchestra/Sir Thomas Beecham
EMI mono
Beecham made three recordings of Sea Drift, but this one (dating from 1951 though not commercially released until 1992) combines the ardour of the first version with the delicate sensibilities of the third. Gordon Clinton's singing is poignant beyond words. There are no serious rivals.

Carl Nielsen (1865-1931)

Springtime in Funen (Fynsk Forår), Op. 42 (1921)
Sunny recollections of childhood fashioned during an especially difficult period in Nielsen's life (the composition of this delightful cantata more or less coincided with that of the searingly dramatic Fifth Symphony – see "The New Symphony", above). Nielsen's marriage was on the rocks at the time and yet the score itself is breezy, tuneful and full of lovely things – not least the emotionally charged tenor solo, "Den milde dag er lys og lang" (The gentle day is bright and long). The first performance involved 900 singers.

Inga Nielsen (soprano), Peter Grønlund (tenor), Sten Byriel (bass-baritone), St Anne's Gymnasium Children's Choir, Danish National Radio Symphony Orchestra/Leif Segerstam
Chandos digital

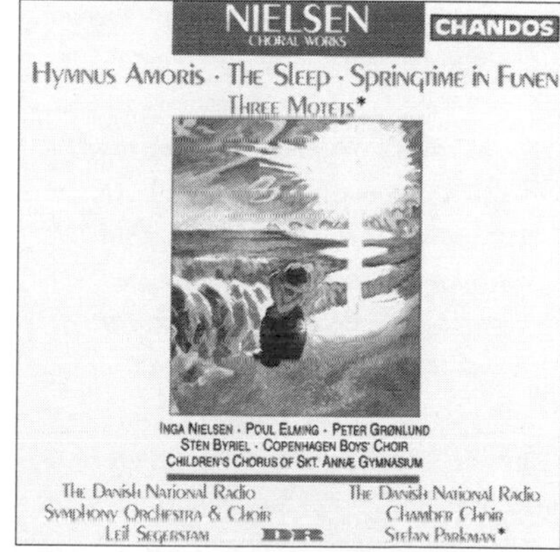

Segerstam's conducting is spirited and sensitive, and although the soloists are a little below par, the performance is certainly good enough to convey the essence of a fine and memorable work. There is, however, an even

finer (analogue) recording, under Møgens Wöldike (Vanguard, and not available at the time of writing), while Aksel Schiøtz's incomparable rendition of "Den milde dag er lys og lang" (Danacord, mono) is sure to bring a tear to your eye.

Sergey Rachmaninov (1873-1943)

The Bells, Op. 35 (1913)

Bells fascinated Rachmaninov throughout his life; they are audibly present in most of his large-scale compositions (even the celebrated C sharp minor Piano Prelude suggests a funereal tolling) while this masterly 'choral symphony' – which sets Konstanin Balmont's translations of Edgar Allen Poe – paints tone-poems of "The Silver Sleigh Bells" (which builds to an especially exultant climax), "The Mellow Wedding Bells", "The Loud Alarum Bells" and "The Mournful Iron Bells". Imagery and music are perfectly matched, while Balmont's words are themselves rich in musical allusions. *The Bells* ("Kolokola", in Russian) might justifiably be deemed Rachmaninov's greatest work.

Yelizaveta Shumskaya (soprano), Mikhail Dovenman (tenor), Alexei Bolshakov (baritone), Russian Republican Capelle, Moscow Philharmonic Orchestra/Kyrill Kondrashin

Melodiya/BMG analogue

If you can get past the first movement (every time I play the CD, I'm tempted to repeat just that one track again and again), you'll discover a reading that's distinguished by a unique blend of warmth and intensity. The sound is perhaps a little edgy (the original was recorded back in 1962), but BMG's careful transfer is reasonably successful. All three singers give passionate performances – the tenor being particularly distinctive. The chorus is superb.

Arnold Schoenberg (1874-1951)

Gurrelieder for soloists, narrator, chorus and orchestra (1900-03, revised 1910-11)

The ultimate post-Wagnerian epic, redolent of *Tristan und Isolde*'s love duet, the Act 2 choruses from *Götterdämmerung* and the lonely soliloquies of *Parsifal* (all included in "Twilit catastrophes", see below). The 'action' takes place in Gurre (Zeeland, Denmark) and concerns King Waldemar, his young lover Tove and her death at the hands of the queen. The texts are by Jens Peter Jacobsen (in a German translation) and musical highlights include a magical evocation of dusk (the highly original Prelude, with its metrical though magical woodwind writing), a sombre "Song of the Wood Dove" and a thrilling "Wild Hunt of the Summer Wind". If you love Mahler's symphonies and Wagner's music dramas, then you'll adore *Gurrelieder*.

Thomas Moser (Waldemar), Deborah Voigt (Tove), Jennifer Larmore (Wood Dove), Bernd Weikl (Peasant), Kenneth Riegel (Klaus the Jester), Klaus Maria Brandauer (Speaker), Dresden State Opera Chorus, Leipzig Radio Choir, Prague Male Chorus, Staatskapelle Dresden/Giuseppe Sinopoli

A live performance (recorded at the Semper Opera Dresden during August 1995), conceived on a grand scale. Sinopoli's attention to detail, his ability to clarify textures, his sense of theatre and his exhaustive knowledge of Schoenberg's style make this one of the most perceptive Gurrelieders ever recorded. The orchestral playing is magnificent, the singing mostly excellent (Larmore's intensely voiced Wood Dove especially) and the sound both 'open' and full-bodied. Best among rivals are Riccardo Chailly (Decca, digital) and Rafael Kubelík (DG, analogue).

Béla Bartók (1881-1945)

Cantata profana, for tenor, baritone, chorus and orchestra, Sz94 (1930)

Subtitled "The Nine Splendid Stags", Bartók's greatest choral work – it plays for a mere 18 minutes – is a moving parable of sons leaving the family nest. The musical language is sometimes harsh, sometimes war-like (try the fiercely syncopated orchestral writing from 3'15" into our recommended recording) but more often than not conjures up feelings of space and timeless mystery. The work falls into three concise sections and the text is Bartók's own adaptation of a Romanian carol.

John Aler (tenor), John Tomlinson (baritone), Chicago Symphony Chorus and Orchestra/Pierre Boulez

Deutsche Grammophon digital

One of Boulez's finest Bartók recordings, with an impressive grasp of the work's three-part structure (Bartók was often preoccupied by

musical symmetry), fine solo singing and a full-throated contribution from the Chicago Symphony Chorus. The balance between chorus and orchestra is first-rate. Best among Boulez's older rivals is a Hungaroton analogue CD featuring tenor József Réti.

Igor Stravinsky (1882-1971)

Les noces – choreographic scenes for chorus, four pianos, percussion and timpani (1923)

The shrill, lamenting cries and pulsing rhythms of the opening tableau set the scene for this most Russian of Stravinsky's stage works. Authentic folk sources are used and *Les noces* ("The wedding") is cast in four sections: "In the Bride's Room", with its kicking syncopations, then "In the Bridegroom's Room", "The Bride's Farewell" and "The Wedding Repast". The chiming retreat of the closing bars is quite unforgettable. Prior to settling for a line-up of chorus, vocal soloists, four pianos and 17 percussion instruments, Stravinsky prepared versions involving alternative instruments (including cimbaloms, harmonium, etc) – but they are generally less effective than the finished masterpiece and very rarely performed.

 ***Pokrovsky Ensemble/Dmitri Pokrovsky***

Nonesuch digital

A talented group of folk-singers with the piano parts re-created on a computer. However, the aggressive, sexy nature of the singing and the rhythmic drive of Pokrovsky's direction make for a thrilling musical encounter. The best of the 'standard' recordings was made in 1964 under the baton of Karel Ančerl (Supraphon, analogue). Stravinsky's own stereo version (Sony, analogue) is also impressive (the four composer-pianists are none other than Aaron Copland, Lucas Foss, Roger Sessions and Samuel Barber), but it's sung in awkward English.

Sergey Prokofiev (1891-1953)

Alexander Nevsky – cantata, Op. 78 (1938)

Alexander Nevsky's "Battle on Ice" is a 12-minute, action-packed evocation of converging armies at dead of winter. The Russian Army confronts Teutonic invaders to music that opens among desolate wastes, gradually gathers momentum and climaxes in a furious battle that raises both the spirits and the temperature. *Nevsky* is a skilful re-working of music that Prokofiev had originally composed for Sergey Eisenstein's film of the same name (itself long regarded as a classic).

 ***Elena Obraztsova (mezzo-soprano), London Symphony Chorus and Orchestra/Claudio Abbado***

Deutsche Grammophon analogue

Abbado's Nevsky faces stiff analogue competition (Reiner on RCA and Ančerl on to Supraphon, both of them excellent) but it still manages to pip even its best rivals to the post. The orchestral playing is truly virtuosic and the chorus (under Richard Hickox, no less) positively maniacal. The 1979 recording is impressively dynamic.

Cantata for the 20th Anniversary of the October Revolution, for narrator, military, accordion and percussion bands, chorus and orchestra, Op. 74 (1936-37)

A colossal piece and a riot of aural excitement culminating in a bludgeoning 'revolution' where the narrator declaims Lenin's words over a pounding accompaniment. Prior to that we hear a noble chorus "The Philosophers", simulated machine-gun fire, an accordion band and some highly characteristic orchestral/choral writing. There's also a *Cantata for the 30th Anniversary of the October Revolution*, but it's much shorter and nowhere near as memorable as its thrilling predecessor.

 ***Gennadi Rozhdestvensky (narrator), Philharmonia Chorus and Orchestra/Neeme Järvi***

Chandos digital

This is one of the very few instances where I'm recommending a particular recording simply because there's nothing else available. It's a fairly reasonable production, exciting in parts but lacking the sort of manic tension that Kyrill Kondrashin generated in his famous (cut) Melodiya analogue recording.

They are Seven – cantata for tenor, chorus and orchestra, Op. 30 (1917-18, revised 1933)

Seven to eight minutes of pure terror – savage, alarming and brilliantly orchestrated. Prokofiev's "Chaldean incantation" sets words by the symbolist Russian poet Constantin Balmont. Both text and music mirror a vision of giant deities, the tenor soloist acting as a sort of master of ceremonies within the context of Prokofiev's most violently modernistic score. The final climax features wild chanting and raucous brass slides, whereas the quiet though sinister closing pages suggest a black void somewhere beyond the boundaries of hope.

 ***Jaroslav Kachel (tenor), Prague Philharmonic Choir, Czech Philharmonic Orchestra/Karel Ančerl***

Praga analogue

Taped live in 1966 and by far the most commanding recorded performance of a rarely-heard masterpiece. The only viable alternative is a Russian studio analogue recording under Evgeni Svetlanov (Melodiya), which is in any case unavailable at the time of writing. They are Seven is urgently in need of fine modern advocacy – and it positively cries out for digital sound.

Carl Orff (1895-1982)

Carmina Burana (1936)

With its images of inebriated churchmen, sex-crazed lovers, gambling and a roasted swan singing, *Carmina Burana* is about as profane as you can get. The poems were written by 'wandering scholars' and gathered into an anthology by a monk at the Bavarian monastery of Benedikbeuern. Orff himself was an ardent educationalist whose experience with amateur choral groups informs his writing: *Carmina Burana* is a vivacious, percussive, tuneful, highly rhythmic and not infrequently lyrical work. Advertising agencies love it (the opening "O Fortuna" has become synonymous with aftershave).

 ***Lucia Popp (soprano), Gerhard Unger (tenor), Raymond Wolansky and John Noble (baritones), Wandsworth School Boys' Choir, New Philharmonia Chorus and Orchestra/Rafael Frühbeck de Burgos***

EMI Eminence analogue

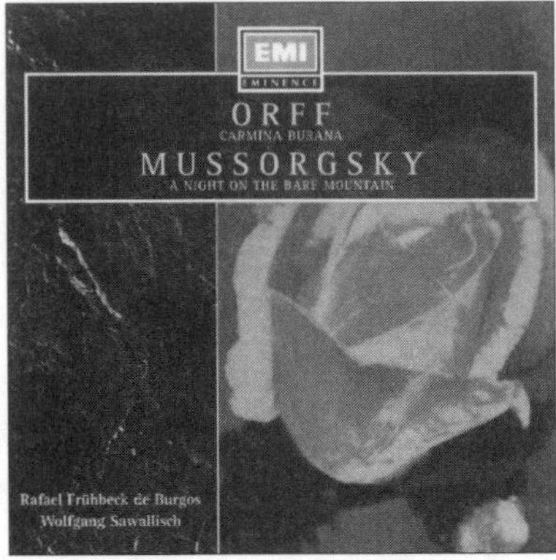

Although somewhat thin in sound, Frühbeck de Burgos's Carmina is among the most exciting and imaginative on disc. Eugen Jochum's famous DG analogue recording (on DG Originals) makes for an excellent – and slightly better recorded – alternative.

Sir Michael Tippett (b1905)

A Child of Our Time (1939-41)

It was in 1938, when Michael Tippett read a newspaper report about a young Polish Jew who had killed a minor official and prompted terrible Nazi reprisals, that a masterpiece-in-the-making finally assumed a potential shape. Tippett's 'message' discredits recrimination and vengeance in favour of compassion and an informed acceptance of our 'darker side'. The score is extraordinarily intense, alternating drama and meditation and incorporating negro spirituals (the closing movement is an especially touching arrangement of *Deep River*).

 ***Jill Gomez (soprano), Helen Watts (contralto), Kenneth Woollam (tenor), John Shirley-Quirk (baritone), BBC Chorus and Symphony Orchestra/Gennadi Rozhdestvensky***

BBC Radio Classics analogue

The most compelling performance on disc (it is taken from a 1980 BBC broadcast), wholly idiomatic and sung with the utmost feeling for the text. The sound might not be quite in the class of the composer's own (Collins Classics, digital) but it certainly passes muster. A further alternative, under Richard Hickox (Chandos, digital), is set at a rather lower temperature.

Opera beginnings (1607-1724)

Opera, or the "union of drama, music and spectacle" as one authority has it, properly started with Monteverdi's *Orfeo* (see below). Later developments included the *tragédies-lyriques* of Lully, the English operas of Purcell and the mature operas of Handel. Early opera is becoming increasingly popular, the French repertoire especially.

Claudio Monteverdi (1567-1643)

L'Orfeo (1607)

An entrancing piece that incorporates a wide range of instruments and numerous choral ballets. *L'Orfeo*, which was probably the earliest opera to win widespread performances in opera houses throughout Europe, concerns Orpheus, who descends to Hades to retrieve the dead Eurydice, loses her and is comforted by Apollo who promises that "in the sun and in the stars shalt thou discover her lovely likeness".

Nigel Rogers (Orfeo), Emilia Petrescu (Euridice), Anna Reynolds (Silvia, Proserpina), Ian Partridge (Shepherd I, Apollo), James Bowman (Shepherd II, Speranza), John Elwes (Shepherd III, Spirit I), Stafford Dean (Plutone, Shepherd IV), Alexander Malta (Caronte, Spirit II), Monteverdi Choir, Hamburg, instrumental soloists from the Camerata Accademica Hamburg, Hamburger Bläserkreis für Alte Musik/Jürgen Jürgens
Archiv analogue

Recorded during November 1973, this delightful performance took what was then the most advanced scholarly approach to a work that still prompts interpretative controversy. Nigel Rogers went on to record the role again (digitally, for EMI), but his earlier performance is notably fresh. Playing and conducting are supremely sensitive; try, in particular, the opening Toccata, the Chorus of Nymphs "Lasciate i monti" (track 4) or "Ma se il nostro giour" (track 6), the latter parading misty harmonies that seem closer in style to the music of our own century.

L'incoronazione di Poppea (1642)

Monteverdi's last – and greatest – stage work more resembles opera as we know it, with dramatic set pieces, sensuous harmonies and attractive tunes. The plot concerns forbidden love and a foiled murder. Nero loves Poppea, whose husband he sends off to Lusitania; Nero's wife orders Poppea's husband to kill Poppea, which he promises to do – though Cupid intervenes, prevents the murder and Nero's wife is banished from Rome (in reality, Poppea was eventually murdered by Nero). The opera ends with Poppea's Coronation.

Sylvia McNair (Poppea), Anne Sofie von Otter (Ottavia), Dana Hanchard (Nerone), Michael Chance (Ottone), Francesco Ellero d'Artegna (Seneca), Catherine Bott (Drusilla), Bernarda Fink (Arnalta), Roberto Balconi (Nutrice), English Baroque Soloists/John Eliot Gardiner
Archiv digital

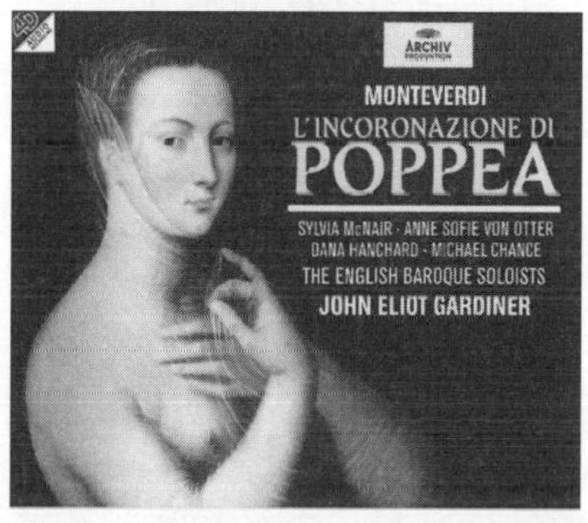

Archiv's star-studded cast assures a minimum high level of vocal refinement (not always the case in early opera recordings), while Gardiner directs a lean, stylish and texturally luminous account of the score. The recording, made during concert performances at London's Queen Elizabeth Hall during December 1993, is excellent. Viable alternatives exist under Nikolaus Harnoncourt (Teldec, analogue) and Richard Hickox (Virgin, digital).

Henry Purcell (1659-1695)

Dido and Aeneas, Z626 (1689)

Purcell's only true opera is based on a libretto by Nahum Tate (the then-Poet Laureate) after Virgil's *Aeneid.* The plot concerns Queen Dido, supposed founder of Carthage, whose love for the Trojan Aeneas is forbidden by the gods. Although modelled in large part on French and Italian styles (Lully's influence is audible in the Overture), *Dido* is quintessentially Purcellian and includes, among many glories, Dido's eloquent lament, "When I am laid in earth".

Dame Janet Baker (Dido), Raimund Herincx (Aeneas), with supporting cast, St Anthony Singers, English Chamber Orchestra (Thurston Dart, harpsichord continuo)/Anthony Lewis
Decca analogue

The young Janet Baker is the undisputed star of this wonderful performance; her account of Dido's Lament is unequalled in its contained emotion, while the remaining singers (not to mention conductor and orchestra) help to focus an immensely strong interpretation. Those in search of a period-instrument performance are directed to William Christie (Erato, digital).

The Fairy Queen, Z629 (1692)

Purcell's masterly 'semi-opera' – which followed in the wake of *Dido and Aeneas* and which is based on Shakespeare's

A Midsummer Night's Dream – is particularly rich in tonal variety. The score includes copious songs and dances, comedy, ceremonial drama (the symphony that opens Act 4) and musical mimicry.

Catherine Bott (soprano), Jeffrey Thomas (tenor), Michael Schopper (bass), Amsterdam Baroque Choir and Orchestra/Ton Koopman
Erato digital

Although a truly 'authentic' Fairy Queen would be near-impossible to realize, Koopman's recording was the first to present the running order as given in the manuscript rather than the printed libretto of the 1690s; it also includes a certain amount of reconstruction and features excellent playing and singing (especially from Catherine Bott). However, there are other excellent recordings under John Eliot Gardiner (DG, digital) and William Christie (Harmonia Mundi, digital), not to mention Benjamin Britten's skilful 'shortened version' (undertaken in collaboration with Peter Pears and Imogen Holst) with an excellent line-up of singers and the English Chamber Orchestra (Decca, analogue).

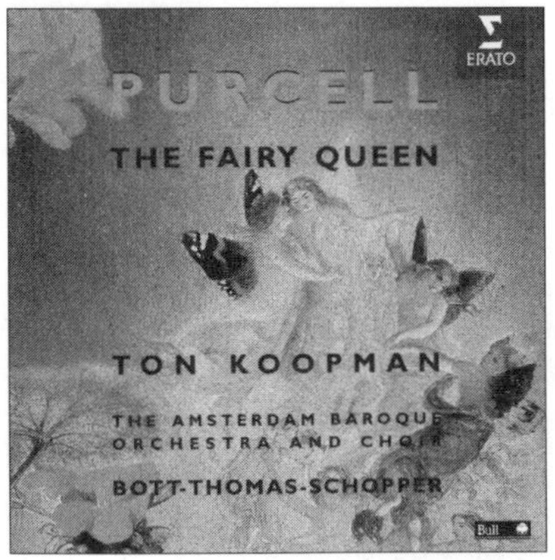

George Frideric Handel
(1685-1759)

Giulio Cesare (Julius Caesar), HWV17 (1724)

The most popular and possibly the greatest of Handel's operas concerns Ptolemy, who presents Caesar with the head of Pompey, much to Caesar's disgust. When Pompey's wife Cornelia tries to commit suicide, battles ensue and Caesar emerges victorious with Ptolemy's sister, Cleopatra. Ptolemy is killed by Cornelia's son as he tries to rape Cornelia's mother. The whole work is both emotionally powerful and physically invigorating, while the best-known excerpts include Cleopatra's aria "Piangerò la sorte mia…" (I shall lament my faith, so cruel and so pitiless").

Jennifer Larmore (Giulio Cesare), Barbara Schlick (Cleopatra), Bernarda Fink (Cornelia), Marianne Rørholm (Sesto), Derek Lee Ragin (Tolomeo), Furio Zanasi (Achilla), Dominique Visse (Nireno), Olivier Lallouette (Curio), Concerto Köln/René Jacobs
Harmonia Mundi digital

The role of Caesar was originally written for a castrato (a male singer mutilated in childhood so his voice wouldn't break), hence the fact that a soprano sings it in this performance. However, such is the vigour of Larmore's performance that the mind's theatre soon adjusts. Cleopatra is in many ways the opera's key figure and Barbara Schlick projects the role with both brilliance and dramatic flair. René Jacobs (himself a singer of some repute) directs an immensely spirited performance and the set also includes 18 minutes' worth of unfamiliar supplementary material. The recording is superb.

Wit, intrigue and lust (1762-1792)

Gluck's version of the Orfeo legend starts us off (it was, after all, a pivotal work in operatic reform), but the main body of this brief section is devoted to some of Mozart's greatest operas, from the sublime flippancy of *Così fan tutte* to the drama of *Don Giovanni*.
Mozart's operas are characterized by the effective fusion of recitative (harpsichord-accompanied linking passages based largely on speech) and individual arias.

Christoph Willibald Gluck
(1714-1787)

Orfeo ed Euridice (1762)

Orfeo is available in Italian, French or German, using – respectively – a contralto, a tenor or a baritone. The music is often extremely poignant (Orfeo's first cries of "Euridice", for example), and the story perennially touching. Orfeo descends to the Underworld to bring his wife Euridice back to life. He sweetens the Furies with his beautiful singing (never more beautiful than on our chosen recording) but makes the fatal mistake of looking at his beloved before they are safely home. Euridice dies again but when Orfeo sings his famous aria "Che farò" (What is life to me without thee?) Amor is so touched that he grants Euridice renewed life.

Dietrich Fischer-Dieskau (Orfeo), Maria Stader (Euridice), Rita Streich (Amor), RIAS Chamber Choir, Berlin Motet Choir, Berlin Radio Symphony Orchestra/Ferenc Fricsay
Deutsche Grammophon mono

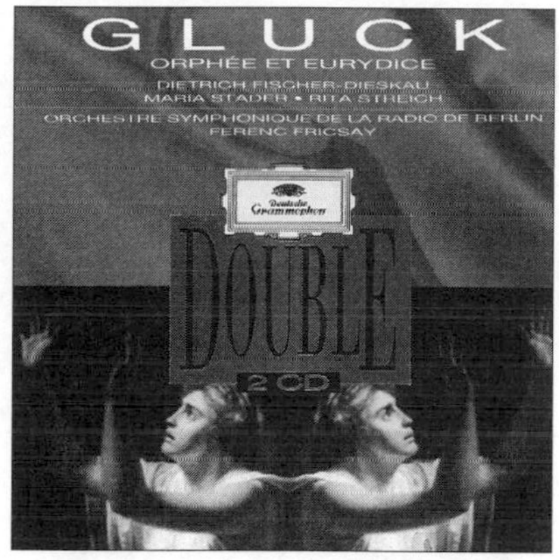

Period-performance devotees will raise their eyebrows at this choice – it's notoriously old-fashioned, both in terms of its text and its performance style – but the singing is extraordinarily beautiful (Fischer-Dieskau surely never made a more memorable operatic recording) and the conducting is both sensitive and stylish. High priorities among digital rivals are two recordings conducted by John Eliot Gardiner – the version by Berlioz (EMI) and Gluck's original (Philips). Toscanini's highly dramatic mono broadcast performance of the Second Act (with Nan Merriman, RCA – it's the Act that includes "The Dance of the Blessed Spirits" but not "Che farò") is also urgently recommended.

Wolfgang Amadeus Mozart
(1756–1791)

Così fan tutte, K588 (1790)
The libretto sets out to prove that 'all women are fickle'. Don Alfonso makes a bet that, if disguised, Ferrando and Guglielmo can seduce the other's fiancées – which they do. All ends happily, and yet the beauty of the music quite transcends the opera's somewhat flippant subject-matter. Among *Così*'s most beautiful numbers is the exquisite Act One trio "Soave sia il vento" (May the wind be gentle, may the sea be calm).

Elisabeth Schwarzkopf (Fiordiligi), Christa Ludwig (Dorabella), Hanny Steffek (Despina), Alfredo Kraus (Ferrando), Giuseppe Taddei (Guglielmo), Walter Berry (Don Alfonso), Philharmonia Chorus and Orchestra/Karl Böhm
EMI analogue

A justly famous set, recorded in 1962, and one that parades singing of such beauty, wit and sensitivity (not to mention first-rate orchestral playing and sympathetic conducting) that no recording since has managed to displace it. An earlier alternative, also under Böhm (1955, Decca – in primitive stereo), features Lisa della Casa, Christa Ludwig and Anton Dermota. Again, the singing is superb and those who would rather dispense with the spoken dialogue may well prefer it.

Die Entführung aus dem Serail (The Abduction from the Seraglio), K384 (1782)
Die Entführung is a delightful – and sometimes menacing – Singspiel (literally 'song play') that, together with the opera *Idomeneo*, marks the onset of Mozart's early maturity as an opera composer. Pasha Selim has imprisoned the Spanish noblewomen Konstanze who – with the help of her betrothed Belmonte – tries to escape, only to be discovered by the Harem-keeper Osmin. All ends well, however, when Pasha releases them. The best-known single items are the sparkling Overture, Konstanze's aria "Marten aller Arten" and Osmin's "O, wie will ich triumphieren".

Wolfgang Reichmann (Selim), Yvonne Kenny (Konstanze), Lillian Watson (Blonde), Peter Schreier (Belmonte), Wilfried Gamlich (Pedrillo), Matti Salminen (Osmin), soloists of the Zurich Opera House Chorus, Mozart Orchestra of the Zurich Opera House/Nikolaus Harnoncourt
Teldec digital

A hugely vivacious performance that has its fair share of distinctive features, not least Harnoncourt's approach to the score's Turkish music (you can hear some of it in the Overture) where "an assortment of carefully chosen percussion and wind instruments" has been creatively employed. The only stumbling-block concerns an approach to fermata (pauses, or prolonged notes) that some readers will find eccentric – although Harnoncourt's recourse to the autograph score serves to support his decisions. Fine alternatives include Ferenc Fricsay (DG, analogue) and Sir Colin Davis (Philips, analogue).

Don Giovanni, K527 (1787)

Donna Anna was virtually raped by him (he killed her father) and Donna Elvira abandoned by him – so it's little wonder that Don Giovanni ends his days in hell. Gounod described the "solemn and powerful opening chords, with their marked rhythm, [that] interpret the just and terrifying power of the Almighty to punish every sin". Fast-moving and dramatic, *Don Giovanni* expresses a depth, cynicism and humour that anticipate the operatic language of a later age.

Eberhard Waechter (Don Giovanni), Dame Joan Sutherland (Donna Anna), Elisabeth Schwarzkopf (Donna Elvira), Graziella Sciutti (Zerlina), Luigi Alva (Don Ottavio), Giuseppe Taddei (Leporello), Piero Cappuccilli (Masetto), Gottlob Frick (Commendatore), Philharmonia Chorus and Orchestra/Carlo Maria Giulini

EMI analogue

Giulini's early stereo Don Giovanni continues to hold its own, not least for the dramatic conducting, consistently fine singing and well refurbished sound. But, as ever, there are plenty alternatives to choose from. Ferenc Fricsay's 1958 recording (with Dietrich Fischer-Dieskau, Maria Stader, Sena Jurinac and Ernst Haefliger, DG) is a personal favourite, while there are superb historical live alternatives under Wilhelm Furtwängler (EMI, mono) and Dimitri Mitropoulos (Sony, mono) – both from post-war Salzburg Festivals.

The Magic Flute (Die Zauberflöte), K620 (1791)

The Magic Flute (or "Die Zauberflöte") – Mozart's last and probably greatest opera – can be appreciated at various levels: as child-like entertainment, as a poetical drama of ideas, as Masonic symbolism or simply as glorious music in its own right (which it is anyway). Roughly speaking, Emanuel Schikaneder's libretto concerns the triumph of love over evil, with much skittish activity to lighten the action.

Nicolai Gedda (Tamino), Gundula Janowitz (Pamina), Walter Berry (Papageno), Lucia Popp (Queen of Night), with supporting cast, Philharmonia Chorus and Orchestra/Otto Klemperer

EMI analogue

Klemperer's Flute (sung without dialogue) is among his most enduring contributions to the catalogue, whether viewed in terms of the singing (female in particular), the conducting (strong but supple) or the first-rate sound production. Good alternatives include the lean but refreshingly original Nikolaus Harnoncourt (Teldec, digital) and a wonderfully transparent mono recording under the great Ferenc Fricsay (DG).

The Marriage of Figaro (Le nozze di Figaro), K492 (1786)

The idea of *Figaro* was an indirect outgrowth of Paisiello's opera, *The Barber of Seville*: a year after hearing it Mozart asked Lorenzo da Ponte to prepare a libretto based on the *Barber*'s sequel, *The Marriage of Figaro* (both plays are by Beaumarchais). The resulting masterpiece makes a hero out of a servant (Mozart had himself known a hostile master) while the actual comedy is both highly complex and extremely funny. The music is consistently delightful.

Sesto Bruscantini (Figaro), Graziella Sciutti (Susanna), Ian Wallace (Bartolo), Monica Sinclair (Marcellina), Risë Stevens (Cherubino), Franco Calabrese (Count Almaviva), Hugues Cuenod (Don Basilo), Sena Jurinac (Countess), with supporting cast, Glyndebourne Festival Chorus and Orchestra/Vittorio Gui

EMI Classics for Pleasure analogue

If you can accept a significant cut (Basilio's Act 4 aria, omitted through reasons of space), you will enjoy one of the most fetching Figaros ever recorded, superbly characterized and very well engineered for 1955 (in stereo). Strong rivals include a lean but vital period-instrument version under John Eliot Gardiner (Archiv, digital) and a fine 1960 recording (DG, analogue) with Dietrich Fischer-Dieskau, Maria Stader and Irmgard Seefried under the characteristically stylish baton of Ferenc Fricsay.

Bel canto (1816-1926)

'Bel canto' (literally "beautiful singing") usually denotes a beautiful tone, an effortless technique and shapely phrasing. Here we use the term to head a whole host of varied Italian operas, some of which, such as the work of Rossini, Donizetti and Bellini, are regularly used as a base for florid vocal display. However, Puccini, Mascagni and the later Verdi, although equally rich in melody, more approximate the passionate music dramas of Wagner (see "Twilit catastrophes", below)

Gioachino Rossini (1792-1868)

Il barbiere di Siviglia (1816)

The Figaros of Mozart and Rossini (both are based on Beaumarchais) inhabit quite different worlds, Mozart gaining in tender melancholy, Rossini, in sparkling wit. Rossini's opera, however, was up against a predecessor by Paisiello and failed miserably at its first performance. The English press was no more enthusiastic, although posterity went on to reverse these judgements and the opera is now loved worldwide – not least for its vivacious Overture, Figaro's spectacular "Largo al factotum" and Rosina's Cavatina "Una voce poco fa" ("The voice I heard just now has thrilled my very heart").

Maria Callas (Rosina), Luigi Alva (Almaviva), Tito Gobbi (Figaro), Fritz Ollendorff (Bartolo), Nicola Zaccaria (Don Basilo), Gabriella Carturan (Berta), Mario Carlin (Fiorello), Philharmonia Chorus and Orchestra/Alceo Galliera

EMI analogue

Callas wasn't exactly renowned for her sense of humour, and yet here she enters fully into the spirit of what is surely one of the best studio recordings of a Rossini opera – not least for Tito Gobbi's Figaro and Alceo Galliera's pointed conducting. The recording – a 1957 Walter Legge production – is superbly balanced.

La Cenerentola (1817)

With no glass slippers and a somewhat unsympathetic father, Rossini's version of the Cinderella tale gains in reality what it looses in magic. The score itself, however, is unalloyed delight, from the sparkling Overture (one of Rossini's finest) to the heroine's celebrated solo work – in particular the closing rondo, "Non più mesta accanto al fuoco", ("No longer sad beside the fire shall I sit alone, singing").

Cecilia Bartoli (Cenerentola), William Matteuzzi (Don Ramiro), Alessandro Corbelli (Dandini), Enzo Dara (Don Magnifico), with supporting cast, Chorus and Orchestra of the Teatro Comunale di Bologna/Riccardo Chailly

Decca digital

Cecilia Bartoli is one of the major vocal discoveries of the 1990s and her virtuosic assumption of the leading role vies in accomplishment with her most fêted predecessors – including Maria Callas (EMI, analogue) and the great Conchita Supervia (Testament, Nimbus or Preiser, mono). Chailly's conducting shows tremendous flair and the whole performance 'lives' in a way that's relatively rare for a studio opera recording.

Gaetano Donizetti (1797-1848)

Lucia di Lammermoor (1835)

Lucia di Lammermoor ("The Bride of Lammermoor") sets a libretto (by Salvadore Cammorano) after Sir Walter Scott that deals with the love between Lucia and Edgar, Edgar's supposed unfaithfulness, Lucia's madness and Edgar's suicide. Among the opera's highlights are a chilling "Mad Scene" (with flute accompaniment) and a glorious Sextet. *Lucia*'s melodies are both simple and indelible.

Maria Callas (Lucia), Giuseppe di Stefano (Edgardo), Rolando Panerai (Enrico), with supporting cast, Chorus of La Scala, Milan, RIAS Symphony Orchestra, Berlin/Herbert von Karajan

EMI mono

Callas made two studio recordings of Lucia (both for EMI), but this live relay is something special, not least for the consistently perceptive conducting of Herbert von Karajan. The Mad Scene is utterly magnificent and although the mono sound is more than adequate (the actual atmosphere is electric), those who require a good studio digital alternative are directed to Cheryl Studer, Plácido Domingo, Juan Pons and the LSO under Ion Marin (DG).

Vincenzo Bellini (1801-1835)

Norma (1831)

Bellini's tragic opera centres on a woman's scorn. Norma, a Druid priestess is forsaken by her Roman lover Pollione, brings down vengeance upon his head but is none the less willing to share his fate. The musical style centres on simple, attractive melodies and straightforward (though effective) dramatic gestures. Best-known are Norma's aria, "Casta diva" (Queen of Heaven), the duet, "Mira, O Norma" (Hear me, Norma) and the First Act's stirring Introduction where Oroveso orders the Druids to climb the hill and wait for the new moon.

Maria Callas (Norma), Franco Corelli (Pollione), Christa Ludwig (Adalgisa), Nicola Zaccaria (Oroveso), Piero de Palma (Flavio), Edda Vincenzi (Clotilde), Chorus and Orchestra of La Scala, Milan/Tullio Serafin

EMI analogue

Controversy reigns as to whether to choose Callas's 1960 recording (our own recommendation) or its 1954 mono predecessor (also EMI). True, there are some signs of vocal decline in the later version, but the presence of Franco Corelli – heard here in magnificent voice – plus the extra clarity of the sound, win the day for the stereo remake. Callas's inspired interpretation of the title-role is common to both, but there's powerful rivalry from Dame Joan Sutherland (Decca, analogue).

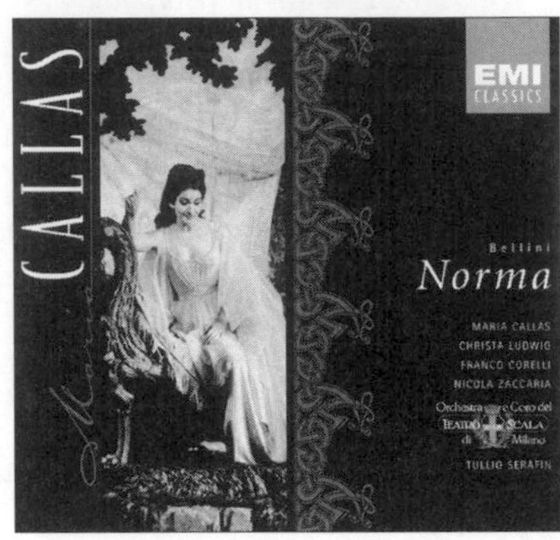

Giuseppe Verdi (1813-1901)

Aida (1871)

Aida was commissioned by the Khedive of Egypt for festivities in connection with the opening of the Suez Canal, although the first performance was postponed by a year. The story concerns the love of the Ethiopian King's daughter (a prisoner at the Egyptian court) for an Egyptian captain of the guard which is further fuelled by the Egyptian princess Amneris, who also loves the captain. *Aida* contains many highlights, not least Radames' "Celeste Aida", Aida's declamatory "Ritorna vincitor!", a stirring "Triumphal March" near the Gates of Thebes, and the closing "Tomb Scene".

Maria Callas (Aida), Richard Tucker (Radames), Fedora Barbieri (Amneris), Tito Gobbi (Amonasro), Giuseppe Modesti (Ramfis), Nicola Zaccaria (King of Egypt), Elvira Galassi (Priestess), Franco Ricciardi (Messenger), Chorus and Orchestra of La Scala, Milan/Tullio Serafin

EMI mono

The tensions between Aida and Amneris have never been more vividly conveyed (at least not on disc), while both Serafin and his supporting cast pull out all the stops for what is surely the classic recorded version of the opera. Connoisseurs of great Verdi conducting will also want Toscanini's 1949 broadcast performance (RCA, mono), but the singing is nowhere near as good as on this 1955 EMI set.

Un ballo in maschera (1859)

If I were to choose three Verdi operas for my desert island, they would be *Falstaff*, *Otello* and *Un ballo in maschera* ("A masked ball"). One of the greatest of the so-called middle-period operas, *Ballo* tells the story of a King who is warned (by a fortune-teller) that the next man to shake his hand will kill him (it's actually his friend Renato). Musically, *Ballo* is consistently inspired, from the tension and wholehearted lyricism of the Prelude, to the sinister music that accompanies the fortune-teller's prophecies and the tragi-comic scherzo-ensemble "E scherzo, od è follia" (superbly done on track 17 on the first disc of our recommended version).

Jan Peerce (Riccardo), Herva Nelli (Amelia), Robert Merrill (Renato), Claramae Turner (Ulrica), Virginia Haskins (Oscar), George Cehanovsky (Silvano), Nicola Moscona (Sam), Norman Scott (Tom), John Carmen Rossi (Judge, Servant of Amelia), Robert Shaw Chorale, NBC Symphony Orchestra/Arturo Toscanini

RCA mono

Good Ballos are legion, but this performance is one in a million – witty, dramatic, wonderfully played, very well sung and imbued with a feeling of animated chamber music.

This was Toscanini's last opera performance: "I began by hearing a performance of Un ballo in maschera at the age of four, up in the gallery," he once said; "and I've finished conducting it at 87". The 1954 recording, although somewhat drier than the norm, still sounds marvellous. Those who fancy the idea of a German-language Un ballo might like to try an almost equally superb performance under Fritz Busch (again in fine mono sound – with the great Martha Mödl as Ulrica, on Bayer).

Don Carlo (1867, revised 1884 [Paris])

The greatest of Verdi's 'middle-period' operas deals with both personal and political tragedy. The original libretto was in French (*Don Carlos*, as opposed to *Don Carlo*) but the more substantial Italian version is generally better-known. Among the more celebrated highlights are the Act 1 duet between Carlo and Rodrigo ("Oh God … Thou must kindle within our hearts a desire for liberty") and the great Act 3 aria where King Philip soliloquizes about his loveless marriage ("She never loved me! No, her heart is closed to me …").

 ***José Carreras (Don Carlo), Mirella Freni (Elisabetta), Agnes Baltsa (Eboli), Nicolai Ghiaurov (Philip II), Piero Cappuccilli (Rodrigo), Ruggero Raimondi (Grand Inquisitor), with supporting cast, Chorus of Deutsche Oper Berlin, Berlin Philharmonic Orchestra/Herbert von Karajan***

EMI analogue

Quite aside from its fine singing, Karajan's 1978 recording (which, incidentally, sounds fairly opulent on CD) is fairly unique in the way it projects the sheer power of Verdi's inspired vision. Karajan's handling of Philip's Act 3 aria is especially commanding, but if vintage vocals are essential then either set featuring Boris Christoff (one – in mono – on EMI, the other on DG, analogue) should also be heard.

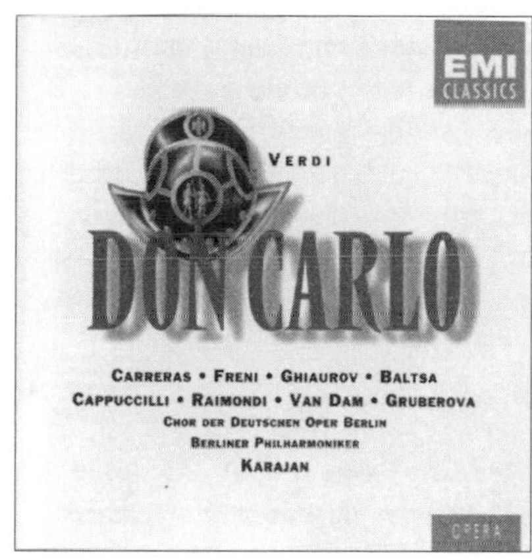

Falstaff (1893)

Verdi's last – and perhaps greatest – opera took up the challenge of comedy and Boito's masterly libretto (adapted from Shakespeare) by merging melody, recitative and orchestral commentary into a fast-moving, indivisible whole. In fact, *Falstaff* rather resembles chamber music with words, such is the urgency of its dialogue and the economy of its orchestration. The story concerns Sir John Falstaff, who sends the same love letter to two married women and earns himself a spell in the Thames (in a dirty laundry basket) and the indignity of being made to wear antlers in Hearn Wood.

 ***Giuseppe Valdengo (Falstaff), Herva Nelli (Mistress Alice Ford), Nan Merriman (Mistress Meg Page), Cloe Elmo (Mistress Quickly), Frank Guarrera (Ford), with supporting cast, Robert Shaw Chorale, NBC Symphony Orchestra/Arturo Toscanini***

RCA mono

"No opera is more beautiful, more complete, newer and more Latin than Falstaff … Think for a moment about how many musical means – beautiful ones, to be sure – Wagner requires to describe the Nuremberg night [in Die Meistersinger]. And look at how Verdi achieves a similarly evocative effect at a theatrically similar moment using three notes." So wrote the Wagnerite Toscanini who was otherwise engaged (he was 26) when Falstaff was premièred in 1893. He never conducted the opera for Verdi, though the ageing composer did at least hear about his 'perfect' performance. This particular production – where the octogenarian conductor pays tribute to the octogenarian composer – is a miracle of precision, spontaneity and affectionate phrasing. It is, in a word, unique.

La forza del destino (The force of destiny) (1862)

A highly theatrical drama that centres on vengeance and confused identities, *The force of destiny* – which Verdi composed for the Imperial Theatre in St Petersburg – marks a further step away from the standard 'string of arias' formula towards greater dramatic continuity (the duets are particularly gripping). Best-known are the magnificent Overture, Leonore's aria "Pace, pace, mio Dio" and the final scene – a virtual masterpiece in itself.

 ***Leontyne Price (Leonore), Plácido Domingo (Don Alvaro), Sherrill Milnes (Don Carlos), with supporting cast, John Alldis Choir, London Symphony Orchestra/James Levine***

RCA analogue

A fine 1977 recording that continues to hold its own, not least for Leontyne Price's thrilling Leonore, Plácido Domingo's ringing Don Alvaro and the lithe, shapely profile of James

Levine's conducting. An earlier RCA analogue recording (1964, under Thomas Schippers) finds Price in marginally finer voice, but Levine's performance is the more consistent of the two. As to digital alternatives, Giuseppe Sinopoli's magnificently recorded DG version (with Rosalind Plowright and José Carreras) earns top billing.

Otello (1887)

Shakespeare's tale of obsession, cunning and corrupted innocence as rendered musical with a degree of subtlety and dramatic flair that equals the finest in Wagner's music dramas. Passages such as Iago's "Credo", the love duet between Otello and Desdemona, Otello's rabid outbursts and death scene, contain some of Verdi's most riveting music. The action is fast and tight, the orchestration powerful but never overstated. In this writer's opinion the two greatest Romantic operas are Verdi's *Otello* and Wagner's *Tristan und Isolde* (see "Twilit catastrophes", below).

Ramón Vinay (Otello), Herva Nelli (Desdemona), Giuseppe Valdengo (Iago), with supporting cast, NBC Symphony Orchestra and Chorus/Arturo Toscanini

RCA mono

It would be all too easy to base one's recommendation simply on historical fact, i.e. that Toscanini played second cello in Otello's world première and that Verdi himself was something of a Toscanini fan. What really matters, however is the sheer heat and passion of this 1947 broadcast performance, that all the singers – none of them major 'stars', even in their day – give of their very best and that Toscanini's conducting has unique authority. No other recorded Otello even begins to approach it.

Rigoletto (1851)

"I had imagined *Rigoletto* without arias, without any formal climax or tableau, rather as a long series of duets, because that is a form that satisfies me." Verdi's own words don't quite reflect the subtle dramatic workings of this 'middle-period' masterpiece (where a hunchback jester and his daughter are victims of a curse) although *Rigoletto* includes two of Verdi's most famous tenor arias, "Questo o quella" and "La donna è mobile". The Third Act in particular is absolutely thrilling.

Maria Callas (Gilda), Tito Gobbi (Rigoletto), Giuseppe di Stefano (Duke of Mantova), with supporting cast, Chorus and Orchestra of La Scala, Milan/Tullio Serafin

EMI mono

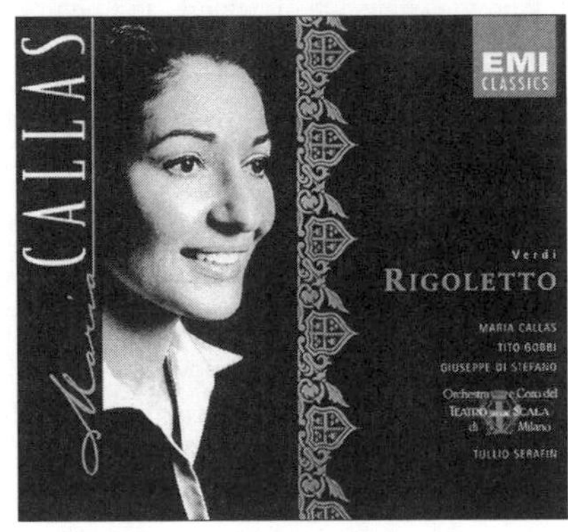

Tito Gobbi's Rigoletto combines top-grade acting with artful 'bel canto' (Gobbi was in his vocal prime during the early- to mid-1950s) and although Callas's Gilda is perhaps slightly over-projected, the intensity of her characterization is consistently compelling. Tullio Serafin's direction is well-nigh ideal and the recording is remarkably clear. Those who require digital sound are directed to Giuseppe Sinopoli's DG recording with Edita Gruberová and Renato Bruson.

La traviata (1853)

The libretto deals with the courtesan Violetta, her love for Alfredo and her ultimate sacrifice of that love. While in Paris in 1852, Verdi had seen the play *La Dame aux Camélias* by Alexandre Dumas the Younger (which was said to be at least partially autobiographical) and immediately thought of making it into an opera. Francesco Piave prepared the libretto and although the first performance was greeted – unbelievably – with almost total incomprehension, Verdi's response was "am I or the singers to blame for this? The future will decide." *La traviata*'s best-known highlights include the First and Third Act orchestral preludes, the Brindisi and the heart-rending final scene.

Ileana Cotrubas (Violetta), Placido Domingo (Alfredo), Sherrill Milnes (Germont), with supporting cast, Bavarian State Opera Chorus and Orchestra/Carlos Kleiber

Deutsche Grammophon analogue

A performance of the utmost vivacity and excitement, one that in terms of dramatic flair is second only to Toscanini's celebrated mono NBC broadcast from the late-1940s (RCA). There are two live Callas recordings on EMI (both are in mono – one under Giulini, the other under Ghione) which, although artistically significant, are sonically under-par.

Amilcare Ponchielli (1834-1886)

La Gioconda (1876)

Described by one commentator as "a tangled story of passion, intrigue, violence and eventual tragedy", Ponchielli's Venetian melodrama is best-known for the heroine's thrilling Act 4 aria "Suicidio!" and the colourful masque from Act 3 scene 2 where dancers represent the Hours of Dawn (the celebrated "Dance of the Hours"). As *bel canto* 'blockbusters' go, *La Gioconda* still packs a fair punch!

Maria Callas (La Gioconda), Fiorenza Cossotto (Laura), Irene Companeez (La Cieca), Ivo Vinco (Alvise), Pier Miranda Ferraro (Enzo), Piero Cappuccilli (Barnaba), with supporting cast, Chorus and Orchestra of La Scala, Milan/Antonino Votto

EMI analogue

It was during the sessions for this famous (stereo) recording that Maria Callas announced her separation from Giovanni Meneghini and her "profound friendship" with Aristotle Onassis. The performance itself is shot through with passion, while the sound – although a little 'hissy' – has plenty of body.

Ruggiero Leoncavallo (1857–1919)

I Pagliacci (1892)

One of the most concise examples of so-called *verismo* (or 'realistic') opera and a setting of a true story about the clown Canio who murders his wife and her lover at a *commedia dell' arte* performance. Often accused of being a direct imitation of Mascagni's *Cavalleria Rusticana* (the other work played at *I Pagliacci*'s premiere), 'Pag' is none the less often paired with 'Cav' – both on disc and in the opera house. Highlights include the Prologue and Canio's celebrated aria "Vesti la giubba" ("On with the motley").

Giuseppe di Stefano (Canio), Maria Callas (Nedda), Tito Gobbi (Tonio), Nicola Monti (Beppe), Rolando Panerai (Silvio), Chorus and Orchestra of La Scala, Milan/Tullio Serafin

EMI mono

Tito Gobbi's account of the Prologue should be enough to convince most listeners that this will indeed be a great Pagliacci, and when it comes to Callas – that promise is more than fulfilled. Karajan's DG La Scala version with Carlo Bergonzi, Giuseppe Taddei and Joan Carlyle provides a more refined – and better recorded – analogue alternative.

Giacomo Puccini (1858–1924)

La bohème (1896)

Anyone who has known love or loss (or both) will surely find this tragic tale of a penniless poet in love with a consumptive seamstress quite overwhelming. *La bohème* is uncompromisingly direct in its emotional appeal; its melodies are indelible, its scoring masterly and its theatrical impact – even away from the stage – extremely powerful. Much grew out of it, not least the purple-cloaked film scores of Erich Korngold and Max Steiner.

Licia Albanese (Mimì), Jan Peerce (Rodolfo), with supporting cast, NBC Symphony Orchestra/Arturo Toscanini

RCA mono

Voice aficionados will baulk at my choice, preferring – with some justification – the greater vocal refinement of Victoria de los Angeles and Jüssi Björling under Sir Thomas Beecham (EMI, mono) or Mirella Freni and Luciano Pavarotti under Herbert von Karajan (Decca, analogue). However, this 1946 recording was a special event that marked the fiftieth anniversary of the world première – also conducted by Toscanini. Then in his late seventies, the fêted Maestro inspired a performance of unprecedented passion and power; the singing is ardently sincere (Peerce is virile, Albanese, vulnerable) while Toscanini's croaky voice bursts in at key climaxes. An unforgettable experience.

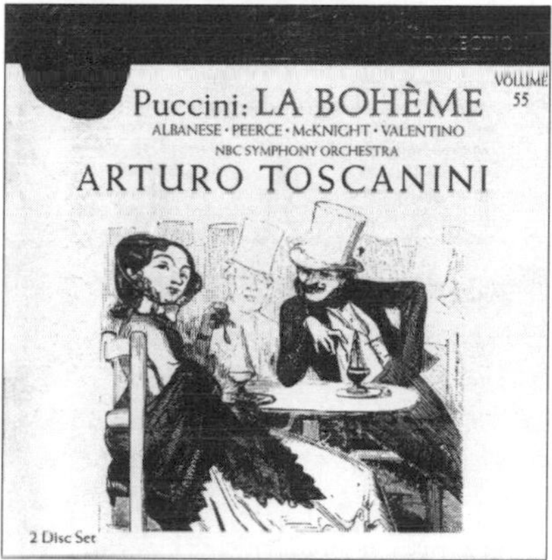

Madama Butterfly (1904)

"Louder, louder, you swine! Go on – shout! Tear your lungs! You will see who is right in the end! This is the best opera I have ever written!" So shouted Giacomo Puccini through the whistles and hisses that greeted *Butterfly*'s stormy La Scala première, although the revised version (first presented at Brescia) was a resounding success. Passionate, touching and exquisitely scored, *Madama Butterfly* tells of a young Geisha girl who kills herself when her American lover returns to Nagasaki with his American wife and takes her child.

Maria Callas (Butterfly), Lucia Danieli (Suzuki), Nicolai Gedda (B. F. Pinkerton), Luisa Villa (Kate Pinkerton), Mario Borriello (Sharpless), with supporting cast, Chorus and Orchestra of La Scala, Milan/Herbert von Karajan

EMI mono

Callas's acting carries the day (no bad thing with opera on record), while Gedda is a consistently convincing Pinkerton and Karajan's conducting has genuine charisma. The mono sound is clear and compact, but there's a fine stereo alternative, also under Karajan, with Mirella Freni and Luciano Pavarotti (Decca, analogue) while those in search of a good digital recording should consider Freni and José Carreras under Giuseppe Sinopoli (DG).

Manon Lescaut (1893)
Manon is coerced into leaving her beloved Des Grieux for the wealthy Geronte; she tries to escape (taking Geronte's gifts with her), but is deported as a thief and a prostitute. Of course, she dies and Puccini's score – it was his very first international success – reflects her plight with beautiful melodies and skilful orchestration.

Licia Albanese (Manon Lescaut), Jüssi Björling (Des Grieux), with supporting cast, Rome Opera Chorus and Orchestra/Jonel Perlea
RCA mono

One of those cases where arguments about sound quality are silenced by the quality of the singing, specifically that of Björling whose princely, trumpeting tenor and emotional delivery are unforgettable. Try track 7 on disc 1, where Des Grieux approaches Manon for the first time, and if you're not completely won over, then best opt for a digital alternative – Pavarotti and Freni (under James Levine on Decca) being as good a choice as any.

Tosca (1900)
Puccini had seen Sardou's play *La Tosca* with Sarah Bernhardt in the leading role and thought it highly suitable for operatic treatment. The action takes place in Rome around 1800; Napoleon has advanced into Northern Italy and supporters of the French Revolution are regularly under threat of the death sentence. Tosca attempts to save her Republican lover Cavaradossi from execution but fails and eventually commits suicide. *Tosca* is among the most concise and dramatic operas in the repertoire and includes such riveting arias as Cavaradossi's "Recondita armonia" ("Strange harmony of contrasts") and Tosca's "Vissi d'arte" (Love and music, these I have lived for).

Maria Callas (Floria Tosca), Giuseppe di Stefano (Mario Cavaradossi), Tito Gobbi (Scarpia), with supporting cast, Chorus and Orchestra of La Scala, Milan/Victor de Sabata
EMI mono

De Sabata's Tosca ranks with Toscanini's Otello and Furtwängler's Tristan as one of three greatest operatic recordings ever made. Callas was ideally suited to the role and in this particular version (a stereo remake isn't as effective) she receives compelling support from di Stefano and Gobbi (especially). The mono sound stands up remarkably well.

Turandot (1926)
The winning of Turandot by Calaf depends on his answering three riddles (which also allows him to escape execution). Puccini's last opera is also among his greatest (certainly in terms of its orchestration and harmonic inventiveness) but was left unfinished. Franco Alfano prepared the completion, Toscanini conducted the première and its most famous single aria is "Nessun dorma". *Turandot* is a complex drama that makes ingenious use of Chinese-style melodies.

Joan Sutherland (Princess Turandot), Luciano Pavarotti (Calaf), Montserrat Caballé (Liù), Tom Krause (Ping), Pier Francesco Poli (Pang), Piero De Palma (Pong), Sir Peter Pears (Emperor Altoum), Nicolai Ghiaurov (Timur), Sabin Markov (Mandarin), Wandsworth School Boys' Choir, John Alldis Choir, London Philharmonic Orchestra/Zubin Mehta
Decca analogue

With Pavarotti at the very height of his powers, Sutherland a regal Turandot and Caballé a highly sympathetic Liù (Turandot's slave-girl), this 1972 recording remains the most secure all-round recommendation. The actual sound is still virtually state-of-the-art and Mehta explores the full range of Puccini's astonishing tonal canvas. Perhaps the most compelling rival is a famous 1957 recording with Maria Callas and Eugenio Fernandi under Tullio Serafin (EMI, analogue).

Pietro Mascagni (1863-1945)

Cavalleria Rusticana (1890)
This first-prize winner at a 1889 one-act opera competition (organized by the publishing firm Sonzogno) tells of the seducer Turiddu and the vengeance of one

of his victims, Santuzza. Often paired with Leoncavallo's *I Pagliacci* (see above), *Cavalleria Rusticana* was composed at break-neck speed and scored an instant hit at its Rome première. Favourite highlights include Turiddu's "Siciliana" with the celebrated "Intermezzo sinfonico" and "Easter Hymn".

Maria Callas (Santuzza), Giuseppe di Stefano (Turiddu), Rolando Panerai (Alfio), Anna Maria Canali (Lola), Ebe Ticozzi (Mamma Lucia), Chorus and Orchestra of La Scala, Milan/Tullio Serafin

EMI mono

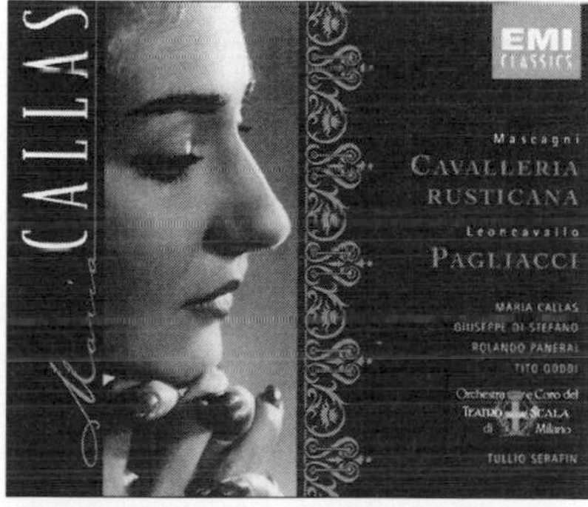

The part of Santuzza could have been written especially for Callas, so utterly convincing is her fiery interpretation. However, there's an almost equally fine RCA recording (stereo, albeit analogue) with Renata Scotto and Plácido Domingo. Karajan's analogue DG La Scala recording (coupled with his I Pagliacci) is also recommended.

From Faust to Hector's Ghost (1856-1892)

***Carmen* is the most popular attraction here, although no opera of the period quite equals the scope and imagination of Berlioz's *Les Troyens*. Romantic French opera is characterized by its emotive plots, choral extravagance and colourful orchestration.**

Hector Berlioz (1803-1869)

Les Troyens (1856-58)

An astonishing four-hour *tour de force* that triumphs with vivid tone painting and a spellbinding theatrical impact. *Les Troyens* is in fact two operas in one, "Les Troyens à Carthage" and "La Prise de Troie" – although the actual composition of the whole (which Berlioz never lived to hear performed) was anything but systematic. As to highlights, there are many – but if you want a thumb-nail sampling of *Les Troyens* at its most compelling and atmospheric, then sample the percussively rousing end of Act 3, where Aeneas leads his men off to war, or the celebrated orchestral "Royal Hunt and Storm" from the beginning of Act 4.

Gary Lakes (Aeneas), Deborah Voigt (Cassandra), Françoise Pollet (Dido), Gino Quilico (Chorebus), with supporting cast, Montreal Symphony Chorus and Orchestra/Charles Dutoit

Decca digital

With sprightly tempos, fine vocal characterization (especially from Gary Lakes and Deborah Voigt) and a spectacularly fine digital recording, Dutoit's Les Troyens makes for splendid living-room theatre. Sir Colin Davis's analogue Philips recording makes for an obvious second choice (some find it even more involving than Dutoit's).

Charles Gounod (1818-1893)

Faust (1859-69)

Initially conceived as an operetta with spoken dialogue, *Faust* was re-cast as a 'grand opera' and – as such – achieved enormous success (certain episodes, including the "Soldiers' Chorus", were relatively 'late arrivals').Gounod himself wrote after the first performance, that "what at first wins the favour of the public is the obvious which lies on the surface, but it is that which lies under the surface that makes the work live and establishes it". Gounod's score includes many well-known episodes (there are good tunes galore), not least being Méphistophélès's "Le veau d'or" (The calf of gold), Faust's cavatina "Salut! demeure" (All hail, thou dwelling pure and lowly!), Marguérite's "Jewel Song" and an extended "Ballet Music".

Nicolai Gedda (Faust), Victoria de los Angeles (Marguérite), Boris Christoff (Méphistophélès), with supporting cast, Chorus and Orchestra of the National Theatre of the Paris Opéra/André Cluytens

EMI mono

A vocal connoisseur's performance (Boris Christoff is magnificent) with classic French orchestral sonorities under Cluytens, although the 1953 sound has its shortcomings. Those in search of a digital alternative are directed to Carlo Rizzi's Teldec recording (with Jerry Hadley, Cecilia Gasdia and Samuel Ramey).

Jacques Offenbach (1819-1880)

The Tales of Hoffmann (1881)

Offenbach's only 'serious' opera was left unfinished at the time of his death and completed by Ernest Guiraud (the man who had also completed the orchestral suites from Bizet's *L'Arlésienne* - see "Suites and dances", see above). The plot concerns the poet E. T. A. Hoffmann whose supposed lovers turn out to be so many aspects of the one woman. Effervescent in the extreme, *Hoffmann* includes many well-known numbers, not least Hoffmann's "Legend of Kleinsach", Olympia's "Doll's Song" and the celebrated "Barcarolle".

Plácido Domingo (Hoffmann), Dame Joan Sutherland (Olympia, Giulietta, Antonia, Stella), Huguette Tourangeau (Nicklausse, Muse), Gabriel Bacquier (Lindorf, Coppélius, Dapertutto, Dr Miracle), with supporting cast, Suisse Romande Chorus and Orchestra/Richard Bonynge

Decca analogue

Sutherland's handling of the four principal female roles is matched by Bacquier's of the demonical figure who appears - again in four roles - as Hoffmann's enemy. What with Domingo's ringing tenor, Bonynge's stylish conducting and the useful inclusion of spoken dialogue, this beautifully recorded set sweeps the board. However, there's an 'old-time' runner up in André Cluytens' sparkling 1948 recording from the Opéra Comique (EMI, mono).

Camille Saint-Saëns (1835-1921)

Samson et Dalila (1877)

It was Franz Liszt who first appreciated Saint-Saëns's *Samson et Dalila*, a stirring yet lyrical work that transformed from an oratorio into an opera and was premièred not in France, but in Weimar, Germany. The biblical story concerns the seduction of Samson by Dalila, Samson's strength through prayer and the ensuing destruction of the Temple of Dagon. The most famous highlights are Dalila's arias "Printemps qui commence" and "Mon coeur s'ouvre à ta voix" (Softly awakes my heart) and the thrilling orchestral "Bacchanale".

José Luccioni (Samson), Hélène Bouvier (Dalila), Paul Cabanel (Grand Priest), Charles Cambon (Abimélech), Henri Medus (Messenger), Chorus and Orchestra of the National Theatre of the Paris Opéra/Louis Fourestier

EMI mono

Even remembering Jon Vickers and Rita Gorr on EMI and Plácido Domingo and Elena Obraztsova on DG (both of them recommendable analogue recordings), Fourestier's classic 1946 set stands out for the extraordinarily high quality of its vocal contributions. The conducting is vigorous and the mono sound constricted but clear.

Georges Bizet (1838-1875)

Carmen (1875)

If ultimately less 'great' than Verdi's *Otello* and Wagner's *Tristan und Isolde* (possibly the finest operas ever composed), Bizet's masterpiece is virtually as compelling, certainly in terms of its dramatic impact. It is also one of the most elegant operatic scores in the repertory. The libretto concerns the fateful attraction of a gipsy girl for a young corporal and the score itself inspired lavish praise from, among others, Wagner, Tchaikovsky, Wolf, Delius and the German philosopher Friedrich Nietzsche. 'Hit' numbers are far too numerous to list individually, though Carmen's Habanera and Séguedille are among the most famous.

Victoria de los Angeles (Carmen), Nicolai Gedda (Don José), Janine Michaeu (Micaëla), Ernest Blanc (Escamillo), with supporting cast, French Radio Maîtrise, French Radio Choir, French Radio National Orchestra/Sir Thomas Beecham

EMI analogue

Beecham's Carmen has long been considered a classic, partly because of los Angeles's stylish singing of the title-role, but equally on account of Beecham's

beautifully pointed conducting. Strong rivals include Marilyn Horne under Bernstein (DG, analogue), Callas under Prêtre (EMI, analogue) and an especially dynamic (mono) account with Risë Stevens under Fritz Reiner (RCA). Also, there is a stunning series of excerpts recorded pre-war by the finest Carmen on record, Conchita Supervia (EMI, Nimbus, etc, mono).

Jules Massenet (1842-1912)

Werther (1892)

Based on Goethe's novel, *The Sorrows of the Young Werther*, Massenet's passionate four-act opera – a tragic tale of love, obsession and suicide – vies with *La bohème* in its emotional impact. There are various high points, not least a number of characteristic orchestral passages (including a delicate evocation of moonlight) and *Werther*'s famous Third-Act aria, "Pourquoi me réveiller", "Why awaken me, O breath of spring?".

Nicolai Gedda (Werther), Victoria de los Angeles (Charlotte), Mady Mesplé (Sophie), with supporting cast, Orchestre de Paris/Georges Prêtre

EMI analogue

Although Sir Colin Davis's analogue Philips recording (with Frederica von Stade and José Carreras) boasts a greater level of refinement, Prêtre's forthright approach soars to the heart of the drama and provides an appropriate context for Victoria de los Angeles's wonderfully eloquent Charlotte. The 1968-69 sound is lively though just a little brash.

Prisons and pantomimes (1814-1893)

Something of an 'originals' gallery before we venture on to Wagnerian territories. Beethoven's only completed opera is shot through with noble idealism, Weber's *Der Freischütz* has many of the musical ingredients that Wagner would later exploit and Humperdinck recalls Wagner from the lighter side. The sequence is completed with some delectable lightweight masterpieces by Johann Strauss, Smetana and Sir Arthur Sullivan.

Ludwig van Beethoven (1770-1827)

Fidelio, Op. 72 (1814)

An uncompromised idealism informs Beethoven's operatic masterpiece, where Leonore, disguised as the boy Fidelio, rescues her husband Florestan from wrongful imprisonment and certain execution. The First Act includes Leonore's vehement recitative and aria ("Abscheulicher!" – an invocation to hope), while the Second Act begins with a chilling Introduction followed by the delirious Florestan's "Gott! Welch Dunkel hier!". The exhilarating finale celebrates the day and the hour "long yearned for but unforeseen".

Christa Ludwig (Leonore), Jon Vickers (Florestan), Rocco (Gottlob Frick), Don Pizarro (Walter Berry) with supporting cast, Philharmonia Chorus and Orchestra/Otto Klemperer

EMI analogue

The strength and nobility that inform Klemperer's best Beethoven symphony recordings extend to this benchmark version of Fidelio. Those in search of an extra shot of vitality are directed to Leonard Bernstein and Ferenc Fricsay (both are analogue and on DG, the former in stereo, the latter, mono), while there are riveting live (mono) performances from Wilhelm Furtwängler (EMI, Salzburg) and Bruno Walter (various 'pirate' editions, recorded at the Met during the Second World War). Both live recordings feature the great Kirsten Flagstad as Leonore.

Carl Maria von Weber (1786-1826)

Der Freischütz (1821)

Seven magic bullets should be enough for Max to win the shooting contest (winning means marriage to his beloved Agathe), but when the seventh kills the evil Huntsman Kaspar only a Hermit's wisdom ensures a joyful ending. *Der Freischütz* is a compelling music drama, concise, tuneful, colourfully orchestrated and with intimations of Wagner everywhere, not least in the chilling "Wolf's

Glen scene" in Act 2 where invisible spirits wail and the amplified voice of "The Black Huntsman" is heard in dialogue with Kaspar. More famous still are Agathe's Act 2 aria "Leise, leise, fromme Weiser" (Waft softly, gentle air) and the Overture.

 ***Elisabeth Grümmer (Agathe), Rudolf Schoeck (Max), Lisa Otto (Aennchen), Karl Christian Kohn (Kaspar), Hermann Prey (Ottokar), Gottlob Frick (Hermit), with supporting cast, Berlin Deutsche Opera Chorus, Berlin Philharmonic Orchestra/Joseph Keilberth***

EMI analogue

Keilberth's 1958 performance has first-rate singers and a genuine sense of theatre. Carlos Kleiber (DG, analogue) is virtually as exciting and Rafael Kubelík (Decca, analogue) – although deemed somewhat underpowered in some quarters – achieves a fine balance of drama and clarity.

Bedřich Smetana (1824-1884)

The bartered bride (1866)

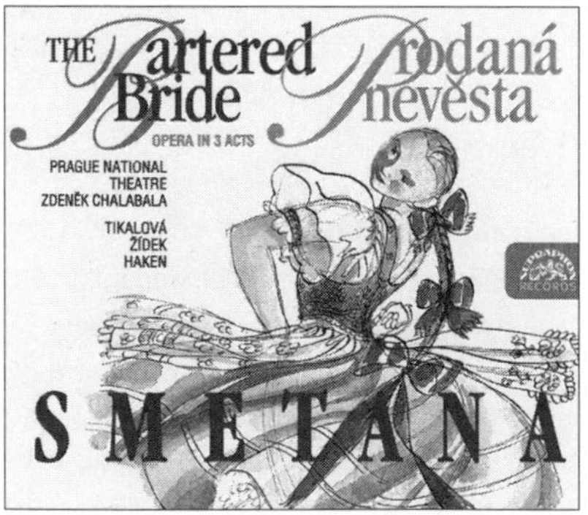

Two farmers agree that the daughter of one will marry the son of the other – although which son (there are two, one being a far better catch than the other) isn't stipulated. The upshot of all this is a tale where love triumphs over greed and cunning, but the real triumph is in a score that is charming, tuneful and imbued with an unmistakably Czech vivaciousness. *The bartered bride* was Smetana's second opera.

 ***Drahomíra Tikalová (Marenka), Ivo Zídek (Jeník), with supporting cast, Chorus and Orchestra of the Prague National Theatre/Zdenek Chalabala***

Supraphon analogue

The first-ever stereo Bartered bride is directed by a skilful conductor whose extensive experience with the Brno Opera and National Theatre Opera in Prague tells in every bar. The cast, too, is excellent, while Supraphon's spacious 1959 recording transfers to CD with remarkable clarity. However, those in search of the familiar Overture, Polka, Furiant and Dance of the Comedians are directed to a classic analogue recording by the Cleveland Orchestra conducted by George Szell (Sony).

Johann Strauss II (1825-1899)

Die Fledermaus (1874)

A delightful distillation of Straussian charm which, according to a contemporary report, found the composer "[throwing] himself into the work with all the enthusiasm of a man in love". Ths story, which had been drawn from a German comedy, concerns a practical joke, some humorous near-disasters, a pantomime and a happy ending. As to highlights, there are so many to choose from – but perhaps the most famous are the vivacious Overture (a skilfully woven pot-pourri of themes from the main body of the operetta) and the brilliant finale to the Second Act.

 ***Josef Protschka (Josef), Barbara Bonney (Adele), Edita Gruberová (Rosalinde), Werner Hollweg (Eisenstein), Waldemar Kmentt (Dr Blind), Marjana Lipovšek (Prince Orlovsky), with supporting cast, The Netherlands Opera Chorus, Royal Concertgebouw Orchestra/Nikolaus Harnoncourt***

Teldec digital

Sparkle and high spirits galore, though the specifically Viennese element isn't exactly underlined – Schwarzkopf and Karajan (EMI mono) are preferable on that score. The virtues of Harnoncourt's set are elegance, vivacity, stylish phrasing, superb playing, characterful singing and excellent sound. Spoken dialogue is replaced by a separately tracked German narration (which can easily be 'programmed out' of your listening).

Sir Arthur Sullivan (1842-1900)

The Yeomen of the Guard (or the Merryman and his Maid – words by W. S. Gilbert) (1888)

The nearest thing to a G&S 'serious opera' (which is not to descry the team's lighter masterpieces). As Arthur Jacobs has remarked, "in the libretto, there is nothing of paradox, nothing of turning things inside out, nothing of present social satire concealed as comment on some remote event (as in other operettas)". The mounting phrase heard at the beginning of the Overture stands for the Tower of London and has an almost Elgarian nobility.

Denis Dowling (Sir Richard Cholmondeley), Richard Lewis (Colonel Fairfax), John Cameron (Sergeant Meryll), Alexander Young (Leonard Meryll and First Yeoman), Geraint Evans (Jack Point), Owen Brannigan (Wilfred Shadbolt), John Carol Case (Second Yeoman), Elsie Morison (Elsie Maynard), Marjorie Thomas (Phoebe Meryll), Monica Sinclair (Dame Carruthers), Doreen Hume (Kate), Glyndebourne Festival Chorus, Pro Arte Orchestra/Sir Malcolm Sargeant

EMI analogue

A star-studded cast in a fine production of the complete musical score (Sargeant includes the duet "Rapture, rapture" which is usually omitted from stage performances), although the spoken dialogue is not included. The CD transfer, taken from a late-1950s stereo original, is first-rate and the set includes a full libretto.

Engelbert Humperdinck (1854-1921)

Hänsel und Gretel (1893)

Two hours of pure delight, cast in the shadow of Wagner (*Die Meistersinger* rather than *The Ring* – see "Twilit catastrophes", below) and with a narrative Overture that's a masterpiece in itself. The story-line is the familiar one about a brother and sister who wander into the woods, are lured to a candy cottage, fall prisoner to a witch but are saved when Gretel stuffs the witch's head into the oven. The score reflects the friendly complexion of German folk music, while its most famous movement is Hänsel and Gretel's dancing duet in the First Act.

Elisabeth Grümmer (Hänsel), Elisabeth Schwarzkopf (Gretel), Maria von Ilosvay (Mother), Josef Metternich (Father), Anny Felbermayer (Sandman, Dew Fairy), Else Schürhoff (Witch), Loughton High School for Girls Choir, Bancroft's School Choir, Philharmonia Orchestra/Herbert von Karajan

EMI mono

Karajan's magical account remains the best sung and probably the best-conducted version in the catalogue. Stereo rivals include Jeffrey Tate's digital EMI recording (with Anne Sofie von Otter and Barbara Bonney) and a lovely 1964 analogue recording – also on EMI – where André Cluytens conducts the Vienna Philharmonic in a cast that includes Irmgard Seefried and Anneliese Rothenberger.

Twilit catastropes (1843-1882)

Of all the composers who wrote for the stage, Wagner was unquestionably the most musically innovative. His revolutionary harmonic and orchestral ideas totally transformed the music of the next two or three generations, and continue to reverberate even to this day. The music dramas themselves (the term 'opera' suggested the vapid stage spectaculars that Wagner was reacting against) are all-embracing, highly dramatic tone-poems that, generally speaking, sit more comfortably in the imagination than on the stage of the average opera house.

Richard Wagner (1813-1883)

The Flying Dutchman (1843)

Wind and sea-spray bombard us in a masterly Overture that anticipates the thrilling action-music of Wagner's first mature music drama (in this respect alone, *The Flying Dutchman* is probably closer in spirit to *The Ring* than the slightly later *Tannhäuser*). The plot concerns a Dutch sea captain who has been condemned to sail the world until the Day of Judgement and who is redeemed only by his loved one's desperate suicide. Aside from the Overture, the *Dutchman*'s most celebrated episodes include Senta's Ballade ("Yohohoe! Yohohohoe! ..."), the Dutchman's recitative and aria "Die Frist ist um..." ("The time is up"), and a stamping chorus of Norwegian sailors (beginning of Act 3).

Franz Crass (Dutchman), Anja Silja (Senta), Josef Greindl (Daland), Fritz Uhl (Erik), Res Fischer (Mary), Georg Paskuda (Steersman), Bayreuth Festival Chorus and Orchestra/Wolfgang Sawallisch

Philips analogue

Choosing between this thrilling though fairly swift Dutchman (a 1961 production in still-vivid stereo) and a more measured – though equally exciting – 1954 Bayreuth production with a classic cast that includes Ludwig

Weber, Astrid Varnay, Wolfgang Windgassen and Hermann Uhde under Hans Knappertsbusch (Music & Arts, mono) is next to impossible. Sawallisch 'wins' merely by dint of marginally superior sound – but do try to hear the Knappertsbusch set as well.

Lohengrin (1850)

Wagner's mastery of the orchestra surfaces triumphantly in this, his most popular opera. *Lohengrin* (Parsifal's son and the Knight of the Grail) sails into view on a swan-drawn boat to claim the troubled kingdom of Brabant. He promises to marry Elsa (who has been accused by Count Telramund of murdering the heir to the kingdom) provided she asks neither his name nor his origins. Lohengrin kills Telramund in self-defence and sails away in a boat drawn by a dove of the Holy Grail. Highlights of *Lohengrin* include an ethereal Prelude (the string-writing is exquisite), a brief but thrilling Third-Act Prelude (ending, in the opera, with what most people will know as "Here comes the bride"), a tender love duet, and Lohengrin's 'aria', "In fernem Land" ("A distant land").

James King (Lohengrin), Gundula Janowitz (Elsa), Karl Ridderbusch (King Henry), Thomas Stewart (Friedrich von Telramund), Gwyneth Jones (Ortrud) with supporting cast, Bavarian Radio Chorus and Orchestra/Rafael Kubelík

Deutsche Grammophon analogue.

A difficult choice but, I think, a strong one – primarily for Gundula Janowitz's radiant Elsa and Rafael Kubelík's vital, clear-headed conducting (how I wish he'd recorded a complete Ring!). The Third Act is a good place to sample (even the Prelude is given one of the most cleanly incisive performances on disc). James King's heroic Lohengrin does occasionally show signs of strain, and Gwyneth Jones's Ortrud is prone to wobble – but the recording is excellent (the Munich brass sounds magnificent) and the performance as a whole, warmly considered. Wilhelm Schüchter's mono EMI recording with Rudolf Schock as Lohengrin is a viable historic alternative.

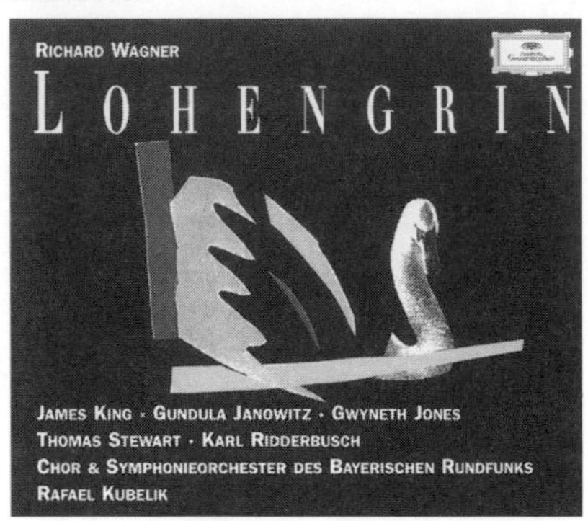

Die Meistersinger von Nürnberg (1868)

The most genial and accessible of Wagner's mature operas celebrates all that is best in German life and art. Walther von Stolzing wants to win the hand of Eva, but also needs to win the Mastersinger's song contest (an event held by the Guild of Mastersingers during the fifteenth century). Hans Sachs (a German shoemaker, poet and mastersinger) helps him compose the winning song and snub the carping critic Beckmesser. Among *Die Meistersinger*'s best-known highlights are the majestic Overture, Walther's "Prize Song", the "Fliedermonolog" and the sublime Quintet.

Ferdinand Frantz (Hans Sachs), Gottlob Frick (Pogner), Gustav Neidlinger (Kothner), Rudolf Schock (Walther), Gerhard Unger (David), Elisabeth Grümmer (Eva), Marga Höffgen (Magdalene), Chorus of the German Opera Berlin and German State Opera Berlin, Choir of St Hedwig's Cathedral Berlin, Berlin Philharmonic Orchestra/Rudolf Kempe

EMI mono

Good Meistersingers on CD are legion (recording-wise, it has been by far the luckiest of Wagner's operas). The vintage/historic department alone boasts such star conductors as Furtwängler (Grammofono, mono), Abendroth (Preiser, mono), Böhm (Preiser, mono), Knappertsbusch (Decca, mono), Eugen Jochum (DG, analogue or Myto, mono), Karajan (EMI, analogue) and Kubelík (Myto, analogue – an especially fine performance). Rudolf Kempe's performance is distinguished by great warmth of delivery, consistently good singing (Frantz's Hans Sachs and Grümmer's Eva are especially memorable), excellent orchestral playing and well-balanced 1956 mono sound.

Parsifal (1882)

Parsifal is the 'Pure Fool made Wise through Pity' who rebuffs seduction, becomes King of the Holy Grail (which he retrieves from theft) and, through his actions, heals the former guardian of the Grail, Amfortas. Wagner's last completed music drama contains some of the grandest, most noble music in the operatic repertory, not least the expansive Prelude, the "Transformation" music from Acts 1 and 3 (the first, which accompanies a scene-change from woodlands to the castle of the Holy Grail, is quite unforgettable), the "Good Friday" music from Act 3 and the whole of the final scene. *Parsifal*, together with *Tristan und Isolde*, is one of the most profoundly influential scores of the late-nineteenth century (Debussy's *Pélleas* is unthinkable without its influence).

 ***Jess Thomas (Parsifal), George London (Amfortas), Martti Talvela (Titurel), Hans Hotter (Gurnemanz), Gustav Neidlinger (Klingsor), Irene Dalis (Kundry), Chorus and Orchestra of the 1962 Bayreuth Festival/Hans Knappertsbusch***
Philips analogue

Hans Knappertsbusch was the pre-eminent interpreter of Parsifal during and immediately after the Second World War; his broad pacing, long-breathed phrasing and innate dramatic sense helped to illuminate every meaningful gesture in Wagner's magnificent score. However, some critics prefer an earlier Knappertsbusch recording, made at the post-war re-opening of the Bayreuth Festival in 1951 (which, like our present recommendation, was taped live). And although that mono Decca recording (available now on Teldec) is, in some respects, even more intense than its successor (the singing, viewed overall, is rather better), Hans Hotter's eloquent Gurnemanz – plus Philips's vastly superior sound – incline me towards the 1962 performance. However, digital-only collectors are well served by Daniel Barenboim's excellent Teldec recording with the Berlin Philharmonic.

Der Ring des Nibelungen (The Ring of the Nibelung) (1848-74)

The story of *The Ring*, which is far too complex and multi-faceted to précis with any accuracy, concerns man's malignant lust for power (and of course gold, the base-metal of the Ring itself) and the contrast between loveless relationships and unconditional love (whether between siblings – as with the brother and sister Siegmund and Sieglinde – or between two independent spirits). As Wagner-scholar Barry Millington has written, "[*The Ring*] is not merely a tale about the adventures of gods, giants, dwarves and dragons, it is an allegory of the conflicts that arise when civilization and power politics obtrude on the innocent world of nature". *The Ring* is sub-divided into four separate works which, although frequently heard in isolation, are the music drama equivalents of the four movements of a massive symphony (which, incidentally, plays for some 15 hours). The first, or "preliminary evening" is *Das Rheingold* (the shortest of the four), the second, or "first day", *Die Walküre*, the third, or "second day" *Siegfried* and the fourth and final "day", *Götterdämmerung*, or "The Twilight of the Gods". *The Ring* is a veritable treasure-trove of action music, nature music and compositional ingenuity (each character or place has its own *leitmotif*, or "leading motif"), whether painting the waters of the Rhine, the fearsome Ride of the Valkyries, the nobility of Wotan's Farewell to his daughter Brünnhilde, the machinations of the dwarves Mime or Alberich, the confrontation of the hero Siegfried with the dragon Fafner, the love of Brünnhilde for Siegfried, Siegfried's death or the inevitable destruction of Valhalla.

 ***Birgit Nilsson (Brünnhilde), Wolfgang Windgassen (Siegfried), Hans Hotter/George London (Wotan), Gustav Neidlinger (Alberich, Fafner), Gerhard Stolze (Mime), Gottlob Frick (Hagen, Hunding), James King (Siegmund), Régine Crespin (Sieglinde), Kirsten Flagstad/Christa Ludwig (Fricka), with supporting cast, Vienna State Opera Chorus, Vienna Philharmonic Orchestra/Sir Georg Solti***
Decca analogue

Any single choice of The Ring on CD is likely to prove controversial and Sir Georg Solti's – which was recorded between 1958 and 1967 – is more controversial than most. The reason for this is that Solti jabs, speeds and thunders rather than sweeps a generous musical line (as, say, Wilhelm Furtwängler does in his two riveting live recordings – from La Scala [in 1950, Music & Arts] or Rome Radio [in 1953, EMI]). The singing, too, is variable: Hans Hotter, a magnificent Wotan in his prime, was by this time past his best and many will find Gerhard Stolze's hectoring Mime decidedly over-the-top. However, Birgit Nilsson is a commanding Brünnhilde (she was at the peak of her powers when these recordings were made) and John Culshaw's 'Soundstage' recording is the aural equivalent of a Spielberg movie – instrumental/vocal imaging is extraordinarily vivid, there are sound effects galore and the stereo production is a source of excitement in itself. If you're approaching The Ring for the first time and have no particular preconceptions about singing, performance style or, dare I say, Sir Georg Solti – then the Decca set should prove immensely compelling. There are, however, numerous fine alternatives: aside from Furtwängler (whose La Scala Ring is marginally more spontaneous than its better considered – and vocally more consistent – Rome Radio alternative), Herbert von Karajan (DG, analogue) is meticulously observant over details of scoring; Karl Böhm (Philips, analogue – live from Bayreuth, 1966 – also with Nilsson) is swift and energetic; Clemens Krauss (1953, Foyer, mono – again from Bayreuth) is more lyrical and has a superb cast (including Hotter in his prime) and Daniel Barenboim conducts what is probably the best all-round digital version (Teldec – another live production from Bayreuth, 1991).

Tannhäuser – music drama (1845)

Wagner's first fully-fledged music drama concerns the knight Tannhäuser, who has been excommunicated by the world and the church but who can be saved by the pure love and self-sacrifice of Elisabeth (the antithesis of the heathen goddess Venus). Musical highlights include an Overture headed by the celebrated "Pilgrim's chorus" and extended, in the version that Wagner wrote for Napoleon III and the Paris Opéra, to incorporate a thrilling "Bacchanale" (the two are often performed together). Almost as famous are "Elisabeth's Greeting" and Tannhäuser's "Rome Narration".

Wolfgang Windgassen (Tannhäuser), Anja Silja (Elisabeth), Grace Bumbry (Venus), Josef Greindl (Hermann), Eberhard Waechter (Wolfram), Gerhard Stolze (Walther), with supporting cast, Bayreuth Festival Chorus and Orchestra/Wolfgang Sawallisch

Philips analogue

Recorded live in 1962 at Wagner's own theatre, Sawallisch's performance has tremendous energy (sample the Overture and Bacchanale, complete with shouts and dancing feet). The cast, too, is excellent, especially Wolfgang Windgassen, who is captured towards the end of his best vocal period. The sound is a little dry but very immediate.

Tristan und Isolde – music drama (1865)

Tristan's Prelude revolutionized music for the twentieth century, opening doors – via its weighted harmonies and rich colouring – for all manner of extravagant orchestral canvases. *Tristan und Isolde*, however, is the greatest of them all, a fervent love poem that casts a spell every bit as powerful as the potion that the lovers themselves fall victim to. The Second Act's "Liebesnacht" is a particular highlight, whereas Tristan's Third Act delirium (he scours the horizon for Isolde's ship) has the capacity to re-awaken one's first pubescent infatuations.

Ludwig Suthaus (Tristan), Kirsten Flagstad (Isolde), Dietrich Fischer-Dieskau (Kurwenal), with supporting cast, Chorus of the Royal Opera House, Covent Garden, Philharmonia Orchestra/Wilhelm Furtwängler

EMI mono

Seamless, sonorous and with an inspiring sense of majesty, Furtwängler's epoch-making Tristan (recorded in 1952) remains a firm top recommendation. Flagstad's Isolde is mature but magical, Suthaus's Tristan, manly and vulnerable, while the orchestra rises to climactic peaks with a combination of ease and emotional fervour. A swifter, more animated performance under Carlos Kleiber (DG, digital) has Margaret Price as a fine Isolde whereas some 'unofficial' labels (Acanta, Fonitcetra, mono) have issued substantial portions of a live 1947 performance under Furtwängler (again with Suthaus, but with an undistinguished Isolde) that adds a further perspective on an already overwhelming experience.

A Russian trio (1874-1890)

The founding father of Russian opera was Mikhail Glinka, whose operas *A Life for the Tsar* (1836) and *Ruslan and Lyudmilla* (1842) pay a small debt to Italian models. Tchaikovsky's operas contain some of his greatest music, while *Boris Godunov* is unquestionably Mussorgsky's masterpiece.

Modest Mussorgsky (1839-1881)

Boris Godunov (original version) (1874)

Boris Godunov speaks volumes, both in terms of its libretto (Mussorgsky's own, concerning a tsar who murdered the true heir to the throne) and its vivid projection of the pre-Communist Russian psyche. However, *Boris* has a long and complex history, starting with the raw first versions, then progressing through Mussorgsky's own revisions, to the colourful (and for a long time highly popular) re-orchestration by Rimsky-Korsakov.

Controversy still reigns as to which version is best, although current thinking veers towards Mussorgsky's stark, naturalistic original.

 ***Anatoly Kocherga (Boris), Sergei Larin (Grigory), Marjana Lipovšek (Marina), Samuel Ramey (Pimen), Gleb Nikolsky (Varlaam), Philip Langridge (Shuisky), with supporting cast, Slovak Philharmonic Choir, Berlin Radio Choir, Tölz Boys' Choir, Berlin Philharmonic Orchestra/Claudio Abbado***

Sony Classical digital

A problematic choice, especially as the finest singers tend to appear in the context of Rimsky's revised version of the opera. Kocherga is a good rather than outstanding Boris, but Abbado's conducting of the original score is magnificent. Those in search of a 'great' Boris are directed to either of Boris Christoff's analogue EMI recordings (under André Cluytens in stereo or, preferably, under Issay Dobrowen in mono), while the magnificent Mark Reizen sings under Nikolai Golovanov (rough sound on Arlecchino or Melodiya, mono) and there are riveting 1928 live Covent Garden extracts featuring the incomparable Fyodor Chaliapin (the greatest Boris of all – EMI, mono).

Pyotr Il'yich Tchaikovsky
(1840–1892)

Eugene Onegin (1878)

Tchaikovsky preferred the title "lyrical scenes" to "opera", an option that speaks volumes about the nature of the piece. Furthermore, because the first performance (which pleased its composer) was undertaken by amateurs in modern dress, the reaction was largely negative. However, this gripping tale of love and remorse inspired some of Tchaikovsky's most attractive music (the actual libretto is a Pushkin-Tchaikovsky synthesis), not least Tatyana's Letter Scene, Lensky's aria ("What can I look for, from this morning?") and two celebrated orchestral excerpts, the "Waltz" and "Polonaise".

 ***Galina Vishnevskaya (Tatyana), Yevgeny Belov (Onegin), Sergey Lemeshev (Lensky), Ivan Petrov (Prince Gremin), with supporting cast, Bolshoi Theatre soloists, Chorus and Orchestra/Boris Khaikin***

Melodiya mono

A dramatic, unindulgent performance featuring Galina Vishnevskaya as a great Tatyana near the beginning of her career and Sergey Lemeshev as a great Lensky near the end of his. Supporting roles are all extremely well sung, Khaikin's conducting is admirably natural and the mono sound is close but clear. Digital-fanciers are directed to Semyon Bychkov's Paris recording on Philips.

The Queen of Spades (Pique Dame) (1890)

"I hoped that the surges of passionate feeling and the fears felt by its composer would strike a chord in the hearts of the audience." Tchaikovsky had initially rejected the idea of setting Pushkin's drama to music (his previous opera, *The Sorceress*, has been a flop), although he later changed his mind and even became excited by his 'work in progress'. The plot concerns love, obsession and suicide, but what really matters is the music itself, which approximates the depth, creative originality and burning emotion of the Fourth and Fifth Symphonies. Tchaikovsky wrote nothing greater for the stage.

 ***Gegam Grigorian (Herman), Maria Gulegina (Lisa), Irina Arkhipova (Countess), Nikolai Putilin (Count Tomsky), Vladimir Chernov (Prince Yeletsky), Olga Borodina (Pauline), with supporting cast, Kirov Theatre Chorus and Orchestra/Valery Gergiev***

Philips digital

Finely honed, vigorous conducting, good singing and a realistic sound-stage (the balance between voices and orchestra is admirable). Although Gergiev's Queen of Spades is, generally speaking, the best available, note should also be made of Seiji Ozawa's RCA digital version with Mirella Freni as Lisa.

Further listening *Rimsky Korsakov's Sadko includes "The Song of the Viking Guest" and "The Song of the Indian Guest", and is best heard in a stupendous performance under Nikolai Golovanov (Arlecchino, mono). Also, keep an eye out for Mark Reizen in Mussorgsky's Khovantschina (Melodiya, mono) and various collections devoted to old opera stars, most notably "Singers of Imperial Russia" (Pearl, mono). There's much to be learned from studying 78s of great singers, and all the operatic recordings listed in the Guinness Classical 1000 could be profitably supplemented by CDs of 'vintage' excerpts.*

Psychologists and psychoses (1902-1957)

Some modern composers would tell you that opera – as a potential creative genre – is dead; others, continue to exploit it. Most works in this section take up the story where Wagner left off, delving ever deeper into the human psyche and exploring all manner of drama, imagery and fantasy. The twentieth century has also witnessed considerable developments in the opera composer's use of the orchestra: most of the works included are enjoyed as much for their vivid instrumentation as for the power of their vocal writing.

Leoš Janáček (1854-1928)

The Cunning Little Vixen (1924)

Janáček's love of nature glows especially bright through some extraordinarily vivid writing, not least in the quietly rustic Prelude, the 'Dawn' sequence when the Vixen appears in her animal shape and such charming episodes as the Little Foxes' ballet steps in the opera's penultimate scene. The libretto concerns, on the one hand, a school teacher and parson who contend for the love of a gipsy girl and, on the other, a Forester who makes off with a fox cub, tries to bring her up but when she causes havoc in the farmyard, rather welcomes her escape. The Vixen then marries Goldmane the fox, bears him offspring but dies at the hands of a poacher. The Forester's spirits lift when he encounters the Vixen's daughter and the life-cycle is seen to be renewed.

 ***Zdenek Kroupa (Forester), Helena Tattermuschová (Vixen), Eva Zikmundová (Fox), with supporting cast, Prague National Chorus and Orchestra/Bohumil Gregor***
Supraphon analogue

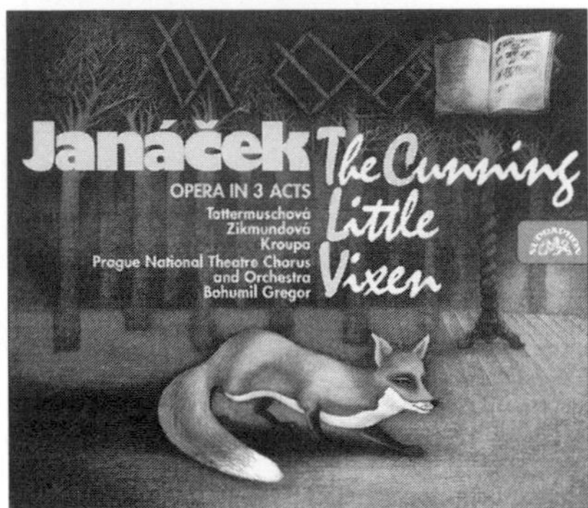

The star attraction here is Helena Tattermuschová's bright, mischievous Vixen – the best that this listener has ever heard (Tattermuschová is a brilliant coloratura soprano). Gregor's conducting is both atmospheric and idiomatic (the Czech violins' silvery timbre is an added bonus) and the recording – which won a "Grand Prix du Disque" in 1974 – comes up remarkably well on CD. Sir Charles Mackerras's digital Decca recording (with Lucia Popp as the Vixen) is an obvious second choice, whereas those who fancy sampling the orchestral Suite – and there's more than enough orchestral tone painting in the opera to justify one – should try Gennadi Rozhdestvensky's 1976 recording (Melodiya, analogue).

The Makropulos Affair (1926)

Anyone attracted to Janáček's quirky and multi-coloured instrumental works cannot fail to respond to his operas – at least four of which (the two featured here, plus *Jenufa* and *Káta Kabanová*) fully justify the 'masterpiece' accolade. Right from its opening Prelude, Janáček's tale of a 342-year-old heroine preserved by a magical elixir casts a powerful spell. The libretto is based on a play by Capek, while the music is typically breathless, dramatic and highly coloured. In fact, one's interest is held as much by the orchestration as by the vocal writing.

 ***Elisabeth Söderström (Emilia Marty), Peter Dvorsky (Albert Gregor), Vladimir Krejcík (Vitek), with supporting cast, Vienna State Opera Choir, Vienna Philharmonic Orchestra/Sir Charles Mackerras***
Decca analogue

Marvellous characterization from Söderström, with excellent vocal support (especially from Dvorsky). Sir Charles Mackerras's long-term experience as a Janáček specialist informs virtually every page while the Vienna Philharmonic provides a sumptuous orchestral backdrop. There's a bonus too in the guise of Janáček's attractive Lachian Dances, keenly dispatched by the London Philharmonic under François Huybrechts. The recordings are superb.

Claude Debussy (1862-1918)

Pelléas et Mélisande (1902)

A haunting narrative, sombre in mood, rich in musical half-lights and where various orchestral interludes help to intensify the spell. A prince finds a young girl weeping in a wood; he takes her back to his grandfather's castle, marries her but, when she establishes a relationship with another man, the prince murders him. *Pelléas et Mélisande* is a compelling 'tone-poem with voices' that is as responsive to the imagination as to the physical stage.

 ***Irène Joachim (Mélisande), Jacques Jansen (Pelléas), Henri Etcheverry (Golaud) with supporting cast, Yvonne Gouverné Chorus and Symphony Orchestra/Roger Desormière***

EMI mono

Like Furtwängler's Tristan and Toscanini's Otello, Desormière's Pelléas established interpretative standards that have never been matched: the singing is extremely poignant (Joachim is a fragile though animated Mélisande), the conducting both sensitive and urgently dramatic and the recording – made during the dark days of the Nazi Occupation of France – remarkably good. There are countless worthy alternatives, with Ernest Ansermet (Decca, mono) and Claudio Abbado (DG, digital) heading the list – but Desormière's is the version to hear first.

Frederick Delius (1862-1934)

A Village Romeo and Juliet – lyric drama, RT1/6 (1907)

The story follows the expected path of forbidden love between the offspring of warring families. Musically, Delius's score runs the gamut from exquisite tenderness (the celebrated "Walk to the Paradise Garden" is typical but by no means unique) to passages of great passion and dramatic impact. Although it might seem a little misleading to label *A Village Romeo and Juliet* a 'suburban *Tristan und Isolde*', the opera's sum effect does rather suggest the parallel. Note, also, that the original libretto was in German, the first performance in Berlin and the story-line based on a specific event said to have occurred in Germany during the mid-nineteenth century.

 ***Denis Dowling (Manz), Frederick Sharp (Marti), Margaret Ritchie (Sali as a child), René Soames (Sali), Dorothy Bond (Vreli), Lorely Dyer (Vreli as a child), Gordon Clinton (Dark Fiddler), Chorus, Royal Philharmonic Orchestra/Sir Thomas Beecham***

EMI mono

A combination of heartfelt singing (intimate rather than overtly operatic), felicitous instrumental phrasing and candid drama make this a performance of a lifetime – and streets ahead of various partially-successful stereo successors. The transfer – from 1948 originals – is superb.

Richard Strauss (1864-1949)

Elektra, Op. 58 (1909)

A classic tale of vengeance, dominated by the ghost of Agamemnon and orchestrated with such imagination, dramatic skill and harmonic daring (Strauss calls for 111 players, carefully sub-divided) that even Mahler found it hard to swallow. Strauss himself referred to the 'unending climaxes' in the scenes between Elektra and either Chrysothemis or her mother Klytemnestra. Just try the passage where Elektra and Orestes suddenly recognize each other (disc 2, track 8 on our recommended version) and the complex web of emotions thereafter, so superbly expressed in Strauss's music.

 ***Birgit Nilsson (Elektra), Regina Resnik (Klytemnestra), Marie Collier (Chrysothemis), Gerhard Stolze (Aegisthus), Tom Krause (Orestes), with supporting cast, Vienna Philharmonic Orchestra/Sir Georg Solti***

Decca analogue

A thrilling collaboration between singers, orchestra, conductor and producer (John Culshaw), and probably Sir Georg Solti's greatest recording. Various live versions also lobby for attention, but mention should also be made of a superlative sequence of excerpts where Inge Borkh sings Elektra and Fritz Reiner conducts (RCA, analogue).

Der Rosenkavalier, Op. 59 (1911)

Opulent, warming and a dizzy synthesis of Viennese charm (there are waltzes galore) and Straussian sophistication. The libretto, by Hugo von Hofmannsthal, concerns the young Sophie who is betrothed to Baron Ochs, falls in love with young Octavian and helps trick Ochs into abandoning his intentions. *Rosenkavalier* is full of musical high-points: in addition to various orchestral suites, there is the Letter Scene, the Presentation of the Silver Rose to Sophie and the Waltz Sequences from Acts 2 and 3.

 ***Elisabeth Schwarzkopf (Die Feldmarschallin), Otto Edelmann (Baron Ochs), Christa Ludwig (Octavian), Eberhard Wächter (Faninal), Teresa Stich-Randall (Sophie), Ljuba Welitsch (Marianne), Paul Kuen (Valzacchi), Kerstin Meyer (Annina), Nicolai Gedda (Italian Tenor), Philharmonia***

Chorus and Orchestra/Herbert von Karajan
EMI analogue

With an absolutely superb cast (the women especially), fine conducting, stylish orchestral playing and an impeccable EMI/Walter Legge production, this remains one of the classic opera recordings of all time. The CD transfer is first-rate (although Schwarzkopf herself much prefers the mono original) and the only recorded performance that approaches it is a pre-war sequence of highlights with Elisabeth Schumann and Lotte Lehmann, under Robert Heger (EMI, mono).

Salome, Op. 54 (1905)

"An active volcano is at work under a heap of slag, a subterranean fire – not merely a firework." So wrote Gustav Mahler on Strauss's grizzly but infinitely subtle setting of Oscar Wilde's play about Salome's sexual obsession with John the Baptist and Herod's with Salome. *Salome* is a tone-poem with voices, decadent yet delicate and with many passages of great lyrical beauty. The final scene, where Salome kisses the lips of John the Baptist's severed head, is one of the most devastating in all opera – no, in all music!

 ***Birgit Nilsson (Salome), Gerhard Stolze (Herod), Grace Hoffman (Herodias), Eberhard Wächter (Jokanaan), Waldemar Kmentt (Narraboth), with supporting cast, Vienna Philharmonic Orchestra/Sir Georg Solti***
Decca analogue

Magnificently produced by the late John Culshaw, Solti's Salome is truly electrifying, not least for the sheer power of Nilsson's singing, the orchestra's virtuosity and the sonic impact of – in particular – the "Dance of the Seven Veils" and the ensuing final scene. Subtler renditions exist (Karl Böhm, DG, analogue; Christoph von Dohnányi, Decca, digital, and Erich Leinsdorf, RCA, analogue, being just three), but none delivers a surer punch.

Hans Pfitzner (1653-1713)

Palestrina (1917)

Some of the century's noblest music is contained in this, Hans Pfitzner's masterpiece. The libretto (by the composer himself) concerns the Council of Trent's ruling (1563) that Palestrina's music was too florid and therefore unsuitable for liturgical use. The style of writing makes audible reference to early modes (albeit in a modernized form) while the opera's dramatic conflicts reflect contemporary tensions in Pfitzner's own creative life.

 ***Nicolai Gedda (Palestrina), Karl Ridderbusch (Pope Pius IV), Bernd Weikl, Heribert Steinbach, Karl Ridderbusch, Dietrich Fischer-Dieskau (Cardinals), Hermann Prey (Graf Luna), Helen Donath (Ighino), Brigitte Fassbaender (Silla), with supporting cast, Bavarian Radio Chorus and Symphony Orchestra/Rafael Kubelík***
Deutsche Grammophon analogue

It would be difficult to imagine a more perceptive, flexible or sensitively sung performance, with Kubelík – a composer himself who was surely familiar with the conflicts inherent in musical creativity – proving Palestrina's ideal conductor. The 1970s recording remains excellent.

Arnold Schoenberg (1874-1951)

Erwartung, Op. 17 (1909)

Schoenberg's nightmare 'monodrama in one act' (it plays for under half-an-hour) is based on a poem by Marie Pappenheim that tells of a women running through a wood at the dead of night in search of her lover. Suddenly, she stumbles across his body – but was she the murderer? *Erwartung* is cast in a grainy, acerbic musical language (the idiom is securely atonal), though the score also includes many tender moments. It is remarkable to think that *Erwartung* was completed before Elgar's Second Symphony!

 ***Phyllis Bryn-Julson (soprano), City of Birmingham Symphony Orchestra/Sir Simon Rattle***
EMI digital

Sir Simon Rattle plumbs Erwartung's complex psychology, while Bryn-Julson balances terror with humanity and compassion. The recording is both detailed and dynamic (qualities that also apply to Rattle's performance): the penultimate climax (track 14, 2'34") has all the power of Bartók's internment of Judith (in Bluebeard's Castle, see below).

Moses und Aron (1930-32)

Moses the philosopher is portrayed by a bass using *Sprechstimme* (a cross between speech and singing), whereas the materialist Aron is sung by a tenor and God is ingeniously represented by a multi-perspectival chorus. The score includes a highly graphic "Dance Around the Golden Calf", but Schoenberg never lived to complete the final scene – the words of which (his own) are usually printed in the CD booklet. *Moses und Aron* (so-named because the letters in Moses und Aaron – i.e. with Aaron claiming his second 'a' – would have totalled the dreaded number 13) vies with Berg's *Wozzeck* for achieving an almost ideal marriage of words and music. Its 'masterpiece' status is due as much to its philosophical ideas as to its complex but riveting score.

Günter Reich (Moses), Louis Devos (Aron), with supporting cast, Chorus and Orchestra of Austrian Radio/Michael Gielen

Philips analogue

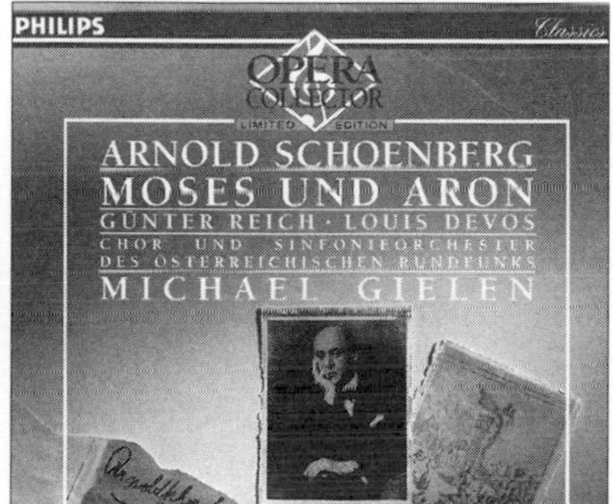

The singing is good, but the conducting is great – not because it's especially dramatic (Solti – on Decca, digital – has the edge in that respect), but because Gielen makes sense of every phrase; he clarifies the score's shape and logic. The early-1970s recording is clean and full-bodied. Pierre Boulez (DG) provides strong digital rivalry.

Maurice Ravel (1875-1937)

L'enfant et les sortilèges (1925)

"The Child and his Spells" is not only a masterpiece, but the ideal vehicle for introducing young people to the concept of opera – especially if they've previously been saddled with tiresome arias and squally sopranos. A bored and disobedient child wreaks havoc on his surroundings but gets his come-uppance when his victims – which include a sofa, a cup, a teapot, an armchair, pet animals, etc – get their own back. The score is evocative, sensual and witty, while the ending is both consolatory and indescribably beautiful.

Françoise Ogéas (Child), with supporting cast, French Radio National Orchestra/Lorin Maazel

Deutsche Grammophon analogue

The best-sung stereo version with superb solo playing, vivid characterization and a recording that, although some 35 years old, still sounds amazing. A good digital alternative is conducted by Charles Dutoit (Decca), while Ernest Bour's Award-winning French recording (Testament, mono) rates as an all-time great.

Béla Bartók (1881-1945)

Bluebeard's Castle, Sz48 (Op. 11) (1911)

A tale of male privacy and female curiosity loosely based on a well-known fairy tale. Judith finds herself in Duke Bluebeard's Castle; she has heard distant rumours of 'murdered' wives and persuades him to reveal what lies behind each of seven doors – his torture chamber, armoury, treasure-trove, magic garden, mighty domain and lake of tears, all of them painted in incredibly vivid orchestral colours. The last door guards Bluebeard's previous wives who are barely alive and who Judith is destined to join.

John Tomlinson (bass), Anne Sofie von Otter (mezzo-soprano), Berlin Philharmonic Orchestra/Bernard Haitink

EMI digital

Tomlinson's Bluebeard is inscrutable and not a little arrogant, whereas von Otter's Judith is vulnerable but determined. Bernard Haitink directs a thoughtful though dramatic account of the score and the recording – made live in the Berlin Philharmonie early in 1996 – presents an imposing sound picture. There are fine analogue alternatives under Pierre Boulez (Sony), Antál Dorati (Mercury) and János Ferencsik (his mono version, Hungaroton).

Igor Stravinsky (1882-1971)

Oedipus Rex (1925-27, revised 1948)

A granitic, deeply impassioned "opera-oratorio", rhythmically driven and theatrically effective – both on stage and on record. The famous tale of Oedipus, who claws out his own eyes when he realizes that he has unwittingly slain his father and married his mother, makes for a musical drama of superhuman psychological force. The adaptation is by Jean Cocteau and the work has a narrator declaim the various stages of the story.

 ***Ivo Zidek (Oedipus), Vera Soukupová (Jocasta), Karel Berman (Creon), Eduard Haken (Tiresias), Zdenek Kroupa (Messenger), Antonín Zlesák (Shepherd), Jean Desailly (Narrator), Czech Philharmonic Chorus and Orchestra/Karel Ančerl***

Supraphon analogue

A superb performance that employs some of Czechoslovakia's finest post-war singers. Ančerl's conducting is lithe and dynamic, while the recording – which dates from 1965 – holds up remarkably well. Best among Ančerl's rivals are Stravinsky himself (either of his Sony recordings, the one with Peter Pears and Jean Cocteau – in mono – being the better of the two), Leonard Bernstein and the Boston Symphony (Sony, analogue) and a remarkable German-language recording under Ferenc Fricsay (DG, mono).

The Rake's Progress (1951)

Stravinsky's only full-scale opera also marks the crowning glory of his Neo-Classical phase. The music refers back to Mozart and Verdi (of *Falstaff*), as well as to various of Stravinsky's own works (at one point *Apollo* makes a brief entrance). The libretto, by W. H. Auden and Chester Kalman, concerns Tom Rakewell, who learns from Nick Shadow that he has inherited a fortune, is induced to take Shadow on as his servant and loses his sanity to the Devil (who, as it turns out, is Nick Shadow).

 ***Robert Lloyd (Trulove), Dawn Upshaw (Anne), Jerry Hadley (Tom Rakewell), Samuel Ramey (Nick Shadow), Anne Collins (Mother Goose), Grace Bumbry (Baba the Turk), Steven Cole (Sellem), Roderick Earle (Keeper), Chorus and Orchestra of Lyon Opera/Kent Nagano***

Erato digital

With Jerry Hadley an extraordinarily vivid Rakewell and Samuel Ramey a characterful Nick Shadow, this proves a most satisfying performance – much aided by Kent Nagano's stylish conducting (just try his sensitive handling of the brief but beguiling chorus "How sad a song", on disc 1, the beginning of track 19). However, there's significant rivalry from Robert Craft (Music Masters, digital – a very swift but extremely invigorating performance) and Stravinsky himself (with the excellent Alexander Young as Tom Rakewell, Sony analogue).

Alban Berg (1885–1935)

Wozzeck, Op. 7 (1925)

It took 137 rehearsals to prepare the first performance of Berg's greatest masterpiece, an opera in three acts and 15 scenes based on a play by Büchner (*Woyzeck* was the original title) about a Private who kills his mistress Marie for fraternizing with the Drum Major. The score presents astonishing musical reportage of varied states of mind, from rage, pride, passion and confusion (Marie's orphaned child on her rocking horse) to the eerie gurgling that describes Wozzeck's accidental drowning – one of the most deeply disturbing episodes in the whole of twentieth-century music.

 ***Dietrich Fischer-Dieskau (Wozzeck), Fritz Wunderlich (Andres), Gerhard Stolze (Captain), Evelyn Lear (Marie), Karl Christian Kohn (Doctor), Helmut Melchert (Drum Major), Chorus and Orchestra of the German Opera, Berlin/Karl Böhm.***

Deutsche Grammophon analogue

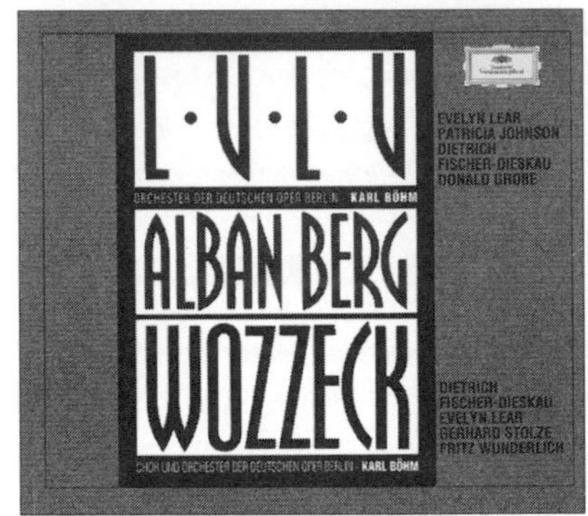

Although Claudio Abbado's digital Vienna recording (also DG) is immensely compelling, this 1965 analogue version under Karl Böhm (a somewhat unpredictable recording artist who is here heard at white heat) has the advantage of Fischer-Dieskau's masterful characterization. The recording too is amazingly good for its years.

Lulu (first performed incomplete in 1937)

Lulu's catalogue of decadent acts has to be heard to be believed. The plot (after plays by Wedekind) concerns a seductress, her three husbands and her lesbian admirer, all of whom meet their deaths – the protagonist herself at the hands of Jack the Ripper. *Lulu* was left unfinished at the time of Berg's death and completed (i.e. the Third Act, which was only partially orchestrated) by

Friedrich Cerha (first performed in 1979). A Symphonic Suite includes some of the score's most imposing music, though not enough to excuse not listening to the whole opera – preferably with Cerha's Third Act orchestration.

Teresa Stratas (Lulu), Franz Mazura (Dr Schön), Kenneth Riegel (Alwa), Yvonne Minton (Countess Geschwitz), Robert Tear (Painter), with supporting cast, Paris Opéra Orchestra/Pierre Boulez

Deutsche Grammophon analogue

A strong performance from all concerned, one that includes Cerha's orchestration of the Third Act. There's compelling annotation from Boulez himself, but if you'd rather stay with 'Berg and only Berg', then Karl Böhm's 1968 Berlin Opera recording is still pretty impressive (DG, analogue).

Sergey Prokofiev (1891–1953)

War and Peace, Op. 91 (1944)

Thought by many to be Prokofiev's masterpiece (not least by the composer himself), *War and Peace* – his longest work – is divided into two halves, the first of which (Peace) contains atmospheric love music and lavish ball sequences, and the second (War), menacing battle scenes. The closing scene is rich in patriotic allusions.

Galina Vishnevskaya (Natasha), Lajos Miller (Prince Andrei), Nicolai Gedda (Anatole Kuragin), with supporting cast, French Radio Chorus, French National Opera/Mstislav Rostropovich

Erato digital

Erato's booklet includes a touching but brief reminiscence by Rostropovich in which he explains how the dying Prokofiev asked him to make War and Peace known the world over. Rostropovich's 1970 Bolshoi production was lavishly praised (especially by Shostakovich); "two hours before the performance," he writes, "I put my arms around Prokofiev's tombstone and kissed it. At this crucial moment, I felt that I must be in communication with him." Sixteen years on and this live recording – although not absolutely perfect on all fronts – conveys a generous measure of that love.

Erich Wolfgang Korngold (1897–1957)

Die Tote Stadt, Op. 12 (1920)

An astonishing achievement for a composer still in his early twenties, studded with aural glitter (Korngold's orchestration vies with Richard Strauss's in its brilliance and imagination). The story is set in Bruges towards the end of the nineteenth century where Paul mourns his late wife, meets a dancer who resembles her – but when the dancer mocks his wife, he strangles her (with a lock of his wife's hair). The most famous aria by far is Marietta's entrancing "Glück, das mir verblieb" ("Joy sent from above, hold me close, my faithful love").

René Kollo (Paul), Carol Neblett (Marietta; The apparition of Marie), Benjamin Luxon (Frank), Hermann Prey (Fritz), with supporting cast, Bavarian Radio Chorus, Tölz Boys' Choir, Munich Radio Orchestra/Erich Leinsdorf

RCA analogue

A world première recording featuring especially poignant characterization from Carol Neblett (her singing of "Glück, das mir verblieb" is equalled only by Leontyne Price [RCA, analogue], Maria Jeritza [RCA, Preiser, mono] and Lotte Lehmann [Preiser, Nimbus, EMI, mono]). Erich Leinsdorf, a fine Straussian, directs a strong, well-centred reading of the orchestral score and the 1975 recording reports more-or-less the full range of Korngold's lavish tonal canvas.

George Gershwin (1898–1937)

Porgy and Bess (1935)

Gershwin's last major work employs a libretto by his brother Ira, a tale set amidst the slums of Charleston, North Carolina, where Bess deserts the violent Crown for the cripple Porgy, but Crown bucks and Porgy murders him. Even more than Gershwin's epoch-making *Rhapsody in Blue* (1924 – "The Twentieth-Century Concerto", see above), *Porgy* helped bridge the gap between jazz and so-called 'classical' music: its hit numbers include "Summertime", "It Ain't Necessarily So", "Bess, You is My Woman Now", and "I Got Plenty of Nuttin'", while Robert Russell Bennett's cleverly arranged "Symphonic Picture" brought copious 'themes from the opera' into the concert hall.

Willard White (Porgy), Cynthia Haymon (Bess), Damon Evans (Sportin' Life), Harolyn Blackwell (Clara), Bruce Hubbard (Jake), Gregg Baker (Crown) with supporting cast, Glyndebourne Chorus, London Philharmonic Orchestra/Sir Simon Rattle

EMI digital

A first-class recording that conveys a genuine sense of theatre – which is hardly surprising, given that it was based on a stage production (Glyndebourne, 1986). Rattle's conducting is consistently idiomatic while both singers and players give their all. However, if you only want highlights, there's a superb analogue selection on RCA with Leontyne Price. The best "Symphonic Picture" is under Eugene Ormandy (Sony, analogue).

Dmitry Shostakovich (1906–1975)

Lady Macbeth of Mtsensk, Op. 29 (1934)
Nikolai Leskov's original short story (published 1865) suggests certain parallels with Ostrovsky's drama *The Storm* (first performed in 1859) which Janáček rendered operatic some 60 years later. The adulterous Katerina Izmailova murders her first father-in-law, then her husband and her husband's nephew before drowning both herself and the prisoner who has taken away the lover she has married. Initially hailed a masterpiece, the work was later condemned by the Communist authorities. It's a phenomenally powerful score, one that's fully on a par with the innovatory Fourth, Fourteenth and Fifteenth Symphonies.

 ***Aage Haugland (Boris Izmailov), Philip Langridge (Zinovi Izmailov), Maria Ewing (Katerina Izmailova), Sergei Larin (Sergei), with supporting cast, Chorus and Orchestra of the Bastille Opera/Myung-Whun Chung***
Deutsche Grammophon digital

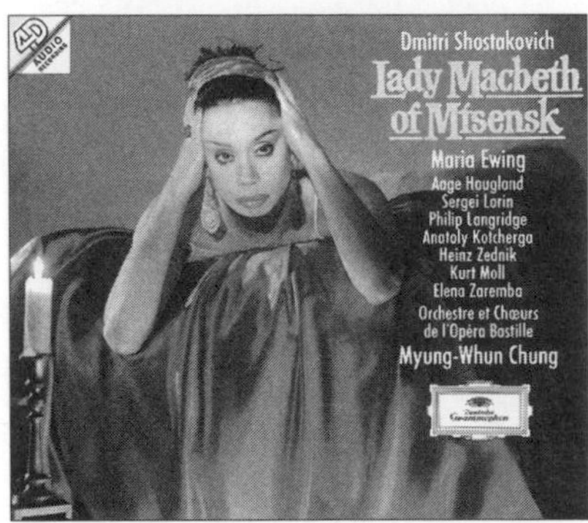

More refined than Rostropovich's famous EMI analogue recording (with Galina Vishnevskaya) and with some remarkable vocal acting, not least from Ewing and Haugland. The conducting is superb, and so is the recording – but Rostropovich is equally recommendable.

Benjamin Britten (1913–1976)

Peter Grimes, Op. 33 (1945)
Peter Grimes, a Suffolk fisherman, is the perennial outsider – and many commentators have drawn active parallels between his tragic plight and Britten's ostracizing homosexuality (such as it would have been, in the 1940s and 1950s especially). The story – fashioned after Crabbe with a libretto by Montagu Slater – concerns Grimes, his intended wife Ellen and two apprentices who have accidentally been killed. Quite apart from its riveting action and moving soliloquies, *Grimes* includes some of Britten's most powerful orchestral writing – principally in the Sea Interludes, Storm and Passacaglia, all of which enjoy a parallel existence in the concert hall.

 ***Anthony Rolfe Johnson (Peter Grimes), Felicity Lott (Ellen Orford), Thomas Allen (Captain Balstrode), with supporting cast, Chorus and Orchestra of the Royal Opera House, Covent Garden/Bernard Haitink***
EMI digital
Some will want to stand by the composer's own recording (Decca analogue, and still sounding marvellous), largely on account of Peter Pears's superb Grimes – although it's interesting to note that Britten had originally intended the role for a baritone. Rolfe Johnson's excellent performance isn't quite so distinctive, but Haitink's handling of Britten's chilling orchestration is second to none (a sampling of the Storm should be enough to convince anyone). The sound is superb.

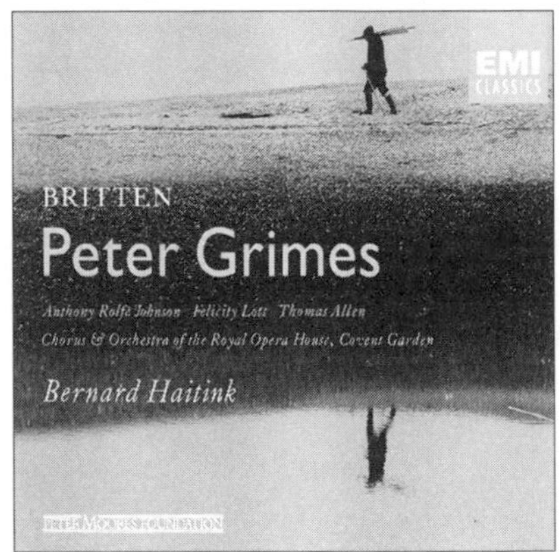

Leonard Bernstein (1918–1990)

West Side Story (1957)
A musical show in an opera section? Absolutely. Bernstein's masterpiece features top-rate arias ("Maria", "I Feel Pretty", "A Boy Like That"), duets ("Tonight", "Somewhere", "One Hand, One Heart") and ensemble pieces ("Jet Song", "Cool", "America", "Gee, Officer Krupke") – not to mention thrilling work for orchestra (Overture, Prologue, "Dance at the

Gym", "The Rumble"). But isn't that equally true of other musicals? Yes and no – 'yes' in a literal sense (they too have solos, duets, etc), 'no' in that Bernstein's music has the weight and originality of a fully-fledged concert score. It is surely among the finest vocal works of the post-war period.

Marni Nixon (Natalie Wood/Maria), Jim Bryant (Richard Beymer/Tony), Russ Tamblyn (Riff), Betty Wand (Rita Moreno/Anita), George Chakiris (Bernado), with supporting cast and orchestra/Johnny Green

Sony Classical analogue

A digital alternative under Bernstein himself (with Kiri Te Kanawa, José Carreras, etc – on DG) is more overtly 'operatic' but the film sound track (our choice) has an ardour, directness and dramatic impact that the studio version lacks. Sony's latest CD incarnation includes a good deal of music not contained on the original LP.

Swans, princes and toys that come to life (1870-1899)

Ballet, as we understand the term today, originated in the courts of France and Italy during the sixteenth and seventeenth centuries. However, it was Delibes's *Coppélia* that marked the artistic high-point of early Romantic ballet, while Tchaikovsky's 'Big Three' (see below) crowned the genre in the late-nineteenth century.

Léo Delibes (1836-1891)

Coppélia (1870)

Swanhilda is jealous because her fiancé blows kisses to a beautiful girl (Coppélia) in the toy-maker's window. She sneaks into the workshop (so does her fiancé), puts on Coppélia's clothes and, in pretending to be the doll come to life, dazes the doll-maker. There's the inevitable reconciliation and a final scene which includes the inauguration of a new bell which the lord of the manor has given to the people. Delibes' score is tuneful, well-crafted and mostly familiar.

Orchestra of Lyon Opera/Kent Nagano

Erato digital

Imaginatively characterized and very well played – but if you don't fancy the whole ballet, there's also a generous single CD of excerpts taken from the same performance. An older, drier recording by the Minneapolis Symphony under Antál Dorati (a dab hand at ballet scores) has plenty of energy but not much subtlety.

Sylvia (1876)

A grand, mythological ballet that established Délibes' superiority in dance music. The shepherd Amyntas nurses a secret passion for Sylvia, leader of Diana's huntresses. Diana refuses to pardon Sylvia for falling in love, until Eros reveals that she too loved a shepherd and all ends happily ever after. *Sylvia* was the first new ballet to be presented in the currently existing Paris Opéra, the first to provide a whole evening's entertainment and the only mythological ballet of the period in the current repertory.

London Symphony Orchestra/ Anatol Fistoulari

Mercury analogue

Excellent playing from a vintage LSO (1958 – most especially among the woodwinds), vigorously and idiomatically conducted. The recording was always exceptional and still sounds good (at the time of writing, it's coupled on three CDs with Dorati's Minneapolis Coppélia – see above).

Pyotr Il'yich Tchaikovsky (1840-1893)

The Nutcracker, Op. 71 (1892)

Tchaikovsky himself felt certain that his latest (and, as it happened, his last) ballet would not equal his earlier successes – a verdict that was initially borne out by an unsuccessful first performance. And yet *The Nutcracker*, based on the tale, *The Nutcracker and the Mouse King*, conjures up Christmas, children and toys that come to life with such vividness and imagination that it's difficult to imagine critical disapproval. Highlights include various 'characteristic dances' (of the Reed-Pipes, Sugar-plum Fairy, etc – included in the celebrated *Nutcracker* Suite) and the Battle between the Nutcracker and the Army of the Mouse King.

 ***London Symphony Orchestra and Chorus/Antál Dorati***

Mercury analogue

If only all ballet recordings were as spontaneous as this! Dorati's experience with various ballet companies pays high dividends, and the playing itself is amazingly characterful and incisive. My only quibble concerns some audible tape edits – and if that is likely to bother you, then try Seiji Ozawa's excellent digital Boston Symphony recording for DG.

The Sleeping Beauty, Op. 66 (1888-89)

The scenario is similar to the Grimm brothers' version of the same story. Tchaikovsky was very pleased with his work, writing to his patron Madame von Meck, "it seems to me that the music for this ballet will be one of my best works. The subject is poetic, so well suited to musical treatment that I was quite carried away while composing it ...". Stravinsky's admiration for *The Sleeping Beauty* – Tchaikovsky's most musically inventive ballet score – extended to making his own arrangements of various movements from the work.

 ***Concertgebouw Orchestra/Antál Dorati***

Phillips analogue

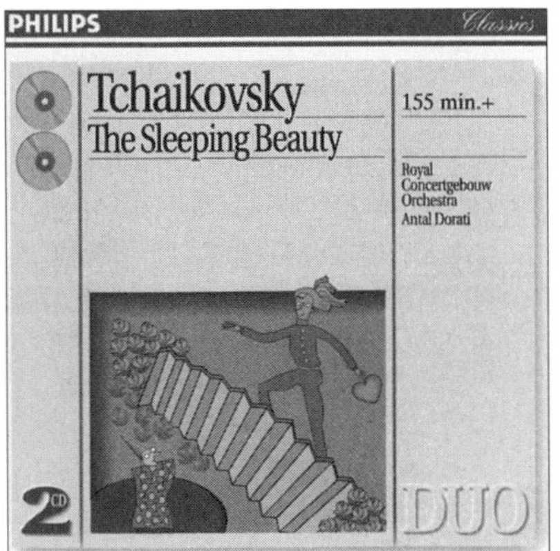

Dorati's second recording (his first, with the Minneapolis Symphony for Mercury, is in mono) is both graceful and dramatic. It is also superbly played, though one musn't forget Evgeni Svetlanov's more theatrical (though less refined) Russian analogue recording (Melodiya/BMG).

Swan Lake, Op. 20 (1877)

When Taneyev chided Tchaikovsky for writing a symphony (his Fourth) in the style of ballet music, the vexed composer replied "I cannot accept that the expression of ballet music should in any way be pejorative". And while Tchaikovsky's symphonies do undoubtedly incorporate much that is balletic, *Swan Lake* – the first of his three ballet masterpieces – is positively symphonic in its sweep, especially in the Fourth Act, where the broken-hearted Princess Odette dies in the arms of Prince Siegfried.

 ***Russian State Symphony Orchestra/Evgeni Svetlanov***

Melodiya/BMG digital

Although a little hard-sounding (at least by the best digital standards) and occasionally raucous, Svetlanov's Swan Lake has an excitement, personality and dramatic intensity that help qualify it for a top-rating. If, however, rasping Russian textures offend, then try Charles Dutoit (Decca) or Michael Tilson Thomas (Sony). Both are digital.

Alexander Glazunov
(1865-1936)

The Seasons, Op. 67 (1899)

The loveliest possible follow-up to Tchaikovsky's Big Three, a sweeping, kaleidoscopic score, superbly orchestrated and consisting of one jewelled miniature after another. The earliest performances of Glazunov's stage masterpiece took place in St Petersburg in 1900 with a cast that included the 19-year old Anna Pavlova. The ballet itself follows the course of the seasons with a set of variations for winter, a bouquet of melody for spring, a "Waltz of the Cornflowers and Poppies" for summer and a thrilling Bacchanale – *The Seasons*' most celebrated single movement – for autumn.

 ***Concert Arts Orchestra/Robert Irving***

EMI analogue

Definitive in virtually every respect: instrumental solos are exquisite, the pacing is perfectly judged (Irving was an experienced ballet conductor) and the sound generally excellent. Strong rivals – all of them analogue – include Ernest Ansermet (Decca), the composer himself (recorded in 1929 but still sounding fairly impressive – Pearl or EMI, mono) and a scintillating sequence of excerpts under Evgeny Mravinsky (Russian Disc, mono).

Puppets and pagans (1912-1947)

The twentieth-century ballet has enjoyed a 'double life' as music for the stage and repertory for the concert hall, with Stravinsky's rhythmically propulsive *Rite of Spring* (which caused a riot at its first stage performance in 1913) having served as a major catalyst. Most of the scores included in this section are both dramatically compelling and extraordinarily inventive.

Claude Debussy (1862-1918)

Jeux (1912)

Possibly the subtlest and most complex of Debussy's orchestral scores (a Diaghilev commission) evokes manifest fun and games as a young man forgets to retrieve his tennis ball and decides instead to engage the interest of two young girls. The interplay of action and suggestion is both erotic and entertaining, while the music itself packs a wealth of incident into a mere 18 or so minutes.

South West German Radio Symphony Orchestra/Michael Gielen

EMI digital

If Jeux is to succeed, its rhythms need to be carefully gauged, its textures properly clarified and the shift from one section to another effected almost by stealth. Gielen and his players qualify on all counts, although Bernard Haitink's Concertgebouw recording (Philips, analogue) runs it close and there's a superb – and seductive – mono version conducted by Victor de Sabata (Testament).

Erik Satie (1866 1925)

Parade (1917)

Jean Cocteau set the theme, whereas Satie's *ballet réaliste* has a cock-eyed, Chaplinesque charm that's at once dated and perennially amusing (*Parade*'s scoring features among its ranks a typewriter, a siren and gunshots). The 'Parade' itself precedes a circus: there's a fairly sober chorale, followed by a wryly humorous – and piquantly characterized – sequence that includes a Chinese juggler, a little American girl dancing ragtime and a pair of acrobats.

London Symphony Orchestra/Antál Dorati

Mercury analogue

Dorati's is a no-nonsense, incisive and superbly played account, recorded during the LSO's 'golden age' by a company famed for its high fidelity. The CD reissue is interesting in that it incorporates other French twentieth-century delights by Milhaud, Auric and Françaix.

Albert Roussel (1869-1937)

Bacchus et Ariane – Concert Suite No. 2 from the ballet, Op. 43 (1932-33)

A drier, more acerbic alternative to Ravel's *Daphnis et Chloé* ballet (see below) – colourful, rhythmically pungent and with plenty of atmosphere. The story concerns Theseus's abandonment of Ariadne on the island of Naxos, while the Second (and more famous) of the two orchestral suites includes some of the ballet's wittiest and most dramatic music.

Lamoureux Orchestra/Igor Markevitch

Deutsche Grammophon analogue

A master ballet conductor in a performance that combines a vivid sense of orchestral colour with genuine theatrical flair. The recording dates from 1959 and still sounds well, though there are compelling analogue alternatives under Václav Neumann (Supraphon) and Charles Munch (RCA, mono). Those who want to investigate the whole ballet (a worthwhile option) are directed to either the French National Orchestra under Georges Prêtre (EMI, digital) or Yan Pascal Tortelier and the BBC Philharmonic (Chandos, digital).

Le festin de l'araignée – ballet-pantomime, Op. 17 (1913)

Delicate music, hyperactive and just a little astringent. *The Spider's Feast* shows Roussel's distinctive but subtle composing style off to fine advantage. The 'plot' concerns a hungry spider who lures a colourful butterfly into his net but is in turn killed by a praying mantis. The scoring makes especially imaginative use of strings and woodwinds (there's even the odd screeching premonition of Bernard Herrmann's score for the film *Psycho*!) and there are some cracking good tunes.

Prague Symphony Orchestra/Václav Smetáček

Supraphon analogue

Smetáček's recording is pure thistle-down: textures are light, definition crystal-clear and the playing spot-on. Recommended alternatives include the Paris Conservatoire under André Cluytens (EMI, analogue) and an extremely fine performance under the composer's own baton (EMI, mono).

Maurice Ravel (1875–1937)

Daphnis et Chloé (1912)

Rich food for the mind's theatre, and a work that opens with a balmy Nocturne and ends with a thundering "Danse générale". The story concerns the goatherd Daphnis, who loses his beloved Chloé to invading pirates. However, when the god Pan comes to the rescue, he releases her. *Daphnis et Chloé*'s most celebrated episodes are in the so-called 'Second Suite' (which includes the colossal crescendo of "Dawn"), but you really need to hear the whole score – such is its dramatic continuity and wide range of sonorities. Ravel's unaccompanied choral writing is exquisite, while the chorus's contribution to the wild "Danse guerrière" helps to intensify the already heated atmosphere.

Royal Opera House Chorus, London Symphony Orchestra/Pierre Monteux

Decca analogue

Pierre Monteux conducted Daphnis's first performance. His innate sense of theatre, supple control of rhythm and acute feeling for texture make this a prime recommendation (the 1959 recording still sounds impressive). Still, the digital field is especially rich in this area and there are fine rival versions from Claudio Abbado (DG) and Kent Nagano (Erato).

Ma mere l'oye (1911)

Quintessential Ravel – delicate, warming and exquisitely coloured. Ravel's intention was to convey "the poetry of childhood": there's an exotic Empress of the Pagodas, a touching "Pavane for the Sleeping Beauty" and "The Fairy Garden", a sublime evocation of a charmed world that children of all ages will instantly recognize. However, beware of the differences between the Suite and the complete ballet – less in terms of timing (there's actually not much in it between the two) than in the latter's additional 'interludes', all of which help cast the spell.

London Symphony Orchestra/Pierre Monteux

Philips analogue

Over 30 years on, and Monteux's recording of the complete ballet is still in a class of its own – a transparent, beautifully played and powerfully atmospheric production conducted by the man who led the world première of Ravel's Daphnis et Chloé ballet (see above). The couplings are fine performances of Boléro and La valse.

Manuel de Falla (1876–1946)

El Amor Brujo (1915)

An extraordinarily vivid score that alternates vibrant orchestral drama (the celebrated "Ritual Fire Dance") with an almost Impressionistic sensitivity to mood and texture (the eighth-movement "Pantomime"). *El Amor Brujo* is a 'ballet-pantomime' that tells of a young widow whose husband claims his posthumous marital rights. The closing pages are rapturously beautiful while Falla's sensual orchestration is fully on a par with the best work of Debussy or Ravel.

Leontyne Price (soprano), Chicago Symphony Orchestra/Fritz Reiner

RCA analogue

Reiner's performance of the delicious "Pantomime" is second-to-none, while Price's fiery assumption of the title-role (four of the movements feature a vocal part) is highly distinctive. With refined orchestral playing and good sound, this is something of a classic – although rival versions under Charles Dutoit (Decca, digital) and Rafael Frühbeck de Burgos (Decca, analogue) aren't too far behind it.

The Three-Cornered Hat (1919)

A riot of rhythm and colour, "The Miller's Dance" and "Danza finale" in particular providing a dramatic evocation of the region. The plot concerns a Corregidor who tries to woo the wife of a miller but ends up being tossed in a blanket while the miller and his wife are reconciled. Most recordings of *The Three-Cornered Hat* are limited to one – or both – of the Suites, whereas the complete ballet includes a wealth of humorous and evocative music that's still virtually unknown away from the theatre.

Colette Boky (soprano), Montreal Symphony Orchestra/Charles Dutoit

Decca digital

Dutoit brings a combination of refinement and virtuosity to both this and the El Amor Brujo coupling, but if the Suites will suffice (they contain the best-known music in the score), then there are plenty of options: Carlo Maria Giulini and the Philharmonia and Artur Rodzinski with the Royal Philharmonic (both EMI) inspire felicitous phrasing, although their (analogue) recordings are of an older vintage (1950s).

Béla Bartók (1881-1945)

The Miraculous Mandarin – ballet-pantomime, Op. 19 (1919-25)
A compelling tale of back-street thuggery, deception and compassion that depicts a hapless Mandarin lured to his death by a captive decoy. Bartók's score mirrors city chaos, seduction, robbery and murder in music of unprecedented delicacy and rhythmic power. A Concert Suite – prepared by Bartók himself – truncates the story, but the complete ballet (which is longer than the Suite by a mere 12 minutes or so) is far preferable.

 ***Ambrosian Singers, London Symphony Orchestra/Claudio Abbado***
Deutsche Grammophon digital

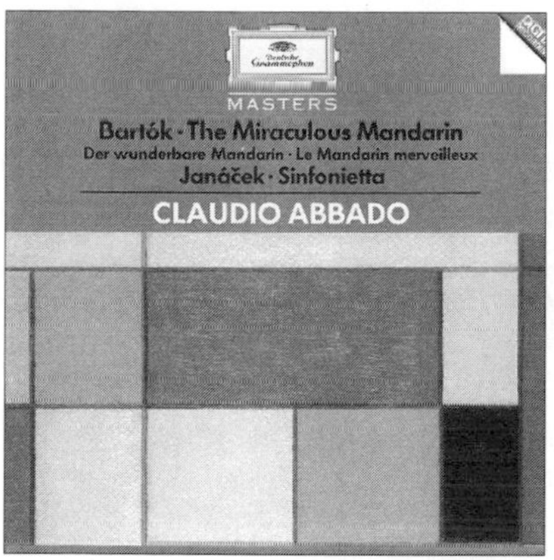

Abbado drives hard but still manages to underline the score's many subtleties. The opening has colossal energy, the so-called "Seduction games", tension to spare and "The chase" (the score's most famous episode), reckless abandon. The closing sections of the ballet, where the girl allows the Mandarin to embrace her, are both tender and mysterious.

Igor Stravinsky (1882-1971)

Apollo (1928, revised 1947)
The most elegant and serenely beautiful of all Stravinsky's ballets is "founded on moments or episodes in Greek mythology plastically interpreted by dancing of the so-called classical school". Scored for strings alone, *Apollo* is a revised version of *Apollon Musagète*, or "Apollo as the Master of the Muses". Highlights include a lively variation for Polymnie, a magical "Pas de deux" and a jaunty, jazz-inflected coda.

 ***Stockholm Chamber Orchestra/ Esa-Pekka Salonen***
Sony Classical digital
Salonen directs a crisp, vividly pointed account of the score, expressive in the slower variations (such as the "Pas de deux") and with an irresistibly buoyant account of the syncopated "Coda". The sound is excellent, but there are fine analogue alternatives under Stravinsky himself (Sony) and Sir Neville Marriner (Decca).

The Firebird (1910)
A fantastic tale of magic and enchantment, the Firebird herself traced in the subtlest of colours, the wicked magician Kastchei with violent, syncopated rhythms. The impresario Diaghilev had originally intended that Anatol Liadov (another musical magician) should compose the score, but it was the young Stravinsky's 42-minute ballet – the first of his major compositions to be performed – that prompted *The Firebird*'s immensely successful maiden flight.

 ***London Symphony Orchestra/ Antál Dorati***
Mercury analogue
The late 1950s witnessed something of a rebirth for the London Symphony Orchestra and this classic 1959 recording reveals lightning precision, taut rhythms and a keenness of attack that no later version quite matches. Dorati's experience as a ballet conductor tells in every bar, although if you're after more modern sound, you might try Charles Dutoit's Montreal recording (Decca, digital). As with Bartók's Miraculous Mandarin, the Suite (or Suites – there are various versions) omits some of Stravinsky's most inventive music.

L'histoire du soldat (1918)
The Soldier's Tale is one of Stravinsky's snazziest stage works – lean and lively with hints of jazz and many lyrical episodes. It's scored for three narrators and seven instrumentalists (violin, double bass, clarinet, bassoon, cornet, trombone and a range of percussion). The story-line (by C. F. Ramuz) centres on a soldier who gives his violin to the devil in return for wisdom, loses his soul in a card game then, ultimately, returns home to surrender himself to the devil. Memorable numbers include the grotesque opening March, a syncopated "Ragtime", a touching "Chorale" and a thrillingly percussive "Triumphal March of the Devil".

 ***Jean Cocteau (Narrator), Peter Ustinov (Devil), Anne Tonietti (Princess), Instrumental Ensemble/Igor Markevitch***
Philips analogue
A class act, stylishly narrated, with an especially supple account of the instrumental score and subtle 'audio stage' effects. Although recorded as long ago as 1962, the actual sound is first-rate. Leopold Stokowski's Vanguard recording and DG's with Sir John Gielgud and the Boston Symphony Chamber Players are viable alternatives, whereas if the Suite suffices (the complete work does after

all contain rather a lot of 'chat'), then no one beats the composer himself (Sony). All recommendations are analogue.

Jeu de cartes (1937)
Stravinsky was a dab hand at straight poker and conjured this dry, jazz-tinted score in three deals (each of which is announced, musically speaking, by a haughty 'linking' theme) for American Ballet. The finale sees the Joker beaten by a "Royal Flush" in Hearts – and the 'game' itself incorporates amusing references to Rossini, Delibes and Johann Strauss.

 ***London Symphony Orchestra/Claudio Abbado***
Deutsche Grammophon analogue

Abbado's eagle eye doesn't miss a trick – in fact, one half imagines him looking over the players' shoulders, calculating each move well in advance of the action. Like the Pulcinella coupling (see below), this is a precision-tooled production, superbly played and very well recorded.

Petrushka (1910-11, revised 1947)
Stravinsky's most colourful score tells of a hapless puppet-sprung-to-life whose love for the ballerina leads to jealousy, fierce frustration and, eventually, death. The stage context is a village fair, replete with stalls, side shows, wet-nurses, coaches, gipsies and all manner of orchestral incidents – from a simple *Ländler* by Joseph Lanner (played on a trumpet) to the raging outbursts in "Petrushka's Room". No other work by Stravinsky parades quite so much emotional intensity.

 ***New York Philharmonic Orchestra/Leonard Bernstein***
Sony Classical analogue
Bernstein's first Petrushka (he re-recorded the work in Israel for DG) is especially spirited and rich in personality. Recommendable alternatives include some that favour the original (and marginally brighter) 1911 version of the score – Charles Dutoit (DG analogue or Decca digital) and Claudio Abbado (DG, digital) being among the best.

Pulcinella (1920, revised 1947)
'Old wine in new bottles,' of Baroque vintage (the original music is by Giovanni Pergolesi) with a colourful, slighty astringent bouquet. The story – based on a character from the Italian *commedia dell'arte* – depicts a cheerful country bumpkin as lover, mock-murder victim and deceiver. The complete ballet is a joy, although the shorter Suite is more frequently performed in concert (and on disc).

 ***Teresa Berganza (mezzo-soprano), Ryland Davies (tenor), John Shirley-Quirk (baritone), London Symphony Orchestra/Claudio Abbado***
Deutsche Grammophon analogue
A sparkling production that combines Baroque-style elegance with Stravinskian acerbity; it's extremely well sung and considerably enhanced by first-rate late-1970s sound. The coupling is a superb Jeu de cartes (see above), but if you're after the Suite (which omits the rather charming songs), then best opt for the decidedly up-tempo St Luke Chamber Orchestra under Robert Craft (Music Masters, digital).

The Rite of Spring (1913, revised 1947)
The Rite's effect on the musical world was rather like a raging dinosaur gatecrashing a conventional stage set. The Paris première (under Pierre Monteux) caused a riot but thereafter Stravinsky's ear-splitting dissonances, savage rhythms and explosive orchestration influenced all and sundry. The story-line concerns a solemn pagan rite where sage elders watch a young girl dance herself to death. There are two parts, "The Adoration of the Earth" and "The Sacrifice", the former in particular parading a breathless sequence of dramatic episodes.

 ***Detroit Symphony Orchestra/Antál Dorati***
Decca digital
Dorati's recording (his third) has plenty of punch yet keeps the aggression under control. The sound is superb, but there are excellent alternatives from Eduardo Mata and the Dallas Symphony (slow and detailed – Dorian, digital), Igor Markevitch and the Philharmonia (extremely fiery but in rather opaque sound – EMI/Testament, analogue) and the composer himself (perceptive but less physically exciting than some – Sony, analogue).

Sergey Prokofiev (1891-1953)

Romeo and Juliet – a ballet in three acts with epilogue, Op. 64 (1938)
Initially dubbed "undanceable" by the Bolshoi, Prokofiev's finest ballet score is an orchestral masterpiece. The grim resolve of "Montagues and Capulets", the fury of "Tybalt's Death", the tender love music (often

swelling to epic grandeur), the devastating "Tomb Scene" and the wit of Prokofiev's smaller characterizations – all contribute to one of the four most compelling musical evocations of Shakespeare's tragedy, the others being by Tchaikovsky, Berlioz and Bernstein.

Excerpts from the Suites Royal Concertgebouw Orchestra/Myung-Whun Chung
Deutsche Grammophon digital

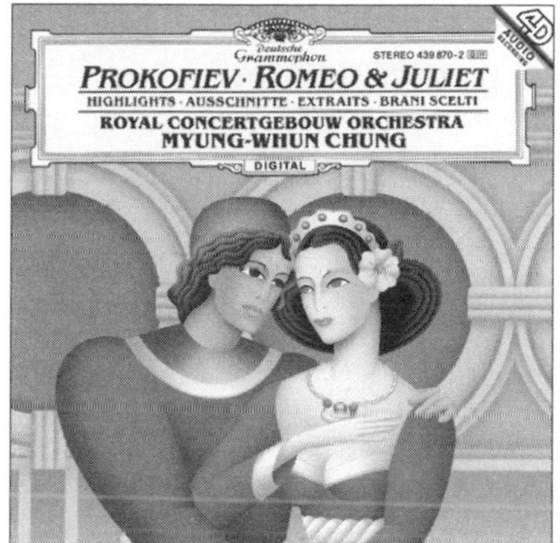

Fifteen numbers, including all the great ones (save, perhaps, the charming "Dance with Mandolins") in performances that combine panache, swagger, lyricism and virtuoso orchestral playing. The recording is magnificent, but those who want the complete ballet (on two discs) are directed to Seiji Ozawa's Boston recording, also on DG (digital).

Darius Milhaud (1892-1974)

Le boeuf sur le toit, Op. 58 (1919)

"The bull on the roof" or, to quote its English subtitle, "The Nothing Doing Bar" is a "cinéma-fantaisie, imagined and arranged by Jean Cocteau". Milhaud had served as an attaché at the French Embassy in Rio de Janeiro during the last year of the First World War and was influenced by Brazilian music. It's little surprise, then, that there's a Brazilian Scene – not to mention a policeman's waltz and a sketch ridiculing American Prohibition. Jazz finds its way in there too and the maddeningly catchy recurring 'main theme' will buzz around in your head for days.

London Symphony Orchestra/Antál Dorati
Mercury analogue

A keen, snappy performance, brilliantly played – though less idiomatically 'jazzy' than Milhaud's own (analogue/stereo) recording on an EMI "Composers in Person" CD that also includes his 78rpm version of La création du monde (see below). Additional options include Leonard Bernstein (EMI, analogue) and the Lyon Opera Orchestra under Kent Nagano (Erato, digital).

La création du monde, Op. 81 (1923)

"The creation of the world" or "The creation of jazz"? Milhaud's immensely witty though concise ballet (it plays for just a quarter of an hour) pre-dates Gershwin's *Rhapsody in Blue* (see "The Twentieth-Century Concerto", above) by a year and yet shares something of its near-neighbour's 'showbiz' musical language. It was in fact the very first symphonic work based on jazz rhythms. Milhaud had been asked to write a score for a scenario dealing with the African creation myth and responded with a jazz ballet "de sentiment classique". The are 19 instrumental soloists, and the work includes a jazz fugue, blues, and a whole host of catchy tunes. It's a riot of a piece!

Soloists/Darius Milhaud
EMI mono

Milhaud's racy, expertly played performance pronounces 'The Twenties' in every bar. If, however, you're allergic to pre-war recordings (although this one sounds remarkably good), then there are spirited alternatives under Leonard Bernstein (EMI, analogue), Charles Munch (RCA, analogue) and Kent Nagano (Erato, digital)

Aaron Copland (1900-1990)

Appalachian Spring – concert suite (1945)

A tuneful, open-air score that tells of a springtime celebration around a farmhouse built for a newly married couple in nineteenth-century Pennsylvania. The title comes from Hart Crane (though not the plot) and the ballet is dedicated to Martha Graham, whose dance company gave the first performance. *Appalachian Spring* represents Copland at his purest and most direct, with a closing melody (borrowed from a pious religious sect, the Shakers) that praises simplicity.

Boston Symphony Orchestra/ Aaron Copland

RCA analogue

A strong, unaffected performance, as warm and sincerely felt as the ballet itself and remarkably well recorded for 1959 (a touch of 'over-modulation' notwithstanding). The best alternatives come from Leonard Bernstein (Sony, analogue, or DG, digital) and Antál Dorati (Mercury, analogue).

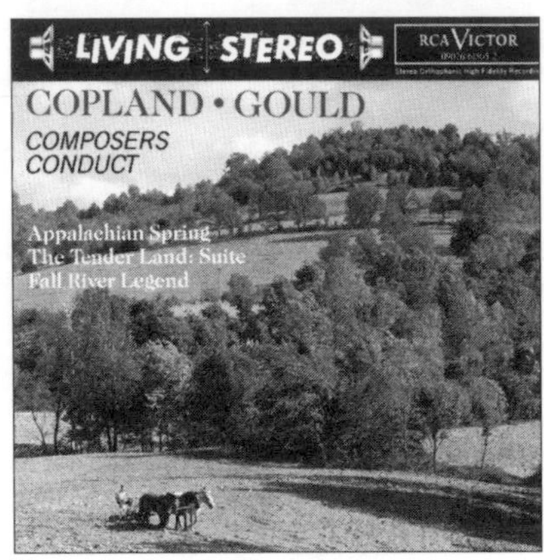

Billy the Kid – ballet (1938)

Copland had the right credentials for composing a Cowboy ballet. Both he and William Bonney (the outlaw 'Billy the Kid') were born in New York and Copland's father once hired Frank James, brother of Jesse James. Furthermore, Copland's manly, 'open' style evokes precisely the right atmosphere and the ballet itself abounds in Cowboy-style tunes. There's also a thrilling "gun battle" (featuring the orchestra's big drums), a disarmingly tender "Billy's death" and a view of the open prairie that anticipates Leonard Bernstein's music from the Elia Kazan's film *On the Waterfront* (see "Narratives in Sound", above).

Baltimore Symphony Orchestra/David Zinman

Argo digital

Fine playing, superb sound and the unquestionable advantage of having the complete ballet rather than the more familiar Suite. The CD also includes the complete Rodeo ballet (again, less well-known than the Suite, or Four Dance Episodes).

Aram Khachaturian (1903–1978)

Gayaneh (1942)

Gayaneh's dramatic goings-on take place, at least for the most part, on a collective cotton farm. The score itself is raw, tuneful and colourfully orchestrated, with the once-ubiquitous "Sabre Dance" as its most popular representative and a whole host of follow-up hits including "Lezghinka", "Dance of the Kurds" and "Dance of the Rose Maidens". The complete ballet is fairly rich in exotic tone-painting, but the individual dances are rather more memorable.

London Symphony Orchestra/ Antál Dorati

Mercury analogue

Dorati conducts a crisp, characterful performance, brilliantly played by the LSO (this was in 1960) and granted ample 'Living Presence' by Mercury's engineers. There are eight items in all, although there's formidable rivalry both from Gennadi Rozhdestvensky with the Leningrad Philharmonic (another virtuoso tour de force, DG, analogue) and Khachaturian himself (Philharmonia, EMI, mono). Jansug Kakhidze's 1976 recording of the complete ballet (Russian Disc, analogue) is also worth considering.

Glossary a brief glossary of musical terms used in the text

A cappella - Literally 'in the chapel'; used to describe unaccompanied choral music
Adagietto - slightly quicker than an adagio
Adagio - 'at ease, comfortably', i.e. at a slow pace – often very slow
Aleatoric - music that allows a performer to improvise within – or to perhaps partially re-structure – a given text
Allegretto - a little slower than Allegro
Allegro - cheerful, sprightly – fast, but not too fast
Andante - 'a walking pace', i.e. a moderate tempo
Andantino - slightly quicker than an Andante
Antiphon - a liturgical chant sung by two choirs in alternation
Appassionata - impassioned
Aria - a broad, song-like piece, usually for voice or solo instrument
Arioso - to be played in a singing style
Arpeggio - breaking up a chord and playing its notes in quick succession – like a harp
Assai - much, very
Atonal - not written in a definite key (see also twelve-note)
Authentic or Period Instruments - instruments that date from the time of composition, often sounding rather 'scrawnier' than those we're used to and played at a different pitch, often slightly lower
Binary - a piece in two distinct sections
Bel canto - literally 'beautiful singing'; usually used to denote Italian opera from the seventeenth to nineteenth centuries
Bravura - swagger
Cadenza - a virtuoso display by the soloist alone, usually towards the end of a first movement and/or finale of a concerto
Canon - when one melodic strand gives the rule to another, which then imitates the first idea, and so on ...
Cantabile - In a singing style
Capriccio - animated, lively, capricious
Castrato - a male singer mutilated in childhood so his voice wouldn't break
Chaconne - a piece (originally a dance) where the main melody is repeated in the bass, and various embellishments played above it
Chalumeau - early wind instrument
Coda - the end episode or 'home straight'
Con - with
Concerto grosso - a work where a small group of soloists ('concertino') contrasts with the main orchestra ('ripieno')
Continuo - a 'continuous' bass part that runs through a concerted work of the Baroque period, often notated in a basic form that is embellished by the performer
Contrapuntal/Counterpoint - where one melody is added to another, the one is called the other's 'counterpoint' – hence the adjective contrapuntal
Crescendo - growing louder
Development - see 'sonata form'
Dolce - sweet
Early - music usually from the Renaissance (up to around 1600) to the Baroque – a term that's commonly used in conjunction with 'period' or 'authentic' performance
Exposition - see 'sonata form'
Fantasia, fantasie 'fancy' – a piece where form is of secondary importance
Fortepiano - an early piano that sounds a little like a harpsichord
Fugato - a passage in fugal style (see fugue)
Fugue - a piece or passage where an initial theme is imitated by other 'voices' or parts and recurs frequently in the course of the composition
Gigue - Jig
Giusto - strict, suitable
Grave heavy, serious
Grazia, grazioso - graceful
Harmonics - 'secondary' sounds (always higher) that can be drawn from any particular note (on strings they have a rather ghostly timbre)
Intermezzo - interlude
Ländler - a slow waltz from lower Austria
Largo - Slow and dignified
Larghetto - slow and dignified, but less so than a Largo
Leitmotiv - leading motive that recurs throughout the course of a work
Lento - slow
Lied, Lieder - (German) song, songs
Madrigal - generally speaking, a composition for several voices (usually five, and generally from the fourteenth to seventeenth centuries), often unaccompanied
Maestoso - majestic
Masque - a ceremonial entertainment for the aristocracy
Mesto - sad
Metronome - a device which produces regular beats and which can be used to determine the pace/tempo of a piece
Minuet, Menuet, Minuetto, Menuett an unhurried, three-in-a-bar dance
Moderato - moderate
Modulate, modulation - moving from one key to another
Molto - much
Moto - motion
Motto - a short, well-defined theme that occurs repeatedly within a work
Nocturne - a night piece, usually quiet in character

Glossary

Non troppo - not too much
Octave - an interval embracing eight notes of the diatonic scale
Ode - a piece in the style of an address, i.e. an "Ode to …"
Passacaglia - a short theme that's played over and over again with variations, usually above it
Period instruments – see 'authentic …'
Pezzo - a piece of music
Piano - soft
Piano Quartet - Piano, violin, viola, cello
Piano Quintet - Piano, two violins, viola, cello
Piano Trio - Piano, violin, cello
Pianissimo - very soft indeed
Pizzicato - plucked
Poco - a little
Polonaise - a Polish dance in triple-time, usually rather stately
Polyphony, polyphonic - where two or more melodies are combined to make musical sense
Portamento - (usually) an expressive slide from one note to the next
Prelude - usually an introductory piece. Sometimes a shortish individual piece (as with Chopin and Debussy)
Presto - originally 'brisk'. Now indicates fastest speed in normal use
Recapitulation – see 'sonata form'
Recitative - a linking passage in imitation of natural speech
Repeat - where a composer asks for a whole passage to be repeated (usually in a symphony, especially in the first and last movements)
Ricercar, ricercare - in fugal or canonic style (see 'fugue' and 'canon')
Ritornello - a section in a concerto which is played by full orchestra without the soloist
Rondo - a recurring musical idea interspersed with contrasting episodes
Scena - a vocal solo in various sections
Scherzando - playfully
Scherzo - literally, 'joke' – usually the lightest movement in a large work
Scordatura - a form of re-tuning
Second subject - second principle theme in a movement
Semitone - the smallest interval between two notes
Sforzando - forced accent
Siciliano - a flowing instrumental piece (or song – derived from a Sicilian Dance) in 6/8 rhythm
Singspiel - a 'sing-play', i.e. spoken dialogue with interpolated songs
Sonata - literally, 'sounded', but which denotes any number of structures – usually (but by no means always) for just one or two instruments
Sonata form - a movement (usually the first movement of a symphony or sonata) where the themes or 'subjects' are presented in an 'exposition', then 'developed' or 'worked out' then summoned back for a 'recapitulation', culminating in a final section or 'coda'
Sostenuto - sustained
Spirito, spiritoso - spirited
Sprechstimme, sprechgesang - 'speech-voice' or 'speech-song', a type of enunciation poised between speech and song and most famously employed by Schoenberg
Staccato - 'detached', i.e. notes that are played in a short, clipped manner
Sul ponticello - bowing on the bridge of a stringed instrument – a thin, glassy sound
Syncopated - displacing the beat – so it doesn't come quite where you expect it to
Tanto - as much, so much – or 'non tanto', not so much
Tarantella - a quick dance in 6/8 time, originating from Taranto
Theorbo - a type of lute
Toccata - from 'toccare', 'to touch' – usually a quick piece where no single notes are unduly dwelt on
Tremolo, tremolando - a juddering, or shimmering effect, usually produced by the strings (i.e. shaking the bow)
Trio - a piece for three players, or the contrasting 'middle' section of a movement, usually a Scherzo or Minuet
Triplet - a group of three notes in a single beat
Tutti - a passage for full orchestra, usually called tutti in a concerto where the soloist might otherwise take the limelight
Twelve-note, twelve-tone - a twentieth-century system of composition where all 12 notes of the chromatic scale are given equal musical value. It's a fascinating and often powerful method, but difficult to grasp 'instantly' (there is no home key to a twelve-tone piece)
Unison - when two or more notes sound together at the same pitch
Verismo - 'realism' – usually associated with Italian operas that deal with the harsh realities of life
Viola da gamba - an early precursor of the cello
Vivace - vivacious, full of life
Virginal - a small early instrument with plucked strings and two keyboards (the favourite instrument of the 'virgin' Queen Elizabeth 1)

Index with the latest CD catalogue numbers of our primary recommendations

Guinness Publishing would like to thank the following record companies for their assistance and permission to reproduce the CD covers included in this edition.

Biddulph Recordings
BMG (RCA) Entertainment
Chandos Records
Collins Classics
Complete Record Company
Danacord
Discovery Records
Decca
Dutton Laboratories
Edel
EMI Premier Group
Harmonia Mundi
Karusell
Koch International
New Note
Nimbus Records
Pavilion Records
PolyGram Classics
Priory Records
Sony Classical
Testament
Warner
Warner Classics UK

Pages 2 to 7 background image - Richard Smith/Corbis
Pages 8 to 262 background image - R Weller